EMMETT TILL

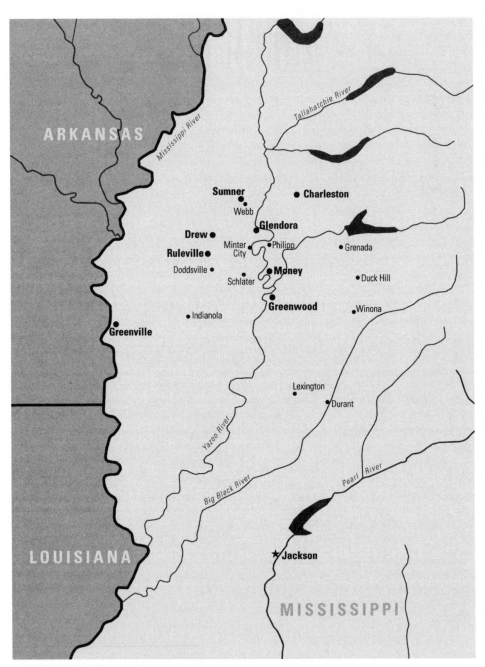

Mississippi Delta. Courtesy of Jason Francis.

EMMETT TILL

The Murder That Shocked the World and Propelled the Civil Rights Movement

DEVERY S. ANDERSON   Foreword by Julian Bond

University Press of Mississippi / Jackson

For Amanda, Tyler, and Jordan,
who have lived with Emmett Till as long as I have

www.upress.state.ms.us

The University Press of Mississippi is a member
of the Association of American University Presses.

First printing 2015

∞

Library of Congress Cataloging-in-Publication Data

Anderson, Devery S.
Emmett Till : the murder that shocked the world and propelled the civil
rights movement / Devery S. Anderson ; foreword by Julian Bond.
pages cm
Includes bibliographical references and index.
ISBN 978-1-4968-0284-2 (cloth : alk. paper) — ISBN 978-1-4968-0285-9
(ebook) 1. Till, Emmett, 1941–1955. 2. Lynching—Mississippi—History—
20th century. 3. African Americans—Crimes against—Mississippi. 4.
Racism—Mississippi—History—20th century 5. Trials (Murder)—Mississippi—Sumner. 6. Hate crimes—Mississippi. 7. Till-Mobley, Mamie,
1921–2003. 8. Racism—Mississippi—History—20th century. 9. United
States—Race relations—History—20th century. 10. Mississippi—Race
relations. I. Title. II. Title: Emmett Till, the murder that shocked the
world and propelled the civil rights movement.
HV6465.M7A63 2015
364.1'34—dc23   2015005681

British Library Cataloging-in-Publication Data available

printed with a grant from
Figure Foundation

vector and square where dots connect

CONTENTS

ACKNOWLEDGMENTS

This work, several years in the making, has been an effort that involved many individuals. Along the journey I have made friends with numerous scholars and students of the Emmett Till case, and all of them have been generous to a fault with their research files and expertise.

I want to thank David Beito and Linda Royster Beito for sharing with me, prior to its publication, portions of the manuscript of their book, *Black Maverick: T. R. M. Howard's Fight for Civil Rights and Economic Power*. They made known to me sources that I had previously been unaware of, and sent me photocopies of hard-to-find documents related to Emmett Till.

Davis Houck at Florida State University opened his newspaper files to me, saving me legwork in locating many Mississippi and out-of-state papers. It was Davis who paved the way for the University Press of Mississippi to publish this book; Davis's friendship has become one of the many rewards of taking on this project. Keith Beauchamp, Hank Klibanoff, and Christopher Metress also sent me important materials at various stages in my research. Amy Chatham went out of her way to provide me with copies of items that had once belonged to her husband's grandfather, Gerald Chatham, the man who prosecuted Emmett Till's accused killers in 1955. Heather McAdams and Patterson Smith sent me a few rare magazines that contained Till-related materials. Plater Robinson also provided me with a copy of a document that I had been trying to get my hands on for years. Scholars such as James Grossman, Stokes McMillan, and Stephen Whitfield were kind enough to answer questions for me by email. Thanks to all of you for your generosity, help, and support.

I must also give a heartfelt thanks to those I have interviewed over the course of my research, and who, after several decades, were able to recount details crucial to the story: Martha Baker, Gerald Chatham Sr., Doris Colon, Roosevelt Crawford, Bobby Dailey, Myrlie Evers-Williams, John Herbers, Gene Herrick, Macklyn Hubbell, Willie [Reed] Louis, Bill Minor, Wheeler Parker Jr., William Parker, Betty Pearson, Bill Pearson, W. C. Shoemaker, Crosby Smith Jr., Bill Spell, Ygondine Sturdivant, Dan Wakefield, Steve Whitaker, Ernest Withers, and Simeon Wright. Others who became part of the Till story did not have to go back quite so far, but their input was just as important. Therefore, thanks go to Jim Abbott, Dr. Jeffrey Andrews, Keith Beauchamp, Phil Benninger, Christopher Benson, Robert Garrity Jr., Susan Glisson, Jim Greenlee, John Hailman, Jan Hillegas, David Holmberg, Dale Killinger, Stanley Nelson, Steve Ritea, Mike Small, and Alvin Sykes. I am extremely grateful to others whom I interviewed or corresponded with who have or once had a relative with some connection to the Emmett Till saga. Most of these people reached out to me first, but I learned about a few of them on my own and contacted them. So I give a special thanks to James Boyack Jr., Randall Bradley, Amy Chatham, Rita Dailey, Robbie Duke, Marsha Gaston, Airickca Gordon-Taylor, Minter Krozer, Allie Ledford, Katherine Malone-France, Mary Lou Ray, Johnny B. Thomas, Ellen Whitten, and Rosalind Withers. Five people I interviewed have asked that their names not be included in this book, but I remain as grateful for their valuable input as I do any of the others I talked to and wish so much that I could publicly recognize them.

I also thank Clare Anderson, Brigid Bennett, Tim Bethea, Guenaëlle Blanchet, Jenny Blue, Shayla Brown, Jimmy Carpenter, Suzy Carter, Norma Chase, Lou Chesterton, Camille Chivers, Ronald Coleman, Cassie Cox, Forrest Crawford, Chris Crowe, Jessica Donaldson, Alan Donnes, Michael Ellery, Amber Etchells, Reena Evers, Ayan Farah, Elizabeth Snyder Fortino, Jim Fox, Mary Francis, Michelle Freeman, Mel Gardner, Whitney Gealta, Devon Geary, Betsy Glick, Isaac Goldberg, Michael Granger, Lisa Gross, John Hatch, John Hays, Tillie Henson, Ronald Herd, Frances Holland, Mark Johnson, Romilly Jones, Ryan Jones, Kurt Kemper, Tony King, Susan Klopfer, Philip Kolin, Rebecca Jane Langwell, Tiffany Littlejohn, Darryl Mace, Deborah Madden, Lee McGarrh, Nick Meakins, Zoe Meakins, Jerry Mitchell, Ed Modestino, Scott Norris, David Nystrom, Neil Padden, Denn Pietro, Virginia Schafer, Mariana Skillen, Priscilla Sterling, Belinda Stewart, Dave Tell, Lois Emily Toole, Timothy B. Tyson, Claire Ward, Kandy Warner, Minnie Watson, Meghan Riley Wheeler, Brian Whitney, John Wilson, former Mississippi governor William Winter, and Dan Wotherspoon for a multitude of kindnesses along the way.

From 1996 until her passing in 2003, I maintained a friendship with Mamie Till-Mobley, mother of Emmett Till. I regret that I did not record every word of the numerous conversations we held, many of which seemed casual at the time, but now, over a decade after her passing, I realize were priceless.

I also express appreciation to staff members at the interlibrary loan department at the J. Willard Marriott Library at the University of Utah in Salt Lake City for processing never-ending orders of microfilm, and to the Salt Lake City Library for its generous policy allowing free photocopying. The staffs at the National Archives offices in Oxford, Mississippi, and Morrow, Georgia, processed orders for me; personnel at the Mississippi Department of Archives and History were most gracious during numerous visits to their facility. I was given equally helpful treatment at the Mitchell Memorial Library at Mississippi State University in Starkville, the Ned R. McWherter Library at the University of Memphis, and the Greenwood Leflore Library in Greenwood, Mississippi. Brittany Bell and Emily Erwin Jones of the Charles W. Capps Jr.

Archives and Museum at Delta State University in Cleveland, Mississippi, were very helpful to me during a two-day visit to their facility in February 2006. Both have since become good friends. The Family History Library of the Church of Jesus Christ of Latter-day Saints in Salt Lake City, Utah, with its seemingly limitless resources, was a treasure trove where I obtained information on many of the players in the Emmett Till story.

Tim Kalich, editor and publisher of the *Greenwood Commonwealth*, was kind enough to search his archives for photos for me; Tom Owen of Archives and Special Collections, University of Louisville, tried hard to find a newspaper article I needed. Brigette Billeaudeaux, Edwin G. Frank, and Christopher Ratliff of the University of Memphis were helpful in providing photos, as were personnel at the *Chicago Defender*. Joel Hornbostel at the *Pitch* in Kansas City took the time to scan and email an article to me from the paper; Clay McFerrin, editor and publisher of the *Charleston Sun*, sent me several obituaries and other items from his paper. Thanks to Stanley Nelson, Alvin Sykes, and Patrick Weems for sending me photos from their own collections, and to Keith Beauchamp for sitting for a photo shoot with my photographer daughter, Amanda Sharise Cooney, while she was visiting in Brooklyn. A special thank you to Jason Francis, who designed the map of the relevant locations in the Mississippi Delta included as the frontispiece in this book.

To friends who critiqued this manuscript, I express my sincere gratitude: Chris Crowe, Jani Fleet, Davis Houck, Ellen Nickenzie Lawson, Erin Metcalfe, and Bill Morgan. I called upon them because I knew their input would be beneficial, and I was right. Although this is a much better book because of their suggestions, I must allow that my own shortcomings have undoubtedly left it an imperfect work. Therefore, I alone am responsible for any errors of fact and interpretation.

It was a great pleasure to work with Cynthia Foster, Craig Gill, Valerie Jones, Courtney McCreary, Leila Salisbury, Anne Stascavage, and Shane Gong Stewart of the University Press of Mississippi. I also appreciate Robert Burchfield for his stellar job at copyediting my manuscript.

Civil rights legend Julian Bond took time out of his busy life to read the manuscript in order to write the foreword. It remains an extreme honor to me that he agreed to do this. A highlight of my involvement in writing this book has been getting to know Mr. Bond and his wife, Pam Horowitz.

Matthew Beachum, Hahn Jackson, and Tracy McKay-Lamb traveled to libraries to look over important collections or hard-to-find microfilm for me, which saved me tremendous amounts of time and money. A former coworker, J. L. Looney, set up my first website on the Emmett Till case in 1999. In 2004, John Hatch and Erin Metcalfe helped me establish a new one, www.emmetttillmurder.com, which has served as a valuable resource for scholars and students worldwide. Both sites opened doors for me that I never could have imagined. Thank you all for your help. Thanks also to Patrick Weems of the Emmett Till Interpretive Center for keeping me updated on current events in Tallahatchie County. This information helped shape the closing chapter of this book.

I enthusiastically give thanks to several friends who helped out financially when it came time to purchase photographs for this book, which was an expensive process. I set up a fund-raiser and they came through quickly and generously. So thank you to my good friends Andrea Alexander, Gary James Bergera, Greg Bragg, Kim Burkart, Cassie Cox, Loyd Ericson, George Fisher, Mel Gardner, Gary Goodell, Mario Hemken, Davis Houck, Romilly Jones, Nick Literski, Tiffany Littlejohn, Ron and Terrie May, Ardis Parshall, and Chris Rohrbach Pedersen.

Special thanks go to Kevin and Christine Elkington for providing much appreciated assistance at a critical phase of my research. Their kindness and support also led to some valuable contacts.

Through my website, I hear regularly from students living in many parts of the world. Several within the United States have made the Till case their subject for National History Day. I want to give a special shout-out to Allie Stutting, Daniel Stutting, Ali Watkins, and Halle Wilmot. Their hard work and dedication took them all the way to the national competition in Washington, DC, in 2013. Many will never forget the Till case because of them.

Last, but by no means least, I want my three children, Amanda Anderson Cooney, Tyler Anderson, and Jordan Anderson, to know how much their patience and support have meant to me throughout the years that this case has consumed me. My two sons probably do not remember life at all without Emmett Till being a major part of it, and all three were taught early in their lives about the racial divisions that have plagued our country. They have taken trips with me to the South and have seen firsthand the places and people of the Emmett Till story. They also read and critiqued the manuscript, for which I am grateful.

I have a passion for historical writing and research, and with the completion of this project, I will take up other subjects that also intrigue, fascinate, inspire, or sadden me. However, I cannot imagine any being more rewarding than this one. The friendships I have developed along the journey have alone been worth it.

FOREWORD

By Julian Bond

I "knew" Emmett Till—even though he was dead before I ever heard of him.

It was because he was dead that I knew him.

I was only fifteen years old, one year older than Emmett Till, when he was brutally murdered in Mississippi because he was believed to have violated the inviolable rule of white southern life. A black teenager, he had approached a white woman, infringing on the sacred canon of a treasured way of life.

I also "knew" his mother, his defenders, and his attackers, that body of white southerners who believed all black males were rapists, "knowing" them through the accounts of black newspapers in my home.

It is hard for us to remember when Till's innocent breach was considered by many so severe as to be worthy of such a harsh reaction. That someone would torture and then kill him for this transgression—indeed, that it was viewed as a transgression at all—seems unthinkable now.

But there was such a time, and because there was and because I lived in the South, I "knew" Emmett Till. Like many, I first saw him in the pages of *Jet* magazine, the black pocket-sized weekly that carried the news of black America to thousands of families like mine.

With a circulation of almost half a million in 1955, and a hand-to-hand pass-along distribution of many, many more in barbershops and beauty shops, *Jet* covered the news and comings and goings of black America's civil rights figures, society leaders, athletes, and entertainers. Each issue had a pretty centerfold beauty, and a few had an ugly photograph of some unfortunate victim of an untimely misfortune.

But none had the ugliness—and the power—of the photograph of Emmett Till's bloated skull.

He was a boy, only fourteen. I was a boy one year older. My family was about to move south again, and I can remember saying, "If they can do that to him, what won't they do to me?" Emmett Till's murder haunted me as it haunted others across the country.

The Till story was a touchstone narrative of my generation. Among many southern horror stories, this was among the most morbid. The Till death picture was proof of white southerners' malevolence. Their refusal to acknowledge the killers' guilt was proof of their acceptance of evil.

Devery S. Anderson has done a marvelous job in putting the Emmett Till story together.

You may think, as I did, that you know the totality of this tale, but you will learn much that is new, as I did. That is because Anderson has tracked down every source; read every testimony, description, and transcript; interviewed every living witness; and read the memories of the departed. He has searched every newspaper and magazine story, including the most obscure, and gathered every conflicting version. Where witnesses conflict, he offers the likeliest version and acknowledges the disagreement.

He places this horrendous crime where it belongs: centrally in the civil rights movement.

He has a focal, but little-known figure, Dr. T. R. M. Howard of Mound Bayou, Mississippi, speaking about Till at a mass meeting at Dexter Avenue Baptist Church in Montgomery, Alabama, a church with a new pastor. One member of the audience is an NAACP activist. Four days later, moved by Dr. Howard's account of Till's death, she refuses to give up her seat on a segregated bus to a white man, and the Montgomery Bus Boycott begins! The new pastor will lead it. She said later: "The news of Emmett's death caused many people to participate in the cry for justice and equal rights, including myself."

This is a courtroom drama, a murder mystery with villains not yet identified. This is a book that covers its subject magnificently.

Above all, this is a labor of love.

PREFACE

At one time, I thought I knew all I needed to about the racial struggles of America because I possessed a general knowledge of slavery and Jim Crow, and was familiar with the stories of Rosa Parks and Martin Luther King Jr. Eventually, however, I received a shocking wakeup call to just how little I really knew.

In the fall of 1994, I was newly transplanted to Salt Lake City and a sophomore at the University of Utah when I made a trip to the City Library, browsed the movie collection, and noticed a six-part PBS series on the American civil rights movement called *Eyes on the Prize*. A year earlier, my history professor at Lower Columbia College in Longview, Washington, Ellen Nickenzie Lawson, taught our class about slavery and its successor, Jim Crow. A timeline she provided recounted the 1963 murder of Medgar Evers, a tragedy that I had never heard of before. Because of that brief lesson, I recognized Evers's name a few months later when I read that his killer was finally convicted on February 5, 1994.

The first episode of *Eyes on the Prize* contained a fifteen-minute segment about the brutal murder of a fourteen-year-old Chicago boy who had traveled to the small hamlet of Money, Mississippi, to spend part of his summer vacation with relatives. Here I heard the name of Emmett Till for the first time and watched in horror as I encountered his story.

From that moment, Emmett Till became a constant presence in my life. At first, the questions I had left me little peace. Whatever happened to this child's mother? Was she still living, or had she died somewhere after a lonely, obscure life? Whatever happened to those who killed young Till? Did they go on to prosper? Were they gloating over the fact they had gotten away with murder? Had they come to feel remorse?

I set out immediately to find out, but because this curiosity preceded my discovery of the Internet by about a year, it took me awhile. I found myself looking through every book I could find on twentieth-century black studies, and I was surprised at how infrequently I encountered Emmett Till. I finally learned that at least one book had been written on the case, Stephen Whitfield's 1988 study, *A Death in the Delta: The Story of Emmett Till*. I shortly learned that there was another, more recent contribution. In May 1995, I happened to read in the University of Utah's *Daily Utah Chronicle* that a woman named Clenora Hudson-Weems was coming to the campus to speak. The brief notice mentioned that she had authored a book, *Emmett Till: The Sacrificial Lamb of the Civil Rights Movement*. Although her lecture was unrelated to the Till case, I still attended, hoping that her book would be available for purchase. It was and I bought it. During her lecture, she briefly mentioned Emmett Till and answered one of my nagging questions by telling the audience that Emmett's mother, Mamie Till-Mobley, was, in fact, still living. She was even scheduled to speak at an event in Memphis for which Hudson-Weems was the chairperson, "From Money, Mississippi, to Union, South Carolina: The Legacy of American Oppression." I was thrilled to learn that Mamie Till-Mobley was still speaking out. During the summer of 1995, I read the Whitfield and Hudson-Weems books to some degree of satisfaction, but I could not get the case out of my mind.

Emmett Till took on an unexpected significance for me in the fall of 1996 after I enrolled in a class on American racism. In early November, I began thinking about my final project for the class, due on December 3. I wanted it to make a real impact, and my first inclination was to center it on Emmett Till. I wondered if there was any way that I could contact Mamie Till-Mobley and interview her. I went to the library, grabbed a Chicago telephone directory from off the shelf, and was surprised to find a listing that read, "Mobley, Gene and Mamie Till." I wrote down both the address and telephone number, and on November 12, I wrote Mrs. Till-Mobley about my project and requested an interview. I gave her my phone number so that she could respond to me quickly.

A few weeks went by, and I never heard back. Because it was getting close to the project's due date, I decided to call her. I nervously dialed the number, and after a few rings, Gene Mobley answered. I asked him if I could speak to Mrs. Mobley, and he put her on the phone. Her friendly tone immediately put me at ease. I introduced myself, reminded her of the letter I had sent her, explained my class project, and asked for the interview. She agreed, and we arranged a time and date for me to call back. After she canceled once to attend a funeral and didn't answer on our second prearranged call, I became nervous. I finally reached her on December 3, the very day the project was due. Luckily, my class met at night, so I had most of the day to transcribe the interview.

Mamie Till-Mobley told me she could spare forty-five minutes, but we conversed for over two hours, with her doing most of the talking. After discussing the kidnapping and murder, we talked about her life in the four decades since Emmett's death. She told me about the Emmett Till Foundation, her years as a schoolteacher, and her current work in training children to recite speeches of the civil rights movement. This call began a friendship that resulted in dozens of telephone conversations over the next six years.

In 1997, I received a telephone call from a budding young filmmaker named Keith Beauchamp. He had seen a brief reference online about some help I was giving Mamie Till-Mobley on a project and asked if I would make an introductory call to her on his behalf, as he wanted to discuss with her a feature film he was hoping to make. I agreed, but for no particular reason, procrastinated in making the call. Soon Keith's mother called and reminded me of her son's request, and then Keith followed up with another call of his own. It became obvious that Keith was serious, and so I finally made the call to Mamie Till-Mobley and explained Keith's interest in talking to her. She told me that she would be happy to speak with him, and I relayed to him that news. After that, I forgot about it.

Nearly two years passed, but on May 1, 1999, Keith sent me an email and reminded me about our earlier conversations. He had not only contacted Mamie Till-Mobley after our earlier exchanges, but he had been working closely with her. She gave a nod of approval not only for his feature film, but she also encouraged him to make a documentary about the Emmett Till story. In time, the latter took precedence, and by late 2002 Keith was showing publicly a rough-cut version of his film, *The Untold Story of Emmett Louis Till*. It was released in theaters in 2005, and in October 2006 it began running on Court TV. By the spring of 2004, the hard work of Keith, victims advocate Alvin Sykes, and others got the attention of the Justice Department, which opened an investigation into the Till murder that lasted eighteen months.

With this unprecedented interest in Emmett Till as my inspiration, I began to think about what my own contributions to this case should be. For some time I had considered writing a book, but rarely gave it serious thought. By the fall of 2004, however, I discovered that there was a book inside of me that needed to get out. Between 1988 and 2004, at least seven books appeared on the case, along with one other documentary, Stanley Nelson's Emmy-winning film, *The Murder of Emmett Till*. Since I started my research, several more books have been released. These include memoirs, novels, and studies of media coverage of the trial. As important as these all are, no one had attempted to write a truly comprehensive narrative of the case, with all of the details that are, in many respects, stranger than fiction. Such a book has been crying out to be written, and the one in your hands is my attempt to provide it.

I began doing newspaper research immediately upon deciding to write, and a few months later, in January 2005, I took my first trip to the Mississippi Delta. In the years since, I have returned over a dozen times and taken three trips to Chicago, where I have worked in archives and conducted interviews. Over the course of my research, I have talked in detail to witnesses of incidents related to the kidnapping and murder of Emmett Till, interviewed reporters who covered the trial, and have even sat down with a spectator who attended it. Around the time I began working on this book, I started a website, www.emmetttillmurder.com, which at the time of this writing has received over one million hits from people in 200 countries. As a result of this attention, I have been invited to speak about the Till story in Florida, Indiana, Mississippi,

Missouri, Nevada, New York, South Dakota, Texas, Utah, West Virginia, Wisconsin, Northern England, and Wales.

I have learned more about the Till case in the last decade of research and writing than I ever thought possible. However, this knowledge has come as a double-edged sword in many respects. More than anything else, my aim has been to tell the story as accurately and thoroughly as I can, and I wanted the depths of my research to be reflected in that. Since the mid-1980s, Mamie Till-Mobley and others who were involved in the case have written or spoken publicly about their experience. As I scoured the earliest newspaper accounts, interviews, and speeches of the principals in this saga, which were provided days, weeks, or just a few months after the events, I have discovered that later reminiscences often conflict with 1955 accounts. Certainly this is to be expected to some degree. If I have learned anything doing this study, it is that memory can be very problematic and is often an unreliable source of history. Memory expert Elizabeth Loftus has demonstrated time and again that "misinformation can influence people's memories when they are interrogated in a suggestive fashion or when they talk to other people who give their version of the events."[1] Sincerity or insincerity has little to do with false memory. Loftus and Daniel Bernstein have pointed out "two types of lying. Some people lie intentionally and for myriad reasons: financial gain, fame, popularity, even mischief. Other people lie without knowing that they are lying. In other words, they think they are telling the truth but they are reporting something that is false—a belief in a false memory."[2] This is rarely obvious to the person incorrectly recalling his or her past experiences. Where stories contradicted each other in my research, my experience as a historian has taught me that, in most instances, it is safest to trust the earliest accounts as the most accurate.

This has not been an easy course to take, and I realize that to some, it may seem a form of sacrilege to take issue with anyone as central to the story as Emmett Till's mother or the cousins who were with Till in Mississippi. Yet to the extent that this happens, it is the result of painstakingly weighing multiple accounts of an incident by the same individual, or equally valid accounts by multiple people who experienced the same thing. If I dispute something said by someone decades after the fact, I am usually agreeing with something that same person said in 1955. Since I cannot accept two (or more) contradictory accounts as accurate, I have had to determine which sources are the most reliable and base my conclusions on that. At no time have I begun with an agenda, nor have I sought to prove any preconceived ideas. It is true that I was not a witness to the events of the Till story and thus lack certain knowledge that an eyewitness would. Yet a historian has his or her own advantages in writing about the past, namely, access to a host of primary sources and a determination to evaluate them fairly. One of the reasons this book has taken longer to write than I had originally anticipated is because my commitment to accuracy has forced a long and laborious creative process.

Wherever I have found contradictions or problems, I have done my best to explain them and make a case for why I reached the conclusions I have. Where these explanations do not disrupt the flow of the narrative or sidetrack from it, I explain them in the text. Where it would distract the reader, I deal with them in the endnotes. For this reason, I encourage readers to consult the notes in the back of this book, as they often contain valuable information beyond mere source citation.

This book is divided into two sections. The first is by far the longest, containing ten chapters. Chapter 1 provides background on the lives of Mamie and Emmett Till up until Emmett's fateful trip to Mississippi. Chapters 2 through 9 deal with the events of the Till case as they unfolded between August 1955 and March 1956. The concluding chapter in part one provides details about the lives of the primary people in the Till case during the years that followed their brief stint in the spotlight.

Part two consists of three chapters and an appendix, which conclude the book. Chapters 11 and 12 deal with the reemergence of the story into the public consciousness after the mid-1980s, through the resulting investigation and closing of the case between 2004 and 2007. Chapter 13 discusses the legacy of Emmett Till. In the appendix, I recap some facts and put forth my own theories about the kidnapping and murder based on all known investigations.

Although I have remained horrified by the Till murder from the time I first learned of it and am sympathetic to the victim as well as his family, all of whose lives were altered as a result, I have tried to keep my emotions out of the narrative. Where the "good guys" in this story made mistakes, I don't shy away from them. No one is one-dimensional, and even those whose evil deeds set off the chain of events in this story need to be understood as best they can. Unfortunately, only two members of the families of the accused killers would talk to me or answer questions. One could tell me very little about their relative in a way that I might better understand him. Hopefully, the families all know by now that I was willing.

PROLOGUE

Through a Glass, Darkly

Saturday, June 4, 2005. Fifty mourners gathered under a white tent and watched solemnly as eight pallbearers unloaded a shiny blue casket from a green hearse at Burr Oak Cemetery in Alsip, Illinois. Those eight, mostly cousins of the deceased, walked the casket to an open grave, placed it on the lowering device, and then paused for a forty-minute service. Afterward, the crowd dispersed, and a fourteen-year-old boy was laid to rest.

For some of those there, this was a moment of déjà vu. Emmett Till, the boy being mourned, had died fifty years earlier. His body was about to occupy this grave for a second time. During two graveside services held a half-century apart, family members in attendance longed for answers. Both times, they longed for justice. The exhumation that led to Emmett's reburial was necessary to help secure both. Two days earlier, medical examiners conducted the first autopsy ever performed on the body, and it would reveal more than had ever been known about just how young Till died all those years ago.

One of those who had twice witnessed the solemn scene at Burr Oak was Wheeler Parker Jr. The first time, he was a shaken sixteen-year-old, still traumatized over the brutal death of his friend and cousin. Now, as a sixty-six-year-old minister, he was there to eulogize Emmett from the perspective of time and some degree of healing. He had spent the day before wondering what to say at the service, and when he closed his barbershop for the night, he went home to seek guidance through prayer.

A large storage shed stood near the cemetery office; and inside was another casket, this one, empty. It was not new and shiny, but had just spent five decades below ground. Its brown exterior had faded from age and the elements. Inside, the once white, soft fabric that lined the lid was torn, brittle, and had become discolored from the rust that had rubbed off the metal. Until just a couple of days earlier, this box had held Emmett Till's remains since 1955.

In February 2007, in the midst of a Chicago blizzard, I visited Burr Oak Cemetery and, knowing that the casket was in storage, I asked Carolyn Towns, the cemetery manager, to let me see it. She kindly obliged and asked a worker to take me into the shed. When we went inside, he removed a thick canvas that covered the casket, opened the lid, and left me to myself. It was an emotional moment as I suddenly felt part of history, as my fingerprints joined countless others left before me that investigators found to be in pristine condition after all these years. Knowing this would likely be the only time I would be given this opportunity, I stood there for what seemed like forever.

Back in September 1955, tens of thousands of mourners had stood in long lines at a Chicago church in order to file by this very casket and see the effects of racism at its extreme. The victim, showing every sign of hate imaginable, had been covered with a clear glass viewing panel so that people could see but not touch the body and be spared of its smell. Suddenly, I became one of those who had touched that same lid, placed my hand on that same glass, and looked inside. Although the casket was empty now, I leaned over and imagined that I was staring at the beaten, bloated, and decomposing face of Emmett Till as had thousands of others so many years earlier. I wanted to feel that same horror. I wanted to be one with them.

Yet when I looked into the casket, however, I found that the glass had also suffered from fifty years below ground. It had darkened to the point that I could hardly see through to the padding upon which Emmett had once lain. Because it was no longer a window but a mirror, I saw something that thousands before me had not—a reflection.

I immediately noted the irony. There I was, looking into a darkened glass, but those who came before me had been looking through a glass, darkly, to borrow the words of the biblical Apostle Paul, even though the glass in a very literal sense had been crystal clear for them. In other words, time had not yet enabled them to grasp the significance of the Emmett Till story in the same way that I, as a historian living in a new era, was able to do. Yet I was sufficiently humbled almost immediately as I tried to make sense of the fact that my seeing Emmett Till through my imagination had been blocked. I could not see *him* because all I could see was *myself*.

This realization forced me to pause for self-reflection as I drove from the cemetery. Yes, I had escaped the racist mindset embraced by most southern whites at the time Emmett Till was buried the first time, but I realized most powerfully that day that this may be so only as a matter of luck. What if I had been born early enough to have been an adult male in 1955 or had been born in Mississippi? The likelihood that I would have seen this tragic murder through different eyes is almost certain. In other words, I am horrified by this tragedy and others like it because I was born at a time and place that allowed me to bypass the prejudices that millions of others could not. As I drove away, I wondered why our common humanity has not been sufficient on its own to stamp out the trappings of cultural conditioning where that conditioning is so deplorable.

Whatever the answer, the questions are important enough that history needs a revisit now and then.

Wheeler Parker finally decided on a theme to eulogize his cousin, Emmett Till, going with the all-important question, "What is life?" As Parker explained it, "We're put on this earth to give back. . . . His life meant far more because of the way he died, his sacrifice. His voice still cries out to us for justice."

The story that follows tells us why.

He's been dead 30 years and I can't see why it can't stay dead.
—Roy Bryant on Emmett Till, 1985

Emmett Till is dead and gone. . . . Why can't people
leave the dead alone and quit trying to stir things up?
—Roy Bryant, 1992

EMMETT TILL

PART ONE

In Black and White

1

Mother and Son

For a few dark and confused hours before the sun rose on August 28, 1955, a fourteen-year-old black teenager visiting Mississippi knew he was hated. Shortly after daylight, as he slipped into unconsciousness, surrounded by white men mercilessly beating him to death, he was more hated than anyone on earth.

That boy, Emmett Till, lost his life tragically in the Mississippi Delta that Sunday morning only because his story began there generations earlier. Although the brash African American youth from Chicago knew little of the region where his life would end, family ties to the South had brought about his fateful visit in the first place. Emmett's mother, Mamie Elizabeth Carthan, had been born near Webb, in Mississippi's Tallahatchie County, on November 23, 1921. Webb is located two miles south of Sumner, one of two seats in the county where Mamie would attend a murder trial nearly thirty-four years later.

Tallahatchie, a Choctaw word meaning "rock of waters," is the name of the river that runs in a southwesterly direction at a length of over 300 miles, rising in Tippah County. It joins the Coldwater, Yalobusha, and Greenwood Rivers and forms the Yazoo in Leflore County. Native American influences notwithstanding, white-black relationships came to characterize the state of Mississippi and laid the foundation for later conflicts. By 1832, one year before the state legislature officially formed Tallahatchie County, white settlers had already come with their slaves.[1] In 1860, over 436,000 African American men, women, and children—or 55 percent of the state's population—were living and working as chattel on plantations and cotton fields throughout Mississippi. The total number of slaves in the South at the start of the Civil War was just under four million.[2]

Memory of life in the Magnolia State would elude Mamie. The only child of Wiley Nash and Alma Smith Carthan, Mamie was just two years old when her family said good-bye to Mississippi and moved north to Summit, Illinois. Summit, more commonly called Argo, is a small suburb on the south side of Chicago, incorporated in 1890. Only six black families had settled there by 1922.[3] The Carthans' arrival two years later was part of what came to be termed the Great Migration, a movement that had already inspired thousands of black families to leave the South and seek a new beginning in northern cities. The migration had begun shortly before World War I, and between 1915 and 1918, 450,000 to 500,000 blacks left their southern homes. Northern destinations were usually determined by the starting point of the migrants. Blacks from southern coastal states generally settled in their northern counterparts, such as New York, Connecticut, Massachusetts, and as far inland as Pennsylvania. Mississippians and those from immediately neighboring states most often boarded a train on the Illinois Central Railroad with Chicago as their destination.[4]

Economic difficulties that followed the war continued to produce staggering migratory figures. During the 1920s, when the Carthans left Mississippi, over 700,000 southern blacks did the same, often with little more than a few possessions and a dream of what the North could do for them and their families. Poignantly, the migration was often couched in religious terms familiar to the Judeo-Christian tradition, in which blacks saw themselves as a chosen people. Theirs was a story that mirrored the ancient Israelites, who triumphed over bondage and persecution by escaping Egypt and finding renewal in the land of Canaan. Such comparisons stimulated an abundance of black optimism, despite the fact that for most of the migrating families, uncertainties about starting over economically were inevitable.[5]

Chicago was especially attractive to African Americans seeking refuge from the oppressive conditions of the South. In the North, they found jobs in a variety of industries. In the early 1920s, the largest employers of blacks were the Armour and Morris stockyards, where a combined total of 3,500 labored. In Argo, African Americans working at Corn Products Refining Company numbered 500.[6]

Although Chicago offered much to blacks who were long accustomed to a repressive life in the South, it was not Utopia. For fifty years prior to the migration, neither whites nor blacks living in Chicago cared much for each other, but any difficulties that the black population endured as a result were still a vast improvement over the institutionalized racism that had been a daily fact of life in the South.[7] As Chicago's black population grew, however, so did white antagonism. This culminated in 1919 in a race riot rooted in job competition in the post–World War I era. The riot began on July 27, when Eugene Williams, a black teenager, swam across an imaginary line on a segregated beach. People on the white side of the beach began throwing rocks, and in the fracas, Williams drowned. Rather than arrest the white man believed responsible for Williams's death, police instead arrested a black man. When blacks protested, whites responded with violence. Fighting erupted on both sides and lasted until August 3. Thirty-eight people died and hundreds more were injured before the uprising was finally quelled.[8]

Five years later, Nash Carthan left Mississippi and sent for his family after a few months. Upon his arrival in Argo, he found work at Corn Products, where most black men in that community aspired to work.[9] The plant also drew several white men at the time, and by 1930, of the 700 workers in the village, nearly half, including Nash, were employed in the refinery industry.[10] Established in 1907, Corn Products was ideally located because Chicago, with its abundant water supply and transportation capabilities, was positioned at the center of the midwestern states, where the majority of US corn is grown.[11]

Mamie's childhood was shaped largely by the influence of her mother. Deeply religious, Alma was also excessively strict and monitored her daughter's every move. This continued even as Mamie grew into adulthood. Alma and Nash separated when Mamie was around eleven, and Nash lost contact with his daughter for over fifteen years. He later remarried and moved to Detroit, while Alma, who stayed behind in Argo, married a man named Tom Gaines in March 1933. Through Alma's dominance, Mamie remained well disciplined in her studies, but was sheltered socially.[12] For her naïveté, she would eventually pay a price.

Because Argo's black population remained relatively small, Mamie attended predominantly white schools. Yet her interaction with students and teachers was mostly positive. "It hadn't occurred to me that I was darker than some of the other people that were in the class," she said, reflecting back on her youth. "I was graded strictly according to my ability to perform and I was never looked down on."[13] She certainly had ample opportunity to develop healthy interracial relationships early on. For instance, Alma played a motherly role to several children in the neighborhood, many of whom were white. After Mamie developed a minor heart condition when she was about twelve years old, she was regularly assisted by a white girl whom Mamie lovingly called her "shadow." This friend accompanied Mamie to school and back, watched over her, and made sure she did not exert herself by climbing steps.[14]

Several white European immigrants also lived in the Carthans' neighborhood. One door down from their house on Sixty-Fourth Street lived John and Mary Nyezprook, from Russia. Two doors up was the home of Stanley and Alvina Lapinski; Stanley was from Poland, while Alvina hailed from Germany. The men in these families also worked at Corn Products.[15] It is not known how well the Carthans knew these neighbors, but some level of interaction in such a tight-knit community can be assumed. Although antagonism often existed in Chicago between blacks and European immigrants as each competed for jobs, for the most part, Argo was able to avoid such conflicts. As an adult, Mamie proudly declared that some of her best friends were white.[16]

Chicago did see its share of discrimination, but unlike the South, it remained de facto, and in fact, illegal. Following the 1919 race riot, a local alderman proposed segregating the city, but the Governor's Commission on Race Relations countered "that measures involving or approaching deportation or segregation are illegal, impractical and would not solve, but would accentuate, the race problem and postpone its just and orderly solution by the process of adjustment."[17] However, as Chicago's black population increased from 44,000 to 492,000 between 1920 and 1950, many worried merchants responded by excluding blacks outright or by resorting to dishonest strategies to keep them away. To discourage blacks from patronizing a restaurant, for example, employees would ignore them, oversalt their food, treat them rudely, or overcharge them. Blacks endured similar treatment in hotels and theaters. Some resisted this breach of the civil rights law with violence, while others sued. Between 1930 and 1940, the National Association for the Advancement of Colored People (NAACP) secured judgments of $7,000 against Chicago restaurants alone.[18]

An episode between Mamie and her high school geometry teacher, Miss Moore, apparently *was* race-related. Moore was not fond of her black students and gave Mamie a failing grade on an assignment that Mamie had completed, but which had been stolen by some boys before she could turn it in. Although the school principal ordered Moore to restore the A grade after Mamie objected, Moore took occasion for revenge when Mamie tried to fulfill the requirements for the National Honor Society. Moore, who was on the board of the society, was also the swimming instructor at Argo Community High and informed Mamie that swimming was a requirement in order to qualify. When Mamie hesitated to get into the water, Moore shoved her in. Terrified, Mamie lost consciousness and began to sink, but was rescued in time by her friend Ollie Colbert. "All the while, Miss Moore stood there laughing," said Mamie several years later. "I'll never forget her as long as I live."[19]

Although this incident ended Mamie's dreams of the National Honor Society, she made the honor roll and claimed to be the first black student at Argo Community High to graduate at the top of her class. This was an accomplishment in itself, but for a black girl at the time, so was graduating at all. Only a few black students had ever received a diploma at Argo before Mamie; most of the girls dropped out in order to marry. Mamie, who had never even dated, felt like romance had already eluded her because at age eighteen, she was still single.[20] Yet her social inexperience created a challenge of its own, and for that, she spent the next decade making mistakes that would teach her valuable lessons for the future. Because dating and dancing had always been denied her, she was left vulnerable by the time she was a young adult and ready for both. When she met Louis Till, a man three months younger and nine inches taller than her own five-foot frame, she was impressed by his sophistication and confidence. Louis, a part-time boxer and skilled gambler, had been born in

Missouri and orphaned as a child. He had recently moved to Argo to work at Corn Products.[21]

For their first date, Mamie and Louis went to Berg's Drug Store, an Argo shop that served, but refused to seat, black customers. They bought banana splits, but instead of taking them out, Louis insisted on eating them there. Mamie nervously went along with Louis on this one, and watched him stand up to store owner Berg, even though Berg threatened to tell Alma what the young couple had done. Mamie admired the Louis Till she saw that night—brave, protective, and standing his ground.[22] Yet Mamie's innocence, contrasted against Louis's worldliness and street smarts, created a dysfunctional relationship from the beginning. "He treated me like I was a little girl and took me for granted like a doll you would set on a shelf and find it there when you came back." Alma saw little that she admired in Louis and persuaded Mamie to break up with him. Later, Louis saw Mamie out with another boy and created such a scene in front of her house that Alma came out and scolded them both. Alma's actions may have finally backfired. "I flared up," declared Mamie, "that I was grown up and wasn't a child anymore. It was then, I guess, that I made up my mind I was going to marry Louis Till." The wedding took place in Alma's living room on October 14, 1940.[23]

Immediately after the wedding, Louis moved in with Mamie and the Gaineses. Mamie was working at the Coffey School of Aeronautics as a typist, and Louis was still at Corn Products. By Mamie's estimation, she conceived their only child on her wedding night, which was her first sexual encounter. As the pregnancy progressed, a family friend began calling the unborn baby by the nickname "Bobo." It stuck, even though Mamie had been favoring "Mickey."[24]

After living with the Gaineses for six months, the Tills rented their own apartment. No one was happier than Louis, who had come to resent Mamie's close relationship with her mother. There was little reason to fault Louis for his attitude. While living at Alma's, the newlyweds felt obligated to ask permission even to go to the movies, an indication of just how controlling Alma was and how ingrained Mamie's submissiveness was in return.[25] Louis hoped the move would free them from Alma's grasp, but in that, he was disappointed. "I was no more prepared for independence than a new-born lamb strayed from its mother," Mamie explained.[26] Consequently, she still turned to Alma for advice and just about everything else, and Louis continued to harbor resentment. Louis, who had been shuffled from home to home while growing up, certainly could not relate to a parent-child bond all that well. He seemed uninterested in the coming baby, but perhaps he just felt out of place. Whatever the reason, he was not present when Mamie gave birth to their child, a boy whom she named after her uncle, Emmett Carthan, and the baby's father. Emmett Louis

Till was born on July 25, 1941, at Cook County Hospital in Chicago. He would forever retain the nickname Bobo, or simply, Bo.[27]

The delivery was not an easy one, and doctors discovered that the child was in a breech position. Due to the harsh instruments used in the birth, Emmett's right hand was swollen and a knee bruised. Doctors told Alma that Emmett's injuries would be permanent, and recommended he be placed in a facility specializing in the treatment of such physical challenges. Mamie believed, however, that she and Alma could help the child overcome any limitations right at home. Emmett recovered, albeit slowly, and by the time he was about two years old he had completely healed from the injuries related to his birth.[28]

Louis showed kindness and patience toward Mamie when she first returned from the hospital, and from Mamie's viewpoint, her husband tried his best. Yet he struggled. Despite the fact that he was easygoing by nature, he also harbored a hot temper, which often caused him trouble. Once, when Emmett was only a few weeks old, Louis came home from work to discover that Mamie was at Alma's. When she returned late, Louis was angry and hungry, and the young couple got into a fight. Mamie went back to Alma's, but the couple shortly reconciled.[29]

Whether any violence occurred that night is unknown, but there were times when Mamie did suffer abuse at the hands of Louis Till. The night she stood her ground essentially marked the end of their marriage. On that occasion, Louis came home drunk and started a fight because Mamie was eating some greens sent over by her mother. She ignored Louis's demands to stop eating, which made him so angry that he jumped on top of her. "I didn't know what to do at that moment, but knew I was no match for Louis Till," she said about the frightening experience. "I found myself on the floor with Louis choking me, squeezing my neck as I coughed up the greens, squeezing harder and harder until I just blacked out."

When Mamie regained consciousness, Louis was gone. Knowing that her enraged husband would return, she took a poker and heated it in the fireplace. She also boiled a pot of water, and waited for Louis in the dark. When he came home, Mamie took the water and threw it at him before he even saw it coming. Screaming, Louis ran to Alma's, where Alma began to peel his shirt—and his skin—from his back. Mamie soon got a restraining order against Louis and moved back in with her mother.[30]

Louis violated the order repeatedly, which forced Mamie to take him back to court.[31] Louis never served time in jail, despite his troubles at home and the occasional fistfights he got into with others, but Mamie's problems were about to be solved, at least for the time being. Around this time Louis decided to join the army. Being separated from Mamie, he listed himself as a single man in his papers. Mamie said later in life that the judge hearing their domestic disputes gave Louis a choice of jail or the military, but her earliest recollections do not indicate that is what happened. "I believed he wanted to go," she explained in 1956. "It meant excitement and travel."[32] Louis entered basic training on July 9, 1942. Beginning August 1, he instituted the required Class F allotment to provide support for his family at $22 per month.[33]

In Alma's home, Mamie returned to the familiar surroundings of comfort and safety that she had always known. There, she could again enjoy her role as a daughter as she moved past the turbulent one she had endured as a wife. Yet this may have added confusion to relationships because now it seemed as though Alma had two children; certainly *she* saw it that way. The changed dynamic between Mamie and Emmett proved to be a positive one for them, however. "We were so much like brother and sister, like friends back then," explained Mamie, "and it added a unique dimension to the mother-son bond we would forge over the years ahead."[34]

In October 1942, young Emmett took his first trip to Mississippi, accompanying Alma to the town of Money in Leflore County. There she tended to her sister, Elizabeth Wright, as Elizabeth gave birth to her ninth child.[35] They had already returned to Illinois when, a month later, Louis suddenly showed up on Mamie's doorstep, unannounced, wearing his military uniform. Despite their troubled past, the Tills had been corresponding prior to this and had decided to reconcile. During this time together, Louis finally began to bond with his son.[36]

The visit came to a halt after the army discovered that Louis had gone AWOL. Military police came to the house, took him away, and sent him to the stockades. Apparently, he never quite learned from this experience. In less than a year after beginning his stint serving overseas on January 14, 1943, he received two more AWOL convictions. In August 1943, he went missing for five-and-a-half hours, and the following December he went absent from his base "without a pass." The brief reunion of the Till family in Argo marked the last attempt of Mamie and Louis to start anew.[37]

In 1943, Mamie began working for the federal government, and for the next few years Louis sent money home regularly. In addition to his family support, he forwarded funds from his boxing and gambling winnings. Mamie turned it all over to Alma for safekeeping, and over time, it grew into a sizable savings account. Mamie's stepfather, Tom Gaines, died in August 1944, and for a time, Mamie had Alma all to herself.[38]

During the summer of 1945, however, Mamie learned that the money she had been receiving from Louis had come to an end. On July 13, she received a telegram from the Department of Defense informing her that her husband had been executed in Italy eleven days earlier for "willful misconduct." Mamie, so overcome with shock when reading this news, fainted. There was no other explanation in the telegram, and none in the letter she received a few days later from a chaplain in Italy.[39]

Louis's untimely death meant that Emmett would never know his father, nor would he ever learn why Louis had been executed. For a time, Mamie knew few of the details either, and just when she learned them is unclear. In 1948, she hired lawyer and family friend Joseph Tobias to write the Department of the Army and inquire about her rights as a widow. The army told Tobias that in cases of willful misconduct, next of kin are not entitled to benefits. She did receive a Social Security stipend of $11 per month for herself, while Emmett received $16. Mamie said that she received this amount until she married again in 1950, at which time Emmett's benefit increased to $38.40.[40] Alma continued the mothering role she had played toward Emmett since his birth, and with Louis's death, promised Mamie that she would help her support her grandson until he turned eighteen.[41] Not long after Louis died, Alma's sister, Elizabeth, came to visit from Mississippi, and when she returned to the South, Alma accompanied her, taking Emmett along. This was the boy's second trip to the South.[42] Perhaps Mamie needed time alone to contemplate her future as a widow.

Mamie maintained that she never received a "satisfactory answer" pertaining to the charges against Louis until the story later went public in 1955. However, army records indicate that in 1948, officials did furnish Tobias with a copy of the court-martial record of trial.[43] These documents would have told Tobias that Louis had been charged with raping two women and killing a third in June 1944 while stationed in Italy.[44] Although it is possible that Tobias did not share the details with Mamie, that is highly unlikely. Therefore, she would have known the reasons for Louis's execution directly from the army by 1948.

It is almost certain that she knew even sooner than that, however. On August 19, 1946, just over a year after Louis's death, Mamie, then twenty-four, married one of Louis's army buddies, twenty-eight-year-old Lemorse Mallory.[45] Very little is known about this marriage, which ended in divorce sometime between 1948 and 1951; Mamie never mentioned it publicly, nor has anyone else for that matter. It would have been odd that her Social Security benefits did not end until she married again in 1950 (this would have been her third marriage) because they should have ceased just after she married Mallory.[46]

Mallory, like Mamie, was from Argo. He entered the army on the same day as Louis Till in 1942, and both men served in the 177th Port Company and were stationed in North Africa and Italy together. The company was made up primarily of Chicago blacks. Mallory was discharged on April 4, 1945, just two months after Louis's trial.[47] Mallory and others in the company may not have learned about the charges officially, but they did hear rumors. In fact, Mallory talked freely to Till family members about Louis's case and told them that he believed there was another side to the story.[48] Because Mallory knew of the allegations against Louis, it is inconceivable that he would not have told Mamie. Mamie's silence is understandable, as nothing regarding Louis's conduct was relevant after Mamie was later thrust into the public eye. However, her silence would only help make Louis's story an embarrassing national headline once it finally leaked out. But that was still a decade away.

Soon after Louis was executed, his personal belongings arrived at Mamie's home in Argo. Among them was a ring, purchased in Casablanca, engraved with his initials, "LT," and the date "MAY 1943." It was the one item of Louis's that Mamie could set aside and one day give to Emmett.

In the fall of 1946, shortly after Mamie and Lemorse married, Emmett started kindergarten at Argo School (later renamed Wharton School), located just across the street from the Mallory home. Although he made friends there, it was the arrival of the Parker family from Money, Mississippi, in early 1947 that brought Emmett his greatest joy. Hallie Mae Parker (Alma's niece); her husband, Wheeler; and their three children moved into the home next door. Alma's brother, Crosby Smith, had vacated the house a few years earlier when he moved back to Mississippi after separating from his wife.[49] Wheeler Jr. soon became Emmett's best friend. Young Wheeler, who was two years older than Emmett, had attended a one-room schoolhouse in Money and now had to adjust to life in the big city. Part of that adjustment meant catching up scholastically. To do so, his mother required that he repeat the first grade.[50]

The boys were inseparable and often at play with Wheeler's two brothers or other children in the neighborhood. Alma sometimes walked with them two miles down the railroad tracks and took them fishing in the Des Plaines River. On one of those outings after Emmett caught a fish, he dipped it back into the water to clean it, only to have it wiggle out of his hands and swim away. Despite losing his hard-earned catch, Emmett simply laughed.[51]

Shortly before Emmett began the first grade in 1947, he started exhibiting lethargic behavior, especially at night. Within a few days, after Mamie and Alma noticed his temperature rising, they began using home remedies in an attempt to nurse him out of the mysterious ailment. When that failed to work, they called a doctor, who made a house call and diagnosed Emmett with polio. Mamie felt sick inside after hearing the news, and Alma very nearly fainted. "Polio was the worst thing that could happen to you back then," said Mamie. "It didn't kill you, but it could take your life away from you just the same."[52]

The doctor advised Mamie to take Emmett to the hospital immediately. This proved nearly impossible because no one would lend her their car for fear of contracting the disease themselves. She was even turned down by an ambulance, but eventually got a ride to the Contagious Disease Center in a police car.[53] Emmett spent the next two weeks there, and once released, was quarantined at home. No one else was allowed in the house, and Alma sat with him constantly while Mamie went to work. Lemorse was probably helpful during this trying time also. Alma was quite fond of her son-in-law, and referred to him proudly as "Sergeant Mallory." He also won the affection of several of Emmett's cousins, who still refer to him as their "favorite husband."[54]

Thankfully, Emmett showed no signs of brain damage or any major problems with his limbs. Finally, on one of his visits, the doctor released Emmett from quarantine and declared him well. The whole ordeal lasted about thirty days. "He had beaten it," said Mamie, who, with Alma, had spent the month praying for Emmett's recovery. "He was up and running again and practically tore a hole in the screen to get out."[55]

Although Emmett's bout with polio could have been worse, it did have a lasting effect upon him in the form of a speech impediment. "When he got excited or nervous, it was particularly bad. Nobody could understand him but Mama and me," explained Mamie.[56] Emmett would later take speech therapy classes, which helped some, and the doctors said he would eventually outgrow the defect. His ankles remained weakened as well, and he began wearing a special shoe for support. The episode brought about a determination within Alma never to have to beg for a ride or face humiliation again should another emergency arise. She was so determined, in fact, that she bought a 1941 Oldsmobile.[57]

Other childhood illnesses followed over the next several years. "He was sick a lot of the time," Mamie recalled, "and he was always catching everything that came around. Measles, mumps, everything, keeping him out of school for days at a time."[58] Yet during his childhood in Argo, Emmett developed the personality for which family and friends would always remember him. Wheeler Parker described his cousin as "outgoing," a "prankster," and always "in the middle of everything" from the time they became neighbors when Emmett was only five years old. People still living in Argo refer to Emmett lovingly as the "bad boy."[59]

Around the time Emmett contracted polio, or shortly thereafter, Mamie began working at the Army Signal Corps but soon took a job with the Veteran's Administration. She became focused on saving money for Emmett's college education, but her work was interrupted for several weeks after she underwent surgery for appendicitis. In 1948, she started a new job as a typist for the Social Security Administration.[60] Things changed for Mamie also in June 1949, when Alma married her third husband, Henry Spearman, and moved twelve miles away to his home in Chicago. Mamie, who may still have been married to Lemorse at this point, stayed behind at the house in Argo. There were other relatives nearby, but life would be different for the Mallorys, this being the first time Mamie had lived any distance from her mother.[61]

Around 1950, Emmett took his third trip to Money, Mississippi, this time with a great aunt, Mamie Hall. At nine, Emmett had no idea that black boys in the South lived by a different set of rules than did those who lived in Chicago, as his actions on this trip demonstrated. When a white man on the plantation asked Emmett for the hammer he was using, Emmett simply told him to get a different one from a nearby shelf.[62] Emmett also got into a fight on this trip, which happened after another boy held his head under water while they were playing in a river. Emmett developed an ear infection as a result, saw a doctor, and was prescribed medicine. Even today, his cousin Simeon Wright remembers vividly the pain Emmett endured.[63]

Mamie and Lemorse separated sometime between 1948 and 1951, putting Emmett in need of a father figure once again. Mamie wanted romance as well, but she found no prospects in Argo. A cousin convinced her that Detroit would be her answer for love and that there she could probably find a man with a good job in the automobile industry. Mamie's father, Nash Carthan—who now went by the name of John—also lived in Detroit, and the move became an opportunity to rebuild their relationship. Although they had recently established some contact, they had not seen each other in years, and John had never met his grandson. John was happy to have them come, and Mamie enthusiastically made arrangements to leave Argo.[64] In 1957, several years after his divorce from Mamie, Lemorse married the woman who had occupied the flat downstairs in the house on Sixty-Fourth Street.[65]

Mamie and Emmett moved in temporarily with John and his wife, Annie, or "A.D." as she was known, and Mamie started working as a typist at the Ft. Wayne Induction Center. The job kept her working long hours, sometimes seven days a week, but John bonded with Emmett and became a caring father to Mamie, something Mamie had longed for. A.D. soon began to resent the inconveniences of having a full house, however, and to appease his wife, John arranged for his daughter and grandson to move in with a family he knew by the name of Harris. The Harrises welcomed them both and doted over Emmett, making the stay in Detroit more tolerable.[66]

Mamie did not forget her mission of finding a man, and soon a cousin introduced her to a friend named Pink Bradley, a twenty-seven-year-old World War II veteran who hailed from Arkansas. He worked for Chrysler, was doing well, and he and Mamie soon began dating. He got along well with Emmett, but Emmett became increasingly unhappy in Detroit and began to miss his friends and family back home. Reluctantly, Mamie allowed him to move back to Argo, where he stayed with his uncle Kid and aunt Marie, next door to the old house on Sixty-Fourth Street. Mamie saw Emmett's move as temporary, and planned to bring him back to Detroit as soon as she found a place of her own.[67]

Meanwhile, her relationship with Pink became serious, and that longing for romance got the best of her. Indeed, she was so flattered by the attention that she easily overlooked all of the warning signs that should have been clear. They were married on May 5, 1951, after dating only a few months. Alma took Emmett to Detroit for the wedding, and he stayed behind briefly. It was not long, however, before he decided to return to Argo once again.[68]

The honeymoon ended quickly with Mamie's third marriage. Pink lost his job soon after the wedding and was in no hurry to find a new one. Mamie took a train back to Chicago to visit Emmett once a month, where she discovered that her son was getting used to a life without her. In November, Alma bought a two-flat home on South St. Lawrence Street in Chicago, and she offered the upstairs apartment to Mamie. She accepted, and the Bradleys left Detroit and moved to Chicago that same month. Mamie had just purchased her first car, a 1947 Plymouth, which the family drove to their new home 300 miles away. Once settled, Mamie found work at the Social Security Administration, and Pink was hired at Corn Products.[69] Emmett, now in fifth grade, began attending James McCosh Elementary. The school, named after a nineteenth-century Princeton University president, had once been equally divided racially, but by 1951 consisted exclusively of 1,600 black pupils and a racially mixed faculty.[70] Although Emmett was no longer in his old Argo neighborhood, the new house in Chicago was in closer proximity to Alma, something that both Mamie and Emmett were happy about.

Pink's relationship with Emmett was good, but they did not become close in the way Mamie had hoped. Although Pink settled in well in Chicago with his wife and stepson, he could barely wait for the weekends, when he would take Mamie's car to visit his friends and family in Detroit. The Bradleys managed to stay together for about a year and a half after the move. Whatever problems they had, they escalated after Mamie overheard Pink making a date with another woman. When he left the house that night, Mamie threw his belongings on the front lawn and changed the locks.[71] They separated permanently in August 1953. For Mamie, this quest to provide Emmett with a new father ended only in heartbreak. "After that it was Bo and me," she said. "Disappointed in my marriage, I intently set myself to make Bo the kind of man every mother wants her son to be."[72]

Over the next few years, Emmett increasingly demonstrated his loyalty to his mother in return. One night that he did so was both dramatic and disturbing. Pink came by the house soon after separating from Mamie, and Emmett, sick with the flu, heard Pink's voice as he approached his room. Emmett, holding a butcher knife, met Pink at the doorway and threatened to stab him unless he left. Mamie stepped in, escorted Pink out of the house, and scolded Emmett for the dangerous thing he had just done. She saw some significance to the episode, however, as she and Emmett grew closer as a result. They even developed a partnership in running the household.[73] Despite this, they had their moments of conflict. When they fought, one of them would usually call Alma to intervene, and she would scold whomever she thought was to blame. "Mama kept us both in check," admitted Mamie.[74]

Mamie eventually left the Social Security Administration and took a better job with the US Air Force, where she had charge of confidential files.[75] Also, love entered her life again, and this time she found what she had always longed for. In 1953, while getting a manicure in a South Side salon, she met a barber named Gene Mobley. Mamie returned to the shop each month for a nail appointment, and after a year or so, Gene finally asked her to dinner. She accepted, only because Emmett was away visiting family, and she did not feel like cooking. After this first date, they saw each other more frequently, and the relationship blossomed.[76] Emmett, then twelve, also developed a close bond with Gene. If Gene asked him to do something or to run an errand, Emmett always came through and left a note for Gene to verify that the project had been completed. Gene had two daughters of his own, and, like Mamie, was separated from his spouse.[77]

On July 25, 1954, Emmett turned thirteen. Five months later, Christmas proved to be the most memorable one the family had ever celebrated. Emmett received a new suit from Mamie and a hat, tie, and coat from Gene, and Mamie hosted a large Christmas dinner for her extended family.[78] She did not own a camera, but a coworker came over to Mamie's house two days later to take some family photos. Most of the images of Emmett Till that the public has seen were taken on that occasion: Emmett in his new suit, a close-up of him in his new wide-brimmed hat, one of him leaning against the family television, and a portrait of him seated with Mamie.[79] Added to all the festivities was the fact that Gene Mobley was now a serious love in Mamie's life.

Not long after the new year got under way, the Christmas bills started coming in. Mamie, whose job rarely provided her with the time or energy to run errands, reluctantly allowed Emmett to take the streetcar into the city, go to the stores, and pay the creditors himself. She returned home that night to see a stack of bills, each stamped "paid," and the leftover change placed next to them. Emmett also left a note explaining that he had taken care of everything.[80] Perhaps it was this side of Emmett that allowed Mamie to sum him up succinctly four decades later. No doubt speaking with a mother's bias, but also after years of interaction with hundreds of children, she said that "to me, Emmett was very ordinary. But as I look at today's youth, I realize that Emmett was very extraordinary."[81]

It would be natural for Mamie to promote and even exaggerate her son's most admirable qualities as she later tried to memorialize him. Shortly after

Emmett turned fourteen in July 1955, others who knew him described him in a variety of ways. He stood between five feet three inches and five feet four inches tall, and, at 150 pounds, was overweight.[82] He had just finished eighth grade at McCosh School, and his friends saw him as a prankster—independent, mischievous, and always the center of attention. To his elders, he was helpful and well mannered. At school, Emmett showed talent in art, science, and spelling, but he enjoyed school mainly for social reasons.[83] His principal, Curtis Melnick, one of several white faculty members at McCosh, said that Emmett was never in trouble and that academically he was "average."[84]

Emmett also loved baseball, and although he was a little too slow for his teammates' liking, he could not resist the temptation to play, even when he knew better. On one occasion Mamie sent him to the store to buy bread, but when he passed a sandlot game on the way home, he set down the bread and started to play. When he failed to return home, Mamie went out looking for him. When she found him, "I whipped him all the way home, and he never said a word."[85] Eva Johnson, a neighbor, witnessed Emmett facing a similar temptation to play when he was supposed to be painting the garage. "He'd paint a while and then run over to [the playground] and play ball a while and then run back to painting. He surely wanted to be painting when his Mama showed up from work."[86]

Emmett was helpful around the house, and even did the laundry and cooking in exchange for Mamie being their provider. He sometimes forgot to do his morning chores, however, and left for school expecting Mamie to do them. She always refused, except when Emmett forgot to feed his dog, Mike. When that happened, Emmett would leave a note where Mamie would be sure to see it. "Mama feed Mike. He's hungry. Poor dog."[87]

Like most kids, Emmett thought about his future, and he talked about becoming a motorcycle cop or a professional baseball player. He had dreams of building his grandmother a new church and even talked of joining the air force after he heard that a boy could sign up at sixteen with a parent's permission.[88]

Religion played a major role in his life, as it did with Alma and Mamie. After the move to Chicago in 1951, Mamie and Emmett resumed their affiliation with the Argo Church of God in Christ, a church Alma had helped found in 1926. Mamie could not always attend because she worked Sundays, but Emmett would go each week, making the hour-long ride on the Sixty-Third Street bus by himself. One Sunday while Emmett was on his way home from his Sunday meetings, he became engaged in conversation and prayer with Bennie Goodwin, son of the church's pastor. It was on this occasion that Emmett found Christ.[89] Even so, he did not appear particularly religious to his friends. As children, "you *had* to go to Church," insisted Wheeler Parker. "That was *every* Sunday."[90]

Religious or not, Emmett was still a teenage boy, and sometimes he could be *all* boy. He loved attention but would get upset when he did not get his own way. "He was kind of a tough guy," said childhood friend Lindsey Hill. "We played marbles together. If he lost, he took all the marbles. I guess you could call him the neighborhood bully. He was bigger than most of us." To others, such as Parker, that description is inaccurate. "No, I would never call him a bully, just a prankster, [who] loved to have fun." Simeon Wright said that Emmett took his pranks so far as to pull the fire alarm at school.[91] He also loved jokes, and would pay playmate Donny Lee Taylor to tell them. Emmett gave Taylor the nickname "T. Jones" after a character in one of Taylor's stories. It is a name Taylor has retained ever since. Parker said that Emmett's outgoing personality made him a "natural-born leader."[92]

Emmett never had a girlfriend, but at age eleven, he went on his first date. He confidently rode the streetcar, picked up the girl, and took her to a movie, although he made her buy her own ticket.[93] Yet in general Emmett showed a shy, less-confident side of himself around girls. "When it came to talking to me, I don't remember him being as forward as some of the other boys," said Phyllis Hambrick, another friend. "He used to come around, not to sit on the porch but more to stand at the end of the sidewalk and talk." Emmett was ridiculed for both his stutter and his weight. "He was a quiet person. I think his stuttering was one of the things that made him shy."[94]

In late August 1955, Mamie's uncle Moses, or "Mose," Wright visited Chicago from his home in Money, Mississippi, to attend the funeral of his daughter Willie Mae's father-in-law. While staying with Willie Mae, Wright, a preacher and sharecropper, talked about country life in Mississippi, fishing, and all of the things young boys like to do outdoors. He invited his grandsons Wheeler Parker and Curtis Jones to go back with him. Mose and Wheeler planned to take the train together, and Curtis would go down the following week. Emmett had already been pressuring Mamie to let him visit the South that summer after he learned that some other friends were heading there. But now that Wheeler was going, a trip to the South was all he could think about.[95]

Mamie granted her son a two-week visit to Mississippi. "I just knew that he was a normal well-adjusted child and that's why I thought that I could let him go," she explained. Yet she still needed peace of mind and admonished Wright to use caution. "When you let the boys go to town, please go with them. Take the car keys. If you get six teenagers together, anything can happen."[96] After Wright accepted responsibility for the boys, Mamie felt at ease. "It was perfectly all right with me to let Bo go in his care because I felt he would be in good hands." Once plans were finalized, Emmett had one week to prepare for his vacation.[97]

Preparation for the trip included lecturing the boys about southern customs. They had to learn about segregation and the laws that kept blacks as second-class citizens. Wheeler received his talk from his parents, and Mamie schooled her own son.[98] Emmett, with his independent and fun-loving ways, had to understand that his personality would not be appreciated or even tolerated by whites in Mississippi. Mamie did not pull any punches and told him that should anything happen down there, "Even though you think you're perfectly within your right, for goodness sake take low. If necessary, get on your knees and beg apologies. Don't cross anybody down there because Mississippi is not like Chicago." For just two weeks, Emmett would need to see the world differently from the way he always had. "No matter how much it seems that you have the right, just forget your rights while you're in Mississippi."[99]

With the trip now a reality, Emmett and Mamie went shopping. Emmett bought new clothes, shoes, and a wallet. While searching through his jewelry box for some cufflinks, he noticed the signet ring that had once belonged to his father. Emmett had not worn it much except when he was younger, and back then, he had to use scotch tape or string to make it snug. As he tried it on now, he discovered that it fit perfectly. "Gee, you are getting to be quite a grown man," Mamie proudly acknowledged. Emmett decided to wear it to Mississippi.[100] Before he left, probably because she too was going on vacation, Mamie gave Emmett's dog, Mike, to the pound.[101]

Mose Wright and Wheeler Parker planned to leave together from the Central Street Station on Saturday morning, August 20. Mamie and a friend, Mary Lee, who was visiting from St. Louis, were going to drop off Emmett there in time to meet up with Parker, Wright, and a female cousin who was heading back to Mississippi on the same train. That morning, however, Mamie and Emmett were running behind schedule. Because they lived closer to the Englewood Station at Sixty-Third and Woodlawn, Mamie decided to board Emmett there instead. Still, they were running late, and once they arrived, Mamie delayed things further by having to stop to buy Emmett's ticket.[102] Wright and Parker, who had boarded at the previous stop, were getting nervous, but were soon relieved when Emmett finally came aboard. "If he'd been five minutes later," noted Wright, "he'd have missed it."[103]

Years later, Mamie spoke of what she said were her final moments with Emmett at the station, and one might suspect that her recollections may well have been shaped by the significance of the events that followed. With no time to spare, Emmett ran up the steps to board the train, with seemingly little thought about his mother, who was still standing at the platform.

"Bo. You didn't kiss me good-bye," she yelled. "How do I know I'll ever see you again?"

Slightly embarrassed, Emmett turned around, went back, and gave her a kiss. As an afterthought, he took off his watch and left it with her, but kept the ring. With that, he was off, barely in time to catch the train. Mamie watched until the train left the station, and once it was out of sight, Mamie and Mary Lee left too.[104] Later that day, Mamie changed her mind about Mike, went to the dog pound, and picked him up. She wanted to surprise Emmett later.[105]

Nobody paid any attention when Emmett boarded the train that day, other than Mamie and Mary Lee. Nobody within the hustle and bustle at the platform had any idea that in addition to the countless trains that had carried blacks north to a new level of freedom since World War I, this one train, heading south, would help play a similar yet more dramatic role in that continued process. Mamie Bradley left the station quietly, unnoticed that day; however, when she went to the Central Street station two weeks later to pick up her son, she was met by a crowd and the media. Americans from around the country, including leaders from the president of the United States on down, knew her name and that of Emmett Louis Till. Yet Emmett would be oblivious to it all. He was returning as a mutilated corpse, the victim of a hate crime. His grief-stricken mother was there to retrieve what was left of him. His murder had become national news, and it would soon make headlines internationally.

That is getting ahead in the story, however. The events that turned this tale into one of the South's most infamous tragedies began shortly after Emmett Till, Wheeler Parker, and Mose Wright arrived at what was called the most southern place on earth—the Mississippi Delta.

2

Mississippi Welcomes Emmett Till

It was an all-day journey on the Illinois Central Railroad for Mose Wright, Wheeler Parker Jr., and Emmett Till before the train arrived at its stop in Winona, Mississippi. Not surprisingly, Wright had a difficult time keeping Emmett in his seat during the 650-mile trip. "He kept telling him to 'sit down' and was trying to make him behave," remembers Parker. "He was all over the place."[1] Somehow during this rambunctious behavior, Emmett managed to lose his shoes, and once he arrived in Mississippi, he had to borrow a pair from a cousin.[2] When the City of New Orleans arrived at the station in the late afternoon, Maurice, Mose Wright's sixteen-year-old son, was waiting with the family car. Mose and the three boys then headed off to Money, a rural, whistle-stop town in Leflore County, named after the late US senator Hernando De Soto Money.[3]

Although he had been to Mississippi three times before, Emmett still knew little about life in the Magnolia State. However, it was very familiar to Mose Wright, who had lived his entire life in the region. For nearly forty years he had worked on the 150-acre plantation owned by Grover Cleveland Frederick, namesake of the US president serving when Frederick was born in 1885. Around 1946, Wright moved to a six-room house on the Frederick plantation, located off a gravel road three miles east of town. The Wrights shared this home briefly with Greene and Gertrude Saffold and their seven children, but the Saffolds left after a few weeks and moved to Stockton, California.[4]

Money sits deep within the Mississippi Delta, the state's northwest region, known for its fertile soil and abundant cotton harvests. The Delta includes all or part of seventeen of the state's eighty-two counties. The area was (and still is) primarily rural, but cities like Greenwood, Clarksdale, and Greenville were welcome respites on the weekends. In 1955, cotton and the field hands who produced the crops gave Money its lifeblood, and the town managed to sustain a population of around 400.

Mose Wright, a small man at five feet three inches, found spiritual strength through his love of God and was strong physically after decades of working cotton. By sharecropper standards, he was also comfortable. He owned a car, an electric refrigerator, and a new washing machine. He maintained an adequate garden and kept several chickens, ten hogs, and three dogs. He even held a checking account in Greenwood at the Bank of Commerce. At the time of Emmett's arrival, Wright's cotton had just become ready to harvest, and he expected to pick as many as thirty bales off his twenty-five-acre share. At $160 to $175 per bale, Wright would clear around $1,000 after settling up his expenses and splitting half of the profits with Frederick. White neighbors described Wright, an ordained minister in the Church of God in Christ, as "a cut above" other blacks in the community because of the articulate way he expressed himself.[5]

Moses Wright was born to William and Ann Safford Wright in Durant, Holmes County, less than fifty miles from Money. His mother died when Mose was only a small boy, and his father went on to raise six children alone.[6] Wright was not always sure about the year of his birth. Discrepancies about age were not uncommon at the time, especially among those raised in rural areas. He stated on his World War I draft registration in 1917 that he did not know his exact birth date, but believed he was then twenty-seven years old. If he was right, then his birth would have occurred around 1890. In 1930, he said he was then forty, which also indicated a birth year of 1890. By the summer of 1955, however, he had come to believe that he was born in 1891. The 1900 US Census lists his birth as April 1892, and when that record became available after 1970, he came to accept this date himself.[7] If correct, this meant that in August 1955, he was sixty-three, not sixty-four as he told reporters a week after returning from Chicago.

On December 16, 1911, the Reverend B. A. Woods married Mose Wright and Lucinda Larry in Holmes County. Wright affirmed by applying for marriage that he was at least twenty-one.[8] He may have believed he was within the legal age for males to marry, but he, like his bride, was probably only nineteen. During their marriage, Lucinda, or Linda as she was known, bore four children before her death in the early 1920s.[9]

Under the provisions of the Selective Service Act of 1917, Mose registered for the draft on August 30 of that year. Once selected for military service, however, he refused to serve on the grounds of conscientious objection. After his defiance landed him in jail for thirty days, news spread throughout the region.[10]

In the 1920s, Wright began leasing land on the Frederick plantation and was working as an itinerant preacher when he married Elizabeth Smith around 1925.[11] The sister of Alma Spearman, Emmett Till's grandmother, Elizabeth, or "Lizzie," bore nine children herself, with eight living to maturity. Through his two marriages, Mose Wright had a dozen living children ranging from twelve to forty-two years of age in 1955. Only the three youngest boys,

Maurice, Robert, and Simeon, still lived at home.[12] For several years Wright led a small congregation at the East Money Church of God in Christ, but stopped preaching in 1949.[13]

The same year that Mose and Lucinda were married, another family—a white one—got its start in nearby Tallahatchie County. On February 7, 1911, William Leslie Milam married Eula Lee Morgan in Charleston.[14] Essley, as he was called, became a farmer. His father, David, had moved to Tallahatchie County from Tennessee, married Adelia Bryan, and raised five children, Essley being the youngest.[15] Although Essley and Eula affirmed by their signatures that they had reached the legal age to marry, they were both, in fact, underage. Essley was just eighteen and Eula fifteen when they wed.[16]

Between 1915 and 1925, Eula bore five sons before Essley died of pneumonia in 1927, an illness brought on after he broke several bones during a gravel pit accident. The pit caved in on him and others working for the Tallahatchie highways; another man died while two others were injured in the accident.[17] A year later, on October 31, 1928, Essley's thirty-three-year-old widow married eighteen-year-old Henry Bryant, and by 1935 Eula had given birth to six more children. Henry, an abusive alcoholic, left Eula in 1947, and the couple avoided any further contact until Eula filed for divorce in 1949. Throughout 1955 and 1956, she used the courts to force Henry to pay the required $15 monthly support for their one minor child, an obligation he had failed to keep on his own.[18]

The large Milam-Bryant clan eventually owned general stores throughout the Mississippi Delta. By August 1955, there was one in Money, owned by son Roy Bryant; Eula ran one in Sharkey County; Henry kept his own store at Curtis Station, eighty miles north of Money in Panola County; and daughter Mary Louise and her husband, Melvin Campbell, owned a grocery in Minter City, Leflore County. Another son, John Milam, known as J. W., had operated his own store in Glendora, Tallahatchie County, but it burned down the year before. Other family stores were operating in Swan Lake, Itta Bena, and Ruleville.[19]

Both the Wright and Milam-Bryant families were large, but here the similarities end—other than the fact that members in each family knew very well their privileges or their place in society. Such rights or limitations were all dependent upon race, and this concept was well ingrained in Mississippians from birth. By quietly accepting their second-class status in southern society and obeying the rules of etiquette forced upon them, African Americans *could* survive peacefully in their communities. Whites often took on a paternalistic role in their relationships to blacks, but this did not imply a belief among Caucasians that the two races were equal.[20]

Emmett Till's visit to the Mississippi Delta would forever link these two families together in the history books of American race relations, despite the fact that they had known little, if any, interaction previously. His timing in coming to the Delta could hardly have been worse. He arrived in Mississippi just before voters decided the 1955 gubernatorial race. All five candidates who sought the governor's office over the course of the election had based their platform on the preservation of segregation.[21] This was all in response to the recent Supreme Court decision in *Brown v. Board of Education of Topeka, Kansas*, which had ruled in May 1954 that segregation in public schools was unconstitutional.[22]

The white backlash to *Brown* was immediate, and dozens of chapters of Citizens' Councils arose all across the state. Their aim was to overturn *Brown* and maintain segregation forever.[23] Lynchings, which had long plagued Mississippi and the South in general, returned after a four-year hiatus, and those seeking any semblance of black equality quickly became targets.[24] On May 7, 1955, fifty-one-year-old Rev. George W. Lee, active in the NAACP and black voter registration in Belzoni, Humphreys County, was shot in the face as he drove home from a dry cleaner's shop at around midnight. His assailant was never caught.[25]

Three months later, on August 13, 1955, World War I veteran Lamar Smith, sixty-three, was shot dead on the courthouse steps in Brookhaven, Lincoln County, as he passed out voting literature to black citizens. His murder occurred in front of witnesses in broad daylight. Three men were arrested, but when witnesses refused to talk, a grand jury failed to indict.[26] Clearly, in the aftermath of *Brown*, racial tensions were on the rise and getting uglier.

After the first primary election on August 2, Mississippi's race for the governorship narrowed to two candidates. Paul B. Johnson and J. P. Coleman battled it out for the next three weeks, and on August 23, Coleman won.[27] "The five candidates for governor of Mississippi and the newspapers of the state had a field day this summer using the Negro, the C.I.O., the Supreme Court, the NAACP, Communists, intermarriage, and other topics as whipping boys in the election race," noted a September 1955 NAACP press release summarizing the campaign soon after the election. "Race hatred was whipped to fever pitch in the scramble for votes."[28]

Perhaps the most outspoken southerner to rail against *Brown* was Judge Tom P. Brady, who predicted dire consequences and a weakened white world as a result of desegregation. In his book, *Black Monday*, which appeared immediately after the Supreme Court decision, he predicted that "the fulminate which will discharge the blast will be the young negro schoolboy, or veteran, who has no conception of the difference between a mark and a fathom." Writing thirteen months before Emmett's trip to the Delta, Brady's words became eerily prophetic as he described how this explosion would occur: "The supercilious, glib young negro, who has sojourned in Chicago or New York, and who considers the council of his elders archaic, will perform an obscene act, or make an obscene remark, or a vile overture or assault upon some white girl."[29] Such was the climate and level of fear at the time Emmett Till went south from Chicago in August 1955.

Emmett likely did not hear about nor would he have cared about the heated issues that had turned the South against the Supreme Court of the United States. He would have noticed that Mississippi was nothing like Chicago, but for reasons other than race, and they no doubt appealed to him. Emmett loved the outdoors, and nothing in Chicago compared to the open space and inviting adventure of the Mississippi Delta. The fifteen-mile region around Money alone boasted several lakes and streams, all excellent for fishing.[30] Yet Emmett was still a city boy, unfamiliar with country living. The farm animals, most of which served to provide for the subsistence living the Wright family was accustomed to, became nothing less than pets to Emmett. "He would buy peanuts and feed them to the chickens, saying they were hungry," explained Mose Wright.[31]

After Emmett Till and Wheeler Parker arrived in Mississippi on Saturday afternoon, August 20, they spent most of the evening talking with their cousins, and even stayed home from church the following day. It was the last weekend before the cotton harvest began, and starting early Monday, everyone in the family, including Emmett, was to work in the fields. However, the weather was so hot that they only labored half of each day. "Daddy couldn't take the heat," recalled Simeon, "and he wasn't going to send us out in it." Emmett did not take to the cotton fields at all and spent most of the time around the house helping his aunt Elizabeth with her chores.[32]

After finishing their work in the fields, the boys spent the second half of their day playing together. Across the road, they swam in Lake Never Fail, competing about who could dive to the bottom. Those who claimed to go all the way had to prove it by bringing up handfuls of mud. Once they even raided a neighbor's watermelon patch.[33] One night out by the church, Maurice Wright and a neighbor boy hoped to create some mischief with Parker and a teenage girl by trying to coax the two of them into the car to "hook up." However, Maurice said that Emmett had his eye on the local eighteen-year-old.[34] Emmett showed off his own mischievous side sometime during the week by buying firecrackers and lighting them in the street, an unlawful act in the city limits.[35]

On August 23, J. P. Coleman won the Mississippi governorship by carrying sixty-four counties.[36] Emmett may have heard talk about the heated race and landslide victory, but he likely paid little attention. The next day, Wednesday, August 24, as Coleman's win was headline news throughout the state, Emmett, Parker, and the Wright boys once again picked cotton in the morning and early afternoon.[37] That evening, Maurice drove his parents to a service at the tiny East Money Church of God in Christ.[38] Because Maurice did not have a driver's license, the boys were supposed to venture out no farther than the country store nearby. Without permission, however, they decided to drive into Money, three miles away.[39] The group consisted of Emmett; brothers Maurice and Simeon Wright; Wheeler Parker; Roosevelt Crawford and his niece, Ruth; and Wheeler's cousin, Thelton "Pete" Parker.[40] Elizabeth had already warned her sons not to take Emmett into Money, knowing that locals would not appreciate his northern manners or fun-loving personality. Despite his mother's instructions, admitted Maurice later, "we went down [anyway]."[41]

The events that unfolded over a twenty-minute visit into Money that evening would shortly bring Emmett Till and those with him out of obscurity and into an international spotlight.[42] Exactly what transpired that evening, however, has been the subject of much debate, faulty memory, and even wishful thinking. Therefore, an examination of the sources is crucial in order to piece together the controversial story and set aside fact from fiction. The earliest accounts appeared in newspapers and were based on interviews with some of Emmett's cousins who were with him that night. Others came from statements made by Mose Wright and local law officers. Most were dictated or published within a few days of the incident. In some cases, witnesses talked to multiple journalists.

Wheeler Parker returned to Chicago on Monday, August 29, just five days after the youths took their trip into downtown Money.[43] After his arrival home, he talked to reporters from the *Chicago Daily Tribune*, the *Chicago American*, and two black weeklies, the *Chicago Defender* and *Jet* magazine. Parker told the *Chicago American* on September 1 that at 8:00 P.M. on Wednesday, August 24, the group drove into Money. The town's business district consisted of a few stores, a post office, and a cotton gin, all lined on one street. At first they tried to visit a café but discovered that it was closed. As they began to head home, Maurice noticed a checkers game in progress in front of the Bryant's Grocery and Meat Market and wanted to join in.[44]

Maurice parked the car between the store and the Ben Roy filling station to the south, and everyone walked over to the group already gathered outside the two-story brick building.[45] It was not unusual for local blacks to congregate in front of Bryant's, even though the store was owned by a white couple. In fact, Roy and Carolyn Bryant catered mainly to a black clientele—field workers who regularly purchased supplies and refreshments on credit.[46] Twenty-one-year-old Carolyn was working behind the counter that evening. In the back of the store, in the cramped living quarters, her sister-in-law, Juanita Milam, was tending to her two boys and the two belonging to the Bryants. Although Juanita later denied that she was there, circumstantial evidence suggests that she probably was.[47]

Wheeler Parker told the *Tribune* on August 30 about something that happened outside the store that set the events of the evening into motion. "One of the other boys told Emmett there was a pretty lady in the store and that he should go in and see her."[48] Parker does not say what, if anything, Emmett may have said to prompt this boy to tease Emmett this way, but a few months later, a reporter named William Bradford Huie, claiming to have interviewed Emmett's cousins, said that Emmett had been showing off a picture of a white girl and claimed that she was his girlfriend. This prompted someone present to dare Emmett to go inside the store and ask Bryant for a date.[49]

None of the witnesses who were interviewed in the days after the event mentioned anything about Emmett showing a photo, or that anyone had dared Till to say anything to Bryant. Roosevelt Crawford had been part of the group that drove to town and was standing with the others outside the store. His recollections agree with Huie's, although his first public statement about what happened came nearly fifty years later. He said that Emmett took a photograph of a white girl out of his wallet and that "several of the group" dared Emmett to say something to the woman inside the store.[50] There is no reason to necessarily doubt Crawford, but because his reminiscence is so late it is possible that his memory about the photo was shaped by what he eventually read in the Huie account. However, years after the incident, Mamie Bradley acknowledged that her son had possessed a photo of a white girl but insisted that it came with the wallet and was actually a picture of actress Heddy Lamar.[51]

Whether or not Emmett carried this photo, the argument that he boasted about relationships with white girls was independently strengthened just after the release of the Huie piece. A series of articles critical of Huie but sympathetic to Emmett Till appeared in the *California Eagle*, a black weekly, beginning in late January 1956. The reporter, using the pseudonym Amos Dixon, based his version of events on the investigation of civil rights activist Dr. T. R. M. Howard. Through his own questioning of the youth present that night, Howard learned that Emmett claimed outside the store to have gone to school with white girls and even dated them.[52]

Whatever the catalyst, there is no question that an unidentified boy urged Emmett to go inside the store to at least look at Carolyn Bryant, because three other reporters who independently spoke with Wheeler Parker in Chicago confirmed what Parker said to the *Tribune*, thus eliminating any chance that he was misquoted. In the September 1 *Chicago American*, reporter George Murray summarized his interview with Parker. After Maurice Wright began playing checkers in front of the store, "somebody mentioned the pretty storekeeper, Mrs. Bryant. Till entered the store to see if she was as pretty as they said."[53] Then, in the September 10 issue of the *Chicago Defender*, reporters

Mattie Smith Colin and Robert Elliott wrote, based on their interview with Parker, that "Bo had gone into the store at the urging of one of several companions to 'look at the pretty lady' behind the counter and to buy some bubble gum." This account added, "According to Parker's description of the incident at the store, Bo went in at the urging of an older boy."[54] Finally, in an interview published in *Jet*, Parker told reporters from that publication, "We'd gone into town Wednesday and were watching some boys playing checkers in front of the store. Somebody said there was 'a pretty lady' in the store and Bobo said he was going inside to buy some bubble gum."[55]

Before Emmett's curiosity drove him into the store, Maurice Wright warned him to be careful about what he said inside.[56] After he entered, Emmett briefly remained alone with Carolyn Bryant. The early reports are somewhat contradictory about what happened next, but this may simply be due to reporter error. Some versions suggest that Emmett acted out of line, but they are silent as to what he may have done. An account published on August 29 reports that Emmett began acting "rowdy" and was then taken out of the store.[57] Wheeler Parker was quoted within a week of the incident as saying, "I never went in the store [to check on Till]. But when I heard there was trouble, I sent one of the other boys in to get Emmett."[58]

Parker did not identify what this trouble was, neither does he name the boy who went in to remove his cousin, but one name did shortly surface. William Sorrels, writing for the *Memphis Commercial Appeal* twelve days after the incident, said the person who intervened was twenty-year-old Albert Johnson Jr., of nearby Schlater. Sorrels learned that Johnson entered the store, "grabbed Till by the shoulder and made him come out." This is the only time that Johnson's first name appears in any source, although Mose Wright said a few days later that "all the boys went along" to the Bryant store that night, "together with a Johnson boy from Slarghter [Schlater]." When asked about Johnson in 2007, Wheeler Parker could not recall if Johnson was there, but he remembered he was a local youth. Sorrels learned the name of the young man from Maurice Wright, which makes Johnson an intriguing yet elusive player in the events of the evening.[59]

Other accounts indicate that Parker sent someone in to remove Emmett, but that he did so in order to *avoid* trouble, not stop it. However, Parker was unclear on that point when talking to a different reporter: "After Emmett went in I became worried and I sent another boy to call him out."[60] Leflore County deputy sheriff John Cothran said that after Emmett entered the store, "one of the other boys was worried about him being in there, and went in to get him." The concern was that "Till would say 'yeah' and 'no' to [the woman] and not say 'ma'am.'"[61] Cothran's statement would indicate that the step to remove Emmett was a precautionary one.

T. R. M. Howard, whose previously mentioned investigation was reported in the *California Eagle*, provided details to another author, Olive Arnold Adams. Through interviews, Howard learned that Simeon Wright, one of those with Emmett Till that night, "went with Emmett to the door and waited outside the door while Emmett made the purchase and put the money, in the exact amount, on the counter."[62] If Simeon did not go inside yet saw the transaction, this would indicate that the front door remained open (although the screen doors would have remained shut), which makes sense because the weather was hot and the store would not have had air conditioning. Wright, however, has told his story publicly on numerous occasions and maintains that he did go inside to check on Emmett (yet he said he did so at the behest of his brother, Maurice, not Parker). "I went in right behind Till to make sure he didn't get out of line. I was waiting," he insists.[63] Wright clarified on other occasions that he entered the store after Till but did not do so immediately, estimating that Till may have been alone with Carolyn Bryant for about a minute. "What he said, if anything, before I came in I don't know."[64]

Carolyn Bryant's version about her moments alone with Emmett Till evolved until they painted a malicious and, from a southern white perspective, perverse picture of Till. Nine days after the incident, on September 2, she detailed a relatively mild account to attorneys:

> Wednesday Aug. 24 ^about 7:30 or 8 P.M. (dark)^ boy came to candy counter & I waited on him & when I went to take money he grabbed my hand & said ["]how about a date["] and I walked away from him and he said "what's the matter Baby can't you take it?["] He went out door and said "Goodbye" and I went out to car & got pistol and when I came back he whistled at me—this whistle while I was going after pistol—didn't do anything further after he saw pistol.

For reasons she could not determine, a "boy from outside came in—he went out with him—don't know whether he asked him to come out."[65]

Twenty days later when she testified in court, she again avoided calling Emmett Till by name but this time referred to him as a "negro man" who came into the store. This time, when she held out her hand for him to pay for his purchase, he grabbed it firmly before asking for the date. She jerked free, turned to go to the back of the store, but the man caught her by the cash register and placed his hands on her waist. "What's the matter, baby? Can't you take it? You needn't be afraid of me." She said he then bragged that he had been "with white women before." At that point, "this other nigger came in the store and got him by the arm . . . then he told him to come on and let's go."[66]

Many of the details of Carolyn Bryant's story were called into question immediately after she told them, even to those unaware that she had initially told her attorneys something different. While she was consistent with Maurice Wright's account to reporter Sorrels that another boy went into the store, grabbed Emmett, and escorted him out, no one present mentioned the aggressive actions that Carolyn Bryant attributed to Emmett in court. Admittedly, however, none of them would have been in the store to witness what did or did not happen anyway. But Leflore County sheriff George Smith spoke to the press a few days after the incident and noted only minor indiscretions. "The Bryants were said to have become offended when young Till waved to the woman and said 'goodbye' when he left the store," Smith reported.[67] Two days after that, Smith elaborated, saying that "Till made an ugly remark to Mrs. Bryant."[68] This was likely a reference to Till's asking Bryant for a date.

In 2004, however, Carolyn Bryant held to the embellished version of the story when talking to the FBI, saying that when Till touched her she kept screaming for Juanita Milam to help her. Yet in what is perhaps the most important development in Bryant's story, in 2010 she admitted to the historian Timothy B. Tyson that the forceful behavior that she had attributed to Till inside of the store was false and that she relayed a story concocted by Bryant family members and her attorneys.[69]

What happened next occurred outside in front of several witnesses. Maurice Wright echoed Sheriff Smith that as Emmett left the store, he waved and said "Good-bye" to the woman—not "Good-bye ma'am," which, minus the wave, would have gone unnoticed. Bryant then walked out of the store and toward a car. In that instant, Emmett blew "what some people call a wolf whistle."[70] Parker, in talking to *Jet* reporters, agreed with Maurice but said that Till whistled before Bryant went to her car: "After a while, we went in and got Bobo but he stopped in the doorway and whistled at the lady. She got angry and followed us out, then ran toward a car. Someone hollered, 'She's getting a gun' and we ran." Maurice confirmed the gun story as well.[71] To the *Chicago American*, Parker added one more detail: "After he whistled and the lady got mad, some of the local boys told us we'd better get out of town fast." Emmett and the others then jumped into the car and left.[72]

Simeon Wright, who shortly after talked with reporter Clark Porteous, echoed Maurice. Carolyn Bryant followed Emmett to the door; at that point, Emmett gave a "wolf whistle," which Simeon demonstrated for Porteous.[73] Wheeler Parker and Maurice Wright elaborated on this to other reporters as well. On September 1, Parker told a Chicago newsman about "the wolf call he [Emmett] whistled at a pretty . . . white lady in a store last Wednesday."[74] Maurice explained to William Sorrels that "I was outside and I heard him [Emmett] whistle at the lady (Mrs. Bryant). It was a wolf whistle. When he came out of the store I told him, 'Boy, you know better than that,' and he just laughed."[75]

Certainly, Emmett's conduct was consistent with the personality for which he was known. "He had a habit of whistling and hollering at girls," Mose Wright acknowledged, having observed his nephew's behavior for several days, "but he only did it for fun. He didn't mean any harm.... He didn't mean any harm not saying 'ma'am' and 'sir' to white folks."[76] Echoing what the others said, Deputy Sheriff Cothran told the *New York Post* that as Emmett left the store, he "said goodbye to Mrs. Bryant. Then, after he got outside, she saw him turn around in the direction of the store and give a whistle. She called it a wolf whistle."[77]

The local youth who witnessed this knew immediately that Emmett Till broke one of the oldest taboos in southern race relations. Emmett and his companions frantically fled the store and sped back toward the church. As the car drove east on Dark Ferry Road, the teens thought they were being pursued by two cars following closely behind. As they neared the church, they parked, jumped out, and hid in a field behind some trees. Simeon, however, remained in the car alone, hiding in the backseat. To everyone's relief, the cars were driven by blacks who passed on by. After Emmett and the others got back into the car, they sat and talked about the incident further.[78]

Sorting through these early sources, a probable scenario at the Bryant store emerges. On whole, those present said that Emmett Till's behavior involved more than just a whistle, but not much more. Clearly, as several black youths stood outside the store playing checkers or watching the game, Emmett boasted about dating white girls in Chicago and may have shown off a photo. Aware of the pretty woman inside the store, an unidentified "older boy" urged Emmett to go inside and look at her. That Parker did not identify the boy but only referred to him as "older" would indicate that he was not any of those who drove to the store with Emmett and that Parker did not really know him. Only one of those in the car, eighteen-year-old Thelton Parker, was older than Wheeler.[79]

Although Emmett's actions inside the store are not certain, they involved nothing more than him touching Carolyn Bryant's hand and asking for a date. In that case, Simeon Wright would have seen Carolyn pull her hand away from Emmett and alerted Parker that there was "trouble." Parker then sent another boy inside—probably Albert Johnson—to bring him out. If Emmett did ask Carolyn Bryant for a date, his actions were only meant as a prank for the benefit of those outside. What may have been a joke to Emmett, however, was not funny to Carolyn Bryant. Bryant followed Emmett to the door, and, once outside, Emmett waved and said "Good-bye," which prompted Bryant to go toward the car. At that moment, Emmett whistled.

Wheeler Parker said years later that in the hurry to flee the store, Maurice Wright dropped a burning cigarette on the floor of the car and refused to drive off until he found it. "Till was furious," Parker remembers. "He was stuttering, saying, 'let's go, let's go.'"[80] The group decided not to tell Mose Wright about the incident and hoped that it would simply blow over. The following day, however, Ruth Crawford assured the others that they "hadn't heard the end of it."[81]

Unfortunately, revisionist attempts to explain Emmett Till's encounter with Carolyn Bryant at the Bryant store and the motive for his whistle have trickled in for decades, and some have been popularized in documentaries and memoirs. This has only added confusion to the historical record, making it necessary to deal with them here.

The first appeared shortly after the incident. Although it was well known that Emmett Till's childhood bout with polio had left him with a stutter, the *Baltimore Afro-American*, a popular black weekly, reported in its September 10, 1955, edition that "the boy made a whistling sound in his effort to pronounce words. This sound, apparently, was misinterpreted by Mrs. Bryant, who thought he was giving her a 'wolf' whistle of admiration." The source for this interpretation, surprisingly, was Maurice Wright, who completely contradicted what he had told reporters earlier. Continuing on, the article insisted that Maurice "steadfastly denied that his cousin had either spoken insolently or whistled at Mrs. Bryant."[82]

There is no explanation for why Maurice suddenly changed his story and felt a need to sanitize Emmett Till's behavior. But it seemed to die quickly, as evidenced by what his father, Mose, summarized for a reporter a month later, which only backed up the original version, although a few of the details are out of sequence: "Simmy [Simeon] said after Bo bought the bubble gum from the lady he said goodbye." Bryant then went to get her gun from the car. "When she came back Bobo was standing there. Simmy said Bobo whistled twice. That's all was said and done. They called it a wolf whistle."[83]

Thirty years later, Mamie Bradley, who was not present to witness the incident, resurrected elements of Maurice Wright's revised story and added a few of her own. Emmett's whistle on this occasion was deliberate, she explained, but only because it helped him stop his stutter and pronounce his words.[84] Significantly, she did not espouse this idea early on, at least publicly. In fact, a month after Emmett's encounter with Carolyn Bryant, Mamie contradicted what Maurice Wright said and even what she would say later: "He had polio when he was in the first grade and although he overcame it, he had a bad speech defect and couldn't whistle at all. I often laughed when he tried and said I could whistle better than he could."[85] A lesser-known theory later came from Roosevelt Crawford, who said that Emmett indeed whistled outside the store, but that it was not directed toward Carolyn Bryant. Instead, it was aimed at a bad move someone made on the checker board.[86]

Wheeler Parker and Simeon Wright have always dismissed these alternate explanations not only because they also witnessed the wolf whistle but because they remember Emmett's reaction. "He knew he had done something wrong, because he begged us not to tell daddy," said Wright. Parker agrees. "Everyone knew a wrong had been committed."[87] In light of all of the many eyewitness accounts of Emmett Till's whistle as reported in August and September 1955, together with what Parker and Wright still vividly recall, it is clear that Mamie Bradley's and Roosevelt Crawford's explanations are without merit.

Ruth Crawford, also present that evening, said in 1979 that she never knew Emmett Till or anything about the story.[88] When interviewed again over twenty years later, however, she was more talkative. She said that on that August night in 1955, she was looking through a window at the Bryant store while Emmett was inside making his purchase. All Emmett did to offend Bryant was put his money in her hand instead of on the counter. Bryant then jerked her hand back. Crawford did not hear the whistle, but she acknowledges that others outside did.[89] Although Huie learned that the teenagers present were peering through the window to watch Till, Simeon Wright insists that Crawford's recollections are inaccurate because the counter was at the opposite end of the store and thus hidden from view. However, Carolyn Bryant's own description placed the candy counter on the south side, about one-third of the way into the store, and the cash register farther back.[90] This likely accounts for the discrepancy between what Ruth Crawford said she saw and what Simeon Wright remembers about the layout of the store.

The day after his encounter with Carolyn Bryant, Emmett wrote a letter to his mother, and if the contents are any indication, the trouble from the night before had already been forgotten. "I am having a fine time[.] will be home next week. please have my motor bike fixed for me," he instructed. He also promised to pay her back for the cost. Elizabeth Wright included a letter of her own in the envelope, written to her sister, Alma Spearman. "The boys is enjoying them selves fine and we are enjoying them," she wrote. As for Emmett: "He is certainly a nice kid. He is just as obedient as you want to see." Upon getting Emmett's letter, Mamie determined *not* to fix the motorbike, assuring herself that, for Emmett, who was probably either too careless or unskilled to ride it safely, it would be "certain suicide" for him if she repaired it. Alma was so pleased with her sister's description of Emmett that she proudly hung the letter on the refrigerator and said it could serve as his obituary. Sometime during that week, Mamie sent Emmett a letter of her own and gave him the good news that she had picked up Mike from the dog pound.[91]

Within a few days, Mose and Elizabeth learned about the trouble from Wednesday night. Elizabeth heard it directly from the boys. "Grandma knew about the 'incident' because we'd told her and not Grandpa, who would have gotten angry at us," said Wheeler Parker just after he returned to Chicago. Mose later said he heard about it from an "outsider" sometime before the weekend.[92] As the family picked cotton again on Thursday, Friday, and Saturday, however, they all forgot about it. At the end of the week, the boys received their payment, calculated at $2 for every hundred pounds picked. Emmett only earned $4, a reflection of his dislike for the fields. Wheeler Parker's earnings totaled around $8, and the more experienced Simeon Wright pocketed about $15.[93]

On Saturday, August 27, sixteen-year-old Curtis Jones, another grandson of Mose, arrived in town, having driven down from Chicago with an uncle. Like Till and Parker, he came to spend a portion of his summer vacation with the Wrights and was anxious to work in the cotton fields. Although he would later say that he had witnessed the store incident and even provided what he claimed were firsthand details, his story proved to be a fabrication.[94]

The day that Jones came to town, the boys went fishing, and Emmett, ever the prankster, threw a log into the water to create a loud splash. "That was a big fish just jump up over there," he yelled, just before he broke down laughing. Echoing Parker's description of their cousin, Jones said Emmett "loved to be what you call the center of attention."[95]

During a typical evening, the Wright family stayed home, relaxed, and listened to the radio.[96] On the weekends, however, they often went into Green-wood, and on this Saturday night, Mose, his three sons, the three boys from Chicago, and some of the Crawford children went into the city for an evening of fun. Maurice, Wheeler, and Emmett drove together, and Mose and the others rode with twenty-two-year-old John Crawford.[97] While Mose visited his own friends gathered at the railroad tracks, the boys walked the busy streets, gazed at the nightclubs, and looked with amazement at the large crowds that had gathered that night. John Crawford bought the boys some wine, and they also drank White Lightning and beer. Later, they broke away to visit a plantation party north of town.[98] For the Chicago boys, it was a nice break from the isolation of East Money. They left Greenwood after midnight and arrived back home around 1:00 A.M.[99]

While driving back to East Money in the late-night darkness, Maurice accidentally struck a dog. Those in the car saw a soft side to Emmett, who started crying and pleaded for Maurice to stop. Suddenly, Emmett was not the show-off or cocky prankster that everybody knew. This was the first time that they had even seen him cry.[100] Maurice kept driving, however, and moments after they arrived home, they all went to bed. The family had plans to visit Elizabeth's brother, Crosby Smith, in Sumner later that morning.[101]

By 2:00 A.M., all eight people in the Wright household were asleep. Simeon Wright and Emmett shared a bed, while Robert and Maurice Wright slept in another in the same room. Wheeler Parker and Curtis Jones were in the west room off the front porch. Mose and Elizabeth slept nearby in the east front room.[102]

Suddenly, Mose was awakened by a loud knock at the door and a voice calling out, "Preacher, Preacher." When Mose asked who was there, a man answered and identified himself as "Mr. Bryant." He said he wanted to talk to Wright and "the boy." Elizabeth, who by then knew of Wednesday's store incident, was also awakened. She realized immediately that the boy Bryant wanted was Emmett. She got up, went to Emmett's bedroom, and attempted to get him up and out the back door to hide in the cotton fields. "We knew they were out to mob the boy," she soon explained. "But they were already in the front door before I could shake him awake."[103]

When Mose Wright opened the door, he saw a large man in front, holding a pistol and a flashlight. Behind him was another man who said, "I'm Roy Bryant." Those were the last words Bryant spoke, and the other, larger man took over from there. Wright saw a third man outside behind the other two. "I think it might have been a colored man, but I didn't see his face. He didn't want me to see him," Wright said. To hide his identity, the man covered his face with his hands.[104]

The two men in front pushed their way into the house, leaving the third, shadowy figure outside. The man with the gun told Elizabeth to get back into bed and to "keep your yap shut." He asked Mose if he had two boys there from Chicago. When Wright acknowledged that he did, the man said he wanted the one who "did the talking at Money." The house was dark, except for the beam from the flashlight held by the larger intruder. He told Wright to turn on the lights, but all except one of the sockets were empty; the only bulb still in place was burned out.[105]

Wright did not know which room Emmett was in, so he led the men first to the room occupied by Parker and Jones. The loud voices had already awakened both boys, but Jones fell back to sleep almost immediately. Parker, however, was still awake when the men came into the room. When he saw the gun, he was certain that he was about to be killed. "I was literally shaking." Seeing that neither boy was the one the men wanted, Wright led them through the next room, which was vacant, then on to the room occupied by Emmett and the three Wright boys. The gunman told Wright, "If it is not the right boy, we are going to bring him back and put him in the bed."[106]

After Wright awakened Emmett, the large intruder spoke directly to the Chicago teen.

"Are you the one who did the smart talk up at Money?"

"Yeah," answered Emmett, still half asleep.

This angered the gunman. "You say 'Ya' again and I'll blow your head off."

The man ordered Emmett to get up and get dressed, which he did while sitting on the side of the bed. He put on a white T-shirt, charcoal gray pants, and black loafer shoes. Simeon Wright woke up as Emmett was getting dressed. He could not make out who anyone was in the room because the only light he could see came from the flashlight. Before the men led Emmett out of the room, the one in charge turned to Wright.

"How old are you?"

"Sixty-four," replied Wright.

"Well, if you know any of us here tonight, then you will never live to get to be sixty-five."[107]

Emmett showed no outward fear of the men or what might happen to him as they led him out of the room.

"This was my sister-in-law, and I'm not going to stand for it," the angry gunman shouted. Still, Emmett remained relaxed through the entire ordeal.[108]

As Wright, Emmett, and the two other men passed through the east bedroom, Elizabeth got back up. Once again, the gunman told her to "get back in bed, and I mean, I want to hear the springs." In a final attempt to spare Emmett of whatever fate the men had in mind, Mose begged them not to take the boy. He explained that because of Emmett's bout with polio, he did not "have good sense." (Wright later clarified to a reporter that he was referring to Till's speech impediment, and that his nephew possessed normal intelligence.)

"Just take him outside and whip him," he pleaded.

Elizabeth even offered to pay them money for the "damages." In each instance, the pleas were futile. Mose then asked the men where they were taking the boy.

"Nowhere if he's not the right one," replied the larger man.

The men then led Emmett outside to a vehicle parked between twenty and twenty-five feet from the front door. The third man who waited outside was no longer visible. While standing on the porch, Wright heard one of the men ask someone waiting if the boy was "the right one." A voice, which Wright said sounded like a woman's voice, answered that he was. That was all the men needed to hear before loading Emmett into what was either a car or a truck—Wright could not make it out. With the headlights off, they drove west, toward Money.[109]

Mose Wright stood silently on his doorstep for about twenty minutes. As one who had never had any trouble with white people in a lifetime in the Mississippi Delta, he fully expected the car that had whisked Emmett Till away to soon return, with his nephew suffering only a whipping for the "talk" he had done three days earlier.[110]

Elizabeth was not as patient, however, and left Mose on the porch while she fled frantically across the fields to the home of William Chamblee, a white neighbor. Mrs. Chamblee wanted to assist the terrified woman, but for reasons unknown, her husband resisted. Getting no help there, Elizabeth returned home and demanded that Mose take her to her brother's house in Sumner. Leaving their three sons and two grandsons behind, they got into the car, stopped for gas, and drove the thirty miles to Crosby Smith's house in neighboring Tallahatchie County. In his hurry to appease his wife, Mose never even told the five boys still in bed that they were leaving.[111]

Meanwhile, Wheeler Parker got up, slipped on his shoes, and then got back into bed. In case the men returned, he wanted to be ready to run to the fields and hide. Simeon, now alone in the bed he had shared with Emmett, lay awake also. Robert and Maurice Wright and Curtis Jones all stayed asleep. For Wheeler and Simeon, the rest of the night was sleepless as they lay silently in their rooms, in total darkness, for what seemed like eternity. "Nobody said anything to anybody," said Parker about the horrifying experience. "It seemed like day would never come."[112]

3

Murder Heard Round the World

Mose and Elizabeth Wright arrived in Sumner around sunrise Sunday morning, still shaken. Crosby Smith was shocked to see his early morning visitors and listened intently as they rehashed the nightmare they had witnessed at their home a few hours earlier, where strangers burst in and kidnapped their nephew, Emmett Till, at gunpoint.[1]

They had not been in Sumner long before Mose drove back home, with Smith following in his own truck. Elizabeth, however, stayed behind. In fact, she was so traumatized that she never again returned to Money—not even to retrieve her belongings. When Mose and Smith arrived at the Wright home that morning, they saw that Emmett was still missing but found the remaining boys safe.[2] The two men then kept watch on the front porch, holding out hope that their abducted nephew would soon return unharmed. That prospect grew dimmer with each passing minute, however, and there was a ghostly silence while they waited in vain. "I guess we was out there from around 8:00 in the morning 'til way past noon," Smith noted, "and not even a dog walked past that house."[3]

When Curtis Jones woke up that morning, he vaguely recalled the commotion from the night before, but thought for a moment he may have dreamed it. He went out onto the porch, learned what had happened, and immediately went to the home of a neighbor to call Chicago and report the abduction to his mother, Willie Mae. It would fall to her to pass the news to Mamie Bradley.[4]

Talk of the abduction began spreading throughout Money Sunday morning, and soon, both white and black neighbors began congregating at the Wright home to comfort the distraught preacher. "The people kept coming," Mose Wright said, "and we prayed and prayed."[5]

Mamie Bradley had not left for her trip to Omaha yet. She felt tired after Emmett left for Mississippi and wanted to take a day just to relax first. That day turned into seven, and she spent much of the week sleeping and simply feeling lonely for her son. By the weekend, she decided she would not leave until she first heard from him. On Saturday, August 27, she received his letter, which lifted her spirits. That night, she went out with a friend until around 11:00 P.M., then hosted several others who dropped by her house. They talked and laughed until early in the morning.

After her company left, she laid down, intending to get up for church, but at 9:30, her phone rang, and with that call came the news that would change her life. The caller, crying, could say very little.

"This is Willie Mae. I don't know how to tell you—Bo—they came and got him last night."

With that, the caller abruptly hung up, leaving Mamie alone to process the words she had just heard, words that came out of nowhere, but which left her stunned and confused. She tried to collect herself, but Willie Mae's evasive message left her with more questions than answers. At the same time, it was frighteningly clear that Emmett had been kidnapped and was presumably still missing in Mississippi.[6]

By instinct, Mamie immediately phoned her mother. Alma began to panic also but told Mamie to come right over. Too upset to drive, Mamie phoned her boyfriend, Gene Mobley, who agreed to drive her. However, after waiting for what seemed like forever, Mamie started to leave by herself. As she backed out of her driveway, Gene finally arrived, got into the car, slid behind the wheel, and together they headed to Alma's. At Sixty-Third Street and Halstead, Mamie again lost patience, made Gene pull over, and traded places with him. After racing through red lights and stop signs, they arrived at Alma's house at 1626 West Fourteenth Place.[7]

Mamie discovered upon arriving that Alma had already made some phone calls but so far had learned nothing. After the mother and daughter took time to comfort each other, they tried to get a call to Mose Wright by phoning his landlord, Grover Frederick, but this proved useless. "The man said he was too old to hear," said Mamie about that frustrating experience. "He didn't have a pencil. He didn't know where the paper was. He was just in a helpless condition. He couldn't even call anybody to the phone who could take the message."[8] Later, Alma called her brother, Crosby, who told her all he knew. By this time, family began to arrive at Alma's, including Willie Mae, who shared what little else her son Curtis had told her about the kidnapping. Mamie now learned for the first time that her son had allegedly whistled at a white woman.[9]

The Argo Temple Church of God in Christ, Mamie's congregation, received word of the kidnapping and said a prayer for the family during its Sunday service. But for Mamie and Alma, this Sabbath would remain a day of waiting and worry, with no apparent comfort on the horizon. Mamie began calling Chicago newspapers and reported the abduction, which proved to be a wise move. Soon, the family members gathering at Alma's were joined by local newspaper reporters, who took immediate interest in the story. "I told them the only thing I knew at the time," Mamie later wrote. "My son, Emmett Till, had been taken away in the middle of the night by white men who came into my Uncle Moses Wright's home in Money, Mississippi."[10] Mamie stayed near the phone in case Wright tried to call. She and Alma also sought help from other friends and family in Mississippi, but this proved disappointing. "They, too, had other business," Mamie said.[11]

After his many visitors left, Mose Wright went into Greenwood and reported the abduction to Deputy John Cothran, who promised to tell County Sheriff George Smith.[12] It remains unknown exactly what Wright said to the officer, but he certainly provided what details he could. After all, one of the men who went to Wright's home identified himself at the door as "Mr. Bryant." Wright did not know the man and had never been in Bryant's store, but he knew that the incident that started Till's troubles had occurred at the Bryant's Grocery and Meat Market the previous Wednesday. That was enough to provide the sheriff's office with at least one suspect—Roy Bryant, the husband of the woman working behind the counter.

Wright and Crosby Smith may have gone to see the sheriff together, or perhaps Smith went first and reported it because he later recalled a conversation he had at the sheriff's office that day. After Crosby related the kidnapping, Sheriff Smith seemed sure of the suspects right away.

"Don't you reckon that's Bryant and Milam?" he asked his deputy. "They done something like that in Glendora once." Sheriff Smith did not elaborate on what that "something" was. Besides Roy Bryant, Sheriff Smith had in mind Bryant's half-brother, John "J. W." Milam.[13]

The two brothers were known as peckerwoods, or poor whites despised by those of a higher social status. They were part of a large clan that was said to "work, fight, vote, and play as a family." Milam, thirty-six, weighed 235 pounds, was bald, stood six feet two inches, and was a decorated World War II veteran. He had been awarded several medals during the war, including a Purple Heart and Silver Star, and won a battlefield commission by the Seventy-Fifth Division. He would not leave his penchant for fighting and shooting behind after his discharge from the army, but kept his Colt .45 pistol and knew how to use it. "Best weapon the Army's got," he would later say. "Either for shootin' or sluggin.'" He married Mary Juanita Thompson in 1949, and by 1955 the Milams had two sons.

Roy Bryant, twenty-four, married Madge Carolyn Holloway in 1951, after their paths crossed during one of her many visits to Tutwiler to visit her married sister, Frances Reed. Carolyn was a former high school beauty queen who also won several beauty contests as a baby. By 1955, Roy and Carolyn had two young boys. Roy served as a paratrooper during the Korean War, but never left the United States during his service.[14] After Bryant moved to Money and took over this family store in early 1954, he got into a dispute with a neighboring white merchant who had agreed to close his grocery each day in the early afternoon. When the man reneged, Bryant threatened him at gunpoint.[15]

Sunday afternoon, Sheriff Smith and Deputy Sheriff Cothran set out to question Bryant in Money. When they arrived at his store at 2:00 P.M., they learned he was still asleep in the living quarters. His wife and sons were gone, but other family members were present. In the apartment upstairs lived Money's postmaster, but it is unknown if she was present at the time. Cothran brought the suspect outside, and Smith questioned Bryant alone while they sat in the patrol car.

Smith, who reconstructed their conversation a few days later, did not pull any punches. "What did you want to go down there and get that little boy for?" he asked.

"I don't know, but I went and got him," admitted Bryant.

"What did you do with him?"

"My wife said he wasn't the right one and I turned him loose at the store," claimed Bryant.

Smith thought that was odd. "Why didn't you take him back home?"

"I thought he knew the way home."

Bryant's confession was enough for Smith to arrest him on kidnapping charges and book him into the Leflore County jail. Bryant went willingly after Smith allowed him to change clothes.[16]

Milam's arrest occurred the next day after he went to the sheriff's office at around noon.[17] He went to Greenwood on his own that day, and Cothran spotted him outside the window.

"Lookey yonder George," urged Cothran to his boss.

Sheriff Smith looked through the window and saw that this was their man. "Oh dog gone let's go get him. That's Milam."[18]

Milam had gone to Greenwood with the intent of turning himself in to authorities in order to keep Bryant from "running his mouth" off and deviating from the story that they had rehearsed.[19] Cothran questioned him on the way to the jail, and Milam admitted abducting the boy but, like Bryant, claimed he let him loose. Milam also failed to implicate anyone else, not even his jailed brother. He was then booked and placed in a separate cell on a different floor from Bryant. Sheriff Smith also issued an arrest warrant for Carolyn Bryant, based on Mose Wright's statement that he heard what sounded like a woman's voice outside during the kidnapping.[20]

That same day, news of the abduction appeared on the front page of one Chicago newspaper and several others in Mississippi. The *Chicago Daily*

Tribune's story, prepared on Sunday after reporters visited Mamie at her mother's home, quoted Deputy Cothran, who said that Till "reportedly had had an argument with Mrs. Bryant at the Bryant store." Mississippi papers reporting the story on Monday included the *Clarksdale Press Register, Delta Democrat-Times, Greenwood Commonwealth, Jackson Daily News, Laurel Leader-Call, McComb Enterprise-Journal*, and *Jackson State Times*. Most of them reported that Till was kidnapped because he had allegedly made "ugly remarks" to the woman. They also noted that three men were involved, two of whom entered the house and abducted Till at gunpoint. The *Delta Democrat-Times* said that Till "said something to offend Bryant's wife." Only one paper, the *Greenwood Commonwealth*, identified J. W. Milam as a second suspect, reporting his arrest just before press-time by placing the breaking news in a paragraph above the story. The *Commonwealth* also named five of the youth who were with Till on the evening of the incident at the store. The *Tribune* failed to mention the presence of a woman in the car who identified the boy, as did some of the Mississippi papers. In these first reports, no one mentioned the wolf whistle. With all the focus on Milam and Bryant, the third man who accompanied the suspects to Wright's home remained unknown and was, in fact, still at large.[21]

Mamie Bradley likely read the *Chicago Daily Tribune* article, which provided some hope that the men who took her son had released him, as they claimed. "In the back of my mind was the hope that Bo had slipped away from his abductors and was hiding, afraid, in the home of some colored people," she said, "and I kept hugging this hope close to me." Yet Deputy Cothran's suspicion, quoted in the same paper, that he feared "some harm has been done to the boy" meant that Mamie had to prepare for the worst. However, Monday proved too busy to dwell on that as she continued to seek information about her missing son. She was not alone. Her stepfather, Henry Spearman, enlisted the help of his nephew, Rayfield Mooty, a local union leader and competent organizer, who introduced Mamie to officials at the local NAACP office. They provided her access to their own legal counsel, attorney William Henry Huff, who was also an expert on extradition cases.[22]

All of this was helpful, but Mamie was over 600 miles from her son's last-known whereabouts. Feeling restless, helpless, and growing more impatient, she nearly boarded a train to Mississippi herself before her uncle Crosby persuaded her to wait until he attempted one last time to try to arrange contact with Mose Wright.[23] That evening, more information came as sixteen-year-old Wheeler Parker arrived back in Chicago.

Parker, who had accompanied Emmett Till to Mississippi nine days earlier, had left the Delta on the 4:30 A.M. train, too scared to stay any longer.[24] His uncle Thelton Parker Sr. had taken him to the home of another uncle, William Parker, in Duck Hill, where Wheeler boarded the train for home. When the train stopped in Memphis, young Parker unknowingly started for a restroom marked "White Only," until someone yelled out, "Don't go in there!" Parker, overwhelmed at the size of the station, thought it looked too much like Chicago for Jim Crow to exist. At sixteen, and all alone, "I got scared all over again."[25] Once safely home, however, he began talking to family and reporters.

In Mississippi, Mose Wright and his sons spent Monday and Tuesday picking cotton, and Mose also gathered wood for the winter. "But I was listening and hoping I could hear something about Bobo." With hope fading, however, he called a daughter in Chicago to let her know there had been no developments. She in turn informed Mamie.[26] Elizabeth wrote Mose on Tuesday, fearing for the safety of their three young boys. She pleaded for him to join her in Sumner, and in the meantime, to not let their sons go into Money. Wright had no choice but to stay on the plantation, however, as most of his twenty-five acres were still full of cotton.[27]

That same day, Mamie finally got through to Wright on the telephone. Wright told her that he had visited the Bryant store soon after the kidnapping and that someone there told him that Emmett had been released unharmed, which backed up Milam's and Bryant's story.[28] In Chicago, Parker's account of the store incident and the kidnapping appeared in the *Chicago Daily Tribune*. Now, for the first time, news of the wolf whistle was known in the North.[29]

While out running errands, Mamie stopped at the NAACP office, where she learned that Huff, already acting on her behalf, had sent telegrams to US attorney general Herbert Brownell, Illinois governor William Stratton, and Mississippi governor Hugh White, urging them all to conduct a thorough investigation.

When Mamie returned to Alma's, she found that her mother was waiting with unbelievable news. Three calls purportedly from the Chicago police department reported news from Mississippi that Emmett was alive and on his way home. As on the morning of the abduction, however, Mamie was once again full of questions, but no one in the house had any answers. She called the police herself, but all they could do was refer her to the Missing Person's Bureau. When she talked to them, she quickly learned that they knew nothing. Devastated all over again, Mamie could only conclude that the calls had been a hoax.[30]

Indeed, in Mississippi, officials had nothing new to report either. In fact, having suspected foul play from the beginning, they had been searching the Tallahatchie River since Sunday. Deputy Sheriff Cothran scoured a thirty-mile stretch on Monday alone.[31]

Mamie again called her uncle Crosby in Sumner. He asked her to give him just a few more hours to find her son, after which she could then board the

City of New Orleans for Mississippi the following morning if she wished.[32] The waiting and wondering continued. "We stood there. We sat there. We waited for . . . three days trying to find out what had happened to Emmett," Mamie said. This took its toll on Alma, who finally collapsed in an emotional climax to the three-day ordeal. It was at this moment, recalled Mamie, "when I realized for the first time in my life, I was going to have to stand up on my feet and be a woman. A real one."[33]

Beginning Wednesday, August 31, she would need all the strength she could muster. That morning, between 6:30 and 7:00, near the town of Philipp in Tallahatchie County, seventeen-year-old Robert Hodges was fishing in the Tallahatchie River near a spot called Pecan Point. While inspecting his trotline, he noticed something in the distance. It was a pair of human legs protruding up above the surface of the water. Hodges checked on his lines, went home, and told his father of his awful discovery. The senior Hodges got word to his landlord, B. L. Mims. Someone else then notified County Sheriff H. C. Strider.[34]

Tallahatchie County deputy sheriff Garland Melton was the first official to arrive at the scene. Mims came, bringing his own boat, and he and Melton took it out to try to retrieve the body. Robert Hodges and Mims's brother, Charlie Fred, followed in another boat. When they approached the half-submerged corpse, Mims could see that it was that of a black person. Realizing they would need a rope to help free it from a snag, they sent one of the boats back to get one. Shortly, with rope in hand, Mims and Melton began the arduous job of retrieving the body by tying the rope around the feet and ankles, pulling the body loose, and then towing it to shore. Melton held the rope, and Mims steered until they arrived at a shallow area near the riverbank. As they brought the body to land, they discovered that barbed wire had been wrapped around the neck and tied to a cotton gin fan in an obvious attempt to weigh the body down. As they placed the body in a boat, part of the skull fell off onto the floor. The head had obviously been crushed in by something—or someone.[35]

Sheriff Strider arrived at the river about 9:15 A.M. and then notified the Leflore County sheriff's office.[36] Sheriff George Smith was in Jackson for the opening day of the annual Tennessee and Mississippi Sheriffs' and Peace Officers Association convention, but office deputy N. L. McCool informed Smith's deputy, John Cothran, of the situation, and Cothran left right away, arriving at the river about 10:00 A.M. The officers immediately assumed that the body retrieved from the Tallahatchie River was that of Emmett Till, now missing for three days.[37]

As Strider approached the body, he was met with an odor so strong that he could not get near enough to examine it. He summoned the black undertaker Chester Miller, manager of the Century Burial Association in Greenwood, who came to the scene to lend a hand. When Miller arrived, he set off two deodorant bombs to rid the scene of the smell, and even sprayed the entire corpse with a deodorizing liquid.[38]

What the authorities saw in the boat was ghastly. The body was naked, had been badly beaten, and, due to the effects of the river, was heavily decomposed and bloated. Strider said the head had been penetrated by a bullet hole above the right ear, and that the face was "cut up pretty badly like an ax was used." It appeared to him that the body had been in the river about two days.[39] He described the tongue as sticking out of the mouth three inches, and that "the left eyeball was almost out, enough to almost fall out. And the right one was out, I would say, about three-quarters of an inch."[40] The river and the force of debris obviously caused some damage to the body, and the weight of the gin fan may have caused many of the fractures to the head, yet there was no mistaking that the victim had been tortured. One officer at the scene said that in his eight years of law enforcement, this was the "worst beating I've seen."[41]

Mose Wright was gathering wood when Cothran and Tallahatchie deputy sheriff Ed Weber brought him news of the discovery. Wright accompanied them back to the river to perform the dreaded task of identification. The deputies also picked up a boy in Philipp whom they did not know but who was able to guide them to the right location at the riverbank.

When they arrived, they saw Melton; Strider; Strider's twenty-three-year-old son, Clarence; and another Tallahatchie County deputy named A. K. Smith all waiting. Wright approached the scene solemnly. Walking toward the body, he told Cothran even at a distance of around fifteen to twenty yards that it "show looks like him," but as he got closer, with the corpse positioned face-down, he could not be sure.[42] Someone there turned it over so that Wright could get a better look.

"That's him," Wright said immediately. He elaborated several weeks later as he reflected back on that moment that "I never saw anything like that in my life." He thought about the fun-loving boy who had just spent a week at his home. "There was Bobo who used to have such a good appetite and who never sassed in my house, not once. There he was dead with his head looking like he had been hit with a sledge hammer."[43]

Wright watched as Miller's assistant, Simon Garrett, removed a silver ring from the middle finger of the right hand and gave it to his boss. Miller then placed it on the floor of the ambulance. Two black men took the heavy gin fan and put it into Cothran's car, soiling the car with mud and water. When Miller learned that there was a relative of the victim present, he asked Wright if he would identify the body for him, as he had for the sheriff. Wright told Miller that the body was indeed that of Emmett Till.[44]

Miller and Garrett began the process of removing the body, first by wrapping it in brown paper and placing it in a casket. Because the body was so swollen, they were unable to fully close the lid. They then placed the coffin in a metal container and loaded it onto the ambulance.[45] Before leaving, Wright asked Miller for the ring, and Miller obliged. When Wright returned home, he held it up and asked his sons Simeon and Robert if they recognized it.

"Yes, that's Bobo's ring," said twelve-year-old Simeon. "He promised to give it to me."

Wright then turned it over to Cothran as evidence.[46]

It was not long before the *Chicago Daily Tribune* learned of the discovery through its wire service. Unsure if Mamie had been told, someone from the paper called her and casually asked if she had learned anything new about her son. She replied that she had not heard a thing. Rather than tell her over the phone that her son had been found dead, the reporter called Mamie's best friend, Ollie Williams, gave her the news, and asked her to break it to Mamie. Williams put it off as long as she could but finally called from her job at Inland Steel and got Mamie on the phone. Williams was nervous and hesitated, which alerted Mamie that something was wrong.

"For God's sake, whatever it is, let me have it, because I can probably take it better than anybody around here anyway," she demanded.

Williams then carefully and sensitively told Mamie what she had just learned. Emmett had been found dead in the Tallahatchie River. He had been beaten and weighed down with a cotton gin fan tied around his neck.[47]

Mamie calmly wrote down these details, and then read them to her mother and an aunt, Marie Carthan, who were waiting nearby. Carthan immediately became hysterical.

"Take her out of here," yelled Mamie. "Don't let her start."

Indeed, a mother's worst nightmare had begun. "As I sat there, I suddenly divided into two different people," Mamie said as she described that moment when she heard the news. "One was handling the telephone. The other was standing off telling the other what to do. Or helping me to keep myself under control. And this second person told me [']you don't have time to cry now—you might not have time to cry tomorrow.[']"[48]

Indeed, tears—even mourning—would have to wait. With her son still in the Deep South, Mamie had work to do, and it would be no easy task to get the body home. The family had a connection with the A. A. Rayner & Sons Funeral Home in Chicago, and Marie Carthan called immediately to begin arrangements for shipping the body north. Alma called Crosby Smith in Sumner and told him that Emmett had been found dead.[49]

In Mississippi, an inquest into the brutal death was scheduled for the afternoon. "We're just waiting until the inquest determines that he died in our county, as we are sure he did," Sheriff Strider told the *New York Post*. "As soon as that's official, we're going to charge those men with murder."[50] After Miller and Garrett laid the body out at their funeral home, police photographer Charles A. Strickland arrived and snapped some pictures. Greenwood pathologist Luther Otken also came by and gave the body a brief examination.[51] Overall, the investigation was informal and hurried. A Leflore County justice of the peace explained a few days later that "it was not exactly an inquest," instead calling it "more of a postmortem. We decided he was dead, killed by a bullet."[52] There was no attempt to perform an autopsy. If the idea was discussed at all, Mississippi officials likely rejected it, believing that the heavy state of decomposition made such an examination impossible.

With their so-called inquest over, law enforcement officials released the body to Emmett Till's Mississippi relatives. Unaware of Mamie's intent to ship it home, Chester Miller, with Till's remains in his hearse, was soon on his way to the East Money Church of God in Christ, with instructions to bury the body immediately.[53] With little time to prepare, Mose Wright summoned men from the church to help dig a grave while he prepared for a brief funeral service. This was all happening within three hours of the discovery of the body, and no one in Chicago knew anything about it.[54]

Curtis Jones was picking cotton at a relative's field when Maurice Wright pulled up in the family Ford to tell him that Emmett was dead. Jones got into the car, and the boys drove out to the church. While the crew was digging, Jones convinced his grandfather that Alma would be opposed to the local burial. Wright agreed to halt the digging and called Chicago.[55] A series of calls got the news to Mamie, who became outraged at this attempt to bury her son in Mississippi without her permission or even her knowledge, and she became all the more determined to get him home. Alma called Crosby Smith again, alerting him to the situation. Smith agreed to intervene and promised to get the body to Chicago if he had to pack it with ice, put it into his truck, and drive it there himself.[56] He then drove to Money. "I got there and had the deputy sheriff with me. He told them that whatever I said, went." And it was just in time—the coffin was still in the churchyard, and the grave was partly dug. "They were getting ready to spill the body into that two-foot hole. He hadn't even been embalmed."[57]

With the local burial thwarted, Smith asked Miller to prepare the body for shipment. Feeling terrified over the situation and fearing the possibility of repercussion, Miller refused to keep it overnight. "They gave me strict orders not to bring this body back to town, and I'm not going to take it back to town," he declared adamantly.[58]

It is not entirely clear why officials in Mississippi were so anxious for such a speedy burial. Over the years Mamie Bradley accused Sheriff Strider of ordering an immediate interment in order to spare Mississippi from the embarrassment of the brutality of the murder. Although there is little reason to doubt such a motive, Strider justified his actions by citing more practical concerns. An attendant at the Century Burial Association said the body "was in such bad shape [meaning embalming was an impossibility] it couldn't be shipped."[59] This seemed to be Mose Wright's understanding as well. Miller told him that they would have to hurry things up because "the body was in such shape it wouldn't keep."[60]

Miller did reluctantly take Till's corpse back to Greenwood, but soon an attendant from a funeral home in Tutwiler came by prearrangement to retrieve it. Chick Nelson, the white mayor of Tutwiler and manager of the mortuary, agreed to prepare the body and also made shipping arrangements with A. A. Rayner in Chicago. Crosby Smith contacted the railroad.[61] Unaware of this intervention, the *Jackson Clarion-Ledger* erroneously reported the next day that Emmett Till had been buried in Money.[62]

The discovery of the body set off a storm of protest, anger, and sympathy, and the kidnapping-turned-murder became a national story. Dr. T. R. M. Howard, civil rights leader and founder of the Regional Councils of Negro Leadership, talked to reporters while on business in Chicago. "There will be hell to pay in Mississippi. Decent citizens are not going to continue to be treated like this."[63] Howard himself was a Mississippian living in the all-black town of Mound Bayou. The NAACP field secretary in Mississippi, Medgar Evers, simply cried. Each murder he dealt with affected him, but because Till was so young, Evers actually shed tears.[64] Shortly before 4:00 P.M., Roy Wilkins, executive secretary of the NAACP, sent a telegram to Mississippi governor Hugh White, stating that his organization, "together with all decent citizens throughout the Nation call upon you to use all the powers of your office to see that the lynchers of 14-year-old Emmett Louis Till are brought to justice." He added that "we cannot believe that responsible officials of the state of Mississippi condone the murdering of children on any provocation."[65]

That same day, Wilkins used less restraint in a public statement. "It would appear from this lynching that the State of Mississippi has decided to maintain white supremacy by murdering children." If that was not enough to get the southern blood boiling, he tried a little harder. "The killers of the boy felt free to lynch him because there is in the entire state no restraining influence of decency, not in the state capital, among the daily newspapers, the clergy nor any segment of the so-called better citizens." Unable to resist a further jab at White, Wilkins continued: "We have protested to Governor

White, but judging by past actions of the state Chief Executive, little action can be expected."[66]

White did not comment on the murder Wednesday because, as he explained it, he had not been officially notified.[67] The following day, however, he sounded determined to act. Although he usually ignored communications from the NAACP, he responded to Wilkins's telegram with one of his own. "Message received. Parties charged with murder are in jail and I have every reason to believe the courts will do their duty in prosecution," he said, assuring Wilkins that "Mississippi does not condone such conduct."[68]

Wilkins was not the only voice demanding justice, and Mississippi officials were not the only ones under pressure. Chicago mayor Richard Daley telegraphed President Dwight Eisenhower, urging him to utilize the federal government in seeking justice.[69] William Henry Huff also wrote Governor White, asking him to act. "If those in the upper class or in authority will have the courage to speak out against these brutal conditions, such conditions will cease to exist."[70]

The grieving mother also talked to the press, which had understandably sought her out. She did not hold back. "The State of Mississippi will have to pay for this. I would expect that down there if the boy did something wrong he might come back beaten up. But they didn't even give me that." Some reports also included Mamie's assessment of Mississippi as a "den of snakes," whose citizens "will do these things with hardly any provocation—they don't even need provocation."[71]

The US Justice Department soon announced that it had no jurisdiction in the matter, thus placing the investigation strictly in the hands of the state of Mississippi. There were a few reasons for this. First, there was no evidence that the abductors had crossed state lines while committing their crime.[72] Also, as FBI director J. Edgar Hoover explained on September 2 to the editor of the black newspaper, the *Chicago Defender*, the "facts pertaining to the murder of Emmett Louis Till have been submitted to the Civil Rights section of the Department which has ruled that they do not constitute a violation within the investigative jurisdiction of the FBI." Hoover and his colleagues would repeat these explanations numerous times over the next several months.[73]

Statements Thursday from Mississippi officials sounded optimistic that justice would prevail under their authority anyway. Governor White held a press conference to reiterate what he had privately telegrammed to Wilkins, saying, "Mississippi deplores such conduct on the part of any of its citizens and certainly cannot condone it." He also rejected the notion that the killing was a lynching, which would certainly have been an unwelcome label recalling Mississippi's dark, but not too distant, past. Instead, he called it "straight out murder."[74] Tallahatchie County sheriff Strider said that he would "seek speedy prosecution" of Milam and Bryant.[75] Leflore County deputy sheriff Cothran told the *New York Post*: "None of them are getting any sympathy around here. Everybody's upset about this. They don't understand how anybody could be so lowdown as to do such a thing—and for such a little cause, too." However, there was irony in his attempt to clear up northern misconceptions about southern race relations. "Northerners always think that we don't care what white folks do to the niggers down here, but that's not true. The people around here are decent, and they won't stand for this. We're going to get to the bottom of this. And we're going to get a conviction, too."[76]

The Tuskegee Institute, which had not recorded a lynching since 1951, announced that it was probing the Till case to determine whether it would be so classified (it was also investigating the recent murders of Rev. George Lee and Lamar Smith).[77] The last thing Mississippi needed, while in the national spotlight, was new lynching statistics, as Governor White knew very well. It is not surprising, then, that Robert Patterson, executive secretary of the proseg-regationist Citizens' Council, sought to distance his group from any perceived involvement. He stated publicly: "This is a very regrettable incident. One of the primary reasons for our organization is to prevent acts of violence." He denied that the murder was connected to his or any similar group. Luckily for Patterson, neither Milam nor Bryant was a member of the Citizens' Council.[78]

Not sure yet under whose jurisdiction the investigation would fall, Governor White separately wired District Attorneys Gerald W. Chatham, of Tallahatchie County, and Stanny Sanders, of Leflore County. White was, he said, "very much distressed over reported murder of Till Negro. If in your district, I urge complete investigation and prosecution of guilty parties."[79] Sanders told the press that a thorough investigation would continue until they could determine where the murder occurred. However, jurisdiction was transferred to Chatham almost immediately because the body had been discovered within Tallahatchie County borders. Because it was found ten miles into the county, Sheriff Strider reasoned, it was probably dumped there. "It couldn't have floated up the river."[80] Chatham, of the Seventeenth Judicial District, was already planning to present the case to a grand jury early the following week. He responded immediately to White: "I am in constant touch with officials of Tallahatchie and Leflore Counties and am confident that we have sufficient evidence to justify indictments against accused in Till murder when grand jury convenes in Sumner Monday."[81]

Chatham announced publicly that the grand jury would hear the evidence and make its decision no later than Tuesday. Because the fall court would begin in early September, he believed that a trial in the Till case would likely not take place until the spring term of court, which would not start until March 1956. Chatham, who did not run for reelection, would by then be out of office.[82]

Reporters descended upon the Leflore jail Thursday to get a look at the suspects in the case now making waves throughout the nation. Neither Bryant nor Milam would speak to them, however, and even refused to allow photos. "I haven't a thing to say," said Bryant, who added, politely, "I'm glad to have met you all." Milam, nearly naked in his sweltering cell, responded similarly, telling reporters, "It's hot in here," and referring them to Greenwood defense attorney Hardy Lott. When questioned, Lott said that he had not been retained, but had consulted with the two men. It was probably on Lott's advice that the suspects refused to speak to the press. In fact, they were not speaking to anyone. Although they admitted to the kidnapping at the time of their arrests, once a body surfaced they went silent. "We don't know what Till is supposed to have said to Mrs. Bryant, as we can't find her, and the two men won't tell us a thing," said Cothran to reporters.[83]

Emmett Till's corpse still lay in a mortuary in Tutwiler. When it arrived the day before, Chick Nelson saw that it was in much worse shape than he had anticipated. Had he known, he insisted, he would never have agreed to prepare it. His embalmer, Harry D. Malone, had to use twenty times the standard amount of embalming fluid in an attempt to preserve the body.[84] Malone later explained that because the normal intravenous procedure was impossible, he instead immersed the corpse in formaldehyde for thirty-six hours and cut several incisions in the flesh in order to release the gases and allow the preservative to enter. Once that process was completed, the body was placed in a plastic bag and enclosed in a casket that Malone described as the "finest" that they had.[85] It was then covered with padding, and placed into a large redwood box for shipping. Chester Miller drove to Tutwiler and helped load the box tagged "Emmett Till" on the train. By late evening Thursday, it was on its journey home, accompanied by Crosby Smith, Elizabeth Wright, and Curtis Jones. It was scheduled to arrive in Chicago the following morning.[86]

On Friday, Illinois governor Stratton added his voice to the growing number of high officials speaking out, and instructed his attorney general, Latham Castle, to urge Mississippi authorities to thoroughly investigate the murder.[87] Indeed, law enforcement officers in Leflore and Tallahatchie Counties were still searching the area where Emmett Till had been found, looking for new clues in the crime. Sheriff Smith and District Attorney Stanny Sanders, who both covered Leflore County where the kidnapping occurred, asked the *Greenwood Commonwealth* to publicize a photo of the cotton gin fan used to weigh down the body in an attempt to locate the owner and zero in on the crime scene. The photo appeared in Friday's paper.[88] Officers also went door-to-door, questioning residents living near the river, in an effort to locate anyone who might have seen the suspects. "We haven't been able to find the murder weapon or anything," Strider reported, but he insisted that "we are not leaving a stone unturned."[89]

Sometime that weekend, officials found what was believed to be hair and blood on a bridge in Tallahatchie County. Strider became convinced that the body had been dumped into the river from this bridge, located about four-and-a-half miles north of the spot where it had been discovered.[90] Strider sent the specimens to Greenwood, and on September 5 police chief R. R. Shurden forwarded them to FBI director J. Edgar Hoover for testing. On September 9, the FBI wired Shurden the results, which revealed that the hair was not human, but of unknown animal origin. The substance thought to be blood was something unidentifiable.[91]

On Friday, September 2, readers of southern papers got their first look at the accused murderers. Because Milam and Bryant had declined to have their pictures taken after their arrests, older photos of the men, smiling in their military uniforms, graced the front pages. These hardly looked like the faces of killers, and an accompanying article in the *Memphis Commercial Appeal* probably helped convince more than a few southerners of the innocence of the pair. "They were never into any meanness," said their mother, Eula Bryant, interviewed from her store in Sharkey County. "I raised them and I'll stand by them." She also praised Milam for his military honors and Bryant for his service as a paratrooper. Milam's wife, Juanita, visiting at her mother-in-law's store, added: "He's an ideal father. The children worship him. And all the Negroes at Glendora . . . liked him like a father. They always came to him for help." The following day, the same paper quoted Bryant's fraternal twin, Raymond, who declared his brother innocent (he did not mention his half-brother, J. W. Milam), and said the charges against Roy were "all a matter of politics." The *Jackson State Times*, also trying to portray a different side to Bryant, reported that the previous January he had spotted two duck hunters whose boat had capsized on Six Mile Lake, jumped into the icy water, and saved them from drowning.[92]

On Friday, Rev. H. Thomas Primm, bishop of the African Methodist Episcopal Church in Mississippi and Louisiana, called for two days of mourning to protest the murder. He encouraged everyone in Mississippi to wear a strip of black ribbon three inches long on September 8 and 9. But some southern newspapers had already gone out of their way to reassure readers that Mississippians were indeed outraged over the crime. On Saturday, the *Memphis Press-Scimitar* gathered several quotations from Mississippi papers condemning the killing, as did the *Jackson Daily News*.[93]

That said, the Mississippi press was also quick to voice contempt for the condemnations hurled by outsiders—most noticeably the NAACP—which seemed to indict all Mississippians in the killing. A front-page editorial appeared in the *Greenwood Commonwealth* on September 2 responding to the harsh statements made by Roy Wilkins and Mamie Bradley just after the body had been discovered. "This deplorable incident has made our section the target of unjustifiable criticism, thoughtless accusations, and avenging threats," it declared. To Mamie, "we offer our sympathy and express our deep regret that this terrible thing has happened to her." However, "her determination to see that 'Mississippi is going to pay for this,' charging the entire state with the guilt of those who took the law in their own hands is evidence of the poison selfish men have planted in the minds of people outside the South."[94]

For the NAACP, there was no sympathy at all. The writer blasted Wilkins's attacks upon his state, but had apparently forgotten that there had been two other racially motivated murders recently committed in Mississippi: "On the basis of one murder it [the NAACP] has judged the character, honor and integrity of the entire population." With this rebuke of Wilkins and Mamie Bradley, the Mississippi press, which had been reporting community outrage over the murder in its stories since Wednesday, became defensive and, going forward, notably less sympathetic. Resentment clearly developed over what most white southerners saw as outside agitation, and Mississippi journalists began carefully orchestrating what they wrote and juxtaposed images in such a way as to shape negative public opinion toward Till in the weeks ahead.[95]

The *Chicago Sun-Times* announced on Friday morning that Emmett Till's body would arrive at the Central Street Station at 9:00 A.M. When Mamie Bradley arrived to meet the box carrying her murdered son, the station was already filled with onlookers and reporters. Entering the station in a wheelchair, Mamie was escorted by a support team consisting of her father, John Carthan (who had come in from Detroit); Gene Mobley; Bishop Louis Ford; Bishop Isaiah Roberts; and some cousins, including Rayfield Mooty. When the train arrived, Mamie got up from her wheelchair and quickly crossed three sets of tracks to meet the baggage car that held her son's remains. Press photographers snapped pictures of the grief-stricken mother as she collapsed. "My darling, my darling. I would have gone through a world of fire to get to you. I know I was on your mind when you died," she cried. The family formed a ring and watched solemnly as men removed the large pine box from the train and loaded it onto a flatbed truck. Mamie spoke again, assuring her deceased son that he "didn't die for nothing." The box was opened as it sat on the truck, and the casket removed and placed into a hearse for the trip to Rayner's.[96]

Mamie had already talked to Ahmed Rayner by telephone and said she wanted to see the body once the casket arrived. Rayner at first refused, stating his own obligation, by verbal and written promise, not to break the seal from the state of Mississippi. Yet Mamie kept insisting, and Rayner reluctantly relented.[97] The family also requested an autopsy, and Rayner agreed to see that the request was honored, providing that the condition of the body would allow it.[98] It is unknown if there was further talk about that once Rayner and his staff saw the remains, but the autopsy did not occur—nor would it until fifty years later.

After the casket left the train station, Mamie, her father, Mooty, and Mobley followed Rayner to his mortuary.[99] Simeon Booker, correspondent for *Ebony-Jet* magazines, and David Jackson, photographer for the same publications, were waiting outside. They had been there since midnight, not knowing when Till's body was going to arrive. Finally, the hearse pulled up, followed by Mamie's party. After Mamie got out of the car and walked into the building, Booker and Jackson followed behind.[100]

Mamie waited with her family in a separate room while Rayner opened the casket. Now a witness to the body's condition himself, he again tried to dissuade Mamie from viewing it. After this failed, Rayner acquiesced. Rayfield Mooty went in first, looked at the mangled corpse, and then went back for Mamie. With her father on one side and Gene Mobley on the other, she made her approach to the room containing her son. "The first thing that greeted us when we walked into the parlor was a terrible odor. I think I'll carry that odor with me to my grave," she said a few months later. As she neared the casket, she could see her son, naked, covered with lime. "What I saw looked like it came from out of space. It didn't look like anything that we could dream, imagine in a funny book or any place else. It just didn't look like it was for real."[101]

Standing over the casket, Mamie began to examine Emmett's right side. She first noticed a large gash in his forehead, which she assumed had been made with an ax. The mouth was open and the tongue was protruding. "His lips were twisted and his teeth were bared just like a snarling dog's," she said. Then she saw the gunshot wound. "I wondered why they wasted a bullet because surely it wasn't necessary." Some features she recognized, such as the nose and forehead. One eye was missing, probably lost during the embalming process, but the other, despite being detached, was the right color. Still looking at the right side, "I found that part of the ear was gone, and the entire back of the head had been knocked out." Mamie then asked Rayner to remove her son from the casket so that she could examine the left side also. He agreed, but asked her to go home first, send some clothes back, and then finish viewing the body once it was dressed.[102]

Although Mamie left, Booker and Jackson stayed behind and watched as attendants lifted the body from the casket and placed it onto a slab. In that instant, they were horrified to see a piece of Till's skull fall off and bits of his brains come out. "Calmly, Dave replaced the skull," explained Booker, "like putting on a hat."[103]

Mamie and her party returned to the mortuary an hour or so later. When she approached her son this second time as he lay clothed on a slab, she saw, for the first time, the left side of his face. "It looked as if somebody had taken a criss-cross knife and gone insane. It was beaten into a pulp."[104]

David Jackson took photos of Till's battered face, with Mamie present, which would appear in *Jet* in its September 15 issue. They would be reprinted in several black newspapers in the coming weeks, which greatly impacted national news coverage of the murder and public outrage. *Jet* publisher John Johnson, hesitant at first to print such graphic images, consented in the end. The 400,000 print run sold out.[105]

Although Mamie remained horrified by what she saw upon her return, Rayner had, in fact, touched up the body slightly while she was gone. He closed the mouth, and sewed the gash in the jaw and forehead. Mamie, already having seen enough evidence of indescribable torture, knew that she could never explain it to anyone; others would have to see it too. After Rayner had done what he could, Mamie determined to have an open-casket funeral, to "let the people see what they did to my boy."[106]

Mamie also asked Rayner's permission to hold her son's wake at the funeral home in order to allow as many people to view the body as possible. He agreed, and by that evening, word was out that fourteen-year-old murder victim Emmett Till was on display, and a crowd began gathering. Newspapers estimated that between 10,000 and 50,000 people viewed the body that night, many of whom fainted or were otherwise taken ill after seeing the badly beaten, partially decomposed corpse. Till's body, under a thick, clear glass covering, was dressed in the dark suit and white shirt he had received the Christmas before. Mamie taped photos from that happy holiday to the inside lid of the casket so that people could contrast the mutilated face before them to the handsome young man who was so full of life only a week earlier. At one point, the number trying to enter the funeral home became so great that a chapel window was accidentally broken by the throng. Some newspapers reported that the place was in a "shambles" due to the push of the large crowd. At 2:00 A.M., the doors were closed.[107]

By the following morning, reports of the viewing and large crowd gathered in Chicago had made their way to Mississippi, and with them, rumors spread that protests and violence were about to erupt in the Delta. George Saucier, chief administrative assistant of the Mississippi Highway Patrol, dismissed the stories, as did the Greenwood police department, which found none but the usual number of out-of-state cars in town during a holiday—this being Labor Day weekend. The rumors were based on traffic checks in Clarksdale (fifty-eight miles north of Greenwood), where fifty or so vehicles with Illinois plates were stopped during a ninety-minute surveillance on Saturday morning. At least a dozen drivers, all black, appeared before Justice of the Peace Mary Martin and were fined for traffic violations. One received an additional $25 penalty for carrying a concealed weapon. Because the violations were so minor, officials remained unalarmed.[108]

That same day, however, Sheriff Strider reported that members of the Bryant family had been forced off a Mississippi road by Illinois cars. He also said he had received letters from people in Chicago threatening Till's accused killers, and that one even targeted James Bryant, a brother serving at a New York naval base. "We are going to kill your son in New York," the letter, addressed to Roy Bryant, read. "We are going to kill the first Hill Billy that say he is kin to you up here." Because so many of the letters were "filthy and vicious," explained Strider, he asked the FBI to investigate.[109]

Then came Strider's bombshell. Out of nowhere he announced that he did not believe the body found in the Tallahatchie River the previous Wednesday was that of Emmett Till. He even postulated that the Chicago youth might still be alive. Four days after he examined the corpse and released it to Till's relatives, Strider had completely changed his tune. Although he stated at the river that the body had probably been in the water just two days, now, without any further examination, he insisted that it had been submerged at least ten— much longer than to have possibly been Emmett Till. He also said that the body appeared to be that of an adult. Most bizarre, however, was his claim that "the whole thing looks like a deal made up by the National Association for the Advancement of Colored People." Roy Wilkins, learning of Strider's revelations from his New York office, wasted no time in firing back, yet surprisingly, he used uncharacteristic restraint. "The sheriff evidently knows nothing about the NAACP. We don't go in for murder."[110]

Mamie Bradley, learning of Strider's announcement, was understandably disturbed, but she remained adamant that "it is my son lying there in the church. If the state of Mississippi says he is not my boy, the burden of proof rests upon that state."[111] Rayfield Mooty, echoing Mamie, accused Strider of a "cover up," but said the family would release the body back to Mississippi officials if doubt about its identity remained.[112]

There was nothing surprising in hearing the NAACP and Emmett Till's family criticize Strider's announcement, which they clearly saw as outlandish. However, law enforcement officials in Leflore County were quick to dispute it as well. Deputy Cothran told reporters he was in complete disagreement with Strider. "Emmett's uncle, Moses Wright, definitely identified the body as the boy. I was with him when he did it," he said. District Attorney Chatham was also shocked by this new development. "When we took over the case, I was assured by Stanny Sanders . . . that there was no question of corpus delecti." He now worried that Strider's statement might erode the murder case, because the evidence was only circumstantial to begin with; without the body of the victim, there could be no evidence of a homicide. "You would certainly have to prove a death," he said.[113] In just two days, Strider would testify before the grand jury. It was not entirely clear what led to his conjectures, but his announcement about threats to the accused and their families and his own accusations against the NAACP were all rooted in Mississippians' disdain for outside interference.

Leflore County officials told the press on Saturday that they were still investigating the original charge of kidnapping, which had occurred in their county. Yet despite the fact that the sheriff had issued a warrant for Carolyn Bryant, Stanny Sanders said that there were no plans now to arrest her. He explained that although they knew where she was and could apprehend her if needed, they did not believe she was involved in the crime. In fact, even Sheriff Smith stated flatly: "We aren't going to bother the woman. She's got two small boys to take care of." Officials were still considering the involvement of at least one other person, however, someone whose identity was still unknown. "We believe there was another man," confirmed Cothran, who declared confidently that "we will get him before we are through." Smith also planned to search the Bryant store, which had been locked since Roy Bryant's arrest. It remains unknown if that ever occurred.[114]

Despite Strider's public doubts about the identity of the body being mourned in Chicago, Emmett Till's funeral service began Saturday morning as scheduled. The casket was moved from Rayner & Sons to the Roberts Temple Church of God in Christ on State Street. People came several hours early for a seat, and by the time the funeral began, the church, which held 1,800, was packed to overflowing. Outside, another 3,000 people gathered. Several police, under Sergeant Frank Heimowski's anti-Communist detail, were dispatched and remained outside throughout the service. Communists had passed out literature in front of the mortuary the night before, and authorities worried that left-wing groups would continue to sensationalize the case during the funeral.[115]

When Mamie arrived at the church, she was escorted first by her cousin Crosby Smith Jr. (on leave from Ft. Campbell in Kentucky), and then by the Reverend Charles Poole and his sister, evangelist Mattie Poole. Mamie took her seat with other family members in the front row.[116]

The boy who only a week earlier was unknown to anyone except his immediate circle of family and friends was next memorialized in what resembled a state funeral. Isaiah Roberts, pastor of Roberts Temple, presided at the service and read Emmett's last letter to his mother, sent from Mississippi. Henry Louis Ford, the forty-one-year-old bishop of St. Paul's Church of God in Christ and presiding bishop of the denomination, preached the eulogy, basing his sermon on Matthew 18:6. "But whosoever shall offend one of these little ones which believe in me, it was better for him that a millstone was hung about his neck and that he be drowned in the depths of the sea." He also addressed the racial division in the South. "Our country is spending millions trying to win the good will of colored people in Africa and India," he told the audience. "Our President and Vice President Nixon and Secretary of State Dulles ought to be seeking the good will of colored people in Mississippi, Alabama and Georgia." Ford also named all of the Chicago newspapers and asked God's blessings upon them for the thorough coverage they had given the case.[117]

Archibald Carey, a minister and former Chicago alderman, also spoke, reminding those gathered that "it is not for us to avenge. A mob in Chicago is not better than a mob in Mississippi." Illinois state senator Marshall Korshak, expressing sympathy to the family on behalf of Mayor Daley, called Till "a martyr and inspiration to God-fearing people." Others on the program included Maybelle Campbell, Till's teacher at McCosh Elementary, who called her student a "fine upstanding pupil," and evangelist Goldie Haynes, who sang "I Don't Know Why I Have to Cry Sometimes." A twenty-five-voice women's choir provided the rest of the music. Throughout the funeral, Rev. Cornelius Adams, of Greater Harvest Baptist Church, sat near the casket, where he collected money for a special fund established by the NAACP. "Contribute your money so that this will not happen again," he told the crowd.[118]

Mamie announced sometime on Saturday her decision to postpone burial of her son until Tuesday at 10:00 A.M. so that people could continue to view the body. After the funeral, a line formed and viewing resumed. Emmett Till would also remain on display Sunday and Monday from 6:00 A.M. until midnight. Thousands more came over the next few days, waiting in line for over an hour. People continued to react emotionally as they looked into the casket. Many cried, and others appeared to be in shock. Chicago resident Doris Colon went to the church with friends. "I wasn't expecting the body to look like it did. It was horrifying," she later said. "If I had known what it was going to be like I wouldn't have gone. I had nightmares. I could see him in my sleep."[119]

Things were still tense in the Mississippi Delta over the weekend. Sunday in Greenwood, Sheriff Smith received two calls from an unidentified black man, whom he described as "apparently friendly and just trying to give us a tip," urging Smith to "make preparations for there was going to be serious trouble." With rumors of a black invasion still in the back of his mind from the day before, Smith played it safe and secured authorization from Governor White to call out the National Guard. In all, sixty guardsmen of the 114th National Guard Field Artillery Battalion, under Major Shelton Wood, began patrolling the courthouse, weapons in hand, with a charge to protect the prisoners and head off any trouble. Most of them were Greenwood area youth with no combat experience; however, Major Hartley T. Sanford of Indianola, provided help, as did Major General W. P. Wilson of Jackson, who served as Mississippi's adjunct general.

Sheriff Smith and his deputies remained armed and present throughout the night as well. Scores of Greenwood residents gathered and watched in amazement, wondering what was going to happen next. Unbeknownst to the public, however, Smith had secretly moved Milam and Bryant to Greenville, fifty-five miles away in Washington County. Although the watch was free of incident, the presence of the Guard was evidence of the tense climate in the Delta, which only served to fuel an already growing resentment.[120]

In that atmosphere, previously reluctant or uninterested attorneys now came to the aid of the defendants. Newspapers announced Sunday that the entire legal force in Sumner had been retained to represent Milam and Bryant. After first setting their fee at $5000, which was well out of reach of the defendants, partners Jesse J. Breland and Johnny Whitten lowered it to $2000, half of which the family was able to pay up front. The attorney's came on board because they had become sensitive to how outsiders were constantly criticizing the state. Two other attorneys, partners C. Sidney Carlton and Harvey Henderson, also joined the team, as did thirty-four-year-old J. W. Kellum. The involvement of these well-known and respected lawyers helped further erode public sympathies for a conviction.[121]

Ed Cochran, president of the Greenwood chapter of the NAACP, aware of the sentiment developing among Mississippi's white citizens, went out of his way to praise local law enforcement officials for doing their best to seek justice. He also countered some of the fallout caused by Roy Wilkins's criticisms with an emphatic reminder that the murder of Till "is condoned by none of the people in Mississippi, white or colored."[122]

Although it was the Labor Day holiday on Monday, an eighteen-man grand jury began meeting in Sumner, the county's western seat, to consider cases for the upcoming term of court. That morning, prior to the jury hearing evidence against Milam and Bryant, District Attorney Chatham gathered everyone involved in the investigation for a conference and went over the evidence—a move prompted by Sheriff Strider's public doubts about the identity of the body. Strider still was not letting down. "It just seems that evidence is getting slimmer and slimmer," he said Monday. "I'm chasing down some evidence now that looks like the killing might have been planned and plotted by the NAACP."[123]

At 2:10 P.M. the grand jury began listening to testimony in the Till case. Four witnesses testified, providing conflicting opinions about the body: Sheriff Strider and Deputy Sheriff Garland Melton of Tallahatchie County, and Sheriff George Smith and Deputy Sheriff John Cothran of Leflore County. At 4:00 P.M., testimony ended for the day.[124]

That same day, the interracial Urban League branded the Till slaying as a lynching at its forty-fifth annual conference in Milwaukee, Wisconsin. The 150 delegates from sixty chapters passed a resolution stating that the Urban League found itself "confronted by the brutal kidnap-lynching in Mississippi, compounded by a tragically irresponsible attitude of substantial elements of the state and its leaders." The lynching "hits all America between the eyes. It brings into focus a deterioration of civil liberties and an alarming growth of hate and contempt for human dignity, which we have come to associate not with America but with certain other parts of the world."[125]

Edwin E. Dunaway, the white president of the Little Rock chapter, agreed with the resolution but took exception to some of its wording. "It seems to me that we could express our outrage without a blanket indictment of the people of Mississippi. The words 'irresponsible attitude' overlook the fact that every responsible newspaper in Mississippi had come out and demanded that whoever committed this crime be punished."[126] What Dunaway did not allude to was that those demands for justice were clearly fading away. Yet with the grand jury still in session and presumably still undecided about Milam and Bryant, Dunaway's dissent may have been a politically wise counter to the Urban League's sweeping denunciations.

Tuesday morning in Chicago, after tens of thousands of people had filed past Emmett Till's casket since Friday, 200 family members and friends came together at the Roberts Temple for a brief service. A large crowd once again gathered outside, this time estimated to be between 1,000 and 2,000 people. Bishops Roberts and Ford both spoke briefly, and the mourners recited in unison, "The Lord hath given and the Lord taketh away. Blessed be the name of the Lord." Mamie collapsed as she took one last look at her son's remains, and demanded that the pictures displayed inside the casket be removed and given to her. Before proceeding to Burr Oak Cemetery in Alsip, six men recruited from among the spectators carried the casket out of the church and into a hearse, as six friends of Emmett's acted as honorary pallbearers. Fifty cars and 100 policemen led by Captain Albert Anderson followed the hearse. After the procession arrived at the cemetery, the casket was carried to the gravesite.

Emotions remained high. "We'll meet you in the sky, Emmett!" his mother screamed. Five women, along with Rev. Luke Ward, the twenty-six-year-old white junior pastor at Roberts Temple, fainted at the gravesite. In this emotional setting, Emmett Till was buried.[127]

That morning, testimony before the grand jury resumed in Sumner at 10:00 and concluded an hour later. Dr. Luther B. Otken was the most worrisome witness from the prosecution's standpoint. Otken, who viewed the body in Greenwood, told Chatham on Monday and the grand jury on Tuesday that he did not believe the body he examined could have decomposed so extensively in only three days. Besides Otken, Greenwood mortician Chester Miller also testified. The state had issued subpoenas for Mose Wright and his twelve-year-old son, Simeon, but neither was called before the jury.[128]

Once all testimonies had concluded, jury foreman Jerry Falls issued the final report to Circuit Judge Curtis M. Swango. After hearing the testimonies of thirty-five witnesses for various cases, they returned nine indictments. At 11:00 A.M., four of those, two for each defendant, were handed down against J. W. Milam and Roy Bryant for the kidnapping and murder of Emmett Till. As to the kidnapping, "Roy Bryant and J. W. Milam did willfully, unlawfully, feloniously, and forcibly, seize, kidnap and confine Emmett Till, a human being, against his will," and did "willfully, unlawfully, and feloniously, injure the said Emmett Till of his liberty." The murder charge read, "Roy Bryant and J. W. Milam did willfully, unlawfully, feloniously and of their malice aforethought kill and murder Emmett Till, a human being."[129]

At 4:50 P.M., the defendants, clean-shaven and nicely dressed, were arraigned before Swango and pleaded "not guilty" to the charges. Gerald Chatham told the press that his team was confident about the identity of the body, based on the statements of Mose Wright and Leflore County law enforcement officials, and that there were no plans that he knew of to delay Till's burial for any testing.[130]

Defense attorney Sidney Carlton told reporters that he was hoping for a "prompt trial," and Sheriff Strider said he expected it to begin during the current term of court, which had just begun the day before. Because the trial itself would probably begin within the next few weeks, Milam and Bryant were transferred to the Tallahatchie County jail in Charleston, without asking for bond. In Mississippi, both murder and kidnapping convictions carried a maximum punishment of death in the gas chamber.[131]

Although the trial was yet to come, the indictments were enough for local officials to boast that Mississippi was capable of handling its own affairs and, more important, in seeking justice in this case. Sheriff Strider declared immediately after the indictments: "As far as any racial issue, this element does not enter into the picture. This case, as well as others presented to my office, receive due consideration regardless of race, color or creed involved." He had words for Chicago observers and NAACP officials, however: "At no time has Tallahatchie [County] ever made any suggestion as to how Cook County, Illinois, or the NAACP should run their business, nor do we intend for them to tell us how we should run ours."[132] Implicit in these assurances by Strider was that his doubts about the identity of the body would not thwart his efforts at justice, nor were they based on racial prejudice. That, of course, would remain to be seen.

The same day that the indictments were issued, the Tuskegee Institute finally reached a decision in the Till murder, and like the Urban League, classified the death as a lynching. Jessie Guzman, director of the records and research division, explained that the institute defined lynching as a murder involving at least three individuals. In addition to the presence of J. W. Milam and Roy Bryant, Guzman said that there was sufficient evidence of the involvement of Carolyn Bryant. This conclusion was based exclusively on statements by Mose Wright, but it was also contrary to what Leflore County officials now believed. "The woman might not have had a part in the actual slaying, but she was along when the boy was kidnapped," Guzman explained.[133]

If Carolyn Bryant was present that night, it was the last time her whereabouts were known by anyone willing to talk about it. Finally, however, family members confirmed that she was in seclusion with her two boys. Her mother-in-law explained that Carolyn "went all to pieces after the incident. She has been unable to sleep and has had to take sedatives."[134] As her husband and brother-in-law sat in jail and indicted for murder, the eyes of the nation were watching, and all of Mississippi knew it. Accusations and rumors were heard everywhere, hurled at and from within the Magnolia State, and it was a week like no other in the Mississippi Delta. The *Jackson Clarion-Ledger* even noted that the murder of Emmett Till had "set off racial fireworks throughout the nation," an assessment that was hardly an exaggeration.[135] And it was only the beginning.

4

Countdown

Following Emmett Till's burial in Chicago, all attention turned to Mississippi. The "not guilty" pleas of Till's accused killers meant that prosecutors and defense attorneys had to prepare for what was sure to be the most sensational trial ever to hit the Delta. In fact, it was the biggest racial story anywhere since the Scottsboro, Alabama, trials over twenty years earlier. In that internationally known case, nine African American males between thirteen and nineteen years of age were tried and convicted of raping two white women while hoboing on a train between Chattanooga and Memphis, Tennessee. The eight oldest were sentenced to death.

The Scottsboro convictions were soon overturned by the US Supreme Court on procedural grounds, however, and after retrials held between 1932 and 1934, charges against five of the defendants were dropped. Even so, the lives of all involved, including the two young women, were forever altered, as was the legacy of Scottsboro itself.[1] In the Till case, the charge was murder, the defendants were white, and the victim was black. Despite those differences, a crucial element remained the same. That was, of course, sex between the races or, more accurately, any hint of sexual impropriety between a black man and a white woman. In the eyes of most white southerners, that always meant something akin to rape.[2]

After the grand jury issued its indictments on September 6, 1955, J. W. Milam and Roy Bryant were released from the custody of Leflore County, where they had been held on kidnapping charges, and taken to the jail in Charleston, one of the two county seats in neighboring Tallahatchie County. Two courthouses had once been a necessity because severe flooding often kept one of the two towns inaccessible.[3] Because Till's body had been discovered in the county's western district, the trial would be held in Sumner. Although the men had been indicted for both kidnapping and murder, District Attorney Gerald Chatham announced a day later that Milam and Bryant would be tried on the murder charges first.[4]

Chatham also said that he would send a telegram to Mamie Bradley inviting her to Sumner to appear as a state's witness, but would wait until after Judge Curtis Swango set a trial date. "In the telegram, I plan to express my personal regret and the regret of the state concerning the unfortunate death of her son," he explained. "I will tell her that I think it is important to the state's case that she appear and that certain evidence she can give would be very important."[5] Mamie had not witnessed the crime, nor had she been in Mississippi during any of the events that led to it. However, in an era before DNA testing, prosecutors hoped that Mamie could convince a jury that the mangled corpse she examined in Chicago was unquestionably that of her son. A mother's testimony, countering Sheriff Strider's public doubts about the body, just might pull some weight in a southern courtroom.

Even before the grand jury met, people began weighing in on this tragic case, but there was no consensus on just where the tragedy lay. Some voiced their views in the local press, like the editor of the *Yazoo City Herald*, who blamed Till's death on the US Supreme Court for its decision in *Brown v. Board of Education*, rendered just sixteen months earlier. "Some of the young negro's blood is on their . . . hands also," because the Court dared to disrupt "the peace of the Southland." Stated more succinctly, the Court had opened the door to interracial relationships by ruling against segregation in public schools. The editor of the *Scott County Times*, however, placed all accountability squarely on Milam and Bryant and called for "proper punishment for the ruthless men who snatched the negro from his bed and took him away."[6]

Hodding Carter, the most liberal editor of any white newspaper in Mississippi and somewhat of a maverick, wrote a thoughtful piece in his *Delta Democrat-Times* on the day of the indictments. His analysis of Sheriff Strider's doubts about the body's identity was not earth-shattering, but that was his point. Most absurd to Carter was Strider's theory that the corpse had been planted by the NAACP. For that to have happened, Carter explained, someone would have had to have taken Emmett Till's ring and put it onto another body with no knowledge that Milam and Bryant would later kidnap Till. "Such a conspiracy defies even the most fantastic reality," said Carter emphatically.[7]

Other observers, using less analysis and even less restraint, wrote to the judge, attorneys, and sheriff handling the trial. In such a polarizing case, it was not surprising that passions ran deep as people all along the spectrum began to speak out. "KILL THE RATS OR DIE YOURSELVES," demanded one anonymous letter sent to Chatham. "KILL THEM! OR WE ARE BLOWING UP YOUR HOLE GODDAM TOWN—EVERY STINKIN ASS[.]" Another was just as direct: "KILL—THEM YOU DIRTY MISSISSIPPI MOTHER FUCKERS OR ALL DIE[.] WE ARE HERE[.]"[8]

After the indictments, letters continued to pour in to Tallahatchie County, and a sampling of just a few speaks to the racial tensions then coming to a head. Two southerners, writing independently, anguished over how the outcome of the trial might affect Mississippi. One who believed in the likelihood of guilt wrote: "It is not always the most popular thing for a man to advocate justice for the Negro. But I believe that it is right." Trusting that justice would prevail, the writer continued: "If the men are not guilty then I would be among the first to free them. If they are guilty then I would like to see the law applied to the full. The good name of all of us Mississippians is on trial. However, our name is not as important as justice."[9]

The other, also assuming guilt, worried more about what message would emanate from a conviction. Addressing Judge Swango, the writer pleaded, "Please Judge try to keep those Boys [Milam and Bryant], for if we loose [sic] this Round with the Negroes we are gone for sure." Although the writer claimed to be "a mother and a Christian" who did not countenance murder, she was relieved, nevertheless, that "we have a few Red Blooded Americans left and Especially down South[.] I want to ask you and the Jury one question[:] what would you do if you were caught in the same condition these men found there [sic] selves?"[10]

It was not just in the South that emotions were high and words were acrimonious, as letters sent from Chicago spewed venom unmatched anywhere else. Race relations in that northern metropolis had long suffered from their own brand of conflict. The black population in Chicago had nearly doubled to half a million between 1940 and 1950.[11] As a consequence, African Americans who could afford it began to leave their dangerously crowded and unsanitary slums and buy homes in traditionally white neighborhoods. To say they were not welcome is an understatement; between 1946 and 1953, six episodes of rioting involving 1,000 to 10,000 whites followed attempts by blacks to move into segregated communities. Violence against black families who moved into the Trumbull Park Homes between 1951 and 1955, for example, left blacks shaken, unprotected, and monitored by police as the aggressors.[12]

White animosity toward blacks in post–World War II Chicago was generally rooted in these housing conflicts. The slippery slope had begun there, some argued, and would flow rapidly to the South should there be a conviction in the Till trial. Consequently, northern whites began to feel for their southern counterparts. To balance that, the Till case also triggered an unprecedented degree of empathy by African Americans living in the North toward those of their own race struggling under Jim Crow in the South.[13]

Angry Chicago whites saw themselves as victims in a city that was once theirs, with their status diminished and their rights in jeopardy. Under these circumstances, some did all they could to persuade Mississippi officials not to convict Milam and Bryant. One Chicagoan pleaded to Gerald Chatham "not [to] let this bunch of racketeers and cowardly bluffers in Chicago, or anywhere else intimidate you in the least about the killing of that dirty nigger. He probably got what he had coming." People in the North were too afraid to convict blacks of their crimes, the letter-writer insisted, and newspapers were scared even to point out when a criminal was black. In one case in particular, "only by seeing his picture in the paper would any one know it was a negrow [sic] that killed that little eight year old girl here a few weeks ago." This was a reference to the July 4 murder of Mary Manzo by seventeen-year-old Clarence Baugh. Baugh was convicted of the crime a few months later in December 1955. "Please maintain your good old southern tradition in this case of the disappearance of the Chicago nigger. The south will some day have to defend these cowards here against their lovable negroews [sic]."[14]

Another wrote of his abhorrence in regularly seeing "a nigger and some white trash walking arm in arm and living together. Do you want that to happen in your state?" In Chicago, the writer claimed, whites have no rights and are forced to "ride with a nigger, eat with a nigger and often live in the same house with a nigger and cant [sic] complain." The Supreme Court and the NAACP together were trying to create a nation of mulattos. The real issue, however, was clear: "Convict those two white men and every nigger in Mississippi will think that it is open season on white women and there will be nothing you will be able to do about it for you will have set a PRECEDENT." Once again, this would lead to a slippery slope. "From there on there is no stopping, next mixing children in schools, then intermarriage and eventually a race of mulattos in the United States—Remember God did not make a mulatto." There was only one way to stop it:

I believe the two defendants Bryant and Milam, if they did what they are accused of might have been a little rough, but rough tactics were required. Because if that nigger got away with it, word would spread around fast and there would be no stopping the niggers. A thing like that must be stopped right away for once it gets rolling there is no stopping, And if that nigger got away with it, his friends would do the same thing the next time they came to town and every white woman would have to [comply] or cause a race riot.[15]

The guilt or innocence of the defendants was not an issue for these outraged citizens. A conviction of these men, they feared, would forever keep southern white women unsafe from ravenous black brutes. If the gruesome murder of Emmett Till was, admittedly, "a little rough," then that was a necessary evil to maintain southern traditions. Equating the fourteen-year-old from Chicago with the mythical black beast rapist, which in times past had frequently set off the fury of lynch mobs, created the rationale many clung to in justifying an acquittal.

Most white Mississippians would have distanced themselves from such extreme views, but at the same time they were becoming increasingly sympathetic toward Milam and Bryant because they were angered by outside interference in the case. Yet such interference was more perception than reality. For example, a week after the indictments, Mississippi governor Hugh White wrote to a friend, despairing that "there has never been as much meddling in any case as the Till case, and I am afraid that the public has become so aroused over the NAACP agitation that it will be impossible to convict these men."[16] It is true that upon the discovery of Till's body, NAACP executive secretary Roy Wilkins made scathing remarks against Governor White and the state, and, understandably, most white Mississippians took offense. But since his August 31 statements, Wilkins had lain low. If NAACP agitation seemed continuous, it was only because journalists in Mississippi kept those *earlier* condemnations stirring in the minds of their readers.[17]

That said, most white Mississippians likely viewed *any* comments by northern blacks with an affiliation with the NAACP as coming from that organization—warranted or not—and when that is considered, there was more for them to stew about. William Henry Huff, Mamie Bradley's legal counsel, was an NAACP attorney, which may have overshadowed his role as Mamie's adviser in the eyes of white Mississippians. On September 7, Huff announced his intention to file a $100,000 damage suit against Milam and Bryant should a jury fail to convict and sentence them to death in the gas chamber.[18] Surely this put white Mississippians on the defensive. If the Till case was only a local matter, as they believed, then they must have wondered what business Huff had in talking about lawsuits or questioning a jury's decision at all. Or worse, what right did he have to use it as a springboard for further action? A few days later, NAACP lawyer Thurgood Marshall, who had argued the *Brown* case before the US Supreme Court the year before, blamed Till's murder on the prosegregationist Citizens' Councils born in the wake of that landmark case. There had not been any major racial incidents for some time, he pointed out, but since the emergence of the Citizens' Councils, three blacks had been murdered in Mississippi.[19] For his victory in outlawing segregated schools in the South, Marshall had won few white friends there. If citizens of the Magnolia State wanted to find meddlers, in their minds, they did not have to look very far.

The narrative most whites would have approved for public consumption regarding their postindictment sentiments came from one of Milam's and Bryant's defense attorneys, who affirmed that "the people of this area all regret that this awful thing happened. We don't condone such actions, but the people here are not convinced that the boys killed the negro boy."[20] Yet any nagging doubts about guilt soon evolved into full support for an acquittal. This can be gauged by public response to a letter to the editor published in the *Greenwood Commonwealth* the next day, September 8, by local storekeeper A. B. Ainsworth. His letter, addressed "To All White Mississippians," urged locals to donate money to a fund set up for the defendants. "We should not sit idly down and see these two men railroaded and made the object of the combined forces now working against them in the North." Ainsworth accused the NAACP, the Urban League, and "various other groups in the North" of raising money to help prosecute the half-brothers, who, being in jail, were unable to earn a living. He encouraged donors to write checks to the Bryant and Milam Defense Fund and mail them to him or drop them off at his store.[21]

Money began coming in immediately, which helped the defendants toward the $1,000 still owed for retaining the attorneys. The people of Humphreys County banded together and sent in at least three different collections totaling nearly $300, with a covering letter assuring the defendants that they "wish to express our sympathy to you as we feel our actions would be the same as yours under similar circumstances." Even the prosecutor who hoped to convict Milam and Bryant received an inquiry from a man in Florence, South Carolina, who wanted to help "the two white men who have been indited [*sic*] by the Grand Jury in your county for defending their home and the purity of their white womanhood against the insult of an arrogant negro. Some of us in this community would like to contribute a small amount, largely as a token, to the defense fund for these boys." Chatham passed the letter on to the defense attorneys.[22]

Five days after starting the fund, Ainsworth boasted that the drive had been successful, although he declined to say how much money had been raised. He scrapped his original plan to open a bank account for the jailed pair, he explained, because most of the donations had been sent directly to their families. A journalist who came to Sumner to cover the trial recalled in 2006 that he saw money jars for the fund displayed in stores throughout town. After the trial began, the *Jackson State Times* reported that donations were rumored to have topped $5,000, although that was disputed by the defense.[23] Ainsworth's thinking when initiating the drive, as indicated in his call to "White Mississippians," reveals that for him and those who supported his cause, the Till case was the latest battle in a southern white war fought simultaneously against influential blacks in the North and any black progress in the South.

On Wednesday, September 7, Judge Swango scheduled a meeting for the following day for himself and the attorneys to work out the trial date. However, he became ill Thursday and was out of his chambers, but promised to return to court and hold the meeting on Friday. Both the defense and prosecution told the press that they preferred a date within the current term of court.[24]

Perhaps it was the fact that her son had been murdered in Mississippi, or maybe she had heard how Tallahatchie County whites were now rallying around Emmett Till's accused killers, but whatever the reason, Mamie Bradley had mixed emotions about going to the trial. She agreed with her advisers that her presence would aid the prosecution, however, and on Thursday, September 7, attorney Huff announced that Mamie would attend as long as she was "adequately protected" from the time she left Chicago until she returned home. Learning this, Gerald Chatham told the press that he would send Mamie his telegram that day and promised to provide her "any reasonable protection she might feel that she needs."[25]

White Mississippians were certainly bothered by Mamie's fears and saw them as an extension of her August 31 assessment of Mississippi as a "den of snakes," where people "will do these things [commit murder] with hardly any provocation." But Mamie also made enemies in the state for more innocent reasons. One newspaper editor criticized Mamie's decision from earlier in the month to hold an open-casket funeral for her son and for allowing the NAACP to accept donations at the service. Jimmy Arrington, editor of the *Collins Commercial*, became convinced that Mamie's move was motivated primarily by the financial interests of the NAACP. He argued in a September 8 editorial for a federal law prohibiting any public display of dead bodies for the purpose of raising money. Arrington even called upon Mississippi senator James O. Eastland to introduce a bill in Congress to that effect. "Human decency demands such a law and civilized people are entitled to one." Arrington was only thinking out loud in his small-town paper, yet larger publications, such as the *Jackson Daily News*, quoted the editorial, giving it statewide attention. There is no evidence that Arrington pushed this idea any further, and none whatsoever that Eastland considered Arrington's proposal at all, despite Eastland having been a fierce segregationist and hardly a friend to black Mississippians.[26]

Although Arrington's idea died rather quickly, white animosity toward the NAACP did not. A prominent black leader recognized this and tried to ameliorate the situation. In Memphis on Thursday, Dr. Joseph Jackson, president of the National Negro Baptist Convention, introduced a resolution to the 7,000 delegates meeting there to commend Mississippi law enforcement officials for their handling of the Till case. He urged them to "pray that they will continue until their task has been completed." Proclaiming the vicious Till murder as "worse than a lynching," however, Jackson called upon whites and blacks all over the country "to discontinue those methods which breed hate and increase tension." He asked black citizens not to judge the entire state by the actions of just a few. His admonition and counsel were covered in most papers throughout Mississippi.[27]

By Friday, September 9, Mamie Bradley had also become more circumspect in her comments. In fairness, her harshest criticisms of Mississippi were uttered immediately upon learning of her son's murder. Speaking calmly ten days later, she explained that she was "not bitter against the white people. The color of a person's skin has never made any difference to me, and it never will. Some of my best friends are among the white race." She was also touched by the outpouring of support she had received from both black and white Americans. In monetary terms, that amounted to over $4,000 in donations from sympathizers all over the country; to keep that in perspective, her annual salary at the US Air Force was only $3,900. Most of the letters she received were favorable, with only a few "cranks." If Mississippians began to feel a little sympathy for her after reading these sentiments, it probably diminished quickly by her resolve, announced in the same interview, to become an advocate for civil rights. "I was never much active in working for racial equality," she said. "Now I'm going to devote all the time I can. This has made me more aware of the problem."[28] To Mississippians committed to maintaining segregation, a declaration of war on Jim Crow would hardly be welcome from anybody, not to mention an outsider, and especially when white citizens wanted to believe that the murder was a simple case of homicide without any racial overtones.[29]

Mamie was still apprehensive about attending the trial. On Friday, Huff wrote Chatham to learn more about his plans to protect Mamie once she arrived. "I wish to advise that reasonable protection is not enough. Absolute protection is what is needed," he insisted. The nationwide coverage the case had received guaranteed that many onlookers would be present at the courthouse. "Some will, of course, be sympathetic, and others will be everything but sympathetic, and some may have the same malignant hearts and desires as those who committed the atrocious act of murdering this mother's child." Huff expected Chatham to protect not only Mamie but also local family members and witnesses to the kidnapping, in the event that a large riot broke out where only the few policemen present would be powerless.[30] Huff even went beyond Mississippi authorities and sent a copy of the letter to US attorney general Herbert Brownell, whom he had met a week earlier in Chicago. Huff requested that Brownell provide additional protection by the FBI.[31]

On Friday, Swango was back in his office and set the trial to begin on Monday, September 19, just ten days away. He also announced that the jury would be appointed from a list of 125 veniremen (later shortened to 120). Because women could not sit on Mississippi juries and no black men were registered to vote anywhere in the county, this would be, as always, a panel of twelve white men.[32]

Although many Mississippians had spoken out about the case in their local papers, no one was more forthright than Pulitzer Prize–winning author William Faulkner. A native of Oxford in Lafayette County, Faulkner argued in a September 9 UPI editorial written from Rome, Italy, that the Till murder was not just a local issue. The consequences were so wide that even the survival of America was at stake. Because the white race totaled only one-fourth of the world's population, he argued, the rest of the world would not tolerate white America's abuses of its minorities any longer. Would the United States survive another attack like Pearl Harbor if people throughout the world, who differ from its majority, either in skin color or ideology, were aligned against it? Talk about freedom means nothing if it does not include all of humanity, wrote Faulkner impassionedly. His conclusion was powerful and frank:

> Perhaps we will find out now whether we are to survive or not. Perhaps the purpose of this sorry and tragic error committed in my native Mississippi by two white adults on an afflicted Negro child is to prove to us whether or not we deserve to survive.
>
> Because if we in America have reached that point in our desperate culture when we must murder children, no matter for what reason or what color, we don't deserve to survive, and probably won't.[33]

These were not the ramblings of an outsider, but were thoughtful observations from one of Mississippi's most celebrated sons. Mississippi officials were about to respond by showing the world that indeed, they meant business. The same day that Faulkner's letter appeared, Mississippi attorney general and governor-elect J. P. Coleman appointed a special prosecutor at Chatham's request to aid the state in the trial. This was forty-one-year-old Robert Smith III, a Ripley, Mississippi, attorney and former FBI agent. Smith, a graduate of Ole Miss, had worked for the FBI in Washington, DC, and elsewhere for about two years. He served as a captain in the marines during World War II, and returned to practice law in Ripley with an uncle. He was still in practice at the time of the Till trial.[34] Smith and Coleman were friends and "poker buddies." Smith's wife was severely tried over the prospect of her husband prosecuting white men for killing a black youth in such a high-profile case. "I think it had really never been done in the State of Mississippi," said Smith's son, Jak. However, that mattered little to Robert Smith. Years later, Smith's former law partner, Bobby Elliott, insisted that Smith "wasn't afraid of the devil himself. . . . Bobby Smith didn't know fear."[35]

Gerald Chatham, forty-nine, of Hernando, requested the special prosecutor because ill health limited his ability to fully try the case alone. Chatham was a 1931 graduate of the University of Mississippi law school and was set to retire in January after fourteen years as district attorney. He suffered from high blood pressure, heart trouble, and severe nosebleeds, but if anyone had the heart to try a race case in Mississippi, it was Chatham. "My daddy was a fair man. He loved people," said his son, also named Gerald. "It didn't matter about what color your skin was. We were raised to treat everybody alike, everybody equal. That's just the way he lived his life. He treated those black people with respect. They loved him."[36]

This assessment was not motivated wholly by family loyalty. Armis Hawkins, district attorney in Tippah, Robert Smith's home county, assured Illinois attorney general Latham Castle that Smith was "one of Mississippi's ablest and most capable trial lawyers." Likewise, Chatham "is one of the best and most experienced district attorneys in the State." Together, "these gentlemen are the soul of honor, and their integrity is beyond question. You need have no fear of the prosecution in this case proceeding vigorously and capably."[37] Chatham even advised an inquiring reporter with the Memphis-based *Tri-State Defender* to check him out with local NAACP official Sam P. Nesbitt. The reporter asked around not only in Hernando but as far away as Memphis and received a good report. Chatham, who had been reelected to his office three times without opposition, was indeed respected and praised for his fairness.[38]

Playing a lesser role on the prosecution team was J. Hamilton Caldwell, fifty-seven, then serving a fourth term as Tallahatchie County attorney. Like Chatham, he had been battling health problems and had even suffered a heart attack the previous year. He had initially opposed the indictments of Milam and Bryant, believing that a conviction was impossible. Caldwell joined the prosecution just two days before the trial started.[39]

The five attorneys representing the defendants exhausted the entire Sumner bar. Sixty-seven-year-old Jesse J. Breland, who had practiced law in Sumner since 1915, headed the team. His partner, John Whitten, thirty-six, had been practicing for fifteen years. Whitten's first cousin was Mississippi congressman Jamie Whitten, who had served in the House of Representatives since 1941. (Jamie Whitten went on to serve until shortly before his death in 1995, becoming the longest-sitting representative up to that time.[40]) The Milam-Bryant family was already known to the law firm of Breland and Whitten, because Eula Bryant, mother of the accused killers, had retained them when she filed for divorce from Henry Bryant in 1949.[41] Breland had nothing but praise for J. W. Milam and Roy Bryant. "I've known those two boys for years. They're men of good reputation, respected businessmen in the community, what I'd call real patriots ... 100 per cent Americans."[42]

J. W. Kellum, forty-four, had been a Tallahatchie County resident for thirty-five years and was admitted to the Mississippi bar in 1939, despite never having gone to college. He had run for Gerald Chatham's job as district attorney but lost the election just a few days before the Till murder. The two attorneys in the firm of Carlton and Henderson rounded out the defense team. Forty-year-old C. Sidney Carlton started his career in Sumner in 1945, and Harvey Henderson, the youngest of the five at thirty-four, had been in practice for eight years. In 1954, when Eula Bryant returned to court to make a motion for contempt against her ex-husband for defaulting on his child support payments, she hired Carlton and Henderson. That case was still pending while her attorneys prepared to defend her sons, and would not be settled for another five months.[43]

It may have been only a coincidence that in nearby Leflore County on Friday, September 9, Greenwood citizens honored eleven-year-old Dianne Kearney, of Money, for risking her life to rescue her nurse from drowning in the Tallahatchie River back on May 26. Kearny was white; the nurse, Jimmie Arans, was black. Kearney and her sisters had been fishing under Arans's watch when Arans fainted and fell into the river. Shortly before Kearney received her award, an editorial in the *Greenwood Morning Star* blasted the press for making the Till murder a national story while Kearney's courageous act received very little attention outside of Greenwood.[44] Yet it was the white press that had chosen to ignore the Kearney story. Two days after this editorial ran, the Red Cross presented Kearney with its certificate of merit for applying the life-saving skills she had acquired from that organization.[45] Whether or not this recognition had already been planned prior to the Till murder, or even before the *Morning Star* editorial, is unknown, but Mississippians could now contrast the two incidents. Both involved white and black citizens, the town of Money, and a tragedy and near-tragedy in the Tallahatchie River. Moreover, they could point to the actions of people in Money as positive examples of race relations at a moment when the town, not to mention the state, desperately needed it.

Meanwhile, in Washington, DC, Attorney General Brownell forwarded Huff's request for federal protection for Mamie Bradley to FBI chief J. Edgar Hoover. Hoover eventually responded to Huff on September 20 that "it is not within the jurisdiction of the FBI to afford the protection you desire for Mrs. Bradley."[46] By then, the trial had already started. In Mississippi, Chatham had probably already been balking at Huff's demands because he was clearly irritated with Mamie for the same reason. Building on Huff's appeal, Mamie announced that she now wanted two Chicago detectives to accompany her to the South. Upon hearing this, Chatham could hardly contain himself. Calling Mamie's request "absurd," he told the press that "if they're trying to make a farce of this trial that's a good way to go about it. We offered any reasonable protection. She won't need any as far as that goes."[47] In fairness to Mamie, she had received threats even at home, as had Chicago mayor Richard Daley, and Daley quickly assigned a policeman to guard Mamie's residence.[48] Under such circumstances, Mamie was justified in thinking that if she needed protection in Chicago, surely she would need it even more in Mississippi.

Although the FBI could not help Mamie and was not officially involved in the case, it was staying apprised of events in Mississippi and maintained a growing file of correspondence. The FBI's most immediate concern was the American Communist Party and its attempts to sensationalize the case for its own purposes. During the Sixth Congress of the Communist International in 1928, the party had defined blacks in America as an oppressed people and a separate nation. The realization of black equality was crucial to the triumph of the working class in the United States, and that goal made the black cause a focus of the Communist Party's financial and political resources.[49] By the 1950s, the party had become a shell of its former self, having lost support in the post–World War II era, but Red scares at home and the Cold War abroad kept it under close scrutiny. On September 9, a letter to FBI director Hoover and Attorney General Brownell warned that the Communist Party of Illinois and Indiana had issued a leaflet titled "Punish the Child Lynchers!," which laid blame for the Till murder on both the state of Mississippi and Brownell, and called upon President Eisenhower to dismiss Brownell from his post.[50]

The letter also noted that on the same day, the official newspaper of the party, the *Daily Worker*, published an article quoting New York City council-man Earl Brown strongly urging people all over the nation to protest and for blacks to hold mass meetings and speak out against the murder. "Then they ought to throw a picket line around the White House demanding at least moral support from the President in their time of trial," Brown continued, "to dramatize their lot in a country which shoots their children down like dogs." It was this sort of action that brought about *Brown* a year earlier, the councilman argued, and "the Negro must implement his great Supreme Court victory by direct action against the enemy."[51]

The FBI also learned from an informant that the Civil Rights Congress, which since 1947 had been on the attorney general's list of subversive orga-nizations, planned a September 15 demonstration addressing the Till case in northern Philadelphia's black section, complete with a sound truck. The FBI special agent in charge, a man by the name of McCabe, was told to keep the Bureau informed of any important developments. The Bureau shortly sent let-ters to Dillon Anderson, special assistant to the president, and to the assistant chief of staff of the Department of the Army, alerting them to these Com-munist activities and of a rally organized by the local steelworkers' union in Chicago, held on Sunday, September 11. There, leaders launched a petition to President Eisenhower, urging him to "call a special session of congress in order to recommend passage of additional anti-lynch and anti[–]poll tax laws." "Only in this way," it stated, "can we be assured that other Negro Americans will not meet a similar death." The FBI also reported that Rayfield Mooty, cousin and adviser to Mamie Bradley, spoke at this event.[52]

News of Communists and their sympathizers stirring up the emotions of northern blacks fit in nicely with Sheriff Strider's announcement on Sunday. Reminiscent of earlier rumors that mobs of black Chicagoans were racing to the Delta to capture and lynch Milam and Bryant in their cells, Strider told the press that he had received over 150 threatening letters from people in Chicago, Milwaukee, Indiana, California, and Memphis. "I know that many of the letters are sent by cranks, but some of them sound dangerous," he said. "It would be serious if the threats in some of them were carried out." The letters promised various and unspeakable methods of murder and torture by weapons as varied as knives and bombs. Strider turned them over to the postal inspector for further investigation.[53]

Strider also updated the press on the murder investigation, but there was nothing promising to report. The search for Till's clothing had finally been called off after investigators failed to uncover any clues at all. Officers still knew nothing about the origin of the cotton gin fan that had been found tethered to the body.[54]

On Monday, September 12, one week before the trial was to begin, the drawing of the jury list got under way, and attorneys for both the defense and prosecution spoke to the press. Gerald Chatham declined to disclose whether he planned to seek the death penalty, but defense attorney Breland predicted that the prosecution would indeed ask for the maximum punishment. Breland said he was "ready to go to trial right now," and had no qualms about trying both men together. "It's alright with us. The facts are the same." It was more than "alright." One member of the defense team, speaking anonymously to a reporter for the *Jackson State Times* a week later, pointed out that trying the men together allowed them to use Carolyn Bryant to their advantage. "Mrs. Bryant can testify against Milam but she can't testify against her husband. Try 'em together and the state can't force her to testify against either one." Should she take the stand, she would do so as a defense witness. "How else can we get the wolf whistle in the testimony?"[55]

Attorney Breland's buoyancy was based in part on the burden of proof that would fall upon the state. The prosecution's job, as described by Breland, was to prove that Till had been murdered, that it happened in Tallahatchie County, and that Bryant and Milam did it. "It's all circumstantial, which is o.k. when you're returning an indictment but quite different when you've got to prove it beyond a reasonable doubt."[56] In a letter to a supporter written three days later, Breland was even more confident:

These defendants are to be tried by a jury of their peers, all of whom will be good, white, Anglo-Saxon men. Frankly, we do not anticipate that either of the defendants will be found guilty by a jury, on the other hand, we seriously doubt that the State will be able to offer probative evidence which will show their guilt. We seriously doubt that the body taken from the Tallahatchie River in this County was that of Emmett Till. Not only do we believe that the State will be unable to prove this essential fact, but on the other hand, we believe that the proof for the Defendants will convince any reasonable person that the body taken from the River was not that of Emmett Till, but in all probability, the body of a dead man that was transported from some other section to this county.[57]

To counter this theory, as unbelievable as it might seem, was why prosecutors needed Mamie Bradley in Mississippi. On Tuesday, September 13, she was sick in bed in Chicago and still unsure about attending the trial. She had not received the promised invitation from Chatham, but even if she had, she was not sure that she would go. Any decision, she insisted, would require the approval of her family. "Right now they've almost got me in chains to keep me from going. They fear for my personal safety."[58] She would decide once she received Chatham's telegram, "along with assurances beyond a shadow of a doubt that it would be safe."[59] So far, communication between Mamie and Chatham had only been carried out in the press. Chatham may have concluded that this was sufficient, because *Jet* magazine later reported that the telegram never arrived.[60]

By Thursday, September 14, Mamie finally made up her mind that she would attend the trial. She was persuaded to go after having a dream, as she later explained it, "and it seemed to me that my place was in Mississippi, that I had more business in Mississippi than anybody down there."[61] She remained fearful, however, unsure whether she would leave Mississippi alive. Yet her new resolve trumped that worry. "My coming back dead or alive was of less importance than my being there on the scene alive as long as I could maintain life," she said in 1996. "And it was on that basis that I went." That decision left her mother devastated.[62]

After Mamie made her intentions known, Huff announced that his client would take along two friends from Chicago. "Mrs. Bradley assures me that she has no ill will against the citizens of the state of Mississippi." He added that Mamie "knows, as we all know, that the majority of people in that state are opposed to brutalities perpetrated upon her son."[63]

If this seemed like an attempt to downplay her earlier fears, Mamie made it known that she was still keeping her travel plans secret. Her concern now focused on the likelihood of strangers showing up at the airport and her inability to discern who among them might be "friend or foe." Huff was equally uneasy. "We don't know what might be cooked up if they knew her plans."[64] Over the weekend, Mamie revealed that she would not leave Chicago until she could be called as a witness (in other words, she would not be there for jury selection), and disclosed that she had received around fifty letters from Chicagoans warning her not to go at all.[65]

Mamie would have one stop to make before journeying to Mississippi. Earlier in the week she accepted an invitation to appear at a September 18 rally in Cleveland, Ohio, where she would share the stage with NAACP executive secretary Roy Wilkins for the opening of the association's 1955 fund-raising campaign.[66] For the time being, Mamie also kept this part of her itinerary quiet.

By Friday, summonses to the 120-man venire had finally been issued in Tallahatchie County, and from this list the jury would be chosen.[67] In the final days before the opening of the trial, members of the press began arriving in the Delta. A week earlier Sheriff Strider had announced that outsiders would be welcome as long as they did not cause trouble. Sumner had no lodgings to accommodate blacks, and the sheriff emphasized that no special arrangements would be made for any who were visiting. His advice to any coming to town was to go to Clarksdale, twenty miles north of Sumner.[68] Indeed, Clarksdale had three hotels for blacks, totaling forty-five rooms. However, most of the black press was heading to Mound Bayou, to the home of Dr. T. R. M. Howard, Mississippi's most prominent black citizen.[69]

A majority of white reporters checked in at Clarksdale's air-conditioned Alcazar Hotel. Others went to Sumner's Delta Inn, which filled up quickly. Rooms were limited there, because several had been set aside to house the sequestered jury once it was chosen.[70] A few reporters, such as twenty-three-year-old Dan Wakefield, rented a room at a small Sumner boardinghouse. The Till trial was Wakefield's first assignment, which he filled for the *Nation*. Murray Kempton, reporting for the *New York Post*, helped Wakefield secure the job by recommending him to the *Nation*'s editor, Carey McWilliams. McWilliams paid the $42 for Wakefield's bus trip from New York to Sumner, and upon his arrival in the Delta, Wakefield went to work. Somewhat naive to the sentiments of locals and their disdain for outsiders, the budding journalist walked door-to-door, asking for comments about the upcoming trial. Most "simply closed the door or didn't want to talk," he remembered.[71] John Herbers, in town from Jackson to cover the trial for UPI, noted the reaction of one passerby. "You're making a mountain out of a mole-hill," yelled the man who spotted a group of reporters. "The NAACP is really making you work."[72]

Herbers had actually gone up to Sumner a few days early to survey the scene, and he learned quickly that sympathies were stacked in favor of Milam and Bryant. He stopped in Greenwood to see his old boss, *Morning Star* publisher Virgil Adams, whom Herbers described as "a hillbilly from east

Tennessee," who fit perfectly in the mindset of the Mississippi Delta. Herbers asked Adams what people thought of the approaching trial.

"Well, you know, they say that this guy was only fourteen years old, but what they're saying now is that when they showed the body, he had a dong on him like this," replied Adams, who raised his fist in the position of an erect penis.

Herbers concluded immediately that Deltans did not see Till as a boy, but as a man posing a threat to white womanhood.[73] Harry Dogan, incoming sheriff of Tallahatchie County, may have known that talk of sex would play a role in the defense strategy. Betty Pearson, wife of a cotton planter in nearby Webb, was intent on attending the trial and secured two press passes from her husband's uncle, William Simpson, owner of the weekly *Sumner Sentinel*. Learning of this, Dogan warned Pearson that the things she would hear in court would be far too sensitive and encouraged her to stay home.[74]

For the most part, reporters arriving in Sumner that weekend found the town surprisingly quiet. William Street, representing the *Memphis Commercial Appeal*, wrote that Sumner citizens were friendly and even welcoming of their visitors. Most of the people he talked to did not want to be quoted, however, but they shed light on the atmosphere. Sumner was innocent of the murder, one person emphasized, unlike other Delta towns. Yet "no matter the outcome—these other towns will be forgotten. Sumner won't be." Betty Pearson sympathized somewhat with her neighbors, who "felt that they were being spotlighted not only nationally, but all over the world as the place where this horrible crime took place."[75] Neither Milam nor Bryant had ever lived in Sumner, and few of the townspeople knew them well or at all. Another resident spoke positively about race relations in the community, pointing out that whites and blacks had once worked side by side to build the town and trusted each other still. "Why, there are only a few white people in Sumner who would hesitate to leave their children with a trusted Negro woman," an unidentified woman assured reporter Street.[76] Overall, residents seemed calm, if resentful, over the attention their town was getting.

Newsmen arriving in Tallahatchie County also began seeking out the cast of characters in the case for pretrial stories. On Saturday, Milam and Bryant granted interviews from their cell. They spoke freely about themselves and how their incarceration had kept them from working during the cotton harvest, a time when people have money and can enjoy it. Neither posed for photographs, citing exhaustion and their unkempt appearances as their reasons. They were also leery of the television photographers, whose cars had Chicago license plates. "They've got a lot of nasty letters from Illinois," explained one of their attorneys. As expected, neither of the defendants was willing to discuss the case.[77]

Sheriff Strider was not available to reporters on Saturday. Expecting no incidents, he spent the weekend in Atlanta attending the Mississippi-Georgia football game. A county officer, who asked to remain anonymous, said he expected the trial to conclude by Tuesday night or Wednesday because the state did not really have a solid case.[78]

On Saturday, *Chicago Sun-Times* reporter Ray Brennan spoke with defense attorney Carlton, who provided a glimpse into the defense team's strategy, which fell in line with Sheriff Strider's theory that Till was alive and that the murder was a fabrication of the NAACP. Because Till's death had not been conclusively established, at least in the minds of the defense, Carlton believed that the killing had been staged by people trying to stir up racial trouble in Mississippi. When Brennan relayed this to special prosecutor Robert Smith, the lawyer simply smiled and said he would refute such theories.[79] This exchange provided a glimpse into the arguments surely to come before the jury.

Carlton would have more to say on Sunday after leading a group of reporters to the home of the prosecution's star witness, Mose Wright, who had helplessly watched Till's kidnapping and spoke at length with the abductors. Although it was unusual for the defense to seek out a prosecution witness in this manner, Carlton said he arranged the visit to get his first view of the site where the alleged kidnapping had occurred.[80] Wright had said little publicly since shortly after the discovery of the body, and his reemergence was a reminder of the crucial role he would play in the trial beginning the next day. Understandably, the press paid him notice.

When the group arrived, they found Wright napping on a porch swing, but he awoke and welcomed the men into his home, which one reporter described as having been "patched together by World War II clippings from the *Progressive Farmer*." The newsmen and Carlton listened as Wright told details of the early morning hours of August 28, when Emmett Till was abducted, a story Wright planned to repeat in court. He also confirmed that sometime before the kidnapping, he had heard about the Bryant store incident from an outsider, but he could not remember who.[81]

No one had given him any trouble since the kidnapping, Wright insisted. In fact, he said that he had never had *any* trouble with white people in the Delta. Taking no chances, however, he had sent his three boys to stay with relatives, and they came home only for short periods during the day. Even Mose did not sleep at home every night. "Some nights I stay and some nights I gets superstitious and gets out," he told his visitors. All of the lightbulbs in the house were still either missing or burned out, as they were on the night of the kidnapping. Wright revealed that he slept with a loaded shotgun under his bed. "The sheriff [Sheriff George Smith of Leflore County] told me I could have it for my protection and could shoot at anybody that came in here without being invited."

Wright was not sure that he could identify Roy Bryant in court, although Bryant did introduce himself after Wright opened the door that fateful August morning. He was positive, however, that he would have no trouble identifying the other defendant.

"That man was Milam," said Wright to the assembled reporters. "I could see his bald head. I would know him again anywhere. I'd know him if I met him in Texas."[82]

Wright revealed that his wife and others had been urging him not to testify. Elizabeth left Money the night of the kidnapping and had since moved to Chicago. Wright told the reporters that as soon as he finished picking his twenty-five-acre cotton patch, he was going to join her up north and leave Mississippi behind. The income from that harvest would sustain the family throughout the year.

"You can see why I can't go now and leave that crop," he said.[83]

Carlton, standing on the porch with reporters, moved away from their host and predicted to the newsmen that Wright would not leave Mississippi in the end. He was also confident that the witness would not be so sure about the identity of the kidnappers once he was under cross-examination, despite what Wright had just told his visitors.[84]

Carlton also revealed what would be the most damning part of his case—Carolyn Bryant would tell a different story about Till's conduct at the store than the mere "wolf whistle" that had come to characterize the incident. In fact, she would testify that Till "mauled and attempted a physical attack while making indecent proposals." Carlton said that this incident occurred while Bryant and Till were alone in the store.[85]

Carlton's revelation certainly begs several questions—namely, why were these allegations never mentioned earlier? Wright had told the press weeks before that Milam had only accused Till of some "talk" on the night of the kidnapping. Upon their arrests, Milam and Bryant told police that Till had made "ugly remarks" directed at Carolyn Bryant. If Till had attempted to assault her, why didn't the Bryants or Milam accuse him of that early on? Why didn't Carolyn Bryant call the police after the incident? And why was Carlton telling this to reporters now, on the eve of the trial? Clearly he knew that this story, true or not, would influence the court of public opinion, and if told on the stand in front of a jury, would erode the chances for a conviction. Did the defense team believe that their clients had actually kidnapped and murdered Emmett Till in response to Till's alleged assault? Why else would Carolyn Bryant's story be relevant at all?

Carlton also predicted to the assembled group that the trial would last no more than three days, and that Judge Swango might even direct a "not guilty" verdict without sending the case to the jury if the prosecution failed to prove the identity of the body pulled from the river.[86] Carlton, however, did not know that events unfolding elsewhere in the Delta at that very moment would add further drama to the trial and serve to boost the state's case.

Thirty miles away, Sumner was quiet. The only businesses open on this Sunday were a drugstore, an auto garage, and a black-catered café facing Cassidy Bayou. Even the sheriff's office inside the courthouse was closed. Amid that calm, however, a church in town held funeral services for Kid Townsend, a black man who had died of a heart attack a few days earlier. He was well liked by locals of both races, and a dozen whites even attended the funeral in segregated pews. Rev. W. M. Smith of Memphis preached the service. Jay Milner of the *Jackson Clarion-Ledger*, trying to counter the image of racial strife in the town hosting the trial, headlined a story about Townsend's death and the charitable services rendered the family by Townsend's white friends.[87] Although Milner highlighted the funeral as a welcome distraction to the upcoming Till trial, in actual fact the service indirectly played a role in helping the prosecution.

Forty-year-old James Hicks, a black reporter for the *Baltimore Afro-American*, went to town early and, after learning about the Townsend funeral, stopped by the church for the 2:00 P.M. service.[88] Hicks was one of black journalism's most prominent and able reporters, having started his career twenty years earlier with the *Cleveland Call and Post*. After World War II, he joined the *Afro-American* and also became the Washington bureau chief for the National Negro Press Association.

Hicks heard that white mourners would attend the funeral and thought that fact would make a good pretrial story. As he listened to the service from outside, he was suddenly approached by a black man who assumed Hicks was a stranger and probably in town for the trial. The man told Hicks that there was a woman nearby who wanted to speak to him. Hicks approached the woman, who nervously told him she was risking her life by talking. She said that a man known as "Too Tight" had been on the truck the night that Emmett Till was murdered, and that he had since disappeared. She did not know Too Tight's real name but told Hicks that he could learn anything he needed about him if he went to a black dance hall called King's in nearby Glendora.[89]

Hicks wasted no time driving the twelve miles south to the little town in question. At King's, he posed as a friend of Too Tight and learned that he had been in jail since Monday. He also learned from a woman there that Too Tight's real name was Levi Collins, and that Collins lived with her and her common-law husband, Henry Lee Loggins. Loggins, she revealed, was in jail also. "Both of them worked for one of those white men who killed that boy from Chicago and they came and got both of them." Hicks knew he was on to something big. He left Glendora and drove back to his hotel in Mound Bayou.[90]

In Mound Bayou at around midnight that same night, a plantation worker identifying himself as Frank Young knocked on the door of Dr. T. R. M. Howard. Young also had a story to tell, and his matched well with what Hicks had learned in Glendora. Young told Howard that early on Sunday morning, August 28, at around six o'clock, witnesses saw a green pickup with a white top parked outside the headquarters shed on a plantation located three and a half miles west of Drew, in Sunflower County. The plantation happened to be managed by Leslie Milam, brother of J. W. Milam and half-brother to Roy Bryant. Before the truck pulled into the plantation, four white men were seen in the cab, and three blacks were riding in the back. Through photographs, witnesses identified Emmett Till as the one sitting in the middle. Young and others heard the sounds of a beating from inside the closed shed. The screams from the victim gradually decreased until they stopped altogether. Then, a tractor left the shed, and the truck pulled in. When the truck drove away, the back of the vehicle was covered with a tarpaulin.[91] Young apparently did not know the names of the black men seen with Till because Howard was not able to identify them before Hicks returned to Mound Bayou.

When Hicks and Howard compared notes, it was clear that their stories correlated. Howard now had the names of Levi "Too Tight" Collins and Henry Lee Loggins as the men who were allegedly on the back of the truck with Emmett Till the morning after the kidnapping.[92] Because these revelations might place the murder in Sunflower County and not Tallahatchie, Howard had to come up with an effective strategy, and time was running out.

That same weekend, residents in Money were put on alert when a break-in occurred at the Bryant store. The robber stole clothing, cigarettes, and firecrackers. Although no one was identified, neighbors saw one man running away from the scene. Because Roy Bryant was in jail and his wife and children were still in hiding, no one was in the store or living area when the robbery occurred. That same night, Greenwood teenagers driving through Money fired three shots from a gun. It was not clear whether this was related to the robbery, but it was obvious that tensions were high in the hours before the trial was to begin. Police reported four days later that they found the stolen merchandise in a hidden spot near Six Mile Lake, just a few miles east of the store.[93]

Mamie Bradley was unaware of any of the developments unfolding in Mississippi. On Friday, September 16, she spoke to a crowd at St. Matthew's

Methodist Church in Chicago. The rally, sponsored by the North Side branch of the NAACP, drew over 1,500 people, hundreds of whom were forced to listen outside over a loudspeaker.[94] From there, she flew to Cleveland, where on Sunday afternoon she spoke to 2,000 people at the Antioch Baptist Church. In three short weeks, her life had changed forever. She told her Ohio audience:

> Two months ago I had a nice six-room apartment in Chicago. I had a good job. I had a son. When something happened to Negroes in the South, I said, "That's their business, not mine." Now I know how wrong I was. The death of my son has shown me that what happen[s] to any of us, anywhere in the world, had better be the business of all of us. I am not bitter against anybody. But I will fight until the day I die to see that justice comes to all of the people who have been visited with a tragedy like mine.

With that, Mamie was met with two minutes of thunderous applause.[95] Her first two public appearances since Emmett's death were before friendly crowds. Her next would be in front of curious onlookers in a Mississippi courtroom. She had spent the last few weeks dreading and fearing that trip to the Delta. Soon, she would sit down only a few feet from the men accused of murdering her son. Although she had no way of knowing just yet what to expect in Sumner, she could safely assume that her reception there would be nothing like this moment in the sun in Cleveland.

5

Tallahatchie Trial, Part 1

Sumner, Mississippi, looked quintessentially quaint. On Monday, September 19, 1955, when first-time visitors arrived in town, they were struck by the dominance of the two-story courthouse. Built in 1902 and later gutted by fire and remodeled in 1910, it sat under a clock tower overlooking the town square. On the courthouse lawn, a statue of a Confederate soldier erected in 1913 stood as a tribute to "our heroes" from the United Daughters of the Confederacy.[1] Looking beyond the cars, cameras, and crowds, it was clear that Sumner would always be a quiet town where everybody knew one another but that few outside of the Mississippi Delta would ever see. When Joseph Burton Sumner and his followers settled the area in 1872, they knew that cotton would always be king, but anticipated little else for the community.[2] Yet for the next several days, cotton would take a backseat to the courthouse, and Sumner would be anything but sedate.

As the Emmett Till murder trial was about to open, there was surprisingly little notable tension, either in the courtroom or outside, but it would soon be clear to astute observers that it was brewing. Tallahatchie County sheriff H. C. Strider had already deputized and armed sixteen men, who, together with eight regular deputies, were keeping their eyes on things inside the courthouse and around the square.[3] White and black onlookers began gathering outside, fascinated by the dozens of journalists and others arriving in town. Now and then, some locals were seen simply going about their usual business. Out-of-towners had already noted the irony of the slogan posted on a sign near the city limits, "Sumner, a Good Place to Raise a Boy."[4]

To prepare for this deluge of reporters, newsmen oversaw the transformation of the courthouse lower lobby into an editorial office for calling in their stories to newspapers and wire services. This meant installing several teletype machines and long-distance phone lines. Western Union set up a booth overseen by representatives from Clarksdale and Greenville, while five men from Southern Bell Telephone Company maintained their own communications lines.[5]

Upstairs, Strider gathered early arrivals among the press and held a brief conference on protocol. Limited space at the front of the courtroom allowed only twenty-two seats for white reporters. He gave the black press four seats at a card table on the right side of the room, behind the railing separating court officials from spectators. He was unapologetic as he explained that segregation laws applied in court as well as anywhere else in the state. "We haven't mixed the races so far in Mississippi, and we don't intend to," he proclaimed. Yet he assured the black press that "we want you colored reporters to be able to cover this just like anybody else."[6] Alex Wilson, the only black newsman there for the briefing, complained that hearing the proceedings from their distant corner might prove difficult, but Strider told him to be sure to let him know. "We'll have order in this court," he promised.[7]

Fifty-one-year-old Strider, wearing a sport coat and a shirt with an open collar, and chewing on an unlit cigar, was an imposing figure at 270 pounds. Reporter Murray Kempton noted that Strider resembled Hollywood actor Sidney Greenstreet. A wealthy plantation owner with 1,500 acres in nearby Charleston, Strider employed and housed thirty-five black families on his property. Seven cement sharecropper homes, nicely painted, lined the driveway to his house, each with one letter of his last name painted on the roof, spelling S-T-R-I-D-E-R.[8]

Although one journalist described Strider's demeanor as "genial" and "easy going," the sheriff was clearly determined to run the courtroom his way. He told reporters that with the exception of lawyers and other court officials, everyone entering the courtroom would be searched for concealed weapons. "We are nice people down here," he assured them, but he had received over 150 threatening letters and was not going to take any chances. "I don't know if they are just trying to scare me, but I don't scare," he said. "I don't plan on having any Chicago or New York Negroes knocking me off." He also cited recent shootings in Congress as part of his motive. This was certainly an allusion to a March 1, 1954, incident involving four Puerto Rican nationalists who fired thirty rounds from the Ladies Gallery in the US Capitol, wounding several congressmen. Strider was not going to chance something similar happening in Sumner. "If there is going to be any shooting, me and my deputies will do it," he stated.[9] Strider had only a few months left of his four-year stint as Tallahatchie County sheriff. Under Mississippi state law, sheriffs and governors were prohibited from serving consecutive terms.

After everyone lined up single file, deputies began meticulously patting down everyone wanting to see the trial, and even went so far as to search camera cases. International News Service reporter James Kilgallen, father of *What's My Line?* panelist Dorothy Kilgallen, noted that in his forty years of covering high-profile crime cases, this was only the third time that he had been frisked, the other two being the 1933 trial of George "Machine Gun" Kelly in Oklahoma City and the trial of Bruno Hauptmann two years later.[10] After a while, the process became more casual, deputies scaled back their search for weapons, and they were even seen kidding around with friends who passed through the line. In the end, the search yielded nothing, and Deputy Ed Weber joked that the sharpest items he found were pens, pencils, and paper.[11]

The reporters covering the trial quickly became a Who's Who of American journalism. In addition to Kilgallen, Wilson, and Kempton was John Popham, of the *New York Times*; Jim Desmond of the *New York Daily News*; Bill Minor of the *New Orleans Times-Picayune*; Clark Porteous of the *Memphis Press-Scimitar*; Gus Harris of the *Detroit News*; and Bill Goolrick of *Time* and *Life* magazines. Newsmen from the *Chicago Daily Tribune, Chicago Sun-Times*, and *Chicago Daily News* were also present. John Herbers, UPI bureau chief in Jackson, drove up to report on the trial. Younger reporters such as David Halberstam of the *West Point Daily Times Leader* and Dan Wakefield of the *Nation*, cut their journalistic teeth in Sumner. The *Daily Worker*, the paper of the American Communist Party, sent forty-nine-year-old Rob Hall, a native Mississippian born and raised in Pascagoula, Jackson County. As both a Red sympathizer and southerner, the overweight, white-haired pipe smoker intrigued locals throughout the trial. Several Mississippi papers, such as the *Clarksdale Press Register, Delta Democrat-Times, Jackson Clarion-Ledger*, and *Jackson Daily News*, sent representatives. However, most others chose to use the wire services for their coverage instead. Art Everett, Associated Press (AP) reporter who had covered the Sam Sheppard murder trial in Ohio the year before, provided many of those stories. Gene Herrick, an AP photographer, was also present.

Members of the black press represented several publications, most of which were published weekly or monthly. Present were Simeon Booker, Cloyte Murdock, and photographer David Jackson, all with *Ebony* and *Jet* magazines, which fell under the auspices of Johnson Publications in Chicago. Nannie Mitchell-Turner, president of the *St. Louis Argus*, also went to town with two of her staff, reporter Steve Duncan and photographer William B. Franklin. James Hicks of the *Baltimore Afro-American* was a prominent presence among the black press, as was Robert Ratcliffe, editor of the *Pittsburgh Courier*, who took with him a white reporter from New York, James Boyack. In addition to Alex Wilson, the Memphis based *Tri-State Defender* sent a young reporter named Moses Newson and freelance photographer Ernest C. Withers.[12]

Significantly, it was not just the print media that covered the Till trial. CBS and NBC also had newsreel photographers present, and NBC even sent a plane to a field in nearby Tutwiler each day to fly film coverage back to New York in time for the evening news. In all, observers estimated that seventy reporters, photographers, and cameramen flooded Sumner, the most seen anywhere since the Sheppard trial.[13] The 1954 *Brown* decision had elevated interest in the civil rights dialogue to a national audience, and now the Till case was adding a layer of shock and tragedy to that discussion.[14] Journalists from the North and South reported aspects of the case differently, dependent upon one's own level of sympathy with, or rejection of, the Jim Crow South. The black journalists stood out from their white counterparts, especially those from the South, as they were also caught in a culture clash. Several studies of the Till case over the years have focused on how the regionally and racially divided press covered the trial.[15]

The courtroom quickly filled to capacity and beyond. The room, which held 280, had very few spectator seats on this opening day, limited mainly by the 120-man special venire panel, called from throughout the county. A forty-eight-man regular venire, chosen from the western, or Sumner, district, was also seated. Therefore, people were forced to sit on window sills, crowd aisles, and stand along walls. Two rows reserved for blacks in the rear of the room easily filled up, but of the forty-five to fifty black spectators present, several stood or were forced into the hallway.[16] Before the proceedings began, the court excused thirty-two members of the jury pool who had been selected for other cases, while thirty-nine were dismissed for a variety of reasons, such as age and hearing imparities.[17] Missing from the courtroom on this opening day was Mamie Bradley, mother of Emmett Till.[18]

At 9:05 A.M., Circuit Judge Curtis Swango welcomed the press and announced a twenty-minute delay in the proceedings to allow photographers time to take pictures. Swango, forty-seven, was a graduate of the University of Mississippi and served in the state House of Representatives beginning in 1936. In 1950, he was appointed to the bench by then-governor Fielding Wright. Regarded as a fair-minded jurist who "makes you toe the line," Swango received advance praise from both the prosecution and the defense.[19] Eleven white and four black photographers took advantage of every moment granted by the judge, moving unrestrainedly around the courtroom, often standing side by side, on top of chairs, tables, and even a ladder. All of this amused spectators. "Photographers work with that wide-eyed, almost desperate, air," observed *Clarion-Ledger* reporter Jay Milner, "as if 'just one more shot' was a matter of life or death."[20]

When Swango called the court to order at 9:25, he explained that neither photography nor sketching would be permitted while court was in session, but that both could resume during recesses. Two sketch artists, Franklin McMahon from *Life* magazine and John Somerville from the *Jackson State Times*, were present. Judge Swango permitted smoking in the courtroom and invited all the men present to remove their suit coats if they wished. John Popham was the only one to keep his coat on and his tie fastened throughout the day; even Swango finally shed his coat during the heat of the afternoon session. The room was without air conditioning, and two ceiling fans only seemed to stir up the heat as the day went on. The temperature reached ninety-five degrees, but as one reporter noted, an occasional breeze kept the crowded courtroom from becoming "unbearable."[21]

J. W. Milam and Roy Bryant were escorted to Sumner from the jail in Charleston under the watch of Marshall Shorty Wilkie and a deputy, both of whom were armed. The half-brothers sat without handcuffs in the rear of the car.[22] Once in Sumner, they entered the courtroom briefly. Then, probably because business unrelated to the trial was in progress, they walked across the street to the offices of J. J. Breland and John Whitten. Mississippi law required that defendants be present during jury selection, and at 10:15, both men walked back into the courthouse, accompanied this time by their wives, children, and a few dozen other relatives.[23] The room went abuzz upon the entrance of the brothers, followed by a heightened round of picture-taking. Milam seemed willing, even anxious to talk to reporters, but Bryant remained quiet. Those present were just as intrigued by Carolyn Bryant, the target of Emmett Till's now famous wolf whistle.[24] If not for the brief encounter between her and Till in the Bryants' small country store less than a month earlier, none of them would be in that courtroom. Both Carolyn Bryant and Juanita Milam stood firmly by their men, and together issued a statement read by attorney Breland. "We know our husbands are innocent of these charges and are confident that any fair jury will acquit them."[25]

At 10:30, shortly after the defendants took their seats, Judge Swango reached into his Panama straw hat, handed names of prospective jurors to Sheriff Strider, and jury selection began.[26] As the process got under way, District Attorney Gerald Chatham spoke to the jury pool: "This case has received wide publicity. The state is going to take every precaution to see that we have a fair and impartial jury." To do that, he first asked the men if race would be a factor in swaying their verdict. Each replied that it would not.[27] "The burden of the state is to prove beyond a reasonable doubt that the defendants are guilty," Chatham explained, "but that does not mean that you must know that they did it because if you knew they did it, you would be witnesses and not jurors."[28] Chatham also told reporters that because the state's case was based primarily on circumstantial evidence, he would not seek the death penalty. That would also prevent potential jurors who did not believe in capital punishment from excusing themselves. However, if the jury found the defendants "guilty as charged," execution would still be mandatory.[29]

Questioning went uninterrupted for the next ninety minutes. Each side was given twelve peremptory challenges to disqualify potential jurors without cause. The judge could also dismiss any he felt compelled to. Prosecutors were careful, focusing in part on the well-publicized defense fund set up for Milam and Bryant. This fund had become so popular that Leflore County sheriff George Smith came to the courtroom with a $45 donation sent to him by someone from Georgia. Smith turned it over to the defendants' families. Special prosecutor Robert Smith warned that anyone with even a slight connection to the fund would be disqualified immediately. The state dismissed one man after he admitted giving a dollar to someone who came into his store asking for donations. Chatham excused two brothers simply because a relative was involved with the fund. Another man said he allowed a jar to sit in his store but said he attached a disclaimer explaining that the drive had nothing to do with his business. He was also rejected.[30]

Judge Swango allowed prosecutors, over defense objections, to ask the men if they *would* have contributed to the defense fund if they had been asked to. "I might have and I might not have," said Jesse Lay, night marshal of Tutwiler and a former deputy sheriff. Lay, and anyone else who answered similarly, was immediately disqualified.[31] Reporters were impressed with the extent to which prosecutors labored to assemble a fair jury. Rob Hall of the Communist *Daily Worker* said that County Attorney Hamilton Caldwell questioned the men "with the persistence of a ferret to bring out their sympathy for the two white men." Chatham and Smith did the same, noted Hall, "which surprised most of the visiting newsmen."[32] The state queried the jury pool about friendships that might exist between them and the accused, and also probed into possible relationships with the defense attorneys.[33]

There were some humorous moments during jury selection. One man entered the court with two summonses—one as a defense witness, and the other for jury duty. "We'd like to get him on the jury," joked defense attorney Sidney Carlton, "but I doubt if it would work out." Another was called twice because he went by two names. Several others, however, were excused because they had important business to attend to, most notably harvesting their cotton fields.[34]

Reporters were both fascinated and disturbed by the presence of Milam's and Bryant's young sons, although children as props were not unusual in Mississippi courtrooms. The defendants each had two sons, all four dressed meticulously. The boys remained attentive at first, but soon grew bored and restless and began pacing the floor near the press tables, playing with water pistols, pointing them at deputies, and pretending to shoot. Milam and Bryant regularly tried to quiet them by giving them mints and gum while alternately sitting them on the laps of their mothers and grandmother, Eula Bryant.

Before the end of the day, the boys, also suffering in the sweltering heat, went shirtless.[35] Yet the entire scene served an important purpose for the defense team, which hoped to convey to potential jurors that doting fathers such as Milam and Bryant would hardly be inclined to kill other people's children.

By the noon recess, twenty-seven of the venire had been dismissed, while prosecutors had tentatively chosen eleven for the jury.[36] Carlton, who had predicted the day before that the trial would be over by late Tuesday or Wednesday, now admitted that it was sure to last longer. Fellow team member Harvey Henderson, frustrated by the state's laborious process in selecting the jury, joked that it could last the rest of the year. During the business of the morning session, spectators ate sandwiches and drank ice water and soda. Two men openly drank cans of beer, and neither was reprimanded by the judge or bailiffs.[37]

Outside, during the break, friends of Milam and Bryant spotted reporters and gave the defendants some free publicity. Johnny Tupman, who had known Bryant for around ten years, said that Bryant had once served under a black noncommissioned officer during the Korean War. "He didn't seem to mind him. He told us the Negro was a good soldier and that they understood each other." Yet when asked about this later in the courtroom, Bryant denied it, saying that he was a sergeant and that the black corporal had served under *him*. These acquaintances, believing that the brothers were innocent, insisted that both Milam and Bryant were friendly to blacks. One said he and his wife often socialized with Roy and Carolyn Bryant, and that he never saw Roy drink in excess or otherwise act improperly.[38]

During the recess, Milam sang his own praises by insisting that he had been a good neighbor to blacks in his community. One act of heroism came five years earlier when he jumped into the Tallahatchie River to rescue a seven-year-old girl from drowning. Another time he lent his car to a man named Gilbert Henderson so that Henderson could drive his polio-stricken daughter to a doctor. Milam also said that four years earlier he rushed a man named Jack Mammon to a hospital after Mammon had slashed his jugular vein.[39] If these stories were true, would Milam's compassion under one circumstance prohibit him from mistreating and even killing a black stranger under another? Certainly, that was *his* point, yet such an assumption ignores the complexities of racial tension and violence in the Jim Crow South. For most, black neighbors were tolerated and could even be admired to an extent, but tolerance evaporated and violence often erupted when blacks stepped out of what white citizens had long determined to be "their place."[40]

After the lunch recess, neither Sheriff Strider nor his deputies bothered searching the crowd as they reentered the courtroom. However, when members of the press tried to return to their seats, bailiffs required them to enter the room by the front door, making it nearly impossible to push their way through the throng of public spectators. When Strider learned this, he asked a local business, probably the *Sumner Sentinel*, to print press passes, and within thirty minutes he signed them and passed them out to both black and white reporters, assuring them that they could use the rear door in the future.[41]

A deputy, spotting two black reporters, saw things differently. The two men, one of whom was *Jet* magazine's Simeon Booker, watched for ten minutes as the white reporters entered the courtroom through the back stairs. When the two black men tried the same thing, a "pompous, sneering" deputy immediately stopped them and demanded that they enter through the front door. They complied, and their colleagues followed their lead. The deputies never allowed the black press to use the back door throughout the remainder of the trial, even though Sheriff Strider initially told them they could.[42]

Over the next three hours, the prosecution dismissed five of the tentatively chosen jurors and replaced them with six others. At 4:26 P.M., Chatham announced that the state had, after questioning nearly half of the panel, finally accepted twelve men. Breland then queried them on behalf of the defense. Would the large number of reporters influence them? he asked. Would they require the state to prove beyond a reasonable doubt that the body in question was Emmett Till's? Would they also require the state to prove that Milam and Bryant had killed Till? "The fact they have been indicted is no presumption of guilt," he stressed. The defense did not challenge any of the men based on their answers, but excused two anyway because information on their background was either lacking or the attorneys thought they were too young.[43] The ten men selected by the end of court Monday were Howard Armstrong, thirty-three, of Enid; Ed Devaney, seventy-four, of Charleston; George Holland, forty-two, of Glendora; Bishop Matthews, forty-six, of Charleston; Davis Newton, thirty-seven, of Enid; Lee L. Price, sixty-seven, of Charleston; James "J. A." Shaw Jr., thirty, of Webb; Travis Thomas, forty-eight, of Murfreesboro; James Toole, forty-four, of Enid; and Ray Tribble, twenty-eight, of Payne.

The makeup of the jury is significant. The prosecution's strategy was to choose men unfamiliar with Milam and Bryant—those living in the northeast section of the county—thinking it would produce a more impartial jury (Holland was the only exception). Yet people who knew the defendants generally did not like them, were afraid of them, and would have been more likely to convict than would strangers. Most of those they chose were from Beat 1 and ran smaller farms. They were actually less friendly toward blacks because they usually found themselves competing with them. The defense team understood full well what the prosecution was doing.[44]

With only ten jurors accepted into the box, Judge Swango adjourned court at 5:00 P.M.[45] This meant that the selection of the two remaining jurors, plus an alternate, would be the first order of business on Tuesday, delaying the opening of testimony further.[46] The ten jurors, under the watch of four bailiffs ranging from sixty-four to eighty-nine years old, proceeded to the three-story Delta Inn, just 100 yards west of the courthouse, where they remained sequestered throughout the trial. No one was more anxious to leave the stifling heat of the courtroom after the tedious day of jury selection than the defendants.

"Where are our goddamned guards?" an irritated Milam asked as he stood to leave. "We've got to get out of here."[47]

Sometime during the day Monday, Henry Moon, publicity director for the NAACP in New York, issued a statement prompted by rumors about the organization's relationship with Mamie Bradley. Speaking just after Mamie's appearances at NAACP-backed events in Chicago and Cleveland, Moon denied that the NAACP was sponsoring Mamie on a speaking tour. He also said it was not seeking public donations to help with the Till trial (as claimed by A. B. Ainsworth, originator of the defense fund). All legal action, Moon affirmed, rested on the state of Mississippi. Although Till's funeral had been staffed with an NAACP representative soliciting donations near the casket, Moon said the organization received none of it. "We had no hand in funeral appeals in Chicago, nor have we received any moneys reportedly received in Chicago."[48] If the money went to Mamie as a donation, that was not clear.

When Mamie left Cleveland on Sunday, she quietly returned home instead of heading directly south, despite telling the press that she would be arriving in Clarksdale on Monday.[49] Her return to Chicago was either an attempt to mislead the press as to her whereabouts or an indication that, once again, she had second thoughts about going to the trial. Either way, her actions showed she was still worried about her safety, but it was clear that attending the trial was still on her mind. Just after 2:00 P.M. on Monday, she sent Chatham a telegram from Chicago, which he received two hours later. "I am willing to attend the trial of Roy Bryant and J. W. Milam to be held in Sumner, Miss., beginning Sept. 19 for the kidnap lynching of my son, Emmett Louis Till," she affirmed. "Would like to know what protection your office will provide for my protection and safety. Will stay departure pending your instruction."[50]

Chatham, who had not heard from Mamie since publicly inviting her to the trial, was shocked that she had not already arrived in the Delta. Later that evening, he and Robert Smith responded with a telegram of their own, and their frustration was clear:

Press reports indicated you would be in Clarksdale, Miss. today, available as a witness in the case of the State vs. J. W. Milam and Roy Bryant now in progress at Sumner for murder of your son, Emmett Till.

Your failure to make yourself available as a witness for the state is not understandable. No evidence of ill feeling exists here, no incidents have occurred.

Sheriff H. C. Strider has ample assistance to give you any needed protection.

Please reply immediately whether you will be available tomorrow.[51]

When contacted by the press that evening, Mamie Bradley learned of Chatham's response but said that she had not yet received it. However, she confirmed that she was going to the trial and also revealed her true itinerary. She would board a plane for Memphis later that night and then travel to Sumner Tuesday morning by car. When asked if she had followed the first day of the trial, she said she had but, without elaborating, added that she was "not so pleased."[52]

Others were more amazed and, perhaps amused, by the day's proceedings. The informalities in the courtroom, the segregated press and spectators, curious gazes from townspeople, or any number of oddities did not go unnoticed by visitors. After *New York Post* reporter Murray Kempton and the *Nation*'s Dan Wakefield walked out of the courthouse Monday, Kempton looked around, observed the setting, and said, "Faulkner was just a reporter." William Faulkner's novels, set in fictional Yoknapatawpha County, Mississippi, often centered on white abuses of blacks, strange and often violent events, and the decay of the South in the years following the Civil War. "I had always thought of Faulkner as kind of an exaggerator—that he made things more dramatic by his descriptions and his writing about Mississippi," explained Wakefield about his observations in Sumner. "But I saw that no, it was really like that. It was certainly like going into another world and another time."[53]

If the scene in Sumner mirrored something out of Faulkner, events unfolding thirty miles west in the all-black town of Mound Bayou seemed as if they were out of a bizarre suspense novel. Dr. T. R. M. Howard and others were busy deciding how to move with the bombshell dropped into their laps the day before—reports that eye-witnesses could place Emmett Till, and possibly his murder, in Sunflower County on the morning of his abduction.

Howard met with members of the NAACP and the black press to discuss the claim of Frank Young, who had gone to Howard Sunday night with the story that black sharecroppers on plantations near Drew either saw Emmett Till on a truck, heard screams coming from a barn, or noted other suspicious behavior. Although Howard asked those present to keep the information confidential until the witnesses could be identified and taken to safety, reporter James Hicks wanted to run the story immediately. Howard tried to persuade Hicks that any premature publicity would put the witnesses' lives in jeopardy, but Hicks still argued for breaking the story. Ruby Hurley, southeastern director of the NAACP, believed that they already had enough evidence to stop the trial and move it to Sunflower County and that the information they had should be publicized immediately. If testimony began, then wrapped up quickly, forcing the jury to begin deliberations, she argued, it would be too late for any new evidence. Yet Hicks, against his journalistic impulses, yielded to Howard and held off.[54]

Howard and the others met again late Monday to discuss the safest way to relay their story to law officials. After considering how they could best move the rumored witnesses off the plantations, the group, consisting of Howard, Simeon Booker, Hicks, Hurley, and Alex Wilson, decided to trust some reliable white reporters, who in turn would notify authorities. The black reporters would then produce the witnesses.[55]

The group nominated a substantial list of the top journalists gathered in Sumner, but Howard rejected many of them outright. Booker suggested Clark Porteous, of the *Memphis Press-Scimitar*, and Hicks recommended John Popham, of the *New York Times*. Howard called Porteous and asked him to come to Mound Bayou, but neglected to emphasize the secret nature of their meeting. Consequently, Porteous failed to bring Popham but instead brought along two other white reporters—James Featherston and W. C. "Dub" Shoemaker of the staunchly segregationist *Jackson Daily News*, a publication Hicks described as "one of the most inflammatory papers in the state!" To their credit, neither Featherston nor Shoemaker, unlike their editor, Frederick Sullens, was considered hostile, yet their presence put them in the know and could easily jeopardize the investigation.[56]

That became apparent right away. Howard, meeting with the group around a conference table in the Mound Bayou office of the Magnolia Mutual Insurance Company, told Porteous, Featherston, and Shoemaker the incredible tale of Frank Young's visit to his home the night before. The most important witness, he learned, was known as "Chicken Willie," actually an eighteen-year-old sharecropper named Willie Reed. Howard had also heard that since talking to Young, someone at the plantation had tried to clean bloodstains out of the shed. Howard did not bother to obtain promises of secrecy from the white reporters until after he had told them the entire story. Consequently, Featherston brushed aside Howard's plea for confidentiality and vowed to run an article the following day. Porteous, however, intervened and convinced Featherston to hold back, as long as the story was kept from any other reporters.

After gaining Featherston's agreement, the group made plans to have law officers in town at 8:00 the following evening. The black reporters would then bring out the witnesses.[57]

In their discussion of law officers, the Mound Bayou group had no intention of involving Tallahatchie County sheriff Strider, however. Although he had been slated as a state witness, his announcement two weeks earlier that the body pulled from the river could not have been Emmett Till, and his accusations against the NAACP of setting up the murder, meant he was not in their camp at all (in the end, he was only called to testify for the defense). Trust in Strider would disintegrate further as the trial wore on, but his actions so far made him suspect, especially to the black press.[58]

At home in Charleston, Strider got very little sleep that night, but it had nothing to do with the investigation in Mound Bayou. During the night, he was awakened several times by anonymous callers threatening him or the defendants should they be acquitted. One call, at 1:15 A.M., came from Oakland, California; another, at 3:00 A.M., was from Flint, Michigan. Several other calls also came from locals. Strider later said that these threatening calls came every night during the trial. Those who knew Strider said later that the sheriff was scared, despite what he had told reporters Monday morning.[59] Already upset with outsiders, any threats he received would only strengthen his resolve to teach troublemakers a valuable lesson. And he could do that best on the witness stand.

In Chicago, Mamie Bradley also stayed awake as she prepared for her late-night flight to Memphis. She, along with her mother and stepfather, Alma and Henry Spearman; her boyfriend, Gene Mobley; her father, John Carthan; and her cousin Rayfield Mooty, drove together to Midway Airport, followed by Woodlawn Station patrolman Sylvester Rollins. Bradley, Carthan, and Mooty said good-bye to the others and boarded the Delta Airlines plane scheduled to depart at 11:35 P.M. Mamie's attorney, William Henry Huff, remaining in Chicago, explained that prosecution of the defendants was under the jurisdiction of Mississippi officials alone and that his presence was not needed.[60]

Before leaving Chicago, Mamie told the local press that earlier in the evening she had received two threatening telephone calls. One of the callers, a woman, told her, "Don't you dare to come back to Chicago if you go to Mississippi. We've got a bomb ready for you and for Mayor Daley if you do. You've got no business going down there." Mamie said she was not afraid, however, and no longer worried about what awaited her in the South, either. "The state of Mississippi has promised me full protection. Now we'll see what happens." She also revealed that she had tried to hire a private detective agency to provide her with an escort to Sumner, but was assured by the firm that it was not necessary.[61]

The flight landed in Memphis at around 6:30 Tuesday morning. The Reverend Bob Mason and newsman L. O. Swingler, both of Memphis, drove Mamie and her party, by prearrangement, to the home of Dr. Ransom "R.Q." Venson, a Memphis dentist and founder of the Cotton Makers' Jubilee, a celebration started in 1936 as a means of bringing dignity and respect to Memphis blacks. Mooty talked to the reporters who followed them to Venson's, providing background on Mamie and himself. Mooty, a cousin to Mamie by marriage, told newsmen he was president of a steelworkers' union local and worked for Reynolds Metals in Chicago.[62]

Mamie and her company ate breakfast prepared by Dr. and Ethyl Venson, and then Mamie changed clothes and readied herself for the drive to Sumner. She had left home the night before without having received Chatham's telegram, but Mooty called Chicago from the Venson home and learned that it had been received. After breakfast, Mamie, her father, and Mooty began the 100-mile drive south, chauffeured by Taylor Hayes, owner of T. H. Hayes & Sons Funeral Home in Memphis.[63]

The trial resumed that morning at 9:00. When Mamie arrived at the courthouse, reporters flooded her with questions before she even got inside. Pausing to answer them, she said she was not fearful for her life, and so far, no one had bothered her in the South. She was positive that the body she identified in Chicago was her son.

"If I thought it wasn't my boy, I would be down here looking for him now." She spoke of Emmett's childhood bout with polio and the resulting speech impediment.

She also talked about Emmett's father, Louis Till, revealing that he had been killed in World War II, but she carefully eluded the fact that he was executed three months *after* the war ended. She mentioned that she had been born in Webb, just two miles south of Sumner, and that this was her first time back to Mississippi since 1949. She had received over 2,000 letters since Emmett's death, only fifty of which were mean-spirited.[64]

When Mamie entered the courtroom, deputies let her in unchallenged, but did search her father and cousin. The frisking of spectators was heightened by Strider Tuesday after he claimed that two suspicious-looking black men were spotted leaving the courthouse Monday, presumably to avoid being searched. They were next seen putting a gun into their car, a new Pontiac with Illinois plates, before driving away. The men were already gone before deputies could rush downstairs to investigate.[65]

Mamie took her seat at the black press table around 9:15, sitting only twenty feet away from the defendants and their wives. She probably got a glimpse of their children, but at some point during Tuesday's proceedings, the young boys became so hot and restless that they were taken out of the courtroom. Mamie's entry caused such a commotion among the journalists that some were nearly trampled as they ran to talk to her. AP photographer Gene Herrick, reflecting in 2012 back on this scene, described it as "pandemonium." The crowd around Mamie became so thick that photographers could hardly position themselves. "When her face would appear through a gap in the jammed-up reporters, decks of photo flashbulbs would go off in unison," one of the reporters observed. Mamie smiled, seemed at ease, and answered their questions.

"I don't have any vengeance in my heart," she assured them.

As the newsmen took down every word she said, spectators and jury members stared in amazement. Northern reporters addressed her as "Mrs. Bradley," while those from the South avoided addressing her at all, thus dodging their suddenly awkward tradition of calling blacks by their first name.[66]

After querying Mamie for several minutes, the gathered press corps stood back and allowed Strider, who was waiting, to serve Mamie her subpoena. Herrick had already asked Strider not to serve her until Herrick gave him a sign so that he could capture the moment with his camera. As the sheriff handed Mamie the document calling her as a state witness, he addressed her formally.

"You are now in the state of Mississippi. You will come under all rules of the state of Mississippi."

Afterward, Herrick and other photographers captured the moment, and Strider stood quietly and patiently as numerous flashbulbs popped. Swango, who was about to pound his gavel and start the proceedings as Mamie arrived, sat back for twenty minutes and let members of the press have their way. Herrick had encouraged Swango to hold off, knowing that photographers and journalists would swarm the mother of the victim once her presence in the courtroom was known.[67]

It became clear that competition between members of the press contributed to tension, because they, like everyone else inside, were forced to endure what their colleague John Herbers called "an oven-hot, smoke-filled courtroom jammed to the walls with spectators."[68] Tempers began to flare after a photographer took the seat of another newsman who had gone to Mamie's table. Strider ordered the one who stole the seat to vacate it, and a heated argument began. Angered reporters even told Strider that the cameraman had sneaked a picture on Monday while court was in session. Although they promised to take matters into their own hands if the man acted up again, Judge Swango offered a stern warning that any further rule-breaking would result in "proper penalties." Later that afternoon, the white press presented Swango with a petition signed by forty among their number, praising the judge and Strider for their cooperation.[69]

An hour or so after Mamie's arrival, black congressman Charles Diggs Jr., a Democrat from Detroit, entered the courtroom. Diggs, elected ten months earlier to the US House of Representatives, had wired Swango the day before to let him know he was coming to observe the trial, not as a congressman, but as a private citizen. When he got to the courtroom, however, a deputy refused to let him in. Photographer Ernest Withers, standing nearby, noticed the trouble and returned to the black press table to tell reporter James Hicks what was happening. Hicks got up, left the room, and found Diggs, who asked him to take his card to the judge. Hicks went back inside, gave the card to the bailiff, and explained what the deputy had done. He then asked the bailiff to take the card to the judge.

"What did you say his name was?" asked the bailiff, even though the card clearly identified Diggs as the US congressman from Michigan's Fourth Congressional District.

"He is Congressman Diggs, and he is one of three colored congressmen of the United States."

The bailiff then turned to a court attendant standing close by.

"This Nigger here says that there is a Nigger outside who says that he is a congressman and he wants to get in."

"A Nigger congressman?" asked the surprised attendant.

"That's what this Nigger says," replied the bewildered bailiff.

The attendant, more confused than before, wondered out loud, "Is that legal?"[70]

Once word got to Swango, however, Strider escorted Diggs to a seat at a newly constructed black press table just put in place. This one, over twice the size of the card table used Monday, had room for ten.[71]

Diggs had arrived in Sumner with James Del Rio, a Detroit business executive, and Basil Brown, a Detroit attorney, and briefly spoke with reporters, who asked if his presence signaled skepticism of a fair trial. To that, Diggs simply shrugged his shoulders and reiterated that he was there for "general interest," but planned to hold a press conference in Mound Bayou that evening at 9:00. Spectators were flabbergasted to see white reporters shake hands with Diggs and address him as "Mr. Congressman."[72]

The business of completing jury selection lasted about an hour. Several men in the pool were eliminated before thirty-seven-year-old Jim Pennington of Webb and forty-eight-year-old Gus Ramsey of Enid were chosen to complete the jury. The makeup of the twelve-member panel included ten farmers, a carpenter, and an insurance salesman. Swango dismissed six from the pool himself because they had either contributed to the defense fund or said they had fixed opinions about the case. The state used its twelfth peremptory challenge to disqualify A. G. Thomas, whose brother was town marshal of Tutwiler. Communist reporter Hall noted that the prosecution routinely dismissed relatives of law officers, an indication that it had "little faith in the capacity of such persons to render fair and impartial verdicts in this case." Four more men were called and sifted through before the state agreed on fifty-one-year-old Willie Havens of Charleston as the alternate juror. After the process was finally completed, and the jury sworn in, Judge Swango instructed the thirteen men not to talk to anyone but the bailiffs until the trial was over; all messages to outsiders were to be transmitted secondhand.[73]

Chatham next asked a clerk to call the prosecution witnesses. Of the thirteen subpoenaed, eleven were on hand, called to the front, and sworn in. Most were then taken to a room where they remained quarantined until it was their turn to testify, the law officers running the court being the exception. Those subpoenaed were Mamie Bradley, Mose Wright, and Wright's twelve-year-old son, Simeon; Leflore County sheriff George Smith and his deputy, John Cothran; Tallahatchie County sheriff Strider along with his deputy, Garland Melton; B. L. Mims, W. E. Hodges, and Robert Hodges, the three who helped retrieve the body from the river; L. B. Otken, Greenwood pathologist; funeral home managers Chester F. Nelson of Tutwiler and Chester Miller of Greenwood. The defense said they would subpoena all of the state witnesses, plus call three others—Carolyn Bryant, Juanita Milam, and Eula Bryant, mother of the defendants.[74] This list would change substantially through the course of the trial. Garland Melton, W. E. Hodges, Simeon Wright, and Eula Bryant never testified at all, and Strider and Otken were called by the defense. Several additional witnesses for both sides were later subpoenaed as well.

Swango recessed court for lunch at 11:15. The jury, eating together for the first time, enjoyed a meal of barbequed pork chops in the Delta Inn dining room. Milam and Bryant ate with Strider at an air-conditioned café in Webb, something they would do each day of the trial. The black press and Mamie Bradley gathered at James Griffin's Place, a black restaurant and recreational spot on Sumner's Front Street.[75]

The expectations that testimony would begin Tuesday attracted larger crowds, both inside and outside the courthouse. Around 400 people jammed the courtroom, and more than once Judge Swango, fearing a fire hazard, asked bailiffs to clear the aisles. Outside, local merchants capitalized on the crowded town square. Because Sumner's only restaurants were Griffin's and a dining room for guests at the Delta Inn, a drugstore on the square began stocking a large supply of sandwiches. A Clarksdale café owner opened a concession stand in the courthouse lobby, offering fried chicken lunches for $1.25. P. M. Westbrook, another Clarksdale businessman, brought food in a portable icebox and sold ninety ham sandwiches and nearly 600 Cokes. A Sumner clothing store was finally able to sell its supply of expensive sport shirts to out-of-town visitors, items that had hung on racks all summer. Black-owned businesses also supplied merchandise to black visitors.[76]

Amid all of this brisk business, Sumner citizens had nearly all become experts at public relations, reminding newsmen that their little town was simply the home of the trial, not the location of the murder.[77] Some expressed publicly what most were thinking privately—that northern reporters were making a major issue out of a local matter. One Sumner grocer bluntly explained to Dan Wakefield just why that was so. "That river is full of niggers."[78]

Still, many Tallahatchians maintained an irresistible sense of curiosity about the trial, even if they resented the fact that it was occurring at all. *Delta Democrat-Times* reporter Harry Marsh observed that inside the courtroom, "it seems that almost everyone in western Tallahatchie County is anxious to see the proceedings." Shortly before recess, Swango told the men left over from the jury pool that they were free to go home, but none left their seats. Sheriff Strider appeared unconcerned about the growing crowds, however, and when asked, said he had no plans to utilize the National Guard. "When I call out the National Guard it will be because ambulances are hauling people away."[79]

It was probably during this recess that Sidney Carlton began circulating stories of J. W. Milam's heroics. Carlton, who had learned during a phone call on Monday about Milam's rescue of a drowning black girl, denied that the story was "defense propaganda," and said he did not believe it himself until he verified it. Milam's sister, Mary Louise Campbell, similarly boasted of her brother to another reporter.[80]

As Carlton praised his client, he could not resist painting Emmett Till as a criminal. Carolyn Bryant had declined press requests to tell her side of the incident, and Carlton insisted that it would "take a block and tackle to get it out of her" because she felt ashamed. But Carlton told reporters Carolyn Bryant's version himself, echoing what he told some of them at Mose Wright's home two days earlier. As Carlton explained it, Till "propositioned" Bryant, and then tried to "assault her" in the store. "It got so bad that one of the other boys had to go in and get him out. We believe the other boys had egged him on, because of his big talk and told him there was a pretty white woman in the store, to go in and see what he could do." When Till went in the store, insisted Carlton, Till "mauled her and he tussled her and he made indecent proposals to her, and if that boy had any sense he'd have made the next train to Chicago."[81] Only Till and Carolyn Bryant ever knew for sure what happened *inside* the store, but only Bryant was still alive to tell about it. The bigger question, however, was why that story was even relevant if Carlton's clients were innocent.

During the lunch recess, the moment came to notify the prosecution about the news brewing in Mound Bayou since Sunday. Clark Porteous, T. R. M. Howard's trusted white liaison in the press, approached Chatham, Robert Smith, and Leflore County sheriff George Smith, and passed along the news that Howard had dropped on him the night before. In fact, he read, or perhaps handed the men, a statement prepared by Howard that told the story in detail. Sunday night, Howard wrote, a black man came to him with information that Emmett Till may have been killed on a plantation managed by Leslie Milam, brother of the defendants. This plantation, owned by M. P. Sturdivant of Glendora, was located three and a half miles west of Drew.[82] Coincidentally, J. J. Breland had successfully defended Sturdivant and his stepson in 1942 against a murder charge; Gerald Chatham and County Attorney J. Hamilton Caldwell prosecuted that case.[83] Howard had learned sometime on Monday that someone tried to clean bloodstains from the floor of the shed, but that if officers searched it they might still see evidence of the crime. The most persuasive part of Howard's statement linked Till to the shed:

> I am informed that a 1955 green Chevrolet truck with a white top was seen on the place at 6 A.M. Sunday, Aug. 28, the last time Till was seen alive. There were four white men in the cab and three negro men in the back. Photos of Till have been identified. He was in the middle in the back.
>
> There are witnesses who heard the cries of a boy from the closed shed. They heard blows. They noted with anxiety of soul that the cries gradually decreased until they were heard no more.
>
> Later a tractor was moved from the shed.
>
> The truck came out with a tarpaulin spread over the back.
>
> The negroes who went into the shed were not seen at this time and have not been seen around the plantation since.

Porteous assured the men of Howard's promise to produce the witnesses, provided the prosecution proceed cautiously and was present when he did.[84]

Chatham and Robert Smith were understandably shocked over these revelations; they were also agitated, because if Till had been killed in Sunflower

County, it meant that the trial, now in its second day, was in the wrong venue. Sheriff George Smith, hearing this, said he had been looking for the missing blacks (or at least one, the third man seen on Mose Wright's porch behind Milam and Bryant) and the truck since shortly after Till went missing. Chatham, Robert Smith, and Sheriff Smith agreed that Porteous should call Stanny Sanders, district attorney in Sunflower County, and convey the news to him, which he did. Sanders was so surprised by the new developments and their implications that he canceled plans to attend the funeral of fifty-four-year-old Sunflower County sheriff Van Buren Long, who had died the day before.[85]

When the trial reconvened at 1:30, Chatham told Swango the startling news about new witnesses, and made a special request for a recess until the following morning so that his team could meet with them. Attorney Breland objected, saying that such a move was unusual, and that the state could commence testimony with the witnesses it already had. Swango granted the request, however, agreeing that it was reasonable. He also saw the break as a chance to finally deal with the crowded courtroom, and addressed everyone assembled.

"If fire develops any place in this courthouse, great tragedy will take place," he said. Beginning Wednesday, he promised, he would remove anyone standing in the courtroom unless they were there on official business.[86]

With Tuesday's court session suddenly and unexpectedly over for the day, Mamie Bradley obviously had questions swirling around in her mind—namely, who were these people who may have seen her son driven to his death? As she pondered these new developments, she was taken to Mound Bayou by Clarksdale businessman Fulton Ford, brother of Rev. Henry Louis Ford, who had preached Emmett's eulogy three weeks earlier.[87] Both Bradley and Congressman Diggs lodged at Dr. Howard's home for the remainder of the trial. This was Diggs's second stay with the doctor that year. Because Howard—wealthy, black, influential, and courageous—was an outspoken advocate of civil rights, he was hated by a majority of white Mississippians and had received numerous death threats. His property was carefully guarded, with weapons placed strategically throughout the house for easy access if needed. Black reporters who stayed there were surprised at the length Howard went to safeguard his home against possible violence. Mamie Bradley was equally amazed, but also found the atmosphere relaxing enough to spend time playing with the Howards' adopted baby.[88]

Finding the witnesses in Sunflower County would not be easy. The farm where they allegedly saw the truck was, after all, managed by a brother of the defendants. Any suspicious-looking persons, white or black, seeking out field hands were taking a risk. Two neighboring plantations owned by Clint Shurden and Ella Zama, and where other witnesses lived, would also need to be penetrated with caution. After careful planning, Ruby Hurley and Moses Newson, along with Medgar Evers, field secretary of the NAACP in Mississippi, and Amzie Moore, president of the chapter in Cleveland, Mississippi, left Sumner about 12:30 P.M. For Evers, whose job required him to routinely investigate beatings, murders, and shootings, this excursion to Drew was somewhat routine. Driving in Evers's 1955 Oldsmobile, they stopped in Cleveland, where they changed into cotton-picking clothes and went undercover as sharecroppers. Newson wore an extra-large pair of overalls, and Moore and Evers dressed similarly. Hurley donned a Mother Hubbard dress and placed a bandanna on her head. Then they got into another car, an older, less conspicuous model, and drove to Drew.[89]

These three NAACP officers found a few of the witnesses and received assurances that one or two, at least, would be willing to testify. They left with the impression from other contacts at the plantations that the witnesses would be taken to a designated place in Mound Bayou that evening for the 8:00 P.M. meeting. The most important one besides Frank Young was Willie Reed, who lived on the neighboring Shurden plantation and had seen a boy on the truck whom he believed was Emmett Till. He also heard the beating in the shed. Another, Mandy Bradley (no relation to Mamie Bradley), was a tenant on the Sturdivant farm who saw several white men and the truck parked at the shed.[90]

Newsmen present in the courtroom earlier that day did not overlook the fact of a story brewing somewhere, and they wasted little time trying to find it. Talk of a bloodstained red barn did not escape them; neither did a story of a possible witness who cleaned blood out of J. W. Milam's truck. "Left with no proceedings to cover and an unoccupied afternoon, the army of reporters covering the trial scattered in different directions trying to trace down the leads," noted a story in the *Jackson State Times*.[91]

This may have been the same day that Dan Wakefield heard rumors that a witness was being held in jail in a nearby town. Not having a car, Wakefield asked two deputies how he could get there. After looking the reporter over and learning that he was from New York, they offered to let him ride with them because they were going there anyway. Wakefield got into the backseat and rode along for about five miles when the men suddenly stopped the car and told him they had changed their plans.

"This is where you get out, boy," one of them said.

Somewhat stunned, Wakefield got out and walked all the way back to Sumner, arriving just before nightfall. He told fellow reporter Murray Kempton about his strange excursion.

"You know," Kempton replied, "you're lucky that all they did was let you walk back."[92]

Meanwhile, Stanny Sanders called Sunflower County prosecutor Pascol J. Townsend. Governor Hugh White, now aware of the new developments, immediately contacted Gwin Cole, an FBI-trained highway patrol identification officer. Both men were dispatched to Sumner, and from there went to Drew with Sheriff Smith, Deputy John Cothran, and others, where they conducted a casual search of the shed. No scientific tests were made, and they found nothing unusual, except that the floor was covered with cottonseed, which may have been placed there to hide traces of the murder. Chatham told reporters that "there was so much soybeans and corn in there that not much could be determined. However, if he [Emmett Till] had been killed there, those head wounds would have left a lot of blood."

They also visited an abandoned cotton gin in Itta Bena, Leflore County, and discovered that the fan, similar to the one used to weigh down Emmett Till's body in the river, was missing.[93] It is not known why the officers chose to search this particular cotton gin, located along one of two routes between Greenwood and Drew. It may have been just a hunch, or perhaps someone tipped them off.

Sure enough, problems developed on the Drew plantations. Sanders and some officers questioned Willie Reed and the others on Tuesday afternoon, but the Mound Bayou group learned that when the black witnesses saw the white investigators, they misunderstood their visit. After the officers arrived, rumors spread quickly that they were from the FBI, and the witnesses became fearful. Consequently, none of them showed up for the 8:00 P.M. meeting, although the sheriffs of Leflore and Sunflower Counties did. Complicating things further, defense attorneys heard about the investigation and surmised that something was up.[94]

Sheriff Smith was not discouraged, however, and told the black reporters, "These witnesses have a story to tell. We've got to find them if it takes all night. We'll stop court until we find them." At that point, officers began calling the plantations where witnesses lived and told landowners to produce them or face legal consequences. They did not stop there. Smith and the white newsmen each took one of the black reporters with them and began searching. In "Mississippi's first major interracial manhunt," as Simeon Booker called it, he, along with James Featherston and Porteous, followed Smith at speeds up to seventy miles per hour along back roads while they searched for Willie Reed. Booker explained their planned strategy: "The Negro escort would plead with the potential witnesses to testify. There would be no warrants issued. No one would be carted out of his home. We agreed to round up our people and bring them to the State Enforcement Agent's office in Drew."[95]

The group got lost trying to find Reed. With Hicks driving separately, they drove back to Townsend's office, where Frank Young arrived with a white woman, presumably fifty-eight-year-old Ella Zama, his widowed landlady. Young refused to talk to anyone except Howard, who was supposed to follow the others to Drew. For some reason, however, Howard was delayed. After a long wait, Zama grew tired and left, taking Young with her. When the sheriff went to Young's home an hour later, he was nowhere to be found. At 2:00 A.M. they located fifty-year-old Mandy Bradley, thanks to the help of a black minister, Isaac Daniels, and reporter Moses Newson. They pleaded with her for ten minutes to come out, but she refused, saying she did not want to get involved. She even claimed that she knew nothing about the case. The persistence of the preacher and the reporter paid off, however, and Mandy finally agreed to testify. By 3:00 A.M., the group had located Willie Reed; his grandfather, Add Reed, who saw Leslie Milam around the shed the morning after Till's kidnapping; and Walter Billingsley, who was only twenty-five feet away milking a cow when Reed walked by the barn. All of them were scared, but contacts at the plantations promised to have them in Sumner when court convened later that morning. Howard even offered to move them to Chicago after the trial if they feared repercussions for testifying.[96]

Wednesday, four of the new witnesses went to Sumner and were subpoenaed, but Frank Young was not among them. Rumors shortly surfaced that the quiet-mannered Young went to town on Thursday as directed, but soon left after he got confused about entering the courthouse and making himself known. Clint Shurden said he saw Young standing outside the courthouse, but the prosecution dismissed that sighting, believing that Howard, who was actively looking for Young, would have seen him had he been there. Ella Zama, however, later told Porteous that she had heard that Young did go to Sumner. By Thursday night Young still had not returned to the plantation, but he had earlier told his wife that he would be home late. His testimony was important because he, like Willie Reed, had heard the beating at the shed. Yet Young, who had courageously alerted Howard to the plantation witnesses to begin with, was never spotted in Sumner again during the remainder of the trial, and no mention was made of him thereafter.[97]

At 9:00 A.M. on Wednesday, September 21, court proceedings resumed. Four of the five new witnesses were at the courthouse, and, finally, testimony was about to begin. After a few preliminaries, the state called its first witness, Mose Wright, about 9:20. It took Wright several minutes to make his way through the crowd and to the wicker-bottom chair at the front of the courtroom. As he walked to the stand, the room, which had been alive with conversation, suddenly went silent.[98]

Milam and Bryant listened attentively throughout Wright's testimony. The defendants were alone this day, their small sons staying away from the courthouse, and their wives both quarantined in the witness room. The court-room filled up about forty-five minutes early, although it was not the danger-ously crowded spectacle of the day before. Judge Swango held to his word and allowed only limited standing beyond the room's 280-seat capacity. There were more white women in the crowd, and several teenage girls were also present. Seven law students from the University of Mississippi Law School in Oxford took the day off from classes to witness the proceedings. Two journalists giving the case international coverage arrived in Sumner on Wednesday morning in time for the opening of testimony. These were Ronald Singleton of the *London Express* (with five million subscribers) and John Brehl of the *Toronto Star*.[99]

Wright, dressed in black pants, white shirt, black tie, and yellow suspenders, responded in detail to Gerald Chatham during direct examination. The state needed Wright to establish the identity of three people, two still living, one dead, in order to secure a conviction. The defense's job, of course, would be to undermine that testimony. Wright spent about an hour on the stand, answer-ing questions from attorneys on both sides. Court reporter O. C. Taylor, with forty-three years' experience, recorded every word.[100]

Wright spoke clearly and loudly, his voice reaching the far end of the court-room. He maintained a serious expression as he detailed for the jury his now familiar story of the abduction of his nephew, Emmett Till. He had told it to police on the morning after the kidnapping, and again to reporters three weeks later. But here, in front of the jury, was where it mattered.

About 2:00 A.M. on August 28, someone knocked on his door. A man out-side identified himself as "Mr. Bryant." When Wright opened the door, he saw another man standing with him, holding a pistol and a flashlight. A third man, whom Wright assumed was black, stayed on the porch. The man with the gun said he wanted "that boy that done the talking down at Money." Wright led the two men through the house, going room to room until they found Emmett Till asleep in bed. Till was awakened, made to dress, and the men led him out the front door. Wright heard them ask someone in the car if this was the right boy, and a voice that "seemed like it was a lighter voice than a man's" said he was. After they loaded Till into the car, they drove off toward Money. Wright expressed himself vividly on the stand, often cupping his hands to his mouth, waving them in the air, and sometimes pounding his fist for emphasis on a table in front of him.[101]

The most dramatic moment of Wright's testimony came early. The dark-ness had prevented him from getting a good look at Bryant, but he did see the face of the other man and could identify him as J. W. Milam. Chatham asked Wright "to point out Mr. Milam if you see him here."

Wright stood and pointed directly at Milam. "There he is," he said, while spectators sat fixated.[102]

Chatham next asked Wright if he could see Bryant. The witness pointed at that defendant quietly. Bryant showed no emotion at all, but Milam shifted nervously in his chair and puffed away at a cigarette as Wright singled them out as the men who had kidnapped Emmett Till.[103] Not long after the trial, Wright said that he "could feel the blood boil in hundreds of white people as they sat glaring in the courtroom. It was the first time in my life that I had the courage to accuse a white man of a crime."[104]

Ernest Withers defied Judge Swango's orders and managed to secretly photograph Wright at the moment he stood and pointed at Milam. Before Withers even had his film out of the camera, however, a representative from Black Star Publishing Company walked to the black press table and paid him $10 for the entire roll. Withers never retained the rights to the iconic photo, but the widely recognized image has remained an important testament to a rare moment in a Mississippi courtroom.[105]

Fifty years later, some of those present that day vividly recalled that scene, and despite the passage of time, it remains the most dramatic moment of the trial. John Herbers, who immediately ran downstairs to the press room to call in his story, said Wright's testimony was "a shock. It was so graphic." Dan Wakefield recalled the "great sense of dignity and courage" Wright demonstrated. "And he didn't shrink from it. He stood tall in the witness box and said very clearly what had happened and clearly pointed out the two men who came and took the boy." Trial spectator Betty Pearson also remembered the image of Wright standing and pointing accusingly at Milam and Bryant as "just unbelievable. It almost brought tears to your eyes. It was just an amazingly brave thing for a black man of that generation to do."[106]

There was also a moment of unintended humor during Wright's exchange with Chatham. Wright said that after his wife, Elizabeth, got up, Milam told her to "get back in that bed, and I mean, I want to hear the springs."

"What did she do?" asked Chatham.

"Well, she got back in bed." Laughter erupted throughout the room, and Swango pounded his gavel to restore order to the court.[107]

Chatham next questioned Wright about the events of August 31, three days after the kidnapping. Deputies went to see Wright, told him of the discovery of a body, and took him to the Tallahatchie River to identify it. Wright told the court that after looking at the corpse, which was lying in a boat, he identified it as Emmett Till. He also testified that he saw the undertaker, Chester Miller, remove a ring from its finger. Miller later gave the ring to Wright, but Wright gave it to Leflore County deputy John Cothran after Cothran took him home. Chatham now had the ring and handed it to Wright.

"I ask you to tell the Court and Jury if that is the ring that Chester Miller took off of Emmett's finger and gave to you that morning."

"Yes, Sir, it is," answered Wright.

Moments later, Chatham turned the witness over to the defense for cross-examination.[108]

Sidney Carlton rose and approached the witness and began his interrogation. Wright admitted that there were no lights on in the house when Till was taken, that they were never turned on, and that he had never seen either of the defendants before. The only light came from the flashlight held by one of the men.

"Did you ever see this man you pointed out as Mr. Bryant, did you ever see the light shining on his face that night?" asked Carlton.

"I did not," responded Wright.

Carlton asked about Milam. "Did you ever see the lights flashing on his face that night?"

"He had it up to his face. That is the way I know him."[109]

Carlton then reminded Wright of a meeting Wright attended with four of the defense attorneys the week before.

"And isn't it a fact, Mose, that you on that day told each one of those gentlemen and me that the only reason you thought it was Mr. Milam in your house that night was due to the fact that he was a big man and had a bald head? Isn't that true?"

"That's right," admitted Wright.

When asked again a few moments later, however, Wright said that he "noticed his face and his stature. And I knowed his face just like I see him there now."

"Then you have changed your story from what you told us the other day, haven't you?"

"They was at my house," answered Wright.

"And the only thing you saw at your house, the only man you saw, was a bald headed man, is that right?"

"That's right."

"Mose, isn't it a fact that before you saw Mr. Milam up here, you saw Mr. Milam's picture in the newspapers, that is, before he came in here and you saw him up here? Isn't that true?"

"I don't know whether I have or not. I can't remember."

"Now isn't it a fact that you told me and these other gentlemen here last week that you saw him in the newspaper before you saw him here in the courtroom?"

"I don't remember saying that."

"Do you deny that?"

"I don't remember," Wright repeated.[110]

After discussing other items briefly, Carlton returned to the identity of the kidnappers. "Now, Mose, you say that the only reason you identified that man there that night as being Mr. Bryant is that he said he was Mr. Bryant, is that right?"

"That's right."

"And you also say that, the only reason you identified Mr. Milam as being there that night is the fact that he is a big man and bald headed, is that right?"

"That's right."[111]

These were the answers Carlton wanted, and he left it at that. Next, it was crucial to the defense to weaken Wright's identification of the battered corpse. Wright was the first family member to see the body and identify it as Emmett Till. Carlton again tried to demonstrate that Wright's testimony on the stand conflicted with something he said earlier at the law office, but this time, Wright held firm. Now it was Carlton's word against the witness's.

"Now, Mose, isn't it a fact that you told these same four gentlemen that I have pointed out previously—those three gentlemen over there and myself— that you told them that the only reason that you could identify that body in the boat as being Emmett Till was because he was smooth faced?" Carlton repeated himself. "Isn't it a fact that you said because the body didn't have any whiskers and was smooth faced, and because Emmett was missing, then you identified that body there in the boat as being Emmett Till? Isn't that correct?"

"I didn't mention no missing."

"Mose, do you deny that you made this statement to Mr. Breland, Mr. Henderson, Mr. Kellum and me that the only reason you could identify that body in the boat as being Emmett Till was because he was clean faced or smooth faced, and because Emmett Till was missing?"

"I did not say it."

"You did not make that statement?"

"No, Sir, I did not make it."[112]

Reporters noted that the defense scored points during cross-examination, but that Wright remained strong. Murray Kempton wrote that "Moses Wright's story was shaken; yet he still clutched its foundations." Dan Wakefield said that the witness "fumbled several times under cross-examination but he never lost his straightforward attitude or lowered his head." Arthur Everett noticed that Wright "became slightly hesitant in his answers but he lounged back in apparent relaxation and often rested his head on the back of the witness chair." John Popham reported that Wright "stuck doggedly by his identification of the accused men," yet acknowledged that Carlton "elicited a number of answers that were conflicting." James Desmond of the *New York Daily News*, wrote that "it was impossible, sitting in the courtroom, to doubt that Mose was telling the truth as he believed he knew it." However, "the defense shook him badly on cross-examination, drawing from him conflicting statements that seriously weakened the validity of his identification of the two men." The defendants seemed to enjoy the exchange between their attorney and their accuser. "Sidney Carlton roared at Moses Wright," noted Kempton, "and every time Carlton raised his voice like the lash of a whip, J. W. Milam would permit himself a cold smile."[113]

Wright also admitted that it was so dark outside that he could not identify the vehicle, did not know whether it was a car or a truck, did not actually see Emmett Till or anyone else get into it, and never saw any of its lights on. The vehicle never did pull up to the house, Wright said, but was parked "in the space between the road and my house," which was possibly fifty feet away. When it left, however, he noticed it pass the trees, and was sure it drove in the direction of Money.[114]

Carlton also asked Wright about the morning he viewed the body at the river. Wright said he identified it as Emmett Till once it was turned face up. He acknowledged that this was also the first time that he had ever seen the ring.

"Do you mean to say that he [Emmett Till] was there in your home all week and you didn't see that ring?" asked Carlton in disbelief.

"I sure didn't," answered Wright. Yet he knew it was Till's ring because his sons Robert and Simeon identified it after he took it home. However, because Wright did not know firsthand that the ring was Till's, Carlton asked that his statement be disregarded by the jury, a motion Swango sustained.[115]

Several reporters noted an act of defiance from Wright, because he stopped answering "Yes sir" to Carlton and simply responded to questions by uttering "That's right." Although the trial transcript reveals that Wright alternated his response similarly when answering the prosecution or the defense, when responding to Carlton, it seemed more deliberate, Wright's way of striking back against Carlton's assaults upon his integrity. Murray Kempton said it was "the bravest thing a Delta Negro can do. . . . The absence of the 'sir' was almost like a spit in the eye."[116]

Wright was excused from the stand at 10:25 A.M.[117]

After a twenty-five-minute recess, the state called, as its next witness, Chester Miller, the black mortician from Greenwood. Robert Smith questioned Miller about the events of August 31, when Miller and a helper were called to the Tallahatchie River to pick up a body. Miller said that after they had turned the body over on its back, law officers told them to remove a ring from a finger, which they did. Smith next handed Miller a ring and asked if "that is the ring you removed off the finger of that dead body?" Miller said it was. He then detailed how he and his helper had placed the body into a casket and loaded it into the ambulance. When Smith asked him about the cotton gin fan, Miller said that when he first saw it, it was in the boat and was attached to the body by barbed wire wrapped around the neck. Mose

Wright, who was at the scene, identified the body for Miller just as he had for Sheriff Strider.[118]

Smith then asked a question that he certainly knew would prompt an objection. "In your opinion, was the body that was there in the boat that you took out of the boat and put in your ambulance, was it possible for someone who had known the person well in their lifetime to have identified that body?"

"Yes, Sir," replied Miller.

Breland protested, and Swango sustained the objection. The judge instructed the jury to disregard Miller's answer.[119]

After Miller took the body to his funeral home, Charles A. Strickland, of the Greenwood police department, came to photograph it. After that, Miller took the body to Money for burial, as he had been instructed, but learned that there had been a change in plans. He returned to Greenwood, after which he delivered the body to an undertaker at Tutwiler. Miller finished his testimony under direct examination by affirming that he had given the ring to Mose Wright and had not seen it since.[120]

Sidney Carlton had only one question on cross-examination. "Chester, this body that you had there, did you carry it to Tutwiler yourself?"

"No, Sir," Miller acknowledged.

Breland next asked that Miller's earlier statement during direct examination be excluded. Swango disagreed, saying that Miller, as manager of the funeral home, "should know where he sent the body."[121]

Chatham then asked permission to briefly redirect. "Who did you instruct to take the body up there to Tutwiler?"

"Crosby Smith," answered Miller.

When Chatham asked whether the body that Smith took to Tutwiler was the one Miller transported from the river, Miller explained that he went to Tutwiler the next morning to check on the body, and the name "Emmett Till" was tagged on the casket. Swango asked the jury to disregard that statement after Breland objected.[122]

Miller finished by providing an important description of the body, which the defense would later try to refute. According to Miller, it was between five feet four or five inches tall and weighed between 150 and 160 pounds. "And it looked to be that of a colored person." He also believed the victim to be young because of the condition of the flesh on the palm of the hands.[123]

The state's next witness was Charles A. Strickland, identification officer for the Greenwood police department. He had gone to Miller's funeral home shortly after the body arrived there and photographed both the corpse and the gin fan in a back room. Deputy John Cothran accompanied him. Robert Smith, conducting direct examination, handed Strickland the two photos, which

Strickland identified. The state tried to enter both as exhibits to Strickland's testimony, but the defense objected because they contained writing on the back, probably identifying the corpse as Emmett Till. Swango sustained the objection until the writing could be obliterated. The defense also objected to exhibiting the photo of the gin fan, which had not yet been brought in as evidence. "That is not important anyway at this time," said Smith, who then ended his examination. Because the witness had not tried to establish the identity of the body, the defense had no questions, and Strickland was excused.[124]

Although Strickland was a minor player in the proceedings, the state provided protection to his family throughout the week. Two Mississippi state troopers escorted one of Strickland's daughters to and from school at the University of Alabama in Tuscaloosa for the remainder of the trial.[125]

Leflore County sheriff George Smith, who next took the stand, was highly important to the state's case. Chatham began questioning the witness by asking if he recalled any conversation between himself and Roy Bryant around the end of August. Immediately, Breland asked the court "if he [Chatham] is going to bring out any admission or any conversation had with the defendant," he wanted it qualified without the jury present. Swango then excused the jury, and questioning continued.[126]

Sheriff Smith told Chatham that he talked with Roy Bryant in Smith's car on Sunday afternoon, August 28. Chatham asked if Smith had offered Bryant any reward or immunity in exchange for a statement about the death of Emmett Till, or if Bryant was threatened or intimidated in any way. Smith replied that he had not and that Bryant had not been threatened.

"And was the statement he made to you voluntarily made?"

"Yes, Sir."

Chatham believed those answers qualified the statement for the jury.[127]

Before the jury returned, however, Breland got up to cross-examine the witness. Answering Breland's questions, Smith said that he had known Bryant for about two years, but not well. Nor did he know whether Bryant had supported him in his recent run for the state legislature. When he went to see Bryant at his store on the afternoon in question, the two spoke privately.

"And you didn't tell him that you actually came up there for the purpose of arresting him or anything like that, did you?" asked Breland.

"Well, I didn't right at that moment," answered the sheriff.

"I mean before any statement was made to you?" clarified Breland.

"No, Sir."

"In other words," Breland pressed, "when he was talking to you, he thought that he was talking to a confidential friend and in a confidential manner, didn't he?"

"Well, I couldn't answer that question."[128]

Breland then moved that Smith be forbidden to testify before the jury because "any statement made to the witness was made as a matter of confidence, and any statement that was made, whatever it was, would not be competent in this case." Also, because the body had not been established to be that of Emmett Till, "then such admission or admissions that might have been made, as far as any admission of guilt is concerned, that is certainly not competent in this case." Swango decided to hear what the witness's actual testimony was before making a ruling. Chatham then began a round of redirect.[129]

Chatham went straight to the point by asking Smith what statement Bryant actually made to him. Smith said that Bryant admitted getting "the boy" from Mose Wright's home and that he took him to his store in Money. Because he turned out to be the wrong one, Bryant "turned him loose." Bryant did not name anyone else involved, but said he then played cards at a relative's home for the rest of the night.

Swango ruled that before Smith could testify in front of the jury, the state would need to establish evidence of a crime. "There has been no proof of any criminal agency shown here as far as a *corpus delicti* is concerned."[130]

Smith could not testify to that because he was in Jackson when the body was discovered and never actually saw it. Therefore, Chatham called Chester Miller back to the stand, believing his expertise could establish that the body in the river had been the victim of murder.

Miller said he had made only a "casual examination" of the body, but he described its several wounds, one of which he believed to have been made by a bullet. The defense quickly objected to that as speculation, but Miller was allowed to describe the wound as a hole, about a half-inch square, located above the right ear. He said that much of the head had been "crushed in" and that a piece of the skull fell off into the boat. Breland objected when Chatham asked the witness if "the wounds which you described here were sufficient to cause his death." Swango allowed the question to stand, and Miller answered affirmatively.[131]

Under cross-examination, Miller could only say for sure that death came to the victim by "some kind of instrument," but when pressed, could not say for sure if damage to the body occurred before or after death. Once that point was made clear upon Breland's repeated questioning, Miller was again excused. Court then adjourned at 11:45 A.M. for a three-hour recess.[132]

During the break, the defense spent two-and-a-half hours questioning the four new witnesses from Sunflower County. Only three, in the end, would testify, because Walter Billingsley became fearful and told attorneys that he knew nothing about the case. Chatham had assured reporters earlier that morning that the witnesses "will place the defendants with the Negro boy several hours after they took him from old man Mose'[s] house." Robert Smith said that their testimony "could substantially change the case."[133] By the end of the day, Chatham ended speculation that this new evidence, as important as it was, might bring about a change of venue. The victim appeared to have been shot, but because no one on the plantations in Drew claimed to have heard a blast, the prosecution concluded that Till was likely "roughed up" at the barn but killed elsewhere. This meant that the trial would continue in Sumner.[134]

When court reconvened at 2:45 P.M., two witnesses recounted the discovery and retrieval of the body from the river. Seventeen-year-old Robert Hodges told how he had been fishing when he saw human knees and feet protruding from the water. Hodges described the condition of the corpse as having wounds to its back and a gash in the head. Smith asked Hodges about the ring on the finger, which Hodges remembered was silver. Smith showed him the ring with its inscription, but Hodges said he never got close enough before to see what it read.

"But that looks like the ring though?" asked Smith.

"Yes, Sir," responded Hodges.[135]

B. L. Mims, Hodges's thirty-year-old neighbor, gave similar testimony about the scene at the river. He added an important description to bolster the state's case. When he and those with him approached the body, "we could tell by looking at it that it was a colored person. That is all we could see, just from the knee on down, both knees." Neither Mims nor Hodges was questioned by the defense.[136]

Sheriff George Smith returned to the stand and, in front of the jury, told the story of Bryant's confession. On cross-examination, Breland once again sought to make a case for the conversation's confidentiality because Smith had been a friend, did not tell Bryant he was there to arrest him until after they talked, did not have a warrant, and did not tell Bryant that any statement made would be used against him. Upon redirect, Chatham asked Smith one question, which made it clear that none of the above made any difference.

"And when you talked to [Bryant] on this particular Sunday afternoon, he knew you were Sheriff of Leflore County, is that right?"

"That's right, Sir."

Swango allowed Smith's testimony to stand on the same grounds, telling the defense that Smith, as sheriff of Leflore County, had the "duty to investigate any and all crimes and alleged crimes" in his jurisdiction. Smith then admitted to the defense that at no time during his conversation with Bryant was Emmett Till's name mentioned. In fact, neither he nor Bryant was yet aware of the missing boy's identity.[137]

Leflore County deputy John Cothran was the last witness of the day. Once again, Swango excused the jury.

Cothran said he talked to J. W. Milam alone at the Leflore County jail on Monday, August 29, one day after Bryant's arrest. Chatham asked if he promised Milam any rewards or immunity, and if he threatened or intimidated him, all of which Cothran denied doing.

"Was any statement made to you on that day in the Leflore County jail by Mr. Milam?"

"Yes, Sir."

"And was the statement made to you on that day, at that particular time, freely and voluntarily made?"

"Yes, Sir."[138]

Through a series of questions, Chatham brought out the details of Cothran's conversation with Milam, which clearly had been a casual one.

"Mr. Cothran, will you tell the Court in the absence of the jury what your conversation was at that time with Mr. Milam?"

"I asked him if they went out there and got that boy."

"When you said 'they,' did you call them by name?"

"I didn't call anyone by name. I just asked if they went out and got that boy. And then he said, yes, they had got the boy and then turned him loose at the store afterwards; at Mr. Bryant's store."

"Did he say why they turned him loose there?"

"He just said that they brought him up there and talked to him, and then they turned him loose."

"Did he say why he went down to get the boy at Mose Wright's house in the first place?"

"No."

"Did he offer any explanation to you as to why they didn't carry the boy back down to Uncle Mose's house after that?"

"I didn't ask him."

"And he didn't offer any explanation to you about that?"

"No."

Chatham then addressed the court and said, "I believe that is all we have in qualifying the witness for the State."[139]

Carlton, cross-examining Cothran, probed for details about his relationships with Milam, Bryant, and their extended family. Cothran said that he believed the entire family had supported him in his recent unsuccessful campaign for sheriff of Leflore County, and admitted to being "good friends" with Milam. Carlton objected to the admission of Cothran's testimony, claiming any statement Milam made to Cothran was said involuntarily and that Milam had not been advised of his rights. Also at issue was the identity of the body, which had not been shown to be that of Emmett Till. Nor was there proof that the victim died as the result of "any criminal agency whatsoever." Again, Swango overruled all objections, and the jury returned to the courtroom.[140]

Deputy Cothran repeated most of his earlier testimony for the benefit of the jury and added details about the morning of August 31, when he was summoned to the Tallahatchie River. He saw one of the morticians remove a ring from a finger on the body, the same ring that was given to Mose Wright and which Wright gave to Cothran shortly thereafter. Cothran had kept the ring in his possession, knew the inscription, and had no trouble identifying it when Chatham showed it to him on the stand. Cothran also identified the cotton gin fan as the one lying in the boat with the body.[141]

Cothran described the body as he saw it at the river, saying "his head was torn up pretty bad. And his left eye was about out, it was all gouged out in there." Also, "right up in the top of his head, well, there was a hole knocked in the front of it." There was also a hole above the right ear, which "I wouldn't say it was a bullet hole, but some of them said it was." Breland raised an objection to that statement, which Swango sustained. Cothran continued to describe the condition of the body without speculating to the cause of the wounds.[142]

Carlton, for the defense, probed Cothran about Milam's statement at the jail. Cothran said the admission had come before he told Milam he was under arrest, but that it had occurred while the two were walking to the jail. Milam did, however, ask to call his attorney before making his statement, which Cothran allowed him to do from the office. The attorney was probably Hardy Lott of Greenwood, whom Milam referred reporters to shortly after his arrest.[143]

Before excusing Cothran from the stand, Carlton asked him to look over the gin fan, count the blades, and even describe their shape and size. Could the fan itself have caused the gashes on the body's head if it had simply been dropped on the body? Cothran admitted it could have. He also testified, in response to Carlton's questioning, that the body's genitals had not been mutilated and that they were "well developed privates."[144] The implications of those revelations, from the defense standpoint, were twofold. Because the genitals were "well developed," the victim, in life, would have been *capable* of rape, which would have made the jury suspect. At the same time, had the body really been that of a black man accused of insulting white womanhood, he would have been castrated. The latter would imply that neither Milam nor Bryant had any motive to kill him. All of this would work in favor of the defense.

For the dozens of reporters covering the trial, there was much to report on this opening day of testimony. In the courthouse lobby, people staffing the Western Union booth worked overtime. Tommy Woodward, manager of the Greenville office helping out in Sumner, said that on Monday they sent out 19,000 words; Tuesday it jumped to 22,000. Wednesday, with the beginning of testimony, it was shooting even higher. Western Union was the method used by most of the larger papers, but organizations such as UPI, International News Service (INS), and AP used specially installed private phones. In the hustle and bustle of reporting so much news out of the crowded lobby on Wednesday, Bob Denley, of INS, dropped and broke his phone, which created a crisis for him and his news organization until it could be replaced.[145]

On this first day of testimony, the state introduced seven witnesses. Mose Wright clearly demonstrated that two men came into his home and kidnapped his nephew, Emmett Till. One of the intruders said he was Roy Bryant, the other was tall and bald. Both the sheriff of Leflore County and a deputy received admissions from Bryant and Milam that they took the boy, but both defendants said they let him loose. A body found in the river three days later wore a ring that Wright identified, albeit secondhand, as belonging to Emmett Till. Connecting the dots pointed logically to Milam and Bryant as the kidnappers and, presumably, the killers. The defense tried to cast doubt on the actual identity of the kidnappers as well as the body and how it met its demise. That would remain the defense's focus for the remainder of the trial.

So far, Judge Swango had been universally praised for his fairness, and the prosecution was applauded for its persistence in seeking justice. What about the four bailiffs in charge of the sequestered jury? Little is known about how well they kept outside influences away from the men under their watch, and there are some contradictory stories. Shortly after Judge Swango adjourned court on Wednesday, a juror was heard arguing with one of the bailiffs.

"Does a juror wish to ask a question?" asked the judge, who overheard the commotion.

"Yes," replied the juror, sitting in the back of the jury box. "We want to listen to the prize fight tonight and the bailiff says it might raise a racial issue."

This was an impressive insight. The match was between white champion Rocky Marciano and black contender Archie Moore. Yet Swango didn't think it would pose a problem, and he granted the men permission to listen to a radio broadcast of the fight at their hotel. That night, at Yankee Stadium, Marciano won the bout by knockout in the ninth round.[146]

The concern exhibited by the bailiff may have been an anomaly. A few years later, a graduate student interviewing the jurors and others reported "rumors" that members of the Citizens' Council visited each member of the jury during the trial and encouraged them to vote "the right way" when the time came. Whether or not this was true, it is clear that *someone* wanted to influence the jury. Early Wednesday morning a cross was set ablaze between the Delta Inn and the Sumner depot of the Mississippi Valley Railroad. This incident, typically an act of intimidation by the Ku Klux Klan, received little attention, perhaps because local resident Clarence Sumner saw the fire and extinguished it before too many people noticed. In fact, one black reporter said the incident "had less effect on Negroes as a flea bite on an elephant." The blaze may have been set by the Klan or may simply have been what *Greenwood Morning Star* editor Virgil Adams called a "juvenile prank." Either way, a burning cross in front of the hotel where the jury slept obviously had an intended message.[147]

The first day of testimony also coincided with, or perhaps was the cause of, increased resentment among the local citizens. Throughout the day, those gathered outside the courthouse still conversed and laughed together, but there was "a nervous edge not evident before," observed *Clarion-Ledger* reporter Jay Milner. The crowds seemed more deliberately segregated, with blacks gathering on the east side of the courthouse and whites on the west. Milner believed the heightened tensions among locals may have been rooted in the Tuesday arrivals of Mamie Bradley and Representative Charles Diggs. "Many Deltans are convinced the two have hidden motives for being here."[148] There was also animosity toward the press, and people wondered why "those blankety-blank newspapers are making all this fuss." Milner noted that the "tan faces" of the white residents "wrinkle into a kind of helplessly belligerent signal when an expensively dressed Negro reporter or photographer would stride confidently past them." Were the members of the jury feeling the same thing? Milner believed this resentment represented the biggest obstacle for the state in winning sympathy for its case.[149] Similarly, Virgil Adams thought the problem originated with the outside press, and branded those visiting from the North as "radicals" who were "probably spreading vicious propaganda about Miss[issippi] in New York and foreign newspapers."[150]

Perhaps Adams took some satisfaction that Wednesday was not a good day for at least a few of the visiting reporters. When *Baltimore Afro-American* journalist James Hicks went to his car after the morning recess, a deputy approached and promptly arrested him. He escorted Hicks to Justice of the Peace Ralph Lindsey, who, being the linotypist for the *Sumner Sentinel*, was at work at the newspaper office. The deputy refused to tell Hicks the charges against him, even after others came to the scene and vouched for him, including William Simpson, owner of the *Sentinel*. Simpson had come to know many of the reporters, and let them use his office to write their stories. He even entertained several at his home during the week. Only after those present threatened to call Sheriff Strider did the deputy explain to Hicks that he had been reported for passing a parked school bus, which violated Mississippi state law. Luckily for Hicks, Lindsey simply took him into a back room, read to him the law, and let him go.[151]

Perhaps the strangest incident involving a reporter occurred that same day to Ronald Singleton, covering the trial for the *London Express*. Singleton had just arrived in Sumner that morning when Town Marshall Audley Downs saw him in the street and, failing to recognize him, told him to stop. Singleton got scared, began to run, and Downs fired three shots over his head. Later, Singleton accidentally walked into the wrong room at a Sumner boardinghouse, where he was run out. He was so traumatized by all of this that he never returned to the courtroom after the Wednesday morning session. On Thursday, he even refused to come out of his room.[152] Nearly a month later, the Communist *London Daily Express* ran a story claiming that Singleton had been kidnapped and abused while in Sumner, but Sheriff Strider denied this, saying Singleton had been drinking when he walked into the wrong room. After the shots were fired, he ran, but was later overtaken. Strider even maintained that Singleton called him from Sumner and told him he had been picked up for drunkenness.[153]

Reporter Bill Minor independently recalled this incident fifty-four years later, and although he probably remembers some of the details incorrectly, he added a bizarre climax to the whole story. Minor said that one night during the trial, he and several other reporters were drinking together at the Alcazar Hotel in Clarksdale when "this one British reporter" came in with scratches on his body and his clothes torn. The terrified man explained that he and another journalist had gone into a bar just off Sumner's town square, not realizing it was for blacks only. When they left, they ran into some white "toughies" who began chasing them. To escape, they crawled through a cotton patch until they were out of sight. "That's a true story!" said Minor, emphatically.[154] The only coverage of the trial to appear in the *London Express* under Singleton's name reported Wednesday morning's testimony, which backs up the claim that Singleton never went back to the courtroom.[155] Singleton telegraphed the paper's New York office and insisted that another reporter be assigned to cover the remainder of the trial. Following that, Singleton left town.[156]

The most powerful symbol of hostility, however, was in Sheriff Strider, and if he was hiding it before, he wasn't by midweek. In fact, on Tuesday, Strider stared at the black reporters as they returned from lunch and greeted them with "Hello niggers." He went on to address them with this epithet throughout the rest of the week.[157] It did not help that Strider was still receiving hate mail, and on Wednesday he showed reporters an airmail letter with a Chicago postmark that had arrived that morning. It included a photo of J. W. Milam and Roy and Carolyn Bryant, mutilated by holes and a red substance indicating blood and wounds. A note, which included some "unprintable words," also threatened: "If the judge don't find them guilty, look for this to happen to all whites in Money, Miss."[158]

Black reporters also had to deal with abuses from Strider's deputies. William Franklin, photographer for the *St. Louis Argus,* found that from the beginning of the trial, Deputy Ben Selby had taken a disliking to him and singled out Franklin for special frisking every time Franklin reentered the courtroom. Franklin wanted to document Selby's antics and asked Ernest Withers to snap a photo as Selby patted him down. When Withers told Selby that the flash failed and asked if he could take another, Selby replied, "Oh, that's awright. Go on and make another. Take it on up to New York and let them see how we treat you niggers down here."[159]

Even though the black press had been given a larger table Tuesday, they were still relegated to a distant corner and could not always hear the testimony. Steve Duncan of the *Argus* noted wryly, "In keeping with the tradition of this state, Negro newsmen were afforded separate and unequal facilities." They did enjoy the assistance of sixty-six-year-old Anderson Scales, a black employee of the courthouse, who regularly brought them water, and nine-year-old Tommy Wiggins, who brought Cokes to the table and ran stories to the Western Union office and other errands.[160]

If Strider and his deputies created difficulties for the black reporters, internal problems among the white reporters meant that they also experienced their fair share of tension. Reporters were still anxious Wednesday night over the revelations concerning new witnesses from Sunflower County who were set to testify the following day. Several details of the story appeared on Wednesday in an article by Clark Porteous in the *Memphis Press-Scimitar,* which only whetted the journalists' appetites for more. Most of them began following special tips and went out on their own to chase down more information. One said the competition became so great that reporters became suspicious of each other. One newsman leaving the Alcazar Hotel only to buy a pack of cigarettes caused such a commotion that the office switchboard was soon overloaded with curious queries from his colleagues.[161] Porteous tried to scoop them all when he reported that on Wednesday night, investigator Gwin Cole had located the truck believed to have been involved in the murder, but was still trying to determine its ownership.[162] Because Cole appears to have said nothing more after that leak, he may have discovered during further investigation that this was not the right truck after all.

Exacerbating the tensions among locals was the longing for normalcy to return to Sumner, and perhaps an underlying fear that it never would. The oppressive heat helped bring it all to a boil. On the first day of the trial, Murray Kempton strolled by J. W. Milam as he balanced a child on his knee, and casually commented, "Pretty hot today, huh, J. W.?"

Milam, sweating profusely, looked up, and stared at Kempton briefly. Milam's answer certainly had a number of factors as its basis, for weeks of incarceration, the gaze of outsiders, and nationwide scorn had slowly taken its toll.

"Hot enough to make a man feel mean," he barked back.[163]

It was clear by the end of Wednesday that Milam was hardly alone in his sentiments.

In this atmosphere, the trial entered its fourth day on Thursday.

6

Tallahatchie Trial, Part 2

Anyone hopeful that a Mississippi jury might convict J. W. Milam and Roy Bryant of murder could cling to precedent set during three trials held five and a half years earlier in Attala County, 100 miles southeast of Sumner. On December 22, 1949, a white ex-convict, Leon Turner, along with brothers Malcolm and Windol Whitt, broke into the home of a black woman, Sally Ward, and attempted to rape her. That same night, they entered the home of one of Turner's gambling friends, Thomas Harris, also black, and threatened to rape his wife, Mary Ella, and his fifteen-year-old stepdaughter, Verlene Thurman. Although the men were arrested that night and jailed in Kosciusko, they escaped eight days later by digging a hole through a wall, using only a spoon, a can opener, and a metal pipe.[1]

At 1:00 A.M. on January 9, 1950, the fugitives broke into the Harris home once again, this time in a drunken rage to exact revenge upon Thomas, whom they erroneously believed had turned them in two and a half weeks earlier following their attempted rape spree. Gunshots followed, which injured Verlene Thurman and paralyzed Thomas Harris from the chest down. Tragically, seven-year-old Mary Burnside, twelve-year-old Frankie "Sonny Man" Thurman, and four-year-old Nell Harris were killed. Their mother, Mary Ella, managed to escape with her week-old infant son. Malcolm Whitt turned himself in later that day, but Turner and Windol Whitt remained at large. Two days later, on Wednesday, January 11, a posse using bloodhounds found the men in a corncrib, arrested them, and took them to the jail in Jackson. The community was shocked and utterly outraged over the murders.[2]

Trials for Turner and the Whitt brothers began at the courthouse in Kosciusko in March. As with the Till case five years later, these trials also attracted national media and were reported in *Time* and *Life* magazines. Windol Whitt went on trial first, was found guilty of murder, and was sentenced to life in prison on March 16. A week later, Leon Turner, ringleader of the trio, was similarly convicted, but was given three life sentences and denied any possibility of parole. There was drama at the trial when Thomas Harris testified against the killers from a hospital bed that was transported into the courtroom. His wife, Mary Ella, testified from the stand. On Monday, April 3, Malcolm Whitt pleaded guilty to manslaughter and was given ten years in the state penitentiary. In a final, tragic turn of events, Thomas Harris died of his injuries just one week after the third trial.[3]

Circuit Judge J. P. Coleman, who was elected Mississippi governor just four days before the Emmett Till murder, presided over the three trials in Kosciusko and passed down the sentences.[4] It was governor-elect Coleman, as state attorney general five years later, who appointed Robert Smith to aid District Attorney Gerald Chatham in the prosecution of Milam and Bryant in Sumner.

Although the Kosciusko convictions were impressive, this marked the first time that white men had ever been tried for killing a black person in Attala County. Citizens were angered that Turner had not been sentenced to death.[5] But one would have to look back in time sixty-five years to find a case where a white man was given the death penalty for killing an African American anywhere in the state of Mississippi. In 1890, M. J. Cheatham was hanged in Grenada for murdering Jim Tillman, a black man who had testified against Cheatham in a gambling trial.[6] A few Mississippi newspapers publicized these cases while the Sumner jury listened to evidence against Milam and Bryant. One intended message was to give evidence that Mississippians believed in justice in white-on-black crime. Yet an unintended consequence of that publicity served to alert readers to just how infrequent convictions actually were.

On Thursday, September 22, the Sumner courtroom filled to capacity by 8:00 A.M. Spectators passed the time until court resumed by reading newspapers or talking about the trial, which was about to begin its second day of testimony. At 8:30, J. W. Milam and Roy Bryant, who both appeared unshaven, entered the courtroom. A few minutes later Judge Swango appeared and took his seat. The prosecuting attorneys arrived, entering the room in company with the court reporter.[7]

Porters came to deliver mail addressed to the various newsmen present. The defendants received some letters, mainly from Chicago, criticizing the trial and demanding that they be given the death penalty. Photographers snapped several pictures of the brothers, who willingly posed with their threatening letters. There was other business to attend to before the trial resumed. The cotton gin fan, which had been introduced as evidence the day before, was still on the floor; Sheriff Strider asked a deputy to move it out of the room.[8]

Court was scheduled to start at 9:00 A.M., but when the hour came, Judge Swango failed to rap his gavel. For the next fifty-three minutes, attorneys and reporters gathered near his bench, where they learned that the prosecution team, now gone from the room, was interviewing the new witnesses who were set to testify that day. For those reporters with afternoon deadlines, this delay was unnerving. "I feel I should be talking to someone, not just sitting here," said one frustrated Chicago newsman.[9]

Finally, at 9:53 A.M., Judge Swango called the courtroom to order, and spectators took their seats. The first witness was fifty-two-year-old Chester F. Nelson, mayor of nearby Tutwiler and manager of two funeral homes there. Nelson, a former football and baseball player for Millsaps College, spent only a few minutes on the stand, testifying that his mortuary received a body from Chester Miller's funeral home, that an attendant prepared it as best he could, and that they shipped it on to Chicago. Swango overruled defense attorney Breland's objection when Nelson said he learned the body was of a person named Emmett Till. Under cross-examination, however, Nelson clarified that he did not personally know its identity.[10]

The state called its next witness at 10:00 A.M. The testimony of Mamie Bradley, mother of Emmett Till, was one of the most anticipated of the trial, and the courtroom fell silent as she was called to the stand. After walking through the center aisle to the front of the room, she looked around for an opening at the railing. She stood puzzled for a few moments, unsure what to do. "Step over to your right and you will be able to get through," Swango instructed her, after which she made her way to the stand and took her seat. Mamie, the only northerner to testify at the trial, clearly stood out. As a black woman, she was even more of an anomaly, not at all representative of the field hands and domestic workers familiar to most people in the rural Delta. Dan Wakefield, reporter for the *Nation*, noted that "she didn't fit the minstrel-show stereotype that most of Mississippi's white folks cherish." Mamie wore a gray flowered dress, a brown bolero jacket, a black hat, tortoiseshell glasses, and a gold watch.[11]

From the prosecution's standpoint, Mamie Bradley needed to convince the jury that the body she identified in Chicago was her son, and to directly link him to the ring found on that body. During questioning by Robert Smith, she affirmed both facts early in her testimony. Smith addressed his witness as "Mamie" rather than "Mrs. Bradley," something they both knew was a necessity for the sake of the jury.[12] Mississippi custom reserved the salutation of "Mr." or "Mrs." for whites only. Gerald Chatham received reminders of that in at least two letters shortly before the trial. "Since you are so interested in Mamie Bradley's safety and winning her your deepest sympathy—and referring to her as *Mrs. Mamie Bradley*—why not take her home with you and intertain [*sic*] her?" one person asked. Two other Mississippians also advised: "Your statement in [the] Jackson *Daily [News]* and *Commercial Appeal* in Regard to invitation to Mrs. Mamie Bradley of Chicago, as you address Her, may we suggest and urge that you comfort her in your home as it appears you are of the same caliber."[13] Considering the prevailing attitude, there was little reason to risk upsetting the jury by breaking from tradition.

Mamie told Smith that after the body arrived at the Rayner funeral home in Chicago, she examined it twice that day—once while it was still in the casket, and again after it was removed.

"I positively identified the body in the casket and later on when it was on the slab as being that of my son, Emmett Louis Till," she affirmed.

The ring had been sent from overseas with the rest of her husband's personal effects. She described it from memory as being "white, or it looked like some kind of white metal." She testified that Emmett took this ring with him to Mississippi, and that it fit more snuggly now that he was older. Smith handed her the ring and asked if it was once among her husband's belongings. She answered affirmatively.

"And you definitely say that was the ring that he [Emmett] left with?"

"Yes sir," Mamie replied.[14]

Smith, using sensitivity, then showed Mamie the Strickland photos taken after the corpse arrived in Greenwood. When she viewed the body in Chicago, it was a shocking, gruesome sight, yet it had been cleaned and, to the extent possible, embalmed. The Strickland photos were even more horrifying, having been taken only hours after the discovery.

"And I hand you that picture and ask you if that is a picture of your son, Emmett Till."

"Yes, Sir," replied Bradley.

The photos were then passed to the jury at the request of the defense and entered as exhibits 1 and 2 of Strickland's testimony from the day before.[15]

Having just seen for the first time the condition of her son after he was retrieved from the river, Mamie lowered her head, lost her composure, began to weep, and, for a few moments, rocked back and forth. Tears rolled down her cheeks as she removed her glasses and wiped her eyes.[16]

Cross-examination began next. J. J. Breland asked permission to remain seated as he interrogated the witness with a long, odd series of questions. Later, he rose and approached the stand.

First, he probed at length about Mamie's birth, her move to Argo, Illinois, as a child, and even her mother's birthplace. Swango reined him in after Chatham objected, yet he continued the same line of questioning. After further objections, he switched gears and asked about Emmett, the teen's interest in going to Mississippi that summer, and if he had ever been in trouble in Chicago.[17]

Breland also asked several questions about the life insurance Mamie had taken out on her son. How large were the policies? How long had she had them? What insurance companies were they with? Who were the beneficiaries? Had she tried to collect the money yet? Swango allowed most of the questions to stand, despite objections from the prosecution. Mamie said she had two policies on her son, totaling around $400. She was the beneficiary of one, her mother the other. She had not tried to collect on them yet because she was still awaiting a death certificate. Stories had been floating around the Delta that had the policies at anywhere from $10,000 to $15,000. Even though the state had objected to Breland's questions, the unfounded stories were at least debunked.[18]

Breland then queried Mamie about her newspaper subscriptions, and, more specifically, he wanted to know if she read the *Chicago Defender*, a popular black weekly. At that point, Swango excused the jury. He allowed the attorney to continue, however, because Breland insisted the question was crucial in order to introduce some exhibits for Mamie to identify.[19]

Continuing on, Mamie explained that she did not subscribe to the *Defender*, but she bought it regularly and read it. Breland showed her the September 17 edition, which carried a photo of her son. She had not seen that issue yet, she said, but recognized the photo as one she had released to the press herself. Breland handed her a copy of the *Memphis Press-Scimitar*, which had run the same photo. Mamie said that her father had copies of the photos with him in the witness room. Learning that, Breland asked that John Carthan be brought to the courtroom. Shortly thereafter, Mamie was handed an envelope with three pictures of Emmett, which she removed and handed to Breland. She testified that these photos, one of which was of her and Emmett together, were taken two days after Christmas, 1954. Breland handed back the photos, along with one of Emmett in his casket, also featured in the *Defender*. Mamie confirmed that they were all of her son.[20]

Before the jury returned to the courtroom, Swango ruled for competency of the photographs because Mamie testified to the identity in each. They could be admitted as evidence, he said, but the *Defender* photo would need to be clipped, with no reference to its source. Furthermore, he would not allow any questions to Mamie regarding the papers she read or subscribed to. "These pictures are for the benefit of the jury, so that they may see a likeness of Emmett Till during this lifetime, and also a likeness of his body, as the witness stated, as she saw it in Chicago after the body was returned to Chicago."[21]

Breland also wanted to deal with another matter while the jury was still out of the room because he assumed the prosecution would raise an objection. He read a quote, attributed to Mamie, in which she told Emmett how to act while in Mississippi, even advising her son that he should "kneel in the street and beg forgiveness if he ever insulted a white man or white woman." Mamie explained that she had indeed instructed him several times before he left about how to act while in the South and even cautioned him not to get in any fights with white boys. She did not mention it on the stand, but five years earlier, Emmett had tussled with a boy while visiting the Delta. She assured Breland that Emmett had never been in any trouble back home.[22]

Before the jury returned, Judge Swango sustained all of the prosecution's objections about Breland's line of questioning, and reminded the attorney that certain questions would not be acceptable.[23]

When the jury returned, Breland again showed Mamie both sets of photos of her son, which she reaffirmed were of Emmett. She explained that when she first saw the body in the funeral home, it had not been touched up; when she came back later that day, it had been.

"He had a gash in his jaw, and his mouth was open and the tongue was out," she said in describing the body as she first viewed it. "But from this picture here, it seems like his mouth has been closed, and that gash was sewn up, and that place in his forehead up there has been closed up."

After that, Mamie was excused.[24] The jury had heard very little of Breland's cross-examination, except for Mamie's identification of photos. Breland said nothing to challenge her testimony about the identity of the body.

Milam and Bryant faced Mamie as she sat on the stand, and for a moment, she was tempted to look them in the eyes. Despite their close proximity, she managed to resist.[25]

The next three people to take the stand were the surprise witnesses off the plantations in Sunflower County. Since Tuesday afternoon, rumors and vagaries had piqued the curiosity of spectators and newsmen alike. Now, finally, these unassuming field hands would have their say.

First up, and by far the most important, was eighteen-year-old Willie Reed. Reed was called in to testify as Mamie Bradley exited the courtroom, which prompted some overeager photographers to snap pictures of them both. The steady popping of flashbulbs got the attention of the judge, who ordered deputies to remove the erring photographers from the room.[26]

Robert Smith examined Reed for the state. The witness said that he lived on the Clint Shurden plantation (erroneously spelled Sheridan in the trial transcript and various newspaper accounts), and was familiar with both Leslie Milam, who managed the bordering Sturdivant plantation, and codefendant J. W. Milam, Leslie's brother.

"Do you know Mr. J. W. Milam when you see him?" asked Smith.

"Yes, Sir," replied Reed.

"Do you see him here in the courtroom?"

"Yes, Sir."

"Will you point him out, please, sir?"

Reminiscent of what Mose Wright had done the day before, Reed looked at Milam, pointed, and said, "He is sitting right over there."[27]

Reed then gave his account about the morning of August 28. Between 6:00 and 7:00 A.M., he was walking north to a store owned by Glen Patterson, located near the Reed home, three and a half miles west of Drew. As he walked along the road, a green and white 1955 Chevrolet pickup truck passed by. In the front, he saw four white men; in the back were three black men. Two of those were sitting on the side of the truck, while one sat on the floor. Reed said the truck was about as far away from him as the back door in the courtroom was to his seat on the stand. Smith estimated this to be about fifty feet. Reed did not notice the features of anyone in the truck, not feeling any need to pay attention.

"Now, later on," Smith probed, "did you recognize a photograph or anything that indicated to you who the one sitting down in the back end of that truck was?"

"Well, when I looked at this paper, I was sure—well, I seen it, and it seemed like I seen this boy someplace else before. And I looked at it and tried to remember, and then it come back to my memory that this was the same one I seen in the paper."

"And was that Emmett Till?"

"I don't know if that was him, but the picture favored him."

Breland promptly objected, so Smith tried rephrasing the question several more times. Each time, Judge Swango sustained the defense's repeated objections.[28]

Reed then provided the most disturbing part of his testimony. Continuing his walk to the Patterson store, he passed a shed on Leslie Milam's place. He heard noises coming from the inside that sounded like someone being beaten. Smith showed Reed one of the photos already entered as evidence. After a few objections over wording, Swango allowed Smith to ask Reed if he had ever seen the boy in the photo before. Reed said that it was a picture of the boy he saw on the back of the truck. Although Breland objected once again, this time Swango allowed Reed's testimony to stand.[29]

After Reed walked by the shed, he noticed that the truck that had passed him earlier was parked in front. He did not see anyone outside just then, but soon J. W. Milam, wearing a gun on his belt, walked out of the shed. He went to a well, got a drink of water, and returned to the shed.[30]

"Did you see or hear anything as you passed the barn?" asked Smith.

"I heard somebody hollering, and I heard some licks like somebody was whipping somebody."

"You heard some licks, and you also heard somebody hollering, is that right?"

"Yes, Sir," replied Reed.

"What was that person hollering?"

"He was just hollering, 'Oh.'"

Instead of continuing on to the store, Reed went to Mandy Bradley's house and told her about the strange noises in the shed. Bradley had him go out to the well, where he could listen more closely, and then bring her some water. As he approached the well, he heard the screams once again. Reed then went on to the store as he had intended earlier. When he returned, the truck and the men were gone.[31]

Before the defense began its cross-examination, Breland motioned that Reed's testimony be excluded because there was nothing to connect the defendants to what Reed saw at the shed, nothing that identified the person he saw as Emmett Till, and not enough evidence to connect the body pulled from the Tallahatchie River to what occurred at the shed. Judge Swango overruled the request, and cross-examination shortly began. Before turning the witness over to the defense, however, Smith had Reed clarify once again that the events he witnessed on the plantation occurred on the fourth Sunday of August.[32]

J. W. Kellum questioned Reed next. The witness stated that he had seen J. W. Milam three or four times in the past, but had never seen the truck before. On the morning in question, Reed was walking east, then turned north. The truck was heading south, then also turned north. The driver's side passed Reed, but he didn't notice the driver or any of the men in the truck. He affirmed once again that he was as close to the truck as he was from the witness stand to the courtroom door. He met the truck, and then it turned right to go down the hill, where Reed was also headed. He noticed the black men in the back. He also revised his earlier statement and said that the black men numbered four, not just three. Three were sitting on the right side, while one was on the floor.[33]

Kellum then queried about the activity at the barn. He asked repeatedly how far Reed was from the barn, and how far he was from the barn when he saw J. W. Milam come out of it. Reed said over and over again he did not know how far it was.

"Then you don't know whether you were one hundred yards away, or two hundred yards, or five hundred yards from him?"

"No, Sir," replied Reed.

The witness obviously did not understand measurements by yardage, and Kellum took full advantage of that.

Reed said he had already passed the well and was going down the road when Milam came out of the barn to go to the well. Reed had to turn around to see him, which Kellum thought was odd.

"Well, what caused you to turn around and look towards the well?" Kellum asked.

"I just looked back there, and I seen him when he came to the well."[34]

Kellum then referred to a meeting between Reed and the defense attorneys, held the day before, when Reed said he was at least 300 or 400 yards away from both the barn and the well. Kellum asked Reed about the "licks" he heard coming from the barn. Reed admitted that he did not see anyone in the barn.

"And you don't know whether that was somebody hammering there, trying to fix a wagon or a car, or something like that, do you?"

Reed did not back down. "It was somebody whipping somebody."

From over at the defense table, Breland raised an objection, even though the question had come from his own team.

"The objection is sustained," said Swango, "but you will have to be careful in objecting to answers to your own counsel's questions."[35]

What happened in the barn and with whom was obviously the crux of Reed's testimony.

"And you don't know whether Mr. Milam was in the barn or not, do you?" asked Kellum.

"I seen Mr. J. W. when he left the barn."

"But you didn't see him in the barn, did you?"

"No, Sir. But I seen him when he left the barn and went to the well, and then I seen him when he went back towards it."

"But you don't know whether he went in the barn or behind the barn, do you?"

"No, Sir. He was headed straight to the front of the barn."

"And also, if all of the people on the truck were in the barn, then that would make eight, is that right?"

"Yes, Sir."

"That is, four white men and four colored men?"

"Yes, Sir."

"And you weren't able to understand anything that was said in the barn at all?"

"No, Sir."

"Did you report this to anybody after you left there that day?"

"Well, I was talking with the grandfather," replied Reed.[36]

Kellum wondered how Reed could have recognized Till in the truck because Reed had told the defense team earlier that the truck passed him at a high speed. Reed then explained that it was going fast at first but slowed down when it turned down the hill. Once again, Reed said that he was about as far away from the truck as he was from the back of the courtroom.[37]

Reed rarely spoke above a whisper, and throughout his testimony, Swango repeatedly asked him to speak up. Reed was noticeably frightened, yet despite this, he held up well.[38] "Defense counsel put Willie through a stern cross-examination," observed Clark Porteous, "but could not shake his testimony. The most they could do was mix him up on his estimate of distance."[39]

Robert Smith then began a round of redirect, demonstrating that Reed really did not know how to measure the distance between himself and the shed. Reed also made it clear that he saw Milam go to the well and back *after* he heard the screams. After Smith finished, Breland asked that the jury be excused, and Reed stepped down from the stand.[40]

Breland motioned that Reed's testimony be disregarded because nothing about it connected Roy Bryant to the events Reed described. Smith, however, argued that the defendants had a choice of being tried jointly or separately, and that they chose to stand trial together.

"We can't put on proof for just one defendant and exclude the other," he said. "We have to put on any proof that implicates either one of them. And since they made their own decision to be tried together, we feel that it is wholly competent."

Swango agreed, which assured that Reed's testimony would stand. It was then 11:45 A.M., and the judge recessed court until 1:35 P.M.[41]

Add Reed, grandfather of Willie Reed, was the first witness called when court resumed.[42] His testimony was more of a supplement to his grandson's. The senior Reed said that on Sunday morning, August 28, he walked across the bayou that separated his house from Leslie Milam's plantation to get some slop for his hogs. He saw two men, one of whom was Leslie Milam. Around 8:00 A.M., he passed a shed where he saw a white pickup truck.

"As you passed there, Uncle Add, will you tell the court if you heard anything out of the ordinary?" asked Smith.

Breland quickly objected—a motion Swango sustained. Reed, however, still answered.

"Yes, Sir," he said, obviously unaware of the objection.

Surprisingly, Smith did not rephrase the question but promptly turned Reed over to the defense. Sidney Carlton asked only that the witness clarify the direction of his house from Drew. After he answered, he was excused.[43]

Although he was not allowed to state this on the witness stand, Add Reed had told reporters earlier that day that when he walked by the shed on the morning of August 28, he heard beating and groaning sounds "and kept going."[44] This backed up the testimony of his grandson. Unfortunately, the jury never heard it.

Mandy Bradley, the last of the plantation witnesses, was next. Bradley lived on the Sturdivant farm managed by Leslie Milam, perhaps 100 yards from Milam's house, she estimated. She testified that between 6:30 and 7:00 A.M., Willie Reed came over and told her what he had heard at the shed. She looked out her window and saw four white men going in and out of the building. One of those men whom Bradley described as "kind of a tall man and bald headed" went to a well and got a drink of water. Bradley said that the men backed the truck into the shed and then drove off.[45]

The defense had no questions for Bradley. With her testimony over, the prosecution had presented all of its witnesses.

"If the court please," Smith announced, "the State rests."[46]

With that news, reporters made a mad dash to the lobby. John Herbers of UPI was the first to call in the story that state testimony had ended, beating out the Associated Press and International News Service reporters. The operator got him through to the Atlanta office before other newsmen could even connect their calls. During the course of the trial, Herbers ran up and down the stairs so many times to call in his stories that by the end of the week "my leg muscles were bigger than they'd ever been."[47]

At 1:55 P.M., the court took a forty-minute recess to allow the defense to telephone one of its witnesses, Greenwood pathologist Luther B. Otken, to instruct him to come to Sumner. When court resumed, Breland asked permission to present motions, and Judge Swango briefly excused the jury.[48]

In an obviously symbolic gesture, Breland asked the court to dismiss all evidence offered by the state against Milam and Bryant and that the jury be directed to issue a verdict of "Not Guilty."

Swango immediately rejected Breland's plea. "Those motions will be overruled for the reason that the Court is of the opinion that the evidence offered on behalf of the state of Mississippi, that that evidence as a whole presents issues for the determination of the jury."

The thirteen jurors then returned to their seats, and Breland entered into evidence the two photographs Mamie Bradley previously identified as those of her son. The defense then began presenting its witnesses.[49]

Carolyn Bryant was called first. After all of Sidney Carlton's teasers about the incident between the woman at the store and the boy from Chicago, those in the packed courtroom were about to hear Bryant's side directly. Mamie Bradley said years later that she was not present for Bryant's testimony but remained in the witness room. After asking several questions about her family and her husband's military service, Carlton wanted to know about the events of Wednesday, August 24, when she was working in the store. Everything came to a halt, however, when Robert Smith raised an objection to any questions having to do with that night "unless it is connected up" with the crime. Carlton assured the court that he would connect it. Rather than appease either side, Swango once again sent the jury out of the room.[50]

Carlton argued that because the state, through Mose Wright, had provided testimony that one of the men who came into his home "wanted to see the boy that did the talking down at Money," the defendants had a right to have explained just what happened the night in question. The occurrences of August 24 and August 28 were, insisted Carlton, part of "one entire transaction."[51]

Legal arguments ensued for the next several minutes. Smith maintained that the state's "proof started with the occurrence on Sunday morning at two o'clock when two or more persons came to Mose Wright's house for the boy. And we went from there on with our evidence and proof." They had offered nothing from before that date, and nothing about Carolyn Bryant had been brought into testimony, nor had she even been mentioned before now. Also, Smith argued, the Mississippi Supreme Court held that past difficulties between two parties cannot be brought in as evidence. More important, he said, "we contend that anything whatsoever that happened down there on Wednesday is no justification for murder anyway."[52]

Breland, on the other hand, insisted that if it could be shown that "any of the happenings can be connected up and it forms a background for a later happening, then that can be considered as part of an entire transaction. And I believe the Supreme Court has ruled on that several times in the past."[53]

Judge Swango then explained how *he* interpreted the state supreme court decisions on evidence. Prior difficulties can be introduced as long as they can be considered part of the entire incident or transaction. If there were questions about who the aggressor was, for example, evidence would be admissible. "But without such a showing it would not be admissible."[54]

Defense attorney John Whitten took the defense's reasoning beyond the supreme court's decisions about res gestae (meaning "things done" or words spoken that are so closely connected to an event that they are considered part of the event).

"In the first place, the state, by its own witness, has raised in the minds of this jury some question as to whether what happened down there at the store in Money was just mere talk." According to Whitten, that was said at least three times. Because the state introduced this into the testimony, "the accused must have an opportunity to explain it or develop it further to show the jury all the facts."

Swango disagreed. "The Court is of the opinion that any accused in any criminal case can bring out anything relating to a continuation of any part of an alleged crime," he argued. "But the testimony that is being offered here of details of a prior incident, I do not believe that is admissible."[55]

Breland finally acquiesced, but he still wanted the defense to examine Carolyn Bryant so that her testimony could be part of the record. Swango allowed him to proceed. Breland told the press later that this was mainly for appeal purposes should the defendants be convicted. With the jury still absent, Sidney Carlton proceeded to question his witness.[56]

Bryant said that on Wednesday, August 24, 1955, she was working at the store, and Juanita Milam was babysitting in the back. At 8:00 P.M., a "Negro man" came in and stopped at the candy counter at the front left side of the store. Bryant said she walked up to the counter and asked what he wanted. After he told her and she got the merchandise, she put it on the top of the candy case and held out her hand for payment. The man then grabbed her hand with a strong grip and asked, "How about a date, baby?" Bryant said she jerked herself loose and started toward the back of the store. The man followed her and caught her by the register by putting his hands on her waist. Bryant demonstrated how the man held her by taking Carlton's hands and positioning them similarly.[57]

Bryant said that when the man grabbed her, he asked, "What's the matter, baby? Can't you take it?" She freed herself but then he told her, "You needn't be afraid of me." Bryant spoke quietly but clearly and appeared quite emotional.[58] She was hesitant, but Carlton urged her to continue.

"And did he then use language that you don't use?"

"Yes."

"Can you tell the Court just what that word begins with, what letter it begins with?"

Bryant did not answer, but simply shook her head.

"In other words, it is an unprintable word?"

"Yes."

Carlton next wanted to know, "Did he say anything after that one unprintable word?"

"Yes."

"And what was that?"

"Well," Bryant continued, avoiding any further description, but clearly intimating something sexual. "He said, well—'With white women before.'"

"When you were able to free yourself from him," Carlton asked next, "what did you do then?"

"Then this other nigger came in the store and got him by the arm."

"And what happened then?"

"And then he told him to come on and let's go."[59]

The man left with the unidentified male who came into the store, but did so unwillingly, Bryant said. They went outside, where several others were still gathered. As the man left the store, he said "Good-bye." Bryant then said she called to Juanita Milam to watch her as she ran outside to Milam's car to get a pistol hidden under the seat. When she went outside, she saw the man again, now standing on the front porch. He then whistled. Carlton asked Bryant to imitate the whistle; she puckered her lips but could not make a sound. Carlton then gave a very "amateurish" version of a wolf whistle, as Clark Porteous described it (which, the reporter noted, was not as good as the one that twelve-year-old Simeon Wright had demonstrated for him back on August 31). Bryant said that sounded right. After she retrieved the pistol, she saw the man get into a car. She then rushed back into the store.[60]

Bryant said she had never seen this man before or since that evening. She described him as about five feet six inches tall and 150 pounds. He spoke without any speech defect, and she could understand him well.

"What sort of impression did this occurrence make on you?" Carlton asked.

"I was just scared to death," Bryant replied.

Bryant said that she knew all of the blacks in the community and that this man, who spoke with a "northern brogue," was not one of them. Her husband, Roy, had gone to New Orleans to drive a load of shrimp to Brownsville, Texas, she explained, and Juanita Milam was there so that Carolyn would not be alone.[61]

Carlton had no further questions, but argued again that the jury be allowed to hear Bryant's testimony in order "to remove from the minds of the jury the impression that nothing but talk had occurred there." Again, Swango refused. The prosecution had no questions, and Bryant was excused from the stand.[62]

Besides her husband, there was one person in the audience who was especially anxious over Carolyn Bryant's testimony. Her mother, Frances Holloway, a nurse at Sunflower County Hospital, sat inconspicuously with other spectators or sometimes stood in the hall listening. Holloway had secured a leave of absence from her job in order to attend her son-in-law's highly publicized trial. She spoke freely to reporter W. C. Shoemaker about her family and Carolyn's high school beauty contests.[63]

Carolyn Bryant's testimony, although given apart from the jury, clearly provided a motive for the kidnapping (and circumstantially, the murder) of Emmett Till, even though the defense argued at the same time that the defendants were innocent. It was no accident that Carlton failed to have Carolyn

Bryant identify Emmett Till through photographs so that the identity of the "Negro man" could be verified. That the defense wanted this testimony as part of the record for appeal purposes is also telling. From its perspective, Carolyn Bryant's account of the store incident would help overturn a conviction should there be one. Was the backup plan for the defense one that would justify its clients' actions?[64]

Carolyn Bryant's dramatic testimony was followed by that of Juanita Milam, who served strictly as a character witness for her husband. Carlton never asked her to provide an alibi for J. W., nor did he address the murder at all. She was asked nothing about Roy Bryant, other than to clarify his relationship to her husband. She strictly answered questions about her family and J. W.'s military service. The jury learned that J. W. was once awarded a Purple Heart and achieved the rank of lieutenant in the US Army.[65]

The state had only two questions for the witness. After she confirmed that her husband was, in fact, J. W. Milam, Chatham asked, "And what relation is he to Leslie Milam?"

"A brother," answered Juanita.[66]

This brief exchange served as a reminder that there was a connection between the brothers and the plantation in Drew.

After the conclusion of their testimonies, Carolyn Bryant and Juanita Milam took seats next to their husbands for the first time since Tuesday afternoon, when they were called as witnesses and quarantined in another room. The four sons of Milam and Bryant had not returned to the trial since Tuesday, nor would they.[67] Unaware of this, the Westheimer's Employment Service sent Gerald Chatham a telegram Thursday with a kindly offer: "Would like to provide two baby sitters for both Roy Bryant and J. W. Milam's children so that they could be able to be free to concentrate and devote all their thoughts to their trial. Can fly baby sitters to Sumner immediately upon your permission. This service and all expenses will be provided by us."[68] There is no evidence that Chatham passed the telegram on to the defense team, as it remained in his papers. However, he probably found it mildly amusing.

Sheriff H. C. Strider was the next witness, and the first of three in succession of vital importance to the defense. Questioned by John Whitten, Strider told the court about the morning of August 31, when he went to examine a body taken from the Tallahatchie River. By the time he arrived, the body had already been brought to shore. He said that he examined it there as "best I could."[69]

The skin had slipped all over the corpse, and the fingernails were gone from the left hand. "A ring on the right hand was holding the skin that held the fingernails on that hand." The head had a small hole about an inch above the right ear. There were also two or three gashes on the head. Strider said he cut a stick about the size of a pencil and put it into the skull to determine if the hole had penetrated it. The tongue was extending out about two-and-a-half to three inches, and the left eyeball was almost ready to fall out. "And the right one was out, I would say, about three-quarters of an inch." The odor about the body was so bad that he could not get close to it until the undertaker got there and sprayed some deodorizing liquids to neutralize the smell.[70]

Strider said that he was familiar with the Tallahatchie River, and had been since 1935. In late August, the water would have been about seventy degrees at the top, and cooler as it got deeper. He estimated the depth of the river to be about twenty-five to thirty feet. He had taken other bodies from the water that had been submerged for at least six days.

"What then, Mr. Strider, is your opinion based on your past experience in taking bodies from the river, as to how long this particular body that was removed from the water on August 31st had been in the river?"

Strider did not hesitate. "I would say at least ten days, if not fifteen."[71]

If Strider was correct, the body could not have been that of Emmett Till.

Whitten then asked about the race of the victim. "The only way you could tell it was a colored person—and I wouldn't swear to it then—was just his hair. And I have seen white people that have kinky hair." Because of heavy decomposition, Strider was only sure of one thing. "All I could tell, it was a human being."[72]

Robert Smith cross-examined Strider for the state and showed him one of C. A. Strickland's photos taken in Greenwood at the Century Burial Association. Strider told Smith that when the body was taken from the river, it "was just as white as I am," but studying the picture, he acknowledged that some areas on the body had begun to darken.[73] He said nothing under cross-examination about the race of the victim.

Smith next asked Strider about the death certificate, which Strider signed. "And that death certificate certified the fact that it was the body of Emmett Till, isn't that correct?"

"I didn't certify that body as Emmett Till," explained Strider. "I said it was a dead body. I had never seen Emmett Till before, and I couldn't swear it was Emmett Till because I didn't know Emmett Till or what he looked like."

Strider also said that he had Mose Wright brought to the scene to identify the body. When Wright looked it over, Strider asked, "Mose, is this the boy that is missing from your home?" Wright said he thought so, but was not positive. When Strider asked him about the ring, Wright said that he did not recognize it and would have to ask his sons about it. Puzzled, Strider pressed him. "Do you mean to tell me Mose, that he has been staying there at your home for a week with this ring on his finger, and eating there at the same table with you, and you don't even know this ring, or that you didn't notice he had a ring on his finger?" Wright insisted that he would have to check with his sons.[74]

Strider described the condition of the body further. He saw no other wounds besides "a little reddish cast" on the back. Smith then tried to challenge Strider's opinion about the time the body spent in the river.

"You know as a matter of fact, do you not, that a body that is wounded and beaten up and injured will decompose much quicker than a body that has not been?"

"I would think so, Yes, Sir," admitted Strider.

"And you also know that conditions will vary in different bodies which will cause one body to decompose much quicker than another?"

"Well, I wouldn't say too much about that," the sheriff answered. "But I have taken bodies out of the river that were in there much longer than this."

Smith pressed him further. "But circumstances can make a difference, and circumstances can vary as far as a body is concerned, which might cause a body to decompose quicker or faster than another body?"

"Well, I thought it depended on the temperature."

Smith finished by asking Strider about the bullet hole in the head. The sheriff could not say for sure if that wound had been caused by a bullet and could not find where one had actually penetrated the skull.[75]

After a twenty-five-minute recess, the defense called Dr. Luther B. Otken to the stand. Like Strider, Otken would cast doubt upon the identity of the body. Over the years, Otken, a practicing physician since 1917, had examined numerous bodies that had been submerged in water. On August 31, at the request of the Leflore County sheriff's office, he went to the Century Burial Association to examine a body taken from the Tallahatchie River.[76]

Otken's examination was not a pathological one. In fact, he never touched the body. But from what he could see, the body was badly bloated, causing it to weigh, in his estimation, at least 275 pounds. The skin was slipping, the head was mutilated, and the right eye and tongue were both protruding. There was a "terrific" odor about the body, and the corpse was "in an advanced state of decomposition—or putrefaction." Because of its condition, he could not see how anyone could have recognized it. No relative, not even a mother or sibling, could have made a positive identification.[77]

"Doctor," asked attorney Breland, "from your experience and study and your familiarity with the medical authorities, what, in your opinion, had been the length of time that the body had been dead, if it had been in the open air?"

"I would say eight to ten days."

Breland wanted to know whether that would still be the case if the body had been submerged in the river, pushed far below the surface by the weight of the gin fan, where the water was cooler.

"I would still say eight to ten days," replied the doctor. He put the maximum at two weeks.[78]

Under cross-examination by Robert Smith, Otken admitted that different conditions will cause bodies to decompose at different rates. He also admitted that he did not know what the conditions actually were where the body in question was found. Like Strider, Otken said he did not know if the body was that of a white or black person. He confirmed that there was a hole above and just behind the right ear, and that there was an open wound on the forehead.

"And behind the left ear, the head was badly crushed in as if by some blunt object."

Smith wanted to hear more. "Doctor, in your opinion, was the round hole you described over the right ear, was that a bullet hole?"

"I couldn't say."

"What is your opinion as to whether it was or not?"

"That would merely be a conjecture on my part," Otken replied. "It was a round hole that went into the skull."

"Doctor, in your opinion, did the injuries or wounds about the head look as if they might have been sufficient to cause his death?"

"I would say so."

Otken admitted that he, like Strider, signed a death certificate, but did so in blank. He never actually identified the body but "stated that this was a body supposed to have been taken from the river and it had a hole above the right ear and the left side of the skull was crushed in."[79]

J. J. Breland spent a few moments in redirect. "Doctor, do you know any of the parties involved in this particular controversy?" More specifically, Breland wanted to know if he knew Milam and Bryant.

"I do not," affirmed Otken. "You would have to point them out to me."

When asked to elaborate on the wounds, Otken said that he could not say whether the injuries were made to the body before or after death.[80]

Robert Smith stood and re-cross-examined the witness. "Doctor, is it true or not that a person who . . . has a good deal of weight, fat weight . . . that such a body will decompose faster than a body that is more slender and muscular?"

"That's right."

"And that would affect the rate of decomposition?"

"That is right."

Breland took over the witness for more redirect.

"Doctor, observing that body as you saw it, and with the wounds that you saw on it, would that change your opinion on the length of time that the body had been dead, as you saw it?"

To that, Otken simply stated, "No."[81]

In other words, despite his admission that the conditions described by Smith *could* have affected the speed at which the body decomposed, Otken saw the probability as unlikely. With that, he was excused.

Sheriff Strider returned to the stand, where Robert Smith briefly queried him for the state. Because Strider did not believe that the body was or even could be Emmett Till, Smith wanted to know "what efforts have you been making to find out whose body that was?"

"Well," answered Strider, "I have had several reports about a negro who disappeared over there at Lambert. And I went out there and investigated that." That yielded no information, because "one man would tell you that he saw him, or that he said somebody told him they saw him, and then someone else would tell me that someone else had told them something about it. And it would just carry you right around to where you started from."

"But you got no information whatsoever to indicate whose body that was?" Smith pressed. "You have not gotten any information about that as yet?"

"No, I have not."[82]

This, of course, begs the question—with the body buried in Chicago, just how would Strider make a determination as to who the victim was, even if he could confirm that a black male from Tallahatchie County was missing? That issue had not been, nor would it ever be, addressed.

The last witness of the day was Harry D. Malone, the embalmer who worked in Chester Nelson's funeral home in Tutwiler. It was Malone who embalmed the body after it came to the mortuary on August 31.[83] He had been an embalmer for three years, and had handled several hundred bodies, some that had been dead up to fifteen days, others perhaps longer. Malone, questioned by Breland, stated that it was he who prepared the body and also examined it.

"The body was bloated, and it was so bloated that the features were not recognizable," Malone explained. "There was a prevalent skin slip all over the body."

He described, as did many of the witnesses before him, that the skin was slipping, the fingernails were loose, the tongue was protruding, and the "eyes were bulged up." He also said that the hair was loose, that he saw "multiple lacerations about the head. The left eye was hanging from its socket. And the entire body was a bluish-green discoloration." In Malone's opinion, this meant that the victim had been dead for at least ten days. Malone called the condition "advanced putrefaction." The protruding tongue was caused by tissue gas, which also meant that the corpse was in an advanced stage of decomposition.[84]

Malone explained to the court how decomposition follows the process of rigor mortis. Putrefaction would occur faster in a body left in the open air than one placed in water.

"Being in the water would retard putrefaction," he said. Decomposition would take longer in the conditions in which this body found itself. The seventy-degree water, the depth of up to thirty feet, and the weight of the gin fan would all have played a role in that. He reaffirmed that the minimum time span the body could have been in the river was ten days.

"And what would be the probabilities of the length of time that it might have been dead? That is, as to the longest length of time it might have been dead?" Breland asked.

"Somewhere between ten and twenty, or maybe ten and twenty-five days, perhaps."[85]

Malone said that the casket he provided was six feet three inches in length, and that the body, which came close to filling it, was about five feet ten inches. If this was correct, the body would be too tall to be Emmett Till. He could not say, however, how old he thought the victim might have been. He thought it possible for a mortician to repair the body to more resemble itself prior to death and the injuries that so disfigured it.[86]

On cross-examination, Smith asked about the conditions that would speed up the rate of decomposition.

"And isn't it true that a body that is wounded and beaten, and so forth, that such a body will decompose faster than one that is not?"

"Under normal conditions, yes, sir."

"But of course, you have no knowledge of the conditions where this body had been, do you?"

"No, Sir."

"And what you are testifying to is what would happen under normal conditions, is it not?"

"That's right."

"And isn't it true that if a person is fat, or heavy, and has more fatty tissue than the average person, that such a body will decompose at a greater rate than one that is not so fat?"

Again, Malone agreed, but Breland objected, pointing out that nothing had ever been said about this body being fat. Swango overruled the objection, and

Malone's answer stood. Malone's testimony concluded court for the day, and at 5:05 P.M. Swango called a recess until 9:30 the following morning.[87]

That evening, the black reporters learned of an important new development. Shortly after court adjourned, Alex Wilson, reporter for the *Tri-State Defender*, received word that Levi "Too Tight" Collins and Henry Lee Loggins, the two men rumored to have been on the truck with Emmett Till the morning after the kidnapping, had been located.[88] This was obviously an important discovery, and if true, could prove to be explosive for the prosecution. The exact whereabouts of the men had been a mystery since James Hicks first learned of their existence five days earlier. If this piece of the puzzle could finally be solved, it was not a moment too soon.

Several among the press, including Simeon Booker, Clotye Murdock, and David Jackson, along with Basil Brown (Representative Diggs's attorney), began following this lead. They first visited the informant who broke the news. This led them to the woman who had initially reported the sighting. She said that just three days earlier, she went to the jail in Charleston to visit a relative. While there, an inmate she did not know asked her to pass a message to a friend on the outside. When she did so, she learned that the man at the jail was Levi Collins. Collins and Loggins, she learned, were being held for two weeks for "investigation" after having been seen washing blood out of a truck. The men claimed they had killed a deer, but hunting season had not yet started.[89]

The group needed someone to positively identify the men. They wondered—had Strider jailed them under false names until after the end of the trial? After traveling some distance, they found a reliable witness who agreed to go to Charleston and make the identification. Around 2:00 A.M., they called Clark Porteous. He agreed to meet them that morning and to ask Gerald Chatham and Robert Smith for permission to make a check of the jail.[90]

Friday morning, Wilson picked up their "finger-man" and made ready for the trip to Charleston. When Porteous told the prosecutors the story about Collins and Loggins, Smith and Chatham explained that they had already searched for the men at the jail twice and in neither case were they anywhere to be found. Porteous, nevertheless, still wanted to search for the men with someone who could positively identify them. The prosecutors again refused, saying that closing arguments were about to start, and that any further delays in the trial "might result in adverse effect." More important, according to Porteous, they simply did not believe the men were being jailed. Robert Smith later told the *New York Post* that Gwin Cole had not only looked for them in Charleston, but he also searched a jail in another county. In each case, the sheriffs "raised hell" about the invasion of their privacy. Needless to say, wrote Wilson, the whole mission "hit a stone wall."[91]

Day five of the trial proceeded as scheduled, but it was met by a steady, although unwelcome, rainfall. Cotton farmers, who needed rain only through June, worried about the damage this downpour might cause, telling reporters that it could cost them up to $20 per bale.[92]

Each witness who took the stand on Friday spoke to the character of the defendants. Three testified for Milam, four others for Bryant. The first three, friends of Milam, each spent only a few minutes on the stand. J. W. Kellum conducted direct examination of the men. All were cross-examined by Gerald Chatham.

Other than asking a little background information about themselves and their relationships with Milam, Kellum had only one question for each of the men. Did they know Milam's "general reputation for peace and violence," and, if so, what was it? None of them hesitated, and all affirmed that Milam's reputation was good. During his cross-examination, Chatham wanted to hear from each man just where their knowledge came from. Was their court appearance a favor based on a close friendship? Perhaps some kind of repayment?

The first witness, Lee Russell Allison of Tippo had just been reelected as a county supervisor over Beat 4, where Milam lived. Because Milam had supported Allison in this election, Chatham suggested that Allison's testimony was one way to reciprocate.[93]

Chatham took his questioning a step further.

"I want you to tell the jury if it is not an actual fact that he [Milam] was convicted—or he was arrested and pleaded guilty to a charge—"

Before Chatham could finish, defense attorney Breland raised an objection. Chatham was trying to introduce the fact that Milam had, in the past, been arrested and pleaded guilty at least five times to bootlegging.[94]

Swango sent the jury out of the room, after which Chatham explained himself to the court. Because Allison had testified to Milam's reputation, Chatham wanted to know how the witness had come to form his opinion. Swango took issue because Chatham never made that clear during his examination. However, he allowed Chatham to ask the question again with the jury absent before ruling on the objection.

"Mr. Allison," Chatham continued, "what you meant to tell the jury was that you don't know of any act of violence that was ever committed by J. W. Milam, so far as your personal knowledge is concerned? Isn't that right?"

"That is all I can say," replied the witness. "I can just say what I do know."[95]

Breland addressed the court again, explaining that Chatham's question went beyond the focus of the defense's direct examination, and Swango agreed.

"As the Court sees it, this examination is a cross[-]examination, and it will have to be limited to the matters in issue in the charge here. And he has testified that the general reputation of the defendant, J. W. Milam, in the community in which J. W. Milam lives, that the general reputation for peace and violence is good."[96]

Chatham then asked Allison if, in his role as supervisor, he had tried to get to know those in his district and form a friendship with them. Allison said he did. Then Chatham went back to his original question.

"Have you ever heard of Mr. J. W. Milam ever having been convicted of any criminal charge?"

"No, Sir," Allison answered.

Breland protested, and once again, Swango took his side.

"The objection is sustained, and the question is not to be asked in the presence of the jury," he warned Chatham.

The jury returned to the courtroom, but Chatham had no further questions.[97]

Lee McGarrh, owner of a gas station and grocery store in Glendora, was the next witness. During cross-examination, Chatham pointed out that McGarrh was also part of the venire panel from among whom the jury was called, but that McGarrh had disqualified himself. He asked McGarrh if he had ever known Milam to be involved in any wrongdoing.

"No, I have not; not to my knowledge."

"And you, as a close friend of his, you want to help him out of his difficulty, is that right?"

"I didn't come up here to tell a lie," said McGarrh. "I came to tell the truth."

"But that is the reason you are up here this morning, isn't it, because you are a friend of J. W. Milam?"

"Yes, Sir."

Chatham had nothing further.[98]

L. W. Boyce, who lived about three and a half miles out of Glendora, gave the same assessment of Milam as the previous two witnesses, and Chatham, during cross-examination, queried further about the friendship between the two men.

"And he asked you to come up here and testify here in his behalf, and that is the reason you came here as a witness, is that right?"

"No, Sir. He didn't ask me to come here at all."

"Then how did you come here? Why did you come?" asked Chatham.

"I got notice from the lawyers to come up here."

"And no one said anything to you about it?"

"No," said Boyce.

"And they didn't ask you what you were going to say?"

Again, the answer was "no."

Chatham pressed further. "But you did come up here as a friend to tell about his reputation as a friend, and to help him out if you could, isn't that right?"

"I am up here to tell his reputation as I know it."

"But you are up here to help him out, isn't that true?"

"I am up here to tell about his reputation as I know it."

Chatham got all he was going to get from Boyce, and the witness was excused.[99]

Kellum and Chatham next questioned the four character witnesses brought in for Roy Bryant. James Sanders, who lived three miles north of Bryant's home in Money, said he had known Bryant for two years. He also answered positively about Bryant's reputation.

"And you are basing your statement of his good reputation on your friendship for him, and you are up here trying to help him out of his difficulty more than anything else, isn't that true?" asked Chatham, bluntly.

"I am just up here to state the truth."[100]

Harold Terry, also of Money, next took the stand. Bryant had a good reputation, Terry said.

"I want to ask you how many people you heard discuss Mr. Bryant's reputation during the past two years," asked Chatham on cross-examination.

"I haven't heard Mr. Bryant discussed,'" replied Terry.

"Then you haven't heard his reputation discussed?"

"No, Sir."

"Well, then, how do you know what his general reputation is?"

Breland objected. "If the Court please, that is the best reputation a man can have, when nobody says nothing about him." However, Swango thought the question proper and allowed the witness to answer.

Addressing Terry again, Chatham asked the witness to clarify. "Then you just stated what you think it is? Is that what you are stating now?"

"Yes, Sir."

"And that is just your opinion, is that right?"

"Yes, Sir."

"Who asked you to come here to testify today?"

"I volunteered to come up here," insisted Terry.

"And you are in sympathy with Mr. Bryant, is that right, or is that wrong?"

Terry sat silent.

"Why do you hesitate to answer, Mr. Terry?"

Again, Terry said nothing.

Chatham did not belabor the point any further. "You can stand aside."[101]

Grover Duke, a section foreman on the railroad, also lived in Money and testified positively about Bryant. Cross-examining Duke, Chatham asked the same question he had asked Terry.

"How many people have you heard discuss his reputation, Mr. Duke?"

"I never heard it discussed one way or the other."

Establishing the fact that Duke and Bryant were friends, Chatham asked, "as one friend to another, you would naturally come up here today to do what you can to help him out of his difficulty, if your testimony would help, isn't that right?"

"Yes, Sir."

"Who asked you to come up here and testify?"

"I believe it was a brother-in-law of the defendant," Duke answered.

"And he asked you to come up here and testify for him?"

"I volunteered to come."

"And you are in sympathy with him, isn't that right?"

"Yes, Sir."

"That is all."[102]

The last witness was Franklin Smith, a thirty-year resident of Money and a cousin of Leflore County sheriff George Smith. On cross-examination, Chatham asked what Bryant's reputation had been since August 28, but Smith kept quiet after Kellum objected. Smith and Bryant were members of the same church, where Smith said he saw Bryant "occasionally." He had volunteered to come to the trial and testify because of his friendship, he admitted, and also stated that he was "in sympathy" with Bryant.[103]

After Smith's testimony, Breland announced on behalf of his clients, "The defendants rest." The state affirmed again that it had nothing in rebuttal. Then, on behalf of the defendants, Breland made a motion for "the Court to exclude all the evidence for and on behalf of the State of Mississippi, and to direct the jury to return a verdict of Not Guilty." Swango rejected the motions and at 10:23 A.M. recessed court for fifteen minutes.[104]

When court resumed at 10:38, the final phase of the trial began. With all witness testimony completed, attorneys would deliver their closing arguments before the jury. Judge Swango allowed each side to take one hour and ten minutes to present their final summations.[105] For both the prosecution and the defense, it was to be an emotional finale to five long days in the hot, crowded courtroom. The pleas from the attorneys, following three days of witness testimony, would be the last chance to influence the jurors before the twelve men deciding the fate of the defendants would begin deliberation and ultimately make their decision.

Gerald Chatham, on behalf of the state of Mississippi, spoke first. His was a call for justice that nobody in that courtroom, or even on the street below, could ever forget. He spoke so loudly that those gathered outside could hear his plea for a conviction, even through the rain that had not let up all morning. Sweating profusely and occasionally pounding on a table, he spoke, as one reporter wrote, "like a Baptist preacher in a Baptist church." Addressing the issue of outside agitators, Chatham insisted he was "not concerned with the pressure of organizations outside or inside the state. I am concerned with what is morally right or wrong." To the state of Mississippi, this was "just another murder case," he said, stressing to the jurors that if they returned a verdict based on anything other than the evidence, they would "endanger every custom and tradition we hold dear."[106]

Chatham declared forcefully that "the very first word of the state's testimony was dripping with the blood of Emmett Till. What were those words, gentlemen? They were 'preacher, preacher. I want that boy from Chicago—that boy that did the talking in Money,' they said. That wasn't an invitation to that card game they claimed." The murder of Emmett Till was cowardly; Milam and Bryant had taken the law into their own hands and given the boy "a court-martial with the death penalty imposed." Afterward, "to hide that dastardly, cowardly act they tied barbed wire to his neck and to a heavy gin fan and dumped him into the river for the turtles and fish."[107]

Chatham said that when Milam and Bryant kidnapped Till, they were "absolutely morally and legally responsible for his protection." If Till acted up and deserved to be punished, the worst they should have done was to "turn him over a barrel and give him a little beating." "I've whipped my boy. You've whipped yours," he said. "You deal with a child as a child—not as if he is a man." And since the night they took Emmett Till from Mose Wright's home, "he hasn't been seen since."[108]

Chatham addressed the defense arguments about the identification of the body. All it took was someone who knew and loved Emmett Till to identify him, not an undertaker or a sheriff. He then told a moving story about his son, whose dog, Shep, had gone missing. One day the boy came to him and said, "Dad, I've found Shep." The young child led his father to a hollow ravine behind their barn, and showed him a decomposing carcass. "That dog's body was rotting and the meat was falling off its bones," Chatham told the jury, "but my little boy pointed to it and said, 'That's old Shep, Pa. That's old Shep.'" If there was anything left of Emmett Till—a hairline, an ear, or just a part of his nose, "then I say to you that Mamie Bradley was God's given witness to identify him."[109]

Chatham's impassioned arguments brought tears to the eyes of the black journalists, sitting on the right side of the courtroom. Even some white spectators were crying. Milam stared straight down at a newspaper positioned on his lap, cupping a hand to his face. Bryant sat back and smoked a cigar. Carolyn Bryant seemed to listen carefully, while Juanita Milam fidgeted a little. The jurors, however, were fixated on Chatham. One removed his pipe and put it away, and another was so entranced that he let a cigar burn out in his mouth.[110]

Chatham continued criticizing the defense. When the corpse was first found, he said, the sheriff learned that there was a body of a "little nigger boy in the river." Everyone who saw the body said the boy was black. Next, he mentioned Dr. Otken. "Now we have this doctor come up here with all his degrees and titles and tell us that he could not tell whether it was a white boy or a colored boy." If he cannot tell the difference, Chatham believed, the people are wasting their tax dollars sending men like him to medical school. "I want to say this about the doctor—if he can't tell black from white, I don't want him writing any prescriptions for me." That remark brought a ripple of laughter throughout the courtroom.[111]

Chatham again reminded the jury that the most severe punishment Milam and Bryant should have meted out to the boy was a whipping. "But did they do this? No they did not. Willie Reed told you how he saw Emmett Till that Sunday morning on the Milam place and he told you how he later saw J. W. Milam with the pistol in his hand and that Uncle Mose saw him also with a pistol." Then Chatham made an important point.

"If Willie Reed had been lying, the five lawyers for the defense would have had fifty people up here to say he was not qualified to speak," he assured the jury. "But did they do this? They did not. They couldn't do it because Willie was telling the truth. But the next time anyone saw that little boy his feet were sticking up out of the river and he was dead."[112]

During this summation, one reporter raised his camera but was quickly spotted by Judge Swango, who, interrupting Chatham, ordered the erring photographer to leave the room. However, the man simply put down his camera and stayed in his seat. A reporter for the black press called Chatham's remarks "one of the most passionate pleas ever made by a white man in the south on behalf of a Negro." Even Mamie Bradley was impressed, as she turned and whispered to that same reporter, "He could not have done any better."[113]

The defense began its arguments with a brief comment by Harvey Henderson, who reminded the jury that in order to convict, they must be "convinced beyond a reasonable doubt and moral certainty" that Milam and Bryant were guilty. Each man, he said, must make up his own mind, even if no one else agrees with him. The defense, he pointed out, did not have to prove anything. The burden of proof rested solely on the state.[114]

Sidney Carlton spoke next. He, too, was excited, and occasionally shouted, but his emotion never reached the level of Chatham's. In refuting Chatham's arguments, Carlton said that the prosecuting attorney "talked generalities because the facts just don't bear out the guilt of these defendants. Where's the motive? Where's the motive?"[115] Perhaps because the jury did not hear Carolyn Bryant's testimony of the store incident that led to the murder, Carlton thought this was a question he could pose.

The state attorneys, Carlton insisted, were not able to link the defendants up with the victim. "The only testimony that Emmett Till did anything in connection with these defendants was Mose Wright's testimony that he heard the boy had done something." Had Wright known Till had gotten into trouble, Carlton argued, "he would have gotten him out and whipped him himself."[116] Again, Carlton took full advantage of Judge Swango's ruling regarding Carolyn Bryant's testimony.

Carlton reminded the jury that Wright said the house was so dark the night of the kidnapping that the only reason he believed Milam was there was because the man was "big and bald." Bryant, on the other hand, identified himself, which, to Carlton, seemed suspect. "How many Mr. Bryants are there in the state of Mississippi?" he asked. "If any of you had gone to Mose Wright's house with evil intent would you have given your name?" Carlton knew that is exactly what Bryant did, however. In a deposition taken from Bryant on September 6, Carlton learned that his client "did identify self as Mr. Bryant when he went in house. No light ever turned on in house. Both went inside house."

Despite what Carlton actually knew, he wanted the jury to believe the idea that Bryant would provide his name was so absurd that there was "nothing reasonable about the state's theory. If that's identification, if that places these men at that scene, then none of us are safe." Carlton remained silent of the fact that the jury knew that both the sheriff and deputy of Leflore County had received confessions from Milam and Bryant themselves that they had taken a boy from the Wright home. Clearly, Carlton hoped the jury had forgotten that.

Carlton also thought it too preposterous that Milam and Bryant would have abducted Till in Leflore County, gone west to Sunflower County, where state witnesses say Till was beaten in broad daylight, then "double back" to Tallahatchie County where they dumped the body in the river. As Carlton rejected Willie Reed's testimony about the location of the alleged murder, he also found Reed's story of a truckload of accomplices as simply too unbelievable. "We've got two men charged with murder, but he would have you believe seven are responsible."[117]

The real weakness of the murder charges, Carlton insisted, was the failure of the state to prove the identity of the body. Three defense witnesses, including Sheriff Strider, testified that the body had been in the river too long to have been that of someone missing only three days. He pointed out that Dr. Otken was the only one with a medical background to examine the body, and that the embalmer, Harry D. Malone, was "unequivocal" that the corpse could not have been Till.[118]

Carlton also dismissed Mamie Bradley's positive identification of the body she examined in Chicago. "Sometimes mothers believe what they want to believe. I'm sure Mamie Bradley thinks that body was her son, but scientific facts show otherwise. We think we could have rested our case when the State rested. The State didn't prove anything."[119]

Carlton closed his arguments by quoting a line from a Charles Dickens classic. It was the duty of the jury to acquit the defendants, he said, and if they fulfilled that duty, they would feel just like the character in A Tale of Two Cities, who said, "'Tis a far, far better thing I do than ever I did before." He did not mention the character by name, but astute observers such as Clark Porteous noted that it was Sidney Carton, whose name was almost identical to the attorney quoting him.[120]

Carlton sat down, after which J. W. Kellum addressed the jury. He read the indictments against Milam and Bryant that the grand jury handed down back on September 6, but pointed out that these were "no evidence whatsoever of their guilt." He reminded the jury, as did Henderson, that the burden of proof of any wrongdoing lay with the state of Mississippi.[121]

Kellum, like Carlton before him, stressed the importance of Otken's medical expertise. He also sought to embolden the jury by assuring them that they were the "peerage of democracy," and "absolutely the custodians of American civilization." Then, in a dramatic voice, he said: "I'll be waiting for you when you come out. If your verdict is guilty, I want you to tell me where is the land of the free and the home of the brave. I say to you, gentlemen, your forefathers will absolutely roll over in their graves."[122]

Kellum reminded the jury that special prosecutor Robert Smith, "a gentleman I don't know," would have the final argument, and that this was a powerful advantage. He then closed with a dramatic message that the jury's verdict would have eternal consequences.

> I want you to think of the future. When your summons comes to cross the Great Divide, and, as you enter your father's house—a home not made by hands but eternal in the heavens, you can look back to where your father's feet have trod and see your good record written in the sands of time and, when you go down to your lonely silent tomb to a sleep that knows no dreams, I want you to hold in the palm of your hand a record of service to God and your fellow man. And the only way you can do that is to turn these boys loose.[123]

Kellum sat down at 11:55, and Swango recessed court for a two-hour lunch. When proceedings resumed at 1:50 P.M., John Whitten concluded arguments for the defense.

Whitten presented a theory in line with Sheriff Strider's that the "murder" of Emmett Till had been faked by the NAACP. The whole thing was concocted "by organizations who would like to destroy the southern way of life."[124]

For any skeptics on the jury, or perhaps among the press, Whitten assured his listeners that this was "not as fantastic as it may seem," and bolstered his theory by telling of an incident that had occurred thirty-five years earlier, when the bodies of three African Americans were retrieved from the Mississippi River at a time when the Ku Klux Klan had tried to revitalize itself. "A great hue and cry went up about the land. But investigation later proved that those three bodies had been embalmed before they were tossed in the river."[125]

Whitten theorized how a similar plot could have been carried out in the Till case. For the sake of argument, he said, J. W. Milam and Roy Bryant *did* kidnap Emmett Till, but turned him loose three miles away at the store, as they claimed. Suppose Mose Wright got in his car and drove toward Money, finding the boy along the road as he walked home. Wright may have taken him to meet a friend involved with the NAACP, and this friend persuaded Wright to put Emmett Till's ring on a "rotton, stinking corpse" that could later be found floating in the river. That body would then be identified by "simple people" as Emmett Till. Again, according to Whitten, this was very plausible:

> There are people in the United States who want to defy the customs of the South ... would commit perhaps any crime known to man in order to widen the gap. These people are not all in Gary and Chicago; they are in Jackson and Vicksburg; and, if Mose Wright knows one he didn't have to go far to find him. And they include some of the most astute students of psychology known anywhere. They include doctors and undertakers and they have ready access to a corpse which could meet their purpose.[126]

Whitten avoided mentioning him by name, but the latter reference was to Dr. T. R. M. Howard, whose clinic in Mound Bayou could easily have provided a body.[127] Then, in what is perhaps the most polarizing statement of the trial, Whitten assured the jurors that "every last Anglo-Saxon one of you have the courage to free these men."[128]

Mose Wright was not in the courtroom to hear Whitten name him as chief accomplice in an NAACP cover-up, but he must have heard about it. He was spotted in the sheriff's office getting his witness fee after Whitten sat down. Someone asked the aging sharecropper if he was intent on leaving Mississippi.

"I don't know," replied Wright. "I got this country so scrounged down in me that I just don't know."

With that, observed Murray Kempton, "he walked out of the courtroom, a tiny old man in his galluses, and down the road across the bridge all alone and leaving Sumner rotting behind him."[129]

The state had the last word when Robert Smith stood before the jury. He reviewed the case and addressed the issue of outside influences. Yes, there were people who were "trying to destroy our way of life," he acknowledged. "But once we take the life, liberty or pursuit of happiness from anyone we will be put on the defensive and become vulnerable in trying to justify our stand." These agitators actually wanted Milam and Bryant freed, he argued, because it would give them the momentum to raise funds for the next decade and a half. If the jury were to convict, on the other hand, "no one can use this to raise funds to fight us in our defense of southern traditions." He reminded the jury that the body had been identified by Emmett Till's mother and also by the ring found on one of its fingers.[130]

As for the defense theory that Mose Wright and Emmett Till helped stage a murder, Smith said it was "the most far-fetched argument I've ever heard in a courtroom." Wright was, he said, "a good old country Negro and you know he's not going to tell anybody a lie." If the men had, in fact, released Till, "Where is he?" Smith also praised Willie Reed for having the courage to testify. "I don't know but what Willie Reed has more nerve than I have."[131]

With Smith's conclusion, all attention turned to the jury. After listening to twenty-two witnesses over three days, it was now up to them to decide the fate of J. W. Milam and Roy Bryant. Judge Swango had only brief instructions to the men before excusing them, and also provided them a form upon which to write their verdict. He excused the alternate juror, Willie Havens, and at 2:34 P.M. the others filed into the jury room, and the large brown door, missing both its latch and lock, was closed shut behind them. No one else was allowed inside.[132]

Gerald Chatham, speaking privately to reporters, said he hoped the jury would be out for at least an hour. Sidney Carlton told Bryant, who seemed slightly nervous, to expect a deliberation of about twenty-five to forty-five minutes.[133] The black press table took a poll among its members on how long it would take. James Hicks passed around a sheet of paper, and each wrote their names and their predictions. A tally put the range between thirty-five minutes and three hours. Till's mother even got in on the poll, writing, "Mamie Bradley, 49 minutes." Hicks kept the paper as a souvenir. In the end, photographer Ernest Withers won the poll, missing the actual time by only five minutes.[134]

Most of the spectators remained in the courtroom, probably because they expected a quick verdict also. A few, however, left Sumner altogether. Mamie Bradley and her companions, along with Representative Diggs, quietly slipped out the door, downstairs, and into Dr. T. R. M. Howard's Cadillac, where chauffer Ed Ramsey was waiting to drive them back to Mound Bayou.[135] Bradley decided to leave after a reporter asked what she intended to do after the acquittal. This convinced her "that it was sewed up from the day it started." She next turned to Diggs.

"I would like for us to leave now."

Diggs was shocked and asked, "What, and miss the verdict?"

Bradley was adamant. "This is one you will want to miss. The verdict is 'not guilty.'"

The others looked at Bradley as though she had lost her mind. However, they appeased her, and the group returned to Mound Bayou.[136]

The Milams and Bryants remained in their seats most of the time the jury was out. Now and then they got up, went to the judge's bench, helped themselves to ice water from his pitcher, and even conversed with him. Friends occasionally came by to talk. The half-brothers were given stacks of pictures that various photographers had taken over the course of the trial. Milam and Bryant, in turn, passed them around to other family members. Spectators gathered in small groups while reporters were busy downstairs calling their respective newspapers. Some even kept the lines open while the jury deliberated to be sure to report the verdict immediately.[137]

Standing had become common in the courtroom on Friday, even before the jury had begun deliberating. Swango refused to allow overcrowding after Tuesday's recess, and Sheriff Strider said that every available chair was inside the courtroom. Yet for some reason, there were still not enough. Reporters found that when they returned after lunch, recesses, or calling in a story, their chairs went missing. Some finally began taping their names to their seats, while others simply gave up. Circuit Court Clerk Charlie Cox finally sat on a stack of law books, while others sat on the floor. Photographer Gene Herrick sat on the steps of the judge's bench. A local drugstore, aware of the problem, found a way to capitalize on the situation by putting its supply of folding canvas chairs on sale for $2 each.[138]

Eight minutes into their deliberations, the men of the jury grew thirsty and asked for some Cokes. Strider passed the bottles into the room, one by one. No one, not even the four bailiffs guarding the jury, was allowed inside. The courtroom remained noisy, and Judge Swango reminded everyone that they must maintain order once the jury returned with its verdict. Thirty minutes later, the door to the jury room blew open, and spectators instantly fell quiet. After a bailiff quickly shut the door, however, the crowd realized it was a false alarm, and people continued as they were. At some point, the jury asked for more Cokes.[139]

Bill Minor, a reporter for the *New Orleans Times-Picayune*, sat near the jury room and was disturbed to hear laughter from inside. Finally, at 3:42, a knock came from inside the room. Again, the courtroom fell silent. One hour and seven minutes after beginning deliberations, the jury had reached a verdict. By now, the rain had stopped, and the sun shone brightly through a dark overcast.[140]

Judge Swango spoke to the crowd. "Let the courtroom be in order. The courtroom will remain in order when this jury comes in and makes its report. There will be no demonstration and no pictures will be taken. Court is in session."[141]

The twelve men looked somber as they entered the room and took their seats. They were all in their chairs by 3:44, when Swango turned and addressed them formally.

"Have you gentlemen reached a verdict?"

"Yes, Sir, we have," replied James Shaw, the jury foreman.

Swango then turned to Charlie Cox. "Mr. Clerk, will you read the verdict?"

Shaw handed it to Cox, who then read the jury's decision. Two words scratched upon a yellow piece of paper in a rural southern courtroom were about to echo all over the world.

"Not Guilty."[142]

A black woman in the rear of the room immediately shouted out, "Oh, no." Many assumed this was Mamie Bradley, but she was not present. A white woman had a similar reaction. At the same instant, reporters began running down the stairs to get back to the phones and report the verdict. Buzzing in the room stopped immediately after Judge Swango stared into the crowd and gave a stern look of disapproval.[143]

Swango then turned to the jury and explained that the manner in which they wrote out the verdict was technically incorrect. "You had a form to be used for that. But this is not a complete verdict." He gave them a new form and had them go back into the jury room to write out their decision the way they had been instructed. Shaw later said that he had put the correct form in his pocket by mistake.[144]

This was only a formality, however. For the emotional crowd in the courtroom, the various feelings of jubilation, disappointment, or shock had already set in, and nothing else the jury had to say would change that. Yet the courtroom remained orderly, and spectators kept quiet while they waited for the jury to return. Milam and Bryant sat smoking cigars. Clark Porteous noted that they did not change their expression at all after the first verdict was announced, although reporter James Gunter said that both men smiled. The only one to congratulate them after the jury went back into the deliberation room was Sidney Carlton, who shook hands heartily with Milam.[145]

A few minutes later, the jury returned. Neither Gerald Chatham nor Robert Smith had been in the room when Cox read the first verdict, so Swango had Sheriff Strider bring them in. After they took their seats, Swango turned to the jury.

"Have you gentlemen reached a complete verdict now? Has your verdict been made in accordance with the form that was given you?"

"Yes, Sir," stated the foreman.

"Will you give the verdict to the clerk, please, Mr. Shaw."

Charlie Cox then made it official. "We, the jury, find the defendants: Not Guilty."[146]

This ended one of the most sensational trials ever held in the South. As the verdict began making its way around the world, Swango announced Chatham's request to drop the kidnap charges as far as Tallahatchie County was concerned (those would now fall under the jurisdiction of Leflore County, where the kidnapping took place). The court had some minor business to attend to, but Swango thanked the jurors and informed them that their pay warrants awaited them downstairs. No one was allowed to leave the courtroom until after the jury filed out. Once they did, Swango adjourned the court.[147]

Photographers immediately crowded around Milam and Bryant, snapping pictures as they kissed their wives in celebration. Some climbed on chairs and tables to work around or over each other. Gene Herrick shot a few photos before quickly giving the film to his partner with the Associated Press, who transmitted them over the wire. Milam joked with reporters about "getting a wig" because of all the references made during testimony about a tall bald man. Reporters also began asking for statements.

"I was well pleased with the outcome, that's all I'm going to say," said Milam. "If you want anything else, you'll have to talk to my lawyers."

Juanita Milam admitted that she was scared throughout the proceedings. Carolyn Bryant said that "I feel a lot better" now that the trial was over, as did her husband. "We feel so good," Roy said. Carolyn refused to comment when another reporter asked about the pending kidnapping case. "She's not allowed to make any statement," insisted Roy. Regarding the prosecution, the defendants' mother, Eula Bryant, said she "didn't think they had any evidence." A sister, Mary Louise Campbell, cried quietly.[148]

Court spectators also made their way to the acquitted pair, shaking their hands and offering congratulations. Jurors trying to get through the crowd for their $25 pay warrants also received pats on the back and words of approval, such as "good work" and "nice going." Downstairs, people surrounded reporters and listened closely as they called in and dictated their stories. Large crowds also stood around the lobby discussing the case. Sandwiches and soft drinks remained available.[149]

A few of the jury members spoke to the press on Friday, either in person or on the phone, providing some insight into the hour and seven minutes they spent deliberating. The "not guilty" verdict was reached on the third ballot. On the first vote, nine voted for acquittal and three abstained. On the second, ten wanted to acquit, while two held back. No one voted to convict, according to Shaw, but those abstaining wanted to go over the evidence further. On the third vote, the decision to acquit was unanimous. The jury studied two photos—one of Till when alive, and another taken after he was retrieved from the river.[150]

Charles Gruenberg, of the *New York Post*, spoke with a few of the jurors by telephone later that day, and they talked freely about the case. Jim Pennington agreed that Mose Wright and Mamie Bradley were "good witnesses," and that "it would be hard for a mother to make a mistake about her own boy." Yet he believed she was wrong, nevertheless. The state did not have enough evidence "all the way around." Pennington rejected Willie Reed's testimony as unbelievable. "I think he was prompted."[151]

Ray Tribble also dismissed Reed. "It looked like he just had a good story." The dead body in the photo seemed too large to be Till, he thought. "I don't see how the body could be identified." Tribble denied that any of the men were influenced by racist attitudes, "either on white or black," and that the group "was a very fine jury on that particular thing." Bishop Matthews, one of the nine voting for acquittal on the first ballot, said that he too, had difficulty with the corpse. "The body they pulled out of the river didn't look like nobody." As for the eighteen-year-old surprise witness, "I don't think Willie Reed knew what he was talking about."[152]

Jury foreman Shaw spoke antagonistically toward Mamie Bradley in his comments. "If she had tried a little harder she might have got out a tear." He also said the jury found credible the defense argument that Till was alive and that another body was planted in the river.[153] It is not known just how long the jury discussed the evidence during its sixty-seven-minute deliberation. However, one juror revealed to a *Time* magazine reporter: "If we hadn't stopped to drink pop, it wouldn't have taken that long."[154]

District Attorney Chatham, tired after the five-day trial, remained dignified until the end. He told the press that "the only comment I have, [is] that they had a trial by jury, one of the sacred guarantees of our federal constitution. I accept it and I abide by it. I have no further comment." Ill health had prevented Chatham from running for reelection earlier that year. However, he still had one important case ahead before retiring in January. It involved a black man charged with killing a white store owner near the Mississippi-Tennessee state line. This case would be tried in Chatham's hometown of Hernando.[155]

Before long, the courtroom, which had been the scene of an internationally followed trial, stood empty. Window shades had been ripped out of place, and cigarette burns had damaged chairs and tabletops. Cane-bottom chairs were scattered in every direction, while paper cups, cigar butts, and cigarette packages lined the floor. Newsmen left behind telegraph blanks, cardboard film boxes, and used flashbulbs. Forty-five minutes after the verdict, Charlie Cox sat alone in the room sorting through papers, while two young black boys picked up pop bottles. Outside, Ralph Hutto of the *Jackson State Times* observed that "an occasional reporter wandered blankly through the halls, as if not quite convinced that it was actually over and the drama which was there so evidently a short time ago was now gone."[156]

If there was any comfort to be had by those who had hoped for a conviction, it was that Milam and Bryant were not yet free men. After a brief conference at their attorney's office across the street, where a crowd followed and waited outside, Sheriff Strider drove the pair to Greenwood. There, they were booked and jailed on kidnapping charges. They celebrated their first night as acquitted killers still behind bars, back in the custody of Sheriff George Smith and Leflore County.[157]

Mamie Bradley; her father, John Carthan; cousin Rayfield Mooty; Representative Diggs; Basil Brown; and their driver, Ed Ramsey, were about forty-five minutes out of Sumner when they heard the verdict over the car radio. When Mamie arrived at Dr. Howard's home in Mound Bayou, reporters were waiting. She had left Sumner because she expected an acquittal, she explained, "and I didn't want to be there when it happened." She was surprised, however, that the jury reached its decision so quickly. The state "did a very good job," she said. She also kept the belief alive that Emmett's death had not been in vain. "I take what little consolation I can in the hope that Emmett's death and the trial which resulted may deter other such killings."[158]

Diggs said a few words also. He praised the judge as "fair," and the prosecution as "impressive," but believed that "the deep-rooted prejudices of the jurors would not permit any kind of objective consideration of the case." The way to fix this problem was through black voter registration. Jurors come from the voter rolls, but not one black citizen in Tallahatchie County was listed upon them. He now planned to address that problem in Washington by challenging the seats of all of Mississippi's congressmen.

"I think the basis of representation in Congress from Mississippi should be reduced," Diggs declared. "The total population is used for basing the number of Congressmen, but the Negroes, included in the total, are not permitted to vote."[159]

The NAACP, through officers such as Medgar Evers and Ruby Hurley, had been assisting the prosecution all week, and from the beginning, Roy Wilkins, of the national office, had kept his eye on the situation. The NAACP issued a statement, and in responding to the verdict, Dr. Channing Tobias, chairman of the board, did not hold back:

> The jurors who returned [the verdict] deserve a medal from the Kremlin for meritorious service in communism's war against democracy. They have done their best to discredit our judicial system, to hold us up as a nation of hypocrites and to undermine faith in American democracy.
>
> Their intolerance is all the more glaring in the light of Judge Swango's fair and impartial conduct of the trial, the prosecutor's skill and vigor and the full and fair coverage of the trial by press, radio and television.[160]

When the *New York Post's* Charles Gruenberg asked jury foreman Shaw what he thought of the NAACP statement, Shaw simply shot back, "I don't give a damn what the NAACP says."[161]

◆ ◆ ◆

Any accurate assessment of the Till trial needs to acknowledge the fairness of Judge Curtis Swango and the passion of the prosecution toward securing a conviction. Reporters praised them both, and the black journalists who covered the trial signed a memorandum after the verdict commending Judge Swango "for the distinguished, the astute manner in which you presided, under trying conditions, at this trial . . . the sense of fairness and decency was evident in your court."[162]

It has been argued, however, that similar accolades for the prosecution were not entirely warranted, that Chatham and Smith were simply "going through the motions."[163] Dr. Howard said that Chatham told him personally that winning the case on circumstantial evidence would be impossible.[164] However, Mississippi governor Hugh White believed that outside pressure proved the biggest obstacle for a conviction.[165] With two unsolved racial murders in the aftermath of *Brown v. Board of Education*, Mississippi could not afford to whitewash this one, and White knew that. Although the governor's office appointed Robert Smith as a special prosecutor and sent Gwin Cole to investigate, everyone aiding the state, the governor included, was undoubtedly conflicted. The murder troubled them, but the international attention it received also put segregation in the spotlight. And that tradition they were willing to defend. Thus, Milam and Bryant were not being tried alone, observed reporter Bill Minor. On trial with them was "a system as old as the Constitution of the United States, and a way of life which may be older."[166]

Whatever the motivation behind its efforts, the prosecution headed by Chatham was impressive, even if it was imperfect, given the circumstances. However, Howard believed that the state was ill prepared, and addressed his criticisms in an October 8, 1955, *Pittsburgh Courier* interview. The state erred, said Howard, in its failure to utilize fingerprint analysis to identify the body. Similarly, its neglect of scientific testing to pinpoint the victim's age was also a blunder.[167] Each would have invalidated the courtroom testimonies of Sheriff Strider and Dr. Luther B. Otken. Yet when Mississippi officials shipped the body to Chicago, they did so with the understanding that its identity was settled, and law officials had yet to say anything to counter that. When he first saw the body at the river, Strider said it appeared to have been submerged for two days, and that the victim had been killed by either a gunshot or an ax. He also called a black undertaker to take it away. He released the body to Till's Mississippi relatives based on Mose Wright's identification and the statement of Wright's sons, made in front of Leflore and Tallahatchie County deputies, that the ring found on the corpse belonged to Till.

When Otken examined the body at the funeral home in Greenwood that same morning, he did so with Leflore County deputy John Cothran present. If Otken believed then that the body had been dead ten days or more, he never told Cothran. After Strider publicly disputed the body's identity three days later, both Cothran and his boss, Sheriff George Smith, were dumbfounded. Although the defense questioned the manner of death during the trial, a brief inquest on August 31 determined that the victim had died of a gunshot. At some point, Strider signed a death certificate, which gave the same cause of death. Further eroding any doubts that the body was Emmett Till, Strider had it driven to a cemetery at Mose Wright's church for burial.

Even if the prosecution wanted to scientifically examine the body, the shed in Drew, or the truck that allegedly carried Till's mutilated corpse, it would have been difficult, if not impossible, given the county's troubled finances. The *Chicago American* learned that the sheriff's office in Tallahatchie County was not supplied with the equipment needed for "big city crime detection" and that the district attorney, who covered four counties, had no funds for his own investigations.[168] Had the federal government found cause to intervene, it may have been a different story. The only known incident where the FBI did help was when the Greenwood chief of police forwarded a hair and bloodlike sample to the FBI for analysis.[169] A Mississippi newsman was quite matter-of-fact about the amateurish methods of Delta law enforcement. "Lack of facilities and training causes criminal investigations to be bungled almost daily [even] in cases that couldn't possibly be connected to the race question."[170] With little help from Strider as it was, Chatham's job was even more difficult.

Was it a coincidence that Strider waited until the day of Till's funeral to publicly dispute the identity of the body? Mamie Bradley's decision to postpone the burial for three more days came *after* Saturday's funeral services. Strider may have assumed that Till was buried or was about to be when he made his announcement. Had Strider believed, in the beginning, that the identification of the body sent up north was uncertain, he was duty bound to retain it. Certainly it was the body of *someone*, meaning an unsolved murder still lingered under his jurisdiction. Any investigation into missing persons would be futile without a body with which to link them. The fact that Strider was skeptical of the body's identity, yet was content to leave it buried in Chicago was inexplicable, except as evidence that his public statements and testimony were a farce.

Howard also criticized the state's failure to produce expert witnesses who could have made a thorough examination of the body to determine its age, but it was already on its way to Chicago less than twenty-four hours after it was discovered.[171] They apparently did consult pathologists in order to refute defense arguments about the rate of decomposition, however. Indeed, such experts were readily available. Breland admitted several years later that he had talked to pathologists at the University of Mississippi and University of Arkansas medical schools who told him that a body that had been severely beaten would have decomposed at the rate of the one in question in just three days. "I intended to get them to testify, but I sure didn't then!"[172] Although the state blundered by failing to call any experts to the stand, none of them would have actually seen the body. Defense witnesses, on the other hand, had seen or examined it, albeit casually. That advantage would hardly have gone unnoticed by the jury.

Both Howard and Representative Diggs also criticized the prosecution's inability to find witnesses, pointing out that it took the black press, or Howard himself, to locate those on the plantations in Drew.[173] But nobody, not even Howard, had any idea that Sunflower County held any clues to the case until those with information came to him and reporter James Hicks the day before the trial opened. Without a tip, neither the prosecution, Howard, nor anyone else would have had reason to focus on Drew.

Because Howard did not inform prosecutors of the surprise witnesses until two days into the trial, they were left with little time to investigate the plantation more thoroughly, even with the help of Gwin Cole. Had the witnesses come to light before or just after the indictments, time would have been on their side for a few weeks of solid investigation. Either way, postponing the trial until the spring term was out of the question. Smith explained later that the murder, which occurred at the end of Strider's and Chatham's careers, could not have justifiably been handed to their successors for investigation and trial. Also, according to Smith, the press "would have roundly denounced a postponement."[174] Similarly, recessing court for a lengthy investigation two days into the trial would have had the same effect, or worse, especially since the jury had already been called. Truly, an unfortunate combination of poor timing and even poorer finances put the state at a severe disadvantage.

There have been other criticisms, such as the state's failure to call Leslie Milam to the stand.[175] However, such a move would probably have backfired. Surely Milam would not willingly implicate his brothers, and any direct refutation of Willie Reed's testimony would have entirely demolished the young sharecropper's credibility for the jury. Significantly, defense attorneys did not call Leslie Milam either. Perhaps they did not want to face the ethical dilemma of Milam perjuring himself, or worse, addressing the whereabouts of Levi Collins and Henry Lee Loggins. Chatham surely had Leslie Milam in mind above all others when he told the jury during his closing arguments that defense counsel could have produced a parade of witnesses to refute Reed had he been lying.

Certainly J. W. Milam and Roy Bryant had a constitutional right to a defense, and according to their attorneys, the brothers never admitted guilt. Sidney Carlton, in a nine-paragraph defense of the verdict published after the trial, said that the prosecution never proved the body to be Emmett Till's, or that the victim met his death through any "criminal agency."[176] The attorneys did what any defense team would have done by raising doubts about the victim's identity. Yet in his closing arguments, John Whitten clearly crossed ethical boundaries by perpetuating a theory that he knew was false and which no evidence had been presented during the trial to back it up.[177] That was, of course, the idea that the murder was faked. However, the jury found it credible, or so they said. And ultimately, a conviction or an acquittal would come from those twelve men.

If the NAACP had staged a homicide, then Mose Wright would have had to have been involved, just as Whitten theorized. What about Mamie Bradley? J. W. Kellum, also part of the defense, said in *his* closing argument that Mamie believed the body was her son but was mistaken. A synthesis of the two arguments would suggest that Wright did not let her in on the hoax. Did he intentionally let her hold a funeral and continue to grieve? And if Emmett Till *were* still alive, did Till willingly keep that fact from his mother also? If Mamie, on the other hand, *was* in on the hoax, were her tears at the train station, at the funeral, at the grave, and in the courtroom all an act? Did she knowingly bury a different body and go to Mississippi to further perpetuate a fraud, just to embarrass the South and raise awareness of Jim Crow? For the jury members to seriously consider Whitten's theory, these were only some of the questions they would have had to consider. Countering such wild speculation, of course, was Mose Wright's testimony of the kidnapping, Milam's and Bryant's confessions to Leflore County authorities, the ring, Mamie Bradley's familiarity with it, and, last but not least, her positive identification of the body itself. In the end, these failed to bear any weight at all.

Any speculation as to what the jury really thought, however, ended seven years later. As part of his research for his 1963 master's thesis, Hugh Stephen Whitaker interviewed many of the trial participants. "All parties concerned—the judge, prosecuting attorneys, defense attorneys, the jury, and the accused—knew that a verdict of not guilty was certain," wrote Whitaker. His findings revealed that, "of the jurors polled, not a single one doubted that Milam and Bryant, or the Negroes supposedly with them, had killed Emmett Till. Only one juror seriously doubted that the body was Till's." Although they were speaking from the perspective of time, most said their verdict had not been swayed by publicity surrounding the trial. "If the Northern reporters and all those outsiders hadn't intervened," said one, "it might have been different. . . . But it probably wouldn't have affected the verdict."[178]

Whatever their personal belief, it would not form the basis of their verdict. Thirty years later, in 1985, a few of the jurors defended their decision, pinning it all on the lack of evidence by the state. Reaching a verdict was easy, said James Toole, then eighty-four. "We took what came across and they never proved them boys were at that place at that time." For juror Jim Pennington, seventy-seven, the trial was "closed and shut and it should stay that way. The prosecutors didn't bring in any proof and didn't prove nothing." The jurors, said Pennington, "were just doing our civic duty. There was no pressure."[179]

All things considered, it is clear that a jury in Sumner, Mississippi, allowed two men to get away with murder.

◆ ◆ ◆

Friday night, Mamie Bradley and her party took a taxi from Mound Bayou to Memphis, and then boarded a plane to Chicago. After a four-hour flight, they arrived at Midway Airport at 5:40 Saturday morning, where they were met by Alma and Henry Spearman, Gene Mobley, several *Chicago Defender* reporters, and a number of policemen.[180] Diggs took two of the prosecution's witnesses on the plane to start a new life in the North, and, fortunately, both already had connections in Chicago. Willie Reed, who had never traveled more than 125 miles from his home near Drew, boarded the flight with only the clothes on his back, a coat, and one extra pair of pants. After testifying at the trial, he briefly returned to the plantation and then walked or ran for about six miles to a prearranged meeting point, where he was taken to Mound Bayou and driven to the Memphis airport. No one had threatened him, he said a week later. "They didn't have to. I knew what they would do." His grandfather, Add Reed, also a state witness, said he felt safe in Mississippi and decided to stay on the Shurden plantation. His wife was ill, he explained, and he had to care for her. Willie's mother, Edith, had married W. D. Thomas and moved to Chicago three years earlier, and Willie would join them in their apartment on South Michigan Avenue. Reed, who had an interest in science and health, planned to work but also to return to school. He had already received several job offers.[181]

Mandy Bradley's decision to flee Mississippi came at the last minute on Friday night. After she testified Thursday, someone came looking for her, and she became afraid. Friends suggested that she go to her mother's house, but whoever was after her learned of her whereabouts and went there also. Bradley hid under a bed while the men made a threat to her relatives, promising that she would never testify at another trial if they found her. Before she went to the trial in Sumner, Bradley later reported, a white woman warned her mother that the Milams might seek revenge, and urged her "to be careful." When she left Mississippi with Diggs, it was so sudden that she took only the dress she wore and even forgot her eyeglasses. "Paid $45 for them in Greenwood," she said later. "I don't know how I'll replace them." Her husband, Alonzo, stayed behind for the time being. The couple had just finished their third year sharecropping for Leslie Milam, and, according to Mandy, they had never made "one red cent." The year before, Milam told Alonzo that he owed him $11, but offered to call it even if they agreed to stay on. "So we stayed to take another chance with him."[182]

Between the time that Emmett Till's kidnapping made news and the end of the murder trial, Mose Wright received mail from all over, even as far away as Russia, Japan, and France. One letter came from Baier Lustgarten, owner of Middle Island Nurseries in Long Island, New York. Lustgarten had seen Wright on television and was so taken by his story that he offered him a lifetime job and a bungalow for his family. For a time, Wright seriously considered the offer but wanted to stay in Mississippi long enough to secure the income from his remaining cotton, which still sat unpicked on sixteen acres.[183]

However, something happened that Friday night that sped up his decision to leave. After returning home from the trial, he decided to lie down around 9:30 P.M. Feeling restless and fearful, however, he grabbed a pillow, got into his car, and drove out to his church. There, he parked in the cemetery, locked his doors, and slept in the car the rest of the night. When he returned home in the morning, a neighbor told him that shortly after he left, two white men came to the house and shined flashlights all around outside.[184]

Wright was so frightened after this incident that he no longer felt safe in Mississippi. By Sunday, he was gone. He managed to sell a cow and a few chickens, but was forced to leave behind his furniture, tools, and cotton. It was an emotional moment for Wright as he gave away his dog, Dallas. "I have to leave this dog. He's the best dog in seven states," said Wright, as he wiped away a tear. The dog let out a whimper as he was loaded into a car and taken to the home of a neighbor. Wright asked his brother, Will, to try to sell off the corn from his vegetable garden and his 1946 Ford. Yet Will Wright would have to fetch the car from the station at Winona because Mose left it there on Sunday night when he and his sons boarded a train. Mose promised to return to testify at the kidnapping trial, but it was clear that his life in Mississippi was over.[185]

The lives of Mose Wright, Willie Reed, and Mandy Bradley changed forever after they testified in Sumner. That they instinctively fled their homes speaks volumes about black life in a Jim Crow world. It is impossible to really predict what would have happened had they stayed in Mississippi. Perhaps everything would have blown over soon. Yet again, it may be that they were literally fleeing for their lives.

Perhaps this was Faulkner's world after all.

1

Protests, Rumors, and Revelations

The day after the verdict in the Till trial made news around the world, Sumner was quiet, except for the usual business expected at the town square on a Saturday. Joe and Gee Bing, Sumner's Chinese grocers, were back to selling meat and neck bone instead of the large quantities of beer that northern visitors had demanded all week. Even though it was the weekend, Judge Curtis Swango was in his chambers reading over an upcoming arson case. The only visible sign that a crowd had come and gone was the trampled, dying grass on the courthouse lawn, which looked as though it would take years to fully rejuvenate.[1]

Most of the reporters had packed up and left, but at the Alcazar Hotel in Clarksdale, one remained. This was fifty-two-year-old James Boyack, a white New Yorker who had covered the trial for the *Pittsburgh Courier*, a black weekly. He was finishing his story when B. J. Skelton of the *Clarksdale Press-Register* came by for a visit. Boyack, born near London and raised in Ireland, was a former public relations man who spoke five languages.[2] Skelton certainly saw the handsome, charismatic outsider as a sophisticated man of the world, yet he was more impressed, and undoubtedly surprised, by Boyack's pro-Mississippi assessment of the trial.

"Nobody can convince me that the people of Mississippi are lynchers," Boyack assured the Delta-based newsman. "While they have their own local culture based on Mississippi traditions and institutions, they are no different from other people in this country or any other country."

Although he believed that locals had misjudged the northern press as wholesale critics of the South, he affirmed that he had been treated kindly by all of the officials and citizens he had encountered in Sumner. As a matter of fact, Deputy Ben Selby, who had refused to let Boyack in the overflowing courtroom on the first day of the trial, later invited the reporter to go fishing. Boyack praised Judge Swango, who took the "dingy little courtroom" and "turned it into a marble palace" by his fair-mindedness. Boyack agreed with Gerald Chatham's postverdict statement that the right to a trial was a sacred guarantee of the US Constitution. Like Chatham, Boyack accepted the verdict. He was pleased that both sides fought bitterly to the end.[3]

Deltans reading Boyack's sentiments in the *Press-Register* the next day surely gave a nod of approval. Yet it would be a gross understatement to say that he used restraint as he tried to appease Skelton and his local readers. In his *Courier* piece, which he had been writing since Friday night, Boyack described the trial as "the most revolting, the most disgusting, the most callous miscarriage of justice that has been my lot . . . in more than twenty years of crime reporting." Sumner was a "purgatory of racial tension," a "vale of hate, violence, fear." For Boyack, it was also a "hell-hole of American democracy." Far from accepting the verdict as he had assured Skelton, Boyack instead posed a question to his northern readers. "What is the meaning of the phrase: 'Tried by a jury of his peers' . . . when no Negro can serve on a jury in this state, because they are denied the right to vote?"[4]

The anger that Boyack was about to unleash had already been manifest by countless others aroused over the verdict. Technically, neither Boyack nor anyone else could do other than abide by the jury's decision. Because of the US Constitution's double-jeopardy clause, neither J. W. Milam nor Roy Bryant could ever be tried again for the murder of Emmett Till, within the same sovereign, no matter what evidence came to light. But with the verdict came a wake-up call, and with that, an endless stream of protests began. New York City seemed to erupt immediately, and there was no sign that it would soon cool down. On Friday night, the Democratic City Committee of New Rochelle passed a resolution to protest the acquittal, and directed its chairman, Salvatore Tocci, to send a telegram to President Eisenhower, urging that Attorney General Herbert Brownell investigate all violations of the federal civil rights statute. In a separate telegram to Mississippi governor Hugh White, Tocci criticized the jury decision. "It is a shock to learn that some of your citizens still choose prejudice over principle."[5]

On Saturday, September 24, fourteen members of the Bronx Labor Youth League, with only a two-hour notice, gathered in the rain, passed out over 5,000 leaflets, and received 516 signatures assailing the verdict on petitions to be sent to the president.[6] That night, the Harlem Community Clubs of the American Labor Party held three large street-corner rallies where they called upon the Department of Justice to intervene against Mississippi brutalities.[7] This demand was about to echo everywhere.

Milam and Bryant were still in the Leflore County jail Saturday. Their attorneys tried arranging bail but were unable to get bond set over the weekend because it first required a preliminary hearing. With plans shattered for a weekend reunion with their families, the brothers "unhappily" resigned themselves to a few more days in jail.[8] Although Leflore County bordered Tallahatchie, it fell into a different judicial district. The prosecution of Milam and Bryant on their kidnapping charges would fall to District Attorney Stanny

Sanders and Leflore County attorney John Frasier. Should a grand jury indict, Judge Arthur Jordan would preside at the trial.

Mamie Bradley barely had time to rest after returning to Chicago Saturday morning before flying to New York to headline a Sunday rally in Harlem at the Williams Institutional Christian Methodist Episcopal (CME) Church. It was only her third public appearance since her son's murder and the first after the acquittal in Sumner two days earlier. Thousands of people, both black and white, young and old, made their way to the highly publicized gathering sponsored by the New York division of the Brotherhood of Sleeping Car Porters. By 3:00 P.M., the church, which held 4,000, was full. An hour later, a crowd estimated to be between 6,000 and 16,000 filled the street between West 131st and 132nd Streets, with people standing twenty deep. Besides Mamie, others on the program included Brotherhood president A. Philip Randolph; New York City Council member Earl Brown; NAACP executive secretary Roy Wilkins; Rayfield Mooty; Rev. David Licorish of the Abyssinian Baptist Church; and other local religious and labor leaders. A choir, sitting behind the speakers, sang the "Battle Hymn of the Republic."[9]

The *New York Post* described the event as the "most emotion-packed rally since the Scottsboro upheaval in 1931." There was a moment of silent prayer on behalf of President Eisenhower, who had suffered a heart attack the day before. Religious and labor leaders then urged the ailing president to convene a special session of Congress to consider antilynching legislation. They also called upon Brownell and Mississippi governor White to investigate the disappearances of black field hands Henry Lee Loggins and Levi Collins, two possible witnesses or accomplices to the Till murder. Both had been missing since the morning after the kidnapping. The White House and the federal government, rally leaders insisted, should lead in fighting the "reign of terror in Mississippi and other parts of the South."[10]

The crowd was especially anxious to hear Mamie Bradley. Before thousands of anxious listeners, she told her story of viewing her dead child in Chicago, despite promising Mississippi authorities that she would not open the casket. She called the murder trial a "comedy" and let loose other criticisms she had kept to herself while talking to the press in the Delta just two days earlier. "What I saw in that courtroom for the two and a half days I was permitted in it was a shame before God and man," she said. "It's about the biggest farce I have ever seen. It is unbelievable and fantastic." She said that "friendly" whites addressed her, Representative Charles Diggs Jr., and other blacks at the press table as "Niggers," while the unfriendly ones simply glared.[11]

Randolph spoke about the plight of Mississippi blacks and wondered: "If the United States can send its armed forces 6,000 miles across the seas to fight Korean and Chinese Communists, in the interests of world democracy,

Thirteen-year-old Emmett Till poses in front of the family television on December 27, 1954. Copyright © Estate of Mamie Till-Mobley. Reprinted by permission.

Emmett Till and his mother, Mamie Bradley, in a mother-son portrait taken in their home on December 27, 1954. Copyright © Estate of Mamie Till-Mobley. Reprinted by permission.

Bryant's Grocery and Meat Market located in Money, Mississippi. It was here where Emmett Till had a brief encounter with twenty-one-year-old Carolyn Bryant on Wednesday, August 24, 1955, that set off the chain of events that led to his kidnapping and murder. Ned R. McWherter Library, Special Collections, University of Memphis. Reprinted by permission.

Carolyn Bryant. AP Photo.

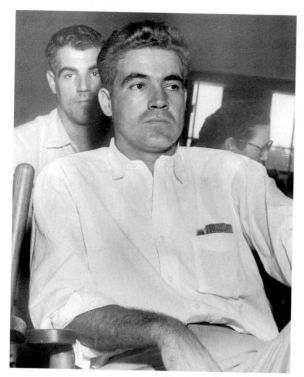

Twenty-four-year-old Roy Bryant, husband of Carolyn Bryant, was tried for kidnapping and murdering Emmett Till. Behind him sits his twin brother, Raymond Bryant. Ned R. McWherter Library, Special Collections, University of Memphis. Reprinted by permission.

Thirty-six-year-old J. W. Milam, half-brother of Roy Bryant, who stood trial for kidnapping and murdering Emmett Till. Ned R. McWherter Library, Special Collections, University of Memphis. Reprinted by permission.

Home of Mose Wright, East Money, Mississippi. Emmett Till was kidnapped from this house in the early morning hours of Sunday, August 28, 1955. Ned R. McWherter Library, Special Collections, University of Memphis. Reprinted by permission.

Mose Wright, holding a pair of pants belonging to his nephew, Emmett Till. He stands in the room where Till was sleeping at the time of the abduction. Ned R. McWherter Library, Special Collections, University of Memphis. Reprinted by permission.

Leflore County sheriff George Smith, who arrested Roy Bryant and J. W. Milam for the kidnapping of Emmett Till. Robert Williams/ *Commercial Appeal*/Landov.

Tallahatchie County sheriff H. C. Strider, under whose jurisdiction the murder of Emmett Till fell. AP photo.

Mamie Bradley collapses at Chicago's Central Street train station as her son's body arrives by train on Friday morning, September 2, 1955. Library of Congress Prints and Photographs Division. Visual Materials from the NAACP Records.

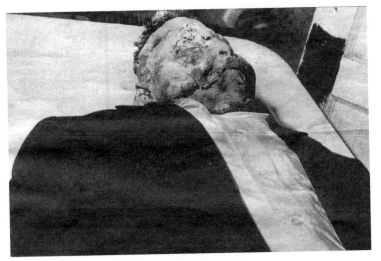

Emmett Till as he appeared in his casket. His mother insisted on an open-casket funeral so that "the world can see what they did to my boy." *Chicago Defender*. Reprinted by permission.

Mamie Bradley buries her son at Burr Oak Cemetery in Alsip, Illinois, Tuesday, September 6, 1955. That same day in Mississippi, J. W. Milam and Roy Bryant were indicted for the kidnapping and murder of Emmett Till. Ned R. McWherter Library, Special Collections, University of Memphis. Reprinted by permission.

Tallahatchie County courthouse in Sumner, Mississippi, where the Emmett Till murder trial was held September 19–23, 1955. Ned R. McWherter Library, Special Collections, University of Memphis. Reprinted by permission.

Circuit Judge Curtis Swango, who presided at the Emmett Till murder trial. He was praised by all sides for his fairness during the proceedings. Ned R. McWherter Library, Special Collections, University of Memphis. Reprinted by permission.

Prosecution team. From left: Tallahatchie County attorney J. Hamilton Caldwell, District Attorney Gerald W. Chatham, and specially appointed prosecutor Robert B. Smith. Robert Williams/*Commercial Appeal*/Landov.

Defense team. From left: J. W. Kellum, C. Sidney
Carlton, Harvey Henderson, John W. Whitten, and
J. J. Breland. These five attorneys constituted the
entire Sumner bar. Ned R. McWherter Library,
Special Collections, University of Memphis.
Reprinted by permission.

Mamie Bradley, her cousin Rayfield Mooty (left), and
Bradley's father, Wiley Nash "John" Carthan (back),
leave Chicago to attend the murder trial in Sumner.
Ned R. McWherter Library, Special Collections, University of Memphis. Reprinted by permission.

The all-white, all-male jury that would decide the fate of J. W. Milam and Roy Bryant. Library of Congress Prints and Photographs Division. NYWT and the Sun Newspaper Photograph Collection.

Members of the black press, crowded around a card table meant to accommodate only four people, sit segregated from white reporters. Although white reporters were allowed to sit behind the jury and closer to the witness chair, black reporters sat on the opposite side of the courtroom behind the railing separating court officials from spectators. Beginning on day two of the trial, Sheriff Strider replaced the table with a new one that accommodated ten seats. From *Shocking the Conscience: A Reporter's Account of the Civil Rights Movement* by Simeon Booker, with Carol McCabe Booker (Jackson: University Press of Mississippi, 2013).

Mose Wright, the star witness for the prosecution, heads into the courtroom to testify on Wednesday morning, September 21, 1955. Robert Williams/*Commercial Appeal*/Landov.

Mose Wright stands and identifies the men who abducted his nephew, Emmett Till, from his home. Corbis/Bettman.

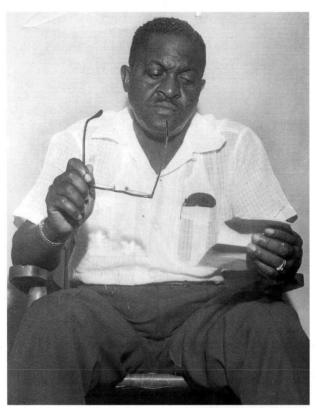

State witness Chester Miller, manager of the Century Burial Association in Greenwood, Mississippi. Miller took Emmett Till's body from the Tallahatchie River to the mortuary, where pathologist Luther B. Otken briefly examined it. Ned R. McWherter Library, Special Collections, University of Memphis. Reprinted by permission.

Defense attorney J. W. Kellum holds a key piece of evidence—the ring found on Emmett Till's finger when the body was retrieved from the Tallahatchie River. Ned R. McWherter Library, Special Collections, University of Memphis. Reprinted by permission.

The cotton gin fan that was used to weigh down Emmett Till's body in the Tallahatchie River. Library of Congress Prints and Photographs Division. NYWT and the Sun Newspaper Photograph Collection.

Surprise witnesses for the prosecution who were located after the trial began. From left: Mandy Bradley, Willie Reed, and Walter Billingsley. Ned R. McWherter Library, Special Collections, University of Memphis. Reprinted by permission.

Shed (on the left) located on the Sturdivant plantation west of Drew, Mississippi, where Willie Reed heard sounds of a beating on Sunday morning, August 31, 1955. The section to the right (behind the truck) with closed door contains a small room where four white men beat and murdered Emmett Till. Ed Clark/The LIFE Picture Collection /Getty Images.

Dr. T. R. M. Howard (center) was the key figure in tracking down witnesses for the prosecu[...] Michigan representative Charles C. Diggs Jr. (right), who attended the trial as a private ob[...] them are John Carthan (left), Walter Billingsley (back), Mamie Bradley, and Mandy Bradley[...] R. McWherter Library, Special Collections, University of Memphis. Reprinted by permission.

Juanita Milam (left) holds son Bill, as her husband, J. W. Milam, balances son Harvey while conferring with attorney J. W. Kellum. Ned R. McWherter Library, Special Collections, University of Memphis. Reprinted by permission.

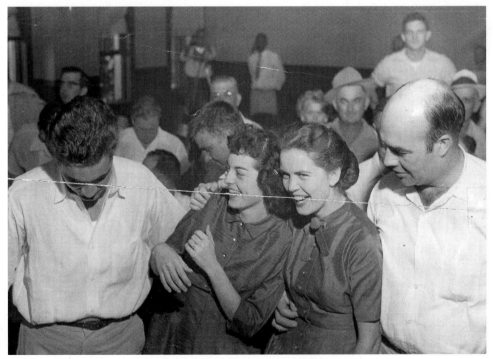

The defendants and their wives celebrate their acquittal for the murder of Emmett Till on Friday, September 23, 1955. From left: Roy Bryant, Carolyn Bryant, Juanita Milam, and J. W. Milam. Ned R. McWherter Library, Special Collections, University of Memphis. Reprinted by permission.

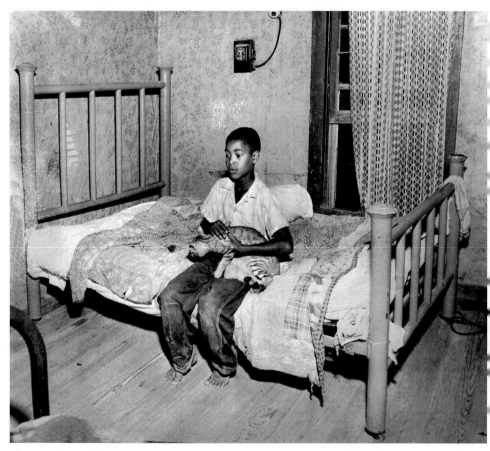

Twelve-year-old Simeon Wright sits on the bed he shared with Emmett Till on the night of Till's kidnapping and murder. The Wright family, like other prosecution witnesses, fled to Chicago after the trial to begin life anew. *Commercial Appeal*/Landov.

it would appear that the federal government should use its vast powers to stop the lynching of Negro citizens by Mississippi racists in the interest of American democracy." The audience interrupted that statement with thunderous applause.[12]

Simultaneous events held in midwestern towns on Sunday also drew large crowds. That afternoon, 10,000 people attended a rally in Chicago sponsored by the NAACP. Mamie Bradley was originally scheduled to speak at this event, but she was persuaded by her cousin and traveling companion, Rayfield Mooty, that the New York rally would guarantee a higher honorarium.[13] The 3,500 people inside the Metropolitan Community Church and 7,000 outside called for a "mass march on Washington." Willoughby Abner, educational director of the United Automobile Workers (UAW) union and chairman of the executive board of the Chicago NAACP, told those gathered: "If this lynching stirs not only Negroes and liberal whites but also the millions throughout this nation and the world, only then can we say that 14-year-old Emmett Till has not died in vain." Simeon Booker, the *Jet* magazine reporter who covered the trial, spoke of his frantic search for witnesses during a late-night rendezvous in the Delta, and introduced one who was present, Willie Reed. Reed, a shy country sharecropper, was out of his element but received a standing ovation before he, too, addressed the crowd. During the meeting, thousands reportedly joined the NAACP.[14]

Representative Diggs held his own rally in Detroit at the Bethel African Methodist Episcopal (AME) Church. Diggs spoke to a crowd of 4,000 inside, while 2,000 lined the street. A block away, 1,000 more people filled Scott Methodist Church. The crowds were kept content by Diggs and NAACP field secretary Medgar Evers, who alternated between the two churches. According to one report, traffic was blocked on dozens of streets. Diggs answered critics upset that he had left his Michigan district to attend the trial. "I am also a representative of all the people, black or white," he explained, "and you can expect me to look into any violation of their rights." Like Mamie, Diggs was far more critical of the trial once he arrived home. He referred to defense arguments as "sheer perjury and fantastic twisting of facts." He intended to gain an audience with the White House to seek the administration's support on civil rights issues. Mississippi "represents a shameful and primitive symbol of disregard for the essential dignity of all persons. Until every Negro is allowed to vote, we intend to challenge the seating of every Mississippi congressman." All of his efforts, Diggs promised, would be done properly, through the American democratic process. He told any Communists present to "stay away from us, we don't need you."[15]

Evers, also speaking at the two churches, assured the audiences that "tremendous good" was occurring in Mississippi because its people have been supporting and donating to the cause, even in the face of abuse by white supremacists. Arthur Johnson, executive secretary for the NAACP's Detroit branch, summed up the meeting in four simple words in a letter to Gloster Current, director of branches: "Wow! What an experience!"[16]

In Baltimore, Dr. T. R. M. Howard hosted a gathering attended by 2,500 people. Howard, fresh from the trial and an exhausting week identifying and gathering witnesses for the prosecution, spoke for over two hours. Addressing not only the Till murder but also the killings of Rev. George Lee and Lamar Smith in May and August, respectively, he noted that it was "getting to be a strange thing that the FBI can never seem to work out who is responsible for killing the Negroes." Howard, being high profile, wealthy, militant, and certainly hated by the majority of Mississippi whites, revealed that he was a "marked man" who kept two bodyguards on duty around the clock.[17]

In addition to the speakers at these highly charged rallies, members of two Jewish groups raised their voices in protest that same day. The Emma Lazarus Federation of Jewish Women's Clubs wired a telegram to President Eisenhower, written by June Gordon, executive director of the organization. After reminding the president that Mississippi was "part of the United States," she asked that he do all that his authority would allow in seeking justice not only for Emmett Till but also in helping Mississippi's black citizens obtain the right to vote. In a separate statement, Adolph Held, national chairman of the Jewish Labor Committee, said that "American democracy has, by this evil, bigoted act, received a serious reversal in the eyes of minority peoples throughout the free world."[18]

The verdict did not affect just minorities, according to New York black congressman Adam Clayton Powell, who weighed in on Monday from the SS *United States*. In an interview with *Chicago Defender* correspondent Ethel Payne, Powell said that the Till murder had disgraced the United States throughout Europe and North Africa.[19] Nowhere was this more evident over the weekend than in Paris, where a headline in *L'Aurore* screamed "Shameful Verdict!" The story read with as much passion as any in the northern cities of the United States. "The two repugnant assassins of the young 14-year-old Negro have been acquitted. Acquitted to the enthusiastic cries of a racialist public and a racist jury." Similarly, *Le Monde* said that the acquittal "proves, if that were needed, that racism is not dead in the United States," even though the US Supreme Court seemed determined to do away with segregation. The *France-Soir* ran a photo of friends consoling Mamie Bradley after hearing the jury's verdict. *Figaro*, often dubbed an "American paper," gave detailed coverage of the trial. The French Communist *Humanite* carried an article on its back page.[20]

Outrage over the verdict did not fade after the weekend. On the contrary, it only escalated, both at home and abroad. New York Democratic congressman

Victor L. Anfuso telegrammed Attorney General Brownell on Monday, September 26, promising that unless Brownell began an immediate investigation into the Till case, Anfuso would take it up with Congress when that body reconvened after the first of the year. In his wire, Anfuso said that "fair-minded Southerners and Northerners" needed all the facts related to the trial "if they are to retain their faith in the U.S. Constitution."[21]

The mood in the South seemed almost subdued by comparison, but not everyone was keeping quiet. Reaction, for the most part, consisted of isolated, individual statements, usually in letters to newspaper editors. One in particular that received publicity came from George W. Hinant Jr. of St. Louis. On Sunday, the *Memphis Commercial Appeal* received a letter and fragments of a Confederate flag that Hinant, formerly of Memphis, had taken with him to battle in Germany during World War II. "I was once proud to be from the South," he wrote, but added, "I've destroyed my beloved battle flag in rejecting the South." To Hinant, the words "liberty and justice for all" now seemed a mockery. "As of today, I am no longer a Southerner. I'm just an American who loves his fellow man whether he be red, white or black."[22]

Northerners also fired off animated letters to Governor White, among others. Grand Sheikh F. Turner, from the National Office of the Moroccan United Organizations, wrote White of the shock Turner felt at both the murder and the acquittal. He worried about the thousands of Muslims in the Magnolia State, telling White that he was "very much desirous of obtaining information as to their status as human beings."[23] Milwaukee mayor Frank Zeidler forwarded a telegram from the Wisconsin conference of the NAACP to Wisconsin governor Walter J. Kohler. Zeidler, concerned about reverberations over the Till case in Wisconsin, asked Kohler to send the telegram to Governor White. "You may reflect my opinion to the Governor of the State that the occurrences in his state, which are recited in this telegram, tend to cause a restiveness and reaction in the people of this community that no public official here wants or desires."[24]

Not surprisingly, Milam's and Bryant's defense attorneys were also targets of both outrage and praise in the days following the acquittal. One unnamed southerner, then living in Los Altos, California, wrote to the law firm of Breland and Whitten: "How frantic your white supremacy must make your peanut minds—when a fourteen year-old boy's prank send[s] you into hysteria! How far below Communists you must have sunk in Mississippi."[25]

A letter directed at John Whitten from Mrs. Frank E. Moore of Littleton, New Hampshire, declared, "If I am ever on trial for murder I want you to be my lawyer. Imagine you saying the body of that little boy killed by Roy Bryant and J. Milam was probably the body of some one else 'planted' where it was found. You should be ashamed, suppose that boy was yours." Moore was so outraged that she momentarily lost all sense of right and wrong herself. "If I was a negro and lived in Miss[issippi] I'd get a mob and kill their [Milam's and Bryant's] kids. Its an awful thing to say but their boys and yours (if you have any) will just grow up to be the same."[26]

Certainly, the worldwide scorn aimed at Mississippi escalated the defense mode that whites had been in since Emmett Till's body first surfaced in the Tallahatchie River. Dana Wier of Phoebus, Virginia, wrote Whitten that she was relieved that "the jury saved the great State of Mississippi from disgrace."[27] A. B. Nimitz of Cordesville, South Carolina, wrote similarly: "Every red-blooded White should sincerely commend you for your defense of Mr. Bryant and Mr. Milam in the Till case. The jury that exonerated Mr. Bryant and Mr. Milam deserve the unstinted praise and gratitude of every red-blooded White Southerner; for the verdict was exactly what it should have been: exactly what was needed. Other Tills will now think twice before insulting our women-folks." Nimitz then blamed everyone but Milam and Bryant for the crime. "If Till was really killed, then the NAACP, it's mongrel leaders, and the abominable excuse for a Supreme Court are solely responsible, due to the trouble inciting acts of the three above named."[28]

The verdict rendered was the only way to strike back at the 1954 *Brown v. Board of Education* decision, as indicated by Athens, Alabama, attorney W. W. Malone, who believed an acquittal would uphold "the southern tradition in the proper defense of our southern womanhood when insulted by a damn brute." Malone, of course, had Emmett Till all figured out. "Encouraged by the recent decision of the nine old buzzards on the United States Supreme Court, I suppose this young savage from the African jungles of Chicago felt like he could do as he pleased in Mississippi and that the NAACP and other South haters would come to his rescue." Writing only hours before the jury announced its verdict, Malone was "sure that a jury of good white men will prefer to believe the evidence of the two defendants ... and acquit these two fine young men."[29]

None of these loyal southerners demonstrated any belief in the innocence of the defendants. Breland's response to Malone, written after the jury had reached its decision, made it clear that in the highly publicized trial, the preservation of Mississippi's way of life was the real issue at stake, not necessarily the exoneration of Milam and Bryant. "It is unfortunate for us that we had to be the place where the NAACP selected in Mississippi to try to drive in an entering wedge in furtherance of their scheme for intergration [sic] and equalization in the State of Mississippi, but we did not hesitate to assume our full responsibility and stopped them cold."[30]

Across the ocean, on Tuesday, September 27, Paris was still seething from the verdict and became the scene of a large protest rally organized by the

International League Against Racialism and Anti-Semitism. Josephine Baker, an American dancer, actress, and French citizen since 1937, served as joint president of the organization. The meeting, held at the French Scientific Society, featured former French cabinet minister Daniel Meyer. Over 1,000 people attended and passed a resolution declaring the verdict in Sumner "scandalous" and "an assault to the conscience of the civilized world." The decision of the jury, the resolution declared, "sanctions legal lynching in the United States."[31]

A *New York Post* reporter interviewing residents of Greenwood, Mississippi, along Howard Street early that same week learned quickly that this approval of "legal lynching" was true in Leflore County. Most of the white people in the city of 18,000 seemed hopeful that Milam and Bryant "will get off scot-free" on the kidnapping charges, although they would not say so for the record. One young secretary at a printing plant told the newsman that the Till case is "all we ever talk about any more." Her hopes for Milam and Bryant were quite matter-of-fact.

"Most everybody is glad they got off on the murder charge, and we all hope they get off on the kidnapping charge, but most of my friends don't see how they can. They've admitted too much already."

On Tuesday, Judge Charles Pollard announced that a bond hearing for the pair would be held that Friday morning.[32]

If guilt was indeed irrelevant, as many believed, there were reasons for that mindset. Perhaps a very small minority were happy about the first acquittal and anxious for another because they truly believed the defense theory that Emmett Till was still alive. Others, of course, still wanted to teach outsiders a lesson or two for interfering in their business, and hence defined justice accordingly. Yet there were those who believed emphatically that the kidnapping and murder were justified, that Milam and Bryant did what any responsible white citizen would do under similar circumstances. As long as supporters backed acquittals for any reason along that spectrum, protesters had every reason to continue raising their voices. One thing that was certain, even among Mississippi white folks, was that the myth characterizing the Till case as only a local matter was now indefensible.

That was quite clear on Wednesday, September 28, in Detroit, the next scene of passionate activism. Walter Reuther, president of the UAW, said that "the lynch slaying of the 14-year-old Emmett Louis Till in Mississippi was a shocking instance of race prejudice and naked lawlessness." That night Mamie Bradley addressed a gathering sponsored by the National Association for Human Justice, held at the Greater St. Peter AME Zion Church. The crowd numbered over 2,000, and the meeting raised between $15,000 and $20,000.[33]

Mamie remained in Detroit to speak at a twenty-four-hour marathon rally held on Thursday and Friday at King Solomon Church. The purpose of the event, called "Operation Justice," was to collect 25,000 signatures protesting the verdict and to send them to the Department of Justice. Twelve black clergymen each ran a one-hour program, with the remaining time taken up by musical numbers and other speakers. The host pastor for the event, Rev. T. S. Boone, assured the people that "we're not rabble rousing. We're merely asking for the rights and privileges of American citizens."[34]

Thursday, things took a bizarre twist when rumors began to spread, claiming Emmett Till was not only still alive but had been spotted in cities such as Chicago and Detroit. When Sheriff Strider weighed in from his office in Charleston, he did not help to quell such stories. As he had before and during the trial, Strider remained adamant that Till was indeed among the living. "As far as knowing anything definite, I don't know it," he stated. "I definitely believe he's somewhere, but I don't know where."[35] Leflore County deputy sheriff John Cothran said he had been bombarded with telephone calls asking if Till had been located. "You couldn't even investigate a cow killing without somebody telling you about a rumor they heard." Cothran said that alleged sightings had also occurred near the Mississippi State Penitentiary (known as Parchman Farm) and as far away as New York.[36]

Mamie Bradley, still in Detroit, declared those sightings "a cruel hoax," and even offered "to have my boy's body exhumed from the vault for a thorough examination if that would dispel these wild rumors."[37]

The stories, however, kept coming. At that moment, Mississippi authorities were investigating the most fantastic one of all, originating out of Washington County. In Alexandria, near Greenville, Mr. and Mrs. John Black reported that their maid, Mozella Brady, told them that Emmett Till visited her on Sunday, August 28, hours after he was reportedly kidnapped. Brady said that Till had come to her home in Greenville at 9:00 A.M., stayed most of the day, allegedly had lunch at her home, and then went to a movie with her fourteen-year-old daughter. Till then told Brady that he was going back to Mose Wright's house in Money before returning home to Chicago the following morning. At first, Brady claimed to be a cousin of Till's, but later denied a relationship.[38]

Stanny Sanders asked Greenville police chief C. A. Hollingsworth to look into the story. When he did, Brady denied everything. Her daughter also said that she had never met Till, and Si Brady, Mozella's husband, insisted that the boy had never come to their house or that Mozella was a relative. In the end, Hollingsworth concluded that the entire story was "a fabrication."[39]

Accompanying the rumors that Emmett Till was still alive were stories that missing black witnesses Levi Collins and Henry Lee Loggins were dead. Some reports permeating the black community in the Delta even claimed that they had been killed and castrated. Leflore County sheriff George Smith dismissed the rumors.

"They are probably just laying low somewhere. Both of them are devoted to Leslie Milam and probably will show up here again when things cool off," predicted Smith. By that, he meant that their return would likely come after the conclusion of the kidnapping trial.[40]

Less dramatic, but at least factual, was a report on Thursday, out of Chicago, that both Mamie Bradley and Willie Reed had been assigned around-the-clock police protection. This was all overwhelming to Reed, who had never even seen a black policeman before. He had no desire to return to Mississippi, but admitted missing his cotton patch and his fifteen-year-old girlfriend, Ella Mae Stubbs. "I feel kind of lonely for Ella Mae," he said, sadly.[41] When this story hit Mississippi newspapers, the *Jackson Daily News* reported almost immediately that its readers were willing to put up the money to move Ella Mae and her family to Chicago, provided they wanted to go. Two anonymous donors seemed most anxious to help out. "Get the arrangements made and I'll send you a blank check," said one. The other told the reporter, Bill Spell, to "just consider the money available."[42] The next day, however, a follow-up story reported that Ella Mae's father had turned down the offer. When contacted at his home on the Roy Clark plantation near Drew, he said that his daughter barely knew Reed and that the family was happy in Mississippi anyway. Reed never saw or heard from Ella Mae again.[43]

It is hard to avoid the plausibility that this southern act of compassion was simply contrived by the Jackson press for the benefit of northerners who might read about it. If the attempted reunion between Willie Reed and Ella Mae Stubbs was nothing more than a publicity stunt from the *Daily News*, it was probably meant to counter the one reporters with the paper believed Chicago police were pulling. If Reed and Mamie Bradley had really fled to safety after the trial, reporters wondered, why were they under police guard now? However, it was not just the fear of revengeful Mississippians that was a concern. Captain Thomas Lyons, chief of the uniformed division of the Chicago police department, said he had ordered the protection as "good policy," due to numerous local racial incidents over the years and because both Mamie and her lawyer had received several crank letters themselves.[44] Reed learned shortly after the trial that, indeed, Chicago had its share of white southern sympathizers. His police protection lasted about four months, during which time he received threatening phone calls. Most of them were from Chicagoans. "At the time, Chicago was just as bad as the South," recalled Reed in 2007. "It didn't take me long to find that out." In fact, most of the callers promised Reed a fate similar to Emmett Till's.[45]

Yet the *Jackson Daily News* still smelled propaganda. Congressman Diggs, the paper reported, was checking out a story that Alonzo Bradley, the husband of trial witness Mandy Bradley, was beaten up and forced off the Leslie Milam–managed plantation after Mandy fled to Chicago. The *Daily News* remained skeptical about that news, as it did with Diggs's story that Mose Wright's sudden departure from Mississippi came after Wright hid out in a cemetery to escape the wrath of "three carloads of white men" who made a late-night visit to his home. "No one has yet said what cemetery," the Jackson paper pointed out. "What was the description of the autos? Where did the incident take place? Or did it take place?"[46] These stories prompted reporter Bill Spell to begin an investigation of his own that would make headlines the following week.

Meanwhile, photographers and reporters gathered at the Leflore County courthouse on Friday, September 30, for the bond hearing scheduled for that morning. Milam and Bryant, accompanied by their attorney, Sidney Carlton, were escorted from their cells by Sheriff George Smith and two deputies. The brothers stood nervously against a wall, smoking during the brief, informal proceeding held in the office of Judge Charles Pollard. Pollard read the court order stating that the men, having entered pleas of "not guilty" to the kidnapping charges, "and the court having heard and considered the evidence and being duly advised in the premises, is of the opinion that said defendants should be and they are hereby bound over to await the action of the grand jury of this county." They were then released on bonds of $10,000 each. Also present at the hearing were Stanny Sanders and John Frasier.[47]

Two Leflore County plantation owners, B. C. Walker and F. B Steinbeck, had put up the money. Deputy Ernest Stowers assured the press that not only had the money been guaranteed for "some time," but Milam and Bryant could have gotten up to a million dollars if needed. A number of planters with means were committed to go all the way for the pair.[48]

The hearing took only fifteen minutes. As they left, the brothers received congratulations from Sheriff Smith and others who had crowded into the office. They left through a side door, Bryant carrying a paper sack with his belongings, while Milam walked out empty-handed. The hearing started and ended so suddenly that most of the newsmen were unaware that it was over, and only a few were able to snap pictures or get statements. Milam told inquiring reporters who spotted him that he was going back to Glendora: "There's some cotton picking I've got to do." Bryant told those gathered that "I plan to open up the store after I rest up a bit." They then climbed into an Oldsmobile driven by a brother, Ed Milam, and headed home.[49]

Milam and Bryant would soon learn, if they had not already, that the Till case was still the biggest news story around. Besides the large and highly publicized rallies in the North and across the Atlantic, many smaller protests had also made waves that week. The National Association of Colored Women's Clubs sent a telegram to President Eisenhower through its leader, Irene McCoy, asking for federal intervention. A small group in Buffalo, New York, did the same. A rally at the Friendship Baptist Church in Milwaukee drew 150 people, while one sponsored by the NAACP in San Jose, California, brought together 100. In Los Angeles, fifteen businessmen from the Westside Republican Club pledged $4,000 and hoped to double that amount in order to hire private investigators and a New York attorney to find "more positive evidence" in the Till case, said club chairman C. Ehrlich Davis.[50] Nothing ever came of this effort, and just how long the group kept its resolve before it waned is unknown.

Labor unions spoke out as well. The UAW Local 333 in Oakland, California; the International Ladies Garment Workers Union Local 22 in New York; the International Longshoremen's & Warehousemen's Union Local 10 out of San Francisco; and the CIO United Steelworkers Local 1104 in Lorain, Ohio, all sent telegrams to President Eisenhower or otherwise condemned the murder and not-guilty verdict. In Berkeley, California, the Seventeenth Assembly District Democratic Club voted unanimously to write officials of the National Democratic Party to urge them to adopt antilynching legislation in the 1956 campaign. The San Francisco Communist paper, the *Daily People's World*, printed 5,000 copies of a September 12 editorial entitled "Punish the Killers," and distributed them all over Los Angeles.[51]

In light of all of the impassioned protests, a letter sent from Mississippi congressman Jamie Whitten to his cousin and the four other men of the defense team seemed eerily out of touch. He insisted that "public reaction" to the verdict "has been excellent indeed." Representative Whitten, hardly isolated from the rest of the country from his office in Washington, DC, certainly knew that millions of Americans outside the southern bubble were unhappy, even outraged that Milam and Bryant were acquitted. Perhaps he meant to dismiss them all when he defined sympathizers toward the defense as "the thinking people of the nation."[52] Yet even Whitten would have had to concede that a September 25 editorial in the *Jackson Daily News*, if he had a chance to read it, proved naive when it insisted that "the Bryant-Milam case be forgotten as quickly as possible."[53] With a second grand jury decision still looming and Americans engulfed in protests throughout the nation, forgetting was not an option, at least not just yet.

On the day that Milam and Bryant were released from jail, the Criminal Division of the US Department of Justice quietly made a request for an investigation into the Till case, explained FBI assistant director Alex Rosen, "in order that we may be in a position to determine whether a violation of the Civil Rights Statute is involved." Although the Department of Justice had announced shortly after the murder that it lacked jurisdiction into the matter, the request was based on a letter from the NAACP that enclosed an article, clipped from the *Washington Afro-American*, reporting that Levi Collins and Henry Lee Loggins had been held in the Tallahatchie County jail in Charleston during the trial in order to keep them from testifying. If true, this would have been a violation of section 242 of the statute, which applies to persons "under color of law." By definition, this meant law officials or those working with them who tamper with witnesses. Under the provisions of the statute at the time, this would have been the only real justification for the federal government to take on the case.[54]

On October 4, F. L. Price wrote a memo to Rosen, authorizing a limited investigation to determine whether the Department of Justice had any jurisdiction. The investigation was assigned to the Memphis office of the FBI, and agents there conducted an interview with trial prosecutor Robert Smith. Smith told the FBI that he had been made aware of the rumors about Collins and Loggins during the trial and had interviewed Sheriff Strider as well as a deputy. Both denied that the men were at the jail. Smith followed up by assigning the highway patrol, led by Gwin Cole, to search the jail and interview each of the black inmates on an individual basis. These officers determined that neither Collins nor Loggins was then, nor had they been, in the jail during the trial. With that, the FBI closed its probe and submitted a report on October 13. Demands for federal intervention increased over the next few months, but after this initial inquiry, the Justice Department never seriously considered jurisdiction in the case again.[55]

On Saturday, October 1, just as the FBI began its brief inquiry, stories out of the Delta reported breaking news that the mysterious whereabouts of Collins and Loggins were finally determined. In fact, an anonymous black leader confirmed not only that the men had been found but that both had been taken out of Mississippi for "safe-keeping."[56]

The quest to find the pair had begun quietly on Monday, September 26. *Tri-State Defender* editor Alex Wilson, stationed in Memphis, heard rumors that Sheriff Strider had contacted Loggins's father, DeWitt, and promised that his son would be back home by Wednesday. If this meant that the two men were about to be released from the Charleston jail where they were rumored to have been, Wilson wanted to have a reporter there to find out and locate them if they suddenly showed up in the community. Wilson left Memphis and headed down to the Delta that night about 8:30, after talking to an unidentified member of what he called the "Mississippi underground."

Over the next few days, Wilson and the others worked tirelessly to find the men but learned on Wednesday that Loggins had gone to St. Louis. This may have been a rumor, because a reporter for the *St. Louis Argus* shortly talked with Loggins by telephone, and Loggins was still in Mississippi. He did say he was going to St. Louis to live with an uncle, Louis Height, and even gave the reporter the address. But when the newsman checked it out, it turned out to be the address for the Adams Bath House. Whether the man on the phone was actually Loggins remains a mystery, but the field hand did have connections to St. Louis and had lived there three years earlier while working as a dishwasher at the Fred Harvey Restaurant.[57]

Wherever Loggins was, he was currently inaccessible, and so Wilson and the "Mississippi underground" focused solely on Collins, who they shortly learned was working in a cotton field in Minter City. Next, they carefully devised a plan whereby they would use a contact—someone known to Collins but who would not arouse suspicion—to convince Collins, who had a fondness for gambling, to go with him to do some betting. This was on Friday, September 30. The plan worked. After Collins and the "Mississippi underground" contact arrived in Minter City, Wilson approached their car and asked Collins for a match. Wilson then revealed his identity and said that he was there to help him out of the state for his own safety.[58]

Collins warmed up to Wilson, but refused to go with him that night. Instead, he promised to have his family at the rendezvous headquarters by seven o'clock the next morning. Wilson left, went back to his room, and got ready for bed. Shortly after, however, he received a call from the "Mississippi underground" leader saying that Collins had changed his mind and was already at the bus station waiting to go to Chicago. Wilson immediately got dressed and went to the station, where he met Collins and his friend. Collins's family, it turned out, did not want to leave the state, but agreed nevertheless that it was best for Levi to go away for awhile. Collins and Wilson then drove to Memphis and at 3:00 A.M. started for Chicago. During the eleven-hour journey, Collins happily helped with the driving.[59]

Meanwhile, Mamie Bradley returned home after the twenty-four-hour Detroit rally but was admitted to Provident Hospital on Saturday night. Reports indicated that she was suffering from a cold and, understandably, nervous exhaustion. During her three-day stay, the media were forbidden from talking to her, but shortly before her release, a reporter for the *Chicago American* was allowed to submit questions through Rayfield Mooty. Mamie, in turn, wrote out her responses, which Mooty then delivered. One question was motivated by reports surfacing since Sunday that University of Chicago pathologists were set to exhume Emmett's body in order to make a positive identification. When asked if she would allow this, Mamie said she could "see no reason for it" at that time. Was she going to Mississippi for the kidnapping trial? "I will follow the advice of my attorney," she replied. From her hospital bed, she also criticized the state attorneys and other investigators who handled the murder investigation.[60]

Mamie was released on Tuesday, October 4, and briefly went into seclusion at the home of some friends.[61] That same day the October 8 issue of the *Chicago Defender* appeared, containing an interview with Collins conducted over a two-day period after his Saturday night arrival up north. Colonel Euclid Louis Taylor, general counsel for the *Defender*, conducted the interview. Also present were Alex Wilson and *Defender* publisher and editor John H. Sengstacke.[62]

For those counting on a confession from the Delta farmhand, or at least something to further implicate Milam and Bryant in the kidnapping and murder of Emmett Till, the interview was a disappointment. Collins denied any connection to the crime and even claimed to have no knowledge of it. He also established alibis for both himself and Loggins. He said that he was home in bed at the hour of the kidnapping and went to Greenwood with a friend later that morning, where they visited some young women until after 10:00 that night. If his story was true, he could not have been on the truck that Willie Reed saw early Sunday. He said that on Monday morning, J. W. Milam came to him, picked him up, and took him to Minter City to run a cotton picker for Milam's brother-in-law, Melvin Campbell.[63] At this point, Roy Bryant would have already been arrested; Milam would turn himself in later that day.

Collins said he did not see Loggins again until Tuesday. During the week of the trial, they were both in Clarksdale driving a gravel truck for Campbell, and Collins was unaware that the trial was even in progress. When he returned to Minter City on Saturday, September 24, he resumed work in the cotton field running the picker. Collins said that it was only then that Campbell told him the trial was over. Taylor then asked Collins if he thought J. W. Milam could have committed the murder.

"No, I believe he was too nice a man to do it," replied Collins. "He treat too many colored people nice. He treat me and all of the rest of the colored people nice. He was mean to white people, though."[64]

The *Defender* had intended to have Willie Reed identify Collins, but Reed, like Mamie Bradley, had entered a hospital due to a nervous condition shortly after arriving in Chicago. Reed was still in Michael Reese Hospital while Collins was in the city, and reporters were forbidden from visiting him.[65] By the time the *Defender* hit the stands on Tuesday, Collins was on his way back to Mississippi. He returned to Memphis with Wilson that day, despite advice from Wilson and others that he not go back to Glendora. In Chicago, Collins had received new clothes and promises of a good job, and was assured a place to live. He wanted to visit his mother first, but promised to return to Chicago on either October 7 or 8. He was then given money to help his mother and pay his way back to Chicago. Unfortunately, he failed to return, and soon word was out that he was missing once again.[66]

Although the *Defender* interview was hardly a bombshell, it clearly showed that Collins was hiding *something*. He could not give the names of the young women he said he had been visiting in Greenwood, even though he had allegedly spent the entire day with them. He also told Taylor more than once that he wanted to talk with Loggins.

"Can you tell us why you want to talk to him?" Taylor asked.

"I just want to talk to him," replied Collins.

"What do you want to talk to him about?"

"I can't tell you what I want to talk with him about. I just want to see him," Collins insisted.[67]

Taylor then arranged for Collins to speak to Loggins by phone, but Collins refused to talk to the lawyer any further until he could see Loggins in person. During the course of the interview, Collins denied knowing Mandy Bradley, but when she entered the *Defender* office and confronted him, he admitted that he had known her for years.[68]

Where was Loggins during all of this? According to the *New York Post*, he had returned to Sumner from St. Louis on Sunday, October 3, and agreed several times to meet with *Defender* reporters there. Unfortunately, those meetings fell through.[69]

To be sure, the Collins interview was important, despite being a letdown in so many ways. It certainly raised some questions, and the answers seemed incredibly elusive. Just what was Collins's and Loggins's involvement in the Till case? Had they really been in jail during the trial, or were they working out of town as Collins claimed? With Collins safe in Chicago, why was he protecting Milam? Was Collins afraid of repercussions against his family, who remained in Mississippi? Reporter James Hicks continued to investigate the two men as he searched for answers. His report, which raised more questions still, would appear a month later.

In the meantime, focus shifted to even more sensational news related to the Till case, and it captivated Mississippians for the next several days. On Wednesday, October 5, the first of three serialized articles by reporter Bill Spell appeared in the *Jackson Daily News*. Spell had just returned from Chicago, where he went specifically to seek out Mose Wright, Willie Reed, and Mandy

Bradley. An editor's note above the first installment explained why. Because of "a flow of conflicting reports" about things the three sharecroppers supposedly said in explaining their move from Mississippi, the paper wanted Spell to learn the facts behind their relocation to Chicago. Spell believed he had evidence to show that they were actually being held against their will. Wednesday's headline did not pull any punches. "A *Daily News* Newspaperman Dared to Penetrate Chicago's South Side: State Negroes Held 'Captive' in Chicago."[70]

Spell, twenty-nine, was a World War II veteran who had been in the news business for about six years. He had just returned to the *Jackson Daily News* after a leave of absence while he worked on the campaign of former Mississippi governor Fielding Wright, who had just sought and lost a second nonconsecutive term for the executive office. Spell, a member of the National Guard, used an official plane to make his Chicago trip. He used the plane to help accumulate required flight hours as part of his training. Flying the plane was thirty-two-year-old crew pilot William J. Chrisler.[71]

Spell and Chrisler flew to Chicago on Monday, October 3. Upon their arrival, they visited the office of police commissioner Timothy J. O'Conner, where they received clearance and were taken by two officers to the Prairie Avenue police station. While there, they learned that Willie Reed had been admitted to Michael Reese Hospital. Spell asked for an escort and was given a police lieutenant named Edward Wolfe to accompany them to the hospital. When they arrived, they found Reed in a four-bed room, shared with one other black patient and two white ones. Reed, whom Spell said was "retching" when they arrived, was under the watch of a tall, black policeman, an obvious anomaly to the two white Mississippians. Wolfe told the officer that Spell had been given permission to talk with the patient.[72] Spell then addressed Reed.

"Willie," Spell said, "I'm from Mississippi. From the *Jackson Daily News*. I came here to get the truth about why you left Mississippi and to find out if you are afraid to go back."

Reed remained silent, but the policeman leaned closer to the bed.

"You don't have to answer me," Spell assured the ailing teen. "I am here to find out who you are afraid of, if you are afraid of anybody."

Reed sat up, but only mumbled.

Spell tried again. "I just want to know if anyone did you any harm before you left."

"No, sir," answered Reed.

"Did anyone threaten you or say they would hurt you?"

"No, sir," Reed replied, his voice gaining strength. "But I was afraid they might."

"Who were you afraid of?" asked Spell.

"Mr. Bryant and Mr. Milam."

"Did they say they would hurt you?"

"No, sir, but after the trial they looked at me hard."

Spell continued to query Reed, who affirmed that he had no desire to return to his former home, even if he was sure no one there would harm him. Reed would not say if anyone had urged him to leave Mississippi or promised to move him from the state in exchange for his testimony.[73]

Spell's second installment ran on Thursday, October 6. After visiting Reed, Spell and Chrisler went to Mamie Bradley's home. Once again, they were met by a police guard. The police presence obviously angered Spell, who noted bitterly that stories "broadcast to the world" had "left the sharp and biting implication that a policeman was needed to protect her from lynch-minded Mississippi 'white men.'" To Spell, this was a myth that many readily believed about his state.[74]

Spell had actually gone there looking for Mose Wright, but he quickly learned that neither Wright nor Mamie Bradley were at the residence. In fact, Mamie was still in the hospital, but Spell probably did not know she had even been admitted. Wright was not living there, but Spell discovered that Mandy Bradley was. The policeman allowed the men inside, and in a few moments, Mandy came into the room and sat down.

"Mandy," began Spell, "I came here to find the truth about why you left Mississippi."

"I left because I was scared," Mandy replied.

"Did anybody do you any harm before you left?"

"No, sir."

"Who were you afraid of, Mandy?"

"Mr. Bryant and Mr. Milam."

"Did they ever say they would hurt you?"

"No, sir."

"Did Mr. Bryant or Mr. Milam ever talk to you?"

"No, sir."

Spell continued to probe, and finally asked, "Is it right that Colored people told you it would be best that you leave?"

"Yes, sir," affirmed Mandy. "But they must have been right because my husband got beat up and run out of Mississippi."

"Do you know where he is now?"

"No, sir."

At that moment, Alma Spearman walked into the room, surprised to see the two Mississippians.

"How did you gain entrance into this house?" she demanded.

"The officer invited me in," explained Spell.

"Who gave you permission to talk to Amanday?"

"She did."

Spearman then turned toward Mandy Bradley, and in a scolding voice said, "Amanday, don't you talk to this man and don't you talk to anybody else unless I have cleared it with the proper authorities."

When Spell asked who those authorities were, both women identified them as the NAACP. Spearman told Spell he could wait until the representatives arrived if he wanted to continue talking, but he declined.

"Never mind. I want Mandy's answers. If she can't give them to me without help from someone else, I don't care to talk with her."[75]

Spell intimated that he left voluntarily, but the *Chicago Defender* later reported that he and Chrisler were ordered off the property by the police guard because Spell had failed to properly identify himself. Spearman immediately called attorney William Henry Huff. Decades later, Spell could still remember that Spearman was "severely perturbed" and "awfully excited and upset."[76]

In a teaser before his third installment, Spell wrote that he next hoped to interview Mose Wright. His aim was to learn the truth about Representative Charles Diggs's story that Wright had escaped the wrath of vengeful white men by hiding out in a cemetery on the night of the trial verdict. "These stories were doing Mississippi no little damage in the eyes of this nation," Spell wrote, and "I wanted to know what Mose himself had to say about this episode."[77]

Spell would learn nothing, but his disappointment became fodder for more conspiracies against the NAACP. To reach Wright, Spell called a phone number where Wright was staying, but someone else answered and questioned Spell about who he was and what he wanted. Spell said that he identified himself by name, and told the person on the other end that he was a reporter for the *Jackson Daily News*.

"I want to find out the truth about why he left Mississippi. If he was beaten before he left and if he is afraid for his life to go back."

The man said he would give Spell an answer later, but the reporter insisted on talking to Wright.

"Now let's get me and you straight," the unidentified man said. "You have given me the questions and I will give you the answers."

After the man failed to get back in touch that night, Spell reached out to him the following morning. He told Spell that he still did not have the answers but would get them later that day. However, the man never called back.[78]

The drama did not stop there. Spell claimed he became the victim of intimidation also, which confirmed to him that the NAACP wielded great power in the North. When he returned to his hotel room after visiting Mandy Bradley, he found several notes under his door. Most were from Chicago reporters wanting to know his motives for coming to town. One was from someone allegedly assigned by the NAACP to check on Spell.[79] In fact, Spell said the

NAACP made several inquiries to the police about him, which led him to a sensational conclusion. "The speed with which the NAACP moved; the thoroughness of their network and other angles they used indicated very strongly that they could reach the highest officials within minutes." Some of his evidence came from conversations with Chicago citizens, the truth of which he could not actually verify. A cab driver, for instance, said that he had to be extra careful in his dealings with black fares, even treating them more courteously than white riders. "At the slightest provocation," reported Spell, "a Negro passenger would 'get word to the NAACP.'"[80]

Apparently, it was not just the NAACP that had its eyes on Spell, who claimed that within an hour of leaving Mamie Bradley's house, black congressman William Dawson queried the police about him and his mission. For Spell, this was ironic. During the Till trial, "scores of newspapermen from all over the world visited in Mississippi. There were no reports that any of them were 'checked' or were even held in suspect." However, "when a Mississippi reporter came to Chicago, even a United States Congressman wanted to know why." Yet Dawson, one of only three black members of Congress, probably had other reasons for checking on Spell. After the three witnesses were relocated to Chicago, Diggs had placed them in Dawson's care.[81]

Spell's Chicago visit lasted only twenty-four hours. Upon returning to Jackson on Tuesday, he traveled to the Delta and found Mandy Bradley's husband, Alonzo. In a separate article that ran parallel to his interview with Mandy, Spell and reporter W. C. Shoemaker challenged the story that Alonzo had been beaten, blaming the rumor on the NAACP. Alonzo, they concluded, had been "used as a propaganda tool" for the organization. The farmhand insisted that "no one has laid a hand on me," and revealed his wife had left Mississippi without telling him good-bye. His only contact with her since then was a letter sent through "some woman in Chicago" to his daughter. Alonzo, however, reported that his wife was "doing alright and being treated royally." Unbeknownst to Alonzo, the *Chicago Defender* had just announced that Dr. N. A. Jacobs of Liberty Optical offered to fit Mandy with free eyeglasses after learning that she left her old pair behind in Mississippi. Alonzo believed his wife would be left alone should she return to the Delta.[82]

Although Alonzo Bradley denied suffering any physical harm, he confirmed that Leslie Milam had indeed ordered him off the plantation and that he was staying with his daughter, who lived just north of Drew. Milam had evicted him, said Alonzo, because Mandy's absence had forced him to take his meals elsewhere, thus making it difficult to fulfill his duties to his crops. A later report, however, claimed that Alonzo had been forced off the plantation at gunpoint just after Mandy left.[83] It seems improbable that Milam would have expelled Bradley so quickly if revenge was not the motive. The beating story, whether true or not, did not originate with the NAACP anyway. If the story was true, Spell and Shoemaker should have understood why Bradley, still residing in the Delta, would be hesitant to talk about it with white Mississippi reporters in the wake of a high-profile racial murder trial at which his wife testified.

After discovering Alonzo's whereabouts, Spell placed a person-to-person call to Mandy to give her the news. Their brief exchange formed the basis of another *Daily News* piece, this one appearing on October 8. After she came to the phone and identified herself, Spell heard someone else pick up an extension. He asked Mandy if she knew anything about her husband's whereabouts, to which she replied, "No." Spell maintained that the voice sounded different, and when he identified himself as a *Daily News* reporter, she quickly hung up. Spell concluded his article by asking rhetorically, "Is Mandy Bradley a free person who can speak without censorship or is she a mental 'captive?'"[84]

The Chicago press tried to answer that question by immediately rebutting Spell's sensational charges. Following Spell's first article, Enoch Waters of the *Chicago Defender* issued a denial that the NAACP was holding the three trial witnesses "captive," and maintained that they had come to Chicago of their own free will. "Chicago is a natural point to gravitate to when people get into trouble in Mississippi," he said. This Associated Press (AP) article also appeared in the *Jackson Daily News* on Thursday, the same day as Spell's second installment.[85]

Mort Edelstein, reporter for the *Chicago American*, published a piece on Friday that not only refuted Spell's theory but also indicated some trickery on the part of both Spell and Chrisler. Edelstein confirmed that the men had flown to Chicago in a National Guard plane, but also learned that they had told Captain Thomas Kelly, of the Prairie Avenue station, that permission to visit Willie Reed had been granted directly from the commissioner's office. "I was led to believe that Spell was a Mississippi policeman and Chrisler was a representative of Gov. White," Kelly said.[86]

Edelstein went to the hospital to get Reed's side of the story. Reed became nervous after Spell left and, unable to keep his food down, had to be fed intravenously. Because reporters were barred from Reed's room, Edelstein was unable to talk to him directly. However, Reed's mother, Edith Thomas, told him later that her son's decision to move to Chicago was his own, although the NAACP helped with expenses.[87]

Edelstein did speak with Mandy Bradley, however, and she was not happy about Spell's charges. "That's the most fantastic story I have heard yet," she said. "Nobody is keeping me here. I wanted to come here and I did, paying my own expenses. I haven't been threatened but I don't want to return to Mississippi." Mose Wright responded similarly. "Well, now I guess I have heard everything. I not only came to Chicago of my own free will, but I brought my wife and my three children, too. I paid all our expenses." Although Wright was too afraid to move back to the South, he made one resolve: "I definitely will testify at the kidnapping trial. They can't do nothing more than kill me."[88]

When Wright talked to an AP reporter a few days later, he confirmed the cemetery story, which he said occurred on the night of September 23. Wright told the story multiple times over the next several weeks, often with inexplicable inconsistencies, but there is nothing to conclude that it originated as NAACP propaganda.[89]

Cora Patton, president of the NAACP's Chicago chapter, was equally troubled by Spell's investigation because all of his accusations came without any attempt to directly contact the association. "If he had, he would have learned that nobody is being held captive as he has charged."[90]

Edelstein's investigation, as detailed in the *Chicago American* on Friday morning, was not overlooked by Spell. An article in the *Jackson Daily News*, which appeared that afternoon, quoted heavily from Edelstein's story, and Spell provided plenty of commentary. Spell was adamant that he never presented himself as a policeman. "I identified myself on every occasion when I felt necessary to do so that I was a staff member of the *Jackson Daily News*. I am sure the Chicago police were smart enough to check my credentials if they doubted my identity." In 2010, Spell explained that he possessed an identification card from his days at the *Jackson Clarion-Ledger* where he covered criminal justice on the police beat and said that he showed this card at the Chicago police station.[91] It is doubtful, however, that Spell could have identified himself as a reporter and still been given access to Willie Reed. Even the Chicago press was forbidden from seeing him.

In his *Daily News* response, Spell said that his only motive was learning whether the three trial witnesses had relocated to Chicago by choice. "I do not believe they left because they were afraid [for] their lives and somebody should defend Mississippi against the wave of propaganda the NAACP is directing toward my state." Responding to Patton's statement, Spell explained that "the entire point of the trip was to reach these people—Wright, Reed and Mandy Bradley—without the NAACP talking for them. The very fact that I could not contact them without the NAACP intervening is further proof that these Mississippi Negroes are held mental captive if not physical captives." Spell was skeptical that Edelstein interviewed any one of them without a "middle man" involved. "I could have interviewed these persons myself by telephone without making the trip to Chicago but I wanted to know the first hand [sic] truth without any interference."[92]

The *Chicago Defender* was outraged over Spell's intrusion upon Willie Reed and demanded in its October 15 edition that the police commissioner,

Timothy O'Conner, look into it. Picking up where the *Chicago American* had left off, *Defender* reporters were determined to find out more about Spell and Chrisler.

On Tuesday, October 11, they found Reed, who had been discharged from the hospital the day before. Reed said he was surprised that Spell and Chrisler had been able to find him at the hospital, but it was more perplexing that they got in to see him. Reed's doctor, William Cunningham, said he had stipulated that Reed receive no visitors and did not learn until the next day that the Mississippi newsmen had even been there. The *Defender* also looked into Chrisler, who police said had claimed to be a representative of Governor White. White's secretary, Lula Carvery, told the paper that she did not know the man, but said he could possibly have been one of 450 honorary colonels that White had named throughout his tenure.[93]

What was the motive behind Spell's investigation? Even a cursory reading of his articles clearly shows that he had an agenda. If NAACP representatives *were* acting as middle men, their motive was understandable. After all, a possible kidnapping indictment against Milam and Bryant was still forthcoming, and these three witnesses could be called back to testify. White strangers from Mississippi would naturally arouse suspicion, especially if the witnesses felt fearful in the first place. All three were transitioning from a lifetime in the rural South to a new beginning in the big city, and naturally, they were overwhelmed. At no time had the NAACP actually intervened and silenced them during Spell's attempts to speak with them, even though Spell tried to convey that impression. Had Spell really wanted to determine NAACP involvement, he could have continued his interview with Mandy Bradley and gauged her behavior before and after attorney Huff's arrival. Clearly, what Spell saw as sinister behavior was, in reality, simply prudence.

In 2010, Bill Spell, a very cordial and pleasant man of eighty-five, recalled those days in Mississippi as "very tense," and called the Till murder "a terrible tragedy and a terrible blow for Mississippi." He insists that he was displeased with the trial verdict, even back when it was rendered. In fairness to Spell, his investigation did not defend the jury, comment on the verdict, try to make a case for the innocence of Milam and Bryant, or accuse Emmett Till of any wrongdoing. It is clear that he was angered by northern depictions of Mississippi and believed that this was due primarily to propaganda by the NAACP. "It was my opinion at the time that without realizing it they [the three transplanted witnesses] were being made part of a story that was bigger than them."[94]

Yet in trying to prove his "mental captive" theory, Spell fell short. If anything, he widened the divide between the North and South, and the suspicions of each side toward the other were further validated. For all of his hard work,

Spell did not stay on the stories or investigate any further. Just days after he returned to Mississippi, he quit the newspaper business altogether to accept a public relations position with an oil company. He later went on to law school and enjoyed a career as an attorney in Clinton, Mississippi.[95]

Most white Mississippians did not need Spell's characterization of the NAACP to continue to harbor distain for the organization, or, for that matter, any pro-black group. Continued protests in the North added layers of animosity to an already sensitive South, as evidenced on Sunday, October 9, when the fall festival of the Wisconsin Civil Rights Congress used the Till murder as its theme. Three hundred black and white citizens attended the event, which made the front page of the *Jackson Daily News*, mainly because it featured prominent Communists such as Geraldine Lightfoot, wife of Claude Lightfoot (previously convicted under the Smith Act); Samuel Horowitz; and Junius Scales. A banner headline read, "Known Communists Using Till Case in Money-Raising Drive."[96] Although the quest to end Jim Crow in the South was not at all welcomed by southern whites, tying Communists to the movement would only ensure white resolve for years to come.

During unrelated Sunday rallies, Mamie Bradley spoke in East St. Louis, Alton, and Lovejoy, Illinois, and it was clear that none of the bad press out of Jackson from the week before had soured people up north. "Every auditorium was filled to capacity," she reported to Roy Wilkins, yet she worried about the toll the long meetings were taking on the standing-room-only crowds. "We feel that there have been *far* too many speakers scheduled to participate in most cases. A program like this can very easily lose its effectiveness when the audience is an overflow crowd with hundreds of people standing for hours on end."[97] The rallies brought in over $3,450, of which $400 went to Mamie. Although she shared the podium with Medgar Evers and *Jet* reporter Simeon Booker, she was clearly the biggest draw. When Gloster Current worried that Mamie might be absent, perhaps due to her recent bout with exhaustion, he instructed organizers to schedule her last on the program and to get donations *before* her speech. In case she did not show, he reasoned, "you do not have to make the announcement until after you have taken up the collection."[98] That people were willing to endure the discomforts that concerned Mamie was a powerful indication that they had not grown tired of Emmett Till.

That same day, miscommunication and poor judgment at a rally featuring Dr. T. R. M. Howard in Los Angeles created near chaos. Advertisements erroneously announced that Mamie Bradley would be in attendance, and Tom Neusom, president of the Los Angeles chapter of the NAACP, booked the Second Baptist Church for the event. The church only held 2,000 people, and projections indicated that thousands more would be in attendance. As a consequence, cars came to a standstill on the street facing the church, aisles in the auditorium were crowded, and a loudspeaker was placed in the overflowing basement. Although the meeting raised over $4,300, disorganization forced hundreds of people to leave the event without donating any money. Organizers also failed to invite labor unions and Jewish organizations, whose members were anxious to attend. "All in all," wrote Tarea Pittman, NAACP West Coast regional field secretary, "a very poor job was done of promoting the meeting in the largest center of population in our region."[99]

Outside of the NAACP, however, some creative voices began displaying their own brand of protest. On October 8, at the Jewish Cultural Club in Cleveland, the Ohio Labor Youth League performed what was probably the first original play about the Emmett Till murder.[100] Reporter James Hicks also began a riveting four-part series in both the *Cleveland Call and Post* and *Baltimore Afro-American*. Hicks enthralled readers with his blow-by-blow account of the trial and his role in the dramatic search for witnesses.

In the midst of this unabated attention, but also in the aftermath of the Spell articles, Edith Thomas, Willie Reed's mother, told the *Chicago American* that she would forbid her son from returning to Mississippi for the Milam and Bryant kidnapping trial for fear that Willie's life would be in danger. Everything he knew was on record from the first trial, she explained, and "is there if they want it." Learning this, Governor White told the *American* that any decision to testify was up to the witness. Thomas's fears, he insisted, were unfounded and "all a lot of propaganda." Edith Thomas, like her son, had been suffering from nervous tension and even quit her job as a laundry worker. "With Willie well, and the few dollars I have saved, we'll manage to get along." William Henry Huff, however, said he would encourage Reed, Mose Wright, and Mandy Bradley to return for the trial and also reiterated his pledge to file $100,000 civil suits against J. W. Milam, Roy and Carolyn Bryant, and, now, Leslie Milam. This he would do, he promised, no matter the verdict.[101]

It was obvious that demand for Mamie Bradley and her story would continue for some time. It was also no secret that fund-raising was the lifeblood of the NAACP. In early October, Mamie and Rayfield Mooty went to New York and visited with Roy Wilkins about how they could work together. At the meeting, Mamie entered into a verbal agreement with Wilkins that her future speaking appearances would be arranged by the association. Plans developed immediately for Mamie to appear at numerous events throughout the month, followed by a West Coast tour starting in November.

Mamie still had two engagements outside of NAACP auspices that she had previously committed to, however. The first would be held in Washington,

DC, on October 16, and the other was scheduled for November 6 in Chicago. Her Washington appearance would conflict with NAACP meetings in Dayton and Columbus, Ohio, but Mose Wright agreed to take her place at these two events. When the Ohio rallies approached, William Durham of the Columbus branch became worried about potential problems should Wright make the long trip from Chicago alone. Durham even reported rumors that claimed that Wright had been kidnapped after the trial, which probably grew out of Spell's sensational "mental captive" articles. Nevertheless, Durham feared that, from such stories, "one might get the idea to really kidnap him and keep him hidden until after the kidnap trial." Durham decided to arrange a police guard for Wright during his stay in Columbus, not only for Wright's safety but also because "it will add to the drama of our meeting."[102]

Wright was visiting in Detroit with Mamie's father when the Ohio arrangements were made. He was willing to speak for $50 per meeting, but Durham offered him $100, plus expenses. However, Annie Carthan, Mamie's stepmother, told Durham that Wright's sudden move from Mississippi left him nearly destitute, and that these speaking engagements were only source of income.

"Can't you make it $150 plus expenses?" she asked. "Uncle doesn't have a suit of clothes. He had to leave everything he had down there, crops and all."

Durham decided to pay Wright $300 for the two meetings. "I am glad that Mrs. Carthan took part in the agreement," wrote Durham to NAACP officer Miley Williamson, "because the family cannot later say that the NAACP took advantage of an elderly old gentleman."[103]

If William Durham wanted drama at his gatherings, certainly the unembellished facts of the Till case were enough to keep the nation talking and the rallies full, and as long as people kept speaking out, interest would continue. Of all the high-profile Americans to do so, none was more influential than Eleanor Roosevelt, who for years had been a thorn in the side of white southerners for her outspoken views on both gender and racial equality. Millions of Americans read her nationally syndicated column, "My Day," which appeared six days a week.[104] On Tuesday, October 11, she shared her thoughts on the Till case. "It is true that there can still be a trial for kidnapping, and I hope there will be," she wrote. "I hope the effort will be made to get at the truth. I hope we are beginning to discard the old habit, as practiced in part of our country, of making it very difficult to convict a white man of a crime against a colored man or woman."[105] The following day, her son, California congressman James Roosevelt, called for a federal law that would help prevent the "brutalities that are presently going unpunished in Mississippi." Roosevelt sought NAACP support for his proposed law, which would allow for federal intervention "when local law officials are patently malfeasant."[106]

That the Till murder would become a rallying cry for civil rights legislation was clear from the beginning, but the verdict in the trial advanced the calls for political action. On October 12, Representative Adam Clayton Powell spoke at a labor rally in New York's garment area, where he proposed a march on Washington to demand antilynching legislation from Congress. He reported to the 20,000 people present that the Till case had damaged the reputation of the United States throughout foreign lands. "In the eyes of Europe," said Powell, who had just returned from overseas, the murder was "a lynching of the Statue of Liberty. No single incident has caused as much damage to the prestige of the United States on foreign shores as what has happened in Mississippi." He then outlined a program to fight the recent surge in racial killings, which, including the murders of Rev. George Lee and Lamar Smith, numbered three in just a three-month period.[107]

To illustrate foreign reaction to the Till murder, the American Jewish Committee released a memorandum quoting newspapers from all over Europe and even Africa that criticized the murder and the subsequent acquittal of Milam and Bryant. "These are only [a] few examples of the unanimous and violent reaction of Europe to the Mississippi trial," the memorandum said in conclusion. "They can be multiplied a hundredfold."[108]

Quite possibly, the fallout over the murder would determine US strategy, but not without a fight from southern politicians. Minnesota representative Eugene J. McCarthy said the Till case had "eliminated what might appear to be a 'go slow' attitude in regards to the civil rights issue," and encouraged the Democratic Party to nominate a liberal ticket for the 1956 presidential election. Black voters were now energized, he believed, and it was time for the party to take a clear stand on racial matters. The election "will be won or lost in the North," and the time to appease the South was over.[109]

With all of the negative attention heaped upon Mississippi, its citizens were more defensive than at any time since possibly the Civil War. None of the protests, rallies, or fund-raisers sat well with its white populace, which was still angry that outsiders cared at all, or worse, wanted to change their way of life. As a result, at least a few decided they were not going to sit back and do nothing. Their means to sway public opinion was to focus on Emmett Till's father, Louis. Although he had been dead for over a decade, the revelations about him would be explosive nevertheless. And when the time came to bring them forth, the *Jackson Daily News* led the pack once again.

It was true that Private Louis Till died while stationed overseas in 1945. Mamie Bradley had told reporters as much upon her arrival in Sumner. But she did not mention that his death came via execution by the US Army. Had she known the story would come out, she probably would have mentioned it herself to soften the blow. She surely felt uneasy when others, such as Ethel Payne, praised the dead soldier, although Mamie was certainly the source of the basic facts and, most likely, the embellishments. Payne wrote passionately about Louis in the *New York Age Defender* shortly after the Sumner trial, although she mistakenly referred to him as Thomas Till. The young soldier, she wrote, "was reported missing in action by the Defense Department in 1945. He died somewhere in the European theater where he had gone to defend his country and make democracy work for his five year old son." "Somewhere in Europe," Payne continued, "Till's body lies mouldering [*sic*] in a lonely unmarked grave and the son he gave his life for lies in a Chicago cemetery, and the picture of the hero father is unclaimed by the boy who couldn't remember him but worshipped his memory."[110]

In one instance where she spoke of her husband, Mamie Bradley was careful to avoid lavish praise, but she still said little about his death. She told the *New York Amsterdam News* for its October 1 edition that Louis wanted to enter the army for the "excitement and travel" of it all. Louis, just like any parent, "would be more than disgusted to learn that two bigoted white men killed his only son." Her words then hinted of unusual circumstances surrounding his death, which may have raised a few eyebrows. "On July 2, 1945, I received a telegram from the War Department telling me my husband had died. I'm still hazy about the details." Astute readers surely caught the fact that the war had ended three months earlier. The headline for the article read, "Father of Young Till Died for His Country."[111]

It was the portrayal of Louis Till in *Life* magazine that got the most attention, however, and that editorial, as brief as it was, seemed to arouse sympathy everywhere but Mississippi. Eleanor Roosevelt even referred to the column, on the whole, as "an appeal to the conscience of all our people."[112] Titled "In Memoriam, Emmett Till," it said in part:

> Men can be forgiven for prejudice, as a sign of ignorance or imperfect understanding of their religion; no righteous man can condone a brutal murder. Those in Sumner, and elsewhere, who do condone it, are in far worse danger than Emmett Till ever was. He had only his life to lose, and many others have done that, including his soldier-father who was killed in France fighting for the American proposition that all men are equal. Those who condone a deed so foul as this are in danger of losing their souls.[113]

It may have been this public praise that aroused some curiosity, or perhaps rumors about the deceased private made their way to Mississippi. Whatever the reasons, reporters for the *Daily News* asked Senators James Eastland and John Stennis to persuade army officials to release Louis Till's records.[114] On

Friday, October 14, Eastland called the office of the judge advocate general of the army for some facts on the former soldier, and he received them verbally through the army records division in St. Louis. A spokesperson for the judge advocate confirmed to the *Chicago Defender* that it was standard procedure to answer questions about specific cases, but that the actual records were confidential. Eastland did not waste any time getting the information to the *Daily News*, because its first story publicizing the scandal came out that same day. Stennis told a constituent the following month that "the matter of getting this information out of the Army was pressed by both of us [he and Eastland] to the limit, as we were glad to do of course, and we were glad to furnish it to the newspapers."[115]

The large, bold headline on the front page of the Sunset edition on Friday said it all: "TILL'S DAD RAPED 2 WOMEN, MURDERED A THIRD IN ITALY." The accompanying article, naming the murdered woman as Anna Zanchi and the two assaulted women as Benni Lucretzia and Freida Mari, noted that Louis Till was tried on February 17, 1945, and hanged four and a half months later on July 2.[116]

An editorial introducing the story when it reappeared in the regular edition on Saturday tried to soften the motive of the reporters who broke it. It assured readers that the *Daily News* was "in complete agreement" with attorney Huff, who said that the story "may be true, but it has no bearing on the case pending." However, the editorial justified its revelation because "NAACP embellishments of the true facts in the case were out of place." Those lies, according to the *News*, went far beyond Louis Till. The NAACP had branded Emmett Till's murder as a lynching "when the facts did not support the 'lynch' label." Mississippi justice was maligned, it said, and the NAACP had collected huge sums of money through "distorted facts" that "painted Mississippi as a virtual battle-ground between the races." None of that, even if true, had any connection to Private Till, yet the paper believed the story still came into play. "It is a fact that Mamie Bradley, in NAACP-sponsored speeches throughout the country, has been saying that her husband and Emmitt [*sic*] Till's father lost his life overseas, leaving the inference that he was one of the Americans who gave his life for his country."[117]

Mamie's response to the story ran in the same article. When she first received her telegram from the War Department in 1945, she insisted, the only thing she learned was that Louis died due to "willful misconduct." She was never given any other details, despite sending letters "to the commanding officer, to the chaplain and to the late President Roosevelt." Roosevelt, however, had died in April 1945, three months before Louis.[118]

As noted earlier, Mamie knew the charges against Louis long before she claimed to have known about them. In 1946, she married Lemorse Mallory, a

World War II veteran who served with Louis in Italy and was still stationed there at the time of Louis's court-martial.[119] Mallory, who had always disputed the army's version of the story, would have been the most immediate source for apprising Mamie of the charges even if the army had not.[120]

Whatever the members of Private Till's company learned, however, came through the grapevine and not official channels, according to a few who served with him. Shortly after the story broke, some of these men spoke out against the army's charges in the November 3 issue of *Jet* magazine. On the night the accusations were first made against Louis, he and three other black soldiers were taken away and placed in a stockade. Later on, all of Louis's records were removed, and no one in the company was allowed to see anything related to the charges. One anonymous former sergeant (perhaps Mallory) said that this occasion was "the first time during our overseas stay that we were plainly ignored." Another said that "Till never confessed to the crime and we felt he was innocent. It is inconceivable that the big, playful fellow could be a criminal. If the facts stood up, the Army should not have been so hush-hush about killing him."[121]

Mamie stated later that she had inquired of the army in July 1948, through attorney Joseph Tobias, about her benefits as a widow but was not given a sufficient answer about Louis's death.[122] Army records, however, show that during that very month, Tobias received the court-martial documents.[123] Those would have spelled out the details behind Louis Till's execution. Tobias's letter to the army may have been prompted not so much by concerns about Mamie's benefits (she had been remarried two years by then), but by the fact that the army had notified Mamie of a July 10, 1948, disinterment directive to move Louis's shroud-wrapped, skeletal remains from the Naples Allied Cemetery in Italy to the Oise-Aisne Cemetery at Fere-en-Tardenois, France. A disposition form listing 122 army personnel who were executed during the war, dated July 14, 1948, stated that their next of kin "have been notified that deaths were due to wilful misconduct and upon their request, further detailed information was given."[124] Considering her marriage to Mallory in 1946 and Tobias's communication with the army in 1948, it is clear that Mamie had known for several years before the story broke in 1955 that Louis had been executed for rape and murder.

Mamie may or may not have known about one source, published three years after Louis's death, that is astonishingly coincidental. Ezra Pound, the acclaimed yet controversial American poet, had been living in Italy since 1924. During World War II, he wrote a series of pamphlets and made several anti-Semitic, pro-Fascist radio broadcasts that included harsh criticisms against the Roosevelt administration. Fifty-nine-year-old Pound was arrested for treason by US Army police on May 24, 1945, and jailed in an outdoor cell at the US Army's Disciplinary Training Center near Metato, a village located just north of Pisa. He was the only civilian held at the facility, which also housed 3,600 military prisoners. The majority of them were black, and 7 percent were accused of rape, murder, or "misbehavior before the enemy."[125] While incarcerated, Pound wrote his *Pisan Cantos*, which makes reference to Louis Till, who had been held at the same prison camp. *Pisan Cantos* was published in 1948, seven years before Louis's son was murdered in Mississippi. In 1949, it won the Bollingen Prize for poetry, awarded by the Library of Congress. In two references to the executed soldier, Pound wrote, beginning on line 170:

> Pisa, in the 23rd year of the effort in sight of the tower
> and Till was hung yesterday
> for murder and rape with trimmings . . .
> "St. Louis Till" as Green called him. Latin!"[126]

In criticizing the military's handling of the Louis Till case, Till's army friends raised a valid point. Several studies of military court-martials document the disparity between white and black convictions and executions during World War II.[127] With that context in mind, a summary of the Louis Till case is in order. His file consists of numerous letters, affidavits, the eighty-three-page trial transcript, and a fifteen-page review by the three judge advocates of the board of review, dated June 13, 1945. Another black private, Fred A. McMurray, was tried with Till on the same charges. McMurray had four previous convictions by summary court-martial, and Till had two. To the present charges, however, they pleaded innocent.

According to testimony given before and during the trial, Private James Thomas and an unnamed British soldier, together with Till and McMurray, raided the homes of the three women. Benni Lucretzia; Freida Mari; her father, Ernesto; and the future son-in-law of Anna Zanchi, the murdered woman, all testified at the trial. Moreover, Thomas gave a statement implicating himself and the others, and McMurray did the same, providing a detailed oral statement that was committed to writing and signed by McMurray in front of witnesses. After the statement was read, the defense declined to offer any counter evidence, and both Till and McMurray remained silent. They were found guilty and were executed together five months later. Thomas was granted clemency for his testimony and released back into his unit and served out his time in the military.[128] It is not known if the British soldier was ever identified.

Whether Louis Till was guilty or not did not matter in the end anyway. If *Daily News* reporters did not see a link between Louis's case and that of his son, they knew that in publishing the sensational details of Private Till's execution, many of their readers would make the connection on their own. It was no surprise that this is exactly what happened. "His son was merely trying to follow in his foot steps and receive the same treatment," wrote Dr. H. S. J. Walker to the editors of *Life* magazine. He also asked for a corrective to *Life*'s October 10 editorial praising Louis Till. "The only difference is that he was caught before he attempted the rape and killed before he could do any harm."[129]

Wade Milam, of Spartanburg, South Carolina (no relation to J. W. Milam), scolded the magazine as well for "lauding this beastly big, 14-year old brute to high heaven." The conduct of Emmett Till was, Milam declared, simply "a case of like father-like son." *Life* did not publish his letter, but Milam did send it to the editor of the *Jackson Daily News*, where it appeared on October 21.[130]

Other letters were forthcoming, making it safe to conclude that Dr. Walker and Wade Milam represented the views of more than a few Mississippi whites. It was probably more acceptable to accuse Emmett of inheriting some deviant trait directly from his father than to publicly accuse all black men of possessing a rapist gene. The latter was still a widely believed notion in the South, however, and here the lines distinguishing one view from the other were easily blurred.

Before the murder trial, the Emmett Till case was all about a "wolf whistle," an innocent flirtation, to be sure, but one that brought to the story an element of sex nevertheless. Once the press coverage of Carolyn Bryant's court testimony emerged, together with the new revelations about Louis Till, it had fast become a case of rape or something just short of it. Just how a grand jury in a Greenwood courtroom would view it was yet to be seen.

8

Clamor, Conflict, and Another Jury

Before agreeing to speak exclusively for the NAACP, Mamie Bradley had already made commitments to address meetings sponsored by two other organizations. The first was a rally in Washington, DC, slated for Sunday, October 16, at the 6,100-seat Uline Arena, organized by the Bible Way Church. On the day of the event, fire marshals and police turned away several thousand hopeful attendees, which inspired a hastily planned second meeting for later that night. Mamie could hardly avoid mentioning the Louis Till controversy, which had been headline news only the day before, but her remarks were brief. "Thank God, Emmett never knew and never asked" about his father's fate, she told her audience. For the crowd of sympathizers gathered to hear her, however, that story was not an issue. The 10,000 or so people she addressed throughout the day donated over $4,000, allowing the host pastor, Reverend Smallwood Williams, to expand into six major cities his grandiloquently named National Prayer Mobilization Against Racial Tyranny and Intolerance in Mississippi and Elsewhere.[1]

Mamie and her entourage, which included Elizabeth Wright, Bishop Isaiah Roberts, and Rayfield Mooty, received a shared stipend of $1,000, plus their expenses paid. While Elizabeth was in Washington, her husband, Mose, was speaking for the NAACP in Dayton and Columbus, Ohio. Wright captivated his audience at the Tabernacle Baptist Church in Dayton with details of the Till kidnapping, but he also took a moment to defend himself against criticisms launched earlier by some of his former neighbors in Money, Mississippi, who had accused him of giving in too easily to the abductors. His answer to them, and anyone else who might be wondering, was certainly cogent. "It didn't make any sense to fight when a man has a .45 in his hand." He shared the stand with *Jet* correspondent Simeon Booker. The meetings were successful, raising $1,000 in Dayton, and $911 in Cleveland.[2]

Before his guests arrived in Washington, Rev. Williams tried to arrange it so that Mamie could appear before the US Senate subcommittee on civil rights, but its chairman, Missouri senator Thomas Hennings, informed them that he was leaving for his home state and that the other two members were out of town. That may have been fortuitous—the chairman of the full Senate Committee on Internal Affairs, which oversaw Hennings's subcommittee, was Mississippi senator James O. Eastland, who had just helped leak the Louis Till story. Hennings apologized, however, and promised to meet with Mamie another time.[3]

Mamie's trip to Washington coincided with more international backlash against the trial verdict, while at home calls for federal intervention continued picking up steam. At the Vatican, the semiofficial newspaper *Osservatore Romano* urged Catholics in the United States to fight the racist atrocities that were becoming more and more prevalent. "Such crimes are so many—one recently involving a youth still remains unpunished. The color of this smudge is so very often the color of blood rather than black."[4] The following day, October 18, New York City Council president Abe Stark addressed a group at an interfaith rally in the Central Park Mall and called on Congress to pass an antilynching law. The Till trial, he said, should push the federal government toward an obligation to all of humankind and inspire a "responsibility to democracy" that could guarantee the civil liberties of everyone.[5]

This was exactly why Mamie wanted to meet with someone in Washington, preferably an official at the White House. Before she left the city, she sought an audience with Maxwell Rabb, Eisenhower cabinet secretary and White House liaison on minority issues, but this, too, was unsuccessful. Rabb, it turned out, was busy preparing for visits to Maryland and New York. This was unfortunate because Rabb was one member of the administration who showed a genuine concern about the conditions of African Americans and other minorities. Later that week, however, Rabb told an audience at a meeting of the United Negro College Fund in Chicago that the Department of Justice was making a "painful" and "careful scrutiny" of the case. The Till murder, he assured the group, had been of "great concern" to the Eisenhower administration.[6]

William G. Nunn, editor of the *Pittsburgh Courier*, suggested in an October 28 letter to Rabb that someone from within the cabinet issue a statement addressing the atrocities surrounding the murder. "If we can get no more than a declaration from Mr. Brownell's office that the [Department of] Justice deplores the Till incident as un-American and vicious and a betrayal of American principles before the world, then we could shake a little story from this." Such an affirmation, Nunn believed, would prove comforting to millions of American citizens.

Rabb's response three days later was sympathetic, yet cautious. "I certainly agree with you that this subject should be tackled in one way or another and I like your suggestion a lot," he assured his friend. However, he believed that "an official statement" could be dangerous. Constitutionally, it might be misconstrued as an infringement upon states' rights, "and even though a statement would not violate this, it makes the problem very touchy." Still, Rabb promised to pass Nunn's suggestion along to the Department of Justice.[7]

President Eisenhower was still recovering from his September 24 heart attack, but he probably would have quashed such a statement had anyone in his administration been inclined to issue it. Although he was far more progressive regarding civil rights issues than he has typically been portrayed, he was nevertheless pragmatic and aware of southern sensibilities.[8]

Nevertheless, pressure for federal intervention in the Till case was mounting. Mamie did not let up either. As she visited the sights of the city following her appearance at the Uline Arena, she found the US Capitol especially meaningful. After she climbed the steps of the building and took a moment to gaze at it, she pointed optimistically at the domed structure. A press photo capturing that moment appeared on page one of the October 22 *Chicago Defender* under the caption, "Maybe I can get help here."[9]

It was this kind of publicity, however, that created uneasiness at the Department of Justice. One official feared that Mamie's speech at the Uline Arena, which sat just two miles from Justice Department offices, might put more pressure on the federal government to take on the case.[10] He was right. Just two days after the meetings, New York representative Edna F. Kelly urged FBI director J. Edgar Hoover to "conduct a complete investigation of the kidnapping and murder of the fourteen year old boy, Emmett Till." Hoover's response was no different from the numerous others he had issued. "For your information, facts relating to the kidnapping and murder of Emmett Louis Till were presented to the Criminal Division of the United States Department of Justice which advised that this Bureau does not have jurisdiction or authority to conduct any investigation in this matter."[11]

That same day, however, the most dramatic call yet for a federal probe occurred right in the nation's capital. Fifty black citizens from Chicago, seven of whom were ministers, demonstrated through Washington all the way to the White House in a protest against government inaction in the case and the plight of southern blacks in general. They carried signs declaring "We have waited 336 years for equal rights" and "Down with the cotton curtain." The delegation, led by C. W. Barding of the Victory Baptist Church was orderly, but asked to meet with Vice President Richard Nixon. When that failed, they tried to see Attorney General Brownell. This was also unsuccessful, but six members of the group gained an audience with Arthur Caldwell, chief of the civil rights department. He assured them that the Department of Justice had no plans to intervene. The protesters, however, promised that they would return in even greater numbers if their demands for an investigation were not met.[12]

All of this was creating a predicament for Hoover. As he continued to stand by the decision of the Justice Department, he also had to respond to recent actions by Mississippi governor-elect J. P. Coleman. Coleman had already vowed to introduce a bill after his January inauguration that would prohibit federal agents from investigating black voter suppression in Mississippi unless the alleged abuses specifically violated the US Constitution. For Hoover, the dilemma meant finding a way to keep the lines dictating legitimate probes crystal clear, while also maintaining an understanding about jurisdictional limitations, especially where such limitations concerned the Till case. Because the public could not understand why the Till murder failed to fall under the federal kidnapping or civil rights statutes, Hoover suggested that Brownell run a series of explanatory articles in major US newspapers.[13]

While federal officials were answering a steady stream of demands throughout the country and protesters continued to cry out for justice nationwide, the first real battle in the aftermath of the Till murder trial had already been won, quietly and without fanfare, in the unlikeliest of places by the most unsung heroes anywhere. A small advertisement appearing inconspicuously in the October 19 issue of the *Greenwood Morning Star* hinted of that victory: "FOR SALE—Grocery Store. Stock and new fixtures. See Roy Bryant, Money, Miss. or M. L. Campbell, Minter City."[14]

Surprisingly, or perhaps not, black sharecroppers in Money who had been Roy Bryant's bread and butter before his arrest now refused to patronize his store. After his September 30 release on bond, he returned to work, but to no avail. "We had it open for three weeks and didn't clear $100," explained Bryant to inquiring reporters thirty years later. "I saw the handwriting on the wall."[15] After the store's closure, the Bryants moved to nearby Indianola, in Sunflower County, and, for the time being, Roy worked odd jobs to scrape out a living.[16]

When she returned home from Washington, DC, Mamie Bradley had only a few days to rest before starting a grueling two-week speaking tour throughout the Midwest and East Coast. Just before she left, Chicago was the scene of a grizzly triple murder involving three young boys. Robert Peterson and brothers Ike and John Schuessler, all between eleven and thirteen years of age, were found naked and beaten in the woods in a suburb outside the city. Mamie, knowing full well the pain consuming both families, took time to wire consoling messages to the grieving parents. "My heart goes out to you in your darkest hours of earthly despair. May God and his Angelic host abide with you and his Holy Spirit comfort you." In the hope that these families could escape the agony of injustice that Mamie had not, she offered her "sincere prayer that justice will inflict its severest penalty upon those criminally responsible." This justice would be long in coming, however, and not before another tragedy occurred. Anton Schuessler Sr., father of two of the murdered boys, died of a heart attack just twenty-six days after the killings while undergoing shock therapy for depression. The murders remained unsolved until 1995, when sixty-two-year-old Kenneth Hansen was tried and convicted for the forty-year-old slayings. Hansen died in prison in 2007.[17]

Mamie Bradley's new role as a public figure who had endured an unspeakable loss no doubt positioned her as a comforter to many others who mourned, as well as an inspiration to people simply anxious to hear her story. Yet her wisdom and judgment over her own affairs soon began to be tested. Sometime between her Washington visit on October 16 and her first tour stop in Gary, Indiana, four days later, Mamie developed misgivings about Rayfield Mooty over what seemed to be his attempt to cash in on her misfortune. Mooty, who had been collecting fees as Mamie's traveling companion, wanted to make his role binding and even permanent. At his urging, Mamie reluctantly accompanied him to the office of attorney Levi Morris to draw up a contract, the provisions of which made Mooty and Bradley partners for the next twenty years. She would receive 50 percent of the monies collected, Mooty would get 40 percent, and 10 percent would go to Morris. Before signing the agreement, Mamie sought the advice of her own lawyer, William Henry Huff. The attorney, later describing the deal as simply "a hustle in the name of Till," instructed Mamie to discharge Mooty immediately, which she shortly did, replacing him with her father toward the end of her tour.[18]

The mother of the victim by herself could not satisfy everyone still anxious to gather and hear about the injustices of her son's murder, and seven NAACP events held around this same time featured speakers other than Mamie. They were successful, collecting nearly $14,000 in donations. Rallies sponsored by labor unions and churches raised countless dollars for other organizations as well. One of those meetings, held on Sunday, October 23, was a small event at New York City's Lawson Auditorium, sponsored by the Cosmopolitan Community Church.

The meeting featured trial witness Willie Reed, who received a standing ovation before answering questions posed by Bishop Robert Hines. Some of Reed's remarks repeated his courtroom testimony, but he also shared a story that did not come out in the trial. A day before Reed testified in Sumner, defense attorneys took him into their offices, where he was asked to identify J. W. Milam, who had his "legs propped on the lawyer's desk, smoking a big cigar." The next day they had him do it again. "They had another big baldheaded man sitting next to him. They tried to mix me up this way, but I told them that [Milam] was the man sitting in the second seat." Reed assured the crowd that he was ready to go back to Mississippi to testify before the grand jury in the kidnapping phase of the case (contrary to his mother's wishes; Edith Thomas had told the press a few weeks earlier that she would not allow him to return). The hearing was scheduled to take place in just two weeks. After the meeting, Reed, with a police guard by his side, shook hands with the entire audience of 400 as each person in attendance filed past him one by one.[19]

After her appearance in Gary, Mamie went on to Grand Rapids, Michigan; Des Moines, Iowa; Omaha, Nebraska; Wichita, Kansas; and then back to Indiana, where she headlined a rally in South Bend. From there, she spoke at three gatherings on the East Coast, then went to Akron, Ohio. To close the tour, she made a third trip to Indiana, this time to a meeting in Indianapolis on November 4. She earned honorariums of well over $1,500 and helped the NAACP take in over $5,600.[20] Four days after the Indianapolis meeting, she was scheduled to begin a fourteen-city West Coast tour in Seattle.

In response to the Till case, the NAACP had already garnered more support than it had over any other incident since its founding forty-six years earlier. New memberships, renewals, and donations were unprecedented, and letters from both black and white supporters flooded the offices. An editorial in the November issue of the *Crisis*, the official magazine of the organization, tried to remind its readers, over a month after the verdict, that "not since Pearl Harbor has the country been so outraged as by the brutal, insensate lynching of 14-year-old Emmett Louis Till. And the unconscionable verdict of the Sumner, Mississippi, jury which freed the boy's accused killers." Not only was this felt in America, "but throughout the world, in Europe as well as in Africa and the Orient."[21] Was there something deeper at play than just this one murder? It seemed that all of the racial crimes and inequities of the past now cried out for justice on the world stage. Something big seemed to be looming just over the horizon.

In that spirit, the Mississippi state convention of the NAACP began in Jackson on Saturday, November 5. Over 2,500 delegates met at the Masonic Temple, where Clarence Mitchell, the organization's chief lobbyist, announced a list of goals that included integration and an end to the poll tax. He defined the Till case as a lynching, and castigated Mississippi law enforcement officials as being "so mired down in prejudice that, even when known criminals are accused of a crime against colored people, juries will not convict them."[22] The meeting, one of the largest gatherings of blacks in the state's history, was undoubtedly a success at one level, but astute supporters could not ignore the fact that in just a few days a grand jury in Greenwood would begin to consider kidnapping indictments against J. W. Milam and Roy Bryant. Southern whites were hardly friends of the NAACP as it was, and now the men about to meet in Leflore County would have on their minds fresh, impassioned criticisms of their way of life, as well as the NAACP's plans to dismantle it.

The following day, Mose Wright and Willie Reed boarded a train for Mississippi for their appearances before the grand jury in Greenwood. Journalists got word that the pair would arrive in Jackson, certainly a convenience, since several reporters were in town for the NAACP convention. However, they got off in Winona instead, arriving at 7:25 P.M. Ruby Hurley arranged a ride and accommodations for the men, but perhaps because of miscommunication, the weary travelers hired a taxi for the twenty-eight-mile drive to Greenwood instead.[23]

That night, the Jackson convention concluded with a powerful speech by Thurgood Marshall, chief attorney for the *Brown v. Board of Education* case from the year before. He called the Till murder a "horrible example of terrorism tactics being practiced against law-abiding citizens." He then put forth the NAACP's strategy to increase the black vote and, on the heels of *Brown*, force integration of the University of Mississippi, including the admittance of blacks to the varsity football team. As to the Till case, he had specific questions for Tallahatchie County law enforcement officers. Since the jury doubted that the murder victim found at the river was Emmett Till, "Whose body was it? What steps are being taken to find out who is guilty of (murdering) whomever it might be?"[24]

On Monday, November 7, the twenty-man panel began considering cases for the upcoming term of court. That morning, Circuit Clerk Martha Lamb swore in Mose Wright, Willie Reed, Leflore County sheriff George Smith, and his deputy, John Cothran, as the only four witnesses slated to testify regarding the Till case. The caseload was so large, however, that they had still not been called before the hearing adjourned for the day. After patiently waiting since morning, Wright and Reed left the courthouse.[25]

That same day, the NAACP announced in a press release that Mamie Bradley had arrived in San Francisco from Chicago for the kickoff of the West Coast tour. She and Ruby Hurley were to hold a 9:00 A.M. press conference in the Cable Car Room at the Hotel Fairmont on Wednesday before flying to Seattle to address the first of eleven scheduled meetings. The finale, in Denver, Colorado, was planned for November 22.[26] Mamie, however, failed to show up in San Francisco, and that temerity on her part began a strange chain of events that would, within hours, sever her relationship with the NAACP.

Sometime that morning, Mamie had telephoned Franklin Williams, West Coast regional secretary for the association, to report that she had missed her flight because she had been out shopping. She also told Williams that she would need more than the $1,100 honorarium that she had previously agreed to, wanted to sell photo books at the events (probably photographer Ernest

Wither's *Complete Photo Story of the Till Case*), and also wanted time to go shopping while in San Francisco. Williams assured Mamie that she would have time to shop and asked her to get on the next plane. The NAACP had already purchased tickets for Mamie and her father. Mamie promised Williams that she would arrive in San Francisco by five o'clock the following morning, and asked that he have breakfast ready for her, which he agreed to do. This would still allow her time to attend the press conference.

Later that day, however, a woman named Anna Crockett spoke by phone with Williams, saying she was Mamie's personal representative and secretary, and that Mamie now wanted a guarantee of $5,000 for the tour, plus expenses, or her original agreement of $100 per engagement, all expenses paid, and one-third of all donations collected at the meetings. After hanging up, Williams frantically called Roy Wilkins and told him of these latest developments.[27]

Wilkins, obviously startled by all of this, called Mamie's home that evening just after ten o'clock. Crockett answered but would not let Wilkins speak with Mamie. She told him, as she had Williams, that she was Mamie's representative and that she would speak on Mamie's behalf. She confirmed the earlier conversation with Williams, including the demand for $5,000. Wilkins listened patiently, then gave Crocket an important message to pass along to Mamie. He was canceling her appearances and would explain it all in a press release. He also explained it all in a telegram sent to Mamie that same night.[28] With the tour already scheduled and ready to begin the following morning at the Hotel Fairmont, Wilkins and his colleagues had little time to make new plans.

The NAACP's New York office immediately prepared a statement and released it the following day, November 8. It revealed Mamie's demands and explained that "the NAACP does not handle such matters on a commercial basis." Ruby Hurley would continue on the tour, but would now do so as the principal speaker. The press release did not state this, but a covering letter from Franklin Williams to the West Coast leadership explained that Williams hoped to secure Mose Wright as Mamie's replacement.[29] Wright was then in Greenwood, Mississippi, waiting to testify before the grand jury and was unaware of the plans being made with him in mind.

As this story played out in the North, the grand jury in Greenwood began listening to evidence in the Emmett Till kidnapping case that afternoon. Wright was the first witness to appear at the hearing, entering the room at 2:20 P.M. After giving testimony behind locked doors for twenty-five minutes, he exited at 2:45. Willie Reed went in next, at about 3:18, and finished at 3:33. Deputy John Cothran and Sheriff Smith each followed. At 4:03 P.M., Mose Wright was recalled for just two minutes.[30]

The jury did not make its decision that day, but Wright could not stay in town long enough to hear about it anyway. His last-minute agreement to substitute for Mamie Bradley on the West Coast gave him almost no time to prepare for his first appearance scheduled for the following night in Seattle. Rather than head immediately west, Wright first flew home to Chicago, where he arrived at around midnight and was met by NAACP attorney Robert Ming, who had worked quickly to secure Wright for the tour. Ming drove the former sharecropper home briefly, where Wright said good-bye to his family and packed some belongings. A few hours later, Ming had him back at the airport to catch his plane to Seattle.[31]

By Wednesday, Mamie had come to regret her falling out with Wilkins. She asked her longtime friend, attorney Joseph Tobias, to call the NAACP leader on her behalf to try to straighten out everything. The phone call was recorded and transcribed by Wilkins's office. Tobias assured Wilkins that he was calling as Mamie's friend and not as her lawyer.

"Mrs. Bradley feels very badly and feels there has been a misunderstanding of what the situation is."

"What situation?" asked Wilkins.

"Whatever little service she can give, she wants to continue," said Tobias.

Wilkins became guarded. "Are you speaking now as a friend of the family or as her legal adviser?"

"As a friend of the family," Tobias assured him.

"Now Mr. Tobias, if it is as a friend I can talk to you."

Tobias told Wilkins that he had read Wilkins's telegram terminating his relationship with Mamie, and he readily acknowledged the one fact at the center of the trouble. "There is no doubt she wants an increased stipend."

Wilkins reviewed for Tobias the various conversations of November 7 involving himself, Franklin Williams, and Anna Crocket. He also detailed the calls among Bradley, Williams, and Crockett regarding Bradley's missed plane and money demands. He refuted any notion that the NAACP was not taking care of Mamie's expenses, and he assured Tobias that Mamie had already expressed satisfaction with the honorarium that they had agreed to.

"There is no misunderstanding as to what has taken place. If there is a change of heart—"

Tobias interrupted. "She feels so distraught about this. Let her say there is a change of heart." She definitely wanted more money, admitted Tobias, "but I would like you to agree to let the cause of your group be served. Let her go up to Ming's office and sign a statement saying what she has just said and let her go and do a job for you."

Wilkins said he would have to get advice from the president, chairman, and legal department of the association before any decision could be made.

However, Mose Wright was about to land in Seattle, and NAACP representatives were meeting him.

"We have changed the billing substituting Moses Wright's name for Mrs. Bradley's name. We had this tour laid out. It cost us money. We made hotel and plane reservations, put out handbills." It was hardly feasible to change plans yet again. "The meeting in Seattle is tonight, and we have made other arrangements."

Wilkins gave Mamie the benefit of the doubt about her motives, however, affirming that she had, in the past, put their common cause over money. Although this had apparently changed, he was still hesitant to blame her entirely.

"She has listened to other people and allowed them to make arrangements for her," he told Tobias. Although doubtful of a resolution acceptable to Mamie, he promised to talk with his officers before 5:00 P.M. if he could.[32]

Whether Wilkins took up the matter with his colleagues or was simply trying to appease Tobias with that assurance is not clear. However, Mamie's admission, through Tobias, that she had in fact wanted more money only served to finalize Wilkins's decision to cut ties with her. That afternoon he sent a telegram to NAACP field secretary Lester P. Bailey, apprising him of the situation:

> We have secured Moses Wright as speaker for West Coast meetings opening in Seattle tonight fresh from grand jury appearance in Greenwood, Miss. November 8. Attempt of agent of Mrs. Bradley to demand five thousand dollars now admitted in effect by principal which means no Bradley appearances henceforth. Judging by Wright reception in Philadelphia, Columbus, Ohio and elsewhere we are confident scheduled meetings on West Coast including Los Angeles will be overwhelming successes. He is not only central hero of case but colorful and articulate speaker. Branch should proceed with November 15 meeting with appropriate publicity as to change of speakers.[33]

That evening, Wright opened the tour in Seattle, telling his audience, among other things, that "Mississippi hasn't got any law. I mean they don't apply the law the same to the Negro and the white man in Mississippi." Leaving the land of his birth had opened his eyes, and the lifelong Deltan could now admit, "Things are pretty bad for the Negro in Mississippi."[34]

Earlier that day, news of the Mamie Bradley controversy hit the papers. At the same time, a small group of reporters were awaiting the grand jury's decision on the kidnapping charges against Milam and Bryant. At 10:00 A.M. the panel began its third workday, and at 3:08 P.M. submitted its report. The men had reached decisions in all of the cases under consideration, but the newsmen present were only interested in one. Judge Arthur Jordan announced the decision to the anxious reporters. Coming on the heels of the internationally publicized, highly shocking, and much-debated verdict in the murder trial forty-seven days earlier, the news out of Greenwood would be anticlimactic no matter the decision. And in the end, it was hardly a surprise.

"Gentlemen," he said, "in the case you are interested in, there was no bill returned."[35]

That was it. Milam and Bryant were no longer simply free on bond but were now free of all charges. And if Jordan's words did not fully sink in, District Attorney Stanny Sanders took over from there. "As far as I know, the case is closed. The Leflore County grand jury has adjourned and did not return indictments in the Emmett Till case. Beyond that I can make no statement." Jury foreman William Henry Broadway Jr., nicknamed "June," told reporters that he wanted to make a statement but was, unfortunately, "sworn to secrecy for six months."[36]

Because grand jury decisions do not require unanimity, it is unknown if the outcome was based only on a simple majority or something else along the spectrum. A granddaughter of fifty-year-old William G. Somerville, a member of the panel, said in 2010 that Somerville was one among the number who voted for an indictment. Family lore has it that Somerville "never recovered" from the outcome of that hearing.[37]

June Broadway, overseer at the Star of the West plantation in Greenwood, died just two years later. He told family members that one day "the world will be shocked at what comes out about this trial." Broadway was well loved by his family, who were shaken in November 1957 when he drove through the plantation, waved at some field hands, turned a corner, and shortly shot himself. Although the death was ruled a suicide, an air of mystery has remained because Broadway died on the same plantation, owned by Luther Wade, where legend places the 1937 death of blues guitarist Robert Johnson. Johnson was said to have been poisoned.[38]

J. W. Milam had been running a cotton picker when he heard the news. He stopped at a gas station in Webb and drank a beer in celebration. "I'm happy about the whole thing," he said, smiling. Bryant was not available for comment.[39] Not smiling, however, was Leflore County sheriff George Smith, who had been in charge of the kidnapping investigation since August 28. Unable to find any new evidence to bolster the case, he blamed the outcome on the dearth of witnesses willing to testify. At least three that he hoped would come forward were Elizabeth Wright, who had witnessed the kidnapping, and two of the boys staying at the house that night, all of whom were now in Chicago.

"I've been in this business for 22 years," he said to a reporter the following day. "I know what you can get and what you can't get" when seeking witnesses. "They have their rights, just like anyone else and if they don't want to talk, I can't make them." Smith, who had worked hard during the murder trial to aid black reporters in rounding up witnesses like Willie Reed, now accused others with crucial testimony of actually wanting the defendants freed as part of a ploy to continue shaming Mississippi.

During a noon recess at chancery court in Indianola, Stanny Sanders expressed similar sentiments as Smith. Sanders insisted that the two witnesses who came down did not even cooperate fully.[40] Since both Wright and Reed *did* testify, it is unclear what Sanders was alluding to. Did he believe they were holding back? Was he blaming Wright for not taking his wife and sons with him? Whatever the case, both Smith and Sanders were clearly frustrated. Unfortunately, their frustration was not focused on the grand jury.

Both Wright and Reed talked to *Jet* magazine about their experience on the stand, and shed a little light on attitudes within the closed courtroom. "The jury members acted peculiar as soon as I got into the room. They wanted to know why I notified Chicago before I called the sheriff" after Till's kidnapping. His grandson, Curtis Jones, had called his mother later that morning, and it was after Mamie Bradley was notified that Wright went to the sheriff. "They kept inferring that I just wanted to start trouble. Then they asked me a lot of questions about why I had left Mississippi. I told them that J. W. Milam had threatened me but they didn't believe it. . . . I knew when I left the room they weren't going to do anything with those men." Reed said that the jury tried to confuse him by showing him several photos and told him to pick from them which ones were of Emmett Till. "I did, and then they tried to say I couldn't tell whether the men on the back of the truck (which went into the barn) were white or colored. I said I could tell colored people from white people. All they did was try to mix me up—and I would not let them."[41]

Although the press corps in the courtroom was relatively small, news of the grand jury decision traveled fast, and reaction was swift. Mamie Bradley, still dealing with her controversial parting with the NAACP, now had to endure a far bigger blow. With the closure of the case, "just about everything has run out on me now. I don't know what to say. I don't see how they could fail to indict those men." She never foresaw a conviction, but believed Milam and Bryant would have at least been indicted. She still hoped to file a civil suit, but was not prepared to pay for it. The NAACP would have to take on that one, she said.[42]

Roy Wilkins also responded to the decision. "The question now arises, since Mississippi jurors have determined that Milam and Bryant did not kidnap and murder young Emmett Till, who did commit the crimes?" Yet the no true bill "comes as no surprise to anyone acquainted with the administration of justice in Mississippi." In Chicago, an editorial in the *Tribune* got right to the heart of the matter. "There was no lack of evidence that would have justified an indictment by any grand jury. . . . Somewhere along the line something went wrong—and it was a shameful, evil thing."[43]

A Mississippi editor saw it differently, however. Virgil Adams of the *Greenwood Morning Star* insisted that the grand jurors were "men who know justice and are capable of making the right decision." The Chicago youth, after all, had "attempted to molest Mrs. Bryant, grabbed her and made indecent proposals. Where is there a husband worthy of the name who would not protect his wife?" Adams predicted that had "Bryant been present and slain Till on the spot there would not be a grand jury in the South who would have indicted him, and many in the nation."[44] Adams believed that Till's behavior at the store, based solely on the testimony of Carolyn Bryant, justified the punishment he received.

Adams's affirmation that any southern jury would agree with him was chilling, yet probably close to the truth. Dr. T. D. Patton of Carthage, Tennessee, unaware that attorneys Breland and Whitten had not been retained to defend Milam and Bryant on the kidnapping charges, sent Whitten some words of advice before the hearing. Patton made four key points that he thought would be helpful in crafting a defense. First, the situation was not at all "a case of kidnapping in the usual sense, without provocation reason, or for ransom." Patton's second point explained why. "Till was guilty of a violent criminal assault and had escaped the scene of the crime." The reaction of the half-brothers, covering Patton's third and fourth points, channeled the mindset of an era that was apparently not really part of the past. "Outraged citizens tracked down the vicious sex criminal and simply made a legal citizen's arrest as any citizen can legally do. The unwritten law decrees sudden execution to such suicidal sex offenders. This fact is well known."[45]

Correspondence between lawyer and future judge Russel D. Moore of Jackson and J. J. Breland seems to indicate further that Patton's view was perhaps the prevailing one among Mississippi's white citizens. Moore had sent Breland a photocopy of a letter that a Confederate soldier and ancestor, S. Blanche Moore, had written his wife during the Civil War. The letter addressed insults that Mrs. Moore and other revered women had been forced to endure from the Yankees.[46] Breland responded the next day and for the first time clearly implicated his former clients in Till's murder. At the same time, however, he fully justified their actions:

The sentiments expressed in the letter of your Ancestor to his wife during the Civil War were, no doubt, the sentiments of Milam and Bryant. When they discovered one of the young married ladies in their family had been grossly insulted by a Chicago negro, their natural reaction was, no doubt, the same that would have been that of "S. Blanche Moore." In fact, their reaction to this gross insult was the same that would have been that of any other true, white Mississippian.[47]

Four witnesses testified against Milam and Bryant on the kidnapping charges, including a sheriff and his deputy.[48] Certainly, the decision not to indict had nothing to do with a lack of evidence. If the grand jury made what Adams called "the right decision," it was a decision based on a system of justice advocated by Adams, Patton, Moore, Breland, and, certainly, a whole host of others.

After he left the Leflore County courthouse, Willie Reed took a train back to Chicago and arrived in the Windy City before the grand jury decision was even announced. He was accompanied by Alonzo Bradley, husband of trial witness Mandy Bradley, who was ready to join his wife up north after a month and a half apart.[49] A resolution passed at the NAACP state convention in Jackson two days earlier provided Alonzo with $200 for new clothing and his train ticket.[50] Alonzo's timing in joining his wife surely lifted her spirits. Mandy was facing difficulties in her new surroundings and was unable to work, due to severe arthritis. At some point, she had moved out of Mamie Bradley's house and in with a family on Chicago's West Side. Although she had been given $50 by the NAACP, she was behind in her rent by several weeks. Overall, Mandy was overwhelmed and disillusioned by the city.

On a brighter note, the Elks lodge had just announced that it had donated $1,000 to an education fund set up for Willie Reed. Should he decide to attend college, he would receive $250 per year over a four-year period. "I feel that this young hero stands as a symbol of our unquenchable faith in God and man," said George Lee, Elks grand commissioner of education. "I feel that this young man is a living symbol of our conviction that no tyrant ever could for long starve or torture average men out of that dream" of freedom and justice.[51]

Unfortunately, things were only getting worse for Mamie Bradley. Following her split with the NAACP, attorney Huff sent her a letter of resignation, thus severing his own relationship with her. Under the circumstances, this was inevitable. As a lawyer affiliated directly with the NAACP, he explained, "it would be impossible for me to continue as your attorney for you being as you are not associated with the organization." By now, the press was seeking Mamie's side to the controversy. Because Wilkins's press release only indicated that Mamie's demand for money was the central issue, she did not address any of the other relevant matters, such as missing her plane to San Francisco, or that her insistence on more money was made at the last minute. Once again, Anna Crockett did all of the talking. Crockett now denied that Mamie had ever asked for the $5,000 but claimed that this figure was suggested by Franklin Williams and Sylvester Odom, a minister and president of the Oakland branch. Speaking by phone from Chicago, Crockett admitted, however, that Mamie had asked for the alternative stipend of $100 per meeting plus one-third of the profits. This increase was necessary because Mamie had accumulated large hospital bills after her nervous breakdown in early October, and because her father quit his job in order to accompany her on her travels. Crockett also told the *Chicago Defender* that in the past, several checks that were to go to Mamie had been turned over to the NAACP instead.[52]

In response, NAACP publicity director Henry Moon calmly countered the latter claim made by Crockett. "We do not wish to enter into a controversy over the matter," he said, "but for the sake of clarification it must be stated that we have not withheld any funds intended for Mrs. Bradley." Moon insisted that NAACP records backed this up.[53]

As Mose Wright was about to take the podium on Wednesday night in Seattle, Mamie wrote Wilkins from her home in Chicago, following up on Tobias's call from earlier that day and hoping that her own words might convince the NAACP leader that her support of the organization's agenda meant more to her than any financial rewards. She was now willing to serve the group on its terms. "I set out to trade the blood of my child for the betterment of my race; and I do not now wish to deviate from such course," she said in this, her first communication with Wilkins since before the trouble began. "I feel very bad that the opportunity to talk for the Association would be taken from me. I know that you have tried very hard and sincerely to see to my day-to-day financial needs. It is unfair and untrue for anyone to say otherwise.... If NAACP is willing to continue to do what it has to defray my travel and living expenses," she assured him, "that should suffice. Please let me go forward with NAACP. It is a duty. I would not want it said that I did anything to shirk it."[54]

After Wilkins received the letter, he presented it to his board of directors on Monday, November 14. He then sent Mamie a personal response the next day. His four-page letter detailed their various conversations, beginning with a meeting back on October 8 during which Mamie had assured him that she wanted to help the NAACP. The two agreed verbally at that time that the association would manage her future speaking engagements and that she would receive a minimum honorarium of $100 per meeting. Rayfield Mooty, who was present, accepted all the terms as well. "It was a shock, therefore, to learn on November 7, the day you were to leave for San Francisco, that Mr. Williams had been informed you had missed the flight on which we had purchased two seats because you were 'busy shopping.'" He reminded her also of the demand, through Anna Crockett, of a guarantee of $5,000 for the eleven-city tour.

Wilkins assured Mamie, as he had Tobias on the phone a week earlier, that there had been no misunderstanding. Although Tobias had tried to persuade Wilkins that Mamie had experienced "a change of heart," Wilkins was troubled that her letter made "no mention of the events of November 7, or of Mrs. Crockett. It does not admit that any such conversations took place, nor does it disavow them or seek to explain them in any way. Instead it implies that we have 'taken' from you the opportunity to talk for the Association." Wilkins explained, as he already had to the press, that his organization could not "enter into any commercial lecture arrangement." Far from shorting her anything, Wilkins insisted Mamie had been paid over $2,100 in honorariums between October 7 and November 4. The real issue, however, was her "ultimatum," through Crockett, which gave him no choice but to cancel her tour. "We could do nothing with Mrs. Crockett and we could not get through to you. It was the last minute of the last hour. We had to act."[55]

This episode was unfortunate for Mamie as well as for the NAACP, because each benefited immensely from the month-long relationship. But the negative press shattered Mamie's image among many who had heretofore supported her. She clearly erred in making her last-minute demands upon the association, thinking that forcing Wilkins into a tight spot would cause him to acquiesce. At the same time, however, she may well have been influenced by others who put her up to it. It is unknown just who Anna Crockett was and why she insisted on speaking on Mamie's behalf. Was the whole plan for more money Crockett's idea? Whoever's idea it was, Crockett's role as a go-between backfired. Had Mamie talked to Wilkins directly, the entire controversy could easily have been avoided.[56]

That said, Roy Wilkins and others in the NAACP may not have been innocent in their treatment of Mamie Bradley while she was affiliated with them. NAACP field secretary Medgar Evers certainly felt that way and told his wife, Myrlie, how furious he was that rather than help Mamie, the association "used her" to advance its cause. Evers even instructed Myrlie that "if anything happens to me, don't let them use you like that."[57] Before long, Mamie was making similar accusations against the organization.

By the time Mamie received Wilkins's letter, however, the sting over her split with the NAACP may have already begun to fade. With her ties to the association severed, she was free to speak for other organizations, and on November 14 she appeared before a crowd of 5,000 in Flint, Michigan. The rally, sponsored by Buick Local 599 of CIO United Auto Workers, took in $1,300, of which $1,000 went to Mamie. That honorarium nearly matched the one she was to receive for her now-canceled eleven-city tour, and was by far the largest she had earned to date for any one engagement. Despite her problems with Wilkins, $100 taken from the profits were also set aside as a donation to the NAACP. It appears that Mamie was still trying to mend fences with the organization, or perhaps wanted to downplay their falling out, as she told her audience that she was working with the association to help raise awareness about the injustices in her son's case.[58]

Meanwhile, many were still fuming over the grand jury's decision and paid little attention to the tiff between Mamie Bradley and Roy Wilkins. On November 10, Illinois governor William Stratton released a letter to Attorney General Brownell. By doing so, Stratton became the most prominent official to call for a federal probe into the Till case. As such, his plea was featured prominently in the press. "It now appears that those responsible for this tragic crime are not being brought to justice," he said, fearing the case might fall off the radar of authorities. "Somebody murdered that boy and should be made to pay for it." A few weeks later Brownell explained that the Department of Justice could have intervened only if local and state officers had participated in the crime (Title 18, USC, Section 242 of the Federal Civil Rights Statute) or if Till had been taken across state lines (as per the Lindbergh Law).[59]

Brownell's personal response to Stratton followed what Justice Department officials surely hoped would be the department's final word on the issue. Whether it was because of Stratton's letter or the 3,000 others sent to his office is unclear, but the Eisenhower administration's answer to the nation at large finally came when Deputy Attorney General William P. Rogers appeared on the ABC television program *College Press Conference* on Sunday, November 20. Rogers, who was not familiar enough with the details of the case "to say exactly where the fault lies," nevertheless called the murder "a real black mark" because Till's killers were still free. Although he would not comment on whether he believed Milam and Bryant had been given a fair trial, he did explain the jurisdictional problems involved that prohibited a federal investigation. He certainly wanted this television appearance to halt public appeals for such action. "We just have no authority to step into a state if we think there is a failure on the administration of justice," he insisted.[60]

One other letter may have also played into Rogers's television appearance, although he did not address it. In the November 19 issue of the *Washington Afro-American*, reporter James L. Hicks published an open letter to Brownell and FBI director Hoover, detailing all of the reasons why he believed the Department of Justice *could* intervene. He had specific information for the FBI in order for it to come to that same conclusion. His instructions to federal agents willing to look into it were precise and were based on investigations that he and Dr. T. R. M. Howard had conducted after the trial.

Hicks assured Brownell and Hoover that the facts would prove that four white men and two black men had participated in the murder of Emmett Till. The key to unanswered questions regarding the case was to be found in the town of Glendora. Agents should talk to both the wife and the father of Henry Lee Loggins. DeWitt Loggins "will be reluctant to talk and when you finally hear his story you will easily understand why he is reluctant to talk." His account would reveal that his son told him that he was on the back of the truck on the morning of the murder. The senior Loggins could also give the FBI the name of a black minister who received a similar confession from Henry Lee.

Hicks next told them what was most relevant in justifying a federal probe. Should the FBI send an agent to the jail at Charleston, he should talk to an inmate named Sarah, who "will tell you that during the Sumner murder trial when Sheriff H. C. Strider was saying that he could not locate Too Tight Collins, actually Collins was at that time locked up in the Charleston jail." Sarah, according to Hicks, was granted various privileges at the jail for performing sexual favors for the inmates as well as for Strider. "I have been informed that Federal Government is looking for an 'in' through which to get into the Till murder case," Hicks continued. "I'm also informed that one of the ways the Federal Government can get into the case is by proving that at the time of the murder trial key witnesses were prevented by law officers from testifying."[61]

The Criminal Division received a photocopy of Hicks's letter on December 6 but declined to investigate further. The revelations about Loggins's alleged involvement in the crime or any newly disclosed evidence about accomplices would not change the jurisdictional problem, and would have been up to the state to pursue. The October interview with Robert Smith by agents from the FBI's Memphis office satisfied them that Collins and Loggins had never been held in Charleston.[62] Still, however, the department would be forced to revisit Hicks's letter a few months later.

Just after the Hicks piece appeared in the *Washington Afro-American*, the West Coast tour featuring Mose Wright and Ruby Hurley wrapped up on November 22 with a gathering in Denver. The eleven meetings brought in over $22,000, with $5,900 more in pledges. Wright, comfortable in front of an audience after years at the pulpit, did not disappoint, and neither did Hurley. Roy Wilkins summarized the tour as "a success in spreading the story of Mississippi terror in the Far West."[63]

With the rallies and Delta trials behind him, Wright began settling in to his new life in Argo, Illinois. If he had entertained any doubts at all about his decision to flee the South after the murder trial, they were about to be swept away. On November 25, in Belzoni, the same town where Rev. George Lee had been shot and killed six months earlier, Gus Courts, president of the local branch of the NAACP, was counting receipts behind the counter at his modest grocery store when someone outside began shooting through the window. Three bullets hit the 250-pound, six-feet-seven-inch Courts in the abdomen and arm before a witness noticed a car, presumably carrying the gunman, slowly drive away. Thankfully, Courts survived. His first instinct was that the assailant was Belzoni Citizens' Council chairman Hezekiah Fly. The Citizens' Council, according to Courts, had been targeting him because of his work toward black equality and for his refusal to step down from his NAACP position. Following the shooting, Courts was taken by car to the all-black Taborian Hospital sixty miles away in Mound Bayou, where his condition was listed as serious. He refused admittance to the local Humphreys County Hospital for fear that his would-be killer might come by to "finish what had been started."[64]

Prompted by this continued violence, E. Frederick Morrow, administrator for special projects in the Eisenhower administration, sent Maxwell Rabb a memorandum lamenting the situation in the South. He also addressed the Till case in particular. Life had not been easy for Morrow, the only black man in the White House, since joining the administration in July. Other staff members were "cold, but correct" in their treatment of him, and as an anomaly in the administration, he was often mistaken as a servant at official affairs.[65] His role and personal experiences made him particularly sensitive to the nation's reaction to the Till murder. He understood that all official responses from the administration had come from the Office of the Attorney General, which reiterated that the federal government lacked jurisdiction in the matter. "However, this particular situation is so fraught with emotion because of the circumstances under which the crime was committed, and the fact that the victim was a youngster, that normal methods of dealing with the usual case of crime are not completely acceptable to all of the interested parties."[66]

Morrow, believing "that we are on the verge of a dangerous racial conflagration in the Southern section of the country," agonized that wherever his duties had taken him throughout the country, "the one theme on the lips and in the minds of all Negroes is the injustice of the Till matter, and the fact that nothing can be done to effect justice in this case." This was creating a situation that could only be described as explosive. "The warning signs in the South are all too clear; the harassed Negro is sullen, bitter, and talking strongly of retaliation whenever future situations dictate." Blacks had formed their own underground to counter unabated discrimination, while Citizens' Councils, on the other hand, were practicing "economic terrorism." The situation was becoming unbearable for Morrow:

As a member of the White House Staff, I am sitting in the middle of this and I have been accused of being cowardly for not bringing this situation to the attention of the Administration, and requesting the President to make some kind of observation on this unwholesome problem. My mail has been heavy and angry, and wherever I go, people have expressed disappointment that no word has come from the White House deploring this situation. I always point out, of course, that our Attorney General has followed this situation with interest and skill and that he will act when and if Federal laws are violated. But this does not still the protestations. There is a clamor for some kind of statement from the White House that will indicate the Administration is aware of, and condemns with vigor, any kind of racist activity in the United States.

Morrow suggested that Vice President Nixon invite several black leaders to Washington to talk together about the problem, and to do it "intelligently and dispassionately." It would reassure the black community that the administration was concerned, while also putting racists on alert that their "un-American tactics" would result in prosecution by the attorney general.

Morrow also noted that thousands still attended large rallies all over the country protesting the Till murder, and that the case was "the subject of numerous Sunday sermons in the pulpits of the land."[67] Unbeknownst to Morrow, one of the most significant of those Sunday gatherings had occurred two days earlier.

Dr. T. R. M. Howard had been scheduled to speak in Montgomery, Alabama, on November 27 for the thirty-fourth annual program of National Achievement Week, sponsored by the graduate chapter of the Omega Psi Phi fraternity at Alabama State College. The speech, scheduled for 7:00 P.M. at the Tullibody Auditorium, promised to tell the "inside story" of the Till case under the theme "Desegregation, a Weigh Station: Integration, Our Destination." The location was later changed to the Dexter Avenue Baptist Church.[68]

The recent Courts shooting added to Howard's outrage and to the list of Mississippi atrocities that he highlighted before the overflow crowd. He had just addressed the shooting in a letter to Brownell, asking that the attorney general pursue Courts's assailants. He went over the unsolved murders of Rev. George W. Lee and Lamar Smith. The FBI had been given evidence on the probable killers of Lee, Howard said. He believed that they were the same ones who tried to take down Courts.[69]

The center of his speech, however, was the Till case. He told the dramatic details, provided little-known facts, and disclosed names, just as he had been doing in speeches since early October. The host for the event, the new pastor of Dexter Avenue Baptist Church, was a twenty-six-year-old Boston University graduate named Martin Luther King Jr. King had gone to Montgomery to lead the church only the year before.[70]

Another local citizen present that night was a forty-two-year-old seamstress named Rosa Parks. She remembered the meeting vividly enough to reflect back on it some thirty years later: "The first mass meeting that we had in Montgomery following his [Till's] death was when Dr. T. R. M. Howard came to speak to . . . a community meeting and he was telling us about it in detail."[71] The Till murder, the protests, and the Courts shooting all contributed to a new resolve. The rest, of course, is history. Four days later, Parks, tired after a long day at work, boarded a bus at Montgomery's Court Square. At the next stop, a rush of passengers overflowed the white section, which left one white man standing. The driver, James Blake, looked at the black passengers in the fifth row, or front row of the black section, and ordered them to "let me have those front seats." Law required black passengers to give up their seats to whites once the white section was full. When no one moved, he spoke again. "Y'all better make it light on yourselves and let me have those seats." The man next to Parks got up and moved, but Parks stayed seated. Blake threatened to arrest Parks, then left the bus and called the police.[72]

Parks's arrest moments later caught the attention of local black leader E. D. Nixon, who wanted to use Parks's case as a means to break down Montgomery's segregation laws. Parks consented, and the day of her trial, Monday, December 5, was designated as a one-day boycott of Montgomery's buses. Local activist JoAnn Robinson prepared 35,000 handbills and recruited students to help distribute them. Monday night, a mass meeting at the Holt Avenue Baptist Church voted to continue the boycott. Rev. King agreed to head the hastily organized Montgomery Improvement Association and lead the boycott, and was the keynote speaker that night. The extraordinary determination of the black citizens of Montgomery to see this protest through to the end produced an unprecedented victory that took 382 days to achieve. It was the first grassroots success (thanks to an eventual decision by the US Supreme Court) of a struggle that emerged as the modern civil rights movement.[73]

It would have been impossible for Parks, secretary of the local branch of the NAACP, to have remained unaffected by the continued outcry following the Till trial verdict that had been announced sixty-nine days earlier. Parks said little publicly that connected Emmett Till with her defiant move, and she does not mention the case at all in her autobiography. Yet, as she explained it in retrospect in 2003, "The news of Emmett's death caused many people to participate in the cry for justice and equal rights, including myself."[74]

Several years earlier, the Reverend Jesse Jackson reportedly asked Parks, "Why didn't you go to the back of the bus?"

"I thought of Emmett Till and I couldn't go back," she responded.[75]

For all that followed, that November evening at the Dexter Avenue Baptist Church proved to be providential. The growing determination, coupled with King's ability to move the masses, provided the guarantee that the citizens boycotting the buses would endure to the end. The federal government thought it could do nothing about Emmett Till. On the other hand, black citizens in Montgomery proved that nothing was impossible.

Dr. Howard did not know it at the time, but his visit to Dexter Avenue served as a passing of the torch to the unassuming Martin Luther King Jr. With King as the new leader of the quest for black equality, a path was about to be emblazoned that would not only burn its way throughout the South, but would be etched permanently across the American landscape.

9

The *Look* Story and Its Aftermath

As December 1955 dawned, media coverage of the Emmett Till case began to wane.[1] The grand jury decision in Greenwood meant that J. W. Milam and Roy Bryant were officially free, while at the same time, jurisdictional issues preventing federal action effectively closed the door to further attempts at justice. Mamie Bradley's controversial parting with the NAACP suddenly took her out of the spotlight, and Mose Wright's West Coast tour had come to an end. In Chicago, Mamie was bracing herself for a Christmas alone, while Wright, Willie Reed, and Mandy Bradley were still adapting to life outside of the South. In Mississippi, the shooting of Gus Courts moved racial violence outside the realm of sex and back to the heated issues surrounding voter registration. Lastly, in Montgomery, Alabama, the bus boycott following the defiant act of Rosa Parks was about to garner steam as well as national attention.

On December 2, one day after Parks's arrest, the Till murder and related southern atrocities were the topics of an Eisenhower cabinet meeting at the White House. The president, still recovering from his September heart attack, was absent, but Vice President Nixon presided in his stead. One issue on the agenda was the upcoming State of the Union address. A planned focus of the speech was the divisive topic of civil rights, with some emphasis on the Citizens' Councils, founded in Mississippi eighteen months earlier in response to the *Brown* decision. Attorney General Brownell wanted to eliminate any language that would anger the South. He believed that threats to investigate alleged efforts to keep blacks from voting lacked solid evidence and were unnecessarily polarizing. Rather than face accusations of "waving the red flag," Brownell reasoned, the administration should limit itself to a short statement in support of the Supreme Court's decision and leave it at that. He also reminded his colleagues that the Department of Justice had been under intense pressure to investigate racial violence in Dixie, particularly the Till murder.[2]

Secretary of State John Foster Dulles listened carefully and offered his own opinions. He called the Till killing tragic, yet he worried about political and constitutional ramifications should the administration get involved. Nixon, however, proposed one way out of the dilemma by suggesting they push the issue on to Congress. If a bill came out of a congressional investigation, southern Democrats would certainly filibuster it, allowing the administration to save face while forcing the Democrats to deal with the fallout. Both Brownell and Dulles liked this idea.[3]

Then, suddenly, it was déjà vu all over again in Tallahatchie County. On December 3, the day after the Eisenhower cabinet discussed and essentially minimized the severity of the southern "Negro problem," a thirty-three-year-old black man named Clinton Melton was at work at a Glendora gas station owned by a local white man named Lee McGarrh. Two other of the town's 175 residents were J. W. Milam and his good friend Elmer Kimbell. Melton had worked for McGarrh for ten years and was popular in the community. Around 9:30 that Saturday night, a drunken Kimbell drove into the station and told McGarrh that he wanted his car filled with gas. McGarrh, in turn, told Melton to go out and take care of it, which he did. The bill came to $4.47, but when Kimbell learned this, he insisted that he had asked for only $2 worth and began threatening Melton. The attendant told Kimbell that he had simply followed McGarrh's orders.

"Suppose I pay by check. Waddaya think you'd do about it if the check bounced?" said Kimbell, angrily.

Melton responded that he did not care how Kimbell paid because he (Melton) only worked there.

Growing more agitated, Kimbell told McGarrh that he had a "smart Negro" working for him, and said he wanted to close out his account. McGarrh sided with Melton and reminded Kimbell that he had indeed asked for a full tank. After things became more heated, McGarrh told Kimbell to "get going."

"I'm going, but I'll be back," said Kimbell. Turning to Melton he promised, "I'm going to kill you." To McGarrh he said, "I'll see you, too."

Kimbell then drove off, leaving behind twenty-nine-year-old John Henry Wilson, a black employee of Kimbell's at the local cotton gin who had been riding in the car with him.[4]

McGarrh, fearing Kimbell would keep his word, urged Melton to go on home. Before leaving, however, Melton paused to put gas in his own car. As he got inside to leave a few minutes later, Kimbell returned to the station. Wilson, knowing what was up, ran out and begged him not to hurt Melton, but Kimbell ignored that plea and threatened to kill them both. Wilson then ran back into the store, begging McGarrh to hide him. Outside, Kimbell fired three shots at Melton, hitting him twice in the head and once in the hand, killing him instantly. McGarrh watched in horror from inside the station.[5]

Although the murder of Clinton Melton was by itself a senseless, tragic act, it was accompanied by a few ghosts of the recent past that gave it a bizarre twist. Store owner Lee McGarrh had been a character witness for J. W. Milam during Milam's murder trial in September. When Elmer Kimbell drove into McGarrh's station that December evening, he did so in Milam's car. Immediately after the shooting, Kimbell drove to Milam's home less than half a mile away, where O. D. Rogers, the town marshal, arrived shortly thereafter. He found Kimbell, who was receiving treatment for a slight bullet wound to his left shoulder. Rogers arrested him, but for reasons that could only make sense in Tallahatchie County, he allowed Milam to first drive Kimbell to a hospital twenty-five miles away in Clarksdale. After doctors spent about forty minutes cleaning and dressing the wound, Kimbell was taken to jail. The mysterious injury allowed Kimbell to claim self-defense by pointing to Melton as the aggressor.[6]

Early on, police seemed to side with Kimbell. Deputy Sheriff A. G. Thomas speculated that Melton, McGarrh, and Wilson had "ganged up" on Kimbell. As he theorized it to the *New York Post*, "It looks very much that way to me. I can't say for sure but it certainly looks like there was a gun duel with three against one." McGarrh, however, insisted that Thomas's theory was "absolutely absurd," and assured police that Melton was unarmed. Indeed, no weapon was found at the murder scene. The officer in charge of the investigation was outgoing sheriff H. C. Strider, who examined the bullet hole in Kimbell's shirt and found no evidence of powder burns. They would be present, he explained, if the gunshot had been self-inflicted or occurred at close range.[7]

On December 24, three weeks after the shooting, Kimbell attended a preliminary hearing in Sumner, where three justices of the peace denied him bond. He was later refused a second time on January 9 by Circuit Judge Curtis Swango after Kimbell's attorney requested bond on a writ of habeas corpus. Swango's decision guaranteed that Kimbell would remain incarcerated until his trial, scheduled for March. Representing Kimbell was J. W. Kellum, one of the five Sumner attorneys who had aided Milam and Bryant during their murder trial three months earlier.[8]

For a brief moment in time, the Melton murder was not touted as a race crime because Kimbell, in his drunken state of mind, could just as easily have taken out his rage on a white attendant. However, the white community quickly made the connection and denounced the slaying. The local Lion's Club issued a statement declaring, "We consider the taking of the life of Clinton Melton an outrage against him, the people of Glendora, as well as the entire human family. We intend to see that the forces of justice and right prevail in the wake of this woeful evil. We humbly confess repentance for having so lived as a community that such an evil occurrence could happen here."[9]

Several local white citizens pledged to help Melton's widow, Beulah, and her four young children, in the wake of the shooting. The National Council of Churches of Christ donated $1,000 to the grieving family. At a meeting of the local Lion's Club, Methodist pastor William A. Harris demanded that the club go on record in protest of the killing. Glendora physician W. C. McQuinn promised Beulah a job, while a local planter, Michael P. Sturdivant, offered to build the family a house.[10] Michael's grandfather, M. P. Sturdivant, had owned the plantation managed by Leslie Milam in Drew where Emmett Till had allegedly been beaten and killed, thus providing another eerie connection to that notorious case. Although M.P. died in 1948, the property remained in the family.

Beulah Melton shortly received a visit from Medgar Evers, but she kindly asked that the NAACP not get involved because "that is why they [the jury in Sumner] did Mrs. Bradly [sic] like they did." In other words, outside agitation had cost Mamie Bradley a guilty verdict, and Beulah did not want to risk the same outcome in Kimbell's case.[11]

Certainly the Melton murder had all the ingredients needed to finally convict a white man for killing a black man in Tallahatchie County. Melton lived locally, was respected by black and white citizens, and was not a known crusader for black equality. Most significant, the sex taboo was not an issue. On March 13, 1956, however, Elmer Kimbell was acquitted of murder after a two-day trial, the jury believing Kimbell's claim that he shot Melton in self-defense. Tragedy preceded the verdict when Beulah Melton's car went off the road and into a bayou on a dark night four days before the trial began. She drowned, but the two children who were with her were rescued, just in time to join their two other siblings as orphans. The drowning was ruled an accident, the sheriff surmising that because Beulah was a new driver, she probably lost control of the car.[12] Others believed that someone close to Kimbell intentionally ran her off the road. Regardless, it was clear by the verdict that in the six months since Emmett Till's killing, things had not changed in the Mississippi Delta.

Meanwhile, Mamie Bradley, like Beulah Melton, wanted little to do with the NAACP, but for entirely different reasons. On December 22, Mamie and her father were in New York, where Mamie was about to headline three rallies hosted by local churches. Still hurt over her rift with Roy Wilkins, she accused the NAACP, during a press conference at Harlem's Hotel Theresa, of profiting off of the death of her son, much as Wilkins had accused her of doing. John Carthan agreed with his daughter's criticisms, declaring that "without any doubt the NAACP is using Emmett Till and his mother." Mamie, however, was more upset that the association dropped its plans of filing a civil suit on her behalf against Milam and the Bryants. When NAACP attorney William Henry Huff resigned as Mamie's legal counsel following the cancellation of her West Coast tour, he saw a conflict of interest in any future representation.

In his November 15 letter to Mamie, Roy Wilkins downgraded the association's willingness to help by extending his hand only for "consultation and advice on matters in connection with your situation."[13]

Because Mamie was now speaking for other organizations and no longer needed the NAACP in that regard, she felt free to offer some new demands should the organization be inclined to take her back. Although reminiscent of Anna Crockett's ultimatum from a month earlier, the new provisions came directly from Mamie herself. She wanted at least $150 per meeting, with a promise that she would not speak at more than three meetings in a week. She also wanted her father to receive $100 per week for traveling with her. Another requirement was that the NAACP pay her household expenses. These included her monthly mortgage payment and a $400 debt left behind by her estranged husband, Pink Bradley. These terms, explained to members of the black press, seemed inexplicable in light of Mamie's earlier attempt to reconcile with Wilkins. Her criticisms, not to mention her preconditions for a renewed partnership, would no doubt serve only to widen the divide. During the press conference, she gave newsmen copies of her November 9 letter to Wilkins and his response from November 15.[14]

It is unclear just how long the demand continued for public appearances. Mamie was scheduled for at least three more meetings in New Jersey on January 15, 1956, sponsored by the Goodwill Progressive Club of the Newark Church of God in Christ.[15] Mose Wright remained willing to speak also, and on January 2 he addressed a crowd in Brooklyn at the First AME Zion Church, hosted by the Baptist Pastors Union. Two thousand people, including fifty ministers, attended the event. Dr. Gardner C. Taylor, who introduced Wright to the crowd, referred to the former sharecropper as not only a black hero but as an American hero who risked his life by testifying in Sumner. The following day, Wright made a surprise appearance at the NAACP annual meeting in New York City.[16]

Although the mass meetings continued to draw large crowds, by the first of the year they had become so routine as to rarely make headlines anymore. And they were about to be overshadowed by an announcement that can only be described as explosive. In early 1956, newspapers ran an advertisement for the January 24 edition of *Look* magazine, and it demanded attention. That the ad was sure to generate interest is evident by the fact that the print run for the issue was two million more than the magazine's usual number.[17] What was so intriguing about this particular ad was that it carried a photo of Emmett Till and included a bold headline that promised "for the first time . . . THE TRUTH about the Emmett Till killing." The accompanying teaser was even more sensational:

Headlines screamed across the Nation. Millions of words were written about it. A trial would be held. Yet the *truth* about the Emmett Till killing in Mississippi remained hidden—until now! Now *exclusively* in *Look* magazine you can read the story—the story that the jury did not hear, that no newspaper reader ever saw . . . the brutal step-by-step *full account* of what happened on that fateful night. You'll read *how* Till was killed, *where, why* and *by whom!* Don't miss this shocking story in *Look*. It will make magazine history the minute it hits the newsstands. Get your copy of LOOK *early!*[18]

Needless to say, the promo promised quite a punch, and on January 10, when the magazine hit the stands, by most accounts, it delivered.

The story had been in the making for three months. The author was William Bradford Huie, a forty-five-year-old nationally known journalist, author, and television personality from Hartselle, Alabama. He was a 1930 graduate of the University of Alabama, and by the time he joined the navy in 1943, he had already worked for the *Birmingham Post* (1932–36), founded *Alabama: The News Magazine of the Deep South* (1937), and published his first book, *Mud on the Stars* (1942). Several other books followed, including *The Revolt of Mamie Stover* (1951) and *The Execution of Private Slovik* (1954), a nonfiction title about a World War II soldier executed in 1945 for desertion; Eddie Slovik was the first to meet such a fate for this charge since the Civil War. For six years, beginning in 1946, Huie served as associate editor and editor of *American Mercury*, and from 1951 until 1953 he hosted the CBS political program *Longines Chronoscope*, described as a precursor to *Meet the Press*. Before his death in 1986, his twenty-one books had sold twenty-seven million copies. *Mamie Stover, Private Slovik,* and four others were adapted into Hollywood movies.[19]

Huie's unorthodox method of paying for stories, known as "checkbook journalism," gave him a reputation among his colleagues that one fellow journalist described as "roguish," "more talented than respectable," "shrewd," and "iconoclastic." A writer who interviewed Huie in 1974 described his subject's long career as one of "chasing stories, exposing injustice, puncturing myths and deflating false heroes." Consequently, "he has made considerable money and no small number of enemies. . . . Prolific, sometimes profane, often provocative, he has led a fast, gadflyish, globetrotting life poking his inquisitive nose into controversy and strife."[20]

Such was the man who set out to learn the facts about the kidnapping and murder of Emmett Till. Huie had been in California on the set of *Mamie Stover* during the trial in Sumner and did not take a real interest in the case until he read newspaper reports later. The coverage, he said, was depressing; the arguments of the attorneys suffered from regional bias, making the trial "a circus." What the case needed, he declared, was the truth, and he believed he was the one who could bring it forth.[21]

In early October, a week or two after the jury in Sumner freed Milam and Bryant on murder charges, Huie left his home in Alabama, drove to Greenwood, Mississippi, and checked in at the Holiday Inn. The next morning, he went to Sumner and at 8:00 A.M. strode into the offices of Breland and Whitten. A five-hour meeting with John Whitten followed.

Huie was frank with the Delta lawyer. "John, I want the truth about the Till case. I want to publish it. Whatever our racial sins down here, I like to think we are less hypocritical than some of our enemies. I like to think that truth serves decent purposes better than mystery or propaganda." He laid out his theory about the murder. Milam and Bryant probably took the boy and meant only to whip him. But they went too far, and in a drunken state, killed him.

Whitten, no longer in the defense mode that won his clients an acquittal, said he did not know what happened to Emmett Till. He never asked either of the men if they were guilty, mainly for his wife's sake, because she became deeply troubled over the murder. He said he only aided them because the Constitution entitled them to a defense.

Regarding Huie's theory, however, Whitten admitted that "my assumption is about what yours is."

Thirty-six-year-old Whitten was more circumspect than his sixty-seven-year-old partner, J. J. Breland, who entered the conversation briefly. Breland's description of his clients was unapologetic:

Bryant and Milam? Sure, they're rednecks—peckerwoods. We've sued Milam a couple of times: he's bootlegged all his life. He comes from a big, mean, overbearing family. He's got a chip on his shoulder. That's how he got that battlefield promotion in Europe: he likes to kill folks. But hell, we've got to have our Milams to fight our wars and keep the niggahs in line. Bryant's a scrappin' pine-knot without a pot. . . . They shouldn't killed that nigger. They should'a just given him Thirty-Nine [thirty-nine licks, the normative punishment for slaves]—and turned him loose. But you know how these things go. They're likkered [liquored] up. They start off whippin' him and he sasses one of 'em, and maybe they hit him with the axe. And then they got to finish the job.[22]

Not one of these men harbored any doubt that Milam and Bryant murdered Emmett Till, but Huie wanted to hear it directly from the killers themselves, and he needed these attorneys to help him. He proposed that Whitten bring J. W. Milam and Roy and Carolyn Bryant to him "in a secret rendezvous in Greenwood" where they would "tell me every last line of the truth."[23] His aim was to write a story about an "approved" murder in the state of Mississippi. In other words, a "community approved murder—a 'policy' murder." Huie would pay Milam and Bryant in cash for their story and the signed releases, plus a percentage of the profits after it appeared in print. He made it clear to Whitten that he would keep their meetings secret, would not testify against the duo in court (at that point, Milam and Bryant were still facing possible indictments on kidnapping), and would carefully avoid writing the story in such a way that it would be perceived as a confession. Breland and Whitten liked the idea and promised to talk with the men. The lawyers were enthused from the beginning, but for reasons of their own. As Huie observed, "Publication of this story, with all its revolting details, is exactly what Breland's group in Mississippi *wants*. They want to 'put the North and the NAACP and the niggers *on notice*.' My proposal strikes them as being a 'good propaganda move.'"[24]

Huie was convinced that Milam and Bryant would talk, and for at least two reasons. First, there was no danger of a retrial on murder charges because they had been acquitted on those. Second, they would simply be swayed by the money. To help raise funds for the payoff, Huie approached Roy Wilkins and asked for $3,000 from the NAACP as a purchase price for the story and the releases. Huie also dropped a bombshell on Wilkins: "Two other men are involved: there were four in the torture-and-murder party. And if I name them I must have their releases—or no publisher will touch it. I know who these men are: they are important to the story; but I have to pay them because of their 'risks.'"[25]

Huie did not say how he learned about these co-conspirators, but it seems clear by the timing that he was tipped off by Breland or Whitten, who would have remembered the courtroom testimony of Willie Reed. Reed had said in court that he saw Emmett Till on the back of a truck in Drew, driven by four white men. Shortly thereafter, he noticed Milam and others at a plantation shed, and heard sounds of a beating coming from inside. As hard as the attorneys tried to refute Reed during the trial, they may well have believed him. It is not likely that the attorneys learned about these other men through Milam and Bryant themselves. If Whitten had never asked the defendants about their own involvement, as he claimed, it follows that the brothers would not have confirmed their guilt by revealing accomplices.

The two mystery men Huie alluded to became the least of his worries, however, because he soon learned that not even Milam and Bryant were both on board. On October 17, Whitten called Huie to tell him that he would get the story, but that only one of the acquitted killers was interested in talking. This limited access may have been Whitten's idea, because, as Huie also explained it, Whitten said it would be "easier" if Huie interviewed and received a signed release from only one of the men. Huie knew that in the end, this would be up to the publisher, but he agreed to push for it anyway. Whitten did not identify which of the two was unwilling to talk, but Huie assumed it was Milam.[26]

Huie envisioned a few outlets for his finished story. One possibility was that it be woven into a book. Another was to sell it as a stand-alone article to a magazine or newspaper. Besides Wilkins, who apparently was not interested, Huie sent the word out to two other influential parties, fifty-year-old Daniel Mitch, longtime editorial director of *Look* magazine, and Basil L. "Stuffy" Walters, fifty-nine, executive editor of Knight Newspapers and former president of the American Society of Newspaper Editors. It did not take long for Phyllis Jackson, Huie's agent at MCA, to call and tell Huie that Mitch was interested.

Huie wrote Mitch that same day and laid out his plans for obtaining and paying for the firsthand account of the kidnapping and murder of Emmett Till. Of concern to Huie, of course, was that he protect himself, Milam, and Bryant, and head off any legal issues for *Look* should the magazine publish it. He made four promises very clear. First, "I will agree never to testify against one of them; that even if I am subpoenaed, I will decline to divulge 'sources.'" Second, he promised never to show the signed release to anyone in Mississippi or with the NAACP. Leaving the door open for a feature film, his only exception would be to "make *confidential* use of it in New York or Hollywood."

In a third stipulation, Huie said he would make no claim that his story was based on a confession by the killers. Although he "may quote directly the words of the murderers at any point in the action, I will not quote them as having said *anything* to me." In other words, Huie continued, "the story will be my version of exactly what happened; exactly what was said; exactly what was done at exactly what date and hour; but I will not state, declare or claim that I had the assistance of any particular person." There was one last issue to consider. The grand jury in Leflore County was set to meet on November 8 regarding the kidnapping charges. Huie predicted (accurately, of course) that there would be no indictment. "However," on the off chance that there would be one, "we will hold up any publication of this story until *after the trial.*"

At this point in time, Mamie Bradley and the NAACP were still on good terms, and the possibility of a civil suit against Milam and Bryant still loomed. "What the Hell do I do?" asked Huie, rhetorically. "Well, I testify to the facts as I established them 'to the best of my ability.' I stand by the story—every line of it. It's the truth. But as to how I came by the truth—I stand on my 'constitutional' right not to reveal any sources."

Huie knew that Mitch had concerns of his own, namely, any potential legal ramifications for *Look*. "It is our *clear* understanding that when I furnish you an original copy of the signed release you will photostat it, return the original to my agent; and then, under *no* circumstances short of the necessity to forestall a legal action, will you ever reveal to anyone that you have it.... But I'm sure you understand that when I tell this murderer that his release will be kept confidential, that I will never use it except to protect you or me from a damage suit, *I mean to do just that.*"

It was now up to Huie and Mitch to decide upon the provisions of the release forms and how many of the men involved in the crime should sign one. "Do you insist that *two* murderers must sign? Or *four*?" Huie had other questions, and the answers were important from a legal standpoint. "Will you insist on a release from *anyone else* whom I reveal as having had a part in the 'case' but not in the abduction, torture, murder, or disposal of the body?" This was clearly a reference to Carolyn Bryant. Regarding actual accomplices, he pointed out "that two of the murderers have been indicted and tried. The other two have never been 'publicly disclosed.' If we do not have their releases, shall we name them in the story or not? Shall we quote them anonymously in any part of the action?"[27]

Mitch made Huie "a substantial offer" for the story, conditioned upon two signed releases. Yet Huie, looking for even greater possibilities—and profits—made an attempt for a better offer, which he outlined in a proposal to Walters. He wanted a $3,000 down payment upon completion of a rough draft, then another $2,000 for the final product. On top of that, he requested half of all profits realized from syndication. With Walters, Huie wanted to avoid Mitch's requirement of two releases, which would work to Huie's advantage. "The cheapest and easiest way for me to proceed is to go with Bryant only. He is the younger; it was his wife who was insulted; and he is flat broke. So I would hope that a publisher would accept him as sufficient." If an agreement with Walters hinged on two signatures, however, Huie could live with that. "I think Milam's release can be obtained if it must." Releases from all four of the men involved, Huie now feared, "would probably be too heavy a handicap."

One advantage to publishing the story in a newspaper was the speed at which it could appear, and if the grand jury failed to indict the men on kidnapping in November, Huie wanted to see it in print the next day. In a worst-case scenario that there was a trial, it should appear immediately following the announcement of a verdict. A magazine, by its very nature, could not be so accommodating. Due to an upcoming Christmas issue then in the works, Mitch could not promise that *Look* could publish the story before January.[28] Whether Walters failed to bite or Mitch countered with something better is unknown, but within a few days Huie sealed the deal with *Look*.

Sometime during the early planning phases, Bryant got cold feet, but Whitten apparently intervened to help alleviate his fears. By October 20, three days before the planned tell-all session with Huie, Bryant made up his mind to talk, and Whitten gave Huie the news. Bryant, whom Huie described as "pretty badly shaken up," had more to lose than he realized, but Huie did not really care. "The poor bastard!" he wrote in a letter to Mitch the next day. "He has already lost his business, and most of those people who 'approve' what he has done will now find ways to avoid him. Three months from now the folks who put up the money for his defense won't speak to him on the street." Huie knew that even though the story would not read as a confession, people would read between the lines and know who his sources actually were.

Within a few days, Milam decided that he would talk after all, and Huie and Mitch made final arrangements concerning the payout. A *Look* attorney would travel from New York to Mississippi with the cash. However, Huie insisted on keeping Breland, Whitten, Milam, and Bryant at ease by falsely representing this attorney as "my lawyer from Birmingham."[29]

On Sunday, October 23, Huie spent the day in Sumner with Milam and Bryant at the Breland and Whitten law office and heard the half-brothers tell their story, in painstaking detail. They held the meeting in the office library, with Milam and Bryant on one side of the table, and Huie and Whitten on the other. Whitten asked all of the questions while Huie took copious notes. Milam did most of the talking.

When Huie returned to his motel in Greenwood that evening, he fired off an enthusiastic letter to Mitch. "This was really amazing, for it was the first time they have told the story. Not one of their lawyers had heard it." Whitten even gave Huie his files on the case so that Huie could make comparisons to the story he had just heard. "Perhaps I am too close to it to appraise it," Huie said as he began to contemplate the aftershocks, "but I can't see how it can miss being one of the most sensational stories ever published."[30]

Huie avoided details in his letter but assured Mitch that "I know every step that was taken—can verify most every word of it—and the manner in which these men operated for five hours before they finally shot this boy and threw him in the river—will make your readers gasp. Particularly, their stark explanation of their motives." The final agreement for payment stipulated that 20 percent of Huie's profits would go to Milam and the Bryants. Huie would pay them $3,150 against that in cash up front. Breland and Whitten would receive 10 percent after Milam and the Bryants received their portion, with a cash payment against that of $1,260. Another 10 percent would be paid out in agency commissions. They scheduled the release signing ceremony for October 28 at the Sumner law office, where a total of $4,410 would be distributed among the various parties.

At some point, Mitch changed his mind and insisted on not just two but three signed releases. Huie confirmed that he would get them from Milam, Roy Bryant, and Carolyn Bryant. Each would also initial copies of Huie's notes wherever needed to verify accuracy. The *Look* attorney and Whitten would officially witness the signing by adding their own signatures to the documents. Huie reassured Mitch that "all this dealing is to be *entirely secret*, with me never divulging to anyone in Mississippi that I have talked with the principals." Huie also planned to spend his week in Mississippi talking to other pertinent people, including Eula Bryant, mother of J. W. and Roy, in an effort to obtain supporting facts.

After explaining all of this to Mitch, Huie made one inexplicable comment that would not only determine the direction of his narrative but would, in effect, shape the Till story for decades to come. "Of this I am now certain: there were not, after all, *four* men involved in the abduction-and-murder; there were only two. So when we have these releases from Bryant and Milam and the woman, we are completely safe."[31]

What led Huie to this new conclusion is unknown, but it clearly came about after his meeting with Milam and Bryant earlier that day. Was he simply taking these two men at their word? Clearly, Milam and Bryant had every motive to protect co-conspirators who could not only be tried alongside them for kidnapping but for murder as well, and Huie was astute enough to know that.[32] He may have backed away from including others because they were not willing to sign releases. Or, in the end, he simply calculated the risks of involving them in the first place.[33] That was certainly a concern five days earlier when he shopped the story to Basil Walters. Even when Huie was adamant that others had conspired with Milam and Bryant, he asked, "Can we safely handle the story with releases from the two men who have been disclosed and tried?" Huie answered his own question. "YES. We can, if necessary, omit the names of the other two. We can even avoid all reference to them; though I would urge any publisher to state that they were present, to quote whatever they said at any point in the action, but not to name them."[34] Whatever the reason, it became easier in the end to simply make them disappear from the story entirely.

On Monday, October 24, Huie met with Milam and Bryant in a second lengthy meeting. Following up with Mitch, he reported that "there is much that I could say about the story as it is developing—but no time or space here. I have had to change some of the conceptions I have conveyed to you in earlier memos. Two long sessions with these bully-boys have been shattering, even to a man like Whitten." Then, easily predicting public reaction to such a sensational story, Huie concluded: "It's an amazing, indefensible murder—and much of our story will be in the cool, factual, manner in which we let the facts indict the 'community.' It will shake people in Mississippi."[35]

The release signing and cash payout occurred as planned in Sumner at the office of Breland and Whitten on October 28 at 7:00 P.M. At present, only the statements signed by Milam and Carolyn Bryant are available, which raises the question of whether Roy Bryant actually signed one. It is possible that Huie persuaded Mitch to go along with Whitten's preference of only two signed releases. Or perhaps Bryant, who had grown hesitant to tell his story before being persuaded by Whitten, backed out at the last minute and left this part of the deal to Milam.

The attorney who joined Whitten as a witness was a man with the last name of Dean of the New York office of John Harding, legal counsel for *Look*. Dean had never been south of the Hudson River before flying to Memphis with the money and the papers, and was scared to death after he landed. Dean was so nervous over the prospect of meeting with two murderers that Huie was worried the entire deal might fall through. Everything went smoothly, however, and after the hour-long signing session, the group celebrated by drinking whiskey. Dean, finally at ease at his point, even chatted with Milam about army weapons, something that each of them apparently knew well.[36]

The releases do not contain admissions of any wrongdoing on the part of Milam or Carolyn Bryant, and there are significant differences between the two forms. For example, Milam confirmed by his signature that he "discussed at great length with William Bradford Huie the abduction and killing of the negro, Emmett Till, in Sumner, Miss.," and goes on to say that "I have also read and fully understand the general rough outline and notes which are to be the basis for the article or story which Mr. Huie proposes to write, which are attached hereto, initialed by me and hereby made a part of this Consent and Release." Carolyn Bryant's says nothing about previous discussions, only that she had read, understood, and initialed Huie's notes. Carolyn was not present during the earlier meetings, thus the signing ceremony appears to be her only meeting with Huie. Her initials were needed to verify the accuracy of Huie's version of the store incident and to satisfy Mitch in that regard.[37]

The signees agreed to a payment of $3,150, to be shared among Milam and the Bryants. Nothing was said about previous arrangements that they were to receive 20 percent of the profits in excess of the lump sum. Each also gave "my consent to William Bradford Huie, to write, (and to anyone else whom he may authorize to publish, produce, dramatize, adapt or otherwise present), an article, story, literary or dramatic work based in whole or in part upon my life and any incidents and episodes therein (hereinafter called 'the work') and, in particular, dealing with the death of Emmett Till in Sumner, Miss." For Milam, this included "the extent of my participation therein." For Carolyn Bryant, it meant "the extent of my connection therewith." For both, "this includes the right to report any or all of the details of my private life and that of my family, and to describe me, my character and actions in such manner as Mr. Huie, in his sole judgment, believes to be accurate." In the case of Milam, "This includes the right to portray me as one of those persons who abducted and killed the negro, Emmett Till, and to portray me, through the use of live actors, in any and all dramatic adaptations of the work." Carolyn Bryant's release differed only by agreeing to allow Huie to portray her "as one of those persons who was in some manner connected with the abduction and killing of the negro, Emmett Till."[38]

As Huie explained it later, for him to publish as fact an account of Milam and Bryant as murderers "would be what we call 'libel per se,' meaning I am libeling these men when I say they murdered because they had already been tried and found not guilty of murder." In other words, "I'll in effect pay them for the right to libel them."[39] Lest anyone misunderstand, the document signed by Milam explained it clearly. "The foregoing consent is in no way to be regarded or considered as an admission by me, express or implied, that I am a killer or possessed of any other reprehensible characteristics, criminal or otherwise, which Mr. Huie may, in the work, attribute to me." Milam also agreed, by his signature, to waive any right by him or his heirs to pursue legal action for this portrayal of him in whatever way Huie planned to use it, such as print media or film.[40]

The corresponding section in Carolyn Bryant's release absents the phrase "that I am a killer." The rest of the paragraph is identical to Milam's. The documents close with the signee stating his or her understanding that the existence of his or her signed release is to remain secret unless a family member or heir decides to sue Huie or those connected with him. To safeguard against this possibility, the attorneys carefully worded the document to protect Huie of any such litigation.[41]

Huie put final touches to the article after taking a trip to Chicago, where he interviewed Mamie Bradley, Mose and Elizabeth Wright, and several of the teenagers who were with Till at the Bryant store in Money. The NAACP put Huie in touch with the Wrights, but because Mamie was on poor terms with Roy Wilkins and his organization by then, Huie talked with contacts at *Ebony* and *Jet* magazines, and they arranged Huie's meeting with the slain boy's mother.[42]

Soon after Huie sent in the completed article to *Look*, he received galley proofs for a chance to make any final corrections. He also passed a copy on to John Whitten for the attorney to look over. Whitten, fearing that town folk might learn of his secret dealings with Huie, sent the journalist some of the firm's envelopes to use for future correspondence. He also asked Huie to avoid using his own return address, and instructed him to mark any correspondence as personal and confidential. "I have had a couple of inquiries about my important mail from Garden City, Alabama," Whitten explained. "When the article appears they may be able to add two and two and reach some conclusions."[43]

Kidnapping charges against Milam and Bryant were dropped on November 9. With the threat of a trial now out of the way, Huie could plan on a release date after the first of the year. After final corrections, the article went to press and appeared in print on January 10.

Nowhere in the four-page tell-all, titled "The Shocking Story of Approved Killing in Mississippi," does Huie mention that he held meetings with Milam and Bryant, nor does he reveal that he ever talked to them personally. Nothing is mentioned regarding a payout for the information contained in the story. All quotations detailing the crime, except one, come from Milam. The one attributed to Bryant centers on a conversation between Milam and Bryant that Milam could have provided himself. This further raises the question as to whether Roy Bryant ever signed a release. As promised, Huie left his readers guessing as to how he had obtained his information, including the direct quotations.

The article includes an original sketch by John Groth portraying Milam, with gun in hand, standing over a naked, nearly prostrate Emmett Till. Roy Bryant and the cotton gin fan are close by. The story starts with background information on the brothers as well as Carolyn Bryant. In addition to running his grocery store in Money, Roy earned income by occasionally driving a truck for a brother. On August 24, the day Emmett Till walked into the Bryant store, Roy was hauling a truckload of shrimp from New Orleans to San Antonio, Texas, and from there he went to Brownsville, Texas.

Huie told how Till, with six other boys and a girl, took a drive in Mose Wright's 1946 Ford and ended up at the store, three miles west of the Wright home. Huie introduced the incident that occurred at Bryant's with a conversation between Till and the other youths standing outside. Till boasts of escapades with white women and shows off a photo of one of them that he kept in his wallet. The others taunt and dare him. "There's a pretty little white woman in the store," one of them said. "Since you know how to handle white girls, let's see you go in and get a date with her."

Huie explained the encounter between Emmett Till and Carolyn Bryant from Carolyn's point of view, most of which was clearly based on her courtroom testimony. Till bought two-cents worth of bubble gum, and when he paid for his purchase, he squeezed her hand and asked for a date. At a break in the counter, he jumped in front of her and told her not to be afraid, that he had been with white girls before. Huie's version adds, for the first time, that Carolyn Bryant and her sister-in-law, Juanita Milam, resolved not to tell Roy and J. W. about what happened. This decision between the women was not mentioned in court and was probably revealed to Huie by Milam or Roy.

Another possibility is that Carolyn told it to Huie on the evening of the release signing ceremony.

Roy was still out of town and did not return from Texas until Friday morning at 4:00. However, "a Negro told him what 'the talk' was, and told him that the 'Chicago boy' was 'visitin' Preacher.'" Knowing now that Roy was aware, Carolyn reluctantly filled in the details. "Once Roy Bryant knew, in his environment, in the opinion of most white people around him, for him to have done nothing would have marked him for a coward and a fool." That night, Milam drove by the store, and Roy asked him to come back early the following morning because "I need a little transportation." At first, Milam objected because Sunday was his only day to sleep late. Once Roy explained what it was all about, however, the protests stopped. Milam promised to be there early.

The account of their arrival at Mose Wright's house early Sunday morning, detailing that they knocked on the door, woke up the Wrights, and demanded the boy from Chicago, all agree with Mose Wright's courtroom testimony. It was probably retold to Huie by Mose and Elizabeth Wright during his interview with them. Here Huie added another detail that was not part of the trial transcript, which he could have received either from Milam or the Wrights. When Milam spotted Till in bed, he woke him and ordered him to get dressed. Till started to put on his socks and shoes.

"Just the shoes," snapped Milam.

"I don't wear shoes without socks," Till shot back, showing little fear. He kept the men waiting while he put on his thick, crepe-soled shoes.

Milam was careful not to indict others. He does not allude to anyone waiting outside who identified Till as the "right one," as Wright had confidently done in court. Milam's version maintains that they were already sure. "Milam and Bryant would have stopped at the store for Carolyn to identify him. But there had been no denial," Huie explained. "So they didn't stop at the store. At Money, they crossed the Tallahatchie River and drove west."

The brothers were not set on killing Till at first. Their plan was simply to "whip him . . . and scare some sense into him." To do that, they drove for three hours looking for a spot that Milam had discovered a year earlier while hunting geese. He called it "the scariest place in the Delta" with a 100-foot drop down to the water and another 100 feet to the bottom of the river after you hit. Milam wanted to teach the big talking black boy a lesson by standing him at the edge and forcing him to look down below. "Brother, if that won't scare the Chicago _____, hell won't." They failed to find the place, however, and drove back to Milam's house in Glendora instead. Till, alone in the back of the truck, never made an attempt to flee, and Huie explained why. "Bobo wasn't afraid of them! He was tough as they were. He didn't think they had the guts to kill him. According to Milam, 'We were never able to scare him. They had just filled him so full of that poison that he was hopeless.'"

Their plans to spare Emmett Till of a brutal death changed, Milam said, after they took him to a toolshed behind Milam's house and began taking turns pistol-whipping him. Even then, Till never cried out or gave in. "You bastards," he screamed, defiantly, "I'm not afraid of you. I'm as good as you are. I've 'had' white women. My grandmother was a white woman."

To Milam, those words signified a death wish. His next decision was rooted in a lifelong rage that he would now take out on a fourteen-year-old boy:

> Well, what else could we do? He was hopeless. I'm no bully; I never hurt a nigger in my life. I like niggers—in their place—I know how to work 'em. But I just decided it was time a few people got put on notice. As long as I live and can do anything about it, niggers are gonna stay in their place. Niggers ain't gonna vote where I live. If they did, they'd control the government. They ain't gonna go to school with my kids. And when a nigger gets close to mentioning sex with a white woman, he's tired o' livin'. I'm likely to kill him. Me and my folks fought for this country, and we've got some rights. I stood there in that shed and listened to that nigger throw that poison at me, and I just made up my mind. "Chicago boy," I said, "I'm tired of 'em sending your kind down here to stir up trouble. Goddam you, I'm going to make an example of you—just so everybody can know how me and my folks stand."

"So big Milam decided to act," Huie wrote. Milam remembered that new equipment had recently been installed at a cotton gin and that there was an old, discarded fan nearby. "When we got to that gin, it was daylight, and I was worried for the first time. Somebody might see us and accuse us of stealing the fan." So Milam made Emmett Till load it. Milam and Bryant then drove the boy out to a spot on the Tallahatchie River, about a mile and a half from the home of his friend L. W. Boyce. Huie did not remind his readers, but Boyce had been a character witness for Milam during the murder trial. Milam forced Till to pick up the gin fan and carry it to the riverbank. "Take off your clothes," Milam ordered. It was now 7:00 A.M., and as Till stood there naked, Milam asked him two final questions.

"You still as good as I am?"

"Ya," Till answered, defiantly.

"You still 'had' white women?"

"Yeah."

Milam next fired a shot point-blank into Till's head. Because the boy moved slightly to the left, the bullet hit him just above the right ear, and he fell to the ground. Next, the men took barbed wire, tied the fan to Till's neck, and rolled him into twenty feet of water. Returning to Milam's, they spent the next three hours holding a bonfire. It took that long to burn Till's crepe-soled shoes.

Huie may have meant to prick the consciences of Mississippians; or, he simply believed he was stating a fact by closing his essay with a scathing assessment. "The majority—by no means all, but the majority—of the white people in Mississippi 1) either approve Big Milam's action or else 2) they don't disapprove enough to risk giving their 'enemies' the satisfaction of a conviction."[44]

The impact of the story was both immediate and immeasurable. This was predicted even before its release. Roy Wilkins became aware of the article and its contents several days before promos began running, as Huie had obviously kept him in the loop. He urged NAACP branch officers to use the article to their advantage to further the association's goals. He gave them a heads-up:

> Next Tuesday, January 10, *Look* magazine will publish a startling article on the murder of Emmett Till in Mississippi. The magazine will be dated January 24, but will go on sale January 10.
>
> This article will be certain to cause fresh nation-wide discussion of the brutal killing of the 14-year-old boy for which no one has been punished.
>
> When the magazine appears and you have seen the article, please write without further delay to both Senators from your state and to the Congressman from your district, reminding them of the Till murder and asking that this session of Congress pass civil rights bills to give the Department of Justice authority to act in such cases as the Till killing.
>
> Ask for an anti-lynching bill. Ask for a stronger civil rights division in the Department of Justice. Ask for laws to guarantee the security of the person.
>
> Ask for the passage of civil rights bills to protect citizens in the right to vote.[45]

On Thursday, January 13, three days after "Shocking Story" went public, Michigan representative Charles Diggs Jr. stood before the House of Representatives. After receiving unanimous consent to speak, he read the piece into the *Congressional Record*. To him, there was no question as to the source of the details in the article. "The stunning revelations are so detailed and stated so positively, the magazine's journalistic integrity and knowledge of libel law is so well established there is no doubt in my mind that the information came directly from the killers themselves, J. W. Milam and Roy Bryant." He theorized that the men, safe from further prosecution, "apparently grasped at the opportunity of selling this exclusive story for an undoubtedly handsome financial reward."[46]

Within days, two southern congressmen responded to Diggs by castigating Huie's summation that the murder had the approval of white Mississippians.

John Bell Williams, a four-term Democrat from Raymond, Mississippi, said the article "contains the most unfair, vicious, vindictive, baseless, scurrilous, scathing, and libelous indictment ever labeled against a State of this Union." It was a "lie out of the whole cloth, embellished with the products of a depraved imagination and is an act of journalistic prostitution of the lowest form." He read into the *Record* a January 11 editorial, published in the *Jackson State Times*, that blasted Huie.[47] South Carolina representative L. Mendel Rivers, during a one-minute speech from the House floor, introduced an article by Davis Lee, black publisher of the *Newark Telegraph*. After a seven-week stay in Mississippi, Lee had become convinced that the Magnolia State "is no worse than any other state in the union," and that the Till murder could have happened anywhere under similar circumstances. Lee's observations convinced him that "white people in Mississippi love and respect their Negro employees."[48] Rivers did not mention that Lee had already become a poster boy for segregationists. After the announcement of the *Brown* decision twenty months earlier, Lee published an editorial criticizing integration, and thus clearly established himself as an appeaser of southern whites. The editor of the *McComb (Miss.) Enterprise Journal* happily reprinted Lee's latest assessment and gave him a renewed voice in the South.[49] Clearly, Lee, a northerner, was a godsend to Dixie whites, but he was hardly representative of its black population.

It was no surprise that in Chicago, Mamie Bradley read the Huie piece immediately. Her instant response was that Milam and Bryant lied about her son. The boy she knew "would never brag about the women he had. How could he? He was only 14." The "Shocking Story" was the most recent in a series of personal blows. The trial verdict in Sumner, the dismissal of kidnapping charges in Greenwood, not to mention the murder itself, all left her devastated. "I don't see how much more I can stand, how I can go on. These terrible lies they tell to try and explain away killing a child in cold blood. They aren't human, they're beasts. And nobody does anything about them." Carolyn Bryant fared no better in Mamie's eyes. "That woman . . . I don't see how she can sleep at night."[50]

Although the article has typically been touted as a "confession," it does not fit that description if remorse and penitence are to be implied by such a definition. Neither did it read as one. Had the signed releases been forced into the open, one would see that Milam only agreed to let Huie *portray* him as a killer, and did so in return for money.

That the acquitted half-brothers immediately distanced themselves from the story further negates the idea that it should be taken as a confession. Newsmen began tracking down the pair right away, but anyone who asked was met with denials by both Milam and Bryant. Unknown to anyone asking, that was all part of the deal. "I don't know a damn thing about it, and you can quote me on that," Milam told newsmen. "There's nothing I can do about someone's imagination but I didn't have nothing to do with killing anyone." Bryant's response sounded more canned. "I haven't seen the article, but if it's anything I am supposed to have said, I deny it. I don't have any comment until we finish talking to our lawyers." Milam also said he was even mulling over the idea of filing a libel suit against the magazine, and claimed to have hired John Whitten to explore the possibility. Whitten, getting in on the act himself, told the press that he was still deciding what to do, but believed a suit, if filed, would be handled by a federal court, through a New York attorney.[51]

Within a few days, however, Milam admitted to reporter Jay Milner that he was not sure if he really had grounds for winning a lawsuit because "that guy that wrote it was careful not to say where he got his information and he didn't quote me directly." Actually, Huie did quote Milam directly, but never mentioned that he heard the story from Milam himself. Milam did note with a smile that the article "was written from a Mississippi viewpoint. I've gotten a lot of letters from people complementing me for what *Look* said I did." He showed the reporter a stack of fourteen that he had received that day alone.[52]

Four years later, Huie revealed that the denials Milam and Bryant made to the press had been carefully crafted by Huie himself.[53] When Huie answered questions from curious reporters following the release of the article, he stood by the story but said little else. In a statement issued through *Look*, he explained, "In researching the Till story for *Look* magazine, I talked to all the important sources in Mississippi." Yet, true to his word, he refused to reveal identities. "I cannot, as a responsible newsman[,] enumerate these sources by name." "For the same reasons," Huie continued, "I cannot answer any questions as to whether or not I personally talked with any particular individuals in the Till case." He insisted that "the *Look* article is completely accurate. *Look* published it only after being thoroughly satisfied of that fact." The magazine's attorney, John Harding, also pointed out that no one connected to the case had contacted the publication to dispute the details.[54]

For most readers, none of that made any difference. However careful Huie was in protecting his sources legally, few saw Huie's "Shocking Story" as anything but an admission of murder by Milam and Bryant. The public denials of the acquitted killers notwithstanding, the article prompted immediate calls for authorities to empanel a new grand jury to once again consider kidnapping indictments against them. Because they had never been tried and acquitted on those charges, they could legally be charged again if there was evidence to warrant it. The loudest voice insisting on a renewed effort was that of Roy Wilkins, who sent a telegram to Mississippi governor-elect J. P. Coleman urging him to act. Coleman was still serving as state attorney general until his inauguration on January 17. "If nothing is done to make them pay for at least one of their crimes, not only is Mississippi disgraced but our country will be held up for international ridicule. Accordingly, we urge you to act promptly to save the good name of our country and to salvage what you can for the State of Mississippi." In a separate letter to *Look*, Wilkins had words for Huie, who raised too many questions by never identifying his sources. "Who stands behind these 'facts,' Mr. Huie?"[55]

The man who had the power to call a grand jury was Arthur Jordan, circuit judge over Leflore County, but even his hands were tied. He explained to the press that in order to proceed, he would have to call a special grand jury with only a twenty-day notice. Because his schedule was already full, this would be impossible. The next term of court for Greenwood was not slated until May, and Jordan still had cases to preside over in four other counties before then. Even so, his only role in the matter would be to empanel the jury. Any decision to indict would be up to the men selected to serve. Jordan was not optimistic. "Nobody will indict anybody just on the basis of an article in a magazine." Should there be an indictment and the case go to trial, it would all be a waste of time without Huie's cooperation anyway. The district attorney could not force him to go to the state to testify, but Huie could do so voluntarily. In a separate interview with the *Washington Afro-American*, Jordan admitted that in that case, testimony from Huie "might carry some weight."[56] For Huie, who had already promised to protect his sources, testifying voluntarily was not an option.

Black journalist James Hicks had stayed on the Till case since the trial, and naturally followed the Huie story with vested interest. It had been two months since he had written his open letter to Attorney General Herbert Brownell and FBI director J. Edgar Hoover, wherein he named probable accomplices of Milam and Bryant.[57] In the January 21, 1956, edition of the *Baltimore Afro-American*, he published another such letter, this time prompted by the Huie revelations. This one was directed to Brownell alone.

Hicks was none too happy with Brownell as it was. Back in December, a delegation of five women from various organizations met with Brownell about the many abuses endured by southern blacks, especially those in Mississippi. Juanita Mitchell, an attorney for the National Council of Negro Women, admonished Brownell to strengthen federal statutes as a means to probe southern racial problems without hindrance. Brownell promised to consider the concerns of the group and offered to meet with them again after the president's State of the Union message in January. One of the women present mentioned Hicks's November letter, in which Hicks named individuals and spelled out a course of action for the FBI. Brownell rejected Hicks's charges as "groundless." Hicks later read about the attorney general's criticisms in a New York newspaper.[58]

Hicks believed, in light of the *Look* article, that he was having the last laugh. To him, however, the situation was not funny. "Mr. Milam is quoted from direct quotes all through the article. Now, Mr. Brownell, you are a lawyer, and you know that if a magazine or any publication charges a man with murder in direct quotes, that man can sue the magazine or newspaper for libel in any court in this nation AND FORCE THAT MAGAZINE OR NEWSPAPER TO EITHER PROVE HE COMMITTED THE MURDER OR COLLECT DAMAGES TO THE AMOUNT OF HARM HE HAS SUFFERED BY SUCH A CHARGE."

Hicks believed that Milam's inaction, despite early threats to sue, was telling. "A Mississippi jury acquitted him of murder and he is in an ideal position to sue. But he is not suing." Hicks said he had even talked with *Look*'s attorney, John Harding, who was sure that *Look* would win a lawsuit in the unlikely event that there would be one. "Mr. Attorney General, you are the highest lawyer in the land—what would be the best guarantee that any editor would want in a case like this? That's right—an affidavit signed by J. W. Milam in which he admits to the magazine that everything in the article is true. That's the only kind of guarantee that any publication with the national standing of *Look* Magazine could accept under the circumstances." Did Harding alert Hicks to the releases signed in Sumner? Harding knew that the statements made no admissions of guilt, but ethical boundaries should have kept him from telling anyone about them at all, especially a loose cannon such as Hicks. Harding may have provided Hicks with a hypothetical scenario, or Hicks's talk of affidavits was all conjecture on his part. Either way, his theory was nearly spot on. "What I now say is that Milam and Bryant have confessed their killing of Emmett Till and there is a strong suggestion that they were paid a handsome sum for the confession." Hicks publicly challenged Brownell to intervene by concluding his letter with six words: "It's your move, Mr. Attorney General!"[59]

Brownell ignored Hicks altogether and was not swayed when former California congressman Sam Yorty wrote and urged, as thousands had before him, that Brownell see "that justice is done in this case." On February 12, Warren Olney, assistant attorney general, responded to Yorty and assured him that the Justice Department shared the congressman's views about the horrific nature of the murder. Regardless, nothing pointed to the crime as anything other than a state matter.[60]

In the end, Huie's "Shocking Story" only confirmed the fact that two men got away with murder. It would not serve as a springboard for justice, and Mississippi officials never tried to prosecute the men again.

The varied responses to the article were hardly a surprise. Huie received around 5,000 letters, and the sentiments of the authors sat anywhere along the spectrum. Some pledged financial support to Milam for doing what was to them an honorable deed. Others accused Huie of being a "nigger-lover." Still others read "Shocking Story" as Huie's attempt "to make a Negro child into something detestable." In its March 6 and March 20, 1956, issues, *Look* published a total of nineteen letters to the editor about the article.[61]

Editorials in northern and southern papers clearly demonstrated these diverse attitudes. The *New York Post* declared that "if a slaying can not only be committed but proclaimed—and that is what the *Look* report suggests—there is no longer any semblance of protection for the civil rights of Negroes in that state. . . . The Till case haunts the national conscience, and this article, until or unless it is successfully disputed, is a sensational and decisive exhibit." The *Greenwood Morning Star* denounced the piece and the magazine that gave it a forum. Huie's claim that the murder was approved by the state of Mississippi was especially disturbing. "It is this insinuation which marks *Look* magazine as the bitter enemy of the South and the South's way of life."[62]

Amid the outcry over the story, one development was completely unexpected, but it demonstrated that Huie planned to cash in on the Till case for some time to come. Within days after *Look* hit the stands, papers reported that Huie, Mamie Bradley, J. W. Milam, and Roy Bryant were all parties in a movie deal with Lloyd Royal, president of Panorama Productions and owner of a movie theater chain in Meridian, Mississippi. When the story broke, Royal was in New York with an associate, T. V. Garroway, to secure a deal with Huie, who was slated to write the script. Huie also contracted with the New American Library to write a book building upon his "Shocking Story."

The film was to be called *The Emmett Till Story*, and Royal hoped to begin shooting in Money and Sumner in less than a month. Till family members had already signed contracts and Royal was in negotiations with Milam and Bryant. Huie was not worried, however. Should the brothers fail to sign on, "we will be willing to take the risks involved. But we intend to use real names and places and the real locale of the killing."[63] If there were any risks to consider, they would have only involved Roy Bryant. The releases that Milam and Carolyn Bryant signed in Sumner already gave Huie and anyone working with him the right to portray them in film. Publicly claiming he still had to negotiate with them was probably necessary to conceal the fact that they had actually given the go-ahead three months earlier.

A follow-up story soon reported that the acquitted pair did sign on, as expected. Twenty-seven-year-old actor and Arkansas native Cecil Scaife told the press he hoped to play Milam in the film, although casting had not yet started.[64] As Royal explained it, "We don't plan to make a documentary. We are going to dramatize a story based on the known facts. We're a Mississippi company and we're not going to do anything to hurt Mississippi. The releases we have obtained give us the final say on what goes into the picture." Royal said he was even working out details for financing and distribution of the film with forty-five-year-old Arthur B. Krim, entertainment lawyer and, since 1951, chairman of United Artists.

Mamie Bradley confirmed after the first reports made the news that she had indeed signed a contract just after the first of the year and hired an attorney to advise her. "My contract gives me the right to pass on the script and I will exercise that right vigilantly to see that it gives a truthful portrayal." Bradley was adamant that she would not allow her son to be portrayed as he had been in the *Look* article. "Emmett was no superman and saying that he took all that beating without begging for mercy or that he kept talking back to them to the very end just isn't true. They were only trying to justify why they did it."[65]

Despite early enthusiasm over this project, the film never came to fruition, and the reasons for that are unknown. Huie did fill his contract with the New American Library, producing the book *Wolf Whistle, and Other Stories* in 1959. The first chapter dealt with the Till case. He finished a screenplay for an Emmett Till film in 1960, but by then Royal was out of the deal and Huie was negotiating with Louis de Rochemont, cocreator of the theatrical newsreels *The March of Time* and producer of such full-length features as *The House on 92nd Street* (1945) and *Windjammer* (1958). De Rochemont, known as the father of the docudrama, may have naturally been drawn to the Till story. However, Huie reported in a 1977 interview that although he had signed a contract with RKO Pictures and had written the script, the producer canceled the project. A footnote to the interview explained that, "given the style of movies at the time, there seemed no way to make a film about two men who casually murder a boy and then escape punishment with the blessings of their peers." The script still sits unproduced in Huie's papers at Ohio State University.[66]

As Huie predicted, his "Shocking Story" eroded the support that Milam and Bryant had gained before and just after the trial. When Huie met up with the pair the following year, he reported that friends had abandoned them and that misfortune was plaguing them both.[67]

Just after the release of the *Look* piece, newspapers began reporting that Mississippi governor-elect Coleman spoke about the case to interviewer Dick Smith of radio station KXOL in Fort Worth, Texas. "So far as I am concerned, they both [Milam and Bryant] should have been convicted and electrocuted." He was quick to criticize the NAACP and Charles Diggs for coming to the trial and stirring up trouble. Had they stayed away, "we would have got the job done."[68]

When news of the interview hit, Coleman denied these statements. A reporter from the *Memphis Press-Scimitar* read Coleman a United Press dispatch in which *Look* attributed the quotes to the governor-elect. Coleman still denied making such statements. "To begin with, Mississippi no longer electrocutes. We use the gas chamber. Secondly, I have been judge and attorney general for so many years I would never make such a statement without having sat in on the evidence. I did not hear the evidence in this case." *Look*, however, insisted that the interview had been recorded and forwarded to New York, where it was released. Coleman admitted that he had talked with Smith by phone several days earlier, but he believed it to have been nothing more than a casual exchange. "I guess I should have declined to talk at all," said Coleman, regretfully. "I didn't regard it as a news release conversation."[69]

Huie's "Shocking Story" has received both undue praise and unwarranted criticism in the decades since it appeared. On the one hand, it convinced many holdouts who would not believe it before that Milam and Bryant were guilty of murder, and it served as a constant reminder to the state of Mississippi that it had, through its court system, delivered an injustice. As such, the acquitted brothers were no longer heroes, but quickly became pariahs in their communities. However, because Huie willingly accepted their version of the story, which portrayed them as the only perpetrators, the article created and perpetuated a false narrative that has unfortunately been given an authoritative status. Its portrayal of Emmett while in the store as attempting to assault Carolyn Bryant, and at the murder site as fearlessly standing up to the men who killed him, has also made his death a little more bearable for many and justified it for not a few.[70]

Huie knew that his article would leave some lingering questions unanswered, especially those raised during the trial by Mose Wright and Willie Reed, who claimed others were present at both the kidnapping and murder. The *Tri-State Defender* reported on the *Look* piece several days in advance of the magazine's release and noted that it "was able to obtain some additional factual information, heretofore unrevealed about the kidnapping and murder." The *Defender* would only state that this information came from an informant. It is clear, however, that the source was none other than Huie himself.[71] This "informant" was already thoroughly familiar with even minute details from Huie's article. For example, the *Defender* source noted that the cotton gin where the men got the fan was called the Progressive Ginning Company, located nearly three and a half miles from the town of Cleveland, in Bolivar County. Huie named the gin in "Shocking Story" as well. Notes in Huie's correspondence indicate that he was likely the source also.[72]

Because the *Tri-State Defender* story had been written in advance of the release of the issue of *Look* containing "Shocking Story," it is clear that Huie initiated the conversation with the paper, and not the other way around, as the *Defender* would not have known that the article was even forthcoming. Huie had already built rapport with *Defender* publications and seemed proud of it. In the letter he wrote to Dan Mitch as he began working out the details for "Shocking Story," Huie asked Mitch to stress some facts to *Look*'s lawyer in case the lawyer had liberal leanings. "Tell him that 16 years ago I was 'honored' by the NAACP; that on my wall hangs a scroll presented me by the *Chicago Defender* for 'symbolizing the best in American democracy'; that the *Pittsburgh Courier* has raised money for me; that the American Civil Liberties Union has field actions on my behalf; and that I have the respect of virtually every literate Negro in the country."[73] Although the last boast was an exaggeration, Huie believed he had standing with the paper.

Many of the details revealed by Huie as an informant to the *Tri-State Defender* were identical to what was forthcoming in *Look*. There is an added detail about the black man who told Bryant about Emmett Till's behavior at his store. "For his own protection, I cannot reveal his name."[74] If protecting the man was an issue, that probably meant that he was still in the South, where his safety would have been jeopardized. This is important because rumors began to surface later that the informant was one of Till's cousins.[75] These relatives were no longer in Money, however, but had all moved to Chicago just after the murder trial ended. Huie knew this as well because he went to Chicago to interview them.

Huie, as informant, completely dismissed Mose Wright's claim that a third man stood on the porch during the kidnapping, calling it "a myth, sheer nonsense," because Milam and Bryant would never take a black man along for a mission such as this. Nor was there a woman in the car. "It is not reasonable to believe that Mrs. Bryant would leave her two children alone in the store at 2 A.M. nor is it logical to think that Mr. Bryant would permit such."[76] Still, Huie does not explain at all how Wright could have seen a third man on the porch and heard a voice from the car if no one was there. Apparently, neither did the *Defender* press him on it.

As to Willie Reed's testimony about the men, the truck, the shed, and the beating on a Sunflower County plantation, "That was a coincidence." As Huie explained it, a truck of the same make and color as Milam's, carrying three whites in front, and a few blacks in back, did drive onto the plantation and into the shed. "This was a fishing party. The truck backed up to the barn and a boat was moved out onto the truck." Huie said the moaning sounds that Reed heard were only noises made by people playing around as they loaded up the boat.[77]

Huie's version of the events surrounding the death of Emmett Till, both in *Look* and in his lesser-known but important account as an informant to the

Tri-State Defender, appeared on the surface to settle the matter. Following a host of rumors, denials, stories of money, greed, and movie deals, the Till case had taken a sensational turn. As Deltans woke up to the fact that two acquitted killers lived among them, most wanted not only to cease talking about the matter but to put it behind them forever.

Shortly after the release of "Shocking Story," a series of articles appeared in the Los Angeles–based black weekly the *California Eagle*, beginning with its January 26 issue. The five-part series claimed to unfold the truth about the Till murder, but the dramatic details differed substantially from Huie's account.[78]

The articles were written by a journalist under the pseudonym Amos Dixon. An introductory note in the first installment described Dixon as a white southerner who had covered the murder trial in Sumner and "talked freely to those who knew what happened."[79] Unlike Huie, Dixon maintained that Milam and Bryant had accomplices, and he names them. His account aligns more closely with the testimonies of Willie Reed, Mandy Bradley, and Add Reed, which "Shocking Story" ignored completely. Midway through publication of the series, a thirty-five-page booklet appeared, titled *Time Bomb: Mississippi Exposed and the Full Story of Emmett Till*, and it told a similar story as Dixon had provided. It was written by Olive Arnold Adams, wife of *New York Age Defender* publisher Julius Adams. A seven-page chapter dealt specifically with the Till case.[80]

Dr. T. R. M. Howard was clearly the driving force behind each of these investigative endeavors, and a primary source of information. Details he provided in published speeches are quoted or paraphrased by Dixon and Adams, but not acknowledged. For example, Howard's revisionist description of Emmett Till's wolf whistle claims that Carolyn Bryant did not even hear it. This is repeated by Dixon and Adams. So, too, are Till's cries of "Lord have mercy, mama save me," which Howard claimed Willie Reed heard the dying boy utter from inside the shed, but which Reed never stated in his courtroom testimony.[81]

Howard had been a columnist for the *California Eagle* in 1933 and 1934, and Loren Miller, who took over ownership of the paper from Charlotta Bass in 1951, had been friends with Howard for over twenty years. Howard also had a connection with Adams, made evident by the fact that he wrote the foreword to *Time Bomb*. He even referred to a book in progress that he and Adams were writing together. For whatever reason, however, that book was never published.[82]

It appears that Adams likely relied exclusively on Howard for her narrative. Dixon, on the other hand, seems to have done some independent research, for at times he differs from both Howard and Adams. Some of the details in each of their works contradicts early statements of witnesses and others, and, unfortunately, the authors never explain why. In that regard, the inconsistencies raise more questions than they answer. However, the most important revelations of Dixon and Adams concern accomplices. The names of Levi Collins and Henry Lee Loggins were well known to the press by the third day of the trial, but Howard later learned of the involvement of another black man. At first, Howard could not identify him by name, but in the month after the trial, he announced from Los Angeles that the mysterious third man on the back of the truck was someone named "Hubbard." Dixon identified him as Willie Hubbard.[83] Hubbard had been a friend of Loggins, and the two men had dated a pair of sisters. When Loggins referred to him in 2001, he remembered him as Joe Willie Hubbard.[84]

Dixon names Loggins and Hubbard as the two on the truck who held down Emmett Till to prevent him from escaping. For reasons unknown, when Adams referred to them in *Time Bomb*, she used pseudonyms, even though their real names had already appeared in the press by this time. Loggins became "Wiggins"; she referred to Hubbard as "Herbert"; and Frank Young, the field hand who first tipped off Howard about the beating of Till on the Drew plantation, became "Fred Yonkers." Dixon says that the white men in the front of the truck with J. W. Milam and Roy Bryant were Leslie Milam "and another brother who has never been completely identified." Adams does not name them, but simply refers to them as "two other persons" who were in the cab of the truck.[85]

Unlike Adams, Dixon reported gruesome details of the beating and death of Emmett Till. The source of this information would have been Loggins's father, Dewitt, who got the story directly from his son. In his open letter to Attorney General Brownell and FBI director Hoover, published in the *Washington Afro-American* the previous November, Hicks identified Dewitt as a reluctant but willing source.[86] For the *Eagle* article, Dixon either talked to Dewitt Loggins or else learned the story from Howard. Either way, Dixon's description is particularly disturbing:

> With Henry Lee Loggins holding the victim, the Milams led by J. W. began beating Emmett about the head with their pistols. He began to cry and beg for mercy. That only whetted their hatred. They smashed his head in, beat it to a pulp.
>
> Emmett fell to the floor, still crying and begging. Their frenzy increased. The blows fell faster. The frenzy mounted higher. The killers kicked and beat their victim. Finally the cries died down to a moan and then ceased.
>
> The Milams and Bryant thought their victim was dead.
>
> A new panic seized them. What to do with the body? J. W. rose to the occasion: throw the body in the Tallahatchie river.[87]

As for Howard, his role in seeking justice in this case was nearing an end. He had recently learned that he was on a "Special Death List" of 100 people slated to be killed off by white supremacists by the first of the year. He had just sold all 720 acres of his property outside Mound Bayou for $200,000, and was spending less time in Mississippi. When rumors surfaced that he was moving from the state, he assured a curious reporter that "I have no intention of leaving Mississippi at this time." By April, however, he decided to move to Chicago.[88]

The Dixon and Adams reports, as sensational as they were, barely caused a ripple, but the alleged involvement of Collins and Loggins in the Till murder was not entirely forgotten, even in the aftermath of Huie, who completely eliminated them from the story. On February 28, 1956, a delegation from the National Council of Negro Women came to the FBI office in Washington, DC, and met with Hoover and Louis B. Nichols, assistant to the director. One of the women, Juanita Mitchell, spoke impassionedly about several issues. With regard to the Till case, she wanted to know why the Bureau had not conducted an investigation in response to Hicks's November letter to Brownell and Hoover. The FBI had decided back in December not to act upon it.

This exchange prompted Hoover to find out why Collins and Loggins had never been interviewed by the Criminal Division, and why this information had never been presented to him in a brief. F. L. Price explained to Hoover about the September 30 memorandum that had requested an investigation to determine whether a civil rights violation had occurred. Price approved the investigation on October 4, and the Memphis office turned in its report eight days later, which was based in part on the Memphis agents' interview with Robert Smith.[89]

Mitchell's comments renewed discussions of Hicks's letter, which had been written after the FBI's October decision to take no action. Price again preferred not to act. "After having read the open letter which Hicks wrote and was published in the *Afro-American* and being subject to Mrs. Mitchell's emotional tirades, I frankly doubt the advisability of interviewing Hicks unless it is a matter of last resort," he wrote. "The very moment that we interview Hicks we can expect to have a story that we are investigating the Till case." Price clearly wanted to avoid that, but he advised Hoover about possible action that the Bureau could take, all of which Price was still reluctant to pursue:

I am wondering if we are on sound ground to send a memorandum to the Attorney General and ask for instructions and then go ahead in the absence of instructions and interview Hicks. It seems to me that if we do want to go ahead and seek to verify whether or not Collins and Loggins were in the Charleston jail as alleged by Mrs. Mitchell, we might do this without interviewing Hicks. After all, Hicks got his information from Dr. Howard and if we interview Hicks we would then have to go to Howard.

If you feel that we should go ahead on this in the absence of a directive from the Department, would it not be better to locate Collins who was interrogated by the attorney for the Chicago defender [*sic*] and whose statement was published in the papers, interview the cook at the jail who allegedly fed these individuals and verify that Collins and Loggins were working in Mississippi while the trial was going on.[90]

No further discussion about possible action exists in the FBI's Till file, which indicates that the entire matter was dropped at this time. However, a few weeks later, black leaders in Mississippi made a last-ditch effort to get Loggins to open up. In mid-March, a writer researching the Till case learned that the field hand had been jailed in Sumner on a theft charge. Loggins was still working for J. W. Milam at the time, and it was Milam who issued the complaint. Apparently Milam had obtained two discarded trucks and kept them on the plantation he was managing. Loggins allegedly sold the scrap metal from the vehicles to R. L. and J. C. Smart, two brothers living in Glendora. When Milam spotted the three black men cutting up the metal with a torch, he confronted them at gunpoint and had all three arrested.[91]

Black leaders hoped that the rift between Loggins and Milam would finally prompt Loggins to tell everything he knew about the Till murder. They immediately devised a plan to clear Loggins of the charge, move him out of the area, and provide him with a home, job, and money. When told about the efforts to help him, Loggins agreed to go along with the arrangement.

Bail for Loggins was set at $700 and was quickly paid. The group retained Abe Sherman, a white lawyer from Clarksdale, to help free Loggins, and the next day Sherman drove to Sumner. When Sherman learned that Milam was involved in the case, he grew reluctant, but kept with his client nevertheless.

Although Tallahatchie County sheriff Harry Dogan tried to release Loggins, surprisingly, Loggins refused to leave the jail. "That boy don't want to come out," Dogan told the group waiting outside. When a black newsman went in to persuade Loggins to leave, Loggins, whom the *Daily Defender* reporter described as "frightened, dirty, and badly in need of a haircut," screamed out, "I don't know you. I want to see Mr. Milam." Loggins finally agreed to leave the cell only if his father came to get him. At that point, Sherman went home to Clarksdale, and reporters went looking for Dewitt Loggins.

After searching for two hours, they found him on a plantation near Minter City. He agreed to go with them to Sumner but wanted to wait until dark. However, when the men went to his home at 7:00 P.M. to pick him up as planned, he was gone. "He had to go away with his boss," his wife, Sarah, informed them. "He told me to tell you he just had to go." While explaining this to the reporters, she made a gesture in the direction of a bayou nearby. The group then went to Glendora to find a friend of Henry Lee's who would go to the jail and try to convince him to leave.

When they arrived back at the Sumner jail, Sheriff Dogan and attorney Sherman were waiting. Loggins's friend went inside and talked to the frightened inmate for half an hour, but Loggins told him to tell the men outside to "come back tomorrow." Dogan, still waiting outside himself, called Loggins to the jail window.

"These folks have spent all day trying to help you," Dogan said. "You can come out if you want to."

"No sir, I don't want to come out," Loggins yelled back.

Dogan, frustrated, told a reporter to try talking to the inmate. The newsman then tried to get Loggins to sign the bond, but Loggins refused.

"Why won't he come out?" the bewildered reporter asked a white official standing nearby.

"It's simple, boy," he answered. "J. W. Milam put him here and told him that when he wanted him out he would get him out."

Loggins remained adamant and told the men that he would not come out, even if they came back for him the next day. Finally, the group left.[92]

The following day, Loggins was arraigned before Judge James McClure and sentenced to six months in jail for obtaining money under false pretenses. J. W. Kellum, attorney for the Smarts, was able to secure the two brothers' freedom by arguing that Loggins alone was responsible for the theft. "These two niggers came to Milam's place in broad daylight with blow torches to cut up that iron, and no nigger in his right mind would come to Milam's place to do wrong." Loggins did not have a lawyer, and Mississippi law did not require that one be appointed for him. As Loggins began his sentence, a relative told the *Daily Defender*, "That boy knows too much about the Till child for his own good. He should leave Mississippi and never come back."[93] Eventually, that is what happened.

That same month, Dr. T. R. M. Howard spoke to a crowd of 3,000 in Chicago at the Greater Bethesda Baptist Church at a meeting sponsored by the United Packinghouse Workers of America. He introduced Willie Reed to the crowd and described him as ill and without friends since moving to Chicago. In response, several in the audience donated cash on the spot to help the struggling teen.

During the meeting, Ralph Helstein, union president and a member of the Civil Rights Committee for the AFL-CIO, called the Montgomery Bus

Boycott, now in its fourth month, a "demonstration of passive resistance in the best tradition of Mahatma Ghandi [*sic*]." Howard also relayed a message from Martin Luther King Jr., who had been leading the boycott almost from the start. King's message through Howard was to "tell the folks in Chicago we have enlisted in this fight for the duration."[94]

King, of course, saw both the fight and its duration in the context of the efforts in Montgomery. But his words would prove prophetic in describing something much larger and grander, a burgeoning movement that would later be defined by a decade of triumph, to be sure, but one also marked by struggle, confrontation, and bloodshed. In time, King would see that bigger picture, and eventually came to foresee his own martyrdom, which would occur just twelve years after the bus boycott began. In doing so, he would link both himself and the boy from Chicago as martyrs in that movement. "Today it is Emmett Till, tomorrow, it is Martin Luther King. Then in another tomorrow it will be somebody else."[95]

The boycott in Montgomery was a continuation of a grassroots momentum that had begun a few months earlier. There was no turning back after the world saw Emmett Till's battered face in Chicago and heard the words "not guilty" echo out of Sumner. For the civil rights movement to succeed, however, it had to move forward and focus on its ultimate goals of freedom and equality for all. As a consequence, the succeeding generation would learn little about the lynching of the Chicago boy. Yet the brutal nature of the crime and the injustice tied to it meant that it could not stay buried forever. A resurrection was inevitable, and Emmett Till eventually reemerged into the public consciousness. This happened simply because it had to.

For some, however, the fourteen-year-old boy from Chicago never really went away. Nor could he.

10

Never the Same

Anyone can speculate on what the likely fate of the Emmett Till case figures would have been had this tragic murder been avoided. The temptation to do so is hard to resist. What if the seven youths who broke from the sweltering heat of the cotton fields on August 24, 1955, had simply arrived in downtown Money *after* the café, to which they were originally headed, had already opened? Would they have bypassed the Bryant's Grocery and Meat Market altogether? If so, would Emmett Till now be a grandfather somewhere in a Chicago suburb? Mose Wright would certainly have lived out the rest of his days in Mississippi, as he had intended, and Willie Reed and Mandy Bradley would have remained as obscure in the rural Delta as they were otherwise destined to be. Perhaps J. W. Milam's only indiscretions would have been the occasional bootlegging for which he was already known. Roy Bryant's store might have stayed open a few more years, but technological advances in cotton harvesting were fast making his field-hand patrons disappear. Carolyn Bryant's fame would have remained local, her only notoriety being her teenage beauty titles, both of which would have been long forgotten by now.

Yet Emmett Till *was* murdered, and his brutal death and the injustice that followed permanently altered the lives and legacies of many. After the verdict was read, once the speeches were over, and the protests had waned, what happened to the key players in this sad southern tale? Some prospered, while others struggled. For a few, life was simply tragic. Among those still living, some are affable when approached, others, aloof. One or two refuse to talk about the case at all.

Mamie Bradley never returned to her job at the air force office in Chicago. Her rift with the NAACP left her tainted in some circles as greedy and exploitive of her son's death. Before she could deal with that, she had other priorities. She had said just after Emmett's death that mourning would have to wait, but the time for unrestrained grief finally arrived in the late fall.

About two months after the trial, Mamie walked downstairs at her home to use her washing machine for the first time since before Emmett's death. The murder, the trial, and the rallies had left her no time for domestic chores, and she left most of them to her mother. As she tried to run the washer on this occasion, the wringer failed to work. "I called my mother crying, telling her that Emmett had broken the machine and he hadn't told me," she said in an interview six years before her death. Blaming Emmett was her attempt to bring him back into her daily routine, as she explained. "I was just so carried away in grief that I guess I was glad to be able to call her and tell her something about Emmett even if it was something that I thought was negative—breaking the wringer and not telling me." Alma instructed Mamie to go downstairs and tighten it. That fixed the problem. "I ran back upstairs, and I cried. I said, 'Mama, it's not broken, it's ok.' It was just such an emotional moment with me."[1]

With this, Mamie found herself on the path toward healing. Speeches sponsored by labor unions kept her in the public eye occasionally through 1956, but it was her serialized memoir, "Mamie Bradley's Untold Story," published in the spring in both the *Daily Defender* and *Chicago Defender* that helped redeem her in the eyes of many. In October 1956, she flew to Washington, DC, as one of 400 women who attended the "Ladies Lunch for Adlai" fund-raiser on behalf of Democratic presidential nominee Adlai Stevenson. There she met former president Harry S. Truman and publicly threw her support behind Stevenson. She also chastised President Eisenhower for ignoring the telegram she had sent him just after Emmett's murder. Stevenson shortly wired Mamie to thank her for her support and assured her that he and his running mate, Tennessee senator Estes Kefauver, were "dedicated to the all-important realization of the democratic rights and guaranteeing the protection of all citizens."[2]

Around this time, Mamie began a self-imposed exile from the national spotlight. This began when she enrolled at Chicago Teachers College in the fall of 1956. She graduated cum laude three-and-a-half years later. Soon after she began her studies, Congressman William Dawson learned that Mamie was in need of a piano for her course work and purchased one for her. When Mamie flew to Washington in October for the women's luncheon, she was so dedicated to her studies that she took a stack of books and did homework on the plane. *Chicago Defender* correspondent Ethel Payne even came to her aid, reading aloud from Mamie's English text.[3] Mamie earned her degree in January 1960 and commenced teaching at Carter Elementary. She later moved to Scanlon School and retired in 1983 after a total of twenty-three years with Chicago's public schools.[4]

On June 24, 1957, thirty-five-year-old Mamie Bradley married Gene Mobley, her boyfriend of three years. The wedding took place in the home of Bishop Isaiah Roberts, who had served as host pastor of Emmett's funeral nearly two years earlier. This union lasted forty-three years, ending only with Gene's death in 2000. Mamie, who became known as Mamie Till-Mobley, never bore another child; instead, she helped nurture Gene's two daughters, Lillian and Yvonne, after their mother moved from Chicago.[5]

Neither Mamie nor her attorneys ever sued the Milams and Bryants as promised throughout the murder trial. However, in January 1958 she filed a $1 million suit against *Look* magazine over two articles written by William Bradford Huie published in January 1956 and January 1957. The first was the "confession" piece; the second was a follow-up on the acquitted half-brothers that appeared one year later. The complaint insisted that both articles were libelous and held Mamie "up to scorn and ridicule." Defendants named in the case were Cowles Magazines, Inc.; publisher Vernon C. Myers; editor Gardner Cowles; and Huie. Seventeen months later on June 22, 1959, a Chicago circuit judge dismissed the suit after he was persuaded by arguments from *Look* attorneys. They insisted that the stories were matters of public interest and also pointed out that the only mention of Mamie noted that she was the victim's mother.[6] She appealed the judgment, but in May 1960 the Illinois Appellate Court upheld the original decision. The following October, she took her case to the Illinois State Supreme Court but did not prevail there either.[7]

In 1960, Mamie sold the home she co-owned with her mother, and in January 1961, one year after her college graduation, she and Gene moved to a new home on Wabash Avenue.[8] By Mamie's own admission, the civil rights movement went on without her, and she watched from the sidelines the triumphs of the Montgomery Bus Boycott, the tragedy of the assassination of Martin Luther King Jr., and everything in between. She did protest one injustice, however, but it was not part of the movement. In 1970, she picketed in front of the National Tea Company store in Chicago where a black man named Alonzo Cushmeer had been killed. Her sign, "National Use Corporate Structure to Corrall [sic] People," indicated that the tea company had taken no responsibility in Cushmeer's death.[9]

In the mid-1960s, Mamie's mother, Alma Spearman, formed the Emmett Till Foundation. The goals of the organization were to build Christian character and a sense of citizenship in young people and to erect an interdenominational and interracial facility called the Emmett Till Center, which would serve to memorialize the slain youth. The foundation held its first annual banquet in Chicago on July 23, 1966. The planned center never came to fruition, but the nonprofit organization began a long tradition of awarding scholarships to deserving youth annually on July 25, Emmett's birthday.[10]

Mamie created an additional way of keeping her son's memory alive by establishing a performing group in 1973. This happened quite by accident after the principal at Carter Elementary assigned her the task of honoring the legacy of Martin Luther King Jr. during a school assembly. She checked out three record albums from the school library that contained King's speeches and became so engrossed in them that she stayed awake all night transferring them to cassette tape while simultaneously transcribing them. Children selected from the fourth, fifth, and sixth grades then memorized the speeches and recited them during the program three weeks later.[11] With this, the Emmett Till Players were born, and over the years they continued memorizing and performing. Older children eventually moved on, while younger ones replaced them. They performed at schools and churches, and a decade after its founding, Mamie estimated that over 200 children had been part of the troupe. In 1984, the group even performed in Mississippi.[12]

Outside of teaching school, running the Emmett Till Foundation, and leading the Players, Mamie remained busy. In May 1973, she helped found the Evangelistic Crusader Church of God in Christ, and two years after that earned a master's degree in administration and supervision from Loyola University, with an additional forty-five credits toward a doctorate.[13]

These first twenty years after the trial had been personally challenging for Mamie, yet they were also rewarding. During the fifteen years that followed, she received validation on three important occasions that Emmett's death had not been in vain. This fact became tangible—cast in bronze, etched in stone, and posted in procession above the hustle and bustle of Chicago's South Side.

This first such occasion occurred in 1976, not in Chicago or in the South, but in Colorado. At a ceremony held on Sunday, September 5, in Denver City Park, local officials unveiled a $110,000, twenty-foot statue designed and cast by Boulder artist Ed Rose. The idea for the sculpture came in 1973 by Herman Hamilton, a Denver bowling alley owner from Money, Mississippi, who was nine years old when Emmett Till was murdered. It depicted Martin Luther King Jr. and Emmett Till standing together. The project had been sponsored by the Martin Luther King Jr. Memorial Foundation, with a grant from the Colorado Centennial-Bicentennial Commission.[14] Till's August 28, 1955, murder and King's 1963 "I Have a Dream" speech occurred exactly eight years apart.

Mamie attended the two-hour ceremony with family and the Emmett Till Players, who performed. The towering statue portrayed a forward-looking King with his arm around the young lynching victim. When Mamie first gazed upon it, she could hardly contain her emotions, and Alma filled in at the podium until her daughter could regain her composure. When Mamie finally spoke, she told the hundreds gathered that "Emmett was too young to fight for his country ... but his death freed a nation from the shackles of fear." Denver was a fitting place for the statue because that city had been "moving with amazing speed toward the promised land of equality and the realization of justice." Governor Dick Lamm and other state and community leaders also attended the event.[15]

Emmett Till was honored once again on November 5, 1989, in Montgomery, Alabama, where Mamie was one of several guests invited to speak at the dedication of the Civil Rights Memorial there. Unveiled on the plaza of the Southern Poverty Law Center, the beautiful $700,000 monument had been conceived two years earlier by Morris Dees, executive director of the center. Dees wanted to honor several lesser-known figures who had died in the struggle for civil rights. The monument was designed by Maya Lin, who also created the Vietnam Memorial in Washington, DC.

The memorial features a fitting quotation from King, taken from Amos 5:24, and embedded in a granite wall: "Until justice rolls down like waters and righteousness like a mighty stream."

Appropriately, water flows down the wall and over the words, as it also does on a granite table, twelve feet in diameter, which sits a few feet away. The table contains a chronology of the civil rights movement and the names of forty of its martyrs. The third name on the list is Emmett Till, identified as a "youth murdered for speaking to white woman." A photo captured Mamie running her fingers over her son's name as she accepted this recognition with reverence.

Five thousand people attended the ceremony. Guests included Rosa Parks, Julian Bond, Martin Luther King III, and Ethel Kennedy. Mamie told the crowd that in the South, Emmett's death was "just one of those things," but this memorial, located two blocks from the site of Jefferson Davis's inauguration as president of the Confederacy, was a reminder to the world "that Emmett's death was *not* just one of those things." Besides Mamie, other speakers included Chris McNair, father of Denise McNair, who was killed in the Sixteenth Street Baptist Church bombing in Birmingham, Alabama, and Carolyn Goodman and Rita Schwerner Bender, mother and widow, respectively, of Andrew Goodman and Michael Schwerner, two of three Freedom Summer workers who were murdered in Philadelphia, Mississippi, in 1964. They all stood together to sing the Civil Rights anthem, "We Shall Overcome."[16]

Perhaps the greatest moment of fulfillment for Mamie came when the city of Chicago renamed a major street after her slain child. On July 25, 1991, Emmett's fiftieth birthday, a seven-mile stretch of Seventy-First Street was renamed Emmett Till Road. A ceremony featured the Emmett Till Players, Chicago mayor Richard M. Daley, former mayor Eugene Sawyer, and Rosa Parks. "I feel if I had the voice of 10,000 angels, I could not express what this day means to me personally, for the city of Chicago and the world," Mamie said at the event. "This is a culmination of a lifetime of dreams." Daley explained to the crowd that the naming of Emmett Till Road "is to commemorate a victim of racial hatred that exists in America, even today."[17]

One of the final highlights for Mamie came on March 7, 2000, when she finally became, at least symbolically, part of the civil rights movement that she had earlier watched from afar. She and Gene, along with hundreds of others, crossed the Edmund Pettus Bridge in Selma, Alabama, as part of the thirty-fifth anniversary of "Bloody Sunday." That original protest, carried out in 1965, was the first of three attempted civil rights marches from Selma to Montgomery, where marchers were halted on the bridge, attacked with tear gas, beaten with clubs, and driven back. Leading the way in the anniversary march, signifying a new America for the twenty-first century, was President Bill Clinton. Ethel Kennedy and civil rights veterans Jesse Jackson and John Lewis were also present. Sadly, less than two weeks later, Gene Mobley became ill and died.[18]

Although widowed, Mamie Till-Mobley's life remained eventful for the next three years as she continued her activities with the Emmett Till Foundation. She also traveled and spoke, despite the heart and kidney problems she had long battled. In fact, it was on January 6, 2003, the eve of a planned departure for an event in Atlanta, that she suffered a heart attack. She died that afternoon at Jackson Park Hospital. She was eighty-one years old.[19]

At her funeral a few days later at the Apostolic Church of God, 2,000 mourners gathered to pay tribute to this largely unsung, yet still emerging heroine. "The struggle for our emancipation is a history of strong, magnificent women," said Rev. Jesse Jackson. He likened her to such notable black women as Sojourner Truth, Ida B. Wells, Fannie Lou Hamer, and Rosa Parks. "In many ways the killers saw (Till's death) as a hole, but Mamie saw an earthquake, and she used the aftershocks of the earthquake to wake up and shake up a nation." Other speakers were Representative Bobby Rush and former Illinois senator and US ambassador Carol Moseley Braun.[20]

Six years before her death, Mamie Till-Mobley described her feelings toward the two men who had killed her son over forty years earlier. "Mercifully, the Lord just erased them out of my mind, out of my sight, with no conscious feelings toward them. Not hate, not love." As she reflected on the different paths their lives had taken in the years following the trial, however, she noted with some satisfaction, "I became a benefactor to society, they became a scourge to society."[21]

As a benefactor, Mamie Till-Mobley gave much in return, and her influence was felt most among the children she mentored. The loss of one child launched her on a path to saving others. One of those, Odel Sterling III, performed at her funeral and told *Jet* magazine, "I had a dream and it was that I wanted to speak." Like Emmett, Sterling had suffered from a speech impediment, but Mamie helped him overcome it by memorizing King's speeches.

Sterling was one of the first to join the Emmett Till Players in the early 1970s. Today, he is a minister and continues to recite those speeches around the country.[22]

Although Mamie Till-Mobley's name has not achieved the recognition of Martin Luther King Jr. or Rosa Parks, students of the civil rights movement know her well. When she insisted on an open casket in September 1955 for the world to see the battered face of her son, she made an impact that can only be described as immeasurable, as visual images preserve in memory what the written word cannot. Even today, those introduced to the Till murder who see those photos feel at one with the shaken crowds who filed past that open casket decades earlier.[23]

Thankfully, Mose Wright lived long enough to hear of the honor his great-nephew received in Denver City Park. For most of the twenty-two years Wright lived in Argo, Illinois, after testifying in Sumner, he did so quietly, outside the public eye. Upon arriving in the North, Mose, Elizabeth, and their three young sons stayed briefly with Mose's daughter, Willie Mae Jones, but soon moved to the second-floor apartment in a house owned by Mose's son, James, which stood next door to Mamie and Emmett's former home on Sixty-Fourth Street.[24]

Wright's speaking engagements, like those of Mamie, lasted only a few months.[25] A year after the trial he reported that he was working odd jobs and had even gained thirteen pounds since moving to the North. "I used to think I couldn't live without seeing cotton stalks. Man, I ain't seen cotton in a year and I'm still living." The former preacher had already come to see the impact of the Till case on the fledgling civil rights movement, and stated, almost prophetically, "What happened down there last year is going to help us all."[26]

Wright eventually found work as a custodian at a nightclub and later as a dishwasher at a local restaurant, working alongside his grandson, Milton Parker.[27] Adjusting to the big city after spending a lifetime in the rural Mississippi Delta was not easy. "At that age you can't really make that adjustment," said his youngest son, Simeon. Mose, who left his car behind in Mississippi, never drove again after his move to Argo, but with the close proximity of stores and schools, and the availability of public transportation, he did not need to. He gave up fishing after leaving the South, but the railroad let him use a little patch of land on which to grow a garden, which he kept up until he was seventy-nine. "That was his joy," recalled Simeon.[28]

Wright returned to Mississippi only one time after his November 1955 appearance before the grand jury in the kidnapping phase of the Till case. In September 1957, he attended the funeral of his older brother, Will Wright, in Greenwood. He often talked with his grandson William Parker about the two of them taking a road trip to the Delta, but that never occurred.[29]

Mose Wright would often debate politics with family members, especially the Vietnam War, which he defended. He was a supporter of John F. Kennedy and Lyndon Johnson. Later, he changed his mind about the war and came to believe that America never should have taken part in it. He sometimes reminisced about the South and how hard he worked in the fields. He remained saddened by the Emmett Till tragedy, but not bitter. He learned several years later that his sister-in-law, Alma Spearman, had harbored bitterness toward him for years for not doing more to prevent her grandson's kidnapping. She confessed this to Wright once she came to realize that there was nothing Wright could have done to prevent it.[30]

In 1964, when Simeon left home to join the army, his parents moved to a smaller home in a low-income housing project on Sixty-Third Place.[31] In 1970, Elizabeth died, and over the next seven years, Mose's health declined. He eventually had prostate surgery, which affected the strength in his legs. Living alone, he enjoyed cooking Jiffy Mix and frozen dinners. In time, his eyesight began to wane, and other health problems made it difficult for him to live on his own. One time while alone in his one-bedroom apartment, he lost his balance and fell. He remained on the floor for a day until his grandson, who had a key to the door, went to check on him. The Wright family eventually placed him in the White Oak Nursing Home in Indian Head Park. He died on August 3, 1977. The *Chicago Defender* ran an obituary acknowledging his role in the Till case.[32] The photo of Wright standing and pointing at two accused killers in Sumner will remain a testament to bravery in a Mississippi courtroom.

The three Wright children living at home during those dark days in 1955—Maurice, Robert, and Simeon—each dealt with the tragedy and its aftermath in his own way. For reasons not fully known, Maurice became plagued with problems. He maintained a good job for a while but developed a drinking problem, which began to consume him. Whenever he was able to return to the church, however, he'd abandon the alcohol; unfortunately, he would always fall off the wagon. One Argo resident remembers him as the town drunk.[33]

In the 1960s, he decided to move to Miracle Valley, Arizona, and affiliate with controversial evangelist and faith healer A. A. Allen. Maurice's brothers, James and Robert, bought him clothes and a bus ticket to get to Miracle Valley, but it is unknown if he ever made it. He did not return home for years, and when he eventually went back to Argo, it was only for an occasional visit.[34] He died in California a homeless alcoholic in 1991. Simeon learned of Maurice's death when a San Francisco hospital called to ask permission to use the body for research purposes. Simeon declined and brought the remains back to Chicago for burial instead. He theorized that unfounded rumors charging Maurice with complicity with Milam and Bryant, and Maurice's inability to shake them, were factors in Maurice's mental breakdown.[35]

If those stories are fabrications, as Simeon insists they are, the rumors originated close to home. Crosby Smith, brother of Elizabeth Wright and an uncle of Emmett Till who lived in Sumner, said in a 1974 interview that it was Maurice who told Roy Bryant about Till's indiscretion at the store in Money. Maurice, Smith said, may have been jealous that his Chicago cousin dressed well and came to town with cash in his pocket. "I don't think Maurice liked Emmett much, but I don't guess he figured what was going to happen to him, either."[36] Smith gave this interview while both Maurice and Mose Wright were still alive. If this story was unknown to the rest of the family at this time, it seems unlikely that Smith would have perpetuated it in print. Then again, his geographical distance from the rest of the family may have forced him to rely on rumors floating around the Delta.

Mamie Till-Mobley backed up the Maurice angle and in 1995 referred back to a conversation she and Wheeler Parker had once shared.

"What is wrong with Maurice?" she asked her cousin. "It looks like he can't hold himself together."

Parker's response was telling. "Maurice said Bo just won't let him alone."[37]

Still, Simeon Wright dismisses the views of Crosby Smith and Mamie Till-Mobley as inaccurate. In 2007, Wheeler Parker denied ever having conversed with Mamie about Maurice or his problems.[38] Even as far back as 1959, William Bradford Huie hinted that the person who informed on Emmett was someone still living in Mississippi. The Wrights had left in September 1955.

Like his brother, Simeon suffered also, mainly from anger and a chip on his shoulder that plagued him for several years after the trial. For him, healing began when he turned himself over to God and married his high school sweetheart, Annie Cole. He also credits schoolteachers in Argo who took him under their wings and helped him adjust to his new life in the North. After graduating from high school in 1962 and then completing his service in the army, Simeon became a pipe fitter for Reynolds Metals, a position he held until his retirement.[39] He has been an active speaker since appearing in the theatrically released documentary *The Untold Story of Emmett Louis Till* (later shown on Court TV) and *60 Minutes* in 2004. In 2010, he published his memoir, *Simeon's Story: An Eyewitness Account of the Kidnapping of Emmett Till*, coauthored with journalist Herb Boyd.

Wheeler Parker, who accompanied Emmett on his fateful visit to Mississippi, also speaks publicly about the murder, was featured in *Untold Story* and the PBS documentary *The Murder of Emmett Till*, and appeared on the *60 Minutes* segment. The tragic death of his cousin changed his life dramatically. When he heard the commotion outside his bedroom after Milam and Bryant entered the house looking for Till, Parker got scared. "I said 'They're going to kill us.' I thought about it. I started praying to God, I said, 'Lord, if you let me live, I'll straighten my life up.'"[40] Parker went on to become a barber, graduating from barber school in 1959. He worked at a shop on Fifty-Fifth Street for several years before buying the Esquire Barber Shop in Argo around 1992. He retired after suffering a minor stroke in 2007.[41]

More significant to his promise to God as he lay frightened in 1955 was his acceptance of Christ in 1961. In 1967, he married Marvel McCain and a decade after that became a minister. He served as an associate minister at the Argo Temple Church of God in Christ, the church that Emmett Till had attended most of his life, and in 1992 became assistant pastor. A year later he was appointed pastor. In 2006, the church celebrated its eightieth anniversary with Parker still at the helm. He and Marvel also organized the nonprofit, interfaith Summit Community Task Force, dedicated to helping troubled youth. Their efforts helped raise funds for the first community center in Argo.[42]

Crosby Smith, unlike the Wright family, remained in Mississippi after the trial, and died in Sumner in 1993. He witnessed a new Mississippi emerge as a result of the civil rights movement, one where white men would no longer be routinely acquitted for killing black men. "Today, I'd say that's one hundred percent changed," he said proudly, two decades after the Till murder. He began voting not long after the Voting Rights Act of 1965 was passed and eventually sat on a jury.[43]

Smith's success in preventing the Mississippi burial of Emmett Till and in personally accompanying the body to Chicago made him a hero in the days following the murder. Yet the case remained a painful subject for him. Other than his 1974 interview and another in 1985, he said little about the case, publicly or privately, in the four decades that he lived to think about it. "When you mentioned anything about it he'd get kind of depressed," said his son, Crosby Smith Jr. "He would stop talking and go into a shell."[44]

Wheeler Parker said that this silence extended to the rest of the family also. "There was never any talk done about it after [the trial] among us, to any degree. Never with anyone, not [even] among ourselves. We never sat down and talked about it." The reasons were simple. "We knew what happened. There was no need to talk about it." They never discussed it with Mamie Till-Mobley or even Mose Wright, for that matter. "He didn't talk," affirmed Simeon. "Not even to me."[45]

It was a traumatic ordeal to witness a kidnapping-turned-murder, and the years of silence among the witnesses signified a lasting pain, not a forgetting. "It's always on your mind," Parker said solemnly fifty-two years after the experience. "It's something that just doesn't go away."[46]

Forgetting was also impossible for Willie Reed, who knew Emmett Till only in death but who remained haunted for decades by the beating sounds he heard emanating from a plantation shed on an August morning in Drew,

Mississippi. His feelings mirrored those of Wheeler Parker. "That's something you never put out of your mind. I remember it like it happened yesterday," he said in 2007.[47]

After speaking at a few rallies following his late-night move to Chicago on the day the jury issued its verdict, Reed dropped out of sight. He had no contact with any of the other witnesses or Till family members for decades, despite living in Chicago and remaining in close proximity to many of them. Wheeler Parker and Simeon Wright even assumed Reed was dead, possibly even lynched for his testimony, until he reemerged for interviews in 1999.[48]

In Chicago, Reed obtained a new identity, or more accurately, reclaimed his old one. From the time he was seven months old until he left Mississippi, he lived with his grandfather, Add Reed, and assumed Add's surname. In Chicago, when Willie obtained a copy of his birth certificate in order to secure a Social Security number, he discovered that his last name was actually Louis, after his father, Joseph Louis. He went by his legal name of Willie Louis from then on, further obscuring his association with the Till case. In fact, most of his friends only learned of his role as a witness after seeing him on television in 2003.[49]

Adjusting to life in the big city was not easy for the eighteen-year-old, who had never been outside of Mississippi before the murder trial. Barely a week after moving to Chicago, he was hospitalized for a nervous disorder and soon suffered further health problems. Sometime during his first year in the North, he underwent surgery for ulcers, a procedure that removed part of his stomach. His police protection ended a few months after the move, and after a year he was still unemployed (despite receiving several job offers after the trial) and contemplated moving to Detroit in order to find work. He never took advantage of the $1,000 scholarship that the Elks lodge offered him should he have chosen to attend college. "I just didn't want to do it," he later said with regret.[50]

Reed quickly learned that, in the North, blacks were still subject to de facto segregation and discrimination. On one occasion he walked to a Walgreen's near his home to buy some cigarettes only to find that it was closed. He then went to a nearby bar instead, and when he went in, he noticed everyone was white. "The people looked at me like they had never seen a black man before in their lives." The bartender asked what he needed, and Reed told him.

"Is Walgreen's closed?" the man asked.

"Yes," Reed replied.

"I'll tell you what I'll do," explained the bartender. "I'll sell you a pack tonight, but make sure next time you go to Walgreen's."

After Reed left the bar, he realized what had just happened, and that this exchange only occurred because he was black.[51]

Things got better, however. Around 1959, he began working as a surgical orderly at Jackson Park Hospital and remained there for forty-seven years before retiring in 2006. While working in the intensive care unit in 1971, he met Juliet Mendenhall, then a nurse's aide. "Hey there. Why don't you come over here and give me a kiss?" he asked upon meeting her. Juliet was taken by the thirty-four-year-old bachelor. "I went over there and kissed him on his jaw." They married in 1976 and made their home in the Englewood area of Chicago. It wasn't until around 1983 that Willie told Juliet about his role in the Till case. Willie suffered from nightmares for several years into their marriage.[52]

Reed appeared in the documentaries *The Murder of Emmett Till* and *Untold Story*, and in the 2004 *60 Minutes* piece. His *Untold Story* interview in 2001 reunited him with Mamie Till-Mobley, whom he had not seen in forty-six years.

On January 6, 2003, Reed was not feeling well and stayed home from work. That day, Mamie died in the emergency room at Jackson Park Hospital. Juliet heard the news around 3:00 P.M. and passed it on to her husband. "If I'd gone to work that day, I'd have seen her," he said regretfully. Yet he accepted it as fate. "They say all things happen for a reason."[53]

After several years of declining health, Willie Reed died of gastronomical bleeding in July 2013 at age seventy-six.[54]

Add Reed, Willie's grandfather and another one of the prosecution's surprise witnesses, remained in Mississippi for several years after the trial. In the late 1960s, he and his wife, Mattie, moved to Chicago. After suffering from an enlarged prostate and other problems, he died of acute renal failure on March 25, 1977, about a week after entering Englewood Hospital. He was ninety-five years old.[55]

Less is known about Mandy Bradley, the third surprise witness at the trial. Her life took a downturn upon moving to Chicago, and she was reportedly "disillusioned" with the city almost immediately. For a brief period after her arrival, she stayed with Mamie Bradley but told the press that she planned to live with her daughter, Mary Brooks.[56] Although Alonzo Bradley began working on a construction project shortly after his move north, upon the first anniversary of the trial, Mandy reported that they had fallen on hard times on Chicago's West Side, where they lived in a two-room apartment. "They haven't treated me right," she said. "Since then [relocating to Chicago] I have really suffered. I've been without food, sick, and unable to find work." Her mother, still in Mississippi, was also ill, and Mandy was frustrated that she could not get back to the South to tend to her. "I'm scared to go back and see about her. I sit here and I cry and I worry and I pray and I ask God don't take my mother, let me see her again."[57]

It is unknown, at present, how Mandy Bradley fared, because she soon fell back into obscurity, and efforts to determine her fate have been unsuccessful. As of this writing, her daughter, Mary, is still living but in poor health. A granddaughter could not recall just when or where Mandy died. She believes it was sometime in the 1960s and that Mandy may have eventually returned to Mississippi.[58]

Levi "Too Tight" Collins never got his life back on track after the case faded from the news. Following the trial, he worked odd jobs in Jackson and Memphis but disappeared again in 1957. Some said he feared revenge from local whites who worried that he might talk or by blacks angry because he had not. "I'm plumb worried about the boy," his forty-six-year-old father, Walter Collins, said. "We used to be close. He'd come over to my place almost daily and we'd chat. Now I haven't seen him but once in three years." That one occasion was when Levi went by the house and the two ate breakfast together. "I haven't heard from him since. The case just ruined his whole life."[59]

On November 8, 1957, Collins's wife, Treola, and their four children arrived in Seattle at the invitation of Treola's sister, Lucinda Burrage, who borrowed $246 from her minister and sent train tickets by way of the Memphis railroad station. "We had to slip off the plantation to catch the train, but we didn't give our right names," Treola explained. "We only had the clothing on our backs. I used an old bedspread for diapers on my six-months-old baby. We had one loaf of bread and one can of peaches to eat."[60]

For a time, both families, with twelve children between them, shared a three-bedroom house in the projects. Treola suffered a nervous breakdown after the move by simply trying to process everything that had happened in the Delta that drove her away. She shortly rented her own house for $45 a month, but it lacked utilities and even a toilet. The state rejected her application for welfare benefits and encouraged her to return to Mississippi, but she remained in Seattle.[61]

Levi apparently surfaced long enough for the couple to divorce, because Treola eventually married Clent Gaston on August 9, 1960. Sadly, Levi never resumed a relationship with his children, all of whom Gaston later adopted. Treola managed to create a new life for herself in Seattle, where she bore five more children. Levi was not so lucky. Family members heard enough to know that the case completely destroyed him. He became an alcoholic and schizophrenic, hearing voices and hallucinating. He died in Jackson, Mississippi, in 1992.[62]

Like Treola, Levi's father, Walter, also moved to Seattle. After his divorce from Levi's mother, he married Elizabeth Tyler, Treola's sister, and maintained a relationship with his grandchildren. Even Treola's children from her second marriage called him "Uncle Walt." He died in Seattle in February 1996.[63]

Clent Gaston eventually became a preacher, and Treola became prominent in the House of Refuse Pentecostal Church in Seattle, the church she
had attended ever since her move there. She became a missionary and served
as the Hospitality Board president. Although she successfully put the painful
past of the Till case behind her, when each of her children turned eighteen,
she sat them down and told them about what had happened. "My mother was
wise for doing that," said her daughter, Marsha Gaston. Treola died of cancer
in Seattle in 1996, her last words being, "Yes, Lord."[64]

Not long after Henry Lee Loggins finished his six-month stint in jail for
theft, he left Mississippi, as his friends hoped he would. At first, he moved to
St. Louis, where he had lived a few years earlier, then moved to Dayton, Ohio,
in 1957. He did not surface publicly until July 2001 when historians David and
Linda Beito found him and interviewed him over the telephone. For years he
made a living in Dayton as a junkman.[65] He later appeared in *Untold Story*
and *60 Minutes,* where he denied any knowledge of, or involvement in, the Till
murder. He insisted that all he knew was what others had told him.

Loggins's wife, Earlean Adams Loggins, died in July 2001 just before Henry
Lee was contacted by the Beitos. Four years later, Henry Lee became incapaci-
tated after suffering a stroke but spent time in a nursing home and later at his
daughter's home recovering.[66] He died in Dayton in October 2009. Since 1982,
his son Johnny B. Thomas has been mayor of the village of Glendora, Mississippi, former home to both Loggins and J. W. Milam.

If J. W. Milam and Roy Bryant followed the news in the decade or so after
their trial, they may have felt some warped sense of justice when, one by one,
the three men who had prosecuted them in Sumner died tragically and much
too soon. District Attorney Gerald Chatham passed away only one year after
his courageous attempt to convict the two half-brothers. Because of notoriety in the Till case, the death of this otherwise unknown country lawyer was
noted in the *New York Times.*[67] Ill health had forced his retirement as district
attorney in January 1956. He suffered not only from high blood pressure but
from nosebleeds so severe that he was often admitted to the hospital, where
doctors had to pack his head in ice to stop them.[68]

In August 1956, Chatham, who had returned to private practice in Hernando, told a reporter that he had not been back to Sumner since the trial and
was happy to be out of his elected office. He no longer received letters related to
the Till case but held on to the 250 that had been sent to him. "It was astound-
ing," he said. "They came from all over the United States, England, France, Italy
and Germany. Most were from cranks, and a few were threatening."[69]

Two months later, on October 9, he introduced a speaker at the afternoon
opening of the Producers Gin of Hernando, Inc., in which Chatham was a
shareholder. Not feeling well, he went home, took a nap, and later that evening

died of a massive heart attack. His family has long blamed his early death on pressures he faced during the Till trial. Two days later, in Batesville, Judge Curtis Swango adjourned the Panola County fall term of court out of respect for his former colleague.[70]

Hamilton Caldwell, the elected attorney for Tallahatchie County, lived for seven years after the trial. He was out of office and serving as vice president of the Bank of Charleston when he drowned in Enid Lake on September 3, 1962. He had been fishing alone in his boat and, for reasons unknown, fell overboard as he headed back to shore. He was sixty-four.[71]

Robert Smith, the special prosecutor sent by the governor's office to aid Chatham in the state's case against Milam and Bryant, went back to his law practice in Ripley, Mississippi, after the trial. He rarely talked about the case, and his sons came to regret that they never asked him about it. "I've come to understand that not a lot of people in those days would have taken that case," said son Fred in 2003. "I know now it took a lot of courage." Bobby Elliot, a former law partner of Smith's, remembered how surprised people were that Smith agreed to do it. "That wasn't the popular thing to do back then."[72]

On December 4, 1967, he was at work in chancery court and appeared fine. Yet privately, he was masking unbearable pain and went home later that morning and shot himself. Although he did not allude to his father's suicide, Smith's son Bruce explained in 2005 that his father had been battling alcoholism. "He had a sad life in a way, in his later years." Smith's obituary noted that he had helped with "important criminal cases" in his career, but it failed to mention the Till trial in particular.[73]

The five defense attorneys who represented Milam and Bryant remained in Sumner. Sidney Carlton, former president of the Mississippi State Bar Association, died first, in 1966, at age fifty after suffering a heart attack. At the time of his death, Carlton was incoming president of the Mississippi Law Foundation and served the Webb-Sumner Methodist Church as a member of the board of stewards.[74] Eighty-year-old Jesse J. Breland, the oldest member of the team, died three years later, in 1969, at Washington County General Hospital in Greenville after a long illness.[75]

J. W. Kellum was one of three members of the defense team who lived for at least four decades after the trial and witnessed Mississippi's transformation to an integrated society. In 1979, he sat for an interview, alongside civil rights activist Amzie Moore, for the PBS series *Eyes on the Prize.* "As far as a fair trial is concerned," Kellum said, there was no proof that his clients "were the criminal agent." Had there been a conviction, he believed the Mississippi Supreme Court would have overturned it. Kellum said this during a new era, however, and he noted with pride that blacks now served on juries, and that more were practicing law. "I would say that Mississippi now is part of the New South."[76]

Kellum, a self-taught lawyer who never attended college, passed the state bar exam in 1939 and practiced law until his death in July 1996. A year before he died, Kellum insisted that, for him, the Till affair was "just another case over the desk." He said that he asked Milam and Bryant early on if they were guilty of the murder, and both denied that they were. "I believed them," he insisted, "just like I would if I was interrogating a client now. I would have no reason to think he's lying to me." Forty years after representing them, he claimed he still harbored doubts about their guilt. "I would have to see something. . . . But they told me they did not [commit the murder]. They told the other lawyers that they did not. I have not seen anything where it was supposed to have been an admission of guilt on their part."[77] Yet Kellum clearly contradicted an acknowledgment made during his 1979 *Eyes on the Prize* session that Milam admitted killing Till in *Look* magazine.[78] His stance sixteen years later may simply have been that of a good lawyer, who could not recall ever seeing the *Look* piece firsthand.

Any infamy Kellum received as a defense attorney in Sumner's famous murder case eventually faded, and his reputation as that of a good man came to the forefront. "Every day, if he could do something and make somebody happy, it made his day," said his wife upon his death. Kellum's motto was "Life's too short. I want to make somebody happy." Two surviving colleagues, both of whom worked alongside Kellum in the Till trial, praised their friend further. "J. W. Kellum diligently represented his many clients," said Harvey Henderson. "He was trusted and respected by the public and members of his profession." John Whitten described him "as a very charitable man. He did what he could do— without any publicity—just because he thought it was the right thing to do."[79]

In 1975, after the fall of Saigon, Kellum and his wife, Ruth, adopted a Vietnamese boy, Duong Nguyen. After Ruth died in 1992, Kellum married Eva Everett. His adopted son, as well as a biological one, Douglas L. Kellum, both became ministers and later presided over their father's funeral at the First Baptist Church in Tutwiler.[80]

John Whitten also practiced law until the end of his life. Betty Pearson, a Sumner resident angered by the acquittal, refused to speak to Whitten for over six months after the trial. Yet in 2006 she remembered him as "a wonderful man," one whom she remained close to for the rest of his life.[81]

At Breland's request, Whitten maintained the firm's name as Breland and Whitten after his partner's death. Whitten's son, John Whitten III, later replaced Breland. The senior Whitten occasionally talked to reporters about the Till case, and the message was sometimes mixed. For instance, he told a

Chicago journalist in 1985 that as a defense attorney, "You do what you have to do and stay within the limits that ethics required you to stay within." That same year, he told another reporter that he never asked Milam and Bryant about their guilt, explaining, "If I went to the moral heart of every case that came to me, I'd starve to death."[82] When asked by another researcher a decade and a half later if he had any regrets about defending the men, Whitten said frankly, "It didn't bother me at all."[83]

The right to defense is one thing; the long-term effect of injustice is quite another, however. In 1994, Whitten told another inquirer that he and his colleagues "suspected they [Milam and Bryant] were guilty the day they walked in here." This prompted a question from his visitor.

"Sir, were you proud of that case?"

"No I was not," answered Whitten candidly, yet seemingly contradicting what he had said before. "I've never been proud of it. Never have. Always wish I'd not been associated with it."[84]

Toward the end of his life, Whitten worked in his law office occasionally, but by then his son did the bulk of the firm's legal work. He had been suffering from Parkinson's disease since the late 1980s and died in February 2003.[85]

The last surviving member of the defense team was Harvey Henderson, who continued to practice law, albeit part-time, up until his death on October 7, 2007. Active in his local community, he was a lifelong member of the Sumner Rotary Club and had also served as its president. The West Tallahatchie School District retained him as its attorney for over fifty years, and he also served as the legal counsel for Mississippi's first chapter of Habitat for Humanity, which was formed in Tallahatchie County.

Outside of law, Henderson directed the Union Planters Bank of Mississippi and was a chairman of the local Red Cross. He was a commander of the American Legion, a Sunday school teacher, and a Sunday school superintendent at the Episcopal Church of the Advent in Sumner.[86] He refused all requests for interviews about the Till case.

Judge Curtis Swango remained on the bench of Mississippi's Seventeenth Judicial District for the next thirteen years. Three years after the Till murder, he presided over another racially charged case, this time in Water Valley. Thirty-six-year-old Yalobusha County sheriff J. G. Treloar had been charged with manslaughter in the beating death of Woodrow Daniels, a delivery man put in jail for bootlegging. It took an all-white jury only twenty-eight minutes to find the sheriff not guilty. The NAACP responded that the verdict "should indicate to negroes in Mississippi that they should expect no justice in Mississippi courts." Daniels's widow, Annie, vowed to leave the state out of fear for her life. Swango officiated over this trial with the same decorum he exhibited during the proceedings in Sumner.[87]

In 1968, a respiratory condition sent Swango to the hospital, followed by several months of treatment for tuberculosis at the Mississippi State Sanatorium in Simpson County. He died there on December 5, 1968. Divorced and without children, he was survived only by his mother and a brother. "He was widely praised for his conduct of the Emmett Till murder case in Tallahatchie County," noted his obituary, "and was recognized as one of the foremost trial judges in the state."[88]

The two sheriffs in the case remained active in the years after the kidnapping and murder, although each was completing his term at the time. After a solid effort in investigating the kidnapping and helping black journalists find witnesses, former Leflore County sheriff George Smith wanted to forget all about his role by the time a reporter asked him about it two years later. "I hate to even mention the case, it was the only thing to mar my four years in office," he said. "Don't quote me on anything. I don't want my name ever printed again in connection with the people involved in this case."[89]

Smith later served a second term as sheriff from 1964 until 1968. This time, he succeeded his former deputy John Cothran, who had helped with the kidnapping investigation and served as a witness for the prosecution.[90]

Smith, an avid outdoorsman, was a member of the Parker-Gary Hunting Club, and was planning a busy season when he died unexpectedly in 1975 at the age of seventy-two. Cothran outlived his former boss by over three decades, dying in 2008 at age ninety-four.[91]

Former Tallahatchie sheriff Henry Clarence Strider planned to run for the office again in 1959 after sitting out the required minimum of one term, but he changed his mind at the urging of his wife after he barely escaped an assassination attempt in 1957. While he sat in his car outside a store in the town of Cowart, someone fired a shot at his head, missing him, but striking the metal piece between the window and windshield. Strider claimed that the shooter had been sent down from Chicago by the NAACP for the express purpose of killing him, and that the would-be assassin was known to black workers living on Strider's plantation. Strider also maintained that the governor of Illinois refused to extradite the mysterious gunman back to Mississippi for trial, thus the entire matter was dropped. Still fearing for his life in 1963, Strider declined to run for his former job yet again.[92]

By 1962, Strider was chairman of the State Game and Fish Commission. In February of that year, state officials tried to keep black student James Meredith from registering at Ole Miss, and the defiance of the governor, Ross Barnett, made national news. Strider, ever the segregationist, announced during the conflict that 250 supervisors and game wardens were ready to aid Ole Miss in preserving its whites-only student body should they be needed.[93]

In February 1965, Strider won a special election to the state senate, where he represented Grenada, Yalobusha, and Tallahatchie Counties for the next five years. In addition to his role with the Game and Fish Commission, he was a member of the Public Property, Transportation, and Water and Irrigation Committees, and chairman of the Penitentiaries Committee.[94]

In July 1968, Strider admitted on the floor of the Mississippi Senate that he had paid for votes during his 1951 campaign for Tallahatchie County sheriff. Strider disclosed this as the Senate debated a bill that provided for absentee voting for teachers and students. "In those days you didn't win elections, you bought them," he told his colleagues. He said that he paid out a total of $30,000 for blank absentee ballots reserved for people who had indicated they would not be present on Election Day. Reporter Bill Minor, who knew the former sheriff, said years later that Strider had paid $25 to each of those willing to cast their ballot in his favor.[95]

Minor also recalled that once Strider was in the legislature, he was not the same man that the world saw in Sumner during the Till murder trial. Although he is remembered for regularly insulting the black journalists in the hot, crowded courtroom in Sumner, his election to the Senate after the Voting Rights Act of 1965 forced him to deal with a black constituency that finally had the power of the ballot. Yet Strider would have been happy to rid the Delta of its black citizens. In February 1966, he cosponsored a bill to relocate Mississippi blacks to other states, as a new farm bill was making it harder for laborers to earn a living. A proposed relocation commission would seek federal funds for the removal of those who wanted to go. "If they (Negro farm workers) feel like they are put upon or have to live in tents and opportunities are brighter somewhere else, we'll be glad to get them there," said Strider's cosponsor, Senator Robert Crook of Ruleville.[96] Nothing ever came of the proposal, however.

Like Sheriff Smith, Strider was a hunter. On December 27, 1970, Strider died of a heart attack while on a deer hunt in Issaqueena County; his body was shortly discovered by others.[97] Governor John Bell Williams flew to Clarksdale to attend the funeral. In 1981, a portion of Mississippi Highway 32 was designated the Henry Clarence Strider Memorial Highway.[98]

It is safe to say that J. W. Milam and Roy Bryant suffered in the years that followed their murder trial, despite the fact that they left Sumner as free men. Milam may have learned about a bizarre story that appeared in the black press shortly after his acquittal, but it is unknown what he thought of it. In October 1955, just a month after the trial, a black minister living in Detroit named Benjamin E. Love, thirty-three, told the *Michigan Chronicle* that Milam had murdered his brother, A. C. Love, back in 1949, when A.C. was helping Milam build a theater in Webb, Mississippi. According to Benjamin, after the two began quarreling over money, Milam shot A.C. and killed him. Milam allegedly told another brother, Clifton Love, that "I'll kill any nigger who argues with me about money."

Benjamin Love said he learned of this incident from his mother, Marie Love, in the early 1950s when he was a student at Leland College in Baber, Louisiana. Love also claimed that he had just recently traveled to Mississippi to move his sister and her family out of state when he learned that his mother, stepfather, and two siblings had been missing for six months, and that Milam was behind their mysterious disappearances. A sister, Gertrude, told Benjamin that the Love parents and siblings left the farm managed by Milam and moved to Arkansas. When Milam found out about it, he took a shotgun and a few friends and drove to the family's new home and took them back to Mississippi. Gertrude and Clifton Love saw Milam take their four family members out to the woods. They then heard screams as though they were being beaten, after which Milam returned without them. After several days, the sister asked Milam where her family had gone. He replied that they were "on a vacation."

Benjamin Love reported the disappearances to the FBI offices in Newark, New Jersey (his former home), and Detroit. The Department of Justice received the report in November and, for whatever reason, failed to act. Agents in Newark told Love not to speak about the case, but two months later, in January 1956, Love went public after he developed "a strange hunch that nothing is going to be done about it by the Justice Department." Love was now convinced that Milam had not only killed his brother A.C. in 1949 but in 1955 murdered the four additional family members whose bodies had never been found. "As a minister, I couldn't make a charge like that unless I was sure."[99] Nothing ever came of this story, however, and the black papers that initially reported it never pursued it further. Benjamin Love later moved to California, where he pastored the Union Missionary Baptist Church in Barstow from 1971 to 1974. He then moved to Inglewood, California, where he died in 1987. His brother Clifton died in Louisiana in 1980.[100] Efforts to find other family members to learn whether they clung to their accusations were unsuccessful.

A year after the Emmett Till murder, Milam was reported to be living on a farm between Ruleville and Cleveland, Mississippi.[101] Several months after that, William Bradford Huie interviewed the brothers for a follow-up article to his "confession" piece from a year before. It, too, appeared in *Look* magazine. In the accompanying photographs, both men appear happy, but it was obvious that the smiles were only a facade. Huie described them as having "been disappointed," explaining further, "They have suffered disillusionment, ingratitude, resentment, misfortune," but as yet, no guilt. Few had pity on them, even those who had earlier been supportive. Milam owned no land and could not get his former backers to rent to him. He was finally able to rent 217 acres in

Sunflower County with the help of his brother-in-law, and secured a $4,000 furnish (the funds to plant a cotton crop) from a Tallahatchie County bank where one of his defense attorneys, John Whitten, sat on the loan committee. Blacks would no longer work for Milam, and he was forced to pay higher wages to whites for the same work. "I had a lot of friends a year ago," he told Huie, reflecting on how the tide had turned.

> They contributed to my defense fund—at least they say they did. I never got half of what they say was contributed. I don't know what happened to it, but we never got it. Since then, some of those friends have been making excuses. I got letters from all over the country congratulating me for my "fine Americanism"; but I don't get that kind of letters any more. Everything's gone against me—even the weather, which has hurt my cotton. I'm living in a share-crop [house] without water in it. My wife and kids are having it hard.[102]

Huie also reported that Milam had been refused a gun permit. After the sheriff learned that Milam was carrying a firearm illegally, he made him give it up, despite Milam's claim that he had been threatened. Sunflower County sheriff E. W. Williams confirmed the report, saying that he told Milam that "no one has a right to carry a gun without a permit." Despite Milam's pleas, "I told him I had been threatened once or twice myself. I didn't see that he was in any danger."[103]

Williams also confirmed that after Milam took up residency near Doddsville, the sheriff's office had been involved in "an incident or two" with him, but Williams did not elaborate. Milam appears to have maintained his penchant for bootlegging, however. According to locals, in 1960 Milam learned of a whiskey still secluded in the eastern hills of Charleston in Tallahatchie County. He went to the spot, assembled it in his truck and trailer, and hauled it away in broad daylight on Highway 32 through Charleston's Main Street and into the town square. "To think of all we did for him," a Till trial juror said in 1962, "and he goes and does something like that." Milam was arrested but not prosecuted.[104]

Ygondine Sturdivant, longtime resident of the town of Glendora, recently recalled her own run-in with Milam not long after Milam's acquittal for murder. Ygondine was the wife of philanthropist Michael P. Sturdivant, who in December 1955 had offered to build Beulah Melton a home after Elmer Kimbell shot and killed Beulah's husband, Clinton, at a Glendora gas station.

Ygondine was working at the polls during a local election when Milam, whom she did not recognize, came in to vote. He told her that he also wanted a ballot for his wife.

"Is she parking the car?" Sturdivant asked, assuming she must be nearby.

"No, she's home. I also want to vote for my mother."

"Is she bedridden?"

"No, she's fine. I've always done it this way. I've always voted for my family," Milam explained.

Sturdivant knew this was a common, yet illegal, practice, but she was determined not to let it happen under her watch. When she refused Milam's request for multiple ballots, he got angry and demanded to talk to her boss, a man by the name of Love.

"Mr. Love isn't here right now," Sturdivant told him.

"I will be back," shouted Milam. "You can count on that!"

When Love returned, Sturdivant told him about the big, angry voter she had just turned away. Love then checked the books and noticed the man's name.

"Do you know who that was? It was J. W. Milam!"

Sturdivant was shocked but had no regrets about holding firm to the law, even when up against someone as intimidating and notorious as Milam.[105]

For three years after the trial, Milam held several menial plantation jobs. In 1958, he was living in a tenant house on a plantation owned by Citizens' Council member J. E. Branton in Greenville. On Valentine's Day, the *New York Post* reported that Milam had been seen standing in a bread line waiting to receive rations from the Welfare Department. The *Pittsburgh Courier*, a black weekly newspaper, picked up on the story also. The director of the Washington County welfare department would not confirm or deny the *Post* report, but Milam adamantly declared it to be false. Despite admitting to hard times a year earlier when talking to Huie, Milam bluntly told an inquiring reporter for *Jet* magazine, "Quote me as saying the *New York Post* is a goddam liar. I'm standing here with'a ass-pocket full of money." Also contradicting what he had told Huie, he insisted, "Everybody in Mississippi has been nice to me." However, "the northern papers have talked about me enough and I'm tired of it." Temporarily disabled with a broken leg, Milam admitted that he had applied for unemployment compensation a few months earlier but had been turned down. "They said a broken leg wasn't reason enough for it. I don't know why." Poor weather had hurt his crops, and he was not working at all, but he claimed that he was about to start a new job managing another plantation.[106]

The Milams later moved to Orange, Texas, but returned to Greenville after only a few years. On Easter Sunday, 1962, Juanita Milam and her five siblings hosted a fiftieth wedding anniversary dinner for her parents, Albert and Myrtle Thompson, at the Thompson home on Purcell Street. Myrtle died the following year while J. W. and Juanita were still living in Texas, but before Albert died in 1965, they returned to Mississippi to help care for him. They would make their home at 615 Purcell Street in Greenville, near the Thompsons, where J. W. would live out the rest of his life. The house was a converted black Methodist church.[107]

Milam would have a few run-ins with the law while living in Greenville. On January 6, 1969, he was convicted in city court for writing a bad check, and fined $55. Three years later, on April 12, 1972, the same court fined him $300 and sentenced him to sixty days in jail for using a stolen credit card. Four months after that, he was convicted of assault and battery, fined $30, and sentenced to ten days in jail.[108]

By the time the Milams returned to Mississippi a decade after the Till trial, the outrage over the murder had subsided, and they were able to live quietly, for the most part. Milam eventually found work as a heavy equipment operator, but that ended due to declining health. A neighbor, Maude Carter, temporarily housed friends at her home at 613 Purcell from June to November 1978 while they were getting ready to buy their own home. The father of that family recalls that the Milams were the only white people living in the neighborhood. J. W. and Juanita's children went to visit periodically, but J. W. seemed passive and stayed to himself. He did not interact with people on the street and spent much of his time outside on the porch. His German shepherd, who roamed the yard enclosed by a chain-link fence, was trained to bark and lunge "like he would tear your head off" if someone walked by while the dog was within the yard area that led to the front door. If the dog was inside the gated area near the driveway, passersby could walk by the house without any reaction from the animal. "I've never seen a dog trained like that in my life," recalled the former neighbor.

As to Milam's life in the black section of Greenville, "That was his place and he seemed satisfied to live there and die there," said the neighbor. Milam appeared to be a shell of the man once so intimidating that he could coax his field hands into helping with murder.[109]

Clearly Milam's health was declining at that time. After a very long and painful illness, he succumbed to cancer two years later on New Year's Eve, 1980, at age sixty-one.[110] He and Juanita were rumored to have divorced at some point, but this was not true. Their marriage was probably not a happy one, however, and the couple maintained separate bedrooms.[111]

Because J. W. never held a permanent job, Juanita began working as a hairdresser at the Greenville Beauty Salon in the 1960s. In 1971, National Beauty Salon week was proclaimed for February 14–20 by Greenville mayor Pat Dunne, and Juanita served as chairwoman. Local Affiliate No. 3 of the Mississippi Hairdressers and Cosmetologists Association sold raffle tickets for a television to raise money for a dialysis machine for Washington County Hospital. In 1975, Juanita served as president of the affiliate. The group raffled off another television that year, this time helping the American Cancer Society.

Juanita told readers of the *Delta Democrat-Times* that the winner need not be present at the April 15 drawing to be held at the Delta Beauty College. Clearly, Juanita felt at ease in her local community. She continued to work at the salon until owner Thelma Wood retired and closed the shop around 1990.[112]

Although she enjoyed a long and steady career, Juanita's life was never the same after the murder of Emmett Till, and she appeared genuinely sad most of the time. Her depression had not been a part of her life prior to the notorious lynching that thrust her family into the spotlight. Despite her personal suffering, she was generous with her family and friends and managed to maintain many of her lifelong interests. She was an avid reader and football fan. An active Methodist, she bought a keyboard and learned to play a few hymns to help her congregation enjoy the benefits of music.[113]

Juanita never remarried after J. W.'s death, nor did she allow herself any further romance. She later sold her home on Purcell Street and moved in with a sister, Carrie Clements, who was widowed in 1984. They later moved together to Ocean Springs, Mississippi, where they lived together in a home Juanita purchased on Old Spanish Trail Road.[114]

After J. W.'s death, Juanita became estranged from Roy and Carolyn Bryant, and they never spoke again. In fact, Juanita and Carolyn (whom Juanita always described as a "drama queen") never considered themselves friends, even before the Emmett Till murder. They saw each other, but did not speak, at the funeral of Milam and Bryant sibling Dan Milam, who died in 1999. Juanita stormed out of the service after Milam and Bryant family members became involved in a confrontation over blame in Emmett Till's death.[115]

Juanita, who was politically liberal, maintained interracial friendships, and her best friend for many years was a black neighbor woman. Juanita suffered a stroke in 2008, and in October of that year, her oldest son, Horace "Bill" Milam, died at age fifty-seven. After several years of declining health, Juanita died in Ocean Springs on January 14, 2014, at age eighty-six. Although she and J. W. had purchased double plots at the Greenlawn Memorial Gardens in Greenville, Juanita was buried in Ocean Springs.[116]

The simple obituary of J. W. Milam that appeared in 1980 escaped media attention. Roy Bryant's death, which came in 1994, would have gone unnoticed as well had it not been for the astute eye of journalist Bill Minor. Minor published a piece that noted Bryant's role in the Till case soon after the *Memphis Commercial Appeal*, and Bryant's local paper, the *Bolivar Commercial*, each ran short, standard obituaries.[117]

Bryant's life, like that of his half-brother J. W., was filled with hardship. After a boycott by blacks forced the closure of his store three weeks after his release from jail, the family moved in with Carolyn's mother in Indianola in Sunflower County. There, Roy reportedly found work as a mechanic. After laboring at odd jobs for seventy-five cents a day, he attended welding school nine miles away in Inverness at the Bell Machine Shop. "Roy'll have it tough," predicted Milam in 1956. "It takes a long time to learn welding and by the time you've learned it, you've ruined your eyes." He was right. In 1985, Bryant reported to the *Jackson Clarion-Ledger* that he was, in fact, legally blind. He suffered from optic nerve degeneration in both eyes, and his left eye was further damaged after a small piece of steel became lodged in it.[118]

Bryant had other ambitions before settling on welding school. In May 1956, the *Delta Democrat-Times*, responding to rumors that Bryant had become an Indianola policeman, learned that he had sought a job with the local force, but was turned away. "He applied with us," confirmed Indianola police chief Will Love, "but he does not work here."[119]

Six months later on November 19, Roy and Carolyn Bryant were riding as passengers in a car driven by Carolyn's eighteen-year-old brother, James Holloway, in Greenville, when they were involved in a head-on collision at about 1:45 A.M. The second vehicle was driven by a black airman named William Macon, who was stationed at Greenville Air Force Base. The Bryants and Macon were all treated for minor injuries at Greenville's General Hospital and released. The four-paragraph article reporting the accident mentioned nothing of the Bryants' notoriety in the Till case, although the *Chicago Defender* shortly learned of the story and reported that fact.[120] That same day, perhaps for reasons brought on by the accident, Carolyn gave birth to her third son, Frankie Lee.[121]

By the fall of 1957, Roy was working as a welder in Morgan City, Louisiana. The Bryants shortly moved to Orange, Texas, where daughter Carol Ann was born on August 14, 1959. Because Carolyn had been sick with the measles during her pregnancy, Carol Ann was born deaf. Sometime later, the family relocated to Vinton, Louisiana, just thirteen miles away, where Roy continued to weld for a steel company. They bought a home there and lived in Vinton until returning to Mississippi in 1973 at the encouragement of Roy's mother, Eula Bryant. For a time, Carolyn's mother, Francis "Frankie" Jones, lived with them in Vinton in a converted apartment in the garage.[122]

The Bryants tried to live a normal, low-key life, and, at one level, succeeded. Their three boys were typical youngsters, regularly bringing home snakes, snails, and lizards, all to the horror of Carolyn, who hated such creatures.[123] Roy Jr. graduated from Vinton High School in 1970, where he played football. He shortly married, and his wife gave birth to the couple's first child, a daughter, in June 1971. This made Roy Sr. a grandfather at age forty and Carolyn a grandmother at thirty-six. Thomas Lamar, a member of the school band, graduated in 1972 and immediately joined the air force. Carol Ann attended the Louisiana School for the Deaf in Baton Rouge from 1965 to 1973.[124]

When Roy, Carolyn, and the two youngest children left Louisiana in 1973 and returned to Mississippi, they relocated to Ruleville, in Sunflower County. Roy went back into the grocery business by taking over a small store that had been run by family members. Son Frank, a football player at North Sunflower Academy, earned his high school diploma in 1975. Carol Ann began attending the Mississippi School for the Deaf in Jackson, but spent every other weekend and holidays at home. She graduated in 1979.[125]

At some point, Roy and Carolyn Bryant's marriage developed serious problems, and it became unbearable for Carolyn. Even her mother-in-law, Eula Bryant, saw it. Eula, whom Carolyn described as tough and outspoken, asked Carolyn in front of Roy many times why she stayed married to him.[126] Eula died in August 1974. A year later on August 15, one day after Carol Ann's sixteenth birthday and one day before Lamar's twenty-second, Carolyn left Roy, and two months after that, she filed for divorce. Their divorce papers describe Roy as having been guilty of "habitual cruel and inhuman treatment of her and of habitual drunkenness." Perhaps Roy's demons had concerned his mother because she had once endured similar abuses from her second husband, Henry Bryant. Carolyn asked for sole custody of Carol Ann, the complaint read, because "said child needs the care and guidance which only a devoted mother can give." Roy failed to dispute any of the allegations. When the divorce was finalized two months later on October 28, 1975, sole custody of Carol Ann went to Carolyn. Roy was granted visitation rights and ordered to pay $75 per month in child support beginning November 1. A lump sum of $6,300 for alimony was due by December 1.[127]

After their return to Mississippi, the Bryants managed to continue a low-profile existence, despite living in close proximity to the site of the Till murder. In fact, in 1977, both Roy and his brother James Bryant were listed as two of five challengers to Ruleville's incumbent aldermen. In the end, the brothers lost, each receiving the least number of votes of all the candidates. James garnered 53, while Roy received only 45. The winners received between 270 and 530 votes.[128] A black man who lived in Ruleville as a youth in the 1980s and saw a film about the Till case in school was shocked to see footage showing Roy Bryant as an accused killer. He had always known Bryant only as a local grocer.[129]

In 1979, Carol Ann graduated from her school in Jackson. One year later on May 17, 1980, ironically, the twenty-sixth anniversary of the *Brown v. Board of Education* decision, Roy married Vera Jo Orman, an accountant at the Mississippi State Penitentiary at Parchman. They remained in Ruleville.[130]

In 1978, Roy Bryant lost his permit to accept food stamps for one year because he was allowing customers to purchase nonfood items with their coupons. In 1982, the inspector general's office of the US Department of

Agriculture learned that Bryant had been purchasing food stamps at a discount for cash and then selling them back to the government at full value. On several occasions between September 2 and December 8, 1982, Special Agent David L. Thomas went to Bryant's store undercover and received cash for hundreds of dollars in food stamps. In October 1983, Bryant was indicted on five counts of food stamp fraud, pleaded not guilty, and was scheduled for a December trial. On December 7, however, Bryant changed his plea to guilty on two counts in exchange for the government dropping the others. He attended a hearing on December 13 in Greenville, Mississippi, presided over by Judge William C. Keady. Before accepting the plea bargain, Judge Keady told Bryant that officers of the probation service would "check out your family, your educational and work background, whether or not you have a criminal record," and would seek to learn "your reputation in the local community from which you come." On February 3, Bryant returned to court for sentencing, and through the pleadings of his attorney, he was given a three-year probation and a $750 fine. Bryant had retained state senator Robert L. Crook of Ruleville as his counsel. Crook had been H. C. Strider's cosponsor of the 1966 bill that proposed to relocate Mississippi's blacks out of state.

Crook told the court that fifty-three-year-old Bryant "is a good citizen of Ruleville, who is disabled and has been in very poor health a number of years, who has attempted to work despite that circumstance, and to be gainfully employed in the course of running his own store." He was caring for both his wife and disabled sister and was an honorably discharged veteran of the army. As to the charges against him, however, "He knows he has made a mistake." Bryant promised to obey the law respecting food stamp regulations going forward.

"Your honor, sir," Bryant said to Judge Keady, "I wouldn't care if I never saw another food stamp."

"All right. It may come to that. I don't know," Keady responded, after which the courtroom erupted in laughter.[131]

Despite his brief moment of humility and penitence, Bryant found himself unable to resist the temptation to repeat the same violations only a few years later. On February 12, 1987, he was again caught purchasing food stamps at a cash discount, and this time, his sister, Mary Louise Campbell, who worked as a cashier at the store, was indicted along with him the following September as a co-conspirator on six counts of food stamp fraud. Bail was set for Bryant at $10,000 and for Campbell at $5,000. Campbell pleaded guilty to one count on November 23, and Bryant pleaded guilty on two counts. Campbell did not receive any prison time, but Bryant, having been convicted four years earlier for the same crime, received a two-year prison sentence and was ordered to turn himself in to the attorney general on April 4, 1988.

Bryant's attorney, John Hatcher, argued for a thirty-day extension so that Bryant could finish converting his store into an apartment building in order that his family might receive income during his incarceration. Bryant also wanted time to train people to run his tree-spraying business during his absence. Judge Glen H. Davidson denied the motion, and Bryant went to prison as scheduled at the federal facility at Fort Worth, Texas. A month later, Hatcher entered a motion that Bryant's sentence be reduced. Since Bryant began his prison sentence, the family had lost income and could not make up for it without Bryant's contribution. Also, "the Defendant is advanced in age, legally blind and has numerous other physical ailments which will not be adequately provided for or properly nurtured in the absence of constant supervision by his family members." Hatcher believed that Bryant either should receive probation, be placed in a supervised work-release program, or have his two consecutive one-year terms changed to two concurrent one-year terms. On August 21, 1989, Davidson denied the motion. In the end, Bryant only served eight months of his term.[132]

Having lived past the thirtieth anniversary of the Till murder when interest in the case reemerged, Bryant received several requests for interviews. He would grant them in varying degrees, but always refused to say much about the case. In 1985, between his two federal convictions, Chicagoans saw film coverage of an aging, overweight, and uncooperative Bryant escorting a WMAQ correspondent from Bryant's Ruleville store. That same year, reporters from the *Jackson Clarion-Ledger* paid Bryant a visit. Fearing belated revenge, he refused to let them photograph either him or his store. "This new generation is different and I don't want to worry about a bullet some dark night. This store is all I have now, that and my disability check."[133]

When speaking to the *Clarion-Ledger* reporters, Bryant sent mixed messages about his role in the Till murder. "I don't know what happened to Emmett Till. I didn't admit to it then. You don't expect me to admit to do it now," he said. Yet he added one caveat, reminding his visitors that the law "couldn't do anything to me if I did." Although he maintained his innocence, he said that "for a bunch of money," he might be willing to talk. He did not elaborate, but insisted that the Chicago teen brought about his own demise. "If Emmett Till hadn't got out of line, it probably wouldn't have happened to him." When pressed by those same reporters, Bryant seemed to show a little remorse about the murder, but even that is not entirely clear. "You mean do I wish I might wouldn't have done it? I'm just sorry that it happened."[134]

That same year, Clotye Murdock Larsson, former reporter for *Ebony* magazine, wrote a sequel to her 1955 article, "Land of the Till Murder," appropriately titled, "Land of the Till Murder Revisited." She and her guide, NAACP officer Cleve McDowell, visited Bryant at Bryant's store, but he refused her request for an interview, saying that he could no longer "trust" reporters. The *Clarion-Ledger* piece, he insisted, had "misquoted me. Claimed I said *money* would jog my memory. I never said nothin' like that. I don't wanta be hard, but this thing has hurt me."[135]

Four years later, Bryant's store was burned down by white arsons, and, having no insurance, he suffered a loss that he estimated to be around $75,000. He opened up a fireworks store near his home, which operated only seasonally, and began selling watermelons out of the back of his truck. He also made money renting his rundown housing units to blacks. On August 24, 1992, thirty-seven years to the day after Emmett Till's encounter with Carolyn Bryant, Roy was again asked the one question that always agitated him. Did he kill Emmett Till?

"Hell no, I didn't do it."

Bryant was puzzled that scholars still viewed him as a criminal. Yet, despite his denials of murder, he hinted that back in 1955, he had a motive to kill.

"Are they saying a man doesn't have the right to protect his wife? A man's got to do what has to be done."

He insisted that he got along well with blacks, did not mistreat them, and would not allow them to mistreat him. "Hell, I got some right here, I guarantee you, would fight for me in a minute." Yet he believed that blacks "still don't know how to act in front of white women." Because of that belief, he refused to permit his second wife to walk alone in the black sections of Ruleville.

Bryant attended the initial town meeting of the administration of Shirley Edwards, Ruleville's first black mayor, and complained of burglaries at his fireworks store and poor performance by police in stopping them. Reminiscent of his actions in his most famous dirty deed, Bryant had no trouble taking the law into his own hands and threatened to do so. "If I catch one out there this big [raising his hands two-and-a-half feet off the floor] I'm going to twist his damn head off." Edwards did not hesitate in telling a reporter that "Bryant is a vicious man," and was bewildered that so many black citizens in town seemed to forgive him of his past. "If my people did not deal or trade with him, he couldn't stay here."[136]

Bryant began battling cancer and diabetes, and not long before his death was left with large lumps growing on his neck and throat. Beginning around September 1993, he underwent radiation treatments for the next year and lost thirty-five pounds. He lived just long enough to learn of the 1994 conviction of Byron De La Beckwith for the 1963 murder of Medgar Evers, and wondered if he (Bryant) was really safe from further prosecution over the Till case. One reason he refused to discuss the case was because he feared that the government might change the Constitution and try him again.[137] But that was probably the least of his worries. John Whitten, who had helped defend Bryant in Sumner so many years earlier, said that in early 1994 Bryant came to Whitten's office, unannounced. "I don't think I'd seen him since the trial. He had to identify himself. He looked terrible. 'I'm old,' he said. 'I'm sick. I can't work.' He wondered if there was anything I could do for him. I told him, 'I don't know, only thing I can tell you, do what you did before: Trade with some of those who might want to write a book about you.' He left and then about six months later he was dead."[138]

Two months before his death he spoke for two hours to a reporter from Florida's *Palm Beach Post*, but refused to say much about the Till case. He again denied that he had anything to do with the murder and matter-of-factly said, "I have no idea" who killed the Chicago youth when the reporter asked. Bryant believed that his acquittal in the Till case meant that people should leave that past alone. The case that brought him worldwide notoriety in 1955 was, to him, "just something in the past. You have to leave it alone, live your life. You can't just sit around and cry over spilt milk." His frustration was caused in part by the occasional threats he received from crank callers. "They say: 'We don't like what you did a few years ago. We're comin' over to get you.' I say, 'Well, bring your goddamn ass on over—what's taking you so long?'"[139]

Bryant died of cancer on September 1, 1994, at the Baptist Hospital in Jackson. When Vera Jo Bryant died in May 2012, her obituary mentioned nothing about her marriage to Roy, and only listed her parents and a brother as family members who had preceded her in death. She was, however, buried next to her infamous husband to whom she was married for fourteen years.[140]

Carolyn Bryant is perhaps frozen in memory as the twenty-one-year-old local beauty working behind a counter in a country store where Emmett Till fatefully crossed her path in 1955. She turned eighty years old in July 2014 and has, for decades, been a devoted mother and grandmother. She remains extremely grateful for both her immediate and extended family.[141] She is equally loved in return by her posterity.

Like Mamie Bradley, Carolyn experienced the pain of losing a child, or, in her case, two. In September 1995, her firstborn, Roy Bryant Jr., passed away of cystic fibrosis. In April 2010, Frank, her youngest son, died of heart failure. Carolyn gives thanks to God that Frank's suffering was minimal. Her faith sustained her through these two losses, and she believes her sons are now together. She places God first and her children second in her life.[142]

Two months after Frank's death, Carolyn put her home in Greenville up for sale and moved to Raleigh, North Carolina, to live with her surviving son, Lamar. She took along her dog, Maggie, a sixteen-year-old Shih Tzu. By July 2012, Maggie had died, but Lamar surprised his mother with another Shih

Tzu that Carolyn named Jack. She has since moved to her own apartment in Raleigh.[143]

Lasting romantic love has eluded Carolyn, however. After her divorce from Roy Bryant in 1975, she remarried at least twice and had another relationship with a man (last name Wren), with whom she lived for a time. On November 21, 1984, she wed Greenville resident Griffin Chandler, an employee at US Gypsum. The marriage ended three and a half years later with Chandler's death.[144] The widowed Carolyn soon married again, this time to former Leland police officer David Donham. In 1988, Carolyn began attending Mississippi Delta Junior College in Moorhead and took classes as a part-time student until 1990. Other than working in her husband's two stores in Money and Ruleville, however, Carolyn never worked outside the home but was content to be a stay-at-home mother. The Donhams lived in Brookhaven for a time, but eventually divorced, and David remarried and later died in 2002. With the help of her brother, Thomas Holloway, Carolyn moved into a small home in Brookhaven after her divorce, where she lived until Thomas died in 2000. After that, she returned to Greenville to be near Frank.[145]

In June 2010, Carolyn joined the social networking site Facebook, under the username "Granny Pike" (after her mother's maiden name), which kept her actual identity hidden. In mid-2014, however, she was forced to close her account because strangers figured out who she was and began to harass her online. Five months after first joining Facebook, however, she both posed and answered the question as to what constitutes the real qualities in a man. Her answer was that he must be ethical and stand up for a good cause. If this seemed to hint of her first husband's attempt to preserve the sanctity of her white womanhood, which propelled both her and him into the spotlight, she was quick to add that a real man will respect others and refrain from bullying.[146] With the encouragement of her daughter-in-law, Marsha Bryant, Carolyn agreed to write her memoir, in which she would tell her side of the painful Till story. However, the emotional trauma surrounding the case and the effect it has had on her made it difficult to continue. Frank Bryant's death in 2010 also took a major toll on her and helped squash the effort. She also suffers from rheumatoid arthritis, which has greatly diminished her physical health. In 2014, she moved back in temporarily with Lamar and his family, who have diligently cared for her during her suffering.[147]

Carolyn has said almost nothing publicly about the Till murder in sixty years, never discussing it with her siblings or extended family members, but had said that the case has kept her a prisoner. For this reason, she has generally avoided social situations out of fear and has preferred to stay home. She has long been the victim of harassment by people who believe she is in some way responsible for Emmett Till's death or otherwise condoned his murder. She has consistently avoided watching any of the documentaries or other television coverage of the Emmett Till case.[148]

For historians, her silence has been frustrating. For many followers of the case, it implies that she has something to hide at best or is suppressing the guilt of an accomplice at worst. It may be, however, that her silence has simply been her attempt at making this painful episode of her past go away.

Some of these people in the Till saga would live long enough to see the case reemerge in the public consciousness after the mid-1980s. None, however, could have predicted a series of events that would one day come to pass, all of which represented an era of healing and renewal. An unanticipated quest for justice would be followed by a second gathering outside the courthouse in Sumner, Mississippi, fifty-two years after that first one in September 1955. It would rival in size the hostile and segregated crowds that had gathered during that sweltering week a half-century earlier, but this time the mood was different. The chain of events that led to this Second Coming in Sumner were years in the making but long overdue, and they followed a complete investigation of the case by the FBI early in the new millennium. That story is next.

PART TWO

In Living Color

11

Revival

On July 11, 1985, at 6:30 P.M., Chicago's NBC affiliate, WMAQ-Channel 5, premiered a half-hour documentary on the Emmett Till case called *The Murder and the Movement*. Written and narrated by reporter Rich Samuels, it was the first of its kind. Samuels had grown up in Chicago's North Shore area but had learned next to nothing about Emmett Till. This changed when he met Mamie Till-Mobley on November 24, 1984, at the funeral of Ben Wilson, a local high school basketball star gunned down four days earlier. Samuels became curious about Mamie's story and began researching the Till case in old newspapers. Inspired by what he learned, he set out to make a film.[1]

With the thirty-year anniversary of the case approaching, Samuels found and interviewed many of the principals in the story. The program featured Mamie, a few journalists who covered the trial, a juror, one defense attorney, and even an attempted interview with Roy Bryant. Samuels was also the first reporter in decades to seek out Wheeler Parker and Simeon Wright. Samuels spoke with random Chicagoans about their memories or knowledge of the fourteen-year-old lynching victim, and their answers were surprising. "Emmett Till? I've never heard of him," said one bewildered black man. Another shook his head in puzzlement when asked what he knew about the Chicago boy who had died so violently three decades earlier. Samuels found that this unfamiliarity was common in the very city where tens of thousands had once filed past Emmett Till's open casket.[2]

In Mississippi, the *Jackson Clarion-Ledger* and *Jackson Daily News*, which published their Sunday editions together, jointly ran anniversary coverage a month later. As in Chicago, memories had faded or held no knowledge at all about Emmett Till. Sumner's town clerk, Bonnie Cheshier, told reporter Joe Atkins that she had never heard of the case, despite the fact that she had lived in town for thirteen years. Like Samuels, reporters in Mississippi spoke with Till-Mobley, Parker, Wright, and Bryant.[3]

At one level, it is hardly a surprise that these Chicagoans and Deltans were uninformed about Emmett Till. Other than Stephen Hugh Whitaker's 1963 master's thesis and an article or two in professional journals, nothing of significance had been written about the case by historians and scholars.[4] However, it had received attention from artistic voices over the years, a strong indication that there was still lingering pain and plenty of healing to be done. Original poems, which began appearing in newspapers even before the murder trial began, are numerous. Less than two months after the acquittal of J. W. Milam and Roy Bryant, Langston Hughes and Jobe Huntley wrote "The Money, Mississippi Blues." Aaron Kramer and Clyde Appleton penned "Blues for Emmett Till," which was published in the November 7, 1955, issue of *Sing Out!* The first song recorded and released as a 78 RPM was by a group calling themselves the Ramparts, featuring Scatman Crothers on vocals. Titled "The Death of Emmett Till," the lyrics were first published in the *California Eagle* in December 1955. The record went on sale the following month.[5]

The most enduring of these early songs came in 1962, and it had name recognition. Given the same title as the Rampart tune, Bob Dylan's "Death of Emmett Till" fit well within the brand of protest lyrics for which Dylan was known, and was even recorded by folksinger Joan Baez a year later. Poet Gwendolyn Brooks, the first black woman to win the Pulitzer Prize, also published two pieces about Till. "A Bronzeville Mother Loiters in Mississippi. Meanwhile, a Mississippi Mother Burns Bacon" appeared in 1960, as did "The Last Quatrain of the Ballad of Emmett Till."[6]

Artistic contributions were not only made in poetry and song but on television and the stage as well. These proved controversial. Rod Serling, who in 1959 would bring *The Twilight Zone* to television, tried just months after the Till trial to dramatize the story in a TV script about a southern racial lynching. "Noon at Tuesday," slated to air on the ABC series *The United States Steel Hour*, was too risky for television executives, however. Fearing that a growing southern television audience would boycott advertisers, network officials forced Serling to rewrite the script and remove any similarities to the Till case. The revised version aired in April 1956. The following year, another network gave Serling the chance to tell the story his way, but once again, opposition forced him to strip the script of anything related to Emmett Till. In the end, it was retooled as a 1940s murder set in a town on the Mexican border. "Noon at Tuesday" became "A Town Has Turned to Dust," and aired on CBS's *Playhouse 90* in June 1958. It was turned into a television movie in 1988.[7]

In 1964, forty-year-old novelist James Baldwin published his play *Blues for Mister Charlie*, which centered on the story of a young black man, Richard Henry, who was murdered by a southern redneck. The killer was subsequently acquitted. Baldwin noted in the preface that his work had been based "very distantly" on the Till case. Dedicated to Medgar Evers, the Evers family, and the children killed in the 1963 Birmingham, Alabama, church bombings, *Mister Charlie* ran on Broadway from April through the end of August 1964. What

Serling could not show to a television audience, Baldwin portrayed from the stage, yet not without criticism. "Mr. Baldwin knows how the Negroes think and feel," wrote a reviewer in the *New York Times* following the premier at the ANTA Theater, "but his inflexible, Negro-hating Southerners are stereotypes. Southerners may talk and behave as he suggests, but in the theater they are caricatures."[8]

Between Serling's attempt to highlight the South's dark side and Baldwin's success in doing so, the southern race issue made its way to the movies when Harper Lee's 1960 novel, *To Kill a Mockingbird*, was adapted for the big screen in 1962. Stark similarities have been noted between the trial in Sumner and the courtroom drama in the case of Tom Robinson, a black man defended against rape charges by country lawyer Atticus Finch.[9] Even if none were intended, audiences were less shocked to see the racial inequities of a Dixie trial portrayed on film because most had already lived through press coverage of J. W. Milam's and Roy Bryant's murder trial in the Mississippi Delta seven years earlier.

Over the next two decades, artists produced more about Emmett Till, but the overall offerings are scant. One must scour hard to find Julius E. Thompson's 1977 poem, "Till," published in the anthology *Blues Said: Walk On*. Four years later, "Afterimages," by poet-activist Audre Lourde, appeared.[10]

Fast-forward once again to 1985. A week before the Samuels documentary aired in Chicago, the thirty-year anniversary of the Till case received national attention on NBC's *Today* show. On July 3, Mamie Till-Mobley appeared on the program, alongside Bill Minor, the Mississippi reporter who had covered the 1955 trial for the *New Orleans Times-Picayune*. Roy Bryant watched and taped the program, and was amused to hear host Bryant Gumbel ask, "Whatever happened to Roy Bryant and J. W. Milam?"[11]

Although the three-minute *Today* segment, which included a few clips from the Samuels film, was hardly substantive, it signified, together with *The Murder and the Movement* and the *Clarion-Ledger* and *Jackson Daily News* articles, that interest in the Till story was reemerging. A new generation would come to know about this pivotal moment in far greater numbers beginning January 21, 1987, when the first episode of a six-part series, *Eyes on the Prize: America's Civil Rights Years*, premiered on PBS. Produced by Henry Hampton's company, Blackside, the documentary was nineteen years in the making and cost $2.5 million, money secured from over forty-five different sponsors. Blackside's team of twenty-five researchers interviewed over 1,000 people for the series, many in just a ten-day period at the John F. Kennedy Library in Boston.[12] The opening segment, "Awakenings," devoted fifteen minutes to the Emmett Till case and showed newsreel footage that most people had never seen. Those interviewed for the piece included Till's cousin Curtis Jones (whose claimed eyewitness account of the Bryant store incident was, unfortunately, fabricated), former congressman Charles Diggs Jr., reporter James Hicks, novelist-journalist William Bradford Huie, and Rev. Fred Shuttlesworth. Others, such as defense attorney J. W. Kellum and Bryant store witness Ruthie Mae Crawford Jackson, were also interviewed, but their stories were cut from the film entirely.[13]

By the time of its premiere, *Eyes on the Prize* was already being hailed as "a television classic, likely to endure as long as whites and blacks live together in America." Just before the first episode aired, Hampton explained how he had long envisioned the series and the place of the Till case within the civil rights movement. "I knew what those [episodes] should be, [and] Emmett Till was the first thing I wanted to have." Civil rights leader Julian Bond, who served as an adviser for the project, narrated all six episodes, off camera, although Hampton gave him a choice to appear on screen. Juan Williams, at that time a reporter for the *Washington Post*, took a sabbatical from the paper in 1985 to write a companion volume to the series, working closely with Hampton's Boston production team.[14]

Both the book and the videocassette release of *Eyes on the Prize* became available a few months apart in 1987. The series, which attracted over five million viewers during its original television run, became popular in college classrooms. Its significance can also be measured by the fact that a Trenton, New Jersey, federal judge ordered a man convicted of burning a cross on the lawn of a black family to view the series with the aim that he develop some level of penitence. *Eyes on the Prize* went on to win four Emmy Awards, a Peabody Award for excellence in broadcast journalism, the International Documentary Award, and the Television Critics Award. It was even nominated for an Academy Award after a brief theatrical release. An eight-part sequel, *Eyes on the Prize: America at the Racial Crossroads*, released in 1990, was similarly honored, winning two Emmys, a Peabody, and three Golden Eagle Awards. It, too, was narrated by Bond.[15]

With the foundation laid by the first *Eyes on the Prize* series, works that focused exclusively on Emmett Till followed. In 1988, Brandeis University professor Stephen Whitfield published the first full-length book on the case, *A Death in the Delta: The Story of Emmett Till*. Whitfield, a southerner himself, first learned of Till's death in *Look* magazine in January 1956 when he was just thirteen years old.[16] In 1994, Clenora Hudson-Weems, an English professor at the University of Missouri–Columbia, published a revision of her 1988 PhD dissertation as *Emmett Till: Sacrificial Lamb of the Civil Rights Movement*, which argued that Till's death was the catalyst for the organized struggle for equality that began just months after the murder.[17]

These works were groundbreaking in many respects. Yet what was missing was a quest for answers, because no one seemed to understand that there were still relevant questions. Studies of the Till case thus far had focused on the horrors of Jim Crow, the racial elements and brutality of the murder itself, and the fact that the accused and tried perpetrators were freed. In his 1963 thesis, Stephen Hugh Whitaker considered the testimony of Willie Reed, which claimed that others were involved, but Whitaker concluded that William Bradford Huie was correct in maintaining that Milam and Bryant had acted alone. Neither Samuels's *The Murder and the Movement* nor Hampton's *Eyes on the Prize* noted that others may have played a role in the killing, although the names of most of Milam's and Bryant's alleged accomplices had appeared in the press at the time of the trial and were known. Whitfield and Hudson-Weems addressed this issue only peripherally.[18]

Although Mamie Till-Mobley went on with life and kept her son's memory alive in local circles through the Emmett Till Foundation and the Emmett Till Players, she never forgot the acquittal in Sumner. In fact, she had always wanted to reverse that injustice in some way. Even though Milam was dead, and Bryant could not be tried again on state charges, she remained optimistic that a probe of some kind was still a possibility. The spark that ignited her hope that justice might be forthcoming occurred in 1990 after prosecutors in Jackson, Mississippi, began a fresh probe into the 1963 murder of civil rights leader Medgar Evers. Two hung juries had kept Evers's killer, Byron De La Beckwith, a free man for twenty-seven years, but because there had never been an acquittal, a third trial remained a possibility.[19]

On December 14, 1990, a Hinds County grand jury handed down a murder indictment against Beckwith, which energized Mamie with a new level of optimism about her son's case. "Where there is a crack in the dam, the water has a chance to get out and other things have a chance to get in," she said. "This has been bottled up for so many years." With the state moving forward in its case against Beckwith, sixty-nine-year-old Mamie acknowledged that she had "been doing serious knocking" regarding a pursuit toward justice for Emmett.[20] In February 1994, a jury finally convicted Beckwith of the murder of Medgar Evers and sentenced him to life in prison.[21]

Rumblings about a possible probe into the Till case began in May 1995 when attorney Johnnie Cochran, in Memphis, Tennessee, for the National Conference of Black Mayors, said in a private conversation that he wanted to launch an investigation himself; the case was personal for him because the injustice in the trial verdict had been his inspiration for going into law in the first place. The following August, as Cochran was nine months into the internationally followed murder trial of O. J. Simpson, in which Cochran helped defend the former football great, people close to the famous lawyer told the *Tri-State Defender* that Cochran planned to look into the Till case later that year or in early 1996. In December, two months after Simpson's acquittal, Cochran confirmed in writing that he had "tentatively agreed to undertake an initial investigation into the circumstances surrounding Emmett Till's death."[22]

This development began the fulfillment of a dream that Mamie Till-Mobley had kept alive for decades. By then, Roy Bryant had also died, but Mamie was not overly concerned about punishing either the living or the dead. Her aim was that a new investigation would "force the state of Mississippi to acknowledge the state's horrible collusion in allowing the men that murdered my only child to go free." At the very least, she wanted the state to pay for the removal of Emmett's body from Burr Oak to Oakwood Cemetery, where several African American notables were buried, including Chicago's first black mayor, Harold Washington. While visiting Emmett's grave in August 1995, Mamie found that the headstone, purchased by singer Mahalia Jackson, was under water, and that both the photograph of Emmett and the flower vase were missing.[23] After Mamie and Cochran discussed Cochran's plans, Mamie told a reporter that success in this endeavor would "serve notice on a lot of people that those days of doing what you want to do to people are over."[24]

For whatever reason, Cochran, who died of cancer ten years later, never pursued the matter further.[25] Although this setback was obviously a disappointment for Mamie, it did not deter her from her goal. She knew, however, that she could not pursue it without help. "I often ask people to send letters to the Justice Department, because justice has not been done," she said in 1996. After four decades, "I am yet trying to bring about justice in this case."[26]

Eventually, others stepped in with the passion and drive needed to help Mamie in her quest. The first was Keith Beauchamp, a twenty-five-year-old Louisiana native who had just moved to New York City in 1996. Beauchamp was interested in a career in film and had big dreams about making a feature on the Till murder. He first learned about Emmett Till at age ten when he saw the *Jet* magazine photos of Till's battered face. He never forgot them.[27]

By the time of his 1989 high school graduation, Beauchamp had come to view Emmett Till as a kindred spirit, due to an unfortunate racial incident that forever changed him. Beauchamp was dancing with a white girl at a party when a bouncer approached, pushed him, and said, "Nigger, mess with your own kind." Beauchamp pushed back, and within moments, a fight broke out. The bouncer called over a man who, Beauchamp learned later, was an undercover police officer, and the fighting continued. Beauchamp was then taken to a back room where he was handcuffed to a chair. The police officer could not resist beating Beauchamp further, knocking over the chair, and nearly fracturing Beauchamp's jaw in the process. During the entire ordeal, Beauchamp could think only of Emmett Till.

The case went to court, but after the officer twice failed to show, the judge dismissed it. Because of this incident, Beauchamp vowed he would devote himself to racial injustice. He enrolled at Southern University at Baton Rouge, majored in criminal justice, and set his sights on becoming a civil rights attorney.

During his junior year, he left his studies but not his passion, and moved to New York, where he joined two friends who had formed a company called Big Baby Films. He began writing and producing music videos and took a second job as a security guard. During a meeting with his Big Baby colleagues, Beauchamp was asked about his interest in writing a script for a full-length film. He decided immediately that he would do something on Emmett Till.[28]

Beauchamp worked diligently on his script. Once a draft was completed, he decided to seek the endorsement of Mamie Till-Mobley, even though he believed that was somewhat of a long shot. He contacted her by telephone in 1997, but he was so nervous after she answered that he immediately hung up. He called back, apologized, and explained to her his lifelong interest in her son's tragic murder. They talked for two hours. Beauchamp was amazed by Mamie's willingness to share her story so passionately with a young stranger.[29]

Beauchamp learned during this first conversation that after four decades, Mamie was still working toward some level of justice for her son, and he decided then and there to help her obtain it. After months of telephone conversations between the two, Beauchamp traveled to Chicago and met Mamie in person, an experience he described as "surreal." When he arrived at her home, a relative, Ollie Gordon, ushered him into the kitchen, where Mamie was baking a pie. "I just hugged her," he recalled fondly.[30]

Proceeding with Mamie became complicated at first, due to the constant presence and zealous oversight of her attorney, Lester Barclay, who wanted Beauchamp to sign a contract with his client. However, Mamie decided to bypass Barclay's well-intentioned efforts to protect her, and she began working directly with the filmmaker.[31]

Although Beauchamp had initially reached out to Mamie regarding a feature film, his focus shifted after he began taking trips to Mississippi. There he learned of, met with, and interviewed people with stories of eyewitness accounts and other information related to the case, and he found himself listening to tales that had never before been told publicly. At first, he began incorporating their stories into his script, but Mamie soon encouraged him to use the footage he was accumulating and produce a documentary as a tool to inspire the government to launch a new investigation.[32]

One of the most dramatic moments for Beauchamp came when he interviewed Shirley Edwards, the first black mayor of Ruleville, Mississippi, home to Roy Bryant for the last twenty years of his life, and to Fannie Lou Hamer, the tireless civil rights activist who died in 1977. Before Bryant's death in 1994, Edwards had long wanted the federal government to find a way to retry the acquitted killer.[33] She apparently believed there were others who could still face prosecution. During Beauchamp's interview with Edwards, which Beauchamp videotaped, an adviser to Edwards came into the room. "You don't know what you are doing. You're putting all of our lives in danger. There are people still alive who were involved in the murder." The man was so concerned that he shut down the interview. "Mr. Beauchamp, you are treading in deep water. You have no idea what you are dealing with." Rather than heed any advice to back off, Beauchamp resolved to continue his research. He had been taking his father along on his trips to the Delta, but out of concern for his safety, he began leaving him behind.[34]

The working relationship between Beauchamp and Till-Mobley soon grew into a close friendship, and she threw her support behind the young filmmaker. "I relate to Keith because when I first met him, I was struck by his youth," she explained. "Then I began to feel his sincerity, his desire to do this job. And it was not a problem to get in step with him and help this project."[35]

The possibilities for a dramatic film continued to develop, however, and in 1999 Beauchamp was approached by Lisa Rhoden, who optioned the script for her fiancé, Cuban director Leon Ichaso. The pair hoped to create a movie for the Showtime network, but executives there shelved that project in the end. Beauchamp, it turned out, was relieved. Losing control of his script felt "like they took my baby away." Beauchamp then set out to do the film on his own, but those plans were soon curtailed due to financial limitations. With no feature film in the immediate future, he focused exclusively on his documentary.[36]

During this early phase of working with Beauchamp, Mamie also labored toward telling her story on the stage. On September 9, 1999, the play *The State of Mississippi vs. Emmett Till* premiered at the O'Rourke Center at Truman College in Chicago and was performed by the Pegasus Players. It was based on Mamie's own version of events, told to thirty-six-year-old playwright David Barr during a twenty-one-month period of collaboration. It ran through October 10. "I've been offered many contracts," explained Mamie to the *BET Weekend* magazine, "but I wanted it told without any lies or enhancements. I have always said that if the story could not be done properly, it would never be done."[37] Although it opened to good reviews, unfortunately, it perpetuated Mamie's belief that Emmett never actually whistled at Carolyn Bryant, a narrative Mamie had long hoped would replace the well-established stories of those who witnessed the event.[38] Despite any shortcomings, this work paved the way for Mamie to eventually write her own memoir and was the first dramatic telling of her story of which she approved and had control.

As Keith Beauchamp persevered on his own project, he began to realize that the interviews he was conducting were sounding more like depositions. In 2000, he contacted Judge Bobby DeLaughter, former Hinds County prosecutor whose tenacity had not only led to the reopening of the Medgar Evers case but also won the 1994 conviction against Beckwith. Beauchamp wanted DeLaughter to appear in the film as trial judge Curtis Swango, but DeLaughter worried about ethics issues and politely declined. However, DeLaughter reviewed Beauchamp's findings and encouraged him to forward the information on to Mississippi attorney general Mike Moore.[39]

Beauchamp also started speaking on various high school and college campuses, and, armed with a half-hour rough-cut of his film, *The Untold Story of Emmett Louis Till*, he began campaigning for a new investigation and for the funds to finish his work. He was optimistic that his film might raise awareness in the same way a 1997 film by Spike Lee had regarding the 1963 Sixteenth Street Baptist Church bombings in Birmingham, Alabama. In Lee's *4 Little Girls*, the witnesses spoke for themselves; the conviction of seventy-one-year-old Bobby Frank Cherry followed five years later.[40]

By mid-November 2002, a longer, although still unfinished, version of *Untold Story* was ready. That same month, the University of Virginia Press released a groundbreaking book edited by Christopher Metress, *The Lynching of Emmett Till: A Documentary Narrative*. Metress, an English professor at Samford University in Birmingham, Alabama, received inspiration for the book from his experience teaching students about the case since 1994. He began putting the volume together three years later, and the result was a compilation of news accounts contemporary to the kidnapping, murder, and trial; it also included investigative pieces, literary contributions, and memoirs.[41] This collection of primary documents was further evidence of a surging interest in Emmett Till, and followed the May 2002 release of the novel *Mississippi Trial, 1955*, written by Brigham Young University English professor Chris Crowe. Geared toward youth, the book was first picked up by the McComb County, Michigan, school district and currently is part of the curriculum in schools throughout the country. In 2003, it won the award for Best Book for Young Adults from the American Library Association, the Notable Social Studies Trade Book for Young People from the National Council for the Social Studies, the IRA Children's Book Award, and the Jefferson Cup. It has been reprinted several times.[42]

Mamie Till-Mobley was pleased with all that was happening, but her gratitude was heightened by the fact that it was coming at a time when her health, which had been failing for years, seemed to be on the mend. She suffered from heart and kidney problems, among other ailments, and her husband, Gene, had died a few years earlier, which made it more difficult for her to live on her own. On two occasions she fell while home alone, and once, unable to call for help, was forced to remain on the floor until she received aid from a relative who came to check on her the following day. Only after consulting with family and organizing a network of loved ones willing to help was she assured the chance to remain in the home she had shared with Gene for nearly forty years.[43]

On November 13, just over a week before her eighty-first birthday, Mamie was thrilled to attend a fund-raiser with celebrity-activist Harry Belafonte, who had requested to meet her. Later that day, in a three-way phone call with radio host Tavis Smiley, Mamie, and Beauchamp talked further about their work. Mamie was upbeat. "So many marvelous things are happening at this point in my life." She revealed that she was writing her own memoir, which would be published in 2003. She was also more active in the causes dearest to her. "I have begun training children again. I train them to do Dr. Martin Luther King's speeches and any other notable speeches. I now have 13 children that I am working with.... So it feels so good to be in the land of the living again."[44]

Although Mamie had tried to write her memoir in the past, the project became delayed several times over the years, most recently when a coauthor abandoned her and retained much of her material after they had been paid an advance. In June 2002, she met Christopher Benson through David Barr, her coauthor for the play *State of Mississippi vs. Emmett Till*. Benson was an attorney and journalist who had published a suspense novel, *Special Interest*, the year before. Barr, Raymond Thomas, director James Moll, and Benson sat down to discuss turning Mamie's story into a film. When Mamie learned that Benson had written a book, she decided he should help her write hers. This met with Barr's approval, who believed that the desired screenplay could then develop out of the book. Benson agreed, and he and Mamie began working together immediately. For the next several months, Benson interviewed Mamie regularly. Two months into the project, after negotiations with her attorney, Lester Barclay, Mamie and Benson signed contracts with Random House on August 28, 2002, the forty-seventh anniversary of Emmett Till's murder. Things moved fast, and by the end of the year the research was finished and Mamie began reviewing chapter drafts.[45]

During the Tavis Smiley interview, Beauchamp revealed that he had talked with an official from the Mississippi attorney general's office who was impressed by the evidence Beauchamp had uncovered and asked Beauchamp to work with his office toward a goal of reopening the case.[46] This was a mixed blessing. Frank Spencer, special assistant attorney to Attorney General Mike

Moore, had first contacted Beauchamp for help in locating the ring taken from Emmett Till's finger after the body had been removed from the Tallahatchie River. Mamie never received it back after the trial, and when she spoke at an assembly at Regina Dominican High School in Wilmette, Illinois, she told the students that if there was anything they could do for her, it would be to find the ring. Inspired by this, Chicago schoolteacher Mike Small put his students in pursuit of the ring by obtaining 300 signatures, which he sent to Senators Dick Durban and Peter Fitzgerald of Illinois; Thad Cochran and Trent Lott of Mississippi; and the governors of both states. Spencer then contacted Small and promised to find out what he could. This led to dialogue between Spencer and Beauchamp, and the Mississippi official sought Beauchamp's help in seeking a photo of the ring.[47]

Because Beauchamp's focus was on pursuing justice, he told Spencer that he had little interest in finding the ring but would work with the state only if officials would commit to opening a new investigation into the Chicago boy's murder. Even then, Beauchamp was hesitant about turning his research and film footage over to the same state that had acquitted Emmett Till's killers so many years before. As Beauchamp mulled over what to do, *New York Times* reporter Brent Staples introduced him to Ted Shaw, president of the NAACP's Legal Defense Fund. Shaw took an interest in Beauchamp and his efforts to reopen the case, and instructed Beauchamp to hold off giving anything to Mississippi officials. Instead, Beauchamp opened his research to Shaw.[48]

Staples had just interviewed Beauchamp for an article that appeared in the *New York Times* on November 11, and the piece served as a turning point. Staples, noting that the last of the Birmingham bombers had finally been brought to justice, believed that Beauchamp's *Untold Story* "could well cause [the Till] case to be reopened." The article highlighted Beauchamp's lifelong interest in the Till story and his success in talking to witnesses speaking out for the first time, and noted that the mother of Emmett Till "has lived half a century with the knowledge that the legal system in Mississippi conspired to disregard her son's murder and let the killers go."[49]

Staples correctly predicted privately to Beauchamp that this article would open doors and that people would come knocking. As the media began to take notice, Beauchamp premiered his ninety-minute rough cut of *Untold Story* on November 16 at the Cantor Film Center at New York University. It was an event sponsored by *QBR: The Black Book Review*, the University of Virginia Press (as part of the launch of Metress's *Lynching of Emmett Till*), and NYU's Institute of African-American Affairs and Africana Studies Department. Till-Mobley and Metress joined Beauchamp for a panel discussion after the private screening. "We have to keep telling the story to raise people's consciousness and until justice prevails," Mamie told the crowd.[50]

The Beauchamp and Metress projects were soon joined by another film documentary, this one to the chagrin of Beauchamp, who was still struggling financially to complete his own. Slated for a January 20 showing on the PBS series *The American Experience*, it would be the first film exclusively about Till to air to a national audience. *The Murder of Emmett Till*, directed by veteran filmmaker Stanley Nelson, was a landmark endeavor. Nelson, fifty-one, had conceived the idea for his project a few years earlier after his wife, Marcia Smith, returned home in tears after listening to a National Public Radio (NPR) interview with Mamie Till-Mobley. After Nelson ordered a tape of the broadcast and listened to it himself, he decided to make Emmett Till his focus. He quickly took his crew to Chicago and interviewed Till-Mobley and Wheeler Parker and came home determined to continue. He had produced an earlier film for *The American Experience*, called *Marcus Garvey: Look for Me in the Whirlwind*, and was anxious to do another. Executives there liked the idea of a Till film and gave Nelson money and the green light to proceed. The film took about a year to complete.[51]

Both the Nelson and Beauchamp documentaries would feature Mamie, Wheeler Parker, and trial witness Willie Reed. Nelson would also include a man named Oudie Brown, who said that he saw and questioned Levi "Too Tight" Collins the morning after the murder when he spotted Collins washing blood out of J. W. Milam's truck. Nelson also found another man, Warren Hampton, who said he had seen the truck pass by while he was playing on the side of the road. Hampton heard screams coming from the back of the truck, which was covered with a tarpaulin. For *Untold Story*, Beauchamp interviewed Henry Lee Loggins in Dayton, Ohio. Although Loggins was believed to have been in the back of the truck restraining Till, he denied those allegations to Beauchamp. In fact, he was adamant that he was never present at any point during the kidnapping and murder. Beauchamp's film also featured Simeon Wright, who had not spoken publicly about the case in fifteen years. Wright also led Beauchamp to Ruthie Mae Crawford and Ruthie's uncle, Roosevelt Crawford. They, like Wright and a few others, had been with Emmett Till at the Bryant store. Beauchamp also interviewed Roosevelt's brother, John, who along with several others had spent time with Till just hours before the Chicago teen was kidnapped. Beauchamp was also the first to talk with Willie Nesley, who, like Oudie Brown, claimed to have seen the blood-splattered truck the morning after the murder.[52]

Although the two films differed from one another, there was enough overlap that Beauchamp was especially disheartened that Nelson's was getting national attention at the same time *Untold Story*, still a work-in-progress, was beginning to make waves. Two Emmett Till films in the news at the same time could easily confuse the public when either was mentioned. Beauchamp and Nelson spoke to each other when their paths crossed in New York City on November 3, 2002. Beauchamp had accompanied Mamie Till-Mobley to a tribute concert for her son, performed by jazz trumpeter Hannibal Lokumbe, at the Schomburg Center for Research in Black Culture. The encounter was awkward.[53] Beauchamp, as a novice documentarian, was working hard to raise every dime he needed to produce his film, while the better-known Nelson avoided that obstacle and glided through to the finish line. In September 2002, just a few months before the release of *The Murder of Emmett Till*, Nelson's talents earned him the MacArthur Foundation's $500,000, no-strings-attached "Genius award."[54]

Nelson had set out mainly to produce a historical film and, unlike Beauchamp, was not actively campaigning for a new investigation into the case. Yet after the first screening of *The Murder of Emmett Till* at Harlem's Schaumburg Library in December 2002, the audience was so affected that they wanted to run to Mississippi, as Nelson later put it, and "burn down the town of Money." Seeing this reaction, Nelson and his wife, Marcia, spearheaded a more constructive way for people to speak out by printing thousands of postcards bearing a photo of Emmett Till and a plea to Mississippi's attorney general to reopen the case. Nelson distributed them at screenings and urged audience members to fill them out and send them in. He estimates that over 10,000 people eventually did so.[55]

The same month that Nelson premiered his film in Harlem, the case got the attention of yet another voice, not a filmmaker or an author but an activist—one with a long history of results. Forty-seven-year-old Alvin Sykes of Kansas City had just read an Associated Press article in the local black weekly, the *Kansas City Call*, and became intrigued. It highlighted the films by Beauchamp and Nelson, as well as the new book by Metress. What especially caught Sykes's eye was the claim that others involved with the murder might still be alive. It quoted Mamie Till-Mobley as saying, "I've been trying to get that case re-opened since 1956." She was determined, the *Call* reported, even though friends and family had long urged her "to let this thing die."[56]

Sykes had been advocating for victims in criminal cases since he was sixteen, and had worked with the Justice Department since age seventeen. In fact, he had worked at some level with every assistant US attorney general for the Civil Rights Division since Drew S. Days III held the position under President Jimmy Carter beginning in 1977.[57]

On the surface, Sykes seemed like one of the unlikeliest voices that those in power would listen to, yet people all the way from the Justice Department to the halls of Congress paid attention. He had been born to a fourteen-year-old mother as a result of statutory rape, and was raised by a friend of the family. Growing up, he suffered from epilepsy and mental problems, made worse, no doubt, by the fact that he was raped by neighbors when he was eleven years old. He dropped out of high school in the tenth grade, as he explained it, in order to get an education, which occurred through what he calls his transition from public schools to the public library. He also sat in on countless courtroom trials, where he learned about the law. At night, he managed the local R&B band, Threatening Weather.[58]

Sykes left the music scene after Threatening Weather disbanded and began to concentrate full time on victims' rights and justice-seeking, although it failed to bring him a steady or sustainable salary. In the late 1980s, he was forced to live for a time in a homeless shelter. Surviving on very little income even in better times, Sykes lived in a small apartment when he could afford one, but stayed intermittently with friends when he could not. He continued to conduct his work from the library and did it all without the benefit of a car or cell phone. Despite any setbacks along his journey, Sykes's experiences prepared him well as a voice for justice in the Till case. In 1980, the racially motivated murder of Kansas City jazz musician Steve Harvey was a turning point. Harvey had become a good friend of Sykes due to Sykes's local music connections. Harvey was practicing his saxophone at Penn Valley Park on November 5 when nineteen-year-old Raymond Bledsoe targeted Harvey because he was black and also because he assumed erroneously that Harvey was gay. Bledsoe attacked Harvey with a baseball bat and beat him to death after chasing him out of a public restroom. The case went to trial in 1981, and Bledsoe was acquitted by an all-white jury. Motivated by that obvious injustice, Sykes formed the Steve Harvey Justice Campaign the following day.[59]

Sykes contacted the Civil Rights Division but was told by an intern there that with Bledsoe's acquittal, double jeopardy laws prevented any further attempt toward prosecution. Sykes persevered, however, spent a day in the library, and ten minutes before closing time found a little-known federal statute, Title 18, USC, Section 245. This statute, called "Federally Protected Activities," prohibited the denial of public facilities because of race. Sykes contacted Richard W. Roberts, an attorney in the Civil Rights Division, and Roberts instructed Sykes to send him everything he had found. In 1983, the case was tried in federal court on the grounds that Harvey's civil rights had been violated. This time, Bledsoe was convicted and given a life sentence.[60]

Harvey's widow, Rhea, mentioned to Sykes on several occasions that her husband's death was the second civil rights murder perpetuated upon her family. Her mother, she explained, was a distant relative of Emmett Till. It would be another two decades before Sykes would have reason to think much more about the Till case, but just before he read of Mamie Till-Mobley's interest in a new investigation, he was working on a case in which a black public utilities worker had been left a hangman's noose at his place of employment.

Sykes investigated the possibility that the incident was a hate crime and heard the victim compare his case to that of Emmett Till. This episode, fresh on his mind, helped Sykes notice the *Call* article featuring Till-Mobley when he happened upon it in late December 2002.[61]

After reading about the new developments in the Till case, Sykes telephoned Wheeler Parker at Parker's church and left a message the day after Christmas. When Parker did not respond, Sykes called directory information for Mamie Till-Mobley and then phoned her at home. She answered, but was at first elusive, asking her own questions and sounding so businesslike that Sykes did not even realize he was talking to Emmett Till's mother until partway through the call, when she revealed herself. He faxed her some information about his success in the Harvey case and then contacted the office of Attorney General John Ashcroft, "in an exploratory way," and let officials there know that he would be looking into the case further. Sykes saw from the beginning that, in going forward, a joint investigation with the FBI and the state of Mississippi would be the wisest course to follow. The response from Ashcroft's office indicated some interest on its part. That same night, Parker returned Sykes's call from earlier that day, and the two men talked.[62]

Sykes was a member of the National Association for Human Rights Workers, as was sixty-three-year-old Donald Burger, a retired official with the Justice Department. The two had known each other from their days of working together on a federal desegregation case in Kansas City some thirty years earlier. Because two of their fellow members were getting married in Detroit, the men arranged to drive to the wedding and then go on to Chicago and meet with Mamie Till-Mobley in person.[63]

They arrived in the Windy City on December 30 and drove to Mamie's home, where they found her frosting a cake for everyone to enjoy as they talked. They were also joined by Chris Benson, who took copious notes at the meeting. They discussed Mamie's interests in a new investigation, and Sykes buoyed up the possibilities of action by telling her that he had already been in contact with Ashcroft's office and that contacts there had responded positively. He further recounted his success in the Harvey case. He emphasized that his goal would be the pursuit of truth, without any preconceived ideas about who may have been involved in her son's death. Sykes assured Mamie that there would be a full investigation into the case, but he could not promise her a conviction.[64]

During the meeting, Mamie talked about Keith Beauchamp, his film, and his own desire to seek a new probe. She immediately believed that Sykes, Burger, and Beauchamp should become allies in this cause. Mamie thought that Beauchamp, who phoned her regularly, might call before the two men left, but when that did not happen, Burger left Mamie his cell phone number.[65]

After Sykes and Burger began the drive back to Kansas City, Beauchamp called Mamie, learned about her two visitors, and in turn called Burger's number and spoke with Sykes. At first, Beauchamp was hesitant to say much about his efforts and explained that he had recently started working with the NAACP Legal Defense Fund.

"Really?" asked Sykes. "Are you working with Ted Shaw?"

"Yes!" replied Beauchamp, surprised that Sykes knew the name.

Sykes then suggested that Beauchamp call Shaw, who would vouch for him and put Beauchamp at ease. When Beauchamp did so, he got a good report. Shaw's connection to both men allowed him to alleviate any concerns either would have had. Shaw suggested that the men work together, and a relationship began.[66]

Sykes and Burger had already thought about proceeding under the umbrella of the Justice Campaign of America, which for nineteen years had functioned broadly on victims' rights. That organization had grown out of the old Steve Harvey Justice Campaign. Upon further thought, however, they opted instead to form the Emmett Till Justice Campaign, with Beauchamp and Till-Mobley as the other two founding members. Sykes would take on the role of coordinator, and Mamie agreed to serve as chairperson. She also approved Sykes's role as her advocate, which included the responsibility of speaking on behalf of the family in the new quest for justice. On January 4, 2003, Sykes called to tell Mamie that the organization had been launched and provided other details.

Two days later, on January 6, Sykes called the Mississippi attorney general's office to determine what it would take from its perspective to reopen the case. He arranged for a conference call for later that day with Sykes, Beauchamp, Till-Mobley, and Special Assistant to the Attorney General Jonathan Compretta, so that the office could verify directly with Mamie that she backed a new investigation and supported Sykes as her advocate. Sykes called Beauchamp and asked him to pass this on to Mamie. Meanwhile, Sykes made other calls in preparation for the conference call.[67]

Mamie had a busy schedule planned for the remainder of the week. She was to leave the following day for Atlanta, where she was scheduled to speak at the Ebenezer Baptist Church as part of its weeklong closing ceremonies for the exhibit "Without Sanctuary: Lynching Photography in America." She was upbeat as she talked to a reporter for the *Atlanta Journal-Constitution* a few days ahead of her visit. "I've got to write my book. To me, the time has come, and I can't wait any longer." She was optimistic about the reality of a new investigation into her son's murder, which "would be the fulfillment of a dream I have had since I left the courtroom. Justice at last will prevail."[68]

Beauchamp, who would be traveling to Atlanta as well to screen *Untold Story* at Ebenezer on Saturday, called Mamie before she left for a dialysis treatment and informed her of the planned conference call for later that day, explaining what the state attorney general's office wanted from her. She was clearly pleased with the news.

"Keith, I told you that you were going to get this case reopened," said Mamie with excitement. She looked forward to seeing Beauchamp in Atlanta.[69]

Sykes waited patiently all day for a response from Beauchamp so that the group could coordinate the time to place the call. Several hours passed, but nothing came. Beauchamp finally called later that evening, and the news he had was devastating.

"She's gone," said Beauchamp, almost in shock.

Sykes was confused. "Who's gone?"

"Mrs. Mobley. She died today."[70]

Mamie had been en route to her dialysis appointment with a family member when she became ill. She was rushed to Jackson Park Hospital, where she died of heart failure at 2:30 P.M.[71]

Nobody who knew and loved Mamie Till-Mobley was prepared for her sudden death, but the timing made it seem all the more tragic. The momentum for reopening the Emmett Till case had been accelerating, and the dedication of others to see it through was firmly in place. Now, the woman who had inspired it all would no longer be part of the journey. Nor would she see the release of her memoir. Chris Benson received the news of Mamie's death while at home working on the book. He called Mamie's home to ask her a routine question but instead was told by her cousin, Airickca Gordon, that Mamie had died. He was still in shock when Mamie's attorney, Lester Barclay, called to encourage him to continue. "She was able to close her eyes and rest in peace knowing that this was going on," he said. Benson called William Morris, his agent, and told him the news. Morris wanted to know if Benson had learned enough from Mamie to continue. Benson assured him that he had, and the two agreed to talk more the following day, along with Benson's editor at Random House. During the meeting they agreed to carry on. Rev. Jesse Jackson, a close friend of Mamie, was also there and offered his help. Benson asked him to write a foreword to the book, and Jackson agreed.[72]

Continuing on was not as easy at first for Beauchamp. Meeting and forming a relationship with Mamie had been life-altering for him, and now, unfortunately, so was losing her. For a time it was almost too much to bear, and he fell into a serious depression. All he could do that first night was lock himself away and write a poem about his beloved mentor.[73]

In his first words to the press after Mamie's death, Beauchamp sounded determined to proceed. Despite his grief, he assured one reporter, "I'm going to go forward with this and definitely get this case reopened." Privately, however, he no longer had it in him. He could not view any of his footage and lost all desire to finish the film. As Beauchamp put it, "I was done."[74]

As shocking as Mamie's death was for Sykes as well, he saw the moment as Mamie's passing of the torch. She had begun this effort herself years earlier, and had just given her nod of approval for others to go with her into the trenches. Sykes and Burger pleaded with Beauchamp to pick up and continue. Beauchamp at first refused but urged the two men to keep working if they wanted to. Should they continue, it would be without him or his unfinished film. Sykes and Burger persevered, however, and their words struck Beauchamp hard.

"If you give up, you're giving up on Mrs. Mobley."[75] Indeed, it was up to those Mamie had entrusted to turn her vision into reality.

Beauchamp forced himself back into his work, but the first screening of *Untold Story* nineteen days after Mamie's death was painful. The screening originally slated for Atlanta on January 11 had been postponed due to her sudden passing but was rescheduled for Saturday, January 25. The 125-seat visitor center theater filled to capacity, forcing staffers at the facility to set up a second screening room where they showed the original thirty-minute version of the film.[76]

As Beauchamp saw Mamie appear on screen, his emotions got the better of him and he broke down. After the screening, he pulled himself together and told the audience about his and Sykes's efforts to persuade Mississippi to reopen the murder case. In fact, Sykes and Ted Shaw, of the NAACP's Legal Defense Fund, planned to carefully scrutinize all of Beauchamp's findings in order to assemble a theory of prosecution. Once that was developed, they would pass that on to the offices of both the Mississippi attorney general and Department of Justice.[77] Federal involvement was desirable over the state going it alone, primarily because the federal government could provide the funds for a vigorous investigation.

As Sykes and Beauchamp began working together without Mamie, Nelson's *The Murder of Emmett Till* gave the case unprecedented publicity, which certainly helped the cause. The film was screened at New York's Gramercy Theater on January 8. On the 17th it premiered at the Sundance Film Festival in Salt Lake City, where it won a Special Jury Award. Three days later, on January 20, 2003, it had its first airing on PBS's *The American Experience*. The following September, at the Shrine Auditorium in Los Angeles, the film received the ultimate recognition when Nelson and Marcia Smith won an Emmy in Directing for Nonfiction Programming.[78]

On April 28, 2003, Beauchamp and Sykes screened *Untold Story* at the National Press Club in Washington, DC. This opportunity came after someone with the organization reached out to Beauchamp with an invitation.[79] The Washington meeting was important because Beauchamp and Sykes, along with Donald Burger and Ted Shaw, were scheduled to meet the following day with Ralph Boyd Jr., assistant US attorney general for civil rights.

Sykes wanted to be ready with answers before meeting Boyd. Prior to the trip to Washington, Sykes tried to clear a few hurdles both with the Till family and the federal government, and these would need resolution before going forward. As Sykes dug deeper into the case, he learned that Emmett Till's cause of death had never been definitively determined; the death certificate noted that Till died either from a gunshot wound or an ax. An autopsy had never been performed but would be a crucial step in a murder investigation. This was important not only to determine how the victim died, but the defense had maintained during the 1955 trial that the body was not even that of Emmett Till. That argument would need to be demolished for good. Yet there had already been some rumblings among Till family members who were opposed to the idea of disturbing the body, even if an examination could lead to solving the case.[80]

Sykes tried to alleviate these concerns immediately and contacted the Armed Forces Institute of Pathology in Washington, DC in a quest to obtain referrals for private forensic pathologists. He was given the name of Dr. Mehmet Yaşar İşcan, professor at the Institute of Forensic Sciences in Istanbul, Turkey, about performing a privately funded examination of the body. Should the government take on the case, an exhumation and autopsy would occur regardless of how the family felt about it, but Sykes thought relatives would be more supportive if they could be in on the procedure. İşcan had worked in the Chicago area and was familiar with local officials, facts that also might be comforting to the family.[81] "I have made a request to the family for both permission for the examination and that you perform the operation," Sykes wrote in an email to İşcan. Sykes had already assured the family that the process would not incur any costs to them personally, but to fully persuade them, Sykes needed information regarding the fees involved and for İşcan to provide an opinion as to why the examination would be necessary. Sykes also wanted to present this information to Department of Justice officials during the April 29 meeting following the Press Club film screening.[82]

İşcan responded that he could do the autopsy for $300 per hour and that the entire process, including the exhumation, would take about four days. İşcan, who had performed autopsies all over the world, assured Sykes that "the remains will provide any injury made to the body and the type of weapons that cause[d] that injury. It can make a distinction between innocence and third degree murders. I believe that if a gun is used and yet no autopsy is made, we can still recover the bullet and assess how it enter[ed] the body. This may even be possible even if it did not hit the bones assuming that remains are not moved later or dismembered." If a bullet penetrated Till's body, "we can reconstruct the way the victim was standing at the time of shooting in relation to the assailant. The skeleton can provide a better explanation of events and cause of death as long as it is shot by a weapon."[83] Continuing opposition from the Till family kept İşcan's services from ever being utilized, but they learned what possible answers the procedure could uncover. Sykes kept preparing for the day when they would be forced to deal with this issue once again.[84]

Sykes had been anticipating another problem and wanted to go to Washington armed with solutions. He foresaw issues that would thwart a federal probe because the statute of limitations for federal charges had expired back in 1960, five years after the crime had been committed. He and Beauchamp had theorized that one way to get the federal government involved was to prove that the gun used to kill Emmett Till was a military weapon issued to J. W. Milam when Milam served in the army. In his 1955 interview with William Bradford Huie, Milam boasted that his .45 pistol was the "best weapon the Army's got." Another option was to look into the highways used to transport Emmett Till, and to determine whether they were federally owned.[85]

Neither one of these ideas panned out, but Sykes thought that the best approach would be for the federal government to partner with Mississippi voluntarily to investigate the case. After the National Press Club screening, Sykes talked with his old friend Richard Roberts, by then a judge in the US District Court for the District of Columbia. Roberts, who attended the event, referred Sykes to a July 28, 1976, opinion of Antonin Scalia that established federal jurisdiction for an investigation into the Kennedy assassination. This same opinion was later used in 1998 to open the door for federal officials to look into the death of Martin Luther King Jr.[86]

Scalia, who was later appointed to the US Supreme Court by President Ronald Reagan in 1987, was a forty-year-old assistant attorney general in 1976 when he penned his memo, "Jurisdiction of the Department of Justice to Investigate the Assassination of President Kennedy." Scalia concluded that public interest was still served when the Department of Justice investigated a crime, even when no one could be prosecuted on federal charges, as long as investigators could *detect* that a crime had indeed occurred.[87] Sykes, Beauchamp, Burger, and Shaw then passed this opinion on to Assistant Attorney General Boyd. Boyd came to the meeting certain that establishing federal jurisdiction would be difficult, if not impossible, due to the expiration of the statute of limitations. Sykes, however, used the Scalia opinion as the "in" that the Department of Justice needed. Jurisdiction for any prosecution would remain with the state. Boyd accepted this reasoning and got on board.[88]

On May 13, two weeks after the Washington meetings, Beauchamp and Sykes presented *Untold Story* in New York at the Dag Hammarskjold Auditorium to the 200 delegates to the United Nations (UN). Gordon Tapper, a friend of Beauchamp and chief of special services at the UN, arranged the event with the help of UN attorney Catherine Caxton. Sykes explained the short- and long-term goals of the Emmett Till Justice Campaign, which expanded far beyond the Till case alone. "First, we are seeking to reopen the investigation into Emmett Till's death," he said, "and secondly, we are seeking to have the Federal Hate Crimes Law modified to bring all racially motivated crimes under Federal jurisdiction."[89]

Sykes was still facing opposition from Till family members about the realization that Emmett Till's body would need to be exhumed and examined should the case be reopened. In June, he traveled to Jackson, Mississippi, and sought out Charles Evers, brother of Medgar Evers. Charles Evers agreed to write a letter to the Till family urging them to finally support the idea of an autopsy. Evers knew firsthand how important this step would be because a June 1991 exhumation and examination of the body of his brother aided the prosecution in finally gaining a conviction of Medgar's killer, even though an autopsy had been performed in 1963. Unfortunately, the record of that first procedure had been lost.[90]

More attention came to the Till story when, in October 2003, Random House released Mamie Till-Mobley's long-awaited memoir, *Death of Innocence: The Story of the Hate Crime That Changed America*. Coming nine months after her death, its publication was bittersweet. Chris Benson finished the work that had begun at Mamie's request in the summer of 2002. During their last meeting together six months later, Mamie told Benson that telling her story to him "has been cathartic for me," and that she was able to reach a new level regarding her own feelings. "I see why it has taken so long," she said, appearing at peace about the project she had envisioned for so many years. Benson and the historian Tim Black were well aware of the void created by her absence as they introduced the book in Chicago on Thursday, October 16, at an event at the Carter G. Woodson Regional Library attended by Mamie's family and open to the public. The auditorium was full.[91] *Death of Innocence* went on to win the Robert F. Kennedy Special Recognition Book Award in 2003 and the following year was awarded the BlackBoard Nonfiction Book of the Year Award.

Beauchamp continued to screen *Untold Story* on college campuses, to civil rights organizations, and to just about any group that would have him. Mamie had given him some advice early on that stuck with him. If he hoped to bring about a new investigation, she insisted, he would need to have the media and those with political power squarely behind him. To spur that on, Beauchamp resolved that whenever the public saw news about Emmett Till, they would see Beauchamp's name also.[92]

Sykes remained busy as well. In addition to his travels, he spent the year writing letters and emails and making phone calls.[93] All of these efforts resulted in a formal review of the case by the state of Mississippi in February 2004. One of Sykes's many phone calls went to John Hailman, a federal prosecutor in Oxford, Mississippi, who had been with the US attorney's office since 1974. By 2004, he was chief of the Criminal Division and, as such, he handled all civil rights cases. Sykes introduced himself and told Hailman that he had met with Ralph Boyd in Washington the previous April and was fully aware that the statute of limitations had run out on the Till case. "However, [Boyd] said your office had a good reputation in civil rights circles and that you might be willing to help persuade the state DA to reopen the case if the FBI will agree to investigate it." Sykes was "calm and low-key but persistent," recalled Hailman. Sykes explained that the trial transcript was missing and that both men who had been tried and acquitted for the murder were dead. However, a good investigation might produce sufficient evidence to prosecute others who were involved. "If not," Sykes said, "at least the family and the nation would finally know what really happened."[94]

Hailman promised Sykes that he would look into the matter further and get back to him. Before they hung up, Sykes told Hailman that he wanted an in-person meeting with the FBI and the district attorney who would have jurisdiction over the case.

Hailman talked to colleagues Jim Greenlee, US attorney for northern Mississippi, and Hal Nielsen, FBI supervisor. Both were doubtful that a probe into a case as cold as the Till murder would yield much, if anything, yet they agreed to listen to what Sykes had to say. Hailman also called Joyce Chiles, district attorney over Mississippi's Fourth Judicial District, to let her know about this renewed interest in Emmett Till.[95] Should the case be reopened, Chiles's office would ultimately decide whether to indict and then prosecute.

Beauchamp and Sykes planned to be in Mississippi showing *Untold Story*, and wanted the meeting with federal and Mississippi officials to coincide with one of those dates. Sykes telephoned Chiles to let her know. Previous to this, she had known nothing about him, but Sykes was direct as he told her about two meetings he had set up in Oxford and Jackson and wanted to know which one she'd like to attend. "Out of curiosity, I chose the Oxford site to see who this person was who was so brazen that he would give me a choice of meeting in two places."[96]

Chiles, forty-nine, had just been elected to office in November and had been serving only one month when Sykes contacted her. The first black district attorney to serve in this section of the Delta, she was elected with 70 percent of the vote after running against a white male opponent. Born just twenty miles from Money in Itta Bena, Chiles was raised on a cotton plantation near Belzoni. She was only a toddler when Emmett Till was murdered in 1955 and grew up hearing very little about the case. She joined the army after graduating from Mississippi Valley State University with a degree in history. She returned to Mississippi after her discharge to work as a counselor at the state prison, and then became an undercover narcotics agent before going on to law school. After earning her degree from the Mississippi College School of Law in 1988, she joined the district attorney's office a year later, eventually serving as assistant district attorney before being elected in 2003 to head the office. Her jurisdiction included Leflore, Washington, and Sunflower Counties.[97]

On Friday, February 6, 2004, Sykes and Beauchamp met with Greenlee, Hailman, Nielsen, Chiles, and others at Greenlee's conference room in Oxford. For over an hour the gathered officials listened first to Sykes and then to Beauchamp, who each explained their reasons for wanting to reopen an investigation. Sykes talked about the need to establish the facts of the case, and of his vision of a joint state and FBI investigation, basing his justification for federal help on the Scalia opinion. "We all listened very attentively to him as he spoke," said Chiles. Sykes convinced Chiles that his priority was learning the truth, but "if justice can be served then it should be." Greenlee remembered Sykes as "organized and logical" in his presentation. "He was meticulous and motivated by facts, not emotion. He almost appeared 'emotionless.'" Hailman recalled Sykes as "focused and very good."[98]

Beauchamp presented the evidence he had uncovered through his numerous interviews with people in the Mississippi Delta and elsewhere. To those listening, Beauchamp's findings, coming forth so many years after the crime, appeared weak from a prosecutorial standpoint. That made it difficult for officials in the room to get on board. Hailman said that at this point, the meeting began "drifting," but Sykes then brought in sixty-one-year-old Simeon Wright, who had been waiting patiently outside. Wright's presentation made all the difference. It was heartfelt and personal, and everyone present was touched. He detailed what he had witnessed at the store in Money, Mississippi, and of witnessing the kidnapping of his fourteen-year-old cousin. After Wright finished, wrote Hailman, "we agreed unanimously, investigators and prosecutors alike, both federal and state, that we had to reopen the case and investigate it as thoroughly as humanly possible."[99]

That being said, Chiles still worried whether they really had a case. With no physical evidence or trial transcript, and Beauchamp's findings problematic for her, she told Sykes bluntly, "I don't know what my office can do with this."[100] Yet she wanted to do the right thing. She turned to Hailman out in the hallway.

"John, I will do what is right. If we have a case, I'll prosecute it, but I won't do it just to satisfy people's feelings."

Chiles knew that should there be an investigation, she would need the Department of Justice to work with her, as she and her staff were not equipped to handle it on their own. She also wanted Hailman to work directly with her office as a specially appointed district attorney. If indictments followed and the case went to trial, she would insist that Hailman be the one to present it in court.[101]

Following the meeting, Greenlee sent a report to the deputy attorney general indicating that the state and federal officials who listened to the evidence wanted an investigation. For Greenlee, the Till case was an open wound and a stain on Mississippi to that day.[102] In order for the federal government to agree to take it on, the state of Mississippi would need to formally request its assistance. Sykes assured Chiles from his past experience that if the Justice Department received a request for help, a joint investigation would be a done deal.[103]

The Oxford meeting was a turning point, and the momentum continued to build. The following day, Beauchamp, Sykes, and Donald Burger held a public screening of *Untold Story* at the Jackson State University campus, where over 200 people attended. Sykes urged those present to call their representatives in Congress to urge them to support an investigation.[104] While in Jackson, the three men learned that Chicago alderman Ed Smith was going to propose a resolution at a meeting of the Chicago City Council Health Committee, urging that the case be reopened. Beauchamp could not attend, but Sykes and Don Burger left Mississippi and drove all night in order to appear before the committee on Monday, February 9.

"We believe that the federal government has a responsibility to investigate and prosecute any individuals who are still alive, who were involved in this case," Sykes told the council.

Burger reminded those present that Mamie Till-Mobley "spent her whole life trying to get justice for her son's untimely death." Alderman Smith made his own plea. "We should bring this case to justice because killers should not be out there walking around after committing such a horrendous crime."

For Smith, who was raised in Mississippi, the Till case was personal. He spoke of his cousin Eddie, and a friend, Henry, the latter whom years earlier had been accused of staring at a white woman. "And when they found them walking down the road, they took both of 'em because they couldn't kill Henry and leave Eddie." The vigilantes "took the two of them. Took these kids and beat them all night. Tied them to a barn and went to work. The next day, they came back and continued to beat them and kill them. And then they cut them up with a chain saw and dropped them in the Mississippi River." The resolution passed.[105]

The message was clearly sinking in. The following day, February 10, Illinois congressman Bobby Rush submitted a resolution in the House of Representatives that stated the facts of the Till case and called on the Department of Justice to investigate the murder as well as the acquittal of J. W. Milam and Roy Bryant. He also asked that the department report the results of its findings to Congress.[106]

In response to Rush, a spokesman at the Justice Department informed reporters from the *Chicago Tribune* that "the statute of limitations . . . barred the department from investigating the case further." This was the argument that Sykes, Beauchamp, and Burger refuted when they met with Assistant Attorney General Ralph Boyd ten months earlier. Rush continued to conduct research through the Legislative Counsel for the House of Representatives and the Congressional Research Service, and on February 27 he sent a letter to Attorney General John Ashcroft with his own refutation, pointing out that federal law USC 3282 stated that "an indictment for any offense punishable by death may be found at any time without limitation." The federal government was looking into or had helped out in numerous cases that were over thirty years old, Rush said, including the Sixteenth Street Baptist Church bombing and the Medgar Evers case.[107]

Such passionate support was crucial, and, fortunately, it kept building in both the House and Senate. In early 2004, Keith Beauchamp met author and history professor Blanche Wiesen Cook through a mutual friend, civil rights activist Connie Curry. Cook then acquainted Beauchamp with attorney Kenneth P. Thompson, who had friends in high places. Thompson introduced the filmmaker to New York senator Charles Schumer and Representative Charles Rangel.[108] Thompson was a former federal prosecutor who had handled the 1997 case of Abner Louima, a thirty-year-old Haitian who had been beaten and sexually assaulted by New York City police officers after they arrested him outside of a nightclub.[109] Schumer, who had already learned much about Beauchamp prior to their meeting, took an immediate liking to the young filmmaker.[110]

By early April, the Department of Justice was already considering the requests out of Mississippi for a joint investigation, but Schumer and Rangel began making public appeals that it act. "The murder of Emmett Till was one of the seminal moments in our nation's civil rights movement," explained Schumer, passionately, "and the failure to bring his murderers to justice remains a stain on America's record for reconciliation." Schumer, a member of the Senate Judiciary Committee, called upon Attorney General John Ashcroft to keep the promises Ashcroft made during his 2001 confirmation hearings to enforce the country's civil rights laws. "In this rare instance, justice delayed may not be justice denied."[111]

On April 6, following the lead of Chicago two months earlier, the New York City Council took up the Till case. Three congressmen joined several city council members and stood outside city hall in support of a resolution calling for a federal investigation. During a press conference arranged by Councilwoman Letitia James, Thompson announced that he had set up a meeting for May 4 with Alexander Acosta, the new assistant attorney general for civil rights. "We intend to present evidence to show that there are people who are still living who may have been involved in the murder of this innocent child," explained Thompson.[112]

The date of the meeting had never actually been finalized, however, and Thompson's announcement was premature. Sykes had arranged for officials at the Department of Justice to meet with Wheeler Parker on behalf of the Till family and was given two possible dates, May 4 being one of them. Neither Sykes nor Parker wanted the date announced publicly, as a safety precaution for Parker. Thompson's announcement forced Sykes to issue an apology to the Justice Department. The meeting was put on hold.[113]

On April 20, Representative Rush sent a second letter to Ashcroft pointing out that "Emmett Till's mother, Mamie Till-Mobley, similarly made numerous requests to the Justice Department and the Federal Bureau of Investigation to investigate her son's murder. Unfortunately, she received only indifference and silence as a rather telling response. I would hope that the Justice Department would not treat a member of Congress the same way it treated Mrs. Till-Mobley 50 years ago—with indifference and silence."[114]

The planned meeting never came about, but Acosta sent his staff to Mississippi to meet with District Attorney Chiles to discuss the possibilities of partnering in an investigation.[115] From there, the Justice Department decided to act, and the announcement it made was historic. On May 10, Sykes was at home in Kansas City but, believing that an announcement about an investigation was probably forthcoming, tried to get to Washington, DC. He called Don Burger to catch a ride with him, but Burger was already packed and about to leave for Washington with someone else to deal with another issue.

"I can feel it is going to happen—maybe today or tomorrow," Sykes told him.[116]

He was right. Acosta announced that day on behalf of the attorney general's office that the Department of Justice, in partnership with the state of Mississippi, was opening an investigation into the kidnapping and murder of Emmett Till. "If indeed others are implicated and they can be identified, they can still be prosecuted," Acosta explained. "While the five-year federal statute of limitations in effect in 1955 has since expired, prosecution can still be brought in state court." He justified the decision by explaining, "Emmett Till's brutal murder and grotesque miscarriage of justice moved this nation.

We owe it to Emmett Till, we owe it to his mother and to his family, and we owe it to ourselves to see if, after all these years, any additional measure of justice is still possible." A 1994 statute provided authorization to the FBI to assist both state and local authorities in this type of investigation under certain circumstances.[117]

Beauchamp was at his girlfriend's home when he learned the news he had been waiting to hear for years. Even though Thompson had told Beauchamp a week earlier that the federal government was beginning to move on the investigation, the news still came as a surprise. The announcement was especially welcome because Beauchamp was then in the midst of a crisis. His girlfriend, Ronnique Hawkins, who had been entrusted with the master copies of *Untold Story*, had accidentally left them on a train. With so many screenings scheduled for the film, Beauchamp sat wondering what he would do next. Just then he received a call from a producer at CNN that did not resolve his dilemma but lifted his spirits nonetheless. He told Beauchamp he was sending a car over to pick him up. Beauchamp wanted to know why.

"Haven't you heard? Keith, we got the Till case reopened. Turn it on CNN."

Beauchamp turned on the television and watched as the network made the announcement.[118] And, as luck would have it, a day before a scheduled screening hosted by Senator Schumer, Ken Thompson, and attorney Doug Wigdor, UPS delivered the master copies of *Untold Story* to Hawkins's house. They had been retrieved from the train and sent to the address left by Beauchamp when filling out the shipping label.[119]

Others' reactions to the news were overwhelmingly positive. Stanley Nelson, whose film had been reviewed for its inclusion of new witnesses, was thrilled. "It's a great feeling, it's an incredible feeling, to be a bit part of this."[120] Till family members were especially happy. "I'm elated," said Simeon Wright. "It's a great decision. Something had to be done." Airickca Gordon, a cousin whom Mamie Till-Mobley helped raise, thought of the woman who had dreamed of this day for so long. "I can see her sitting in the chair with a tissue, and her cheeks rosy red and her eyes full of tears. It would be a happy, relief, burden-lifted type of cry."[121]

Mississippi's highest official as well as prominent black leaders also weighed in. Governor Haley Barbour threw his support behind the decision, stating that the Justice Department would not have acted had it not had good reasons to do so. "It reopens some old wounds," he admitted, "but that's not always counterproductive to reconciliation."[122] The Reverend Jesse Jackson noted the historical significance of the case by affirming, "Emmett Till's death changed the hearts and minds of millions. It was the wake-up call." NAACP president Kweisi Mfume applauded the news but noted that "it is sad that it has taken so long."[123]

To be sure, the news that this forty-nine-year-old case would be investigated by the Justice Department was welcomed in many quarters, yet the decision was only a first step. Federal officials were cognizant of the fact that decades had passed since the murder had been committed. "At the end of the day, there may not be a prosecutable crime, but it's a case of such importance that it's worth taking a chance to see what's there," said one official, speaking to the *New York Times* on condition of anonymity. Beauchamp planned to aid the FBI investigation by providing them over eighty hours of film and stacks of documents that he had accumulated.[124]

For a variety of reasons, not everyone was happy about a new probe into a decades-old racially motivated murder case. Bonnie Cheshier, who had never even heard of the case when Mississippi reporters asked her about it twenty years earlier, was disappointed by the decision. "You're kidding," she said with surprise upon hearing the news. Unlike Governor Barbour, Cheshier, who had served as town clerk for over two decades, believed that opening old wounds *was* counterproductive. "I do not think it's a good idea. It seems like we have a better community here now between blacks and whites. I feel [the decision] focuses on the bad and we need to focus on the good. I've worked real hard to let everyone know we treat all people the same here."[125] A letter to the editor of the *Jackson Clarion-Ledger* no doubt reflected the opinion of other concerned Mississippians. "I can't understand why our tax dollars are being used to investigate this case," wrote Jackson resident Nita Martin. "This happened [forty-nine] years ago and there has already been a trial and the men involved are dead now. So what can be accomplished?"[126]

Martin obviously failed to understand that a probe would not only seek to uncover the facts as they related to Milam and Bryant, but it would also try to determine who else was involved and whether they could be punished. Although Cheshier was correct in her belief that moving forward was an essential step for Mississippi to heal from its tortured past, that would be futile without an attempt toward justice in the case that had haunted the Delta for so long. The fact that there is no statute of limitations on murder said as much. Even if no one could, in the end, be prosecuted, learning the truth would be essential to long-term healthy race relations. Only then could the dark fog be lifted from Tallahatchie County and Cheshier's vision be fully realized. With the decision made and the FBI gearing up to do its work, critics of the decision, supporters, Till family members, and any guilty parties still at large would now pass the time with two things in common—watching and waiting.

12

Seeking Justice in a New Era

Soon after the Justice Department announced its decision to investigate the Emmett Till murder, officials turned the case over to the FBI. Robert J. Garrity Jr., who had been with the Bureau since 1976, transferred to Mississippi in June 2005 as special agent in charge, replacing Ed Worthington, who had retired in March. As special agent in charge, Garrity would lead the field office in Jackson as well as the nine resident agencies scattered throughout the state. Garrity believed strongly that investigating the case was the right thing to do, and a supervisor at the Oxford office assigned the job to an agent there named Dale Killinger.[1] Twenty-four counties made up the territory covered by the Oxford Resident Agency, including those most relevant to the Till case—Leflore, Sunflower, and Tallahatchie.

Killinger, forty-one, was a Pennsylvania native who had been with the FBI for eight years when Garrity placed him in charge of investigating the forty-nine-year-old homicide. Although Killinger had spent his entire career with the Bureau in Oxford, Mississippi, he had never heard of Emmett Till before getting the assignment. He went immediately to the local library to brief himself and checked out the only two books in the stacks, Stephen Whitfield's *A Death in the Delta* and Christopher Metress's documentary history, *The Lynching of Emmett Till*.[2]

The investigation would be a full-time job for Killinger, although an occasional bank robbery or other federal crime required his attention now and then. From the start, he discovered many of the challenges that would make the Till case especially difficult. Most of the participants in the 1955 trial were dead—both defendants, the judge, all of the jurors, and most of the known trial witnesses. Of the eight attorneys who tried the case, the only one still living was eighty-three-year-old Harvey Henderson, a member of the defense team. In fact, Henderson was still practicing law out of the same office in Sumner's town square that he used in 1955. The trial transcript had been missing for decades, and there was no surviving investigative file. Killinger and his team would quite literally be starting from scratch.[3]

During the early phase of the investigation, Killinger sent letters to all of the authorities in the surrounding counties and asked for anything in their files that might help. He also traveled to Chicago to establish a positive relationship with the Till family and met with Wheeler Parker and Simeon Wright, among others. The investigation required extensive background research from the beginning. With the passage of time, much of the landscape of the Mississippi Delta had changed, and it became necessary to re-create the layout of the 1950s. Killinger had to determine where the relevant locations were or had once been, such as Mose Wright's house, the Sturdivant plantation, and the sharecropper homes of Willie Reed and Mandy Bradley. He had to learn who trial witnesses were as well as other key players in the case. This was a time-consuming effort, and as Killinger proceeded, the Justice Department conducted research of its own to ensure that Killinger and his team stayed within the bounds of the law.[4]

A month after the federal officials opened the case, Steve Ritea, a reporter for the *New Orleans Times-Picayune*, traveled to the Mississippi Delta, where he quickly learned that after fifty years, black people living in Money and the neighboring communities were still reluctant to speak about Emmett Till. Ritea's brief probe provided some insight into the challenges Killinger would face. L. C. Dorsey of Mississippi Valley State University assured Ritea that there were "still a lot of older people who are uncomfortable with going out of their place." Seventy-five-year-old Mary Jackson said that there were people who even today kept quiet because "they're still afraid."[5] Killinger learned this himself after some of those he tried to interview refused to speak with him. Their fear immediately became apparent; when he approached one woman whom he thought might have information, she quickly made a 180-degree turn away from him before providing Killinger an alibi for her husband on the night Till was kidnapped.[6]

One who came forward to Ritea and later to Killinger was a man calling himself Willie Lee Hemphill of Darling, Mississippi.[7] Hemphill, who was around the same age as Emmett Till in 1955, had an unusual story that he had kept quiet for decades. He claimed that on the Saturday evening before Emmett Till's kidnapping, he was heading home from the Bryant grocery. As he walked north along Money Road, a pickup truck approached and someone from inside the cab ordered a black man sitting in the back to grab Hemphill and throw him in the truck. The jars of molasses and snuff that Hemphill had been carrying broke into pieces when he landed face down in the bed, as did some of his teeth. He could see J. W. Milam and Roy and Carolyn Bryant sitting in the cab. After Carolyn got a better look at Hemphill, she turned toward the men riding with her. "That's not the nigger. That's not the nigger boy," she said. Hemphill recognized the black man who accosted him but did not provide the name to Ritea. When Hemphill later talked to Killinger, he identified the man as "J. W. Washington." Hemphill actually meant Johnny B. Washington, a twenty-seven-year-old helper at the Bryant store. Hemphill never discussed this strange, frightening encounter with anyone, not even his children. As he explained it to Ritea, "I just didn't want them to know what really happened to Dad, that there wasn't anything done about it."[8] If Hemphill's story was any indication, there was a multitude of secrets in the Mississippi Delta, and peeling back the layers of silence would not be easy.

In August, Killinger, federal prosecutor John Hailman, District Attorney Joyce Chiles, and her assistant, Hallie Gail Bridges, all met at the courthouse in Greenwood to discuss the case and the status of the inquiry. Hailman described Bridges as thoroughly committed to the investigation and "as tough and pragmatic a state prosecutor as I could possibly have wished for." Leflore County sheriff Ricky Banks was also fully supportive, as was retired FBI agent Lent Rice. In an unusual move, Killinger dedicated a room to the Till case at the FBI office in Oxford. It contained photos, old reports, and anything that Killinger's team would accumulate.[9] They worked quietly, but the fact that the investigation was occurring at all attracted media attention. The biggest story prompted by the inquiry was a two-part *60 Minutes* segment that aired on October 24, 2004, five-and-a-half months after the probe began. The piece confirmed to viewers the names of two individuals still living that had become a focus of the FBI.

The highly rated news program would guarantee that millions of Americans would tune in and learn about Emmett Till, most, perhaps, for the first time. In the opening segment, longtime correspondent Ed Bradley provided background for the case and interviewed Wheeler Parker and Simeon Wright, who each recounted the store incident and kidnapping in Money. Bradley also spoke with sixty-seven-year-old Willie Reed, who recalled the beating he heard outside the shed in Drew. The story featured footage of Mamie Till-Mobley from Keith Beauchamp's *The Untold Story of Emmett Louis Till*, which, incidentally, Beauchamp was still trying to complete. In the second segment, Bradley talked with Beauchamp about his research and to Senator Charles Schumer (D-NY) about their push to reopen the case and hopes of punishing any living perpetrators. Bradley interrogated Henry Lee Loggins at Loggins's home in Dayton, Ohio, and, not surprisingly, the former Mississippi farmhand denied any firsthand knowledge of the kidnapping and murder. Bradley's interview occurred before FBI agents had yet talked to Loggins, and Loggins assured Bradley that when they came calling, "I'll tell them the same thing—that I wasn't there."[10]

The most intriguing part of the piece occurred when the public got its first glimpse of Carolyn Bryant in nearly fifty years. Bradley and his producer,

Michael Radutzky, found Bryant, by then known as Carolyn Donham, living in Greenville, Mississippi, near her forty-seven-year-old son, Frank. A cameraman filmed a few frames of Donham, who never emerged from beyond the glass door at her home and refused to talk. Frank Bryant drove up to the home while Ed Bradley was on the property and angrily denied the reporter any access to his mother. He ordered Bradley to leave and then quietly walked toward the house and went inside. All of this footage appeared on the broadcast. Bradley revealed to viewers that Mose Wright's testimony in which he claimed to have heard a woman's voice at the scene of the kidnapping made Donham a target in the new investigation.[11]

The *60 Minutes* piece was well hyped and important in shining a light on Beauchamp's efforts in talking to potential witnesses, working with Mamie Till-Mobley before her death the previous year, and the film that grew out of that, all of which played a major role in opening the new investigation. However, the story was also skewed in many respects because the angle it took—that a novice filmmaker had single-handedly persuaded federal authorities to reopen the case—was not accurate. Bradley failed to interview other crucial players such as Alvin Sykes, president of the Emmett Till Justice Campaign; Donald Burger, who had pushed hard for an investigation and had several notable contacts within the Justice Department; and Stanley Nelson, who had also produced a film, uncovered witnesses, and petitioned Mississippi's attorney general to reopen the case. Producers of the show reached out to Sykes during the early stages of the report, but, unfortunately, miscommunication prevented any follow-up with the tireless activist.[12]

To be sure, Beauchamp had tracked down several individuals claiming to have a direct link to the Till case, knew people who did, or saw suspicious behavior by the killers or their accomplices. An essential part of Killinger's job as lead investigator was to sift through the evidence provided by Beauchamp and anyone else and determine its relevance. Some of it panned out, some did not. In his public speeches, Beauchamp claimed that up to fourteen people had been involved in the kidnapping and murder of Emmett Till, a number that critics believed was inflated. However, Ed Bradley happily passed that figure on to *60 Minutes* viewers, along with a revelation that five of the fourteen were still alive. In a teaser, Bradley promised to name them during the second half of the broadcast, but the only two he identified were Carolyn Donham and Henry Lee Loggins.[13]

Significantly, a similar claim that three other participants were still living was then being made by a fifty-one-year-old filmmaker named Gode Davis, who was trying to produce a documentary he was calling *American Lynching: A Strange and Bitter Fruit*. Davis contacted Keith Beauchamp for help with the Emmett Till segment of his film, and Beauchamp learned that some of the people still living whom he believed participated in the Till murder were the same as those Davis discovered.[14]

In 2003, Davis told journalists Rebecca Segall and David Holmberg about two of his sources. Davis described one of them as "a white man in Mississippi who told a convincing story of his alleged participation in the Till murder." Davis did not provide a name or tell where the man lived but said that six months earlier he had moved "out of the sticks" and into a "residential neighborhood" in an unidentified town in Mississippi. Davis also interviewed someone who identified himself as Billy Wilson, who claimed to have witnessed but not participated in the Till murder.[15]

Oddly, a man named Billy Wilson had once owned a grocery store called Billy's Pak-a-Sak in West Point, Mississippi, and was rumored in the *Southern Patriot* in February 1970 to have bragged to local blacks "about being one of the killers of Emmett Till." Strangely, the article also stated that "Wilson's wife was formerly married to one of the self-confessed but legally acquitted killers, Roy Bryant, and was the woman in the case." John H. Haddock, director of Mississippi's Division of Economic Opportunity, told Governor John Bell Williams that same month that "a very reliable source gave me some information which is not verified and is not known in the West Point community of the white citizens, but which is apparently known by the black community, that Mr. Billy Wilson is the husband of the white lady who was the center of controversy in the Emmett Till case."[16] These 1970 claims that Billy Wilson and Carolyn Bryant were married are clearly erroneous, partly because the Bryants did not divorce until 1975. Additionally, this Billy Wilson had wed Betty Dewberry in 1951, and they remained married until Billy's death in 1991, over a decade before Gode Davis talked with a man with the same name. Jan Hillegas, who wrote the *Southern Patriot* piece, said in 2014 that she later investigated the rumors further but "could find no reason to think that Billy Wilson was other than a local man with another wife."[17] Around the same time the 1970 Hillegas piece appeared, *Jet* magazine also got in on the Billy Wilson rumors, claiming that he had been acquitted for the Till murder. A month later, however, it published a retraction and apology to Wilson after discovering that he had nothing to do with the case.[18]

Dale Killinger also learned of Billy Wilson, probably from Gode Davis, but for privacy purposes, Killinger's report does not provide his source. Killinger only notes that the informant "was conducting research on a lynching in Mississippi" when he learned of Wilson.[19] Killinger also interviewed Betty Wilson sometime during his investigation. The widow told Killinger that she knew about statements her husband had allegedly made about his connection to the Till murder but that she believed that there was likely another man by the same name living elsewhere in the Delta who made those claims.[20] Because the man rumored to have been involved in the Till murder was long dead before Gode Davis began his research, Davis's claim is puzzling. Was there another Billy Wilson, as Betty Wilson claimed, and were the stories that he witnessed Emmett Till's lynching unfairly linked back in 1970 to the man living in West Point? Even if there had been another Billy Wilson, he was never married to Carolyn Bryant. In the end, Killinger was unpersuaded by the Wilson angle and found many inconsistencies when comparing his informant's story with what his own investigation would later turn up. Davis told Killinger that, according to Wilson, the Till murder "had been approved by the local Ku Klux Klan leadership." Killinger, however, could find nothing in the records of Klan activities that backed up that assertion. Wilson also told Davis that up to twelve people were in the shed watching or participating in Till's murder, including a white woman and a twelve-year-old boy. The shed was even said to have contained a set of bleachers, apparently for spectators. Wilson also said that most of Till's teeth were knocked out by the beating and that "there were scraping wounds along Till's ribs." He also repeated a claim made decades earlier that the hole in Till's head was made by a drill. Not only do those elements of the story sound farfetched, they would soon be proven untrue.[21] Sadly, Gode Davis's quest for answers ended when he died unexpectedly in September 2010. Unfortunately, his documentary, still only a work-in-progress at the time, died with him.[22]

Killinger spent much of his time trying to separate fact from fiction as he had in the Wilson story, and was not distracted by the *60 Minutes* episode or other news stories about the investigation; on the contrary, he generally found such media attention to be helpful. Nor did he allow any criticisms to intimidate him.[23] On November 19, 2004, Senators Schumer and Jim Talent (R-Mo.), along with Representatives Bobby Rush (R-Ill.) and Charles Rangel (D-NY), gathered for a news conference in Washington, DC, to make the point that, in their view, the probe was going dangerously slow. "We want to find those who participated in this brutal murder and bring them to justice," said Schumer. "But both they and the witnesses . . . are old and so there cannot be a delay." To spur things on, the four men sponsored a congressional resolution "that calls on the Department of Justice and the state of Mississippi to speed up their investigation of the murder of Emmett Till and the acquittal of Milam and Bryant." They planned to introduce the resolution when Congress reconvened in January and even considered raising the issue at the confirmation hearings of Alberto Gonzales, President George W. Bush's nominee to replace John Ashcroft as US attorney general. "We have moral rectitude on our side," said Schumer.[24]

Senator Talent's presence gave the resolution bipartisan support. Although the Missouri Republican had consistently received failing grades from the NAACP throughout his term for lack of support, he seemed genuinely anxious to see justice in this case and was hopeful that the resolution would "continue to hold the department accountable." Bobby Rush explained that the investigation was personal for him because "it was the brutal murder and torture of Emmett Till that started me on my own personal journey for justice and my own participation in the civil rights movement." Speaking for all four congressmen, Charles Rangel hoped "that the Justice Department would not make the family of Emmett Till [simply] feel good or the people in Chicago or us individually or collectively, but to make the world know that America has the courage to admit when she is wrong and to move forward to say, 'Never, never again.'" Schumer read the nonbinding resolution to the Senate on January 24, 2005, and Rangel presented it to the House of Representatives three weeks later on February 17.[25]

With the 2004 elections over, George W. Bush assured a second term, and both houses of Congress still in Republican hands, one cannot ignore the probability that political motives played a role in the three Democratic politicians speaking out about what they saw as ineptitude within the current Justice Department; Talent also may have wanted to make good with his black constituents. Politics aside, Alvin Sykes was less than pleased with the action of the lawmakers, despite their calls for a speedier investigation. "We appreciate what the Congressmen are doing," Sykes told the press. "But you can't rush justice. One of the worst things they could do is not have enough evidence and risk another acquittal." Sykes explained that the goal of the investigation was not only to prosecute but to clear the names of any innocent parties. "If there are people who were not involved but were accused, then they need to be cleared by this process as well. They don't need this hanging over their heads for generations to come."[26]

During the news conference, Schumer relayed a message from Beauchamp that "if a full investigation is done, the likelihood is there will be new indictments." This was a bold declaration, but Beauchamp's confidence was understandable. He had invested years in this endeavor, which had become personal due to his relationship with Mamie Till-Mobley and his promises to her that he would fight for justice in this case; for the investigation to produce anything less seemed unthinkable. In fact, in February 2005 he told a group of students who had just screened his film at Clark University in Worchester, Massachusetts, that indictments "should be handed down within two months."[27] Killinger, who was still conducting his investigation with no apparent end in sight, may have felt uneasy about such assurances, but they were undeniably frustrating to Mississippi district attorney Joyce Chiles, who would ultimately be the one to decide any action in the case. Feeling the same discomfort, Alvin Sykes repeatedly urged Beauchamp to be circumspect in his public comments.[28]

Killinger remained focused, paid little attention to external commentary, and would not let political pressure or the rumor mill affect his probe. "That doesn't dictate the way the FBI operates," he explained in 2014.[29] Yet there were important developments unfolding, which meant there was no denying the world would soon know more about the murder of Emmett Till. Information that leaked out indicated that Killinger and his team were making headway. For example, they had recently located old Department of Agriculture aerial photographs that honed in on the sites relevant to the case. This allowed investigators to see the land of the Till murder as it looked in 1955.[30] To help further reconstruct the layout of the plantation in Drew, Mississippi, where Till had been beaten and presumably killed, Killinger took Willie Reed to the scene in April 2005. Reed identified the shed, which was still standing, and pointed out the former location of his grandfather's home and the sharecrop house of Mandy Bradley. On May 18, the FBI conducted a thorough search of the shed, which included the laborious job of sifting through the dirt floor for fifty-year-old evidence and spraying luminol in an effort to locate traces of blood spatter. The passage of time alone had diminished the likelihood of finding anything incriminating, but chances were even slimmer because a few years earlier the current owner, local dentist Jeff Andrews, removed and discarded the original floorboards, where bloodstains would at one time have been plentiful. Investigators removed five items that appeared at first glance to be bone fragments, but tests concluded that three of them were animal bones while two were rocks.[31]

Discussions about exhuming Emmett Till's body had been uncomfortable for the Till family, and they had been forced to deal with the issue at some level for over a year before the investigation even began. Then, in October 2004, Killinger traveled to Argo and met with Wheeler Parker, Crosby Smith Jr., and Simeon Wright, to prepare them for the fact that the body would need to be exhumed and autopsied. In response, Parker explained to the press that the family would support an exhumation if mandated by federal authorities, but they would not back a voluntary one. Because the defense in the 1955 murder trial had argued so vehemently that the body claimed and buried by Mamie Bradley could not have been that of her son, laying that theory to rest and determining the cause of death were essential to a complete investigation. At this point, Alvin Sykes was still hoping that the federal authorities would utilize Dr. Mehmet Yaşar İşcan, of Istanbul, Turkey, for the job, but they apparently never looked further into Sykes's recommendation and had the Cook County coroner in mind and saw him as sufficient.[32]

On Wednesday, May 5, 2005, the news hit that Emmett Till's body would be removed and examined. Sykes had been anticipating that day because of the answers he believed doing so would bring, and he summarized that nicely when speaking to a reporter. "The exhumation represents the first and last time for Emmett Till to speak for himself." Many of those answers would come once investigators gathered DNA from the body and ran it against samples donated by living family members. Parker seemed more supportive once plans became official, realizing the procedure "would bring a lot of closure and that he [Emmett Till] would be positively identified. We need to get the whole thing closed."[33]

Unfortunately, the views of Parker, Smith, and Wright were not representative of the entire family, however, and divisions soon arose and went public. Civil rights leader Jesse Jackson even got in on the controversy and quickly arranged a news conference at his Rainbow/PUSH headquarters for Wednesday at noon, where he gathered family members opposed to the exhumation. His initial complaint was that the family had learned of the decision only through media reports, but he quickly began criticizing the entire process. "There is a feeling (among the family) that the FBI is grandstanding," he said. However, Representative Bobby Rush, learning about the plans to exhume the body, immediately parted with Jackson and voiced his support for unearthing the murder victim. "The alternative to me is less desirable, and that is to forget about this case and seeking justice for Emmett Till. The alternative would be disrespectful of the wishes of Mamie-Till-Mobley."[34]

Bertha Thomas, a cousin and president of the Emmett Till Foundation, stood beside Jackson and before the media and made it clear that she was adamantly opposed to disturbing the remains. "We are offended," she said bluntly, citing religious concerns, but for her and those siding with her, an exhumation was also "a useless process at this stage. Why now?" Echoing Jackson, Thomas accused the FBI of simply "grandstanding" and called the entire undertaking "a waste of time."[35] With the media gathered around, Jackson upped his criticisms. "Is the FBI and the Department of Justice making a renewed commitment to racial justice and a national dialogue with civil rights organizations, or is it using Emmett Till as a trophy 50 years after a brutal act of terror?" Jackson even accused the FBI of "trying to prove a nut theory that this is not Emmett Till's body. Rather than pursuing the terrorists, the FBI is searching for positive identification, which is the position that the Mississippi court took." Bertha Thomas went so far as to suggest that the investigation be called off rather than exhume the body. "If I have to, I will fight this and I am more than prepared to fight . . . the FBI, the Department of Justice and anybody else that steps up to the plate."[36]

Although Thomas maintained that her views were in line with most of the family, Simeon Wright insisted that his cousin was "speaking for herself." Thomas's stance was puzzling to Wright and undoubtedly to others. "Why would [the Emmett Till Foundation] want to keep Emmett's memory alive at all if there's something that might be done about the murder and it refuses to do it?" he asked. "That's no different than the jury that let those two men go." Thomas, however, countered that it was Wright who was in the minority. FBI spokeswoman Deborah Madden, weighing in from her office in Jackson, said that none of the relatives she had spoken with shared Thomas's objections.[37] Civil rights leader Al Sharpton also split with Jesse Jackson on this issue and threw his support behind the Justice Department. "I think that it is impera-tive that just as we fought for decades to track down the murderers of [other civil rights victims], that we track down the murderers of Emmett Till," he said. "This cannot be done without completion of his death certificate and the exhumation of his remains."[38]

A few weeks earlier in April, FBI director Robert S. Mueller appointed Jim Garrity to a new post in Washington, DC, and Garrity would vacate his posi-tion as Mississippi's special agent in charge on Friday, June 3.[39] He would not leave before weighing in on the hullabaloo surrounding Emmett Till's exhu-mation, however, and his irritation over Jesse Jackson's accusations led him to fire off a letter to the *Chicago Tribune*, which the paper published in part on May 22. Although the *Tribune* censored Garrity's obvious references to Jack-son, the *Daily Southtown*, published thirty miles south in Tinley Park, printed the letter in full. "The planned exhumation and medical examination of the body of Emmett Till has provoked controversy, misinformation and allega-tions of an ulterior motive on the part of the FBI that I cannot allow to go unaddressed," he wrote. His response to his most vocal and prominent critic was sharp:

> The men and women of the FBI are conducting a painstakingly thorough crimi-nal investigation, not a historical exercise, and it is offensive to their professional reputation to hear the irresponsible statements of those who allege the FBI is grandstanding, posturing or viewing Emmett Till as a "trophy." This investiga-tion, as all FBI criminal investigations, is being conducted with the objective of identifying the facts and unwaveringly following them to their logical conclusion. The exhumation of a body is a delicate issue, and we are sensitive to the emotions that are naturally evoked as a result. However, it is the FBI's absolute obligation to pursue justice wherever the facts may lead, even in the face of dissension. To do any less would be an abdication of our duty, and would doubtless result in accusa-tions of a sloppy investigation or cover-up.

Indeed, the investigation would be stalled without an autopsy. The decision to exhume the remains, Garrity assured his readers, "was not reached lightly, or in ignorance of the potential consequences." Scientific testing would uncover details related to the manner of Till's death and would be used to verify or debunk statements by others, such as defense attorneys or Sheriff H. C. Strider, who all theorized at the time of the trial that the body was not Emmett Till's. Physical evidence such as bullet fragments might also be available for recovery, and the exhumation would allow the vital step of proving identity through DNA testing. In concluding his letter, Garrity charged that "reckless allegations that the FBI is trying to prove a 'nut theory' that the body is not that of Till's are ignorant and ill-informed at best and, at worst, dishonest." He promised that throughout the entire process, "Emmett Till's remains will be treated with the utmost dignity and respect. At the conclusion of the pathological examinations, his body will be made available to the family so they may pay their respects in whatever manner they deem appropriate prior to reinterment."[40]

As the controversy continued, other developments in the case were well received by all, and perhaps gave assurance to skeptics like Jackson that the FBI was carrying out a serious investigation after all. Mississippi officials never retained the transcript of the murder trial in their files, and the only copy known to have existed had been given to Hugh Stephen Whitaker in the early 1960s by J. J. Breland, one of the defense attorneys for Milam and Bryant. Unfortunately, Whitaker's copy perished in a basement flood in the 1970s. The likelihood that a copy still existed somewhere could not be dismissed, and for a few, finding it became an obsession. Off and on, Florida State University professor Davis Houck, who held a deep interest in the Till case, made inquiries about the transcript but did not give the matter serious thought until 2005, when one of his graduate students, Mark Mulligan, took on the task of locating a copy for a class project. Mulligan made calls, followed leads, and spoke regularly with a son of one of the Till trial jurors who also became curious about the document. However, Mulligan's efforts turned up nothing. On February 21, the *Memphis Commercial Appeal* ran a story about Houck and the hunt for the elusive record. The article got the attention of Killinger, who called Houck at his office to learn of any progress.[41]

Killinger did not tell Houck whether FBI investigators had already found the document, but his office had indeed located and logged in a copy five months earlier on September 13, 2004. It would prove to be one of the most significant discoveries of the investigation. Early on, when Killinger sent inquiries out to various law enforcement officers and prosecutors in an effort to obtain information from their files, the only response he received informed him that a man named Lee McGarrh, who lived near Biloxi, Mississippi, owned a copy of the transcript. Killinger was skeptical but drove all the way to the Gulf Coast to talk to McGarrh, but McGarrh was not home. Killinger then assigned someone else to look into it.[42]

Killinger later questioned the investigator who was to follow up and assumed the lead came up empty. Killinger was surprised to learn that not only did McGarrh really own the transcript, but he agreed to loan it to investigators. In fact, it had already been safely logged as evidence and placed in the designated room at the Oxford office. McGarrh had inherited the document from his father, Lee McGarrh Sr., a Glendora, Mississippi, service station owner who died in 2002. The elder McGarrh had served as a character witness for J. W. Milam during the 1955 murder trial. The document, which Robert Garrity described as a "copy of a copy of a copy," was barely legible and missing one page, but investigators were still able to decipher it all and verify its authenticity by comparing it to direct quotes that Whitaker cited in his master's thesis. Two clerks devoted long and grueling hours over several weeks transcribing the document in its entirety, retaining the original line breaks and pagination. On May 18, 2005, the *New York Times* broke the story of the find. The transcript would benefit investigators by resurrecting the testimony of dead witnesses while comparing the recollections of those still living with what they had said fifty years earlier.[43]

By Wednesday, June 1, the Till family united, and Bertha Thomas and any others who had opposed exhuming Emmett's body ceased their efforts to stop it. Even Jesse Jackson affirmed his support and said simply that he was happy that the family was "speaking with one voice." FBI agents were at the Burr Oak Cemetery by six o'clock that morning and covered the gravesite with a large white tent. A few hours later, Ollie Gordon, Crosby Smith Jr., and Simeon and Annie Wright, representing the family, arrived and held a brief ceremony. Following their short service, they watched silently for the next three hours as a backhoe slowly dug down and uncovered the concrete vault containing Emmett Till's casket. The process was done as quietly as possible, and the media were not allowed past the gates during the exhumation. That same day, Frank Bochte of the Chicago FBI office reiterated the Bureau's motive. "The first and foremost thing we're trying to do is to put to rest any theories that the body inside there is not Emmett Till. We would like to settle that issue once and for all." At around noon, the dirt-caked vault was loaded onto a flatbed truck and taken to the Cook County medical examiner's office.[44]

The casket was removed from the vault, then opened, and workers carefully set aside the tight-fitting glass panel that had been placed over the body a half century earlier in order to protect it from the touch of curious onlookers. Witnesses included Dale Killinger and District Attorney Joyce Chiles, who flew in from her home in Itta Bena, Mississippi. Those present were met with the smell of chemicals used to preserve the body a half century earlier. The witnesses who gathered at the coroner's office expected to gaze upon skeletal remains; instead, they were surprised to see a body that was in near pristine condition. Even the clothing was still intact. In addition to an obviously thorough job at embalming the body, preservation was no doubt aided by the glass top, which further protected the remains from outside elements. The vault had also sheltered the casket from the cemetery's large water table. A close examination of both the glass and casket lid revealed a large collection of fingerprints left behind by many of the thousands of mourners who had filed past the body in September 1955. They looked as fresh as they did five decades earlier.[45]

The autopsy, conducted by Chief Medical Examiner Edmund R. Donoghue, began the morning of June 2 and was completed that afternoon. When the body was removed from the casket, examiners discovered newspaper underneath the head, along with a scattering of charcoal and straw that had apparently been placed inside to reduce the smell of the waterlogged corpse.[46] Before the physical examination took place, the body was taken to the John H. Stronger Jr. Hospital of Cook County, where technicians performed a CT scan. This procedure revealed the presence of metallic fragments inside the cranium, a clear indication that the victim had been shot. The massive head wounds described by Mississippi law enforcement officers and Mamie Bradley back in 1955 were also documented, but the scan revealed that both wrists and the distal left femur had been fractured, facts never discovered before.[47]

Tests performed on the teeth of the victim were necessary to determine age and identity. Dental development confirmed that the deceased was around fourteen years old at the time of death. Photographs of Emmett Till taken during Christmas 1954 compared to pictures taken of the body exhumed from Burr Oak Cemetery revealed a small but identical gap in the teeth. "The dental examination concluded that based on a reasonable degree of dental certainty, the dental age, and proximal angle comparisons, are consistent with that of Emmett Louis Till," noted Killinger's summary of the tests. Despite Mamie Bradley's many descriptions of the body as having had most of its teeth knocked out, the autopsy revealed that only one tooth was missing. It also dispelled rumors long afloat that the victim had been castrated. This myth received greater publicity from the reminiscences of John Crawford in *Untold Story*. Crawford said that Mose Wright made the castration claim after Wright identified Emmett Till at the river. Examiners photographed the body's genitals to document that they were still intact.[48]

DNA testing was done by taking a piece of muscle tissue from the body and a blood sample and two buccal swabs from Simeon Wright. Results showed that the mtDNA sequence obtained from both was the same. The mtDNA database, which represented 1,148 African Americans, showed only two instances of this same sequence. In addition to dental testing, an examination of bone development in the growth centers (or epiphyses) indicated that the deceased died at around fourteen years.[49]

Closer examination of the metal fragments found in the cranium showed them to be consistent with spent number 7 or 8 lead shot pellets. The investigation learned that the Remington Arms Company made both the M12 and M15 .45 caliber pistols in the years preceding Emmett Till's death. They were manufactured for the army and both contained number 7 lead shot. A relative of J. W. Milam's confirmed for the FBI that not only did Milam own such a firearm, he knew how to use it. "I can tell ya how good he was with that old pistol. I seen him shoot bumble bees out of the air with it." On March 11, 2004, two months before the investigation began, Keith Beauchamp received an email from a woman who said she had "heard a rumor," which she had not substantiated, "that the gun used by the man who killed Emmett was given to a man in Tallahatchie County," who was then told to "do something with this!!" She said the man's widow still possessed it and that it was a Colt .45 army edition and was kept in a leather holster. She named the woman who allegedly owned the gun and told Beauchamp that she lived in Tippo, Mississippi.[50]

Killinger followed up on that lead, which proved to be legitimate. On November 1, 2004, the woman in Tippo gave Killinger an Ithaca model .45 believed to have been owned by Milam. The serial number revealed that it had been manufactured in 1945. Milam served in the armed forces from 1941 until 1946. Killinger sent the gun to the FBI laboratory in Quantico, Virginia, where firearms experts dismantled and examined it. However, they found no latent fingerprints that matched Milam's or anyone else's involved in the case. Still, this weapon was certainly the gun in question.[51]

After all tests were done and the results were in, Dr. Donoghue concluded that the body was that of Emmett Till and that Till was a victim of homicide, having died from a gunshot wound to the head. Before the exhumation started, a judge at the Cook County Circuit Court signed a court order stipulating that the body be returned to the family by June 6. On June 4, just three days after the process began, Emmett Till was reburied in a new casket during a private ceremony attended only by family members. Just days later, revelations about the discovery of bullet fragments hit the news. Press reports that DNA tests confirmed the body to be that of Emmett Till followed in August.[52]

These very public developments in the investigation satisfied the media, which allowed details that the FBI learned from witnesses to remain largely under wraps. Although Carolyn Donham had refused all requests for interviews about the Till case in the years after the murder, she agreed to speak with Killinger. Family members, with Donham's permission, contacted Joyce Chiles and Hallie Gail Bridges at the district attorney's office, who in turn set up an appointment for Donham at the federal office in Greenville. Killinger interviewed Donham for several hours, during which Donham became emotional. Donham was happy that investigators treated her kindly, and she said, with some relief, "I'm glad this is over with."[53]

Carolyn Donham had, in fact, appeared relieved and anxious to talk. John Hailman, who stayed in direct contact with Killinger throughout the investigation, said that Donham genuinely appeared as though "the case was a dark cloud that had hung over her all through her life" and that this was a chance to lift a burden she had been carrying for half a century. Killinger and Donham spoke over the phone several times and met in person on at least a few occasions over the course of his investigation. During their in-person interviews, Killinger was wearing a wire, unbeknownst to Donham.[54] She answered questions about the store incident and of the events surrounding the weekend of Emmett Till's kidnapping.

As to her encounter with Emmett Till at the Bryant grocery on August 24, 1955, Donham stuck to her courtroom testimony that Till grabbed her. During the trial she said that Juanita Milam was in the apartment at the back of the store babysitting the four boys belonging to the Milams and Bryants. Donham told Killinger that when her customer began to act inappropriately, "I . . . screamed for [her] and screamed for [her] . . . as soon as he touched me I started screaming for [her]." The customer gave her the impression that he would be back. She said, as she had in 1955, that she went to get a gun out of the car Juanita was driving, but in her interview with Killinger, she clarified that she first looked for the weapon under the counter where it was normally kept.

Donham maintained that she was not the one who told Roy about the incident. "I didn't say anything and one of the reasons I, I didn't say, ever say anything more about it, was because I was afraid that, what I was worried about was he's gonna go find and beat him up. . . . I told [Juanita] what had happened, [and] I asked her not to tell J. W., because I didn't intend to tell Roy, because I was afraid of what they would do." When Roy came back to town, she never brought up the subject, but Roy apparently found out from someone. "He waited a long time and he asked me didn't I have something I wanted to tell him and I told him no." Only after Roy became visibly angry did she tell her husband that a black customer grabbed her hand and held her by the waist.

Roy was so outraged over these revelations that when another black youth came into the store that night, Roy began questioning him. Donham recalled that incident. "I don't know, Roy said something to 'em, and I remember telling him to leave him alone that, you know, that wasn't him."

Later that same night, J. W. came around to the back of the store to the apartment door, picked up Roy, and left. "I was there all night by myself. Alone. With two boys," said Donham to Killinger. After the men left and the two boys fell asleep, she became frightened. "I was just scared to death, sittin' there, didn't know what, and I think that was the first time I'd ever been alone at night there."[55]

Before daylight, Donham recalled, she heard what sounded like a black person knocking at her door. She refused to answer, out of fear. Later that same morning Roy, Milam, and a man she called "Kimbrell," or Elmer Kimbell, returned to the apartment. "I think they came back and I think that Kimbrell man was, was with, with 'em." They took Emmett Till for Carolyn to identify. "I think it happened pretty much like he, like they said. I think they probably asked me who, if that was him." Carolyn told them "no that's not him." Roy then told her that "he was gonna take him back."[56]

Killinger does not say that he asked Donham if she accompanied the men to Wright's home, but her insistence that they brought Till to her at the store to identify him would indicate that she claimed or implied that she stayed home. However, Killinger was left with the clear impression that Donham's denial was not true.[57]

Donham told Killinger that after daylight she went down the road and used a phone to call her brother-in-law, Melvin Campbell, to learn Roy's whereabouts. Campbell told her that Roy had been out all night playing poker but would return home later. After Roy was arrested that afternoon, Carolyn began staying with members of the Bryant family. While she was visiting at a store operated by Buddy Milam, one of her husband's half-siblings, Roy's twin brother, Raymond, came in. "I think it was the day the body was found, and I think he told me that and uh, I don't know what I said to him, that Roy, Roy said he didn't do anything to him or something and anyway, Raymond said Roy didn't. It was Melvin." When Carolyn asked why they arrested Roy if he did not kill the boy, Raymond told her that "I was not to tell anybody it was Melvin."[58]

Carolyn Donham's testimony implicating others who either knew about the murder, helped cover it up, or, with the Melvin Campbell allegation, actually fired the shot was a tremendous breakthrough considering she never told her story to anyone for the record before. Parts of her account were problematic, however, and notable discrepancies soon came to light. The first concerns Juanita Milam's alleged presence at the apartment the night Emmett Till went into the store. When Killinger interviewed Juanita, she denied having been there that night. "I thought I was in Greenville," she told him. She also believed that she "would not have been babysittin' for her." In fact, Juanita believed that Carolyn fabricated the entire story about Emmett Till accosting her. "The only way I can figure it is that she did not want to take care of the store. She thought this wild story would make Roy take care of the store instead of leavin' her with the kids and the store." Juanita may be confusing the Wednesday night incident with the kidnapping and murder that occurred on the following weekend. On September 2, 1955, she told defense attorneys Sidney Carlton and Harvey Henderson that "I went to Greenville about 1:30 P.M. on Saturday and got back home about 12 midnight and went to bed."[59]

A second contradiction to Carolyn Donham's story to Killinger would come from Donham herself. While the investigation was still in progress, Donham and her daughter-in-law, Marsha Bryant, began working together on Donham's memoir. Perhaps prompted by the investigation, Donham reached the point where she wanted to tell her side of the story. Around this same time, she reached out to the historian Timothy B. Tyson and told it all to him. She said that she made up the tale about Emmett Till accosting her and did so at the urging of Bryant family members and defense attorneys.[60] Indeed, defense notes written up by Sidney Carlton during an interview with Carolyn on September 2, 1955, quoted earlier, mention only that Till touched her hand, asked for a date, said good-bye, and whistled at her.[61] The fabrications that he did anything else likely took days to concoct, but were clearly in place by Sunday, September 18, when Carlton began telling reporters that Emmett Till "mauled [Carolyn] and attempted a physical attack while making indecent proposals."[62]

An unrelated yet nationally followed case should have caused Carolyn Donham some consternation. On January 6, 2005, seventy-nine-year-old Edgar Ray Killen was arrested on three counts of murder for the June 1964 Freedom Summer slayings of civil rights activists James Chaney, Andrew Goodman, and Michael Schwerner in Philadelphia, Mississippi. Killen had actually been charged, along with seventeen others, on federal civil rights violations in 1967 in the deaths of the three men. Although seven of them were convicted at the time, a hung jury in Killen's case resulted in his release.

After Killen was charged with murder in January 2005, his trial began five months later, on June 13. On June 21, forty-one years to the day of the killings, he was convicted of manslaughter and two days later was given a twenty-year sentence for each count, for a total of sixty years. He would be eligible for parole after twenty, but the mandatory time virtually guaranteed that he would die behind bars, given his age.[63] The Killen conviction, like that of Byron De La Beckwith eleven years earlier for the murder of Medgar Evers, was a reminder that revisiting cold cases was beginning to pay off.

Although Carolyn Donham had spoken to Dale Killinger willingly during his investigation, and to family members did not appear worried, she was in all probability feeling some angst about being a target of an FBI probe and had every reason to fear the worst.[64] On August 7, 2005, two months after the Killen conviction, attorney Richard Barrett, a New Yorker who had moved to Mississippi, visited Donham's son, Frank Bryant, at the Donham home in Greenville. Barrett, founder of the white supremacist organization called the Nationalist Movement, had run unsuccessfully for Congress in 1984. Two years earlier, he authored the book *The Commission*, which argued that the black race (or any nonwhite group) was void of any "creativity of its own." Barrett sought out Bryant to offer "moral support," and to encourage Donham "to go on the offense," after seeing what he believed to be a tremendous outpouring of support for the seventy-one-year-old grandmother. Barrett described his meeting with Frank Bryant as "extremely cordial" and "upbeat." Barrett emphasized that he was only consulting with Bryant as an "ordinary citizen," but would happily get involved in the case should they ask him to.

Barrett discussed the meeting with Greenville's WXVT television station, and did his best to paint Emmett Till as a sexual deviant. Fourteen-year-old Till, Barrett said, had "bragged" that he had raped a white woman and pointed out that Till's father had been executed for raping and even murdering white women. Then, in a rant that sounded like something out of a 1950s segregationist playbook, Barrett insisted that if Donham were to be prosecuted, "the whole drive to invade and integrate Mississippi and to communize and destroy America" should be tried in a courtroom also. When reporters asked Barrett if he knew of any evidence that could lead to a prosecution, he said only that "the real issue is who will rule America, the minorities or the majority." He called the investigation into Donham a "witch-hunt" that "has to be defeated by a fearsome political-defense, based upon love of freedom, reliance upon democracy and appeal to innate justice." Frank Bryant made it clear to Barrett that he not only stood by his mother during this trying time but maintained his father's innocence as well. Barrett described Frank Bryant, who asked the lawyer for a copy of *The Commission*, as "a man of backbone, defiance, vision and spirit." Frank promised that both he and his mother would read the book.

Barrett believed firmly that Mississippi attorney general Jim Hood would seek an indictment, probably because Hood had tried the Killen case personally and showed great passion in seeking a conviction. Be that as it may, Barrett thought that "an early showing of support, bolstered by strong, patriotic public-opinion, for Carolyn Bryant could stave the vampires off." Barrett demonstrated his support for Carolyn by applying biblical language. "As Paul said that he was not ashamed of the Gospel, I am not ashamed of Carolyn Bryant." Frank Bryant seconded that statement wholeheartedly. Barrett had nothing good to say about state officials looking into the case and insisted that "there is a ghoulishness about the Till prosecutors, which needs to take flight before the light of reason and the righteousness of religion."[65] It is unknown if Barrett had any further contact with Frank Bryant or ever spoke directly with Carolyn.

As fate would have it, five years later Barrett was stabbed to death and his body set on fire at his home in Pearl, Rankin County, by a twenty-two-year-old black man named Vincent McGee, whom Barrett had hired to do yard work. McGee pleaded guilty and was sentenced to seventy-five years in prison in 2011.[66]

Killinger and his team were able to learn details from other key players in the case even from beyond the grave. Not long before his death in 1980, J. W. Milam allegedly allowed a young (and, unbeknownst to him, black) woman to question him over the telephone on at least three different occasions. The interviewer, Bonnie Blue, provided Killinger with details of what Milam told her. Blue has since self-published a novelized account of the Till case called *Emmett Till's Secret Witness*.[67] Milam's account, provided to Blue nearly twenty-five years after he first told his story to William Bradford Huie in *Look* magazine, differs substantially from that famous "confession." It does, however, bolster the courtroom testimony of Willie Reed and Mandy Bradley. In his conversations with Blue, Milam confirmed the participation of three other white men besides Roy Bryant and himself—his brother Leslie Milam, brother-in-law Melvin Campbell, and a friend named Hubert Clark—all of whom were dead by 1974. He also verified the involvement of Levi "Too Tight" Collins and Henry Lee Loggins. Both of these former field hands were still living when Milam had his conversations with Blue.

According to Blue, Milam said that he and Melvin Campbell were together from late Saturday, August 27, until early the following morning. Roy Bryant had just returned to town on Saturday and was at home. That night, the three men met up and began drinking when the Wednesday night incident at the Bryant grocery came up in conversation.[68] Milam and Bryant, along with either Collins or Loggins (Milam apparently could not remember which), borrowed Hubert Clark's car, went to the Bryant store in Money, picked up Carolyn Bryant, and drove out to Mose Wright's home, where they abducted Till.[69] After that, they dropped off Carolyn at the store, then drove back to the place where they had been drinking. Milam, Bryant, Collins, Loggins, Clark, and Campbell were all together at this point. There they beat Emmett briefly and then put him into the back of Milam's truck with the intention of taking him to a spot on the Mississippi River to scare him. After driving around at length, however, they failed to find it. Because it was now approaching daybreak, they drove to Leslie Milam's farm in Drew.[70]

Leslie was upset that the truckload of men showed up at his farm unannounced because he had work to do that day. However, he remained present when they took Till into a shed and resumed beating him. During this violent episode, Till's wallet fell out of his pants, and the men discovered that it contained a photo of a white woman. The men were further angered that Till disrespected them by failing to address them as "sir" and by insisting that he was as good as they were.[71]

Till was killed at the shed and stripped of his clothing. Collins and Loggins were told to clean the blood off the floor, which they did twice before spreading cotton seed to cover any remaining stains. The group then divided into two. Milam, Bryant, and Campbell took Till's body away in Milam's truck, stopped to pick up a gin fan, and then threw the body off a bridge and into the Tallahatchie River. Clark, Collins, and Loggins left in Leslie Milam's car to bury Till's clothing. For whatever reason, Till's shoes were accidentally left in the car. After burying the clothes, Collins and Loggins walked home. After Roy was arrested later that day, the Bryant and Milam siblings met at the home of their mother, Eula, and decided that J. W. should turn himself in to authorities in order to keep an eye on Roy and prevent him from veering away from the story they had concocted.[72]

If accurate, Milam's candid account is fascinating, but the stories do not end with him. Indeed, the most significant of all to corroborate his version of events as told to Bonnie Blue came from Milam's best-known accomplice, his half-brother, Roy Bryant. Five years or so after Milam provided his account to Blue, Bryant opened up to a friend who recorded him on audiotape. The source, whose name Killinger kept out of his published report, called Killinger's office and told him of his 1985 encounter with Bryant. The source explained that he had gone to Roy Bryant and that Bryant agreed to ride along to the sites related to the kidnapping and murder. These included the store, the site of Mose Wright's home, and the shed in Drew. Upon meeting the man, Killinger saw that he owned several personal photographs of other Bryant family members, an indication that they were well acquainted. This confidential source handed Killinger the audiotape and encouraged him to "use it as you see fit."[73]

Bits and pieces of the conversation between Bryant and his friend confirmed important details and captured Bryant's lack of remorse regarding the murder of Emmett Till. Like Milam, Bryant admitted that they had been drinking but insisted that "we wasn't drunk . . . wasn't nobody drunk."

Bryant's account of beating and killing Till was especially disturbing. "Well, we done whopped the son of a bitch, and I had backed out on killin' the motherfucker," he said. After beating the fourteen-year-old nearly to death, they thought about taking him to the hospital. However, Bryant explained (laughing) that "carryin' him to the hospital wouldn't have done him no good." Instead, they "put his ass in the Tallahatchie River." Bryant could not explain why they went to the plantation in Drew, other than they were "tryin' to make our minds up." He did confirm that Till was tortured and murdered inside of the shed. Bryant's friend photographed the building in Bryant's presence. Fifty-three-year-old Bryant did not name others who aided him and Milam in the kidnapping and murder, but boasted that "I'm the only one who's living that knows.... That's all that will ever be known."[74] Bryant would be long dead before that last statement would be proven wrong. Unbeknownst to Bryant, his half-brother Leslie Milam had privately confessed his involvement over a decade earlier.

Within a few months of the murder, Leslie was "requested" to leave the Sturdivant plantation because many of the black laborers working there were leaving the farm out of fear of the man. He shortly found a new job on a plantation in the nearby town of Cleveland.[75] Fifteen years later, in February 1971, he was arrested, and four months after that, convicted of illegally possessing over 500 methamphetamine pills, popularly known as speed. He was sentenced to one year at the state prison in Parchman. His defense attorney was J. W. Kellum.[76]

Despite his other problems, the biggest burden he carried throughout his life was his involvement in the tragedy that occurred in a plantation shed in August 1955. On Thursday, August 29, 1974, local minister Macklyn Hubbell received a call from Frances Milam, Leslie's wife. Hubbell, who had been pastor of the First Baptist Church in Cleveland, Mississippi, since 1962, knew the family, and Frances asked him to come to the Milam home at Leslie's request. Hubbell left his office and drove to the address at 201 Oakland Drive. Once inside, he was ushered into a room where he saw Leslie lying on a couch, near death. Frances left the room, and Hubbell pulled up a chair. Leslie, so weak that he could barely whisper, was nevertheless anxious to talk and immediately told Hubbell that he wanted to get something off his chest. He proceeded to confess that he had been involved in the murder of Emmett Till, which had occurred nineteen years and one day earlier. Leslie provided no details of the crime, but Hubbell could see that he was remorseful. Leslie Milam died the following morning at 5:45 A.M. Rev. Hubbell officiated at the funeral a few days later. Retired FBI agent Lent Rice, who was working with Killinger, learned of Hubbell and got the entire story directly from the minister. Because Hubbell was still living at the time Killinger issued his report, his name is redacted from the document. Leslie's wife, Frances, who later remarried a man named Thomas Bryant (no relation to Roy Bryant), owned a beauty shop in Cleveland from 1963 until her death in October 2014. Her obituary said nothing about her marriage to Leslie Milam.[77]

Killinger learned about the involvement of others who were also deceased. Milam's half-sister and Bryant's sister, Mary Louise Campbell, told investigators that her husband, Melvin Campbell, had been with Milam and Bryant on the night of the kidnapping and murder, just as Milam told Bonnie

Blue. The name of local black laborer Otha "Oso" Johnson Jr. never surfaced before or after the trial, but Johnson's son learned directly from his father that he claimed to have driven Milam and Bryant around on the night of the kidnapping. The younger Johnson fully believed the confession of his now-deceased father. Efforts to find Joe Willie Hubbard, who was mentioned in 1955 accounts as having been on the truck, yielded nothing. Killinger learned that Levi Collins died in Mississippi in 1992.[78]

Black field hand Henry Lee Loggins, the only person living besides Carolyn Donham whom the press named as a possible suspect, suffered a stroke in 2005 and lay recovering in a nursing home. It is unclear from Killinger's report if he talked to Loggins directly or spoke only with Loggins's family members. However, in August 2005 *Los Angeles Times* reporter Ellen Barry visited Loggins in Dayton, where Loggins maintained his innocence to the journalist. "I wasn't there. I know people say so, but I wasn't there. I ain't that kind of man," he insisted. Loggins, who first heard about the FBI investigation from his son Johnny B. Thomas, told Barry that as yet, he had not hired a lawyer. Fifty-one-year-old Thomas, mayor of Glendora, Mississippi, had earlier asked state and federal authorities to award his father immunity from any prosecution.[79]

Killinger talked with others who had stories to tell, some more compelling than others. The town of Glendora held many memories of residents who lived near Milam's home and saw blood dripping from the back of his truck on Sunday morning, August 28, 1955. In a few instances, people remembered Levi "Too Tight" Collins, Oso Johnson, or Henry Lee Loggins on or near the truck that same morning. In one case, Milam was said to have shown a curious black man what was underneath the tarpaulin in the back of the green and white pickup. Uncovering Till's body, Milam said, "This is what happens to smart niggers." One man claimed that Collins asked him and a friend to clean the blood out of the truck and paid each of them thirty-five cents.[80]

There were others, such as Peggy Morgan, who claimed that her father, Gene Albritton, and uncle, Bob Moye, both had a hand in Till's death. Morgan also told Killinger that, as a child, she used to accompany her father to the Bryant store when he passed through Money on his way to go fishing. She said that on many occasions, she saw him "kissing and hugging" Carolyn Bryant and sometimes made Peggy and her siblings wait in the car for hours before he left the store.[81] These stories could not be substantiated. Neither could the reminiscences of one man who said that Sheriff H. C. Strider was with Milam and Bryant on the Saturday night before Till's kidnapping and that they went to a gambling spot in Glendora asking for directions to Mose Wright's home. Although Killinger included this testimony in his report, he appeared to pay it little heed. Some stories he did not include at all and concluded his report by explaining why. "While there are other rumors regarding the murder of Emmett Till which have been expressed from time to time, there is insufficient corroboration, lead information or other evidence to warrant further investigation into any of these rumors."[82]

Shortly before the fiftieth anniversary of the murder, Keith Beauchamp completed work on his documentary, *The Untold Story of Emmett Louis Till*. After spending much of the last several years trying to raise funds to finish the project, he was finally forced to use money his parents had set aside for him to attend law school. The costs of obtaining archival film and photographs was expensive, and Beauchamp went from one stock house to the other, dealing with Mississippi archives, Fox Movietone, and CBS. Fox Movietone held a large quantity of footage on the case. He had tried to secure funding from several sources over the years, including prominent civil rights leaders, but none would help. His law school money, taken with the blessings of his parents, finally saved the day. On August 17, 2005, the finished version of *Untold Story* began a two-week run in Manhattan at the Film Forum. It would be distributed nationally in theaters by ThinkFilm after that. The timing of the release seemed perfect. The fifteen-month-old FBI investigation looked promising, and significant progress, unthinkable only a few years earlier, was undeniable as the anniversary occurred on August 28, 2005. That evening, a special screening of *Untold Story* at the Film Forum featured appearances by Simeon Wright and Roosevelt Crawford, who had both been with Till at the Bryant store in Money.[83]

Two days later, the *New York Daily News* announced Beauchamp's continued optimism that as many as five people could be indicted for Emmett Till's murder. Three of them were white men "who are still alive that we're trying to build a case on now." Beauchamp's "gut instinct" was that indictments against individuals would occur within a few months. Hallie Gail Bridges, assistant district attorney in Greenville, tried to remain circumspect in response. "We won't know about indictments or anything else until we get a report from the FBI."[84]

That report would be on its way to Mississippi prosecutors in just a few months. On November 24, 2005, the *Chicago Tribune* announced that after a year and a half, the FBI had finished its inquiry into the kidnapping and murder of Emmett Till.[85] Over the course of his investigation, Killinger talked to dozens of people. He traveled not only throughout the state of Mississippi, but to Alabama, Illinois, Ohio, Tennessee, and Washington, DC. Items once considered lost and probably gone for good—the murder weapon and the trial transcript—were filed safely away as evidence. The whereabouts of the ring found on Emmett Till's finger remained a mystery, and although the gin fan that had been tied around Till's neck was also nowhere to be found, Killinger at least learned of its fate. The fan had been stored in the courthouse basement after the trial but was tossed out when the building underwent renovations in 1973 designed by architect John Eldridge Decell III. A local man who knew the story behind the fan retrieved it and took it home. However, after only three days, he concluded that "there could be no good that could come from me having this." He, too, got rid of it.[86]

Mike Turner, legal counsel for the FBI in Jackson, Mississippi, told the press that he hoped to turn the report over to District Attorney Joyce Chiles in December. It would then be up to Chiles to decide whether to file charges against any possible suspects. Chiles, who had a small staff operating out of three offices in one of the most crime-ridden regions of Mississippi, said it would likely take her and her staff several weeks to examine all of the material and was even gearing herself up to working weekends. "The documentation is that extensive."[87]

It took several months longer for the FBI to finish its report and prepare the documents for transfer. During this time, Killinger worked with attorneys and tied up a variety of loose ends that needed attention. The report was then sent to Washington, DC, where it received the approval of the FBI and then went through a final round of approval at the Justice Department. All of that took about a month. On March 16, 2006, three boxes containing twenty-eight volumes totaling 8,000 pages were transferred to Chiles's office in an unmarked vehicle by US Attorney Jim Greenlee and two FBI agents. The report included the original FBI file kept on Emmett Till between 1955 and 1966, several newspaper clippings, the trial transcript, and the text of Killinger's many interviews, among other items. Killinger then gave Chiles and her staff a full presentation of the case. Although Killinger made no public statements about his findings, Chiles told members of the Till family that Killinger recommended she take a closer look at Carolyn Donham. "She's going to look at everyone involved," explained Wheeler Parker, who talked directly with Chiles, "but Carolyn will definitely be on the list." Once the transfer was made, the Till murder became a state case, and the FBI ceased commenting.[88]

With the files now in her hands, Chiles enlisted others to scour the documents with her. She had been briefed by Killinger periodically during the investigation, but now she would learn all the details. She put together a team of three prosecutors who each examined the report on their own, and by early July, three and a half months after getting the files, they were still reading, each at their own pace. "After everyone reads all the material, we'll make our decision," explained Chiles. Unsolicited advice meant to sway her one way or the other came from strangers, family, friends, and even her doctor. Surprisingly, Chiles received no threatening or racially charged mail. Most of those weighing in, however, encouraged her to prosecute. She remained tight-lipped about the report, saying only that it "dispelled a lot of myths, things I've learned through word of mouth."[89]

Three months later, as Chiles and her team continued to work their way through the material, *Untold Story*, following its theatrical run, premiered on Court TV.[90] It had already won an Audience Award and a Special Jury Award from the Miami Film Festival in 2005 and that same year received the Freedom of Expression Award from the National Board of Review, USA. In 2007, it would be nominated for Best Documentary at the Twenty-Eighth Annual News and Documentary Emmy Awards.[91]

Joyce Chiles, who oversaw three counties as district attorney of Mississippi's Fourth Judicial District, had numerous other cases to deal with as she continued to study the FBI's Emmett Till findings, and was preparing to prosecute several of those, including a murder, a kidnapping, and a sexual assault. As she dealt with the rest of her workload, she managed to keep herself detached from the pressures of dealing with such a historic case as the Till murder. "I know I'm going to do the right thing," she assured a reporter in November 2006. "It's not going to have anything to do with how bad the crime was or that it represents such and such." In this case, as in all others, her decision would come down to "the law and the evidence."[92]

If Chiles managed to keep herself focused and unaffected by the historical significance of the Till case, anxious observers still felt the pressure for her. "If the evidence is there, she'll go forward with it," said Alvin Sykes. "If it's not there, she won't go forward just to satisfy 50 years of anxiety and to appease the political considerations of people wishing her to do so." Keith Beauchamp predicted correctly that "anything she does is going to be seriously controversial."[93]

In December, Chiles, Bridges, Hailman, and others met at the courthouse in Greenwood with Charlie Maris, assistant state attorney general. Maris's expertise in Mississippi state law put him in an advisory position with Chiles and her team regarding how to proceed. One course was to pursue charges against Carolyn Donham for assisting in the kidnapping by identifying Emmett Till at the scene. However, because at that time the statute of limitations on kidnapping was only two years, that charge alone would be impossible to prosecute.[94] Within a few months, Chiles and her team finished the report and believed they could make a case against Carolyn Donham on manslaughter. A careful reading of the Mississippi code showed there was precedent for this. In the 1955 case of *Gibbs v. State of Mississippi*, the court ruled that "one rendering aid to another is presumed to share in the latter's intent and this presumption will persist until overcome by the evidence." In *Smith v. State* (1945), the court held that "it was not necessary to allege and prove that the killing was wilfully done, but it was incumbent upon the state to prove beyond a reasonable doubt that the defendant was guilty of such gross negligence as to envince [sic] a wanton or reckless disregard for the safety of human life, or such an indifference to the consequences of his act as to render conduct tantamount to wilfulness." Such "reckless disregard for the safety" of Emmett Till would have occurred if Carolyn Bryant indeed identified him or even ruled out other youth that night as the right one, if she knew that her husband and brother-in-law would harm him. Also, "if it is shown that the accused was present pursuant to a conspiracy to commit some unlawful act, it has generally been held that his participation in the homicide was sufficient to make him liable for manslaughter." The unlawful act that led to Till's death was the kidnapping.

In an even older case, *Wade v. State* (1939), the court ruled that "there could be no accomplice to manslaughter, but several could act together in committing the offense and it was not error for the court to instruct the jury that the defendant might be convicted of manslaughter, although he did not inflict the fatal wound." These cases helped pave the way for the 2005 conviction of Edgar Ray Killen, who incidentally was not present when the three civil rights workers were murdered in Philadelphia, Mississippi, in 1964.[95]

Although Chiles refrained from making any formal announcements, the *Chicago Tribune* stated on February 22, 2007, that the district attorney had already planned to present evidence in the Till case to a grand jury the following month. Wheeler Parker heard the news and felt hopeful. "We have been waiting for a long time to get some closure to this and we hope this will give us the information we have been waiting on for years."[96]

Little did Parker or the author of the *Tribune* piece realize, but Chiles's grand jury had already met in Greenwood at the Leflore County courthouse on that very day. Even the grand jury members were not aware that they would be hearing evidence in the Till case until they left for their lunch break. When they returned, Chiles and assistant prosecutor Hallie Gail Bridges presented the evidence for a manslaughter indictment against Carolyn Donham to nineteen impaneled citizens of the county. The racial makeup of the group was nearly even between black and white members, seven being men, twelve women. Dale Killinger presented a full PowerPoint presentation of his evidence, which likely would have emphasized that Mose Wright heard what sounded like a woman's voice in the car identify Till when Till was kidnapped from Wright's home. Killinger also would have pointed out that Carolyn aided her husband and J. W. Milam on two other occasions in the hours prior to the kidnapping by confirming that a boy in the store and later, Willie Hemphill, who was walking up Money Road, were not the right boys. Evidence presented in the Till case took up most of the afternoon.[97]

The next day, February 23, the jury reported on several cases. They had deliberated for a little more than an hour on the Till case before they came to a consensus. Their unanimous decision was that the evidence against Don-ham was unpersuasive, and they quietly returned a no bill, essentially closing the case forever. They were not asked to consider evidence against Henry Lee Loggins.[98]

Jackson Clarion-Ledger reporter Jerry Mitchell learned the news first and called Alvin Sykes, whose response was measured. "As painful as it will cer-tainly be to many people around the world, if Carolyn Bryant is truly innocent or there was not sufficient evidence to indict her or anyone else for crimes associated with Emmett Louis Till, then all justice-seeking people should be proud that the grand jury had the courage to do the right thing." Sykes had not been too optimistic anyway, as Chiles had recently confided in him that "knowing what I know now, if I were a juror on the grand jury, and I was going to follow the law, I would not indict."[99]

Sykes called Beauchamp and broke the news to his friend and associate in this four-year endeavor. As expected, the decision in Greenwood was dev-astating to the young activist who had spent a decade dedicated to the case. When contacted by the press, he said he was "extremely shocked" by the deci-sion. "I strongly believe that we should have gotten an indictment in that case. I know a lot of the things that we came across, and I'm questioning now how the case went in the grand jury, what was presented." He was not about to give up. "Our next move is to get the documents to Congress, particularly to Sena-tor Chuck Schumer and Congressman Rangel." Juan Williams, correspondent for NPR, a contributor to Fox News, and author of the civil rights history Eyes on the Prize, took exception to Beauchamp and affirmed that the grand jury, which was racially mixed, did the right thing. Considering also the fact that the prosecutor was black, "I don't know what he [Beauchamp] wants. It's not as if this has been a whitewash by any means."[100]

Simeon Wright was equally distraught over the decision, having lived with the horror of Emmett Till's murder and the effect it had on him and his family for half a century. "They came up with this 50 years ago," he said. "Some of the people haven't changed from 50 years ago. Same attitude. The evidence speaks for itself." Wright told another reporter that despite his disappointment, he "wasn't expecting any indictments" anyway. "Not too much has changed here in Mississippi. I guess that's just about it."

Joyce Chiles weighed in, empathizing with Wright's emotional response but recognizing that there had been tremendous progress in her state. "I am very sorry he feels that way," she said. "I personally feel that a lot has changed. Men's hearts and attitudes have changed over time. This was a very intelligent grand jury, and a good grand jury. They looked at all the evidence that was presented and considered it, and I do respect their decision." Injustice could have worked the other way, Chiles noted. "It would have been very easy for that grand jury to have returned a true bill based solely on emotion and the rage they felt. And I commend them for not doing that." As to Carolyn Donham, Chiles emphasized that "I didn't feel good toward her; I still don't feel good toward her." However, "We are justice-seekers and not headhunters." Reiterating what she had privately told Alvin Sykes, "if I were to follow the law and the evidence as it was presented, I would have had to have returned a no bill."[101]

Federal prosecutor John Hailman, who worked with both Dale Killinger and Joyce Chiles during the course of the investigation, believed that things would have worked out differently with just one more bit of evidence. During the 1955 trial, Mose Wright testified that the voice he heard identify Emmett Till "seemed like it was a lighter voice than a man's," but Wright did not say specifically that it was Carolyn Bryant's. Had Wright have been able to do so, Hailman believed, Chiles probably could have gotten an indictment and been able to prosecute.[102] In that case, would there have been a conviction? That will never be known, of course, and the evidence presented to the grand jury would have been undermined by defense attorneys had the case gone to trial. If Carolyn Bryant was present at the Wright home and identified Till and had aided her husband and brother-in-law in ruling out others who were not, did she know in advance that the men were going to kidnap the boy once she identified him, or did she believe they would only talk to him? Did she accompany her husband and brother-in-law willingly and presumably consent to leave her two young sons home alone, or had Roy or J. W. coerced her? Surely these were issues good attorneys would have raised had the case been tried in a Mississippi courtroom.

Grand jury members were sought out by *Greenwood Commonwealth* reporter William Browning once the six-month gag order had expired and they were free to talk. He spoke with five of them—Otis Johnson, Almeda Luckey, George Smith III (grandson of the former Leflore County sheriff who arrested Milam and Bryant on kidnapping charges in August 1955), Greg Watkins, and Gary Woody. "The fact is," said Woody, a white man, "there is no way to know for sure if she was in that car. And if she was, the question is, was she there on her own free will?" Of course, a grand jury does not need proof before issuing an indictment—that is a later job for a trial jury when considering a conviction. However, Otis Johnson, a forty-seven-year-old black member of the panel, found that sufficient evidence was lacking and that even the motive of the state was suspect. "I feel like the district attorney used us as scapegoats. To me it seems like they just wanted to put on a show and go through the process to make people happy." Johnson insisted that "anybody who sat in there with us would have reached the same conclusion—no matter which side of the aisle you sit on."[103]

Did Joyce Chiles believe that putting the case before a grand jury was warranted when in the end she knew that she would not have indicted Carolyn Donham either? What was not at issue was that Carolyn Bryant *could* have been charged with manslaughter even without being present during the murder if it could be shown that she identified Emmett Till as the one who came into the store, *if* she knew that Till would suffer harm as a result. The problem for the jury was that the evidence used to incriminate her was based on hearsay. Chiles presented the evidence, the grand jury weighed it. In the end, both did their jobs.

On Thursday, March 29, 2007, a month after the grand jury issued its no bill, family members of the slain fourteen-year-old met with FBI officials at its Chicago headquarters and went over the evidence in the case. The following day, the FBI released a 115-page summary of its investigation, along with a copy of the 1955 trial transcript. Both became immediately available online at the FBI's website.[104]

The success of the joint investigation partnered by the FBI and the state of Mississippi should not be measured in terms of suspects indicted, tried, and convicted. Indeed, if evidence is persuasive to bring anyone to justice, then justice should be sought, no matter how many years have passed or how old or repentant any guilty parties are. However, the investigation was as much a fact-finding mission as it was a justice-seeking endeavor. That alone justified the cost in tax dollars and human resources. In the Till case, as in all criminal cases, suspects and convicts die. Yet the truth lives on. The 2004–5 investigation did not uncover all of the answers, but it revealed more than anyone could have imagined about what happened to Emmett Till and who had a hand in his demise. The truth will often incarcerate the guilty, but it will always set the rest of society free.

If there is any consolation in the fact that no one was ever punished for the kidnapping and murder of Emmett Till, it is that the lingering, multilayered injustice tied to the case gives it its power. The horrific details of the crime are exacerbated by the fact that men got away with murder and lived to tell about it. Two were tried and acquitted, while others died before ever seeing the inside of a courtroom. Mamie Till-Mobley turned that tragedy into a positive, as her life's work later demonstrated. Now and then the nation has followed suit. The next phase of the case would set the Till family and the state of Mississippi on a path toward healing, despite the stinging message out of Greenwood that, once again, when it came to Emmett Till, it was "justice denied."

13

The Legacy of Emmett Till

In Webb, Mississippi, just two miles south of Sumner, Highway 32 intersects with Highway 49 E. In 1981, an eighteen-mile section of Highway 32 that stretches east-west from Webb to Charleston was designated the Henry Clarence Strider Memorial Highway. Twenty-four years later, on March 21, 2005, Mississippi governor Haley Barbour signed legislation that renamed thirty miles of the north-south-running Highway 49 E as the Emmett Till Memorial Highway.[1] More than a few have noted the ironies in seeing these two highways come together. The overtly racist sheriff who declared that Emmett Till's murder was all a hoax has been confronted by the young teen whose name on the sign serves as official recognition that the once-beloved lawman, the hero of the defense, was wrong.

Given Mississippi's long, concerted effort to forget the horror and injustice of the Till case, it is stunning that the name change and highway sign honoring the slain Chicago youth came to fruition at all. The proposal came before the Mississippi Senate at the last hour of a Friday afternoon session, its sponsor even giving an unprepared speech.[2] The memorial is not an *announcement* that the defense theory was absurd, but a *reminder*. For better or worse, it is a *constant* reminder. No doubt many a Deltan's blood has boiled during morning commutes on this long stretch of road. The Emmett Till Memorial Highway, unlike the one named for Strider, has the element of collective guilt behind it as much as it does any determination to remember and commemorate. Seeking to right the wrongs of the past can divide people as much as it unifies because people haunted by the past simultaneously live with fear and denial. When haunting evolves into ownership, and then remembrance, peace has a chance to enter the mix—but not without pain and certainly not without controversy.

Over the years, the name "Emmett Till" has provoked anger, bitterness, uneasiness, sadness, guilt, and shame—depending on locale, race, generation, and sometimes even gender. Yet the emotional impact of the case has made it a rallying cry for change. This can be demonstrated in pivotal moments where Emmett Till's name has been invoked in Congress, and once the partisan or ideological wrangling quieted down, there are times when it has made a difference.

This was evident during the debate that ensued prior to passage of the Civil Rights Act of 1957, the first such law passed in over eighty years. Southern resistance to the *Brown v. Board of Education* decision in 1954 focused on a greater resolve among white southerners to stifle black voting rights, and President Eisenhower would not long ignore that. The administration tried and failed to pass civil rights legislation in 1956, but after Eisenhower's reelection in November of that year, Attorney General Herbert Brownell informed Republican leaders that he would introduce the bill again after the first of the year. During his State of the Union speech delivered on January 10, 1957, Eisenhower urged Congress to pass the legislation and outlined to the nation each of its four components. His aim was to form a bipartisan civil rights commission, create a civil rights division within the Department of Justice, expand the authority of the department to enforce civil and criminal proceedings, and authorize the attorney general to protect voting rights through civil suits and preventative injunctions.[3]

Earlier on the same day that Eisenhower addressed the nation, Michigan representative Charles Diggs Jr. read into the *Congressional Record* William Bradford Huie's new *Look* article, "What's Happened to the Emmett Till Killers?," which was a follow-up to Huie's "The Shocking Story of Approved Killing in Mississippi" piece from a year earlier. Diggs saw the local backlash against J. W. Milam and Roy Bryant as recorded in the new article as "evidence of a change in Mississippi, the significance of which cannot be discounted."[4]

Things were not quite that simple, however, either in Mississippi or Washington. Debate about the proposed civil rights bill began on February 4 before a House Judiciary subcommittee, overseen by Brooklyn representative Emanuel Celler, and on February 12 before the Senate Judiciary Committee chaired by Senator Thomas C. Hennings Jr. of Missouri. Brownell tried to reassure the House subcommittee that Part III of the legislation would not trample states' rights; he then sought to persuade Hennings's group that the administration had no intention of sending in federal troops to enforce injunction orders. Southern Democrats believed, however, that if enacted, the law "would result in creation of a Federal gestapo" that would recklessly launch investigations into state affairs.[5]

In addition to their desire to gut Part III of the bill, southern Democrats also came out fighting because Part IV failed to provide for jury trials in cases of criminal contempt in civil rights cases. Advocates of the bill knew that southern juries, all of whom were made up of white men, would never convict anyone in a case involving civil rights. Val Washington, director of minorities for the Republican National Convention, knew how ineffective the courts would be in jury trials and posed a question to Senate majority leader Lyndon B. Johnson. "If a Southern jury would not convict confessed kidnappers of Emmett Till after he was found murdered, why would they convict an election official for refusing to give a Negro his right of suffrage?"[6] Johnson, like southerners before him, had always blocked civil rights legislation that came before the Senate. Now that he was eyeing a presidential run in 1960 and knowing full well that the fate of the national Democratic Party rested partly on its stance on such issues, Johnson came out in favor of a moderate civil rights bill.[7]

Eisenhower and officials within his administration were opposed to the jury trial amendment inserted by southern Democrats and made it clear that they saw this move as a "clever device to nullify the civil rights bill." Several members of Congress went before the Senate committee and used the Till case when weighing in on either side of the argument. On June 14, during a session of the House of Representatives, Republican Marguerite S. Church of Illinois's Thirteenth District, told her colleagues, "I myself have had only one personal experience illustrating the need for such legislation to protect civil rights, but it was a potent one." It had nothing to do with the right to vote "but with the failure adequately to determine and punish those who had taken young life. I refer, or course, to the Emmett Till case. . . . I knew then, Mr. Chairman, that action must be taken to protect the civil rights, at least, of certain of our citizens who are as much American and who are as much entitled to the protection of their rights as anyone who sits in this Chamber as a Member of Congress." Church then launched into an argument against the jury trial proposal.[8]

An opposing view came from Mississippi congressman Jamie Whitten, who represented Tallahatchie County and preceded Gerald Chatham as district attorney in that section of the Delta. He, too, pointed to the Till case but declared, "It is easy to second guess either a jury or a judge when one does not know all the facts or even when the facts are known." He proceeded to tell the story of a case dating back to his days as district attorney when a black man was killed by a white citizen. The white defendant then tried to plead guilty in court. The man's request was denied because the evidence against him was overwhelming and prosecutors wanted him to go to trial instead. "The defendant was tried in that county before a jury of 12 white citizens. That jury brought in a verdict of guilty, which meant he received a death sentence. I mention that case to show what southern juries do when the facts are sufficient to warrant a guilty verdict." However, his colleagues' memories were not as short as Whitten had hoped. In all, six members of Congress brought up Emmett Till during hearings about the bill.[9]

Opponents of the legislation tried unsuccessfully four times to inject a jury trial amendment, and the administration's version passed in the House on June 18 by a vote of 286-126.[10] Two days later, the Senate voted 45-39 to bypass the Judiciary Committee and send the bill directly to the floor. Senate debate opened on July 8, and lawmakers there began working toward a compromise. On August 2, the Senate added an amendment to the bill guaranteeing a right to a jury trial, and passed the amended bill 51-42. Eisenhower, who had always viewed his bill as a moderate proposal, declared immediately that the modifications would damage the entire judicial system of the United States. On August 7, the Senate approved its compromise bill 72-18.

The revised bill was expected to pass in the House, but was immediately rejected by Republican leader Joseph W. Martin, who declared it would be better to have no bill at all than to pass the Senate's watered-down version. More debate followed, and on August 21 House Republicans offered their own Eisenhower-backed compromise that would retain the Democrats' requirement for jury trials for criminal contempt cases but tweaked it to apply only when fines exceeded $300 or imprisonment was set at ninety days or more. Two days later, however, congressional leaders of both parties—Democrat Lyndon Johnson and Republican William Knowland of the Senate, and Democrat Sam Rayburn and Republican Joseph Martin of the House—reached their own deal stipulating that federal judges could determine whether a jury trial would be granted in criminal contempt cases that arose out of federal voting rights injunctions. If judges proceeded unilaterally and convictions surpassed a $300 fine or forty-five days in jail, the defendant could request a retrial before a jury.[11]

On August 27, 1957, the House passed this compromise bill, 279-97. In the Senate, Strom Thurmond, of South Carolina, made a last-minute attempt to kill the bill by initiating a filibuster on the evening of August 28 that lasted for twenty-four hours and eighteen minutes (still the longest filibuster in the history of the Senate), but that body passed the bill late on August 29 by a vote of 60-15. It was signed by President Eisenhower on September 9.[12] Even though the bill had lost many of its original provisions, it was the first civil rights bill passed since Reconstruction, and for that it could be measured as a success. The Civil Rights Division it created is still a vibrant part of the Department of Justice.[13]

Nearly fifty years later, as Dale Killinger worked to uncover the truth about the Till murder, Congress discussed the Chicago teen once again. After Senators Jim Talent and Charles Schumer and Representatives Charles Rangel and Bobby Rush met together in November 2004 to pressure the Justice Department to speed up its investigation, Alvin Sykes called Talent's office to voice his dismay at the resolution because a rush to justice could have adverse effects. Sykes left a message for the senator, who soon responded, and the two men talked.

"At best, your resolution is symbolic. It won't have any impact because they will go at their own pace anyway," explained Sykes. "At worst, it could interfere with the investigation."

Sykes advised Talent that if he wanted to make a difference, he should find a way for the federal government to look into the numerous unsolved civil rights cases that had gone ice cold, the victims of which were mostly unknown to the public at large. Sykes's vision grew out of the quest for justice that he, Keith Beauchamp, Donald Burger, and Mamie Till-Mobley foresaw when they formed the Emmett Till Justice Campaign in 2002. It was hardly feasible to start a justice campaign for each of the many unsolved cases still on the books, but if investigations were centralized and placed under the jurisdiction of the federal government, money would not be an issue.[14]

Talent liked the idea, and he began work on a bill right away. His strategy was to make it a bipartisan effort. Before long he authored the Unsolved Civil Rights Crime Act (S. 1369) and introduced it before the Senate Judiciary Committee on July 1, 2005; California representative Bob Filner brought it to the House four weeks later, on July 28. Unfortunately, it died in committee.[15]

After Congress reconvened in early 2006, Talent reintroduced the bill, which went before the Judiciary Committee on April 27, 2006. It called for the investigation of civil rights violations that had occurred prior to December 31, 1969, that "resulted in death." The committee passed the legislation by a voice vote on August 3, 2006, with an amendment that included the Missing Child Cold Case Review Act. Sponsors tried to pass the bill with "a unanimous consent agreement" before the 109th Congress closed in early December 2006, but that effort failed.[16]

Talent was defeated in the November 2006 elections and was thus out of the Senate when the 110th Congress convened in January 2007. However, Representative John Lewis of Georgia introduced a new version of the bill in the House of Representatives on February 8. Now called the Emmett Till Unsolved Civil Rights Crime Act, it was cosponsored by over sixty members of the House. "Our purpose here today is not to open up old wounds," explained Lewis. "There is a need for those who committed horrible crimes to be brought to justice. This process of seeking justice is not just good for history's sake, but it is good for the process of healing. It will help us put this dark past behind us and to bring closure to the families of the victims of these age-old and vicious crimes." The bill would create an Unsolved Crimes Section in the Civil Rights Division and an Unsolved Civil Rights Crime Investigative Office within the Civil Rights Unit of the FBI. On June 20, less than two weeks after Lewis's proposal, the "Till Bill," as it came to be called, passed in the House by a vote of 422-2. The two votes cast against it came from Republicans Ron Paul (Texas) and Lynn Westmoreland (Georgia).[17]

The Till Bill was expected to glide through the Senate as well, but Alvin Sykes remained skeptical. He explained his concerns while in conversation with *Jackson Clarion-Ledger* reporter Jerry Mitchell, who could not foresee any opposition for the bill under consideration.

"This is America," Sykes retorted. "No civil rights bill ever went through with unanimous consent. I'm waiting for a Bull Connor to emerge." Eugene "Bull" Connor, the commissioner of public safety in Birmingham, Alabama, during the late 1950s and early 1960s, had been the epitome in his day of racist ideology coupled with power.

Sure enough, opposition caused the bill to languish in the Senate for over a year when Senator Tom Coburn of Oklahoma single-handedly placed a hold on dozens of spending bills. "There's our Bull Connor," Sykes declared.[18]

To help persuade Coburn to ease up, Democratic senators Chris Dodd, Dick Durban, and Patrick Leahy took Simeon Wright to Washington to stand by their sides during a press conference held on July 23, 2008. In response to this tactic, Coburn—who was no Bull Conner in that he meant no malevolence—explained that he supported the Till Bill but thought Congress was recklessly passing legislation with little consideration of the costs—the bills in this package amounting to $10 billion. "We ought not be borrowing and expanding the federal government unless we get rid of stuff that is not working," he said.[19]

With the 110th Congress set to close in January, time was of the essence. Sykes called Coburn's office and then flew to Washington to make a direct appeal to the senator. Coburn listened, and the activist was persuasive. On Tuesday, September 23, 2008, after Sykes had returned home, Coburn called him on the phone and left a message encouraging him to get some rest and to expect some good news in the morning.[20] The next day, Sykes turned on C-SPAN and listened as Senate majority leader Harry Reid announced that the Senate passed the Till Bill with unanimous consent. "Today we can be proud that the US Senate has at long last acted to resolve unthinkable, unsolved Civil Rights–era murders like Emmett Till's. I encourage the President to sign this bill as early as possible."[21]

Following the bill's passage, Coburn addressed his colleagues and voiced his pleasure at having lifted his objections. He then paid tribute to the man from Kansas City. "There is a gentleman in this country by the name of Alvin Sykes. If you haven't met him, you should. He is what America is all about," said Coburn. "If you met him, you would fall in love with him. He is [as] poor as a church mouse. He has led this group with integrity. He has been an honest broker. He has not played the first political game with anybody in Washington." The senator continued:

> I think that speaks so well about our country; that one person has truly made a difference, and that one person is Alvin Sykes. I can't say enough about this individual. I can't say enough about his stamina, his integrity, his forthrightness, his determination. All of the qualities that have built this country this gentleman exhibited as he worked to keep the promise to the dying mother of Emmett Till. So I come to the floor now to sing his praises, to recognize him publicly for his tremendous efforts, and all those on his board have made in making this come to fruition.[22]

President George W. Bush signed the Emmett Till Unsolved Crime Act into law two weeks later, on October 7. The bill would appropriate up to $13.5 million annually over a ten-year period to fund investigations into cold civil rights murders prior to 1970.[23] In time, the new legislation could potentially impact countless families and others seeking the truth, something in which the Till family could take pride. However, for relatives of the Chicago teen whose name the act bears, healing had already begun. In 2007, as Congress waited on passage of the Till Bill, citizens in Tallahatchie County, Mississippi, decided it was time to act.

In 2005, fifty-three-year-old Jerome G. Little, president of the Tallahatchie County Board of Supervisors and the first black person elected to that position, formed the Emmett Till Memorial Commission with big dreams of reviving the dying economy in Sumner. The goals of the commission soon became twofold—increase racial harmony and work to secure state, federal, and private funds to renovate the courthouse where the trial took place and restore the courtroom to its 1955 appearance. The committee, with the help of architect Belinda Stewart of Eupora, Mississippi, was able to place the building on the National Register of Historic Places on March 6, 2007, which made it easier to raise funds. Stewart was hired to do the restoration on what was estimated to be a $10 million project. The building would continue to serve as a functioning courthouse but would double as a museum. The unemployment rate in Tallahatchie County was 9 percent, and hopes were that these efforts would increase tourism and bring jobs to the area.[24]

After its formation, commission membership first consisted of six black and three white members, but the white members never attended the meetings because they did not know they had been invited. Eighty-five-year-old Betty Pearson, one of Sumner's few trusted white liberals, became enthusiastic once she received the invitation, and she and Little began getting the word out. Eventually, the committee totaled eighteen members, evenly split between black and white residents from the west side of the county. Pearson and Tutwiler mayor Robert Grayson were elected cochairs of the committee, which met monthly on the second floor of the courthouse. Susan Glisson, executive director of the William Winter Institute for Racial Reconciliation, served as an adviser and facilitator for the group.[25]

Little reached out to Glisson because, in 2004, Glisson became involved with the Philadelphia Coalition, which was a multiracial group in Neshoba County. Philadelphia, Mississippi, had been the site of the 1964 Freedom Summer murders of civil rights workers James Chaney, Andrew Goodman, and Michael Schwerner, and upon the fortieth anniversary of the slayings, those responsible for the murders remained unpunished. The coalition pushed to reopen the case, and the conviction of Edgar Ray Killen followed in 2005. In addition, the coalition helped erect historic markers and created a driving brochure of the sites related to the murders. Little saw the Philadelphia Coalition as an excellent model for his group in Tallahatchie County.[26]

The Till Commission was the first real effort to unite white and black citizens in the community in working together toward a common goal. With little precedent to follow, discussions were sometimes awkward and contentious. For the most part, the black members of the committee wanted to focus on establishing a museum honoring Emmett Till, while the white members were primarily interested in restoring the courthouse. Those two ideas could easily mesh into one, but Glisson advised the committee members that they would need to deal directly with the Till case before any of their other goals could be accomplished.[27]

In January 2007, state senator David Jordan read a resolution to the Mississippi legislature asking the state to apologize for the Emmett Till murder and called "for reconciliation in this matter," but in July his proposal died in committee. The Till Commission decided to draft its own apology on behalf of Tallahatchie County residents and asked Susan Glisson to write it. By May 2007, a seven-paragraph resolution was ready.[28]

Unfortunately, the strongly worded document caused division within the group. Seventy-three-year-old Frank Mitchener, a wealthy cotton planter and perhaps the committee's most prominent member, objected to the use of the word "apology" in the text of the document and refused to sign it. Apologizing was tantamount to admitting guilt, Mitchener reasoned. Neither he nor anyone on the commission took part in the crime, he said, then he got up from the table, walked out of the room, and went home.[29]

Betty Pearson immediately contacted Mitchener at his house and tried to reason with him, but he refused to change his mind. Pearson then asked him to meet with Glisson, and he agreed. Glisson paid a visit to Mitchener, and the two spent several hours talking at his home. There were no arguments; in fact, Glisson spent most of her time listening as Mitchener talked about his personal experiences. His father had treated African Americans well; no one in his family approved of the murder. The crime, as horrendous as it was, did not even occur in the community or anywhere in Tallahatchie County, for that matter. Sumner was the home of the trial only. Why should the commission members apologize for a crime they did not commit?[30]

"What is unfortunate is that the jury that convened was the official body that spoke for your county," said Glisson in response. "No one has ever spoken up and said that they were wrong. It's not fair, but that's how it is."

Glisson left the statement with Mitchener along with instructions to make any changes he wanted. Two weeks later, when the commission met again, Mitchener read his revised proclamation to the members. He had removed the word "apology" and inserted "regret" and "sorry" in its place. He then moved that the proclamation be adopted. The committee approved it unanimously.

An outdoor ceremony had been scheduled for Tuesday, October 2, 2007, at 10:00 A.M., and with the entire commission on board, everything went as planned. Buses of schoolchildren came in from surrounding districts, and at least 400 people attended the event. A stand erected in front of the courthouse was beautifully decorated. Till family members Wheeler Parker, Simeon Wright, their spouses, and Deborah Watts were escorted into town in squad cars. Former governor William Winter was present, and Senator David Jordan served as master of ceremonies. Tallahatchie County sheriff William Brewer and other elected officials were also in attendance. All took their seats in the shade under trees outside of the courthouse entrance.[31]

Commission cochairs Betty Pearson and Robert Grayson took turns reading the resolution, dated May 9, 2007. "We the citizens of Tallahatchie County believe that racial reconciliation begins with telling the truth," the document began. It called on Mississippi and its citizens to take an honest look at its past. That would be painful yet essential in order to "nurture reconciliation and to ensure justice for all." After recounting the details of the kidnapping, murder, and outcome of the trial, and providing a reference to the recent FBI investigation, the statement concluded:

> We the citizens of Tallahatchie County recognize that the Emmett Till case was a terrible miscarriage of justice. We state candidly and with deep regret the failure to effectively pursue justice.
>
> We wish to say to the family of Emmett Till that we are profoundly sorry for what was done in this community to your loved one.
>
> We the citizens of Tallahatchie County acknowledge the horrific nature of this crime. Its legacy has haunted our community. We need to understand the system that encouraged these events and others like them to occur so that we can ensure that it never happens again. Working together, we have the power now to fulfill the promise of "liberty and justice for all."[32]

Till family members enthusiastically addressed the crowd. "I accept your apology," said Simeon Wright. "We want to thank you all today for what you are doing here. You are doing what you could. If you could do more, you would." Deborah Watts said that "it's good to be in Mississippi. The world has been holding its breath for fifty-two years and now it's exhaling." Wheeler Parker pointed out that "Emmett Till spoke louder in death than he would have if he had lived." Former governor Winter and Sheriff Brewer also spoke, while soloists provided music.[33]

The ceremony concluded with Jerome Little unveiling a historical marker in front of the courthouse on the northwest corner of the lawn. The commission worked with the Mississippi Department of Archives and History to work out the language on the sign, the first of several planned markers to be erected at the various Emmett Till–related sites. It noted that after "a five day trial held in this courthouse, an all-white jury acquitted two white men, Roy Bryant and J. W. Milam, of the murder" of Emmett Till. "Till's murder, coupled with the trial and acquittal of these two men, drew international attention and galvanized the Civil Rights Movement in Mississippi and the nation."[34]

Newspaper stories that reported the event repeatedly referred to the commission's statement as an apology; even some of the speakers did so. Frank Mitchener raised no objection. In fact, he was fine with such language if it was used outside of the commission's statement. "If that's the way they want to describe it, it's okay with me."[35]

Renovations to the Tallahatchie County courthouse in Sumner were completed in 2014. The final price tag was around $3 million a substantial savings over what was originally projected. Visitors will not only see the influence of the Till case inside and out, they can also turn around and enter the Emmett Till Interpretive Center on the north side of the town square in what was once the Wong (formerly Bing) grocery store. The purpose of the center is to provide a place where the Till story can be told and its impact understood. Sadly, Jerome Little died of cancer in December 2011 at age fifty-nine and did not live to see the fruits of his labors.

Leaving Sumner and heading south on the Emmett Till Memorial Highway, motorists will shortly pass the Emmett Till Multipurpose Complex. Continuing on, they will see a sign for an Emmett Till museum in Glendora. After visiting the structure, called the Emmett Till Historic Intrepid Center (ETHIC), housed in an old cotton gin, they can cross the railroad tracks and take a stroll through the Emmett Till National Park and Nature Trail. A brochure titled the *Tallahatchie Civil Rights Driving Tour*, created by the Emmett Till Memorial Commission, guides tourists to eight sites in Tallahatchie County, complete with commemorative markers, and another four in Leflore and Sunflower

Counties, all of which bear a direct relationship to the Till case.[36] One day visitors will be able to gaze upon a monument to Emmett Till that will be erected on the courthouse lawn in Greenwood. The memorial was approved by the Leflore County Board of Supervisors in 2005.[37]

Chicago came to recognize the slain youth back in 1991, as noted earlier, when a stretch of Seventy-First Street was renamed Emmett Till Road. On August 28, 2005, a Chicago overpass off of that road crossing the Dan Ryan Expressway was dedicated as the Emmett Till Memorial Bridge. In 2006, McCosh Elementary, the school Till attended in his South Side neighborhood, was renamed the Emmett Till Math and Science Academy. In March of that same year, the Chicago City Council gave city landmark status to the Roberts Temple Church of God in Christ, the site of Till's funeral.[38]

If Mississippi is on the path toward reconciliation, it is not easy to ascertain the distance traveled and the progress made. Sensitivities about how Emmett Till is portrayed and who controls the narrative have been points of contention since the murder occurred. Surely there have been charges—if even in hushed tones—that society is overcompensating for the murder of the fourteen-year-old boy from Chicago. However, the plethora of memorials is indicative of the fact that Emmett Till has become a symbol. For sixty years his death has represented what America has been at its worst and how a tragedy of this nature can arouse a people to action. Even today, when people see the photos of Emmett Till's battered face for the first time, the emotional response is as powerful as it ever was.

An unintended consequence of Emmett Till as a symbol is a continued stream of distrust interwoven within these very public attempts toward reconciliation. For example, retired black preacher G. A. Johnson stood up in public meetings and denounced the work of the Emmett Till Memorial Commission, calling its efforts to bring the courthouse back to its 1955 appearance "blood money." As Johnson saw it, "They slaughtered this boy and now they want to come back and raise money off the death of that child—God forbid." Robert Grayson found that, at his church in Tutwiler, people took a different stand yet still represented an obstacle for the goals of the commission. "A lot of people don't say anything, but when I mention it, you can look at their expressions and know they're thinking, 'I don't know why you have to go back and dig up the past.'" Of the 400 or so spectators at the Sumner ceremony in October 2007, few of them were local whites.[39]

More serious than indifference or even a lack of trust is when hostility and hatred rear their ugly heads. In June 2006, vandals painted the letters "KKK" on the Emmett Till Memorial Highway sign in Greenwood. The sign at the river site where Till's body was discovered was stolen in October 2008. Jerome Little, whose efforts created the signs in the first place, was furious. "We're not going to tolerate them tearing down anything that's marking Emmett Till's murder," he told the press. "I want to send a message: Every time they take it down, we're going to put it back up."[40] That he did, but the replacement sign fared no better. In March 2013, it was found riddled with bullet holes. Eighteen months later it remained unchanged.[41]

While most civil rights memorials have stood unmolested, these defaced signs simultaneously become symbols of reconciliation and division that send a powerful yet tragic message. Although it has become cliché to note that Mississippi has come a long way toward racial reconciliation but still has a long way to go, these signs are dramatic confirmation of that fact.

Emmett Till as a symbol, however, goes beyond signs, commemorations, and legislation. He has been called a martyr and the catalyst that started the civil rights movement. In the last thirty years, he has certainly *become* both in retrospect, but those descriptions need to be qualified. Unlike Martin Luther King Jr., who predicted on more than one occasion that his work would cut his life short, Emmett Till was never a willing martyr and was certainly indifferent to the issues that consumed countless folks before or after him. He was not Rosa Parks, who took a stand and knew there would be consequences. Simply put, he was in the wrong place at the wrong time and paid a heavy price for that. Yet his innocence and naïveté during a harmless flirtation meant that every African American was vulnerable, and that is why his death resonated with so many. It resonated immediately with fearful black mothers all over the North who refused to send their sons down to the South to visit relatives ever again. To say that the murder of Emmett Till started the civil rights movement is to ignore the work of politicians, ministers, grassroots activists, and organizations as early as the 1930s and is an oversimplification.[42] From those early activists to black soldiers who fought for other people's freedom overseas during World War II only to be denied it for themselves when they returned home, all the way to the US Supreme Court's decision in *Brown v. Board of Education*, a movement was brewing. Yet the death of Emmett Till and the injustice that followed galvanized a people like few events have. It got them moving in the direction they were already headed but moved them faster and with greater resolve. The rest is history.

EPILOGUE

Seeing Clearly

From June 2005 until July 2009, the casket that had contained the body of Emmett Till for half a century sat empty and covered in a storage shed behind the office at Burr Oak Cemetery.

From the mid-1990s until her death in 2003, Mamie Till-Mobley had become increasingly dissatisfied with the condition of Burr Oak and the upkeep of Emmett's grave in particular. The grounds, equipment, and offices had suffered from years of neglect; things became so bad that even the clientele became suspect, and office members interacted with customers behind bulletproof glass.[1]

During my first conversation with Mamie Till-Mobley in December 1996, she told me that she had established an Emmett Till Memorial Fund to raise the necessary monies for removing Emmett's remains from Burr Oak and transferring them to the beautifully maintained Oak Woods Cemetery. She also wanted to erect a monument at the new gravesite that would honor her son and those who died in the civil rights struggle. I asked if anyone was helping her in this endeavor, and, to my surprise, she informed me that she was doing it alone. I enthusiastically offered my assistance, and she readily accepted. As I began creating and sending out flyers, the *Deseret News* in Salt Lake City ran an article about Emmett Till, and highlighted my efforts to raise money for the reburial and monument.[2] Donations trickled in, but they were few and far between. Four years later, we were still trying when Mamie faxed me a letter to preface my upcoming remarks at a local school where I hoped to solicit student help with the project. It is clear from her message to the students how much the grave removal meant to her:

Emmett's grave is located above a sewer. Apparently, the pipes burst in winter, flooding his grave site to a depth of 4 to 8 inches. Even in the spring, it is soggy and wet. In addition, the mowers have broken up his headstone until the picture has been smashed and fallen out, the vase which recesses into the headstone will no longer stand up. It's a mess! Personally, I am so depressed when I visit that it takes me days to recover.... If I don't get the job done with the help of you and Mr. Anderson, I can predict that it will never come to pass.[3]

Sometime the following year, Mamie told me that there had been a sudden change in plans. She decided to end the efforts to remove her son to Oak Woods because the new management at Burr Oak offered to raise funds to build a facility on the grounds, to be called the Emmett Till Historical Museum. This seemed like an ideal solution and relieved her and me of the burden of raising the money ourselves; indeed, Mamie seemed satisfied with the change of plans. A company called Perpetua Holdings of Illinois had just taken over the neglected property in July 2001. Slivy Edmunds Cotton, president of Perpetua, committed to make all of the improvements necessary to restore the 150-acre cemetery to its former self. Since 1927, Burr Oak had been an important presence to the black community as one of the first places black families could bury their dead. It had served the growing population of African Americans who had been part of the Great Migration following World War I.[4]

Plans also began taking shape to build a mausoleum within the proposed museum that would hold the bodies of Emmett Till, Gene Mobley, and, one day, Mamie Till-Mobley. The museum would not only tell the story of Emmett but of other African Americans who made a difference in Chicago and elsewhere.[5]

Mamie Till-Mobley did not live to see the facility that was to honor her son come to be, but after her death, plans for the project appeared to remain intact. The cemetery produced a flyer announcing that ground-breaking ceremonies would take place in the spring of 2005.[6] Yet when Emmett's body was exhumed for an autopsy in June of that year, there had as yet been no activity on the project. Till's remains were returned to the ground with the idea that they would once again be unearthed. The day I stood before Till's decaying casket in February 2007, cemetery manager Carolyn Towns assured me that the museum was still a priority and that the coffin would become part of a permanent exhibit.

Nearly two-and-a-half years later, on July 9, 2009, news broke that Carolyn Towns, then forty-nine, and coworkers Maurice Dailey, fifty-nine, Keith Nicks, forty-five, and Terrance Nicks, thirty-eight, had been arrested and charged with dismembering human remains, a Class X felony. Additional charges filed against Towns alleged that a large number of graves had been excavated and the bodies buried or dumped into a vacant part of the cemetery. Towns then allegedly sold the emptied graves to the families of newly deceased individuals and kept the money, which officials estimated to be over $200,000. At the same time, she destroyed all the paperwork relating to the original graves. Authorities believed that over 300 graves were affected.[7]

The scheme came to a halt when Willie Esper, a twenty-eight-year-old gravedigger practicing with a backhoe, began inadvertently excavating bones in what was supposed to be an unused section of the cemetery. After Esper made the discovery, another employee told him to keep quiet or else he would lose his job. Esper kept talking, however, and a co-worker who overheard his story went to the authorities.[8]

As the case unfolded, anxieties that Emmett Till may have been one of the discarded bodies were quickly alleviated. However, authorities began investigating the fund set up for the Emmett Till Historical Museum, which had never gotten off the ground. They also learned that the casket in the storage shed had been neglected and was deteriorating further. In fact, when they first discovered it, a family of possums apparently living inside the shed ran out and scurried away. These revelations were devastating to Till family members and others who believed the casket was being cared for. Rev. Jesse Jackson noted upon hearing news of the scandal that the casket "is as much a part of the civil-rights movement as the bus that Rosa Parks was riding on."[9] That bus sits prominently at the Henry Ford Museum in Dearborn, Michigan.

On August 26, news outlets announced that the Till family had taken possession of the casket and had made arrangements to donate it to the Smithsonian Institution, where it would go on display at the National Museum of African American History and Culture, targeted to open in 2015 (since moved to 2016). Restoration work on the casket was to take place at A. A. Rayner & Sons Funeral Home, where Till's body had been prepared for burial in 1955. On Friday, August 28, the fifty-fourth anniversary of Emmett Till's death, family members gathered at the Roberts Temple Church of God in Christ, where Emmett's funeral service had taken place in September 1955, and made the official announcement. Afterward, they marched across the Emmett Till Memorial Bridge and released white balloons into the air in a symbolic gesture of freedom.[10]

On July 8, 2011, almost two years from the day when the Burr Oak scandal first broke, fifty-one-year-old Carolyn Towns pleaded guilty to several charges related to her grave-selling scheme and was convicted of stealing over $100,000 from Perpetua. Sentenced to twelve years in prison, she was granted a few months to make arrangements for the care of her elderly mother, after which she began serving her sentence on November 1. The cases involving her co-conspirators are currently pending.[11]

On February 22, 2012, President Barack Obama, former First Lady Laura Bush, Congressman John Lewis, Washington mayor Vincent Gray, and others gathered for a ground-breaking ceremony for what would be the nineteenth Smithsonian museum. The site, located on the National Mall between the Washington Monument and the National Museum of American History, sits near what had once been the largest slave market in the nation. President George W. Bush had signed the law creating the museum back in 2003. It was projected to cost $500 million, half of which would be appropriated by Congress. When finished, it would contain seven levels, totaling 323,000 square feet.[12]

Mamie Till-Mobley's death spared her of what would have been another heartbreaking development and final disappointment. She had placed her trust in Carolyn Towns, who promised to honor Emmett Till. Unbeknownst to Till-Mobley, she had put that trust into the hands of a criminal. Burr Oak's reputation became deeply and possibly irreversibly tarnished as a result of the scheme masterminded by Towns. Emmett Till's body, however, remains there to this day. In August 2014, a monument honoring those whose graves were desecrated was dedicated by Illinois governor Pat Quinn and Cook County sheriff Tom Dart.[13]

Although the Emmett Till Historical Museum that Mamie Till-Mobley died anticipating never came to fruition, there was an unexpected triumph. The casket's place in the Smithsonian only came about because of a scandal, yet it will fully cement Emmett Till's role in the civil rights struggle in a way never imagined and that will tell his story to millions who otherwise would have never learned of it. Countless others will become one with those who filed past this same coffin in 1955, as I did in a dimly lit cold shed in February 2007. It will preserve in a new, dignified setting the images that aroused not only a nation, but a world.

The restoration work will make the glass top clear once again so that visitors can look down and see where a tortured body once lay, a vision that was denied to me because time had darkened the original glass. Seeing clearly now, both figuratively and literally, millions will understand and be forever changed by the stories, not only of Emmett Till but of countless others, on what will forever be hallowed ground.

Mamie Till-Mobley in the 1990s. She never gave up the pursuit of justice for her son and always wanted to see his case reopened. Copyright © Estate of Mamie Till-Mobley. Reprinted by permission.

Filmmaker Keith Beauchamp. In the late 1990s, Beauchamp began research for a documentary film project on the Emmett Till case, working closely with Mamie Till-Mobley. Results of his findings, which included interviews with witnesses telling their story on film for the first time, were turned over to the FBI and played a major role in the 2004 decision to reopen the case. His film, *The Untold Story of Emmett Louis Till*, was released in theaters in 2005 and later played on Court TV (now TruTV). Copyright © Amanda Sharise Anderson. Printed by permission.

Stanley Nelson, whose documentary *The Murder of Emmett Till* premiered on PBS's *The American Experience* in January 2003. His film, along with his uncovering of new witnesses, was also reviewed by the FBI. At screenings, Nelson passed out postcards for audience members to send to the Mississippi attorney general's office encouraging officials to reopen the case. The film went on to win an Emmy in 2003. Firelight Media. Printed by permission.

Civil rights activist Alvin Sykes, who contacted Mamie Till-Mobley a week prior to her death and formed the Emmett Till Justice Campaign. His efforts helped get the attention of the federal government, which eventually opened an investigation into the Till case in May 2004. Kansas City Library. Printed by permission.

FBI agent Dale Killinger, of Oxford, Mississippi, conducted a federal investigation into the Emmett Till murder from May 2004 until November 2005. Federal Bureau of Investigation. Printed by permission.

Shed near Drew, Mississippi, where Emmett Till was beaten and killed, as it appears today. In 2005, the FBI tested the shed with luminol and sifted through the dirt floor with hopes of finding fifty-year-old clues to the murder. Copyright © Amanda Sharise Anderson. Printed by permission.

District Attorney Joyce Chiles, whose jurisdiction over Mississippi's Fourth Judicial District included Leflore, Sunflower, and Washington Counties. It would be up to her to decide whether the FBI's findings should lead to the prosecution of any living individuals for the murder of Emmett Till. AP Photo/Rogelio Solis.

Event held on October 2, 2007, in front of the courthouse in Sumner, Mississippi, sponsored by the bipartisan Emmett Till Memorial Commission. On this occasion, the county officially expressed regret and sorrow for the murder and unjust verdict in the Till murder trial. Author's collection.

Simeon Wright speaks at the event in Sumner, Mississippi, on October 2, 2007, and accepts the resolution signed by the fourteen members of the Emmett Till Memorial Commission. Author's collection.

Wheeler Parker Jr. speaks at the event in Sumner, Mississippi, on October 2, 2007. Author's collection.

State senator David L. Jordan, who attended the 1955 Emmett Till murder trial, served as master of ceremonies for the event in Sumner, Mississippi, on October 2, 2007. Author's collection.

Former governor William F. Winter speaks to the crowd at the event in Sumner, Mississippi, on October 2, 2007. Author's collection.

Betty and Bill Pearson, who hosted several members of the press in their home during the 1955 Emmett Till murder trial. Betty Pearson attended all five days of the trial, sitting with the white press, along with her friend Florence Mars. One of Tallahatchie County's few white liberals, she was elected cochair of the Emmett Till Memorial Commission in 2006 and served until moving to Davis, California, in 2009. Copyright © Amanda Sharise Anderson. Printed by permission.

Jerome Little, president of the Tallahatchie County Board of Supervisors, speaks before unveiling a new marker on the grounds of the courthouse in Sumner, Mississippi, on October 2, 2007. Directly behind him stands Robert L. Grayson, Tutwiler, Mississippi, mayor and cochair of the Emmett Till Memorial Commission. Tallahatchie County sheriff William L. Brewer with sunglasses stands to the left. Author's collection.

Till family members pose in front of newly unveiled marker at the Sumner courthouse, October 2, 2007. From left: Wheeler Parker Jr., Marvel Parker, Simeon Wright, and Annie Wright. Author's collection.

Former Tutwiler Funeral Home in Tutwiler, Mississippi, is one of many Emmett Till–related sites in Tallahatchie County that are part of the Tallahatchie County driving tour. Till's body was embalmed here on August 31–September 1, 1955. Author's collection.

Sign on Highway 49 E in Greenwood, Mississippi. The stretch of highway between Greenwood and Tutwiler was renamed the Emmett Till Memorial Highway in 2005. Author's collection.

Emmett Till Historic Intrepid Center (ETHIC), which opened in Glendora, Mississippi, in 2006. The museum is housed in an old cotton gin. Author's collection.

Courtroom in the Tallahatchie County courthouse, August 2014. One of the main endeavors of the Emmett Till Memorial Commission was to secure funding to renovate the courthouse and restore the courtroom to its 1955 appearance as a way of saving the dilapidated building and increase tourism. Eupora, Mississippi, architect Belinda Stewart led the efforts. The final price tag for the restoration was around $3 million. Author's collection.

Jury box in restored courtroom in Sumner, Mississippi. Author's collection.

Patrick H. Weems, director of the Emmett Till Interpretive Center. The facility is located on the north side of the town square in Sumner, Mississippi, and faces the courthouse. It is housed in the old Wong grocery building, serving as an outlet for telling and understanding the impact of the Till murder. Patrick H. Weems. Printed by permission.

Sign in front of the Bryant store in Money, Mississippi, was the first of several dedicated in May 2011 as part of the Freedom Trail, which celebrated the fiftieth anniversary of the Mississippi Freedom Riders. Author's collection.

From left: Attorney General Eric Holder, Wheeler Parker Jr., and Alvin Sykes. The men met in early 2009 to discuss the Emmett Till Unsolved Civil Rights Act with the new Obama administration. The bill had been signed by President George W. Bush in October 2008. Courtesy of Alvin Sykes.

APPENDIX

Piecing the Puzzle

Off and on for sixty years, historians and investigators have sought to uncover the facts behind the kidnapping and murder of Emmett Till. In October 1955, William Bradford Huie sat down with acquitted killers J. W. Milam and Roy Bryant just weeks after their trial and boldly declared in the article based on those interviews that he was revealing "the real story of that killing—the story no jury heard and no newspaper reader saw." Decades later, writer Bonnie Blue proclaimed that her book, based largely on alleged telephone interviews with Milam, "uncovered the total unvarnished truth" about the Till case.[1]

Any assertion that all the facts are in and can be nicely assembled is certainly erroneous and irresponsible. Memories fade and stories become conflated; details often become the storytellers' truth because they want to believe certain things; personal reminiscences are reshaped by what has been suggested to them by others or what people read in the media. In what follows, I examine several relevant questions surrounding the Till case, and although I reach conclusions where I can, that is not always possible. Some of the issues presented here were addressed in earlier chapters in varying degrees but are recapped now to provide a useful summary. Although facts have emerged that were unavailable a decade ago, many of the answers have raised even more questions. Some facts will likely never be known.

What happened at the Bryant's Grocery on August 24, 1955?

The encounter between Carolyn Bryant and Emmett Till at the Bryant's Grocery and Meat Market occurred between 7:30 and 8:00 P.M. on the night in question. Emmett Till and several companions hopped into Mose Wright's 1946 Ford and drove into downtown Money to visit a café. After discovering that the café was closed, Maurice Wright spotted a checkers game going on outside the Bryant store and stopped the car so that he could join in. According to Carolyn Bryant, they parked on the south side between the store and the gas station next door.[2] Several other black youths were already gathered outside on the porch. Wheeler Parker told several reporters on four different occasions upon returning to Chicago that during the bantering outside, an older boy told Emmett that there was a pretty woman inside and that he should go in and look at her.[3] What prompted this boy to say this is unclear, but it was likely due to some conversation about girls initiated by Emmett.

According to William Bradford Huie, who said he later talked to some of Till's cousins, Emmett was showing off a photo of a white girl and claimed that she was his girlfriend. Roosevelt Crawford, who was there, said the same thing when interviewed by Dale Killinger decades later. Dr. T. R. M. Howard, a tireless black civil rights activist then living in Mound Bayou, Mississippi, also interviewed some of the youth who had been at the store that night and learned that Emmett had been boasting of dating white girls, which lends credence to Huie's story.[4] Whatever the exact details, these independent sources confirm that Emmett had been boasting about relationships with white girls. That clearly prompted the unidentified boy to urge him to go into the store to see the woman inside.

After Emmett entered the store, he turned to the left and approached the candy counter, which was about one-third of the way into the store.[5] He asked the clerk, twenty-one-year-old Carolyn Bryant, for two-cents worth of bubble gum. According to an account that Carolyn provided for attorneys C. Sidney Carlton and Harvey Henderson nine days later, Carolyn said that "when I went to take money he grabbed my hand & said [']how about a date['] and I walked away from him and he said 'What's the matter Baby can't you take it?['] He went out door and said 'Goodbye' and I went out to car & got pistol and when I came back he whistled at me—this whistle while I was going after pistol—didn't do anything further after he saw pistol." Emmett Till left the store after another boy went inside. Carolyn said that she did not "know why boy from outside came in—he went out with him—don't know whether he asked him to come out."[6]

In court, Carolyn testified that Emmett's actions went far beyond what she had initially told her attorneys, and this evolution is where fabrications unquestionably crept into the narrative, if not before. She said that her customer held her by "grasping all the fingers in the palm of his hand" and that she had to jerk herself free. At that point he asked for the date, and as Carolyn turned to head to the back of the store, the customer caught her by the cash register and grabbed her by the waist. It was at this point that he uttered the words, "What's the matter, baby? Can't you take it?" She then freed herself and Till said, "You needn't be afraid of me." He then bragged in a crude manner that he had been "with white women before." In her courtroom testimony, Carolyn said that her customer did not just leave peacefully with his friend, but that "this other nigger came in the store and got him by the arm," and when the customer left with him, he did so "unwillingly."[7] Because most of these details were not stated to her attorneys on September 2, it is clear that this aspect of her story developed later for the purposes of gaining sympathy with the jury. Carolyn admitted in 2010 that those more lurid details were later concocted by family members and defense attorneys.[8]

Although no one else was inside the store to corroborate Carolyn Bryant's testimony, the rest was witnessed by those outside. Maurice Wright's account agrees with Carolyn that Emmett waved and said "Good-bye" after he left the store. As Carolyn walked outside and toward her car, Emmett emitted "what some people call a wolf-whistle." Wheeler Parker said basically the same thing, and both he and Maurice affirmed that Carolyn went toward her car to get a gun. Simeon Wright repeated the wolf whistle when a reporter asked him to demonstrate it.[9] After seeing Carolyn Bryant's reaction, Emmett and the group that were with him all got into the car and quickly left the scene. Stories that Emmett whistled in an attempt to stop his stutter or for any reason other than directing it toward Carolyn Bryant are without foundation and contradict virtually all witness testimony as given within days of the incident.

When did Roy Bryant find out about the store incident and who told him?

On the evening Emmett Till visited the Bryant store, Roy Bryant was on a road trip to East Texas hauling shrimp. Nine days later Carolyn told attorneys Carlton and Henderson that "I reported the incident to my husband when he came in about 4:30 A.M. Friday. Had seen J. W. & not told him since he brought company with him. I told Mrs. Milam but she never did tell J. W." After Huie interviewed Milam and Bryant the following month, he wrote that Carolyn and Juanita "determined to keep the incident from their 'menfolks.' They didn't tell J. W. Milam when he came to escort them home."[10] This appears to be true, but it is unclear from the defense notes if their silence was intentional.

"By Thursday afternoon," continued Huie, "Carolyn Bryant could see the story was getting around. She spent Thursday night at the Milams, where at 4 A.M. (Friday) Roy got back from Texas." This story is in basic agreement with Carolyn's statement to her attorneys that Roy returned home early Friday morning at 4:30. Milam or Bryant told Huie that because "he [Roy] had slept little for five nights, he went to bed at the Milams' while Carolyn returned to the store." Carolyn's later recollection to Dale Killinger was that Roy returned home on Saturday.[11] Because the earliest accounts were written within a few days to a few weeks of the event, it is safe to conclude that Carolyn's later version is incorrect.

Although Carolyn said to Carlton and Henderson that she told Roy about the incident after Roy returned home Friday morning, she does not state that she told him immediately or initiated the conversation. In fact, sources independent of each other demonstrate that Carolyn was not the one who first told Roy about the encounter with Emmett Till. In a speech delivered on October 8, 1955, even before Huie interviewed Milam and Bryant, Dr. Howard affirmed that he talked to the people that had gathered on the porch the night of the Till/Bryant trouble. He learned that there was "some two-bit person sitting there who wanted 50 cents worth of credit; that individual told Mr. Bryant that a boy from Chicago, a northern boy, whistled at his wife." Huie learned a similar story. He wrote that after Roy returned to the store sometime in the afternoon on Friday, "a Negro told him what 'the talk' was, and told him that the 'Chicago boy' was 'visitin' Preacher.'" It was then that Carolyn confirmed to Roy what he had already learned had occurred.[12]

Olive Arnold Adams, whose booklet *Time Bomb* relied exclusively on Howard, repeated the same story but claims that the unnamed person got the idea to tell Roy only after Till and his friends returned to the store two days later. During this alleged second visit, the Wednesday night encounter did not come up. However, "The whistle incident was marked by one of the men who was within earshot. It is believed such a person may have sought a favor, or perhaps easy credit at the store, by distorting the story for the benefit of Roy Bryant who had been out of town during the week." In his October speech, Howard said he learned of this information after he spoke with the black people who were sitting on the porch.[13]

Neither Howard nor Adams specifically noted that the person who informed Roy Bryant of Till's indiscretion was black, but another source influenced by Howard does. A reporter writing for the *California Eagle* under the pseudonym Amos Dixon, like Adams, learned that the day after the store incident, "Emmett and some of the kids went back to the store, to 'fool around' and buy cokes and bubble gum." Dixon, like Adams, said that "nobody mentioned the wolf whistle. It had been forgotten, that is forgotten by everybody but one Negro loafer. That one loafer who hadn't forgotten wanted to curry favor with Roy Bryant, either to get some credit, or cadge a favor, or just to keep in good with the white folks." Sometime after Roy's return on Friday, "the Negro snitch told him that the 'Chicago boy' had whistled at Carolyn."[14]

The Adams and Dixon stories are the only instances to claim that Till returned to the store a day or two after the incident, although their common source is clearly Howard. Simeon Wright denies that they ever went back; Carolyn Bryant also maintained that she never saw the "Negro man" again after Wednesday night.[15]

When speaking to Dale Killinger during his 2004–5 investigation, Carolyn affirmed that she did not tell Roy about the incident and the reason was that she feared Roy "was . . . gonna go find and beat him up." She also instructed Juanita not to tell J. W.[16] Carolyn's later story is consistent with what J. W. and Roy told Huie and may have been influenced over the years by what she read in that account. However, Howard's and Huie's independent confirmations that someone else told Roy about the trouble at the store backs up Carolyn's story to Killinger.

If Roy Bryant learned the story from a black "loafer," who was it? As noted earlier, in 1974 Mose Wright's brother-in-law, Crosby Smith, told an interviewer that the informant was Mose Wright's sixteen-year-old son, Maurice. Smith believed Maurice was jealous of Emmett Till because he wore fancy clothes and had spending money in his wallet. Smith said confidently that "Maurice told Bryant how Emmett had told his wife what a good-looking woman she was," but that Maurice "also added a whole lot more to it than there actually was." In 1995, Emmett's mother indicated to George Curry of the now defunct *Emerge* magazine that she believed elements of that story as well. Simeon Wright has repeatedly declared the accusations against his brother to be false and said of *Emerge*, "With stories like that, I can see why the magazine went under."[17] However, Wright fails to note that Curry relied on the Crosby Smith story and that Mamie Till-Mobley also backed the accusation. Nor does he mention that his uncle Crosby was the first to tell that story in print twenty years before that.

Neither Howard, Adams, Dixon, nor Huie place blame on Maurice—at least by name—and by characterizing the person as a "loafer," they seem to take Maurice out of the picture, as Maurice hardly had time to hang around outside the Bryant store during this crucial cotton harvest time. Huie said a few years later that he knew the identity of the person but opted not to reveal his name so as not to jeopardize his safety. Since Maurice was by then living with his family up north in Chicago, he would not have needed protection, at least from anyone in the South. It is possible that Huie wanted to protect him from northern blacks who would have seen him as a Judas. It is also possible that Huie simply wanted to appear in the know concerning this aspect of the story and in reality knew nothing about the identity of the informant.[18]

Keith Beauchamp believes that the informant was Johnny B. Washington, a black employee of Bryant's.[19] This is based on an account made fifty years later by a man who claimed to have seen Washington with Milam and Bryant earlier on the night of Emmett Till's abduction. Robert Wright, son of Mose, revealed years later that his father said he may have heard Washington's voice outside the house during the kidnapping.[20] Still, there is no evidence that Washington was the informant at the store. In summary, it appears that a black male who witnessed the encounter at the store was the first to tell Roy Bryant about it. His identity remains a mystery, although there have been suspicions, and family lore has in the past identified him as Maurice Wright.

Did Mose and Elizabeth Wright learn of the store incident prior to the kidnapping?

Simeon Wright has been adamant that his mother and father knew nothing about what happened on Wednesday, August 24, prior to Emmett Till's kidnapping. "If I had told Dad, he would have done one of two things: either he would have taken Bobo back to the store and made him apologize to Mrs. Bryant or he would have sent Bobo home as soon as possible. Either way, perhaps Bobo would be alive today." He also insists that "Mom didn't know about the incident—it was Bobo who wanted it to remain a secret."[21] This claim is refuted by Mose and Elizabeth Wright themselves. Simeon is correct that *he* did not tell his father, but somebody did. Elizabeth Wright found out even before her husband. Wheeler Parker told *Jet* magazine after he returned to Chicago from Money that "Grandma knew about the 'incident' because we'd told her and not Grandpa, who would have gotten angry at us." Elizabeth made it clear that she had heard about it before the kidnapping because when the men came to their home, she immediately knew what they wanted. She tried to run to Emmett's bedroom to wake him up before they got in the house. "We knew they were out to mob the boy," she explained to a reporter. "But they were already in the front door before I could shake him awake." This backs up Huie's story as published in his book *Wolf Whistle, and Other Stories*. Huie quotes from an interview he conducted with Mose and Elizabeth Wright, which Simeon believes Huie fabricated. "I feel partly responsible for the boy's death," Elizabeth said. "From what I could worm out of the boys, it seemed like a kind'a prank. Bobo shouldn'a done it. I told him so; and Preacher told him so. The boys shouldn'a let him do it. But he didn't know what he was doing—and I guess I thought the white folks'd realize that. And when they didn't come lookin' for him right off, I figgered maybe they'd forget it."[22]

Mose Wright's testimony on the witness stand was clear that he had found out about the store incident, perhaps one or two days after it happened.

"I heard someone say that this boy had done something, or had done some talking down at Money. I think that was on Thursday or maybe Friday," he told attorney Sidney Carlton on cross-examination.

Carlton asked Wright to clarify that statement. "You already knew about it, did you?"

"That's right," the witness answered.

"Had you talked to Emmett about it?"

"I sure did," confirmed Wright.[23]

Defense papers show that attorneys interviewed Wright previous to the trial. Notes from that interview read that "sometime between Wednesday and Saturday night someone told Mose about Till's getting into trouble in Money, but he did not talk to Till about it at anytime."[24] The discrepancy about whether Wright talked to Emmett is inexplicable, but the issue as to whether Wright heard about the trouble before the kidnapping is indisputable. On Sunday, September 18, Wright told reporters that he had heard about the incident from an unidentified "outsider." Roosevelt Crawford said in an interview for Keith Beauchamp's film, *The Untold Story of Emmett Louis Till*, that it was his father, Jonas Crawford, who told Wright. This is probably true, since two of the Crawford children were with Emmett at the store, witnessed the event, and could easily have told Jonas about it. The Crawfords and the Wrights were neighbors.[25]

What happened in the hours prior to Emmett Till's kidnapping?

By Saturday, August 27, Roy Bryant clearly knew about the trouble at the store, was angered by it, and wanted to confront the stranger from Chicago. As part of his investigation, Dale Killinger confirmed from two separate sources that a boy entered the store Saturday and was accosted by Bryant, who thought the boy may have been the one who had insulted his wife the previous Wednesday. Both the boy involved and Carolyn Donham separately recounted the August 27, 1955, incident to Killinger. Because both were still living at the time the FBI released its report, their names are redacted from the published version:

[Source] lived near Money, Mississippi, and had just returned to Mississippi from a summer vacation trip to Chicago, Illinois. [Source] entered Bryant's Grocery & Meat Market, accompanied by his uncle and his mother. When he entered the store, Roy Bryant and [Carolyn Bryant] were inside. Roy Bryant asked [source] where he [source] was on "that Thursday or Friday or something...." "I didn't know what the devil he was talkin' about, so he, he acted like he wanted to do something to me...." [Source's] mother intervened..."and she said what's goin' on? And ah, he just started out off and he say you all got to teach this boy how to say I said yes sir, no sir." At about the same time [Carolyn Bryant] said something to Roy Bryant that [source] could not hear. The next day, [source's] father went and told their landowner about the incident. The landowner went to find out if Roy Bryant had a problem with [source] and learned that Roy Bryant was in jail for kidnapping Preacher Wright's grandson the night before.[26]

Killinger's summary of Carolyn Donham's version is as follows: "On the evening prior to Till's kidnapping, a black boy entered Bryant's Grocery & Meat Market and Roy Bryant was aggressively quizzing the boy. Initially, [Donham] did not recall exact details about the incident." When Killinger interviewed her again later, she remembered more clearly. "'I know that there was a lady and her little boy or her grandson or somebody was in the store and, I don't know, Roy said something to 'em, and I remember telling him to leave him alone that, you know, that wasn't him,' meaning it wasn't Emmett Till."[27]

This story is actually confirmed, with some variation and likely exaggeration, in an overlooked account published in the *Baltimore Afro-American*. In October 1955, Elizabeth Wright told a reporter during a joint interview with Mamie Bradley that on the day before the kidnapping, something happened inside the Bryant store: "A colored boy forgot to say 'sir' . . . and the white man kicked the boy in the body. Everybody thought he would be stomped to death, but only one thing saved him. He begged and pleaded that his life be spared."[28]

As discussed earlier, a man named Willie Hemphill claimed in 2004 that a few hours before Emmett Till's kidnapping, Hemphill was walking home after buying some items at the Bryant grocery. A pickup truck drove up alongside him, stopped, and someone inside the cab ordered a black man sitting in the bed to put Hemphill into the truck. Hemphill could see J. W. Milam, Roy Bryant, and Carolyn Bryant inside the cab. Carolyn told the men that Hemphill was not the right boy, and Washington threw him out of the truck. During the fracas, Hemphill's front teeth were broken.[29] Although the confrontation at the store earlier in the day involving a different boy is corroborated by three separate sources (including Carolyn Bryant), one must rely solely on Hemphill's late recollection for his story. However, it is consistent with the fact that upon finding out about the Wednesday night encounter between Emmett Till and Carolyn Bryant, Roy Bryant became incensed and was determined to find the guilty youth.

Who went to Mose Wright's home early Sunday morning for the abduction and in what vehicle?

Ruth Crawford Jackson, one of the youths who went to the store with Emmett Till and Till's cousins and who lived about 100 yards from the Wright home, told Keith Beauchamp in an interview outtake from his film, *The Untold Story of Emmett Louis Till*, that on the night of the kidnapping, "I heard a lot of cars, just driving real fast. It seemed like to me there ought to have been 200 or 300 cars come down through the gravel road to Wright's home." When Beauchamp asked her to clarify if there was more than one car, Crawford reiterated, "Oh my God yes. More than one car."[30]

In a portion of the interview retained for the film, Crawford said, "I looked out the window and it was just like daylight. And I said 'My Lord,' I said, 'Look at the cars.' But I didn't know where they was going. So at the time I could see this black man get out of the car, went to the back, and the whites went to the front."[31]

If Crawford is describing what she saw on the evening of Till's kidnapping and not confusing a different incident, her testimony contradicts Mose

Wright's, who said that it was so dark outside that he could not tell if the vehicle parked just twenty to twenty-five feet from the door was a car or a truck. If Wright could not make out the vehicle when it was that close and who was in it, it would have been impossible for Ruth Crawford to see the people that she described outside the house, especially being 100 yards away. If she did see numerous headlights coming down the street, the cars obviously did not stop at the Wright home, as Mose heard only one vehicle drive away as he watched from the front porch. He remained outside for around twenty minutes.[32]

From the first reports of the kidnapping, Mose Wright said that when he was awakened by loud knocks on his door, he opened the door to see three men. Two came into the house, and a third remained on the porch. He assumed that the one who stayed outside was black, only because he "acted like" a black person. After Emmett was taken outside, Wright heard a voice that "seemed like . . . a lighter voice than a man's" that identified Emmett as the right one. From Wright's testimony, there were at least four people present. He stood on the doorstep and heard them drive off, but it was so dark that he could only tell which direction they went because he could see the vehicle as it passed the trees.[33]

J. W. Milam allegedly told writer Bonnie Blue that he and Roy Bryant picked up Carolyn Bryant and either Henry Lee Loggins or Levi Collins and that they used the car of a friend named Hubert Clark to drive out to Mose Wright's home.[34] Interestingly, Clark's name appears in an article published in *Jet* magazine in October 1955. "A third man who rode on the ill-fated truck, Hurburt [sic] Clark, has not been located."[35] How Clark's name became associated with the kidnapping at the time and why it was revealed exclusively in *Jet* is puzzling. The reporter gave no explanation as to his source.

When Roy Bryant talked to defense attorneys on September 6, 1955, he admitted to going to Mose Wright's home to kidnap Emmett Till and told them that he "did identify self as Mr. Bryant when he went in house" (a fact that the attorneys never mentioned in court; instead, they berated Mose Wright on the witness stand for mistakenly identifying their clients as the abductors). Notes made by the defense contradict Milam's late statement to Bonnie Blue about the vehicle used because Bryant told the attorneys that he "went out there [to Mose Wright's home] in pickup."[36]

A 1955 green and white Chevy pickup as described in news stories at the time of the trial belonged to J. W. Milam. Dailey Chevrolet in Charleston, Mississippi, was owned by the Dailey family from 1926 until 2009. In April 2012, eighty-two-year-old Bobby Dailey revealed to his family that he was the one who sold Milam the truck. In fact, Dailey said that Milam bought it the Wednesday before the kidnapping, which would have been the same day Emmett Till whistled at Carolyn Bryant. Dailey never told his story before mentioning it to his children when they stopped in Glendora to see their old homestead shortly after his wife's death when they scattered her ashes in Itta Bena. His fear had always been that people would assume he and Milam had been friends or might reach a conclusion that he condoned the murder. Milam financed the truck through General Motors Acceptance Corporation (GMAC).[37]

Amos Dixon, writing for the *California Eagle* and basing most of his story on the research of Dr. Howard, said that "about 2 o'clock Sunday morning, Aug. 28, three full days after the wolf-whistling incident, a Chevrolet truck belonging to J. W. Milam drew up in front of Mose Wright's farm," and that Henry Lee Loggins was in the back. "He lives in Glendora, too, where J. W. lives. He has worked for J. W. for 12 years and whatever J. W. says is gospel as far as Loggins is concerned. He was along to see that Emmett Till didn't jump off the truck and run once he was placed there." Reporter James Hicks revealed later that this and other information about Loggins came from Loggins's father, DeWitt, who Hicks said received a confession directly from Henry Lee, and that Henry Lee also told an unidentified preacher that he was in the back of the truck that night. The significance of Hicks's account, then, cannot be overstated as it seems unthinkable that he and Howard would have fabricated the stories they say came from DeWitt Loggins or that the senior Loggins would have made up tales about his son. Hicks detailed Loggins's involvement in an open letter to Attorney General Herbert Brownell and FBI director J. Edgar Hoover, and published it in the *Washington Afro-American* on November 19, 1955.[38] The risk he ran in jeopardizing the safety of Henry Lee and DeWitt Loggins was serious, but he thought he had a case, and taking it public was the only way the federal authorities might listen.

It is possible that Roy Bryant told the attorneys that he went to Wright's house in a pickup and not in a car so as not to say anything that would incriminate anyone else—in this case, Hubert Clark. Loggins's account came after having been told by Loggins to his father, then to Dr. Howard, and finally, to Dixon. It is possible that some details got muddled as a result or that DeWitt Loggins conflated the story of the kidnapping and, later, the murder by assuming the same people were present for both. Therefore, it is impossible to determine what vehicle was used during the kidnapping and precisely who was in it, but the most likely scenario is that J. W. Milam, Roy Bryant, Carolyn Bryant, and Henry Lee Loggins comprised the group.

What happened just after the kidnapping party left Mose Wright's house?

J. W. Milam told Bonnie Blue that from the Wright home, they drove to the store and dropped off Carolyn Bryant. Carolyn, of course, denied having accompanied the men during the abduction. Defense notes show that she told attorneys on September 2, 1955:

I did not go to this negroe's [Mose Wright's] house on Saturday night but they [J. W. and Roy] did bring him [Emmett Till] to the store later Saturday night or early Sunday morning for me to identify. Roy brought him in—if J. W. was there I didn't see him. Roy brought him to back. He came right ~~in but~~ inside back door. No gun. Negro was scared but hadn't been harmed. He didn't say anything. Roy asked if that was the same one and I told him it was not the one who had insulted me. Roy went out with the negro and I locked the door.

Carolyn told a similar story to Dale Killinger fifty years later. "I think it happened pretty much like he, like they said. I think they probably asked me who, if that was him." Her response was "no that's not him." Roy then told her that "he was gonna take him back."[39] Either scenario means the men drove back to the store, either to drop off Carolyn (if she had, in fact, accompanied them to Mose Wright's house) or to have her identify Till. It is possible that they did both—she may have identified Till at the Wright home with only the help of the flashlight and did so again once she could see more clearly at the store. One must also consider the possibility that when she identified Till at the Wright home, she thought Roy and J. W. might only talk to him or reprimand him. Once he was abducted and they returned to the store, she may have changed her mind and said Till was *not* the right one because she realized at this point that they were going to harm him. Mose Wright definitely heard a voice identify Till at his house. No one else is known to have been in a position to identify Till from his moment with Carolyn other than her.

If she was forced to leave her boys at home during the six-mile round trip to Mose Wright's home, she likely went along unwillingly. Carolyn did make one interesting claim to Killinger. When Roy and J. W. brought Emmett Till to the store for her to identify him, she said, "I think that Kimbrell man was, was with, with 'em."[40] This was, of course, Elmer Kimbell, a neighbor and good friend of Milam's in Glendora. If Carolyn did accompany the men to the Wright home, it may be that Kimbell went inside the store to remain with the boys while she did so. Milam did not tell Bonnie Blue that Kimbell was with them at all that night. However, because Kimbell was still living at the time (he died in 1985), Milam may have wanted to protect him from any possibility of prosecution.

What happened between the kidnapping and when the party was spotted at 6:30 A.M.?

It is unknown how long the group remained at the Bryant store before heading out to begin what ended in the torture and murder of Emmett Till. One story that does not fit the chronology is provided by writer Susan Klopher, who said she talked to someone who was seventeen years old at the time of the murder. Klopher's source told her that one evening in August 1955, at around midnight, her mother and father let Milam and Bryant into their home in Ruleville. "My parents didn't tell me then what was going on at the time. J. W. had a full brother, Bud, and I am very sure he was with them too. I was in bed but I could hear their voices." The woman, who remained anonymous by request in Klopher's report, said her father told her many years later that Milam and Bryant revealed to him that they had killed Emmett Till. When the daughter got up the next morning, the men were gone. "I never knew what happened to them after they left our house. I think they knew the law was going to catch up with them."[41]

The problem with Klopher's story is that the men did not kill Emmett Till until after sunrise Sunday morning, so they could not have gone to the house late Saturday night claiming that their kidnap victim was dead. By the following afternoon, Roy Bryant had been arrested. If Klopher's source is instead thinking of a Sunday night visit, Bryant could not have been there. It is possible that Milam and his brother Spencer Lamar "Bud" Milam went to the home in Ruleville alone on Sunday night, but a late-night visit would not have been necessary at that point. Also, there is no evidence that Bud Milam was involved in any of the events related to the kidnapping and murder. By Monday afternoon, J. W. Milam was in jail himself.

J. W. Milam told Bonnie Blue that after they dropped off Carolyn at the store, they went to a place where they had been drinking earlier in the evening. At this point, Hubert Clark, Melvin Campbell, Henry Lee Loggins, and Levi "Too Tight" Collins were there. They beat Emmett for a while, after which they got back into the truck to take him to a spot on the river to scare him. After driving around for some time, daylight was approaching, and they went to Leslie Milam's farm in Drew.[42]

Milam told a similar story to Huie, but in 1955 he was trying to protect his accomplices who had not been tried. He said that he and Roy planned only to "just whip him . . . scare some sense into him." Milam had discovered a spot the year before while hunting near Rosedale—a place he called "the scariest place in the Delta," with a 100-foot drop straight into the Mississippi River. After driving around for seventy-five miles looking for it, they gave up and went back to Glendora, arriving there at 5:00 A.M.[43]

When a friend of Bryant's asked him in 1985 about taking Till to a bluff on the river near Rosedale, Bryant said only that they planned to "put his ass in the river." This backs up Milam's story to Huie that they went to Rosedale. As to why they eventually went to the shed in Drew, Bryant said they were "tryin' to make our minds up." Bryant also said they "didn't go back to Glendora" as Milam told Huie, but that they "went through Glendora."[44] The Glendora story was Milam's way of diverting attention away from Leslie Milam's farm.

Both accounts are consistent that they spent much of their time trying to find a place to scare or otherwise deal with Till but gave up. Although Milam does not mention to Huie anything about the eventual stop in Drew, he does admit this to Bonnie Blue. Bryant also did so on tape in 1985. All of this would indicate that the four-hour window was taken up by first going to the Bryant store, either to drop off Carolyn or have her identify Emmett Till, and from there going to a spot where they had been drinking earlier and where they initially beat Emmett. From there they drove out to Rosedale to find the spot on the bluff to scare their victim. After getting lost and abandoning that plan, they went to the Drew plantation, arriving around 6:30 A.M. It was about a seventy-mile drive from Money to Rosedale, and from Rosedale it was another thirty-eight miles to Drew. Driving to these locations without any diversions would have taken about two hours. The time they spent giving Till his first beating and then looking for the bluff before giving up could have easily taken up the rest of the time.

Who was in the truck when it was spotted at the plantation in Drew?

What is clear is that the people who went to Drew did not comprise the exact group who had gone to the Wright home and abducted Emmett Till. Willie Reed, who saw the truck pull into the plantation, testified that he saw four white men in the cab of the truck. William Bradford Huie initially said that "two other men are involved: there were four in the torture-and-murder party."[45] James Hicks reported that Loggins's father said "his son has named to him the four more white men—instead of two—who were involved in the kidnapping or murder." Hicks learned that "the other white men involved along with Roy Bryant and J. W. Milam were relatives of Milam, that one of them was a close relative who has already been named by Willie Reed and that the other is a relative who lives at Ita Bend [Itta Bena], Miss." This is somewhat consistent with what Milam told Bonnie Blue, although there is some variation. Besides J. W. and Roy, Milam said that two others who played a role that night or early in the morning were Leslie Milam (whom Reed mentioned in court) and Melvin Campbell, a brother-in-law. Both fit the description as relatives of Milam and Bryant as described by Loggins's father, although Campbell lived in Minter City and not Itta Bena. A brother, Edward Milam, did live in Itta Bena, and could have been present, but his name never surfaced in any of the early investigations. It is unlikely, however, that Leslie Milam was in the truck that night. He would have been at home and was there when the truck unexpectedly arrived. J. W. Milam told Blue that Leslie was upset that the men showed up with Till because he had work to do that day. If Reed was correct that he saw four white men in the truck instead of just three, the fourth man would have been either Hubert Clark, whom Milam said was present, or

Elmer Kimbell, whom Carolyn Bryant said came by the store with her husband and Milam.[46]

Who were the black men in the back? Loggins's father told Howard that Henry Lee confessed to being on the truck. Both Amos Dixon and Olive Adams, using Howard as their source, said that Loggins was indeed on the back of the truck with Emmett Till, but that eventually Loggins needed help restraining him. The men stopped in Glendora to pick up farmhand Joe Willie Hubbard to give Loggins a hand.[47] During interviews later in life, Willie Reed consistently identified the men he saw on the truck as Collins and Hubbard, thus eliminating Loggins altogether.[48] There are problems with Reed's description, however. Reed testified during the trial that there were three black men besides Emmett Till in the back of the truck, not just two, and that "I had never seen them before."[49] Reed could have identified Collins later through a photograph that appeared in the *Chicago Defender* the month after the trial, but photos of Hubbard never appeared. Reed later began naming the men as Collins and Hubbard probably because those names came up in the news at the time of the trial and were mentioned repeatedly by Howard in speeches. On at least a few occasions, Reed accompanied Howard on speaking engagements. In actuality, Reed could not have identified these men. Seeing Collins's photo in the paper is the only way that Reed could possibly associate a name with a face.

If Loggins and Hubbard were on the truck, as Loggins's father told Howard and Hicks, who was the third man? According to Howard and Dixon, Levi Collins was not recruited until after the murder when the truck returned to Glendora, and his role was to help clean blood out of the truck.[50]

In a 2001 telephone interview with the historian Linda Beito, Henry Lee Loggins denied having been present during the kidnapping and murder, but he did provide some clues. "They say Too-Tight, they say he was on the back of that truck and some other boy, named, we called him Oso." During an interview with Keith Beauchamp for *Untold Story*, Loggins repeatedly said he had "heard" that Collins, Hubbard, and Oso were on the truck. "Oso" was Otha Johnson Jr., whom Dale Killinger learned had admitted to his own son that he was with Milam and Bryant that night and even drove them around.[51] Johnson probably did not drive the truck himself, but was certainly one of those in the back. In all probability then, Loggins, Hubbard, and Johnson were the three black men whom Willie Reed saw with Emmett Till. Later, they picked up Collins to help clean out the truck.

Who was at the shed in Drew?

After the truck stopped at the shed, the men went inside and began beating Emmett Till. Willie Reed identified J. W. Milam as the man he saw walk out of the shed and get a drink of water from a well. Reed claimed at the trial that he turned around and saw Milam from a distance after Reed passed the shed on his way to a store. However, Reed said many times during interviews later in life that Milam approached him with a gun on his side and asked if he had heard or seen anything at the shed. Reed, fearing for his life if he gave the wrong answer, nervously told him no.[52] This story, however, is not true. Reed never spoke of any encounter with Milam in his courtroom testimony either during direct or cross-examination, which would have helped the prosecution tremendously. Defense attorneys tried to use the distance issue to paint Reed's identification of Milam as mistaken. If Reed was afraid to speak about the encounter in court, perhaps fearing that the men would seek revenge, he still failed to do so during the several speeches he gave at rallies in the first few months following the trial after he had moved to Chicago. He did mention other facts that did not come out in his testimony, such as an experience at the attorney's office where several of the lawyers and Milam tried to intimidate him and confuse him about seeing Milam at the shed. Unfortunately, Reed's invented account of being confronted by Milam received publicity in Stanley Nelson's *The Murder of Emmett Till*, in Keith Beauchamp's *Untold Story*, and on CBS's *60 Minutes*.[53]

During his own courtroom testimony, Willie Reed's grandfather, Add Reed, said he saw Leslie Milam and another man at the shed not long after Willie would have passed by. Mandy Bradley, looking out her window, said she saw four men walking in and out of the shed.[54]

Stories that there were several other people present, including a small boy and a woman, as one informant told Dale Killinger, do not square with witness testimony from the day of the murder. None reported other cars being present besides the pickup containing four white men inside, which would have been a tight fit as it was, and four black men in back. If there were four men in the truck, then there certainly was a fifth man in the shed, however, and that was Leslie Milam, who would not have been in the truck.[55] Therefore, the white men present at the shed were J. W. Milam, Roy Bryant, Melvin Campbell, Leslie Milam, and either Hubert Clark, Elmer Kimbell, or possibly Edward Milam. The black men were Henry Lee Loggins, Joe Willie Hubbard, and Otha "Oso" Johnson Jr.

Where was Emmett Till murdered and by whom?

Although Emmett Till's body was discovered on the Tallahatchie County side of the Tallahatchie River, there is no evidence that he was actually killed in the county. Milam told William Bradford Huie that he shot Emmett Till near the spot where the body was found, outside of Glendora, off Swan Lake Road, past the house and property of L. W. Boyce. Ignoring that version, however, both J. W. Milam, to Bonnie Blue, and Roy Bryant in 1985, to an unidentified friend, said that Till was killed in a shed at the Leslie Milam plantation outside of Drew, in Sunflower County. Witnesses like field hand Frank Young, who was the first to inform Howard of the activities on the Drew plantation, said that a tractor was removed from the shed, the truck then backed in, and, when it left, something was in the back covered with a tarpaulin.[56] The trial was never moved to Sunflower County because no one reported hearing a gunshot at the shed. However, Willie Reed had already gone to the store, Add Reed had passed by, and Mandy Bradley was inside of her house. It is possible the gunshot was fired from inside the shed and that no one else on the property heard it.

Amos Dixon wrote that after the truck left the plantation and reached the river, Emmett Till, whom his killers assumed was dead, began moving, and so Milam shot him.[57] This may have happened, but if so, it was probably in the shed and not at the river. Again, all of the details that came from Loggins were told to Howard and Hicks secondhand by Loggins's father.

Stories vary as to who pulled the trigger. In the Huie and Dixon accounts, Milam was said to have shot Till. This is probably what happened, although Carolyn Bryant said she was told by her brother-in-law Raymond Bryant that Melvin Campbell actually killed the boy.[58] Raymond may have wanted to find a way to spare his brothers of a murder charge and was less hesitant to implicate Melvin, a brother-in-law, which would have been welcome news to Carolyn. Or perhaps Roy told that to Raymond over the phone from the jail as he proclaimed his own innocence. That, unfortunately, will never be known for sure.

What did the murder party do after killing Emmett at the shed?

Information about what happened after Emmett Till was murdered comes in greatest detail from Bonnie Blue. Milam told her that after they killed Emmett Till, they removed the clothing from his body and that Collins and Loggins cleaned blood from the shed floor and then spread cottonseed to cover traces of the crime. When highway patrol investigator Gwin Cole, Sheriff George Smith, and Deputy John Cothran visited the shed on September 21, 1955, after learning that Emmett may have been killed there, they reported that the floor was indeed covered in cottonseed.[59]

Amos Dixon addressed the attempt to hide the murder but said nothing about cleaning up the shed. He said that they stripped Emmett of his clothing long after they left Sunflower County. They then dumped the body in the river. After that, they returned to the Milam plantation, and, at this point, they recruited Levi Collins to wash blood out of the truck. Someone told Collins that the blood came from a deer and that they wanted to hide evidence from the game warden in case he came around. Collins was also told to burn the clothes, which he did. He tried to burn Till's shoes, but the fire could not consume them. Collins then buried them instead.[60]

Milam told a similar story to Huie, who wrote that "for three hours that morning, there was a fire in Big Milam's back yard: Bobo's crepe-soled shoes were hard to burn." Oudie Brown said that Levi Collins pointed to a shoe on the ground and told him that it had belonged to the murder victim. Henry Lee Loggins, despite denying any involvement, said that someone showed him a partially burned shoe and said that it belonged to a boy Milam had killed the night before.[61] Dixon is clearly wrong that this happened at the Leslie Milam–managed plantation because all witness testimony regarding the shoe points out that they saw it in Glendora. This makes sense, because if Collins was recruited only to clean up the mess, the men would have had to have gone to Glendora to get him. During his investigation, Dale Killinger learned that many people in Glendora recalled seeing the truck, and seeing Collins, Loggins, and Otha Johnson lounging nearby or cleaning up the mess.[62]

The origin of the cotton gin fan used to weigh down the body has never been definitively determined. Milam told Huie that they secured the fan from the Progressive Ginning Company. Huie was specific about the location. "This gin is 3.4 miles east of Boyle: Boyle is two miles south of Cleveland. The road to this gin turns left off U.S. 61, after you cross the bayou bridge south of Boyle." In 1985, Roy Bryant said that the group never went to Boyle, but he failed to say where the fan came from. This was technically true; even if they went to the Progressive gin, it was not actually in Boyle. Dixon said that it was taken from an abandoned gin familiar to Leslie Milam but not to J. W. However, Dixon did not identify it or its location. After law enforcement officials examined the shed on the Drew plantation on day two of the trial, they stopped at an old cotton gin located in Itta Bena and discovered that the fan was missing. It is unknown why they stopped at that particular gin. If they were acting on a tip, that fact was never disclosed, and they never determined that this was the correct gin. In a film shown at the Emmett Till museum in Glendora, former Glendora resident Robert Walker recalled seeing the gin fan thrown into the truck while it was parked near the M. B. Lowe cotton gin, which sat close to Milam's house within that village.[63] The gin now houses the Emmett Till Historic Intrepid Center (ETHIC). A marker placed outside the building states that the "old metal fan" used to weigh down Emmett's body "was taken from this gin." That has never been determined, and, so far as is known, the only statement from Milam or Bryant was supplied to Huie.

When and how were Roy Bryant and J. W. Milam arrested?

There is no confusion about Roy Bryant's arrest, which was detailed in court by Sheriff George Smith of Leflore County and also to defense attorneys before the trial. On Sunday afternoon, August 28, Smith and his deputy, John Cothran, drove to Money and stopped at the Bryant store at about two o'clock. They learned from other family members who were there (not Carolyn) that Roy was still sleeping. Bryant got up, and Cothran took him out to the car, where Smith questioned the suspect. Bryant admitted to taking the boy from Mose Wright's home but said he let him loose after Carolyn told him that he had the wrong one. Smith then arrested Bryant and took him to the Leflore County jail.[64]

Oudie Brown, interviewed for Stanley Nelson's PBS documentary, *The Murder of Emmett Till*, claimed that he witnessed Sheriff Smith arrest J. W. Milam at a store in Minter City.

"J. W., I got a writ for you. Is you goin'?" Smith asked.

"Hell no. That's shit you talking," responded Milam.

The sheriff left but went back within a couple of hours. "J. W. Milam, I come at ya. I'm gonna carry you dead or alive. You just well get ready to go."[65]

This alleged encounter never occurred, however, although it is possible that Brown was remembering another occasion when Milam was arrested, perhaps for bootlegging. On Monday, August 30, the day after Bryant's arrest, the *Greenwood Commonwealth* reported that Milam went to the sheriff's office around noon to turn himself in. This was done, according to what Milam told Bonnie Blue, so that Milam could keep an eye on Bryant and make sure Bryant refrained from "running his mouth off" and stuck to the script they had come up with, which was probably the story that they took Emmett Till but let him go. When Killinger interviewed John Cothran during his investigation, Cothran recalled that on the day of Milam's arrest, he spotted Milam outside the sheriff's office, pointed him out to Smith, and that Smith said, "Oh dog gone let's go get him. That's Milam."[66]

One interesting story recently came to light from Bobby Dailey, who sold Milam his 1955 Chevy pickup. GMAC became worried that with Milam in jail awaiting trial for murder, he would be unable to pay for the truck; to protect themselves, representatives from GMAC called Dailey and informed him that they were going to withdraw financing for the truck. GMAC also knew that the truck had become evidence. After the acquittal with the men out on bail awaiting kidnapping charges, Dailey went to visit Milam at a family store in Itta Bena and tried to work out a different finance plan; Dailey suggested that Milam apply for a loan from the Bank of Charleston instead. To Dailey's surprise, Milam wrote him a check for the full amount, and Dailey never saw him again.[67] Milam probably used the money he had received from William Bradford Huie for his "confession" in *Look* magazine.

Were Levi "Too Tight" Collins and Henry Lee Loggins kept hidden in jail during the trial?

On September 18, the day before the trial began, reporter James Hicks learned of the involvement of Levi "Too Tight" Collins and Henry Lee Loggins in the Till murder and was told while seeking information in Glendora that the two men were being held in jail.[68] Although these rumors persisted over the next several days, by Thursday, September 22, members of the black press covering the trial followed a lead that someone at the jail in Charleston reported seeing Collins there. The informant said that both men were being held for two weeks for "investigation" because they were seen cleaning blood out of the truck that they said came from killing a deer out of season. On Friday morning, September 23, white reporter Clark Porteous, assisting black reporters in the endeavor to verify the accuracy of the jail story, talked to prosecutors Gerald Chatham and Robert Smith about arranging a search at the jail. The two attorneys informed Porteous that they had already searched the jail twice and that neither man was there. They looked not only in Charleston but also searched another jail. The sheriffs of both counties "raised hell" about what they believed was an improper intrusion.[69]

There is no reason not to believe that Chatham and Smith tried but came up empty, as they had demonstrated all week a tremendous effort to secure and interview the surprise witnesses from the Drew plantations and made an examination of the barn, as superficial as that was. It is likely that Tallahatchie County sheriff Strider learned that black journalists had received a tip from an inmate and moved the men somewhere else. One of Milam's and Bryant's defense attorneys, J. J. Breland, told graduate student Hugh Stephen Whitaker in 1962 that Collins and Loggins had been kept in jail during the trial.[70]

One story that has been touted as proof that at least Loggins was in jail during the trial came from Loggins during his interview with Keith Beauchamp. Loggins told a story about how Milam had given Loggins some scrap iron but used that gift as an excuse to charge him with theft. Loggins was at a gambling house in Glendora when someone told him that Milam wanted to see him outside. When Loggins went out, Milam and the Tallahatchie County sheriff were there.

"You're going to jail," Milam said to Loggins.

"Going to jail? For what?"

"You got that iron without my consent."

Loggins was stunned. "J. W., you gave me that iron."

The sheriff sided with Milam, placed Loggins in handcuffs, and took him to jail. He spent the next six months locked up in Sumner.[71]

Loggins did spend six months in the Sumner jail for stealing iron from J. W. Milam, but this did not occur at the time of the trial, but several months later, beginning in March 1956. This was reported in full in the *Daily Defender*. Loggins and two other black men living in Glendora, brothers R. L. and J. C. Smart, were seen by Milam cutting up the metal with a torch. He approached all three with gun in hand and had them arrested. The Smarts, whose lawyer was J. W. Kellum, got off, while Loggins was convicted and sentenced to six months in jail.[72]

In sum, Loggins and Collins were most likely jailed during the investigation and most of the trial, but the iron episode involving Loggins was a separate and much later incident. Loggins never told Beauchamp just when his jail time occurred, at least on film, but the assumption that it was the smoking gun to show where he was during the trial is mistaken. By the time of the interview forty-five years later, Loggins probably did not remember exactly when the theft charge occurred anyway.

NOTES

Preface

1. Elizabeth Loftus, "Make-Believe Memories," *American Psychologist* 58, no. 11 (November 2003): 868.

2. Daniel Bernstein and Elizabeth Loftus, "How to Tell If a Particular Memory Is True or False," *Perspectives on Psychological Science* 4, no. 4 (2009): 371.

Chapter 1

1. Lillie Neely Henry, comp., and Jean Conger May, ed., *A History of Tallahatchie County* (Charleston, Miss.: *The Mississippi Sun*, 1960), 5, 26.

2. Kenneth M. Stampp, *The Peculiar Institution: Slavery in the Ante-Bellum South* (New York: Knopf, 1956), 31–32; Vernon Lane Wharton, *The Negro in Mississippi, 1865–1890* (Chapel Hill: University of North Carolina Press, 1947), 13.

3. Mamie Till-Mobley and Christopher Benson, *Death of Innocence: The Story of the Hate Crime That Changed America* (New York: Random House, 2003), 19; Mamie Bradley, "Mamie Bradley's Untold Story," installment one, *Daily Defender* (Chicago), February 27, 1956, 5; *Illinois Guide & Gazetteer*, Prepared Under the Supervision of the Illinois Sesquicentennial Commission (Chicago: Rand McNally, 1969), 495; *Summit Heritage* (Summit, Ill.: Summit Bicentennial Commission Heritage Committee, 1977), 29.

4. Maurice Isserman, *Journey to Freedom: The African-American Great Migration* (New York: Facts on File, 1997), 62–64; Eric Arnesen, *Black Protest and the Great Migration: A Brief History with Documents* (Boston: Bedford/St. Martin's, 2003), 1. For more on the migration, see Nicholas Lemann, *The Promised Land: The Great Black Migration and How It Changed America* (New York: Knopf, 1991); Isabel Wilkerson, *The Warmth of Other Suns: The Epic Story of America's Great Migration* (New York: Random House, 2010).

5. Arnesen, *Black Protest*, 2.

6. Chicago Commission on Race Relations, *The Negro in Chicago: A Study of Race Relations and a Race Riot* (Chicago: University of Chicago Press, 1922), 361.

7. James R. Grossman, *Land of Hope: Chicago, Black Southerners, and the Great Migration* (Chicago: University of Chicago Press, 1989), 166.

8. St. Clair Drake and Horace R. Cayton, *Black Metropolis: A Study of Negro Life in a Northern City* (New York: Harper and Row, 1962), 65–66. For more on the riot of 1919, see William M. Tuttle Jr., *Race Riot: Chicago in the Red Summer of 1919* (New York: Atheneum, 1970); Chicago Commission on Race Relations, *Negro in Chicago*.

9. Till-Mobley and Benson, *Death of Innocence*, 3.

10. 1930 US Census, Cook County, Illinois, Village of Summit, Enumeration District 16-2193, sheets 1A–22A, Family History Library, Salt Lake City, Utah, film no. 2340237.

11. Forest Preserve District of Cook County (Ill.), Nature Bulletin No. 500-A, September 29, 1973.

12. "Mamie Bradley's Untold Story," installment one, 5; "Mamie Bradley's Untold Story," installment two, *Daily Defender* (Chicago), February 28, 1956, 5; "Mamie Bradley's Untold Story," installment four, *Daily Defender* (Chicago), March 1, 1956, 5; "Mamie Bradley's Untold Story," installment five, *Daily Defender* (Chicago), March 5, 1956, 8; Till-Mobley and Benson, *Death of Innocence*, 46–47, 49. In her earlier memoir, Till-Mobley said her parents separated when she was thirteen, but in her 2003 autobiography she said this occurred when she was eleven. When her mother remarried on March 2, 1933, Mamie was eleven years old. Therefore, her later recollection is the more accurate. For the marriage of Alma Carthan to Tom Gaines, see file no. 1363987, *Cook County, Illinois Marriage Index, 1930–1960* [database online], Provo, Utah, USA: Ancestry.com Operations Inc., 2008.

13. Mamie Bradley, "I Want You to Know What They Did to My Boy," speech delivered October 29, 1955, Baltimore, *Washington Afro-American*, November 5, 1955, 20, and *Baltimore Afro-American*, November 12, 1955, 6, reprinted in Davis W. Houck and David E. Dixon, eds., *Rhetoric, Religion, and the Civil Rights Movement, 1954–1965* (Waco, Tex.: Baylor University Press, 2006), 139 (hereafter, references to this speech will cite Houck and Dixon only).

14. Mary Strafford, "'When I Find Time I'll Cry,' Till's Mother Tells *Afro*," *Baltimore Afro-American*, October 29, 1955, 2.

15. 1930 US Census, Cook County, Illinois, Village of Summit, sheets 16B–17A.

16. "'Not Bitter' Says Mother of Till," *Memphis Press-Scimitar*, September 8, 1955, 27. For more on race relations in Chicago, see Grossman, *Land of Hope*.

17. Drake and Cayton, *Black Metropolis*, 69–70.

18. Drake and Cayton, *Black Metropolis*, 106–9; Wheeler Parker Jr., Crosby Smith Jr., and Simeon Wright, author interview, February 7, 2007, Argo, Ill., comments by Parker.

19. "Mamie Bradley's Untold Story," installment one, 5; Till-Mobley and Benson, *Death of Innocence*, 24–25.

20. "Mamie Bradley's Untold Story," installment one, 5; Till-Mobley and Benson, *Death of Innocence*, 3, 25.

21. "Mamie Bradley's Untold Story," installment two, 5; Till-Mobley and Benson, *Death of Innocence*, 3, 13–14; James G. Chesnutt to William Bradford Huie, November 9, 1956, William Bradford Huie Papers, Cms 84, box 38, fd. 349, Ohio State University Library, Columbus (hereafter cited as Huie Papers).

22. Till-Mobley and Benson, *Death of Innocence*, 14–16. In 1956, Mamie said she and Louis went out for banana splits on their first date, but never mentioned the integration incident. See "Mamie Bradley's Untold Story," installment two, 5.

23. "Mamie Bradley's Untold Story," installment two, 5; "Mamie Bradley's Untold Story," installment three, *Daily Defender* (Chicago), February 29, 1956, 5; Louis Till and Mamie E. Carthan marriage record, file no. 1659634, *Cook County, Illinois Marriage Index, 1930–1960*.

24. Till-Mobley and Benson, *Death of Innocence*, 12, 26, 30, 97; "Mamie Bradley's Untold Story," installment three, 5.

25. Till-Mobley and Benson, *Death of Innocence*, 30. When discussing her marriage in 1956, Mamie did not indicate that she and Louis lived with Alma after their wedding, but only says

that they "got a little place to ourselves, hoping to be as independent of our folks as possible" ("Mamie Bradley's Untold Story," installment three, 5).

26. "Mamie Bradley's Untold Story," installment three, 5.

27. Till-Mobley and Benson, *Death of Innocence*, 4, 6; "Mamie Bradley's Untold Story," installment three, 5.

28. "Mamie Bradley's Untold Story," installment three, 5; Till-Mobley and Benson, *Death of Innocence*, 4, 11.

29. "Mamie Bradley's Untold Story," installment three, 5.

30. Till-Mobley and Benson, *Death of Innocence*, 14–16.

31. Till-Mobley and Benson, *Death of Innocence*, 16. Mamie says that the judge gave Louis a choice between going to jail or joining the army, but Mamie may be misremembering some of the details. In a 1955 interview, she said Louis had been drafted into the army, and she made no mention of military service being an alternative to jail.

32. "Father of Young Till Died for His Country," *New York Amsterdam News*, October 1, 1955, 7; see also "Mamie Bradley's Untold Story," installment three, 5; "Mrs. Bradley Raps 'Expose' on Till's Father," *St. Louis Argus*, October 21, 1955, 1.

33. National Archives and Records Administration, *U.S. World War II Army Enlistment Records, 1938–1946* [database on-line], Provo, Utah, USA: Ancestry.com Operations Inc., 2005; Chesnutt to Huie, November 9, 1956. In 1956, Mamie erroneously said that Louis was drafted in March 1943. See "Mamie Bradley's Untold Story," installment four, 5.

34. Till-Mobley and Benson, *Death of Innocence*, 27.

35. Till-Mobley and Benson, *Death of Innocence*, 28; Federal Bureau of Investigation, Prosecutive Report of Investigation Concerning . . . Emmett Till, Deceased, Appendix A—Trial Transcript, February 9, 2006, 207 (hereafter cited as Trial Transcript).

36. "Mamie Bradley's Untold Story," installment four, 5; Till-Mobley and Benson, *Death of Innocence*, 16–17. Mamie wrote in 2003 that after Louis entered the army, she had no further contact with him until he showed up on her doorstep for his unannounced visit. It was then that they talked of reconciling and that Louis promised to begin sending family financial support. Mamie said she was hesitant about getting back together, and had not made up her mind before the visit ended (Till-Mobley and Benson, *Death of Innocence*, 17). During a question-and-answer session with reporters for the *Washington Afro-American* in October 1955, however, she acknowledged that she and Louis had separated before he went into the army, but said they had patched up their differences through corresponding. "We were going to go back together after his discharge" ("Mrs. Mamie Bradley Routs False Reports," *Washington Afro-American*, November 5, 1955, 21). In her 1956 version of the story, as told to the *Daily Defender* (Chicago), Mamie is consistent with what she told the *Washington Afro-American* in that she and Louis had already decided, through correspondence, to rekindle their relationship shortly after Louis entered the army. Mamie is also incorrect in *Death of Innocence* in saying that it was this visit that prompted Louis to begin sending family financial support. As noted earlier, Louis had signed up for this on August 1, 1942, less than a month after his induction. Mamie thought Louis's visit occurred in 1943, but because she was off by one year regarding his date of induction, I assume that this visit actually took place in November 1942. My assumption is likely accurate because Mamie said that after the MPs discovered that this trip was unauthorized,

they took Louis away and sent him overseas immediately. Louis's records show that he began serving in the European theater of operations on January 14, 1943, making Thanksgiving 1942 the only time when such a holiday visit could have occurred.

37. "Mamie Bradley's Untold Story," installment four, 5; certificate signed by George W. Williams, dated September 8, 1944, in *The United States v. Private Fred A. McMurray and Private Louis Till*, copy of trial transcript and related documents in author's possession; Chesnutt to Huie, November 9, 1956. Louis's army records do not show a conviction for his AWOL visit to Argo, and the story comes only from Mamie. His surviving records, however, appear to deal only with his overseas service.

38. Till-Mobley and Benson, *Death of Innocence*, 17, 98; Tom Gaines death certificate, dated August 29, 1944, Cook County Clerk's Office, Chicago. In both her 1956 and 2003 memoirs, Mamie erroneously gives 1945 as the year of Tom Gaines's death. See "Mamie Bradley's Untold Story," installment five, 8; Till-Mobley and Benson, *Death of Innocence*, 44.

39. "Mamie Bradley's Untold Story," installment four, 5; Till-Mobley and Benson, *Death of Innocence*, 17.

40. "Mamie Bradley's Untold Story," installment four, 5; Till-Mobley and Benson, *Death of Innocence*, 202; "Mrs. Bradley Raps 'Expose,'" 10. When Louis first entered the army, he listed his uncle Lee Green as his next of kin because he and Mamie were separated. This was later changed, as army records eventually listed both Green and Mamie as next of kin.

41. "Mamie Bradley's Untold Story," installment four, 5; "Mrs. Bradley Raps 'Expose,'" 10.

42. Till-Mobley and Benson, *Death of Innocence*, 35; Trial Transcript, 207.

43. "Mamie Bradley's Untold Story," installment four, 5; Till-Mobley and Benson, *Death of Innocence*, 17; James G. Chesnutt to William Bradford Huie, October 18, 1956, Huie Papers, box 38, fd. 349.

44. *United States v. Private Fred A. McMurray and Private Louis Till*. I received the trial transcript and other documents related to the Louis Till execution on August 8, 2010, directly from the US Army, despite having received a letter on May 12, 2008, from Qiana Scruggs, archives technician, National Personnel Records Center, stating that any records related to Louis Till were destroyed in a fire that occurred on July 12, 1973. The letter informed me that nearly all records of army military personnel serving between 1912 and 1959 were consumed. William Bradford Huie received a few of these documents in 1956 and reported details of Louis Till's trial and execution in "Why the Army Hanged Emmett Till's Father!," *Confidential*, May 1956, 8–9, 50, 52, and in *Wolf Whistle, and Other Stories* (New York: Signet Books, 1959), 48–50.

45. Lemorse Mallory and Mamie E. Till, marriage certificate, dated August 19, 1946, no. 1925866, filed August 20, 1946, Cook County Clerk's Office, Chicago.

46. Although Mamie never publicly acknowledged her marriage to Lemorse Mallory, others close to her or who had interviewed her referred to another husband in addition to Louis Till and Pink Bradley, the man whom she had divorced (or was divorcing) before Emmett Till's murder. Mamie's uncle, Mose Wright, speaking to a reporter shortly after Emmett's death, mentioned that Mamie had "twice remarried" after Louis Till (see Clark Porteous, "Grand Jury to Get Case of Slain Negro Boy Monday," *Memphis Press-Scimitar*, September 1, 1955, 4). Reporter William Bradford Huie, writing of his 1955 interview with Mamie (before she married Gene Mobley in 1957), noted that Mamie had married three times (Huie, *Wolf Whistle*, 39). However, when Rayfield Mooty, Mamie's cousin, introduced her to the press upon their arrival in the

South for the murder trial of her son's accused killers, he told reporters that Mamie had married only twice (see John Spence, "Till's Mother Pauses in Memphis on Way to Trial," *Memphis Press-Scimitar*, September 20, 1955, 15. It appears that from the moment she became a public figure, Mamie chose to keep her marriage to Mallory from the public.

47. Mallory's military information was found in *U.S. World War II Army Enlistment Records, 1938–1946*, and in documentation related to his final payment and discharge, photocopies sent to author with a covering letter from Tina Hanson, archives technician, National Personnel Records Center, dated November 20, 2008.

48. This, and information about Mamie's marriage to Lemorse Mallory, initially became known to me during my interview of Parker, Smith, and Wright. All three of these men, cousins of Mamie, remember her marriage to Mallory but could not explain why she failed to mention it in her 2003 memoir. Mallory died on February 9, 2013. He was the grandfather of Aja Evans, American bobsledder who won a silver medal at the World Cup in Sochi, Russia, just days after Mallory's death. An article mentioning her win noted: "Evans was mourning her maternal grandfather, Lemorse Mallory, who died last Saturday at age 95 and had been instrumental in supporting her track and field career. Her mother, Sequocoria Mallory, insisted she stay in Russia to compete" (Philip Hersh, "Ligety Has a Record Day," *Chicago Tribune*, February 16, 2013, 8). The article made no mention of Mallory's connection to Mamie and Emmett Till, and Evans refused to discuss it with me after I twice contacted her. Upon my second inquiry, she asked that I not contact her again (Aja Evans to author, April 28, 2013).

49. Till-Mobley and Benson, *Death of Innocence*, 36; Parker, Wright, and Smith, author interview, comments by Parker and Smith.

50. Wheeler Parker, author interview, July 6, 2013, Argo, Ill.

51. "Mamie Bradley's Untold Story," installment three, 5; Till-Mobley and Benson, *Death of Innocence*, 36–37; Parker, Smith, and Wright, author interview, comments by Parker.

52. "Mamie Bradley's Untold Story," installment three, 5; Till-Mobley and Benson, *Death of Innocence*, 37–38.

53. "Mamie Bradley's Untold Story," installment three, 5; Till-Mobley and Benson, *Death of Innocence*, 38–39.

54. Parker, Smith, and Wright, author interview, comments by all three.

55. Till-Mobley and Benson, *Death of Innocence*, 38–39.

56. Till-Mobley and Benson, *Death of Innocence*, 39–40; "Mamie Bradley's Untold Story," installment three, 5.

57. Till-Mobley and Benson, *Death of Innocence*, 40; "Mamie Bradley's Untold Story," installment three, 5.

58. John Barrow, "Here's a Picture of Emmett Till Painted by Those Who Knew Him," *Chicago Defender*, September 24, 1955, 5; Strafford, "When I Find Time I'll Cry," 2.

59. Parker, Wright, and Smith, author interview, comments by Parker.

60. "Mamie Bradley's Untold Story," installment five, 8.

61. In her 2003 autobiography, Mamie mistakenly says that Alma married Henry Spearman in 1947 (Till-Mobley and Benson, *Death of Innocence*, 44). For the official source, see Henry Spearman and Alma Gaines marriage record, June 4, 1949, file no. 2085599, *Cook County, Illinois Marriage Index, 1930–1960*. The possibility that Mamie and Lemorse were still married at this point comes from Simeon Wright, who visited Argo for Christmas in 1949 and believes

that they were still together (Parker, Smith, and Wright, author interview, comments by Wright).

62. Strafford, "When I Find Time I'll Cry," 2; Trial Transcript, 207. In 2003, Mamie said that the hammer incident occurred during Emmett's second trip to Mississippi, having forgotten that this was actually his third. She also said that it was her mother, Alma, who witnessed the incident. Additionally, she makes no mention at all of an aunt taking Emmett to the South. See Till-Mobley and Benson, *Death of Innocence*, 35. Simeon Wright recalled this 1950 visit but was sure that Emmett went with his aunt Mamie Hall, sister of Alma Spearman (Parker, Smith, and Wright, author interview, comments by Wright). I am assuming that Simeon Wright's memory is the most accurate here, but this is not conclusive.

63. Strafford, "When I Find Time I'll Cry," 2; Parker, Smith, and Wright, author interview, comments by Wright; Simeon Wright, with Herb Boyd, *Simeon's Story: An Eyewitness Account of the Kidnapping of Emmett Till* (Chicago: Lawrence Hill Books, 2010), 38.

64. Till-Mobley and Benson, *Death of Innocence*, 44–46, 49; "Mamie Bradley's Untold Story," installment five, 8. It is not known why Nash Carthan changed his name to John, especially since he had a sibling named John Carthan who was still living. A Detroit newspaper article published less than two weeks after Emmett Till's murder quoted Samuel Gibbons, an acquaintance of Mamie's father, who said that Mamie and Emmett had moved to Detroit in 1948 and stayed until 1952. These dates differ from those that Mamie provided in her book and may or may not be accurate. See "Lynched Boy Lived Here, Early Days on Vinewood Recalled," *Michigan Chronicle* (Detroit), September 10, 1955, 1, 6.

65. Lemorse married Bessie Dixon on August 5, 1957 (file no. 2453272, *Cook County, Illinois Marriage Index, 1930–1960*).

66. "Mamie Bradley's Untold Story," installment five, 8; Till-Mobley and Benson, *Death of Innocence*, 49–52.

67. "Mamie Bradley's Untold Story," installment five, 8; Till-Mobley and Benson, *Death of Innocence*, 52–53; information on Pink Bradley found in *U.S. World War II Army Enlistment Records, 1938–1946*; Randall Bradley, author telephone interview, February 27, 2011.

68. "Mamie Bradley's Untold Story," installment five, 8; Till-Mobley and Benson, *Death of Innocence*, 54.

69. Till-Mobley and Benson, *Death of Innocence*, 54–56; "Mamie Bradley's Untold Story," installment five, 8; "Mrs. Mamie Bradley Routs False Reports," 21.

70. Timuel D. Black Jr., *Bridges of Memory: Chicago's First Wave of Black Migration* (Evanston, Ill.: Northwestern University Press, 2003), 306; Barrow, "Here's a Picture of Emmett Till," 5.

71. Till-Mobley and Benson, *Death of Innocence*, 57.

72. "Mamie Bradley's Untold Story," installment five, 8.

73. Till-Mobley and Benson, *Death of Innocence*, 59–60.

74. "Mamie Bradley's Untold Story," installment five, 8.

75. Till-Mobley and Benson, *Death of Innocence*, 70.

76. "Till's Mother Sues Magazine; Reveals Marriage," *Jet* 13, no. 14 (February 6, 1958): 17; Chester Higgins, "Mrs. Bradley Becomes a Teacher," *Jet* 17, no. 18 (September 1, 1960): 15–16; Till-Mobley and Benson, *Death of Innocence*, 73–77.

77. Clenora Hudson-Weems, *Emmett Till: The Sacrificial Lamb of the Civil Rights Movement*, 4th ed. (Bloomington, Ind.: AuthorHouse, 2006), 141; Till-Mobley and Benson, *Death of Innocence*, 75.

78. Till-Mobley and Benson, *Death of Innocence*, 84–87.

79. Trial Transcript, 197; Till-Mobley and Benson, *Death of Innocence*, 87.

80. Till-Mobley and Benson, *Death of Innocence*, 88–89.

81. Mamie Till-Mobley, author telephone interview, December 3, 1996.

82. A description of Emmett Till was provided by his uncle Mose Wright in court. See Trial Transcript, 49; Eric Stringfellow, "Memories Sketch Varied Portraits of Emmett Till," *Jackson Clarion-Ledger*, August 25, 1985, 1H.

83. Till-Mobley and Benson, *Death of Innocence*, 66–67; Mamie Till-Mobley, interview, in Keith A. Beauchamp, prod., *The Untold Story of Emmett Louis Till* (Till Freedom Come Productions, 2005).

84. Barrow, "Here's a Picture of Emmett Till," 5.

85. "Mamie Bradley's Untold Story," installment five, 8; Till-Mobley and Benson, *Death of Innocence*, 71–72, 80.

86. Barrow, "Here's a Picture of Emmett Till," 5.

87. Strafford, "When I Find Time I'll Cry," 2.

88. Barrow, "Here's a Picture of Emmett Till," 5; Till-Mobley and Benson, *Death of Innocence*, 78–79; "Father of Young Till Died," 7.

89. Till-Mobley and Benson, *Death of Innocence*, 92–93; Hudson-Weems, *Emmett Till*, 149–50; *Argo Temple Church of God in Christ 80-Year Celebration*, program distributed for event held October 8, 2006, 6.

90. Parker, Smith, and Wright, author interview, comments by Parker.

91. Stringfellow, "Memories Sketch Varied Portraits," 1H; Parker, Smith, and Wright, author interview, comments by Parker and Wright.

92. Till-Mobley and Benson, *Death of Innocence*, 81; Wheeler Parker interviews, in Nancy Button, prod., *The Fifties*, vol. 6, *The Rage Within* (History Channel, 1997); Stanley Nelson, prod., *The Murder of Emmett Till* (Firelight Media, 2002); Beauchamp, *Untold Story*.

93. Till-Mobley and Benson, *Death of Innocence*, 94–95.

94. Stringfellow, "Memories Sketch Varied Portraits," 1H.

95. "Mamie Bradley's Untold Story," installment six, *Daily Defender* (Chicago), March 6, 1956, 8; Till-Mobley and Benson, *Death of Innocence*, 98–99.

96. Hudson-Weems, *Emmett Till*, 235.

97. "Mamie Bradley's Untold Story," installment six, 8; Trial Transcript, 192. Mamie later insisted that both she and Alma were initially against the idea of Emmett going down to Mississippi unless he went with one of them, as he had in the past. This may have been partly true due to the fact that Mamie and Gene were planning a road trip in Mamie's new 1955 Plymouth, and they wanted Emmett to go with them. See "Mamie Bradley's Untold Story," installment six, 8; Till-Mobley and Benson, *Death of Innocence*, 98–99.

98. Parker and Till-Mobley interviews, in Nelson, *Murder of Emmett Till*, and Beauchamp, *Untold Story*; "Mamie Bradley's Untold Story," installment six, 8; Hudson-Weems, *Emmett Till*, 235.

99. Hudson-Weems, *Emmett Till*, 235.

100. Trial Transcript, 188; Till-Mobley and Benson, *Death of Innocence*, 102–3. One author, seeing significant symbolism in Emmett receiving his father's ring, writes, "By giving Emmett his father's ring [Mamie] thus acknowledges his growing independence and maturity. Furthermore, she binds him symbolically to his paternity and his patrimony, despite the fact that

irreconcilable differences had torn his parents' marriage apart" (Valerie Smith, "Emmett Till's Ring," *Women's Studies Quarterly* 36, nos. 1/2 [Spring/Summer 2008]: 152).

101. Strafford, "When I Find Time I'll Cry," 2.

102. Till-Mobley and Benson, *Death of Innocence*, 103–4; Hudson-Weems, *Emmett Till*, 129. In 2007, Parker said that two women accompanied himself, Mose Wright, and Emmett Till on the train to Mississippi (Parker, Smith, and Wright, author interview, comments by Parker). I have assumed his earlier remembrance in Hudson-Weems, in which he states that only one woman went along, to be the most accurate. Complicating things further, Simeon Wright wrote in 2010 that Curtis Jones also traveled on the train with Wright, Parker, and Till, but stayed the first week with his aunt in Greenwood. In 1985, Jones said that he drove down with an uncle. Parker, as noted in Hudson-Weems, said in 1986 that it was Wright, Parker, Till, and the female cousin who traveled together that day, making no mention of Jones. See Curtis Jones, interview, conducted by Blackside, Inc., November 12, 1985, for *Eyes on the Prize: America's Civil Rights Years (1954–1965)*, Henry Hampton Collection, Washington University, St. Louis, http://digital.wustl.edu/eyesontheprize/; Wright and Boyd, *Simeon's Story*, 37.

103. Arthur Everett, "Till Nearly Missed His Fatal Journey to Land of Cotton," *Jackson Clarion-Ledger*, September 19, 1955, 1.

104. Till-Mobley and Benson, *Death of Innocence*, 104–5; Till-Mobley interviews in Nelson, *Murder of Emmett Till*, and Beauchamp, *Untold Story*.

105. Strafford, "When I Find Time I'll Cry," 2; "Mamie Bradley's Untold Story," installment six, 8.

Chapter 2

1. "Resume of Interview with Mose Wright," William Bradford Huie Papers, Cms 84, box 85, fd. 346, Ohio State University Library, Columbus (hereafter cited as Huie Papers); Wheeler Parker Jr., Crosby Smith Jr., and Simeon Wright, author interview, February 7, 2007, Argo, Ill., comments by Parker.

2. Mamie Bradley and Elizabeth Wright, interview, in Mary Strafford, "'When I Find Time I'll Cry,' Till's Mother Tells *Afro*," *Baltimore Afro-American*, October 29, 1955, 2.

3. Mamie Till-Mobley and Christopher Benson, *Death of Innocence: The Story of the Hate Crime That Changed America* (New York: Random House, 2003), 106; "Resume of Interview with Mose Wright"; "Leflore County Communities and Their History," unpublished typescript, 5, located at the Greenwood Leflore Library, Greenwood, Miss. Hernando Desoto Money (1839–1912), a Democrat, represented Mississippi in the US Senate from 1897 to 1911. He, like Mose Wright, was born in Holmes County.

4. Information about Grover Frederick comes from US Selective Service System, *World War I Selective Service System Draft Registration Cards, 1917–1918* (Washington, DC: National Archives and Records Administration), M1509, 4,582 rolls, Mississippi, Leflore County, roll 1682936; Parker, Smith, and Wright, author interview, comments by Wright; 1940 US Census, Leflore County, Mississippi, Beat 2, Enumeration District 42, sheet 9B, https://familysearch.org/ark:/61903/1:1:VBSH=GYR; Simeon Wright, author interview, February 4, 2013, Ogden, Utah.

5. Parker, Smith, and Wright, author interview, comments by Wright; Paul Holmes, "Uncle Tells How 3 Kidnapers Invaded Home and Seized Till," *Chicago Daily Tribune*, September 19, 1955, part 1, 2; Arthur Everett, "Till Nearly Missed His Fatal Journey to Land of Cotton," *Jackson Clarion-Ledger*, September 19, 1955, 12; Simeon Wright, with Herb Boyd, *Simeon's Story: An Eyewitness Account of the Kidnapping of Emmett Till* (Chicago: Lawrence Hill Books, 2010), 6–7, 25.

6. 1900 US Census, Holmes County, Mississippi, Enumeration District 47, sheet 10A, microfilm no. 1240811, Family History Library, Salt Lake City, Utah (hereafter cited as FHL); Simeon Wright, author telephone interview, August 31, 2005; Wright and Boyd, *Simeon's Story*, 15.

7. *World War I Selective Service Draft System Registration Cards*; 1930 US Census, Leflore County, Mississippi, Beat 2, Enumeration District 42-5, sheet 6B, microfilm no. 2340890, FHL; "Rites Held Saturday for Moses Wright, 85," *Chicago Defender*, August 8, 1977, 2; William Parker, author telephone interview, April 30, 2014. Simeon Wright also believes the April 1892 date to be correct. See Wright and Boyd, *Simeon's Story*, 15.

8. Holmes County (Miss.) Circuit Clerk, *Marriage Records, 1889–1951*, black marriages, vols. 11–12: 157, microfilm no. 879492, FHL.

9. 1920 US Census, Holmes County, Beat 2, Enumeration District 50, sheet 17b, microfilm no. 1820877, FHL; Wright, author telephone interview; Wright and Boyd, *Simeon's Story*, 17, 19.

10. *World War I Draft Selective Service System Registration Cards*; Parker, Smith, and Wright, author interview, comments by Wright; Wright and Boyd, *Simeon's Story*, 18. For more on the Selective Service Act, see Edward M. Coffman, *The War to End All Wars: The American Military Experience in World War I* (Lexington: University Press of Kentucky, 1988), 25–28. See also Richard V. Damms, "World War I: Loyalty and Dissent in Mississippi during the Great War, 1917–1918," http://mshistory.k12.ms.us/articles/237/World-War-I-the-great-war-1917-1918-loyalty-and-dissent-in-mississippi.

11. Wright and Boyd, *Simeon's Story*, 21.

12. 1930 US Census, Leflore County, Beat 2, Enumeration District 42-5, sheet 6B; Federal Bureau of Investigation, Prosecutive Report of Investigation Concerning . . . Emmett Till, Deceased, Appendix A—Trial Transcript, February 9, 2006, 8 (hereafter cited as Trial Transcript); Wright, author telephone interview; Parker, Smith, and Wright, author interview, comments by Wright.

13. Till-Mobley and Benson, *Death of Innocence*, 109; Parker, Smith, and Wright, author interview, comments by Wright; Wright and Boyd, *Simeon's Story*, 32.

14. Tallahatchie County (Miss.) Circuit Clerk, *Marriage Records of the First District, 1856–1918*, white marriages, vol. 8, 1908–1916: 238, microfilm no. 894882, FHL.

15. William Leslie Milam parents' information, http://trees.ancestry.com.

16. Helen E. Staten Arnold and Nick Denley, comps., *Tallahatchie County, Mississippi Marriage Records* (Carrollton, Miss.: Pioneer Publishing, 1998), 177, 181; 1920 US Census, Tallahatchie County, Mississippi, Enumeration District 132, sheet 2, microfilm no. 1820895, FHL.

17. 1930 US Census, Tallahatchie County, Mississippi, Enumeration District 68-8, sheet 18A, microfilm no. 2340903, FHL; "Two of Three Victims of Gravel Pit Accident Die of Their Injuries," *Mississippi Sun* (Sumner, Miss.), October 13, 1927, 1; "Milam Is Pictured a War Hero Who Also Snatched Negro from Drowning," *Jackson Daily News*, September 20, 1955, 6.

18. Arnold and Denley, *Tallahatchie County, Mississippi Marriage Records*, 153; *Eula Lee Morgan Bryant v. Henry E. Bryant*, Chancery Court of the Second Judicial District of Tallahatchie County, Mississippi, Case No. 2875.

19. "Milam Is Pictured a War Hero," 6; Clark Porteous, "New Angle in Till Case Claimed," *Memphis Press-Scimitar*, September 20, 1955, 4; Federal Bureau of Investigation, Prosecutive Report of Investigation Concerning . . . Emmett Till, Deceased, Victim, February 9, 2006, 23 (hereafter cited as Prosecutive Report).

20. Ellen Whitten, "Justice Unearthed: Revisiting the Murder of Emmett Till" (honor's thesis, Rhodes College, 2005), 9; http://www.rhodes.edu/images/content/Academics/Ellen_Whitten.pdf.

21. Erle Johnston, *Mississippi's Defiant Years, 1953–1973* (Forest, Miss.: Lake Harbor Publishers, 1990), 28–29.

22. For excellent studies on the *Brown* case, see James T. Patterson, *Brown v. Board of Education: A Civil Rights Milestone and Its Troubled Legacy* (New York: Oxford University Press, 2001); Charles J. Ogletree Jr., *All Deliberate Speed: Reflections on the First Half-Century of Brown v. Board of Education* (New York: Norton, 2004); Clare Cushman and Melvin I. Urosky, eds., *Black, White, and Brown: The Landmark School Desegregation Case in Retrospect* (Washington, DC: Supreme Court Historical Society/CQ Press, 2004).

23. For a full account of the Citizens' Councils, see Neil R. McMillen, *The Citizens' Council: Organized Resistance to the Second Reconstruction* (Urbana: University of Illinois Press, 1971). For more on the black response to the councils, see J. Todd Moye, *Let the People Decide: Black Freedom and White Resistance Movements in Sunflower County, Mississippi, 1945–1986* (Chapel Hill: University of North Carolina Press, 2004).

24. Julius E. Thompson, *Lynchings in Mississippi: A History, 1865–1965* (Jefferson, N.C.: McFarland, 2007), 142. Two scholars note, "By the time of Emmett Till's murder, lynching was no longer an acceptable public spectacle, though it was still an acceptable community practice. That is, by 1955, lynching had become an invisible public event: everyone in town would know what happened, to whom, and 'why,' but it was no longer performed before a large crowd in the public square" (Christine Harold and Kevin Michael DeLuca, "Behold the Corpse: Violent Images and the Case of Emmett Till," *Rhetoric & Public Affairs* 8, no. 2 [Summer 2005]: 269).

25. Jack Mendelsohn, *The Martyrs: Sixteen Who Gave Their Lives for Racial Justice* (New York: Harper and Row, 1966), 1–20.

26. "Grand Jury, District Attorney Rap 'Cover-Up' in Brookhaven Case," *Clarksdale (Miss.) Press Register*, September 21, 1955, 6; M. Susan Orr-Klopfer, with Fred Klopfer and Barry Klopfer, *Where Rebels Roost: Mississippi Civil Rights Revisited*, 2nd ed. (Parchman, Miss.: M. Susan Orr-Klopfer, 2005), 240–48.

27. "Gov. White Orders Crackdown on Wide-Open Gambling," *Greenwood (Miss.) Morning Star*, August 25, 1955, 1.

28. NAACP press release, September 1955, in Papers of Medgar Wiley Evers and Myrlie Beasley Evers, Mississippi Department of Archives and History, Archives and Library Division, Special Collections Section, Manuscript Collection, Accn. no. Z2231.0005, box 3, fd. 1.

29. Tom P. Brady, *Black Monday* (Winona, Miss.: Associations of Citizens' Councils, 1955), 63–64.

30. "Leflore County Communities," 5.

31. Clark Porteous, "Grand Jury to Get Case of Slain Negro Boy Monday," *Memphis Press-Scimitar*, September 1, 1955, 4.

32. Till-Mobley and Benson, *Death of Innocence*, 111–12; Parker, Smith, and Wright, author interview, comments by Wright; Wright and Boyd, *Simeon's Story*, 45.

33. Parker, Smith, and Wright, author interview, comments by Wright. In my interview with Wright, he could not recall specifically what day this or any of the events occurred that week other than Till's encounter at the Bryant store and Till's kidnapping three days later. For his book, Wright assigned dates to the various events for clarity. For Wright's account of the week, see Wright and Boyd, *Simeon's Story*, 41–66.

34. Parker, Smith, and Wright, author interview, comments by Parker; William Sorrels, "Guards Called to Protect Men Held in Youth's Death," *Memphis Commercial Appeal*, September 5, 1955, 8.

35. Parker, Smith, and Wright, author interview, comments by Wright. In his book, Wright said the firecracker incident happened on Sunday, August 21, the day after Till's arrival. See Wright and Boyd, *Simeon's Story*, 42.

36. "Gov. White Orders Crackdown," 1.

37. Wheeler Parker Jr. interviews, in Stanley Nelson, prod., *The Murder of Emmett Till* (Firelight Media, 2002), and Keith Beauchamp, prod., *The Untold Story of Emmett Louis Till* (Till Freedom Come Productions, 2005); Parker, Smith, and Wright, author interview, comments by Parker.

38. Trial Transcript, 58; Porteous, "Grand Jury to Get Case," 4–5. Simeon Wright said in 2007 that his parents did not go to church that Wednesday night, and that the story was fabricated by some unknown person. His recollection is that the family attended church on Tuesday nights instead (Parker, Smith, and Wright, author interview, comments by Wright). However, because Mose Wright stated on at least two occasions that he had been at church that Wednesday evening, it is clear that his version is the accurate one. Simeon does not address this at all in his book when discussing the events of Wednesday, August 24. See Wright and Boyd, *Simeon's Story*, 49–53.

39. Porteous, "Grand Jury to Get Case," 4–5; George Murray, "'Wolf Call' Blamed by Argo Teen," *Chicago American*, September 1, 1955, 4; "Resume of Interview with Mose Wright."

40. Sorrels, "Guards Called to Protect Men," 8; "Chicago Negro Youth Abducted by Three White Men at Money," *Greenwood (Miss.) Commonwealth*, August 29, 1955, 1; Mattie Smith Colin and Robert Elliott, "Mother Waits in Vain for Her 'Bo,'" *Chicago Defender*, September 10, 1955, 2, reprinted in Christopher Metress, ed., *The Lynching of Emmett Till: A Documentary Narrative* (Charlottesville: University of Virginia Press, 2002), 31. Simeon Wright is inconsistent when providing names of those present. In a 2004 article written by the coauthor of his book, Wright lists the same names I do, which mirrors Wheeler Parker's list from September 1955. However, in his book Wright insists that Ruth Crawford was not with them. He also told me in 2007 that he does not recall Roosevelt Crawford having been there either. See Herb Boyd, "The Real Deal on Emmett Till," *New York Amsterdam News*, May 20, 2004, 3; Wright and Boyd, *Simeon's Story*, 134; Simeon Wright, author interview, October 2, 2007, Money, Miss.

41. Sorrels, "Guards Called to Protect Men," 8.

42. The length of the visit is an estimation by Simeon Wright to the author during Parker, Smith, and Wright, author interview.

43. Clenora Hudson-Weems, *Emmett Till: The Sacrificial Lamb of the Civil Rights Movement*, 4th ed. (Bloomington, Ind.: AuthorHouse, 2006), 133; Parker, Smith, and Wright, author interview, comments by Parker.

44. Murray, "'Wolf Call' Blamed by Argo Teen," 4. Neither Parker nor Wright remembered in 2007 that their purpose in going into Money was to visit the café (Parker, Smith, and Wright, author interview). In his book, Wright said that after they got into town, "we went directly to Bryant's grocery store" (Wright and Boyd, *Simeon's Story*, 49). I am judging Parker's August 1955 statement to be more accurate, however. William Bradford Huie, a journalist who later claimed to have interviewed several of the youth who were with Till at the Bryant store, learned from one of them the same story that Parker told the *Chicago American*. Huie said that the teens "were in the '46 Ford going to a 'jook.' But the 'jook' wasn't open yet, so they stopped in front of Bryant's." Because that fact had only been made known one other time, by Parker, it strengthens the argument that Huie did talk to the teens as he claimed, something that Simeon Wright maintains today never happened (Wright and Boyd, *Simeon's Story*, 133–34). For Huie to have referred to such an obscure and relatively unknown part of the story, he would have had to have learned about it from someone who had been in the car with Emmett Till that night (see William Bradford Huie, *Wolf Whistle, and Other Stories* [New York: Signet Books, 1959], 40; Devery S. Anderson, "A Wallet, a White Woman, and a Whistle: Fact and Fiction in Emmett Till's Encounter in Money, Mississippi," *Southern Quarterly: A Journal of Arts & Letters in the South* 45, no. 4 [Summer 2008]: 11–12).

45. Defense notes from interview with Carolyn Bryant, September 2, 1955, Huie Papers, box 85, fd. 346; Wright, author interview, October 2, 2007; Murray, "'Wolf Call' Blamed by Argo Teen," 4.

46. William Bradford Huie, "The Shocking Story of Approved Killing in Mississippi," *Look*, January 24, 1956, 46.

47. Huie, *Wolf Whistle*, 18; Trial Transcript, 268–69. In her testimony to the FBI during its 2004–6 investigation, Juanita Milam stated that she was not babysitting at the store that Wednesday night, but was probably in Greenville (Prosecutive Report, 42). The evidence that Juanita Milam *was* at the store the night of the Till-Bryant encounter, in addition to Carolyn Bryant's testimony, was that there was a car present, to which Bryant went to retrieve a gun. Bryant also testified in court that the car she walked to belonged to Juanita Milam (Trial Transcript, 276). The Bryants did not own a car; the Milams did.

48. "Kidnapped Boy Whistled at Woman," *Chicago Daily Tribune*, August 30, 1955, 2.

49. Huie, "Shocking Story," 46.

50. Prosecutive Report, 44. Crawford's name is redacted from the report for privacy purposes.

51. Till-Mobley and Benson, *Death of Innocence*, 102

52. Amos Dixon, "Mrs. Bryant Didn't Even Hear Emmett Till Whistle," *California Eagle*, January 26, 1956, 2. Dixon's identity has never been identified with certainty. His articles will be dealt with more fully in a later chapter. Another source that backs up the claim that Emmett Till bragged about relationships with white girls comes from John Milton Wesley, who was a youth at the time who lived twenty-five miles east of Money in the town of Ruleville. Wesley later wrote an article for the *Washington Post* in which he claimed to have known Emmett Till as "one of those kids who came from 'up North' every summer to join us in the cotton fields. . . .

He could keep us spellbound with stories of white girlfriends, the forbidden fruit." Although Till had been to Mississippi three previous times, the 1955 trip was his first trip in five years and the only time he was old enough to pick cotton. If Wesley was spending time in Money during the week Emmett was there, they could have met, but their interactions would have been brief. It is unlikely that Wesley shared the intimacy with Till that his article suggests. See John Milton Wesley, "The Legacy of Emmett Till," *Washington Post National Weekly Edition*, September 4–10, 1995, 21.

53. Murray, "'Wolf Call' Blamed by Argo Teen," 4.

54. Colin and Elliott, "Mother Waits in Vain," 2; Metress, *Lynching of Emmett Till*, 31.

55. "Nation Horrified by Murder of Kidnaped Chicago Youth," *Jet* 8, no. 19 (September 15, 1955): 8.

56. "Two Armed White Men Break into Negro Worker's Home," *Greenwood (Miss.) Morning Star*, September 1, 1955, 1.

57. "Two White Men Charged with Kidnapping Negro," *Delta Democrat-Times* (Greenville, Miss.), August 30, 1955, 1.

58. Murray, "'Wolf Call' Blamed by Argo Teen," 4.

59. Sorrels, "Guards Called to Protect Men," 8; Parker, Smith, and Wright, author interview, comments by Parker; "Resume of Interview with Mose Wright."

60. "Kidnapped Boy Whistled at Woman," 2.

61. Porteous, "Grand Jury to Get Case," 4.

62. Olive Arnold Adams, *Time Bomb: Mississippi Exposed, and the Full Story of Emmett Till* (Mound Bayou, Miss.: Regional Council of Negro Leadership, 1956), 17.

63. Hudson-Weems, *Emmett Till*, 132.

64. Eric Stringfellow, "Memories Sketch Varied Portraits of Emmett Till," *Jackson Clarion-Ledger*, August 25, 1985, 1H; Hudson-Weems, *Emmett Till*, 132; Nelson, *Murder of Emmett Till*; Beauchamp, *Untold Story*; Parker, Smith, and Wright, author interview, comments by Wright; Wright and Boyd, *Simeon's Story*, 51.

65. Defense notes from interview with Carolyn Bryant.

66. Trial Transcript, 269–75; Huie, *Wolf Whistle*, 20.

67. "Two White Men Charged," 1.

68. Porteous, "Grand Jury to Get Case," 4.

69. Timothy B. Tyson, emails to author, March 31 and July 26, 2014; Patricia Spears, "Timothy Tyson Sheds Light on His Novel," *Duke Chronicle* (Durham, N.C.), January 26, 2014, www .dukechronicle.com/articles/2014/01/26/timothy-tyson-sheds-light-his-novel#.VJNIrCvF -Ec. Carolyn decided to talk to Tyson after she read one of his books, likely *Blood Done Sign My Name* (New York: Crown, 2004), the true story of the 1970 murder of Henry Marrow, a twenty-three-year-old black Vietnam War veteran. Marrow's accused killers were acquitted by an all-white jury; the book focuses on the protests that followed. *Blood Done Sign My Name* became a feature film (Mel Efros, producer, Paladin, 2010). Tyson will be providing details of his interviews with Carolyn in his own book, still forthcoming as of this writing.

70. "Two Armed White Men," 1.

71. "Nation Horrified," 8; "Two Armed White Men," 1.

72. Murray, "'Wolf Call' Blamed by Argo Teen," 1.

73. Porteous, "Grand Jury to Get Case," 5.

74. Murray, "'Wolf Call' Blamed by Argo Teen," 1.

75. William Sorrels, "'Tall Man Came' with Companion, Say His Cousins," *Memphis Commercial Appeal*, September 1, 1955, 4.

76. Porteous, "Grand Jury to Get Case," 4.

77. "Negro Boy Was Killed for 'Wolf Whistle,'" *New York Post*, September 1, 1955, 12. For more perspective on the whistle, see Rebecca Mark, "Mourning Emmett: 'One Long Expansive Moment,'" *Southern Literary Journal* 40, no. 2 (Spring 2008): 130–31.

78. Sorrels, "Tall Man Came," 4; Hudson-Weems, *Emmett Till*, 132; Stringfellow, "Memories Sketch Varied Portraits," 1H; Parker, Smith, and Wright, author interview, comments by Wright; Wright and Boyd, *Simeon's Story*, 52.

The name of the road that leads to East Money has, apparently, never been certain. Simeon Wright recalled its name as Darfield Road. However, the FBI called it Dark Ferry Road in the summary of its 2004–6 investigation. Wright told me in 2007 that this was news to him, as he had always called it Darfield Road. In his book, however, he referred to it as Dark Fear Road, explaining that it was given this name due to its reputation as "one of the darkest places in the world, filled with menacing woods and snake-infested lakes. But old-timers say it also got its name from the many lynchings that took place in the area" (Wright and Boyd, *Simeon's Story*, 25). Leflore County witnessed 125 documented lynchings between 1882 and 1955. See Thompson, *Lynchings in Mississippi*, 23, 36, 49, 65, 84, 98, and 142 for charts breaking down the numbers by each decade. It is unclear how many, if any, occurred on the road in East Money. I have found no evidence from any other source that the name of the road was Dark Fear.

79. Establishing evidence that the boy who dared Till was not one of Till's cousins is important, not only to understand the facts but also to address Wright family sensibilities. Simeon Wright has been very vocal that nobody dared Till at all. "If we had put Emmett up to that, we'd be no better than Milam and Bryant," he said in 2007 (Parker, Smith, and Wright, author interview, comments by Wright; Anderson, "A Wallet, a White Woman, and a Whistle," 18). Certainly none of the youth present who may have challenged Till can be blamed for contributing to the actions of those who later killed him.

80. Parker, Smith, and Wright, author interview, comments by Parker. Simeon Wright remembered this incident also. See Wright and Boyd, *Simeon's Story*, 51.

81. Murray, "'Wolf Call' Blamed by Argo Teen," 1; "Negro Describes Boy's Abduction," *Jackson Clarion-Ledger*, September 2, 1955, 1; Hudson-Weems, *Emmett Till*, 130; Wright and Boyd, *Simeon's Story*, 53.

82. "3rd Lynching of Year Shocks Nation," *Baltimore Afro-American*, September 10, 1995, 2.

83. Moses Wright, "I Saw Them Take Emmett Till," *Front Page Detective*, February 1956, 29.

84. A sampling of interviews with Mamie Till-Mobley, during which she maintained her son's whistle was only an attempt to stop his stuttering, are "Time Heals Few Wounds for Emmett Till's Mother," *Jet* 66, no. 5 (April 9, 1984): 55; Stringfellow, "Memories Sketch Varied Portraits," 1H; Evan Ramstad, "Youth's Murder for Flirting Stimulated Civil Rights Drive," *Tupelo (Miss.) Daily Journal*, September 2, 1995, 1F; Till-Mobley, interview, in Beauchamp, *Untold Story*, rough-cut version of film, copy in author's possession. In her 2003 memoir, she not only puts forward this theory but also considers the account of Roosevelt Crawford (discussed later) that Emmett was only whistling at a bad move made by someone on the checkerboard (Till-Mobley and Benson, *Death of Innocence*, 122). However, in the early 1990s

she provided a different possibility altogether: "As they [Emmett and another boy] came out of the store, according to the accounts I heard from some of the boys, someone asked Emmett, 'How did you like the lady in the store?' They said Emmett whistled his approval" (Studs Terkel, *Race: How Blacks & Whites Think & Feel About the American Obsession* [New York: New Press, 1992], 20). In her comments to the press in the days after the store incident, and in her recorded speeches and interviews granted in the months following the murder trial, she never argues for any of these scenarios in order to explain the whistle. In fact, she rarely mentioned the whistle at all. See Mamie Bradley, speech delivered October 28, 1955, South Bend, Ind., in Hudson-Weems, *Emmett Till*, 229–42; Mamie Bradley, "I Want You to Know What They Did to My Boy," speech delivered October 29, 1955, Baltimore, *Washington Afro-American*, November 5, 1955, 20, and *Baltimore Afro-American*, November 12, 1955, 6, reprinted in Davis W. Houck and David E. Dixon, eds., *Rhetoric, Religion, and the Civil Rights Movement* (Waco, Tex.: Baylor University Press, 2006), 132–45.

85. Ted Poston, "'My Son Didn't Die in Vain,' Till's Mother Tells Rally," *New York Post*, September 26, 1955, 22.

86. Beauchamp, *Untold Story*, rough cut. See also Crawford's testimony (although his name is redacted) in Prosecutive Report, 43–44. Crawford also espoused his view in a conversation with the author on August 28, 2005, in New York City, and in a telephone interview with the author on October 21, 2006. Crawford abruptly stopped our telephone interview after having previously agreed to it because he wanted money for all future interviews.

87. Parker, Smith, and Wright, author interview, comments by Parker and Wright.

88. Rutha Mae Crawford Jackson and Willie Hill Jackson, interview, conducted by Blackside, Inc., August 29, 1979, for *Eyes on the Prize: America's Civil Rights Years (1954–1965)*, Henry Hampton Collection, Washington University, St. Louis, http://digital.wustl.edu/eyesontheprize/.

89. Rutha Mae Crawford Jackson, interview, in Beauchamp, *Untold Story*. Jackson did not respond to my request for an interview.

90. Huie, *Wolf Whistle*, 20; Parker, Smith, and Wright, author interview, comments by Wright; Trial Transcript, 269; Defense notes from interview with Carolyn Bryant.

91. Harry Raymond, "Cousin Tells How Negro Youth Was Kidnapped," *Daily Worker* (New York), September 2, 1955, 1; Till-Mobley and Benson, *Death of Innocence*, 114 (Till's letter is reproduced in photograph inset between pages 136 and 137). Till's letter and Elizabeth Wright's letter to Alma Spearman are both at *American Experience*, http://www.pbs.org/wgbh/amex/till/filmmore/ps_letters.html. Till-Mobley said in her 2003 memoir that she placed a call to Mose Wright's neighbors and talked to Emmett while he was in Mississippi (Till-Mobley and Benson, *Death of Innocence*, 114). However, during a joint interview with Mamie Bradley and Elizabeth Wright in October 1955, Bradley asked Wright how Emmett reacted to Bradley's letter telling him she had retrieved his dog from the pound. There would have been no reason to ask this had she spoken to him herself. Therefore, I conclude that Bradley's memory is incorrect, and that she wrote to her son, but did not call him (Strafford, "When I Find Time I'll Cry," 2).

92. "Nation Horrified," 8; Porteous, "Grand Jury to Get Case," 4; Trial Transcript, 39; Huie, *Wolf Whistle*, 41. Simeon Wright insists that his parents never found out about the incident, because if they had, they would have sent Till back to Chicago or made him apologize to Carolyn Bryant. "Either way, perhaps Bobo would be alive today" (Wright and Boyd, *Simeon's Story*, 52). It is clear, however, based on repeated testimony, that Mose Wright learned about

the store encounter prior to Till's kidnapping. During his courtroom testimony, Wright said he heard about the trouble at the store and talked with Emmett about it. However, notes taken by the defense during a deposition given by Wright before the trial state that "sometime between Wednesday and Saturday night someone told Mose about Till's getting into trouble in Money, but he did not talk to Till about it at anytime" ("Resume of Interview with Mose Wright"). Whether or not he talked to Till, Wright was aware of the incident prior to the kidnapping.

93. Wheeler Parker, interview, in Nelson, *Murder of Emmett Till*; "Events Night of Kidnaping Told by Slain Boy's Cousin," *Jackson Daily News*, September 1, 1955, 12; Porteous, "Grand Jury to Get Case," 5; Parker, Smith, and Wright, author interview, comments by Parker and Wright.

94. In a separate interview, published in August 1985 in the *Jackson Clarion–Ledger/Jackson Daily News*, Jones admitted that he was not yet in Mississippi the night Emmett went into the Bryant store, but he reaffirmed the details as he would have heard them from the others: "The boys had dared him. He was trying to show them that he wasn't afraid. He wasn't the type that scared easily." Jones also told these papers that Emmett had pictures of two white girls in his wallet. See Stringfellow, "Memories Sketch Varied Portraits," 1H. Because Jones's story came thirty years after the incident and he was not a witness to it in the first place, he may be recalling the photo incident not from memory but from reading the Huie account, which had become the most commonly told and accepted version of the events at the Bryant store.

95. Curtis Jones, interview, conducted by Blackside, Inc., November 12, 1985, for *Eyes on the Prize*. Even though he is deceptive about the store incident, Jones may be trusted for other details, such as his arrival date in Mississippi and how he got there. Simeon Wright says that Jones had been staying with an aunt in Greenwood the week previous, and that they met up with him there that Saturday night. It was *then*, according to Wright, that Jones came to stay in Money (see Wright and Boyd, *Simeon's Story*, 59; Parker, Smith, and Wright, author interview, comments by Wright). However, if Jones is correct that he was fishing with Till Saturday, he would have been in Money sometime during the day.

96. Till-Mobley and Benson, *Death of Innocence*, 113–14.

97. Trial Transcript, 10; Wright, "I Saw Them Take Emmett Till," 29; Parker, Smith, and Wright, author interview, comments by Wright. Simeon Wright said his brother, Robert, stayed home that night, opting to listen to the radio broadcast of *Gunsmoke*. An episode of the popular western did run on Saturday, August 27, 1955, and was titled "Doc Quits." Mose Wright testified in court, however, that only his wife, Elizabeth, remained at home that night. Wright and Boyd, *Simeon's Story*, 54. For the radio broadcast history of *Gunsmoke*, see http://comp .uark.edu/~tsnyder/gunsmoke/gun-radio1.html.

98. Crawford, interview, in Beauchamp, *Untold Story*; Parker, Smith, and Wright, author interview, comments by Parker and Wright; Wright and Boyd, *Simeon's Story*, 54–55. Simeon Wright believes he spent part of his evening in Greenwood at a movie.

99. John Crawford, interview, in Beauchamp, *Untold Story*; Trial Transcript, 10.

100. Till-Mobley and Benson, *Death of Innocence*, 115; Parker, Smith, and Wright, author interview, comments by Parker.

101. Trial Transcript, 10.

102. Holmes, "Uncle Tells How 3 Kidnapers," 2; Trial Transcript, 32–33. Wheeler Parker and Simeon Wright said that Parker was in the bed with Maurice Wright, not Curtis Jones, and that Jones and Robert Wright shared a bed in a different room altogether. However, because Mose Wright testified to the sleeping scenario, first to reporters and then at the murder trial a few

days later, I assume that his testimony is more accurate than the later recollections of Parker and Simeon Wright. Their account is in Hudson-Weems, *Emmett Till*, 208; Beauchamp, *Untold Story*; and Parker, Smith, and Wright, author interview, comments by Parker and Wright. However, the fact that Mose Wright had to go from room to room in order to find Till when the kidnappers came to the house to take him away is an indication that the sleeping arrangements were spontaneous and changed from night to night. If so, this may account for the discrepancy between Mose Wright's testimony and how Parker and Simeon Wright have come to recollect the night decades later.

103. Porteous, "Grand Jury to Get Case," 5; "Details Told of Lynching of Emmett," *Baltimore Afro-American*, September 17, 1955, 14.

104. Porteous, "Grand Jury to Get Case," 5; Holmes, "Uncle Tells How 3 Kidnapers," 2; Wright, "I Saw Them Take Emmett Till," 28; Trial Transcript, 38; "Resume of Interview with Mose Wright."

105. Holmes, "Uncle Tells How 3 Kidnapers," 2.

106. "Resume of Interview with Mose Wright"; "Uncle Tells How 3 Kidnapers," 2; "Slain Boy's Uncle Recalls Fatal Night," *Chicago American*, September 19, 1955, 4; Trial Transcript, 18, 19, 39; Wright, "I Saw Them Take Emmett Till," 29; Jones, interview, for *Eyes on the Prize*; Hudson-Weems, *Emmett Till*, 133; Porteous, "Grand Jury to Get Case," 5.

107. Trial Transcript 19; Porteous, "Grand Jury to Get Case," 5. Simeon Wright told defense attorneys shortly after the kidnapping that he thought he recognized one of the men present as Roy Bryant, having seen him before at the store. Upon further questioning, however, "He said he really couldn't tell who anybody was that night." Later in life, however, Wright said that he saw and recognized Bryant but not Milam. See "Resume of Interview with Simmy Wright," Huie Papers, box 85, fd. 346; Simeon Wright, interview, in Beauchamp, *Untold Story*.

108. Holmes, "Uncle Tells How 3 Kidnapers," 2; Porteous, "Grand Jury to Get Case," 5; Hudson-Weems, *Emmett Till*, 132.

109. "Resume of Interview with George Smith," Huie Papers, box 85, fd. 346; "Resume of Interview with Mose Wright"; Everett, "Till Nearly Missed His Fatal Journey," 12; Huie, *Wolf Whistle*, 24–25; Holmes, "Uncle Tells How 3 Kidnapers," 2; Ray Brennan, "Till's Uncle Sticks to Guns, Says He'll Relate Kidnapping," *Chicago Sun-Times*, September 19, 1955, 3; Porteous, "Grand Jury to Get Case," 5; Trial Transcript, 18–21; Wright, "I Saw Them Take Emmett Till," 29.

110. James Kilgallen, "Wright Tells Story of Negro's Kidnapping," *Memphis Commercial Appeal*, September 22, 1955, 11; Wright, "I Saw Them Take Emmett Till," 29.

111. Wright, "I Saw Them Take Emmett Till," 29; Till-Mobley and Benson, *Death of Innocence*, 125; "Resume of Interview with Mose Wright"; Brennan, "Till's Uncle Sticks to Guns," 3; Holmes, "Uncle Tells How 3 Kidnapers," 2 (Holmes erroneously refers to William Chamblee as William Chandler); Hudson-Weems, *Emmett Till*, 131; Parker, Smith, and Wright, author interview, comments by Wright; Huie, *Wolf Whistle*, 25; Wright, author interview, October 2, 2007.

112. Parker, Smith, and Wright, author interview, comments by Parker.

Chapter 3

1. Paul Holmes, "Uncle Tells How 3 Kidnapers Invaded Home and Seized Till," *Chicago Daily Tribune*, September 19, 1955, part 1, 2; Joe Atkins, "Slain Chicago Youth Was a 'Sacrificial Lamb,'" *Jackson Clarion-Ledger/Jackson Daily News*, August 25, 1985, 20A.

2. Moses Wright, "I Saw Them Take Emmett Till," *Front Page Detective*, February 1956, 29, 69; Holmes, "Uncle Tells How 3 Kidnapers," 2.

3. David A. Shostak, "Crosby Smith: Forgotten Witness to a Mississippi Nightmare," *Negro History Bulletin* 38 (December 1974–January 1975): 322.

4. Curtis Jones, interview, conducted by Blackside, Inc., November 12, 1985, for *Eyes on the Prize: America's Civil Rights Years (1954–1965)*, Henry Hampton Collection, Washington University, St. Louis, http://digital.wustl.edu/eyesontheprize/. Just after Till's murder, reporters in Chicago also interviewed Jones, who said that he heard Mose Wright trying to plead with the kidnappers not to take Till. He said that Elizabeth Wright even identified the men as Milam and Bryant (see "Kin Tell How Murdered Boy Was Abducted," *Chicago Daily Tribune*, September 3, 1955, 11). Jones's later retelling of the events of the night, although it came thirty years later, appears to be the most accurate. In the 1955 interview, he inserted himself into the story as an eyewitness but in actuality he learned what had happened from his grandparents because he stayed asleep most of the time while the kidnappers were present.

5. Clark Porteous, "Grand Jury to Get Case of Slain Negro Boy Monday," *Memphis Press-Scimitar*, September 1, 1955, 4; Wright, "I Saw Them Take Emmett Till, 69."

6. Mamie Bradley, "Mamie Bradley's Untold Story," installment one, *Daily Defender* (Chicago), February 27, 1956, 8; Mamie Till-Mobley and Christopher Benson, *Death of Innocence: The Story of the Hate Crime That Changed America* (New York: Random House, 2003), 117.

7. "Mamie Bradley's Untold Story," installment six, *Daily Defender* (Chicago), March 6, 1956, 8; Till-Mobley and Benson, *Death of Innocence*, 118; Clenora Hudson-Weems, *Emmett Till: The Sacrificial Lamb of the Civil Rights Movement*, 4th ed. (Bloomington, Ind.: AuthorHouse, 2006), 231.

8. Mamie Bradley, "I Want You to Know What They Did to My Boy," speech delivered October 29, 1955, Baltimore, *Washington Afro-American*, November 5, 1955, 20, and *Baltimore Afro-American*, November 12, 1955, 6, reprinted in Davis W. Houck and David E. Dixon, eds., *Rhetoric, Religion, and the Civil Rights Movement, 1954–1965* (Waco, Tex.: Baylor University Press, 2006), 133 (hereafter, references to this speech will cite Houck and Dixon only); "Chicago Boy, 14, Kidnaped by Miss. Whites," *Jet* 8, no. 18 (September 8, 1955): 4.

9. "Mamie Bradley's Untold Story," installment seven, *Daily Defender* (Chicago), March 7, 1956, 8; Hudson-Weems, *Emmett Till*, 232; Till-Mobley and Benson, *Death of Innocence*, 118, 120.

10. Till-Mobley and Benson, *Death of Innocence*, 118.

11. "Mamie Bradley's Untold Story," installment seven, 8; Hudson-Weems, *Emmett Till*, 232.

12. Wright, "I Saw Them Take Emmett Till," 69. Deputy John Cothran indicated in an interview with defense attorneys that Mose Wright had reported the kidnapping by eight o'clock Sunday morning ("Resume of Interview with John Ed Cothran, Deputy Sheriff of Leflore County, Mississippi," William Bradford Huie Papers, Cms 84, box 85, fd. 346, Ohio State University Library, Columbus [hereafter cited as Huie Papers]).

13. Till-Mobley and Benson, *Death of Innocence*, 120; William Bradford Huie, *Wolf Whistle, and Other Stories* (New York: Signet Books, 1959), 25; Shostak, "Crosby Smith," 322. If Crosby Smith's recollection of Sheriff Smith's comments is correct, it remains unknown just what crime Bryant and Milam had previously committed. However, in an article in the *Chicago Defender*, a news story on the abduction reports that "Bryant was implicated in the death of a Negro who was beaten and left in a ditch last year." Attributing this revelation to Sheriff

George Smith of Leflore County, the article also quotes Smith in a telephone conversation with Alma Spearman as saying "Bryant is a mean, cruel man." By reputation, this more accurately describes Milam, and this may be who Smith had in mind. See Mattie Smith Colin and Robert Elliott, "Mother Waits in Vain for Her 'Bo,'" *Chicago Defender*, September 10, 1955, 2.

14. Confidential source C, author interview, August 19, 2014; "Milam Is Pictured a War Hero Who Also Snatched Negro Girl from Drowning," *Jackson Daily News*, September 20, 1955, 6; William Bradford Huie, "The Shocking Story of Approved Killing in Mississippi," *Look*, January 24, 1956, 46–47; Huie, *Wolf Whistle*, 16–23.

15. Wheeler Parker Jr., Crosby Smith Jr., and Simeon Wright, author interview, February 7, 2007, Argo, Ill., comments by Wright; Hudson-Weems, *Emmett Till*, 135; Simeon Wright, with Herb Boyd, *Simeon's Story: An Eyewitness Account of the Kidnapping of Emmett Till* (Chicago: Lawrence Hill Books, 2010), 83.

16. "Resume of Interview with George Smith, Sheriff of Leflore County, Mississippi," Huie Papers, box 85, fd. 346; Federal Bureau of Investigation, Prosecutive Report of Investigation Concerning . . . Emmett Till, Deceased, Appendix A—Trial Transcript, February 9, 2006, 131 (hereafter cited as Trial Transcript).

17. "Chicago Negro Youth Abducted by Three White Men at Money," *Greenwood (Miss.) Commonwealth*, August 29, 1955, 1.

18. Federal Bureau of Investigation, Prosecutive Report of Investigation Concerning . . . Emmett Till, Deceased, Victim, February 9, 2006, 68 (hereafter cited as Prosecutive Report).

19. Prosecutive Report, 91; Bonnie Blue, *Emmett Till's Secret Witness: FBI Confidential Source Speaks* (Park Forest, Ill.: B. L. Richey Publishing, 2013), 252–56, 290–94. Blue served as a confidential source for the FBI during its 2004–5 investigation into the Till case. She claimed to have interviewed Milam over the phone several times shortly before his death in 1980, during which she extracted a candid admission of his role in the killing as well as several details about the murder. This is discussed in more detail in later chapters.

20. Trial Transcript, 137–49; Porteous, "Grand Jury to Get Case," 4; F. L. Price to Mr. [Alex] Rosen, September 2, 1955, FBI FOIA release to Devery S. Anderson, 2006, re Emmett Till (hereafter cited as FBI file on Emmett Till).

21. Monday's headlines, mentioned above, were: "Armed Trio Seizes Visitor in Mississippi," *Chicago Daily Tribune*, August 29, 1955, 1; "Leflore County Officers Checking Kidnap Charge," *Clarksdale (Miss.) Press Register*, August 29, 1955, 1; "Charge Greenwood Storekeeper with Abducting Youth," *Delta Democrat-Times* (Greenville, Miss.), August 29, 1955, 2; "Chicago Negro Youth Abducted by Three White Men at Money," *Greenwood (Miss.) Commonwealth*, August 29, 1955, 1; "White Storekeeper Held in Abduction of Negro Youth," *Jackson Daily News*, August 29, 1955, 1; "Charged Negro Boy Abducted," *Laurel (Miss.) Leader-Call*, August 29, 1955, 1; "Delta Officers Study Abduction of Negro Youth," *McComb (Miss.) Enterprise-Journal*, August 29, 1955, 1; "Kidnapping Charges as Boy Seized," *Jackson State Times*, August 29, 1955, 1.

22. "Mamie Bradley's Untold Story," installment seven, 8; Till-Mobley and Benson, *Death of Innocence*, 119–20.

23. "Mamie Bradley's Untold Story," installment seven, 8.

24. Hudson-Weems, *Emmett Till*, 212; "Kidnapped Boy Whistled at Woman," *Chicago Tribune*, August 30, 1955, 2; Till-Mobley and Benson, *Death of Innocence*, 121.

25. Parker, Smith, and Wright, author interview, comments by Parker.

26. Wright, "I Saw Them Take Emmett Till," 69.

27. "A Wife in Hiding Writes Back to Hubby—'Come On Up Here,'" *Tri-State Defender* (Memphis, Tenn.), September 17, 1955, 5.

28. "Mamie Bradley's Untold Story," installment seven, 8.

29. "Kidnapped Boy Whistled," 2.

30. "Mamie Bradley's Untold Story," installment seven, 8; Till-Mobley and Benson, *Death of Innocence*, 126.

31. "Muddy River Gives Up Body of Slain Negro Boy," *Memphis Commercial Appeal*, September 1, 1955, 4; Clark Porteous, "Mississippi Hunt for Clews [*sic*] Goes On," *Memphis Press-Scimitar*, September 2, 1955, 5.

32. "Mamie Bradley's Untold Story," installment seven, 8; Till-Mobley and Benson, *Death of Innocence*, 126.

33. Houck and Dixon, *Rhetoric, Religion, and the Civil Rights Movement*, 133.

34. Trial Transcript, 102, 111. Hodges said in court that after he told his father about the body he found in the river, his father told Mims, and that Mims in turn told the sheriff. Robert Hodges would have no firsthand knowledge of what happened after he told his father about his discovery. Since Mims said he was told about the body by a boy in the area, and that someone else called the sheriff, it is safe to assume that Mims's version of events is the more accurate.

35. Trial Transcript, 99, 114–17.

36. Trial Transcript, 285; "Missing Chicago Negro Youth Found in Tallahatchie River," *Greenwood (Miss.) Commonwealth*, August 31, 1955, 1.

37. Trial Transcript, 149–50; Porteous, "Grand Jury to Get Case," 4.

38. Trial Transcript, 287.

39. James Featherston, "White 'Deplores' Slaying in Note to NAACP Which Is Creating National Issue," *Jackson Daily News*, September 1, 1955, 1.

40. Trial Transcript, 287.

41. "Muddy River Gives Up Body," 4.

42. "Missing Chicago Negro Youth," 1; Trial Transcript, 151, 173–75; "Resume of Interview with John Ed Cothran." Cothran's interview was not the only source indicating that Strider's son was there, as the younger Strider affirmed this to filmmaker Stanley Nelson as well. However, Clarence Strider overplayed his role when talking to Nelson and claimed that he used his boat and, with others, went into the river to get the body out. No source contemporary to the event backs up his story; court testimony is very specific about who got into the boat and whose boat was used. See Stanley Nelson, prod., *The Murder of Emmett Till* (Firelight Media, 2002).

43. "Resume of Interview with Mose Wright"; Wright, "I Saw Them Take Emmett Till," 69.

44. Trial Transcript, 70–71, 73–74; "Resume of Interview with John Ed Cothran." For more on the role of the black undertaker who "is always and forever called to handle things after the white man slaughters somebody," see Rebecca Mark, "Mourning Emmett, 'One Long Expansive Moment,'" *Southern Literary Journal* 40, no. 2 (Spring 2008): 126.

45. Trial Transcript, 71–72, 153.

46. Wright, "I Saw Them Take Emmett Till," 69; Trial Transcript, 155.

47. Houck and Dixon, *Rhetoric, Religion, and the Civil Rights Movement*, 135; Hudson-Weems, *Emmett Till*, 236; "Mamie Bradley's Untold Story, installment seven, 8; Till-Mobley and Benson, *Death of Innocence*, 126–27.

48. "Mamie Bradley's Untold Story," installment seven, 8; Till-Mobley and Benson, *Death of Innocence*, 126–27; Houck and Dixon, *Rhetoric, Religion, and the Civil Rights Movement*, 135; Hudson-Weems, *Emmett Till*, 236. For an analysis of the role of motherhood as an integral part of disseminating and shaping the story of Emmett Till, see Ruth Feldstein, "'I Wanted the Whole World to See': Race, Gender, and Constructions of Motherhood in the Death of Emmett Till," in *Not June Cleaver: Women and Gender in Postwar America, 1945–1960*, ed. Joanne Meyerowitz (Philadelphia: Temple University Press, 1994), 263–303.

49. Houck and Dixon, *Rhetoric, Religion, and the Civil Rights Movement*, 135–36; Hudson-Weems, *Emmett Till*, 236–37; Till-Mobley and Benson, *Death of Innocence*, 130.

50. "Negro Boy Was Killed for 'Wolf Whistle,'" *New York Post*, September 1, 1955, 5.

51. Trial Transcript, 76, 77, 84–86, 298–304.

52. "Sheriff Believes Body Not Till's; Family Disagrees," *Jackson Clarion-Ledger*, September 4, 1955, 4.

53. Trial Transcript, 76–77.

54. Wright, "I Saw Them Take Emmett Till," 69; Houck and Dixon, *Rhetoric, Religion, and the Civil Rights Movement*, 135.

55. Jones, interview, for *Eyes on the Prize*.

56. "Mamie Bradley's Untold Story," installment seven; Till-Mobley and Benson, *Death of Innocence*, 130.

57. Joe Atkins, "Emmett Till: More Than a Murder," *Jackson Clarion–Ledger/Jackson Daily News*, August 25, 1985, 20A; "Slain-Boy's Body Arrives Here; Sets off Emotional Scene at Depot," *Chicago Sun-Times*, September 3, 1955, 4.

58. Jones, interview, for *Eyes on the Prize*. Mamie Bradley, speaking in 1955, said that Miller refused to keep the body in his funeral home overnight, and quoted him as saying, "I wouldn't have any place in the morning and perhaps I wouldn't be alive by morning" if he did (Houck and Dixon, *Rhetoric, Religion, and the Civil Rights Movement*, 136). Bradley obviously heard this story from someone in Mississippi, perhaps Jones or Mose Wright, but it is consistent with what Jones said in 1985. Mississippi state senator David Jordan recalled a similar fear in Miller while Miller testified at the murder trial. "He was respected and looked up to by all of us, but when I saw him that day he was scared to death. . . . He was just giving a description of the body, but his shirt was wet, like someone had just poured water on it" (Mamie Fortune Osborne, "An Interview with David Jordan on Emmett Till," *Southern Quarterly: A Journal of Arts & Letters in the South* 45, no. 4 [Summer 2008]: 140. See also David L. Jordan, with Robert L. Jenkins, *David L. Jordan: From the Mississippi Cotton Fields to the State Senate* [Jackson: University Press of Mississippi, 2014], 58).

59. "Body of Negro Found in River," *Jackson Clarion-Ledger*, September 1, 1955, 1.

60. Wright, "I Saw Them Take Emmett Till," 69.

61. Trial Transcript, 77–80, 181–82; "Slain-Boy's Body Arrives Here," 4.

62. "Body of Negro Found in River," 1.

63. Mattie Smith Colin, "Mother's Tears Greet Son Who Died a Martyr," *Chicago Defender*, September 10, 1955, 1; "Protest Mississippi Shame," *New York Age Defender*, September 10, 1955, 1.

64. Myrlie Evers-Williams, author telephone interview, April 23, 2014.

65. Roy Wilkins, telegram to Governor Hugh White, August 31, 1955, James P. Coleman Papers, Accn. No. 21877, box 23, fd. 3, Mississippi Department of Archives and History, Archives

and Library Division, Special Collections Section, Manuscript Collection, Jackson (hereafter cited as Coleman Papers).

66. "Body of Negro Found in River," 1; "Find Kidnaped Chicago Boy's Body in River," *Chicago Daily Tribune*, September 1, 1955, 2.

67. H. L. Stevenson, "Fisherman Finds Body of Chicago Negro Boy in Tallahatchie River," *Greenwood (Miss.) Morning Star*, September 1, 1955, 1.

68. Hugh White, telegram to Roy Wilkins, September 1, 1955, Coleman Papers, box 23, fd. 3.

69. "Mayor Daley Protests Slaying of Chicagoan," *Chicago Sun-Times*, September 2, 1955, 3; "Ask Ike to Act in Dixie Death of Chicago Boy," *Chicago Daily Tribune*, September 2, 1955, 2.

70. "Ask Mississippi Governor to Denounce Killing of Boy," *Chicago Daily Tribune*, September 1, 1955, 2.

71. "Body of Negro Found in River," 1; "'A Den of Snakes' Youth's Mother Calls Mississippi," *Delta Democrat-Times* (Greenville, Miss.), September 1, 1955, 2.

72. "Muddy River Gives Up Body," 4; "Body of Negro Found in River," 1. For a thorough treatment on why the federal government did not intervene, see Jonathan L. Entin, "Emmett Till and the Federal Enforcement of Civil Rights," unpublished paper presented at Stillman College, September 16, 2005, copy in author's possession.

73. J. Edgar Hoover to John H. Stengstacke, September 2, 1955, FBI file on Emmett Till. Correspondence in this file reveals that Hoover and other FBI officials responded to numerous letters calling for a federal investigation, basically citing the same reasons as those in the Stengstacke letter.

74. "White Calls Boy's Death 'Murder; Not Lynching,'" *Jackson Daily News*, September 2, 1955, 14; "Kidnap Murder Stirs Delta," *Clarksdale (Miss.) Press Register*, September 2, 1955, 1; "Boy's Slaying Held Murder by Gov. White," *Chicago Daily Tribune*, September 2, 1955, 1.

75. George Murray, "'Wolf Call' Blamed by Argo Teen," *Chicago American*, September 1, 1955, 4.

76. "Negro Boy Was Killed for Wolf Whistle," 12.

77. "Tuskegee to Probe Slayings of Three Negroes in State," *Jackson Daily News*, September 1, 1955, 12.

78. "Kidnap-Murder Case Will Be Transferred to Tallahatchie," *Greenwood (Miss.) Commonwealth*, September 1, 1955, 1; "Muddy River Gives Up Body," 4; "White Orders Full Probe of Delta's Kidnap-Murder," *Jackson Clarion-Ledger*, 2; J. Todd Moye, *Let the People Decide: Black Freedom and White Resistance Movements in Sunflower County, Mississippi, 1945–1986* (Chapel Hill: University of North Carolina Press, 2004), 84.

79. Hugh White, telegrams to Honorable Gerald W. Chatham and Honorable Stanny Sanders, September 1, 1955, Coleman Papers, box 23, fd. 3.

80. "Muddy River Gives Up Body," 1, 4.

81. Gerald Chatham, telegram to Honorable Hugh L. White, September 1, 1955, Coleman Papers, box 23, fd. 3.

82. "Officer Fears Actions Build Up Resentment," *Jackson Clarion-Ledger*, September 4, 1955, 1.

83. Porteous, "Grand Jury to Get Case," 4.

84. Chester Marshall and James McBroom, "White Men Face Double Indictment for Kidnapping, Murdering Till Boy," *Jackson Daily News*, September 6, 1955, 3.

85. Hugh Stephen Whitaker, "A Case Study in Southern Justice: The Emmett Till Case" (Master's thesis, Florida State University, 1963), 118, reprinted as Hugh Stephen Whitaker,

"A Case Study in Southern Justice: The Murder and Trial of Emmett Till," *Rhetoric & Public Affairs* 8, no. 2 (Summer 2005): 195. The 2005 autopsy report verified that Till's body had been embalmed and that "numerous venting incisions" were made in the skin and on the bottom of his mouth. See Prosecutive Report, 109. See also Mark, "Mourning Emmett," 126.

86. "Charleston Sheriff Says Body in River Wasn't Young Till," *Memphis Commercial Appeal*, September 4, 1955, 2; Huie, *Wolf Whistle*, 26. A photo exists of men taking the casket out of the pine box to load onto a hearse after it arrived in Chicago. Because padded paper covered the casket, one writer at the scene reported that "five men lifted a soiled paper wrapped bundle from a huge, brown wooden mid-Victorian box at the Illinois Central Station in Chicago Friday and put it into a waiting hearse" (Colin, "Mother's Tears Greet Son," 1; Christopher Metress, ed., *The Lynching of Emmett Till: A Documentary Narrative* [Charlottesville: University of Virginia Press, 2002], 29). The writer obviously thought that the "bundle" was Till's body, and did not realize that what the men were actually carrying was a casket under padded paper. The padding was probably used to protect the casket during the journey and to allow a more secure fit within the pine box.

87. "Stratton Acts in Dixie Killing," *Chicago American*, September 2, 1955, 1.

88. "No Developments in Negro Slaying," *Greenwood (Miss.) Commonwealth*, September 2, 1955, 1.

89. "Try to Determine Spot Where Negro Was Slain," *Greenwood (Miss.) Morning Star*, September 3, 1955, 1; "Officers Press Hunt in Slaying of Negro," *Memphis Commercial Appeal*, September 4, 1955, 19.

90. "Muddy River Gives Up Body," 1, 4.

91. R. R. Shurden to J. Edgar Hoover, September 5, 1955; Mr. Tolman to Mr. Parsons, September 9, 1955, both in FBI file on Emmett Till.

92. "'Were Never into Meanness' Says Accused Men's Mother," *Memphis Commercial Appeal*, September 2, 1955, 35; "Bryant's Brother Claims Charges Are All 'Politics,'" *Memphis Commercial Appeal*, September 4, 1955, 19; "Suspect Credited with Saving Lives," *Jackson State Times*, September 1, 1955, 11A.

93. "Negro Bishop Asks 2 Days' Mourning as Slaying Protest," *Jackson Daily News*, September 2, 1955, 1; "Newspapers Over State Blast Murder of Negro," *Jackson Daily News*, September 3, 1955, 1; "Mississippi's Reaction to Boy's Death," *Memphis Press-Scimitar*, September 3, 1955, 11.

94. "A Just Appraisal," *Greenwood (Miss.) Commonwealth*, September 2, 1955, 1.

95. "Just Appraisal," 1; Davis W. Houck, "Killing Emmett," *Rhetoric & Public Affairs* 8 (Summer 2005): 234. For an excellent treatment of the changing position of Mississippi journalists in reporting the case, see Davis Houck and Matthew Grindy, *Emmett Till and the Mississippi Press* (Jackson: University Press of Mississippi, 2008).

96. "10,000 at Bier of Slain Boy," *Chicago American*, September 3, 1955, 1; "Murdered Youth's Kin Hysterical at Station," *Chicago Sun-Times*, September 2, 1955, 3. Knowledge that the pine box was opened at the train station comes from a photograph that shows that the lid and front panel had been removed, while men position themselves to lift out the casket. Removal from the box was obviously necessary in order for the casket to fit in the hearse. This scene is further collaborated in the eyewitness account cited earlier that erroneously called the padded casket a "soiled bundle" that the author believed was simply Till's body (Smith Colin, "Mother's Tears Greet Son," 1; Metress, *Lynching of Emmett Till*, 29).

97. Till-Mobley and Benson, *Death of Innocence*, 131.

98. "Stratton Acts in Dixie Killing," 1.

99. Houck and Dixon, *Rhetoric, Religion, and the Civil Rights Movement*, 136.

100. Simeon Booker, "Best Civil Rights Cameraman in Business Dies," *Jet* 30, no. 2 (April 21, 1966): 29; Simeon Booker, with Carol McCabe Booker, *Shocking the Conscience: A Reporter's Account of the Civil Rights Movement* (Jackson: University Press of Mississippi, 2013), 59. In his later memoir, Booker said that he and Jackson waited all night at the train station. In 1966, he said they waited at the funeral home. I am using his earlier recollection here in telling his story.

101. Hudson-Weems, *Emmett Till*, 238; Houck and Dixon, *Rhetoric, Religion, and the Civil Rights Movement*, 136.

102. Houck and Dixon, *Rhetoric, Religion, and the Civil Rights Movement*, 137; Trial Transcript, 185, 211–12. Decades later, whenever Mamie Till-Mobley talked about the day she viewed the body, she told several details differently from those I provide in the text above. In her 2003 autobiography, she said that she could smell the odor of her son's decomposing body several blocks away as she and her companions drove toward the funeral home. In a speech given in the fall of 1955, cited above, however, she said she began to notice the odor after she entered the room where she viewed it. This sounds much more reasonable, although admittedly, not as dramatic. It is possible that she could smell the body outside as she approached the funeral home the second time, because by then, the casket had been open for some time, but she was not likely several blocks away. Her later recollections about examining the body also differ from her earliest ones. In her memoirs and other interviews after the mid-1980s, she says that she began her examination at Emmett's feet and worked her way up. In her earliest speeches, she indicates that she started with his face. See Till-Mobley and Benson, *Death of Innocence*, 132–36; see also her statements in two documentaries: Nelson, *Murder of Emmett Till*, and Keith Beauchamp, prod., *The Untold Story of Emmett Louis Till* (Till Freedom Come Productions, 2005). Because her earlier descriptions in speeches and on the witness stand agree with each other but not with her later ones, I have concluded that her recollections decades after the fact are less accurate.

103. Booker, "Best Civil Rights Cameraman," 29; Simeon Booker, *Black Man's America* (Englewood Cliffs, N.J.: Prentice Hall, 1964), 3; Booker and Booker, *Shocking the Conscience*, 60.

104. Houck and Dixon, *Rhetoric, Religion, and the Civil Rights Movement*, 137.

105. John H. Johnson, *Succeeding against the Odds* (New York: Warner Books, 1989), 207, 240; Brian Thornton, "The Murder of Emmett Till: Myth, Memory, and National Magazine Response," *Journalism History* 36, no. 2 (Summer 2010): 100.

106. "Mamie Bradley's Untold Story," installment one; Till-Mobley and Benson, *Death of Innocence*, 140; "Slain-Boy's Body Arrives Here," 4. For various interpretations about the meaning and effects of Mamie Bradley's decision to show her son's body, see Jacqueline Goldsby, "The High and Low Tech of It: The Meaning of Lynching and the Death of Emmett Till," *Yale Journal of Criticism* 9, no. 2 (Fall 1996): 245–82; Christine Harold and Kevin Michael DeLuca, "Behold the Corpse: Violent Images and the Case of Emmett Till," *Rhetoric & Public Affairs* 8, no. 2 (Summer 2005): 263–86; Mark, "Mourning Emmett," 126–28; Courtney Baker, "Emmett Till, Justice, and the Task of Recognition," *Journal of American Culture* 29, no. 2 (2006): 111–24; Valerie Smith, "Emmett Till's Ring," *Women's Studies Quarterly* 36, nos. 1–2 (Spring/Summer 2008): 151–61.

107. "Mourners, Curious Mingle at Till Rites," *Clarksdale (Miss.) Press Register*, September 3, 1955, 1; Houck and Dixon, *Rhetoric, Religion, and the Civil Rights Movement*, 138; Harold and DeLuca, "Behold the Corpse," 273. For more on the role black mortuaries played in the civil rights movement, see Suzanne E. Smith, *To Serve the Living: Funeral Directors and the African American Way of Life* (Cambridge, Mass: Belknap Press of Harvard University Press, 2010). For how this relates specifically to the Till case, see 124–29. In summarizing, Smith notes that "by the mid-1960s, the civil rights funeral, a tradition that had begun with Emmett Till's ceremony in 1955, became a central stage on which the dramas and internal tensions of the movement played themselves out" (166–67).

108. "Negro Mass March Call Rumor," *Jackson State Times*, September 4, 1955, 1.

109. "Grand Jury Considers Charge in Till Case as Suspects Guarded in Greenwood Jail," *Clarksdale (Miss.) Press Register*, September 5, 1955, 1; Marshall and McBroom, "White Men Face Double Indictment," 1.

110. William Middlebrooks, "Sheriff Says Body Thousands Viewed May Not Be Till's," *Delta Democrat-Times* (Greenville, Miss.), September 4, 1955, 1–2; "Mississippi Sheriff Voices Doubt Body Was That of Till," *Greenwood (Miss.) Morning Star*, September 4, 1955, 1; "Sheriff Believes Body Not Till's," 4.

111. "2500 at Rites Here for Boy, 14, Slain in South," *Chicago Daily Tribune*, September 4, 1955, 2.

112. "Sheriff Believes Body Not Till's," 4; "Charleston Sheriff Says Body in River Wasn't Young Till," 1.

113. "Sheriff Believes Body Not Till's," 1, 4.

114. "Officer Fears Actions," 1, 8; "Mourners, Curious Mingle at Till Rites," 1; "Officers Press Hunt in Slaying of Negro," *Memphis Commercial Appeal*, September 4, 1955, 1.

115. "Urge Tolerance at Boy's Funeral," *Chicago Sun-Times*, September 4, 1955, 3.

116. "Urge Tolerance," 3; Parker, Smith, and Wright, author interview, comments by Smith.

117. "100,000 at Last Rites on S. Side for Kidnapped Boy," *Chicago American*, September 3, 1955, 3; Glen Bludeau, "10,000 View Casket of Slain Negro Boy," *Jackson State Times*, September 4, 1955, 1.

118. "2500 at Rites Here for Boy," 2; "100,000 at Last Rites," 3; "Urge Tolerance," 3.

119. "2500 at Rites Here for Boy," 2; Doris Colon, author telephone interview, January 5, 2007. In her interview with me, Colon said that several of her friends refused to let their children travel to Mississippi to visit relatives after the Till murder. This was not uncommon, although Harold and DeLuca note ("Behold the Corpse," 276) that this was not limited to the South. "African American communities have added the story to their folklore tradition in order to pass along an important lesson: 'never forget what can happen to a black person in America.'"

120. George Harmon, "'Jail Raid' Has Area Tense," *Jackson State Times*, September 5, 1955, 1, 10A; "Troops Posted in Delta as Mob Violence Feared in Aftermath to Slaying," *Jackson Daily News*, September 5, 1955, 1.

121. Whitaker, "Case Study," 126–27, reprint, 197–99; J. J. Breland to Thomas L. Miller, September 15, 1955, Huie Papers, box 85, fd. 347; William M. Simpson, "Reflections on a Murder: The Emmett Till Case," in *Southern Miscellany: Essays in History in Honor of Glover Moore*, ed. Frank Allen Dennis (Jackson: University Press of Mississippi, 1981), 181.

122. Whitaker, "Case Study," 126–27, reprint, 197–99; Jay Milner, "Doctor's Testimony May Alter Inquiry," *Jackson Clarion-Ledger*, September 6, 1955, 12.

123. "Grand Jury Calls Several Witnesses in Till Murder Case," *Greenwood (Miss.) Morning Star*, September 6, 1955, 1.

124. William Sorrels, "Grand Jury Weighs Officers' Reports in Death of Youth," *Memphis Commercial Appeal*, September 6, 1955, 1.

125. Clay Gowran, "Urban League Asks Action in Till Case," *Chicago Daily Tribune*, September 6, 1955, 8.

126. Gowran, "Urban League Asks Action," 8.

127. "Mother Hysterical at Victim's Rites," *Chicago American*, September 7, 1955, 4.

128. "Accused White Men Plead Innocent of Murder and Kidnap," *Greenwood (Miss.) Morning Star*, September 7, 1955, 1; Milner, "Doctor's Testimony," 1; "Wolf Whistle Kidnap Pair Indicted on Murder Count," *Memphis Press-Scimitar*, September 6, 1955, 7; Parker, Smith, and Wright, author interview, comments by Wright. One newspaper says that Otken was summoned but did not testify, and that Mose and Simeon Wright did; see William Sorrels, "Defendants Enter Pleas of Innocence in Slaying of Youth," *Memphis Commercial Appeal*, September 7, 1955, 3. I conclude, based on Simeon Wright's recollections, that he did not testify, and that Sorrels is incorrect.

129. "Wolf Whistle Pair Indicted on Murder Count," *Memphis Press-Scimitar*, September 6, 1955, 7.

130. "Wolf Whistle Pair Indicted," 7.

131. "Grand Jury Makes Report and Adjourns," *Sumner (Miss.) Sentinel*, September 8, 1955, 1; "J. W. Milam and Roy Bryant Indicted Sept. 6," *Sumner (Miss.) Sentinel*, September 8, 1955, 1; Marshall and McBroom, "White Men Face Double Indictment," 1; "Body of Negro Found in River," 1.

132. Sorrels, "Defendants Enter Pleas," 3.

133. "Killing of Till Listed as Lynch in Records," *Greenwood (Miss.) Morning Star*, September 7, 1955, 1.

134. Sorrels, "Grand Jury Weighs Officers' Reports," 8.

135. Milner, "Doctor's Testimony," 1.

Chapter 4

1. For more on the Scottsboro case, see Dan T. Carter, *Scottsboro: A Tragedy of the American South*, rev. ed. (Baton Rouge: Louisiana State University Press, 2007); James Goodman, *Stories of Scottsboro* (New York: Random House, 1994).

2. James Fairfield, "Deadly Discourses: Examining the Roles of Language and Silence in the Lynching of Emmett Till and Wright's *Native Son*," *Arizona Quarterly* 63, no. 4 (Winter 2007): 64.

3. William Street, "Emmett Till Case Suddenly Thrusts Little Sumner into Limelight," *Memphis Commercial Appeal*, September 18, 1955, 10.

4. "Till Slaying Trial May Be Set Thursday," *Delta Democrat-Times* (Greenville, Miss.), September 7, 1955, 1.

5. "Slain Boy's Mother Will Get Invitation to Trial of Deltans," *Jackson Clarion-Ledger*, September 8, 1955, 1; "Mother of Slain Negro Is Asked to Aid in Prosecution," *Jackson Daily News*,

September 8, 1955, 6; "Slain Boy's Mother Invited to Trial," *New York Post*, September 8, 1955, 3; "Mother of Slain Chicagoan Urged to Attend Trial," *Chicago American*, September 8, 1955, 4.

6. "Random Thoughts by the Editor," *Yazoo City (Miss.) Herald*, September 8, 1955, 1; "An Even Bigger Crime," *Scott County Times* (Forest, Miss.), September 8, 1955, 4, as quoted in Davis W. Houck and Matthew A. Grindy, *Emmett Till and the Mississippi Press* (Jackson: University Press of Mississippi, 2008), 48, 50.

7. "Lynching Post-Facto," *Delta Democrat-Times* (Greenville, Miss.), September 6, 1955, 4.

8. Letter to Gerald Chatham, unsigned, postmarked Cleveland, Ohio, September 2, 1955; undated, unsigned letter, both in Gerald Chatham Papers, Charles W. Capps Jr. Archives and Museum, Delta State University, Cleveland, Miss. (hereafter cited as Chatham Papers).

9. J. Noel Hinson to Gerald Chatham, September 6, 1955, Chatham Papers.

10. Mrs. G. Lee to Judge Curtis Swango, September 6, 1955, Chatham Papers.

11. Otis Dudley Duncan and Beverly Duncan, *The Negro Population of Chicago: A Study of Residential Succession* (Chicago: University of Chicago Press, 1957), 97.

12. Adam Green, *Selling the Race: Culture, Community, and Black Chicago, 1940–1955* (Chicago: University of Chicago Press, 2007), 181–84.

13. Green, *Selling the Race*, 182.

14. Unsigned letter sent to Gerald Chatham, September 7, 1955, Chatham Papers; "Sex Slayer Confesses," *Jet* 8, no. 14 (August 11, 1955): 48; Richard C. Lindberg and Gloria Jean Sykes, *Shattered Sense of Innocence: The 1955 Murders of Three Chicago Children* (Carbondale: Southern Illinois University Press, 2006), 347n4; "Deaf Mute Convicted of Rape-Slaying," *Spencer (Iowa) Daily Reporter*, December 13, 1955, 2.

15. Unsigned, undated letter, sent from New York, to Gerald Chatham, Chatham Papers.

16. Hugh White to Armis Hawkins, September 14, 1955, James P. Coleman Papers, Accn. no. 21877, box 23, fd. 3, Mississippi Department of Archives and History, Archives and Library Division, Special Collections Section, Manuscript Collection, Jackson (hereafter cited as Coleman Papers).

17. Houck and Grindy, *Emmett Till and the Mississippi Press*, 46.

18. "Speedy Trial Planned in Kidnap-Slaying Case," *Greenwood (Miss.) Commonwealth*, September 7, 1955, 1; "Plan Suit If 2 Escape Death in Boy Lynching," *New York Post*, September 7, 1955, 5.

19. "Marshall Blames Citizens Council for Till Slaying," *Jackson Daily News*, September 12, 1955, 1. The other two murders were those of the Reverend George Lee, on May 7, 1955, and Lamar Smith, on August 13, 1955, just two weeks before the murder of Emmett Till.

20. "Speedy Trial Planned," 1.

21. A. B. Ainsworth, "To All White Mississippians," *Greenwood (Miss.) Commonwealth*, September 8, 1955, 8; see also Houck and Grindy, *Emmett Till and the Mississippi Press*, 53.

22. Citizens of Humphreys County to Breland and Whitten, attorneys, September 9, 1955, three separate letters with multiple signatures sent on this date; Thomas R. Miller to Gerald Chatham, September 12, 1955, all in William Bradford Huie Papers, Cms 84, box 85, fd. 347, Ohio State University Library, Columbus (hereafter cited as Huie Papers).

23. "Backer Says Bryant-Milam Fund Is Growing Rapidly," *Clarksdale (Miss.) Press Register*, September 13, 1955, 1; Dan Wakefield, author telephone interview, November 20, 2006; Ralph Hutto, "Sheriff Won't Call Guard to Preserve Order," *Jackson State Times*, September 21, 1955, 8A.

24. "Slain Boy's Mother Will Get Invitation to Trial of Deltans," 1; "Slain Youth's Mother to Testify at Trial," *Delta Democrat-Times* (Greenville, Miss.), September 8, 1955, 1.

25. "Slain Youth's Mother to Testify," 1.

26. "Collins Editor Asks U.S. Law on Dead Bodies," *Jackson Daily News*, September 8, 1955, 1.

27. "Negro Leader Hails Officers for Handling of Till Slaying," *Memphis Commercial Appeal*, September 9, 1955, 1. Jackson's praise of Mississippi law enforcement officials was certainly not aimed at Sheriff Strider, whose allegations of an NAACP conspiracy, together with his belief that Emmett Till was still alive, placed him in the corner of the defense. If Jackson was not simply trying to appease white Mississippians in his remarks, then he likely had Leflore County sheriff George Smith and his deputies in mind. It was those officers who had quickly arrested Milam and Bryant after Till's uncle, Mose Wright, reported the kidnapping.

28. "'Not Bitter,' Says Mother of Till," *Memphis Press-Scimitar*, September 12, 1955, 27; "Wolf Whistle Trial Date Set Sept. 19," *Memphis Press-Scimitar*, September 9, 1955, 34.

29. Houck and Grindy, *Emmett Till and the Mississippi Press*, 59–60.

30. William Henry Huff to Gerald Chatham, September 9, 1955, Coleman Papers, box 23, fd. 3; FBI FOIA release to Devery S. Anderson, 2006, re Emmett Till (hereafter cited as FBI file on Emmett Till).

31. William Henry Huff to Honorable Herbert Brownell, September 9, 1955, FBI file on Emmett Till.

32. "Judge Curtis Swango Draws Jury List," *Jackson Clarion-Ledger*, September 13, 1955, 1; "Delta White Men to Go on Trial September 19," *Jackson Daily News*, September 9, 1955, 1.

33. "Faulkner Pictures Till Case as Test of Survival of White Man, America," *Jackson Daily News*, September 10, 1955, 1; "Hypocrisy Is Attacked by Writer," *Jackson State Times*, September 10, 1955, 1, 12A.

34. "Coleman Names Assistant to Aid Delta Prosecution," *Jackson Clarion-Ledger*, September 10, 1955, 1; "Till Prosecutor Will Have Help," *Memphis Press-Scimitar*, September 10, 1955, 11; "Special Prosecutor Named in Till Case," *Memphis Commercial Appeal*, September 10, 1955, 1; "Prominent Local Attorney Dies," *Southern Sentinel* (Ripley, Miss.), December 7, 1967, 1.

35. Jak and Bruce Smith Oral History Interview (OH289), May 17, 2005, Charles W. Capps Jr. Archives and Museum, Delta State University, Cleveland, Miss.; Danny McKenzie, "Ripley Attorney Played Major Role in Till Case," *Tupelo (Miss.) Daily Journal*, September 21, 2003, 6A.

36. Gerald Chatham Sr., Oral History Interview (OH293), January 19, 2005, Charles W. Capps Jr. Archives and Museum, Delta State University.

37. Armis E. Hawkins to Honorable Latham Castle, September 10, 1955, Coleman Papers, box 23, fd. 3.

38. "Here's Cast for Sumner, Miss. Trial," *Tri-State Defender* (Memphis, Tenn.), September 24, 1955, 2.

39. "Here's Cast for Sumner," 2; Hugh Stephen Whitaker, "A Case Study in Southern Justice: The Emmett Till Case" (Master's thesis, Florida State University, 1963), 130, reprinted as Hugh Stephen Whitaker, "A Case Study in Southern Justice: The Murder and Trial of Emmett Till," *Rhetoric & Public Affairs* 8, no. 2 (Summer 2005): 200.

40. David Binder, "Jamie Whitten, Who Served 53 Years in House, Dies at 85," *New York Times*, September 11, 1995, D13. On June 7, 2013, Whitten's time in the House was surpassed by John Dingell, Democratic representative from Michigan.

41. *Eula Lee Morgan Bryant v. Henry E. Bryant*, case no. 2875, Tallahatchie County, Mississippi.

42. "Prosecution Doesn't Say If Death Penalty Sought in Trial of White Men," *Jackson Daily News*, September 12, 1955, 1.

43. *Eula Lee Morgan Bryant v. Henry E. Bryant*.

44. "Why Didn't They Get the Same Publicity?," *Greenwood (Miss.) Morning Star*, September 7, 1955, 4.

45. "Girl Honored for Saving Negro Nurse," *Clarksdale (Miss.) Press Register*, September 10, 1955, 1.

46. J. Edgar Hoover to William Henry Huff, September 20, 1955, FBI file on Emmett Till. Huff may have received an earlier response, perhaps from Brownell, denying the requested protection, as he announced to the press on September 16 that his request had been denied. See "Mother of Till Has a Secret," *Memphis Press-Scimitar*, September 16, 1955, 3.

47. "State Calls Special Counsel to Assist with Prosecution," *Clarksdale (Miss.) Press Register*, September 10, 1955, 1.

48. See also Mamie Till-Mobley and Christopher Benson, *Death of Innocence: The Story of the Hate Crime That Changed America* (New York: Random House, 2003), 149.

49. Fraser M. Ottanelli, *The Communist Party of the United States: From the Depression to World War II* (New Brunswick, N.J.: Rutgers University Press, 1991), 36–37.

50. FBI letter to Herbert Brownell and J. Edgar Hoover on Communist Party, USA, the Negro question, and internal security, September 9, 1955, FBI file on Emmett Till.

51. FBI letter to Brownell and Hoover, September 9, 1955; "Councilman Brown Urges Picketing of White House to Protest Lynching," *Daily Worker* (New York), September 9, 1955, 1.

52. Office memorandum to Mr. A. H. Belmont, September 14, 1955; Letter to Honorable Dillon Anderson, September 13, 1955; John Edgar Hoover to Assistant Chief of Staff, Department of the Army, n.d., but sent September 14, 1955, all in FBI file on Emmett Till.

53. Whitaker, "Case Study," 137, reprint, 203. Whitaker examined the letters himself and even retained possession of them until they were destroyed in a basement flood.

54. "Threats Are Voiced as Trial Date Nears," *Memphis Commercial Appeal*, September 11, 1955, 13.

55. "Strategy of Defense Attorneys Violates Every Rule in Books," *Jackson State Times*, September 19, 1955.

56. "Prosecution Doesn't Say If Death Penalty Sought," 1; "Wolf Whistle Jury Panel Will Be Selected Today," *Memphis Press-Scimitar*, September 12, 1955, 13.

57. J. J. Breland to Westbrook Pegler, September 15, 1955, Huie Papers, box 85, fd. 347.

58. "Till's Mother Unsure on Attending Trial," *Jackson Clarion-Ledger*, September 14, 1955, 1; "Asks FBI Guard Mother of Slain Boy," *New York Post*, September 13, 1955, 8.

59. "Mother of Negro Boy Advised to Stay in Chicago," *Delta Democrat-Times* (Greenville, Miss.), September 12, 1955, 1; "Till's Mother Is Being Urged Not to Testify," *Jackson Daily News*, September 12, 1955, 1.

60. "Lynch Victim's Mom Asked to Avoid Miss. Trial," *Jet* 8, no. 20 (September 22, 1955): 4.

61. Mamie Bradley, "I Want You to Know What They Did to My Boy," speech delivered October 29, 1955, Baltimore, *Washington Afro-American*, November 5, 1955, 20, and *Baltimore Afro-American*, November 12, 1955, 6, reprinted in Davis W. Houck and David E. Dixon, eds.,

Rhetoric, Religion, and the Civil Rights Movement, 1954–1965 (Waco, Tex.: Baylor University Press, 2006), 140–41 (hereafter, references to this speech will cite Houck and Dixon only).

62. Mamie Till-Mobley, author telephone interview, December 3, 1996; Till-Mobley and Benson, *Death of Innocence*, 149.

63. "Mother of Till Finally Agrees to Testify," *Delta Democrat-Times* (Greenville, Miss.), September 13, 1955, 1; "Mother of Till Will Attend Trial as State Witness," *Jackson Daily News*, September 13, 1955, 3; "Mother to Testify in Kidnap Trial," *Memphis Press-Scimitar*, September 13, 1955, 1; "Mother of Till to Testify in Murder Trial," *Greenwood (Miss.) Morning Star*, September 13, 1955, 1.

64. "Till's Mother to Testify, She Says; To Come Quietly," *Delta Democrat-Times* (Greenville, Miss.), September 16, 1955, 1; "Till's Mother, 'Wary of Foes,' Keeping Her Route to Trial Secret," *Jackson Daily News*, September 16, 1955, 1; "Mother of Till Has a Secret," 3.

65. "Till Youth's Mom to Delay Appearing at Murder Trial," *Delta Democrat-Times* (Greenville, Miss.), September 18, 1955, 1.

66. Marty Richardson, "Mother of Lynched Boy Here to Open 1955 NAACP Drive," *Cleveland Call and Post*, September 17, 1955, A1.

67. "Delta Veniremen Called; Mother to Attend Trial," *Jackson Clarion-Ledger*, September 16, 1955, 1. For the complete list, see "State v. Roy Bryant and J. W. Milam List of Special Venire," Huie Papers, box 85, fd. 347.

68. "Threats Are Voiced as Trial Date Nears," *Memphis Commercial Appeal*, September 11, 1955, 13.

69. Street, "Emmett Till Case," 10; David T. Beito and Linda Royster Beito, *Black Maverick: T. R. M. Howard's Fight for Civil Rights and Economic Power* (Urbana: University of Illinois Press, 2009), 120.

70. "Defendants Refuse to Pose Before TV," *Jackson State Times*, September 19, 1955; Paul Holmes, "A Way of Life Going on Trial in Till Case," *Chicago Tribune*, September 18, 1955, 6.

71. Wakefield, author telephone interview; Dan Wakefield, email to author, June 20, 2009.

72. John Herbers, "Sleepy Sumner Surprised by Way World Watching Pending Till Trial Today," *Delta Democrat-Times* (Greenville, Miss.), September 18, 1955, 1; "Defense Predicts State Cannot Prove Murder," *Greenwood (Miss.) Morning Star*, September 18, 1955, 1.

73. John Herbers, author telephone interview, December 15, 2006. Herbers's story is also told in Paul Hendrickson, *Sons of Mississippi* (New York: Knopf, 2003), 319. In his interview with me, Herbers said he had forgotten the name of the *Morning Star* publisher, and he does not mention it in Hendrickson either. However, Houck and Grindy point out that the man in question was Virgil Adams, who at the time of the Till trial was still with that paper. In an article published in the *Morning Star* four days after the trial concluded (discussed later), Adams accused Emmett Till of attempted rape. See Houck and Grindy, *Emmett Till and the Mississippi Press*, 181; Virgil Adams, "A New Wrinkle in the Vilification of Mississippi," *Greenwood (Miss.) Morning Star*, September 27, 1955, 6.

74. Betty Pearson, author interview, Sumner, Miss., February 6, 2006.

75. Pearson, author interview.

76. Street, "Emmett Till Case," 10.

77. Holmes, "Way of Life Going on Trial," 6; "Defendants Refuse to Pose," 8A.

78. Sam Johnson, "Jury Selection Starts Climax on Noted Case," *Jackson Daily News*, September 18, 1955, 4. This may have been county attorney and prosecution member Hamilton Caldwell, who admitted several years later that he had harbored similar concerns.

79. Ray Brennan, "2 on Trial in Till Slaying; Defense Questions Body Identity," *Chicago Sun-Times*, September 18, 1955, 3.

80. Murray Kempton, "Preacher, Preacher," *New York Post*, September 19, 1955, 3; Paul Holmes, "Uncle Tells How 3 Kidnapers Invaded Home and Seized Till," *Chicago Tribune*, September 19, 1955, part 1, 2.

81. Arthur Everett, "Till Nearly Missed His Fatal Journey to Land of Cotton," *Jackson Clarion-Ledger*, September 19, 1955, 1, 12; Holmes, "Uncle Tells How 3 Kidnapers," 2; Kempton, "Preacher, Preacher," 3, 30; John N. Popham, "Slain Boy's Uncle Ready to Testify," *New York Times*, September 19, 1955, 50; "Slain Boy's Uncle Recalls Fatal Night," *Chicago American*, September 19, 1955, 4; Ray Brennan, "Till's Uncle Sticks to Guns, Says He'll Relate Kidnaping," *Chicago Sun-Times*, September 19, 1955, 3.

82. Everett, "Till Nearly Missed His Fatal Journey," 1, 12; Holmes, "Uncle Tells How 3 Kidnapers," 2; Kempton, "Preacher, Preacher," 3, 30. Simeon Wright, Mose Wright's son, said that he and his brothers slept at home each night after the kidnapping (Wheeler Parker Jr., Crosby Smith Jr., and Simeon Wright, author interview, February 7, 2007, Argo, Ill., comments by Wright). However, because his father's story is contemporary to the event, and Simeon's memory is over fifty years old, I accept Mose Wright's account as the most accurate. In a later interview, Mose Wright said that his sons stayed with his brother, Will Wright (Moses Wright, "I Saw Them Take Emmett Till," *Front Page Detective*, February 1956, 29).

83. Brennan, "Till's Uncle Sticks to Guns," 3; Holmes, "Uncle Tells How 3 Kidnapers," 2; Everett, "Till Nearly Missed His Fatal Journey," 12.

84. Holmes, "Uncle Tells How 3 Kidnapers," 2; Everett, "Till Nearly Missed His Fatal Journey," 12; Kempton, "Preacher, Preacher," 30.

85. Brennan, "Till's Uncle Sticks to Guns," 3. Sidney Carlton had told reporter Paul Holmes a day earlier that he had evidence that Till had "made an indecent proposal" to Carolyn Bryant, which still went beyond the wolf whistle, but this may have been in line with early reports that Till had made "ugly remarks" to Bryant. If Carlton said anything to Holmes about Till attempting to "maul" Bryant, as Brennan relates, Holmes did not report it. See Holmes, "Way of Life Going on Trial," 6.

86. Everett, "Till Nearly Missed His Fatal Journey," 12.

87. Jay Milner, "Negro's Funeral at Sumner Takes Spotlight from Trial," *Jackson Clarion-Ledger*, September 19, 1955, 1; James L. Hicks, "Lynch Trial Begins; Mother Arrives with Her Pastor," *Baltimore Afro-American*, September 24, 1955, 2.

88. Christopher Metress, ed., *The Lynching of Emmett Till: A Documentary Narrative* (Charlottesville: University of Virginia Press, 2002), 156–57. Hicks's investigative articles ran in the *Baltimore Afro-American*, the *Cleveland Call and Post*, and the *Atlanta Daily World*. Metress uses the *Call and Post* articles as his basis, and includes omitted portions that appear in the other two publications in brackets. All three were prominent black newspapers. For convenience, I cite Metress's synthesis rather than the original sources. For Metress's explanation of his editorial method, see Metress, *Lynching of Emmett Till*, 154; Hicks, "Lynch Trial Begins," 2.

89. Metress, *Lynching of Emmett Till*, 156.

90. Metress, *Lynching of Emmett Till*, 159–61.

91. Clark Porteous, "Officers Work All Night on Searches," *Memphis Press-Scimitar*, September 21, 1955, 1, 7; T. R. M. Howard, "Terror Reigns in Mississippi," speech delivered October 2, 1955, Baltimore, *Washington Afro-American*, October 1, 1955, 19, and *Baltimore Afro-American*, October 8, 1955, 6, reprinted in Houck and Dixon, *Rhetoric, Religion, and the Civil Rights Movement*, 125–27; Beito and Beito, *Black Maverick*, 120–21.

92. Metress, *Lynching of Emmett Till*, 162.

93. "Bryant's Store in Money Robbed Sat. Night; Boys Fired Guns," *Greenwood (Miss.) Morning Star*, September 20, 1955, 1; "Recover Merchandise Believed Stolen from Bryant Store at Money," *Greenwood (Miss.) Morning Star*, September 22, 1955, 1. The latter story says the robbery occurred on Sunday, not Saturday.

94. "1500 Hear Till's Kin Speak at Rally," *Chicago Defender*, September 24, 1955, 3.

95. Marty Richardson, "Clevelanders Rally Behind Mother of Lynching Victim," *Cleveland Call and Post*, September 24, 1955, 1A, 5A.

Chapter 5

1. Clark Porteous, "Jury Being Chosen in Till Trial," *Memphis Press-Scimitar*, September 19, 1955, 4; Arthur Everett, "Till Nearly Missed His Fatal Journey to the Land of Cotton," *Jackson Clarion-Ledger*, September 19, 1955, 12. In 1979, J. W. Kellum said that the courthouse was built in 1903 and burned in 1909. See J. W. Kellum and Amzie Moore, interview, conducted by Blackside, Inc., August 29, 1979, for *Eyes on the Prize: America's Civil Rights Years (1954–1965)*, Henry Hampton Collection, Washington University, St. Louis, http://digital.wustl.edu/eyesontheprize/.

2. William Street, "Emmett Till Case Suddenly Thrusts Little Sumner into Limelight," *Memphis Commercial Appeal*, September 18, 1955, 10.

3. James Featherston, "Delta Courtroom Is Packed as Murder Trial Opens; Evidence 'Circumstantial,'" *Jackson Daily News*, September 19, 1955, 14.

4. Featherston, "Delta Courtroom Is Packed," 14; Street, "Emmett Till Case Suddenly Thrusts Little Sumner," 10. According to Clark Porteous, Sumner adopted its town slogan after a restaurant owner there complained about lackluster business but noted, "it's a good place to raise a boy" (Clark Porteous, "Proud, with Reason at Sumner," *Memphis Press-Scimitar*, September 21, 1955, 2).

5. Harry Marsh, "Hundred Newsmen Jam Scene of Till Trial," *Delta Democrat-Times* (Greenville, Miss.), September 19, 1955, 1; Harry Marsh, "Communist Writer at Trial Lauds Citizens," *Delta Democrat-Times* (Greenville, Miss.), September 23, 1955, 1; B. J. Skelton, "Testimony at Bryant-Milam Trial Has Left Many Questions Unanswered," *Clarksdale (Miss.) Press Register*, September 23, 1955, 7.

6. Jay Milner, "Bryant Didn't Mind His Negro Non-Com during Korean War," *Jackson Clarion-Ledger*, September 20, 1955, 12.

7. L. Alex Wilson, "Picking of Jury Delays Opening," *Tri-State Defender* (Memphis, Tenn.), September 24, 1955, 1. Davis Houck and Matthew Grindy say that, initially, Strider was not even going to allow the black press inside the courtroom, but after arguing the issue with Judge

Swango, he relented (Davis W. Houck and Matthew A. Grindy, *Emmett Till and the Missis-sippi Press* [Jackson: University Press of Mississippi, 2008], 73). They do not cite a source for this claim, but it was also made by David Halberstam in 1993. Halberstam cites a statement purportedly made by John Popham of the *New York Times*: "'There ain't going to be any nig-ger reporters in my courtroom,' he [Strider] told Popham in their first struggle over media privileges. 'Talk to Judge Swango,' Popham answered. Strider did and only reluctantly allowed the blacks to be seated" (David Halberstam, *The Fifties* [New York: Villard Books, 1993], 439). Halberstam does not identify the source for his anecdote, but in surrounding notes he cites interviews he conducted with other journalists who attended the trial, such as Jay Milner, Mur-ray Kempton, and Bill Minor. It is possible that the comments purportedly made by Popham come from late reminiscences of one of these reporters. In Popham's coverage of the trial, he notes that the white and black journalists were segregated but says nothing about an attempt by Strider to keep black reporters from attending the trial (John N. Popham, "Trial Under Way in Youth's Killing," *New York Times*, September 20, 1955, 32). It is clear that the black press table had already been set up before the Monday morning briefing. James Hicks arrived in Sumner the Friday before the trial and reported that Strider had already ruled that black reporters would be sitting in a segregated area of the courtroom (James L. Hicks, "Reporters Segregated," *Baltimore Afro-American*, September 24, 1955, 1). Strider would have no more to say about the subject before Monday because he went to Atlanta on the weekend to attend a football game. See Sam Johnson, "Jury Selection Starts Climax on Noted Case," *Jackson Daily News*, September 18, 1955, 4.

8. Paul Holmes, "A Way of Life Going on Trial in Till Case," *Chicago Tribune*, September 18, 1955, 6; Murray Kempton, "Heart of Darkness," *New York Post*, September 21, 1955, 50; Gene Roberts and Hank Klibanoff, *The Race Beat: The Press, the Civil Rights Struggle, and the Awak-ening of a Nation* (New York: Knopf, 2006), 96–97.

9. James L. Kilgallen, "Spectators in Dixie Court Searched for Weapons," *Chicago Ameri-can*, September 19, 1955, 1; John Herbers, "Till Trial Bogs Down in Jury-Picking Job," *Delta Democrat-Times* (Greenville, Miss.), September 19, 1955, 1; Milner, "Bryant Didn't Mind," 12; Rob F. Hall, "Kidnapers' Friends Fill Panel as Trial Opens in Mississippi in Child's Murder," *Daily Worker* (New York), September 20, 1955, 1; Paul Holmes, "2 Go on Trial in South for Till Murder," *Chicago Daily Tribune*, September 20, 1955, 2. For more on the Capitol shootings, see Clayton Knowles, "Five Congressmen Shot in House by 3 Puerto Rican Nationalists," *New York Times*, March 2, 1954, 1; Irene Vilar, *A Message from God in the Atomic Age* (New York: Pantheon, 1996). The shooters were later tried and convicted in federal court but pardoned by President Jimmy Carter in 1978 and 1979.

10. "Newsmen and Photographers Are Frisked for Weapons," *Memphis Commercial Appeal*, September 20, 1955, 17.

11. Popham, "Trial Under Way," 32; "Newsman and Photographers Are Frisked," 17.

12. Milner, "Bryant Didn't Mind," 12; Clark Porteous, "Big Names in Nation's Press Are at Trial," *Memphis Press-Scimitar*, September 20, 1955, 1, 2; "8-Man Team Covers Till Case Trial," *Chicago Defender*, September 24, 1955, 5; "Here's Cast for Sumner, Miss. Trial," *Tri-State Defender* (Memphis, Tenn.), September 24, 1955, 1, 2; Roberts and Klibanoff, *Race Beat*, 90–94; David T. Beito and Linda Royster Beito, *Black Maverick: T. R. M. Howard's Fight for Civil Rights and Economic Power* (Urbana: University of Illinois Press, 2009), 121; Gene Herrick, author

telephone interview, January 27, 2012. For an analysis of how the Communist paper handled the case, including the trial, see Matthew A. Grindy, "Mississippi Terror, Red Pressure: The *Daily Worker*'s Coverage of the Emmett Till Murder," *Controversia: An International Journal of Debate and Democratic Renewal* 6, no. 1 (2008): 39–66.

13. Roberts and Klibanoff, *Race Beat*, 90–94; Beito and Beito, *Black Maverick*, 121; Milner, "Bryant Didn't Mind," 12; Ralph Hutto, "Dynamic Personalities Form Till Trial Cast," *Jackson State Times*, September 20, 1955, 2A; "70 Newsmen Cover Trial in Sumner," *Clarksdale (Miss.) Press Register*, September 20, 1955, 1; "Newsmen and Photographers Are Frisked," 17; "Daily Worker's Reporter at Trial Is Mississippian," *Jackson Daily News*, September 20, 1955, 6; Marsh, "Communist Writer at Trial," 1; W. C. Shoemaker, "Reporter for Commies Relates How He Shifted to 'Left'—Says Trial 'Fair,'" *Jackson Daily News*, September 21, 1955, 14.

14. Halberstam, *The Fifties*, 436–37.

15. See, for example, Warren Breed, "Comparative Newspaper Handling of the Emmett Till Case," *Journalism Quarterly* 35 (Summer 1958): 291–98; Charles Ealy, "The Emmett Till Case: A Comparative Analysis of Newspaper Coverage" (Master's thesis, University of Texas at Dallas, 1996); John R. Tisdale, "Different Assignments, Different Perspectives: How Reporters Reconstruct the Emmett Till Civil Rights Murder Trial," *Oral History Review* 29, no. 1 (Winter/Spring 2002): 39–58; Craig Flourney, "Reporting the Movement in Black and White: The Emmett Till Lynching and the Montgomery Bus Boycott" (PhD diss., Louisiana State University, 2003); Michael Olby, *Black Press Coverage of the Emmett Till Lynching* (Koln, Germany: Lambert Academic Publishing, 2007); Margaret Spratt et al., "News, Race, and the Status Quo: The Case of Emmett Till," *Howard Journal of Communications* 18, no. 2 (2007): 169–92; Houck and Grindy, *Emmett Till and the Mississippi Press*; Yolanda Denise Campbell, "Outsiders Within: A Framing Analysis of Eight Black and White U.S. Newspapers' Coverage of the Civil Rights Movement, 1954–1964" (PhD diss., University of Southern Mississippi, 2011); Rebecca Miller Davis, "Reporting Race and Resistance in Dixie: The White Mississippi Press and Civil Rights, 1944–1964" (PhD diss., University of South Carolina, 2011); Darryl C. Mace, *In Remembrance of Emmett Till: Regional Stories and Media Responses to the Black Freedom Struggle* (Lexington: University Press of Kentucky, 2014).

16. Featherston, "Delta Courtroom Is Packed," 14; Hutto, "Dynamic Personalities," 2A.

17. B. J. Skelton and Sam Johnson, "Prosecution Says Case Depends on Circumstantial Evidence," *Clarksdale (Miss.) Press Register*, September 19, 1955, 1; William Sorrels, "10 Jurymen Are Selected for Trial of 2 White Men in Slaying of Negro Youth," *Memphis Commercial Appeal*, September 20, 1955, 15.

18. In her 2003 memoir, Mamie Till-Mobley said that she was at the trial on its opening day. Because nearly fifty years had elapsed between the trial and her book, either she forgot just when she went to Sumner or her coauthor, Christopher Benson, who finished the book after Mamie's death, erroneously assumed that she was there. See Mamie Till-Mobley and Christopher Benson, *Death of Innocence: The Story of the Hate Crime That Changed America* (New York: Random House, 2003), 158–60.

19. "Judge in Mississippi Case Has Long Service Record," *Memphis Commercial Appeal*, September 18, 1955, 10; Ellen Whitten, "Justice Unearthed: Revisiting the Murder of Emmett Till" (Honor's thesis, Rhodes College, 2005), 20, http://www.rhodes.edu/images/content/Academics/Ellen_Whitten.pdf.

20. Milner, "Bryant Didn't Mind," 12; W. C. Shoemaker, author interview, August 21, 2009, Kosciusko, Miss.

21. Herbers, "Till Trial Bogs Down," 2; Featherston, "Delta Courtroom Is Packed" 1, 14; Art Everett, "10 Tentative Jurors Chosen in Till Trial; Will Not Ask Death," *Jackson Clarion-Ledger*, September 20, 1955, 12; Popham, "Trial Under Way," 32–33; "Judge Limits Sketching of Murder Trial," *Jackson State Times*, September 20, 1955, 2A; Harry Marsh, "Unanswered Questions Nag Newsmen at Trial," *Delta Democrat-Times* (Greenville, Miss.), September 20, 1955, 2.

22. Featherston, "Delta Courtroom Is Packed," 14.

23. Sam Johnson, "State Will Not Ask Death Penalty in Trial of White Men at Sumner," *Greenwood (Miss.) Commonwealth*, September 19, 1955, 1; Holmes, "2 Go on Trial," 2.

24. Marsh, "Unanswered Questions," 2.

25. James Kilgallen, "Expect Trial to Be Short, Tense," *Tri-State Defender* (Memphis, Tenn.), September 24, 1955, 2.

26. Sorrels, "10 Jurymen Are Selected," 1.

27. Herbers, "Till Trial Bogs Down," 1.

28. Featherston, "Delta Courtroom Is Packed," 1.

29. Skelton and Johnson, "Prosecution Says Case," 1; Popham, "Trial Under Way," 32; Porteous, "Jury Being Chosen," 1, 4; James L. Kilgallen, "Jury to Go Out as State Rests Case," *Chicago American*, September 23, 1955, 1.

30. Ralph Hutto, "Sheriff Won't Call Guard to Preserve Order," *Jackson State Times*, September 21, 1955, 8A; Clark Porteous, "New Angle in Till Case Claimed," *Memphis Press-Scimitar*, September 20, 1955, 5.

31. "'Money Jars' for Defense Delay Trial," *Jackson State Times*, September 20, 1955, 2A; Hutto, "Sheriff Won't Call Guard," 8A; Herbers, "Till Trial Bogs Down," 1.

32. Rob Hall, "Sumner, a Good Place to Raise a Boy," *Daily Worker* (New York), September 21, 1955, 8.

33. Porteous, "New Angle in Till Case," 5.

34. "'Money Jars' for Defense," 2A.

35. Everett, "10 Tentative Jurors Chosen," 1, 12; Milner, "Bryant Didn't Mind," 1, 12; Featherston, "Delta Courtroom Is Packed," 14; Murray Kempton, "The Baby Sitter," *New York Post*, September 20, 1955, 5; John Herbers, "Testimony Opens Today in Till 'Wolf-Whistle' Murder Trial," *Delta Democrat-Times* (Greenville, Miss.), September 20, 1955, 2.

36. Featherston, "Delta Courtroom Is Packed," 1.

37. Ralph Hutto, "Defense Sees Longer Trial Than Expected," *Jackson State Times*, September 19, 1955, 1.

38. Milner, "Bryant Didn't Mind," 12; "Milam Is Pictured a War Hero Who Also Snatched Negro from Drowning," *Jackson Daily News*, September 20, 1955, 6; James Gunter, "Wives Serious, Children Romp as Trial Begins," *Memphis Commercial Appeal*, September 20, 1955, 14.

39. Gunter, "Wives Serious, Children Romp," 14.

40. For a good discussion, see John Arthur, *Race, Equality, and the Burdens of History* (New York: Cambridge University Press, 2007), 8–51.

41. "Newsmen and Photographers Are Frisked," 17.

42. "Sidelights of Till Trial," *Tri-State Defender* (Memphis, Tenn.), October 1, 1955, 5; see also Till-Mobley and Benson, *Death of Innocence*, 162.

43. Skelton and Johnson, "Prosecution Says Case," 1; Sorrels, "10 Jurymen Are Selected," 1, 15; Rob Hall, "Lynched Boy's Mother Sees Jurymen Picked," *Daily Worker* (New York), September 21, 1955, 8; Porteous, "New Angle in Till Case," 5.

44. Hugh Stephen Whitaker, "A Case Study in Southern Justice: The Emmett Till Case" (Master's thesis, Florida State University, 1963), 142–44, reprinted as Hugh Stephen Whitaker, "A Case Study in Southern Justice: The Murder and Trial of Emmett Till," *Rhetoric & Public Affairs* 8, no. 2 (Summer 2005): 205–6; Hugh Stephen Whitaker, email to author, June 22, 2005; Sorrels, "10 Jurymen Are Selected," 1, 15; Arthur Everett, "Hint New Witnesses May Shed More Light on Killing," *Jackson Clarion-Ledger*, September 21, 1955, 5.

45. Sorrels, "10 Jurymen Are Selected," 1; Marsh, "Unanswered Questions," 2; "Ten Accepted on Till Jury," *Jackson State Times*, September 20, 1955, 8A.

46. Holmes, "2 Go on Trial," 1.

47. Holmes, "2 Go on Trial," 1; Skelton, "Testimony at Bryant-Milam Trial," 7; Kempton, "Baby Sitter," 32.

48. Henry Lee Moon to Mrs. Ruby Hurley, September 19, 1955, Papers of the NAACP, Part 18: Special Projects, 1940–1955, Series C: General Office Files, microfilm reel 15 (Bethesda, Md.: University Publications of America, 1995). According to reporter Steve Duncan, "some individual or organization capitalizing on the Till tragedy, used the name of the NAACP to raise funds for personal gain" (Steve Duncan, "NAACP Disavows Support of Till Fund Raising," *St. Louis Argus*, September 23, 1955, 1).

49. Porteous, "Jury Being Chosen," 4. This article may have been the source for later accounts that incorrectly report Bradley's arrival date. See Till-Mobley and Benson, *Death of Innocence*, 152; Houck and Grindy, *Emmett Till and the Mississippi Press*, 76.

50. "Mother of Till Due Here Today on Way to Trial," *Memphis Commercial Appeal*, September 20, 1955, 15.

51. "Mother of Till Due Here," 15.

52. Everett, "10 Tentative Jurors Chosen," 12; "Mother of Till Boy Goes to Mississippi for Trial," *Chicago American*, September 20, 1955, 4.

53. Dan Wakefield, author telephone interview, November 20, 2006.

54. Christopher Metress, ed., *The Lynching of Emmett Till: A Documentary Narrative* (Charlottesville: University of Virginia Press, 2002), 162–64; Beito and Beito, *Black Maverick*, 122.

55. Metress, *Lynching of Emmett Till*, 164; Simeon Booker, "A Negro Reporter at the Till Trial," *Neiman Reports*, January 1956, 14; Beito and Beito, *Black Maverick*, 122.

56. Metress, *Lynching of Emmett Till*, 164; Booker, "Negro Reporter at the Till Trial" 14; Beito and Beito, *Black Maverick*, 122; Roberts and Klibanoff, *Race Beat*, 93.

57. Metress, *Lynching of Emmett Till*, 166; Booker, "Negro Reporter at the Till Trial," 14; Beito and Beito, *Black Maverick*, 123; L. Alex Wilson and Moses Newson, "Story of the Search for New Witnesses," *Chicago Defender*, September 24, 1955, 1, 2; Shoemaker, author interview.

58. Metress, *Lynching of Emmett Till*, 163.

59. Harry Marsh, "Anonymous Telephone Calls Kept Sheriff Strider Awake at Night," *Delta Democrat-Times* (Greenville, Miss.), September 20, 1955, 1; Whitaker, "Case Study in Southern Justice," 137, reprint, 203.

60. John Spence, "Till's Mother Pauses in Memphis on Way to Trial," *Memphis Press-Scimitar*, September 20, 1955, 15; "Huff Tells Why He Didn't Attend Trial," *Chicago Defender*,

September 24, 1955, 2. Bradley said years later that Huff stayed home due to a foot ailment. See Till-Mobley and Benson, *Death of Innocence*, 151.

61. "Mother of Till Boy Arrives in Courtroom," *Chicago American*, September 20, 1955, 4.

62. William Sorrels, "New Trial Evidence Disclosed by State in a Dramatic Turn," *Memphis Commercial Appeal*, September 21, 1955, 1; Spence, "Till's Mother Pauses," 15. For more on the Cotton Makers' Jubilee, see Dr. R. Q. and Ethyl H. Venson Cotton Makers' Jubilee Collection, Memphis and Shelby County Room, Memphis Public Library and Information Center, Memphis, Tenn., http://memphislibrary.contentdm.oclc.org/cdm/ref/collection/p13039coll1/id/39.

In her 2003 memoir, Till-Mobley mistakenly says she flew in to Memphis on Friday, September 16. She does recall going to the home of a Memphis dentist upon her arrival, but does not mention his name. She also says, erroneously, that she went on to Clarksdale, Mississippi, the following day, September 17. She apparently forgot that she had been a speaker at a Cleveland rally on Sunday, September 18, and also fails to mention that she sent Chatham the telegram (quoted above) while still in Chicago on Monday, September 19 (Till-Mobley and Benson, *Death of Innocence*, 152).

63. Spence, "Till's Mother Pauses," 15.

64. B. J. Skelton and Sam Johnson, "Court Completes Jury for Bryant-Milam Trial," *Clarksdale (Miss.) Press Register*, September 20, 1955, 5; Arthur Everett, "Hint New Witnesses May Shed More Light on Till Killing," *Jackson Clarion-Ledger*, September 21, 1955, 5; James Featherston, "Negro Congressman Eyes Trial—His Role Not Clear," *Jackson Daily News*, September 20, 1955, 1; Herbers, "Testimony Opens Today," 2.

65. James Gunter, "Jokes, Threats Are Blended at Tension-Packed Sumner," *Memphis Commercial Appeal*, September 21, 1955, 8.

66. Herrick, author telephone interview; Hutto, "Sheriff Won't Call Guard," 8A.

67. Herrick, author telephone interview; "Defendant Carried Gun—Witness," *Chicago American*, September 22, 1955, 4; Skelton and Johnson, "Court Completes Jury," 5; Featherstone, "Negro Congressman Eyes Trial," 1, 7; Herbers, "Testimony Opens Today," 2; "Arrival of Victim's Mother Causes Stir," *Jackson State Times*, September 20, 1955, 1; Marsh, "Anonymous Telephone Calls," 1; Hutto, "Sheriff Won't Call Guard," 8A.

68. Herbers, "Testimony Opens Today," 1.

69. Jay Milner, "Sumner Folk Already Plenty Bored with All This Ruckus," *Jackson Clarion-Ledger*, September 21, 1955, 5; "Arrival of Victim's Mother," 1; "Judge's Skilled Handling Draws General Praise," *Jackson State Times*, September 21, 1955, 8A.

70. "Unbelievable!," excerpts of an address delivered to the Richmond, Virginia, branch of the NAACP on Monday, November 7, by James L. Hicks, published in the *Baltimore Afro-American*, November 12, 1955, 2; James L. Hicks, interview, conducted by Blackside, Inc., for *Eyes on the Prize*.

71. Herbers, "Testimony Opens Today," 1.

72. Featherston, "Negro Congressman Eyes Trial," 7; "Arrival of Victim's Mother," 1.

73. Hall, "Lynched Boy's Mother," 8; Hutto, "Sheriff Won't Call Guard," 8A; William Sorrels, "New Trial Evidence Disclosed by State in a Dramatic Turn," *Memphis Commercial Appeal*, September 21, 1955, 1, 8.

74. Paul Holmes, "Hunt Shadow Witnesses in Till Slaying," *Chicago Daily Tribune*, September 21, 1955, 1.

75. Everett, "Hint New Witnesses," 1, 5; Hutto, "Sheriff Won't Call Guard," 8A.

76. Clark Porteous, "Instead of Lunch, Surprises," *Memphis Press-Scimitar*, September 21, 1955, 2; W. C. Shoemaker, "Sumner Citizens Turn Public Relations Experts While Spotlight Beams at Them," *Jackson Daily News*, September 20, 1955, 6.

77. Shoemaker, "Sumner Citizens Turn Public Relations Experts," 6.

78. Dan Wakefield, *Between the Lines: A Reporter's Personal Journey through Public Events* (New York: New American Library, 1966), 161.

79. Harry Marsh, "Judge Swango Is Good Promoter for South," *Delta Democrat-Times* (Greenville, Miss.), September 21, 1955, 1, 2; Hutto, "Sheriff Won't Call Guard," 8A.

80. "Milam Is Pictured a War Hero," 6.

81. Porteous, "New Angle in Till Case," 1, 4; Virgil Adams, "State Granted Recess to Produce New Witnesses in Till Case," *Greenwood (Miss.) Morning Star*, September 21, 1955, 1.

82. Clark Porteous, "Officers Work All Night on Searches," *Memphis Press-Scimitar*, September 21, 1955, 1, 7; Louis E. Lomax, "Leslie Milam Quits Farm Home," *Daily Defender* (Chicago), March 5, 1956, 5.

83. See "Sturdivants and Stepson Held for Trial," *Mississippi Sun* (Sumner, Miss.), August 20, 1942, 1; "Sturdivant Trial Postponed Till March," *Mississippi Sun* (Sumner, Miss.), September 17, 1942, 5; "Sturdivants Now on Trial at Sumner," *Mississippi Sun* (Sumner, Miss.), March 11, 1943, 1; "Sumner Jury Acquits Sturdivants in Alexander Slaying," *Mississippi Sun* (Sumner, Miss.), March 19, 1943, 1.

84. Porteous, "Officers Work All Night," 1, 7.

85. Porteous, "Officers Work All Night," 7; "Sunflower County Sheriff Is Dead," *Greenwood (Miss.) Commonwealth*, September 19, 1955, 1.

86. Everett, "Hint New Witnesses," 1, 5.

87. Till-Mobley and Benson, *Death of Innocence*, 152. Till-Mobley wrote that she arrived in Clarksdale on Saturday, September 17, and that this was when Fulton Ford drove her to Mound Bayou and left her in the care of Dr. Howard. However, this could not have happened before Tuesday, September 20, that being the morning she arrived in Mississippi.

88. Beito and Beito, *Black Maverick*, 120, 123.

89. Myrlie Evers, with William Peters, *For Us, the Living* (New York: Doubleday, 1967), 172; Metress, *Lynching of Emmett Till*, 167; Wilson and Newson, "Story of the Search," 1, 2; "A Journalist's Perspective of the Civil Rights Movement," E. Artz, interview of Moses J. Newson, http://collections.digitalmaryland.org/cdm/compoundobject/collection/saac/id/20059/rec/1; Moses Newson Oral History, interview by Marshland Boone, http://knightpoliticalreporting .syr.edu/wp-content/uploads/2012/05/Moses_Newson_oral_essay.pdf; Myrlie Evers-Williams, author telephone interview, April 23, 2014.

90. Beito and Beito, *Black Maverick*, 123; Wilson and Newson, "Story of the Search," 2.

91. "Rumors Send Newsmen on 'Wild Goose' Chase," *Jackson State Times*, September 21, 1955, 8A.

92. Wakefield, author telephone interview.

93. Porteous, "Officers Work All Night," 7; Ralph Hutto, "NAACP Leader Says Two Witnesses Disappeared," *Jackson State Times*, September 23, 1955, 6A.

94. Clark Porteous, "Mrs. Bryant on Stand," *Memphis Press-Scimitar*, September 22, 1955, 4; Porteous, "Officers Work All Night," 7; Booker, "Negro Reporter at the Till Trial," 14; Metress, *Lynching of Emmett Till*, 168; Beito and Beito, *Black Maverick*, 123–24.

95. Booker, "Negro Reporter at the Till Trial," 14; Metress, *Lynching of Emmett Till*, 169.

96. Booker, "Negro Reporter at the Till Trial," 14–15; Metress, *Lynching of Emmett Till*, 169–70; Porteous, "Officers Work All Night," 1; Wilson and Newson, "Story of the Search," 2; "Whistle Killing May Go to Jury Today," *New York Post*, September 23, 1955, 3; Clark Porteous, "Kidnap Trial Delay Sure," *Memphis Press-Scimitar*, September 23, 1955, 1.

97. Porteous, "Kidnap Trial Delay Sure," 1; Beito and Beito, *Black Maverick*, 125.

98. James Gunter, "Judge Raps Gavel as Witness Provokes Laughter at Trial," *Memphis Commercial Appeal*, September 22, 1955, 33; John Herbers, "Wright Tells of Kidnaping of Till Boy," *Delta Democrat-Times* (Greenville, Miss.), September 21, 1955, 1.

99. Arthur Everett, "Defendants Admit Kidnaping Till Boy but Deny Murder," *Jackson Clarion-Ledger*, September 22, 1955, 18; John Herbers, "Cross-Burning at Sumner Went Almost Unnoticed Yesterday," *Delta Democrat-Times* (Greenville, Miss.), September 22, 1955, 1; Gunter, "Judge Raps Gavel," 33; Porteous, "Instead of Lunch, Surprises," 2; John Herbers, "Uncle Identifies Boy's Abductors," *Jackson State Times*, September 21, 1955, 8A.

100. James Kilgallen, "Uncle Tells Story of Negro's Kidnaping," *Memphis Commercial Appeal*, September 22, 1955, 11; Herbers, "Uncle Identifies Boy's Abductors," 1; Hutto, "Sheriff Won't Call on Guard," 8A; Everett, "Defendants Admit Kidnaping Boy," 18.

101. Federal Bureau of Investigation, Prosecutive Report of Investigation Concerning . . . Emmett Till, Deceased, Appendix A—Trial Transcript, February 9, 2006, 7–23 (hereafter cited as Trial Transcript); John Popham, "Slain Boy's Uncle on Stand at Trial," *New York Times*, September 22, 1955, 64; Everett, "Defendants Admit Kidnaping Till Boy," 18.

102. Trial Transcript, 12. Mose Wright's exact words on the stand have been a source of controversy since 1987, thanks to reporter James Hicks. In his *Eyes on the Prize* interview, recorded in 1985, Hicks said that when Wright stood and pointed out Milam in court, he said, in broken English, "Dar he" (meaning "There he is"). This portrayal of Wright has offended his son, Simeon, who insists that his father would never use such an expression. He believes that Hicks perpetuated this story because "it was more colorful and stereotypical to make him sound like an illiterate country farmer. But that wasn't the case. My father was a preacher and very articulate" (Roberts and Klibanoff, *Race Beat*, 424n40). Most of the newspaper coverage of the trial—even that written by Hicks—report Wright saying "There he is," as does the official trial transcript. None report the words "Dar he," "Thar he," or similar expressions. Hicks appears to have originated this story in the mid-1980s, and since then, a few others have echoed him. Reporter John Herbers said in 2006 that he definitely recalled Wright saying, "Thar he," as does trial spectator Betty Pearson (John Herbers, author telephone interview, December 15, 2006; Betty Pearson, author interview, February 6, 2006, Sumner, Miss.). Because all sources contemporary to the event report Wright saying "There he is," Herbers's and Pearson's memories were likely shaped by Hicks's recollection after *Eyes on the Prize* aired, and is evidence of how malleable memory can be. The *Eyes on the Prize* series, originally televised over thirty years after the Till murder, was the first source to give the case national attention in the years after the trial and, as such, is considered authoritative, which explains why the Hicks recollection has been accepted uncritically. For more of Simeon Wright's criticisms of Hicks, see Simeon Wright, with Herb Boyd, *Simeon's Story: An Eye Witness Account of the Kidnapping of Emmett Till* (Chicago: Lawrence Hill Books, 2010), 130–32.

103. Herbers, author telephone interview; Wakefield, author telephone interview; Pearson, author interview.

104. "How I Escaped from Mississippi," by Rev. Moses Wright (as told to *Jet*), *Jet* 8, no. 23 (October 13, 1955): 7.

105. Ernest C. Withers, author interview, at the Ned R. McWherter Library, University of Memphis, February 8, 2006.

106. Herbers, author telephone interview; Wakefield, author telephone interview; Pearson, author interview.

107. Trial Transcript, 89; Gunter, "Judge Raps Gavel," 33.

108. Trial Transcript, 24–32.

109. Trial Transcript, 41–43.

110. Trial Transcript, 44–45.

111. Trial Transcript, 55–56.

112. Trial Transcript, 56–57. Wright was not able to hear Carlton's questioning at all times. One reporter noticed that when the defense attorney asked Wright if it was "true that the only reason you could be sure that the body taken from the river was that of Emmett Till was that he was smoothfaced didn't have whiskers and that Emmett was missing?," Wright, "in a voice audible only to a few newsmen replied, 'I never made whiskey in my life.'" See James Featherston, "Slain Boy's Uncle Points Finger at Bryant, Milam but Admits Light Was Dim," *Jackson Daily News*, September 21, 1955, 14.

113. Kempton, "He Went All the Way," 5; Dan Wakefield, "Justice in Sumner, Land of the Free," *Nation*, 181, no. 14 (October 1, 1955): 284; Everett, "Defendants Admit Kidnaping," 18; Popham, "Slain Boy's Uncle," 64; James Desmond, "Old Negro Points to White Pair, Says 'That's the Men,'" *New York Daily News*, September 22, 1955, C3.

114. Trial Transcript, 64. Rutha Mae Crawford Jackson, then an eighteen-year-old neighbor, was interviewed for Keith Beauchamp's film, *The Untold Story of Emmett Louis Till*. She said that she was home the night of Till's kidnapping, saw multiple cars going to the Wright home, and even saw the white men go to the front of the house while a black man went around to the back. By Mose Wright's estimate, the Crawford home was at least 100 yards to the east. If it was too dark for Wright to see anyone, or even make out the vehicle in his yard as it drove away, it would have been impossible for Jackson to have seen what she claimed, making her sensational recollections suspect and certainly inaccurate. This discrepancy is also discussed in Terry Wagner, "America's Civil Rights Revolution: Three Documentaries About Emmett Till's Murder in Mississippi (1955)," *Historical Journal of Film, Radio and Television* 30, no. 2 (June 2010): 197. If Crawford is intimating that Milam and Bryant may have visited the Wright home earlier, on Saturday, perhaps while the Wrights and Till were in Greenwood, she does not make that clear. This theory is discussed in a later chapter.

115. Trial Transcript, 53–55.

116. Kempton, "He Went All the Way," 5; Everett, "Defendants Admit Kidnaping," 18; Desmond, "Old Negro Points to White Pair," C3.

117. Trial Transcript, 65–66.

118. Trial Transcript, 68–75.

119. Trial Transcript, 75.

120. Trial Transcript, 75–78.

121. Trial Transcript, 78–79.

122. Trial Transcript, 81–82.

123. Trial Transcript, 82–83.

124. Trial Transcript, 83–87.

125. Katherine Malone-France, email to author, March 1, 2006. Malone-France is the grand-daughter of Strickland. Her mother, Millicent A. Malone, still living in 2006, is Strickland's daughter.

126. Trial Transcript, 88–89.

127. Trial Transcript, 89–90.

128. Trial Transcript, 90–93.

129. Trial Transcript, 93–94.

130. Trial Transcript, 94–95.

131. Trial Transcript, 96–101.

132. Trial Transcript, 101–2. Future state senator David Jordan recalled that Miller was nervous during questioning. "When it was time for cross-examination, the white attorney began drilling Miller and sweat poured profusely from the funeral director's face. It looked as if someone had poured a bucket of water on top of his head" (David L. Jordan, with Robert L. Jenkins, *David L. Jordan: From the Mississippi Cotton Fields to the State Senate, A Memoir* [Jackson: University Press of Mississippi, 2014], 58. See also Mamie Fortune Osborne, "An Interview with David Jordan on Emmett Till," *Southern Quarterly: A Journal of Arts & Letters in the South* 45, no. 4 [Summer 2008]: 140).

133. "Undertaker's Story Heard," *Jackson State Times*, September 21, 1955, 12A; John Herbers, "Uncle Identifies Boy's Abductors," *Jackson State Times*, September 21, 1955, 8A.

134. Paul Holmes, "Jurors Hear of Confession in Till Trial," *Chicago Daily Tribune*, September 22, 1955, 11; William Sorrels, "Uncle of Slain Boy Points Out Milam, Says Body Was Till," *Memphis Commercial Appeal*, September 22, 1955, 10.

135. Trial Transcript, 103–9.

136. Trial Transcript, 110–15.

137. Trial Transcript, 119–35.

138. Trial Transcript, 139.

139. Trial Transcript, 139–40.

140. Trial Transcript, 140–44.

141. Trial Transcript, 144–58.

142. Trial Transcript, 159–62.

143. Trial Transcript, 163–65, 171; Clark Porteous, "Grand Jury to Get Case of Slain Negro Boy Monday," *Memphis Press-Scimitar*, September 1, 1955, 4.

144. Trial Transcript, 165–68, 171, 176. Mose Wright's neighbor, John Crawford, interviewed for Beauchamp's *Untold Story*, made several erroneous statements that went unchallenged in the film. First, he said he was the one who took Mose Wright to the river to identify the body, even though Wright and Cothran testified differently in court. Simeon Wright also says that Crawford drove his father to the river, but he is probably using Crawford's memory as his source (Wright and Boyd, *Simeon's Story*, 63). Crawford also said that Mose Wright told him that Till's "privates had been cut off," something that Cothran, on the stand, and Till's mother later denied. Such stories as Crawford's were also disproved during Till's 2005 autopsy (Federal Bureau of Investigation, Prosecutive Report of Investigation Concerning . . . Emmett Till, February 9, 2006, 99–110). Nowhere in its summary of the autopsy, including its description

of the body, is any evidence of castration mentioned. Dale Killinger, the FBI agent in charge of that investigation, told me that the autopsy conclusively proved that Till had not been castrated (Dale Killinger, author telephone interview, April 29, 2014).

145. Marsh, "Communist Writer at Trial," 1.

146. Holmes, "Jurors Hear of Confession," 1; Popham, "Slain Boy's Uncle on Stand," 64; Joseph C. Nichols, "Marciano, Floored in Second Round, Stops Moore in Ninth to Keep Title," *New York Times*, September 22, 1955, 37; Desmond, "Old Negro Points to Accused Pair," 6.

147. Herbers, "Cross-Burning at Sumner," 1; Virgil Adams, "Resentment Rising against Radicals at Trial," *Greenwood (Miss.) Morning Star*, September 22, 1955, 6; "Sidelights of Till Trial," 5.

148. Jay Milner, "Jittery News Men at Sumner Kept in a Dither by Rumors," *Jackson Clarion-Ledger*, September 22, 1955, 2.

149. Milner, "Sumner Folk Already Bored," 3, 5.

150. Adams, "Resentment Rising," 6.

151. James L. Hicks, "Hicks Arrested in Mississippi," *Baltimore Afro-American*, October 1, 1955, 8; "Dismiss Traffic Charge Against Reporter Covering Sumner Trial," *Clarksdale (Miss.) Press Register*, September 22, 1955, 1.

152. Harry Marsh, "Editors Eye Clock in Awaiting Verdict," *Delta Democrat-Times* (Greenville, Miss.), September 23, 1955, 1.

153. Marsh, "Editors Eye Clock," 1; "Says Reds Lie About Arrest in Sumner," *Jackson State Times*, October 17, 1955, 2A.

154. Wilson F. Minor, author interview, August 24, 2009, Jackson, Miss.

155. See Ronald Singleton, "Dey' Done Took Him, says Old Mose," *London Express*, September 22, 1955, 2. Articles reporting Thursday's and Friday's trial coverage were written by others. See "Murder Trial Jury Hears Wolf Whistle," *London Express*, September 23, 1955, 1, attributed to an "Express Staff Reporter" in New York; James Cooper, "'Wolf Whistle' Men Are Freed," *London Express*, September 24, 1955, 1.

156. "Says Reds Lie," 2A.

157. Kempton, "Heart of Darkness," 5; "The Strange Trial of the Till Killers," *Jet* 8, no. 22 (October 6, 1955): 8.

158. Gunter, "Jokes, Threats Are Blended," 8.

159. William B. Franklin, "Staff Photog Tells Own Story of Trip," *St. Louis Argus*, September 20, 1955, 19; Ernest Withers, *Complete Photo Story of Till Murder Case* (Memphis, Tenn.: Withers Photographers, 1955), 13.

160. Steve Duncan, "Argus Pres. On-the-Scene," *St. Louis Argus*, September 23, 1955, 13.

161. Milner, "Jittery News Men at Sumner," 2.

162. Porteous, "Mrs. Bryant on Stand," 4.

163. Wakefield, *Between the Lines*, 146; Wakefield, author telephone interview; Kempton, "Heart of Darkness," 5.

Chapter 6

1. See Stokes McMillan, *One Night of Madness* (Houston: Oak Harbor Publishing, 2009), for a thoroughly researched, detailed treatment of this tragedy. For a contemporary account, see

"Attala Desperadoes Captured after Killing 3 Negro Children," *Kosciusko (Miss.) Star-Herald*, January 12, 1950, 1, 6.

2. "Attala Desperadoes Captured," 1, 6; "Brilliant Defense Counsel Named for Three Men Accused of Massacre," *Kosciusko (Miss.) Star-Herald*, January 26, 1950, 1, 3; "Preliminary Hearing Set Friday for Men Accused of Mass Killing," *Kosciusko (Miss.) Star-Herald*, February 2, 1950, 1. Windol Whitt died in 1992 at age sixty-seven, Malcolm Whitt died in 1996 at seventy-four, and Leon Turner was fifty-seven when he died in 1968.

3. "Mississippi: Shooter's Chance," *Time* 55, no. 4 (January 23, 1950): 17; "Trial of Revenge Murderers to Be in National Spotlight," *Kosciusko (Miss.) Star-Herald*, March 9, 1950, 1; "Windol Whitt's Trial Opens Today in Attala," *Jackson Clarion-Ledger*, March 15, 1950, 1; Bill Keith, "Windol Whitt's Trial Rusumes [*sic*] Today with Surprise Testimony," *Jackson Clarion-Ledger*, March 16, 1950, 1, 7; "First of Trio Goes on Trial Here for Revenge Massacre of Children," *Kosciusko (Miss.) Star-Herald*, March 16, 1950, 1, 6; Bill Keith, "Windol Whitt Gets Life Term," *Kosciusko (Miss.) Star-Herald*, March 17, 1950, 1, 16; "Attala Court Judge Overrules Mistrial Motion by Defense," *Jackson Clarion-Ledger*, March 21, 1950, 1, 10; Bill Keith, "Turner Guilty, Jurors Disagree on Penalty," *Jackson Clarion-Ledger*, March 22, 1950, 1, 16; "Leon Turner Gets Life Imprisonment without Hope of Pardon," *Kosciusko (Miss.) Star-Herald*, March 22, 1950, 1; Bill Keith, "No Parole for Leon Turner, Thrice Murderer," *Jackson Clarion-Ledger*, March 23, 1950, 1, 16; "Whitt Gets 10 Years for 'Manslaughter,'" *Jackson Clarion-Ledger*, April 4, 1955, 7; McMillan, *One Night of Madness*, 301–64.

4. McMillan, *One Night of Madness*, 286.

5. McMillan, *One Night of Madness*, 360.

6. "White Man Was Hanged 65 Years Ago in Grenada for Murdering Negro," *Columbian-Progress* (Columbia, Miss.), September 29, 1955, 2.

7. James Gunter, "Early Crowd Fills Courtroom, Unrest Mounts at Late Start," *Memphis Commercial Appeal*, September 23, 1955, 1.

8. Gunter, "Early Crowd Fills Courtroom," 1.

9. Gunter, "Early Crowd Fills Courtroom," 1.

10. Clark Porteous, "Mrs. Bryant on Stand," *Memphis Press-Scimitar*, September 22, 1955, 4; Federal Bureau of Investigation, Prosecutive Report of Investigation Concerning . . . Emmett Till, Appendix A–Trial Transcript, 180–83 (hereafter cited as Trial Transcript).

11. Porteous, "Mrs. Bryant on Stand," 3; Dan Wakefield, "Justice in Sumner, Land of the Free," *Nation* 181, no. 14 (October 1, 1955): 284.

12. Mamie Till-Mobley and Christopher Benson, *Death of Innocence: The Story of the Hate Crime That Changed America* (New York: Random House, 2003), 178.

13. Telegram from B. M. Bammett and M. E. Steel to Gerald Chatham, n.d.; J. H. Ashley to Gerald Chatham, September 13, 1955, both in Gerald Chatham Papers, Charles W. Capps Jr. Archives and Museum, Delta State University, Cleveland, Miss. (hereafter cited as Chatham Papers).

14. Trial Transcript, 189.

15. Trial Transcript, 189–90; Porteous, "Mrs. Bryant on Stand," 3.

16. Porteous, "Mrs. Bryant on Stand," 3.

17. Trial Transcript, 190–92.

18. Trial Transcript, 193–94; Porteous, "Mrs. Bryant on Stand," 3. Although Mamie Bradley correctly remembered this questioning as an attempt by defense attorneys to insinuate that she

had been party to her son's death, or perhaps had a hand in faking his death in order to collect life insurance money, decades later she misremembers other defense theories that she says were posed to her while she was on the stand. One was the claim that the NAACP planted a corpse in the river in order to fake the murder. In reality, that was part of the defense's closing arguments to the jury, not to her. She also wrongly remembered that attorneys accused her of sending Emmett, who they believed was still alive, to live with his grandfather in Detroit. Defense attorneys did not make this accusation at all, but alleged sightings of Till had their origins in posttrial rumors publicized in the press. Bradley responded to the rumors at the time. See "'A Cruel Hoax': Till's Mother," *Memphis Press-Scimitar*, September 29, 1955, 4; "Rumors Flying That Till's Alive Somewhere in Detroit," *Jackson Clarion-Ledger*, September 30, 1955, 1; Jack Stapleton, "Query Lingers: Is Till Dead?," *Clarksdale (Miss.) Press Register*, September 30, 1955, 1; "Yarn About Till Being in City Is Denied by Negro," *Delta Democrat-Times* (Greenville, Miss.), September 30, 1955, 1. For Bradley's later, erroneous recollections, see Keith Beauchamp, prod., *The Untold Story of Emmett Louis Till* (Till Freedom Come Productions, 2005); Till-Mobley and Benson, *Death of Innocence*, 179–80.

19. Trial Transcript, 195. Mamie Bradley mentioned Breland's question in her later memoir: "Well, everybody knew where he was about to go with that" question. "The *Defender* was about as bad as the NAACP to those people. He wanted to try to prejudice the jurors against me" (Till-Mobley and Benson, *Death of Innocence*, 180).

20. Trial Transcript, 195–99.

21. Trial Transcript, 204–5.

22. Trial Transcript, 205–8.

23. Trial Transcript, 209.

24. Trial Transcript, 210–12.

25. Till-Mobley and Benson, *Death of Innocence*, 180.

26. Porteous, "Mrs. Bryant Called on Stand," 3.

27. Trial Transcript, 213.

28. Trial Transcript, 214–20.

29. Trial Transcript, 220–22.

30. Trial Transcript, 220–24. Reed's account of his experience at the shed changed substantially as he told it later in life, resulting in many conflicting statements. A crucial part of Reed's court testimony was that he saw J. W. Milam with a gun strapped to his side after Milam exited the shed where Reed heard the beating. He saw Milam get a drink of water from a well and then reenter the shed. Reed never claimed to have been close enough to Milam to talk to him, and was very specific that he saw all of this from a distance, which allowed the defense to challenge Reed's identification. After the trial and Reed had moved to Chicago, he spoke at a few protest rallies and said nothing to contradict his courtroom testimony, although he did provide other minor details that did not come out at the trial in Sumner.

David T. Beito and Linda Royster Beito were the first in decades to contact Reed when they interviewed him in 2001 for their book, *Black Maverick: T. R. M. Howard's Fight for Civil Rights and Economic Power* (Urbana: University of Illinois Press, 2009). This brought Reed back into public view, and other interviews followed, three of which were filmed and featured in Stanley Nelson, prod., *The Murder of Emmett Till* (Firelight Media, 2002); Beauchamp, *Untold Story*; and Michael Radutzky, "The Murder of Emmett Till," *60 Minutes* (CBS, October

24, 2004). In each of these, Reed claimed that Milam actually confronted him after Milam left the shed. Milam asked the young sharecropper if he had heard anything, which was an obvious reference to the beating. Reed, seeing the gun on Milam's side and fearing for his life, denied that he had. When I interviewed Reed in 2007, he told me, as he had Beauchamp, that Mandy Bradley was with him when Milam confronted him and asked them separately if they had heard or seen anything (Willie Reed, author interview, February 6, 2007, Chicago). That Reed never mentioned any conversation with Milam in court (which would have bolstered the prosecution's case) or even in his speaking engagements once he was safely out of Mississippi makes these later recollections extremely suspect. He may have come to conflate this imagined experience with one he did have with Milam at the defense attorney's office the day before he testified in court. The attorneys had Milam and another bald man present to see if Reed could correctly pick out Milam. Milam appeared intimidating and had his legs propped up on a desk. This will be discussed in a later chapter.

To complicate things further, Mamie Till-Mobley said in an otherwise very important filmed interview for *The Chicago Project* in 2001 that Reed was looking through a crack in the shed's wall and witnessed the men inside split open Emmett's head with an ax, something Reed had never claimed before ("Interview with Mamie Till-Mobley," https://sites.google.com/site/mamietillinterview/). When I asked Reed about this in 2007, he assured me that Mamie was incorrect. He had never heard this version of his story before.

31. Trial Transcript, 225–27.

32. Trial Transcript, 227–28.

33. Trial Transcript, 229–33.

34. Trial Transcript, 237–39.

35. Trial Transcript, 239–41.

36. Trial Transcript, 241–42.

37. Trial Transcript, 242–43.

38. Betty Pearson, author interview, February 6, 2006, Sumner, Miss.

39. Porteous, "Mrs. Bryant on Stand," 2.

40. Trial Transcript, 244–46.

41. Trial Transcript, 247–48.

42. One indication of Willie Reed's poor memory when reflecting back on the trial was that he forgot his grandfather had been a witness at the proceedings. In my interview with Reed, he insisted that Add Reed never testified, even after I pointed out that he had (Reed, author interview).

43. Trial Transcript, 248–52.

44. William Sorrels, "Uncle of Slain Boy Points Out Milam, Says Body Was Till," *Memphis Commercial Appeal*, September 22, 1955, 1.

45. Trial Transcript, 253–58.

46. Trial Transcript, 258.

47. Harry Marsh, "Editors Eye Clock in Awaiting Verdict," *Delta Democrat-Times* (Greenville, Miss.), September 23, 1955, 1; John Herbers, author telephone interview, December 15, 2006.

48. Trial Transcript, 258–59.

49. Trial Transcript, 259–60.

50. Trial Transcript, 261–63; Beauchamp, *Untold Story*. Although Mamie told Keith Beauchamp that she did not hear Carolyn Bryant's testimony, her memoir is written as though her report is firsthand. See Till-Mobley and Benson, *Death of Innocence*, 185–86.

51. Trial Transcript, 263–64.

52. Trial Transcript, 263–65.

53. Trial Transcript, 265.

54. Trial Transcript, 266.

55. Trial Transcript, 266–67.

56. Trial Transcript, 267–68.

57. Trial Transcript, 268–73.

58. Trial Transcript, 273–74; Clark Porteous, "Till Murder Case Goes to Jury," *Memphis Press-Scimitar*, September 23, 1955, 2.

59. Trial Transcript, 274–75.

60. Trial Transcript, 275–77; Porteous, "Till Murder Case Goes to Jury," 3.

61. Trial Transcript, 277–79.

62. Trial Transcript, 279–80.

63. W. C. Shoemaker, "Mrs. Bryant Won 2 Top Beauty Honors—Mother Loyally Stays at Trial," *Jackson Daily News*, September 22, 1955, 11.

64. This thesis of justifiable homicide has been persuasively argued by researchers David Houck and Matthew Grindy. The prosecution seemed aware, yet worried that this would thwart their effort for a first-degree murder conviction. In *Emmett Till and the Mississippi Press* (Jackson: University Press of Mississippi, 2008), 96, Houck and Grindy write:

> Perhaps the more important question is[:] Why did the prosecution object to Carolyn Bryant's testimony in the first place? If she was going to testify to a possible sexual assault, wouldn't this work to its advantage? Upon cross-examination, wouldn't the prosecution try to show that the offending person in question was in fact Emmett Till? If so, wouldn't this make liars out of her husband and half-brother [who told Leflore County law officials that they let the boy go after Carolyn said he wasn't the right one]? At this point, wouldn't the prosecution case be even stronger? Had the prosecution made a mistake in not beginning its case at the Bryant's Grocery and Meat Market? If members of the Wright and Crawford families could describe what happened when Emmett entered the store, wouldn't such testimony force Carolyn to take the stand and admit that the offender was Emmett Till? In hindsight it seems that the prosecution was unusually careful in steering clear of what happened on August 24; it stands to reason that they actually feared a justifiable homicide defense—even if they had caught the perpetrators in a big lie.

65. Trial Transcript, 280–82.

66. Trial Transcript, 283–84.

67. James Gunter, "Judge Raps Gavel as Witness Provokes Laughter at Trial," *Memphis Commercial Appeal*, September 22, 1955, 33; Gunter, "Early Crowd Fills Courtroom," 1; Arthur Everett, "Defendants Admit Kidnaping Till Boy but Deny Murder," *Jackson Clarion-Ledger*, September 22, 1955, 18; Arthur Everett, "Trial in Leflore Must Await Action by Grand Jury," *Jackson Clarion-Ledger*, September 24, 1955, 8.

68. Telegram from Westheimers Employment Service to Gerald Chatham, September 22, 1955, Chatham Papers.

69. Trial Transcript, 284–85.

70. Trial Transcript, 285–87.

71. Trial Transcript, 287–89.

72. Trial Transcript, 290.

73. Trial Transcript, 290–91.

74. Trial Transcript, 291–93.

75. Trial Transcript, 293–94.

76. Trial Transcript, 298.

77. Trial Transcript, 298–300.

78. Trial Transcript, 300–301.

79. Trial Transcript, 301–4.

80. Trial Transcript, 304–5.

81. Trial Transcript, 305–6. Years later John Whitten reflected back on Otken's testimony. "He testified [that] the body . . . pulled from the river had been in the river at least two weeks, and this Till boy had been in the river just three or four days. It could have been anybody. That's what made me question, not whether the crime had been committed, but whether they had the right corpse. He was a well-respected doctor" (Ellen Whitten, "Justice Unearthed: Revisiting the Murder of Emmett Till" [Honor's thesis, Rhodes College, 2005], 21, http://www.rhodes.edu/images/content/Academics/Ellen_Whitten.pdf).

82. Trial Transcript, 306–8.

83. Trial Transcript, 309–11. In recent years there has been some question about who actually embalmed Emmett Till. Malone was called to testify about the condition of the body because, as the embalmer, he was familiar with it. When graduate student Hugh Stephen Whitaker conducted research in 1962 for his master's thesis on the case, he interviewed Malone, who described the unique embalming process that he was forced to use because heavy decomposition had made the intravenous process impossible. See Hugh Stephen Whitaker, "A Case Study in Southern Justice: The Emmett Till Case" (Master's thesis, Florida State University, 1963), 118, reprinted as Hugh Stephen Whitaker, "A Case Study in Southern Justice: The Murder and Trial of Emmett Till," *Rhetoric & Public Affairs* 8, no. 2 (Summer 2005): 195.

In a study published in 2003 that touches briefly on the Till case, Paul Hendrickson of the *Washington Post* interviewed a man named Woodrow Jackson who claimed that he was the one who embalmed Till. He also said that he was the attendant who drove to Greenwood to pick up the body from the Century Burial Association and took it to the Tutwiler funeral home where the embalming took place. "Oh, Lord, look what I got here," he said after he first saw the battered corpse. He then worked on it from four o'clock that afternoon until five the following morning, taking "a few drinks" to make the process more bearable. He then put the body into a wooden casket and drove it to Clarksdale, where it was loaded onto a train bound for Chicago (Paul Hendrickson, *Sons of Mississippi* [New York: Knopf, 2003], 310–11). A marker placed in front of the now-abandoned funeral home in Tutwiler also credits Jackson with the embalming. Others, such as filmmaker Keith Beauchamp, also interviewed Jackson, and Jackson held to this story. Jackson may have indeed been the attendant who retrieved the body, and then assisted Malone from there. However, in his closing remarks to the jury, Robert Smith said that Malone was not competent enough to determine just how long the body had been in the river. As paraphrased in a report by the *Chicago Defender*, "Malone is supervising two funeral homes, a colored and white one." "A Negro is during [doing] his job," said Smith, and urged "that Malone should be fired" ("Sidelights of Till Trial," *Tri-State Defender* [Memphis, Tenn.], October 1, 1955, 5). If Smith had gleaned some knowledge about the funeral home, this may mean that Malone simply oversaw the embalming and that perhaps Jackson did the actual physical work. Jackson died in 2007; Malone died fourteen years earlier in 1993, and thus any verification of the specific role of each is now impossible.

84. Trial Transcript, 310–14.

85. Trial Transcript, 315–19.

86. Trial Transcript, 319–21.

87. Trial Transcript, 322–23.

88. L. Alex Wilson, "Reveals Two Key Witnesses Jailed," *Tri-State Defender* (Memphis, Tenn.), October 1, 1955, 2.

89. Wilson, "Reveals Two Key Witnesses," 2.

90. Wilson, "Reveals Two Key Witnesses," 2.

91. Wilson, "Reveals Two Key Witnesses," 2; Murray Kempton, "They Didn't Forget," *New York Post*, September 26, 1955, 22.

92. James Gunter, "Milling Throng in Courtroom Kept Eyes on Juryroom Door," *Memphis Commercial Appeal*, September 24, 1955, 4.

93. Trial Transcript, 325–27.

94. Trial Transcript, 327; Murray Kempton, "2 Face Trial as 'Whistle' Kidnapers—Due to Post Bond and Go Home," *New York Post*, September 25, 1955, 16.

95. Trial Transcript, 327–28.

96. Trial Transcript, 328–29.

97. Trial Transcript, 329–30.

98. Trial Transcript, 330–33.

99. Trial Transcript, 333–36.

100. Trial Transcript, 336–38.

101. Trial Transcript, 340–43.

102. Trial Transcript, 343–46.

103. Trial Transcript, 347–49.

104. Trial Transcript, 350–51.

105. Trial Transcript, 351; John Herbers, "Wolf Whistle Murder Case Goes to Jury in Sumner Circuit Court," *Delta Democrat-Times* (Greenville, Miss.), September 23, 1955, 7.

106. "Called Lynch-Murder, 'Morally, Legally' Wrong," *Cleveland Call and Post*, October 1, 1955, 10C; Jay Milner, "Defendants Turned Back to Face Kidnap Charges by Leflore County Jury," *Jackson Clarion-Ledger*, September 25, 1955, 8; James Featherston and W. C. Shoemaker, "State Demands Conviction; Defense Says No Proof Presented, Asks Acquittal," *Jackson Daily News*, September 23, 1955, 1; W. F. Minor, "Two Not Guilty of Till Murder, Jury Declares," *New Orleans Times-Picayune*, September 24, 1955, 5; Kempton, "2 Face Trial, 16; Herbers, "Wolf Whistle Murder Case Goes to Jury," 1; Christopher Metress, ed., *The Lynching of Emmett Till: A Documentary Narrative* (Charlottesville: University of Virginia Press, 2002), 101–2, 110.

107. Featherston and Shoemaker, "State Demands Conviction," 1; William Sorrels, "Two Mississippians Acquitted in Slaying of Chicago Negro; Jurors Out Only 67 Minutes," *Memphis*

Commercial Appeal, September 24, 1955, 1; Everett, "Trial in Leflore," 8; "Jury Acquits Bryant, Milam of Murder Charge as Trial Ends," *Clarksdale (Miss.) Press Register*, September 23, 1955, 3.

108. Everett, "Trial in Leflore Must Wait Action," 8; Featherston and Shoemaker, "State Demands Conviction," 1; "Called Lynch-Murder," 10C; Metress, *Lynching of Emmett Till*, 104; "Jury Acquits Bryant, Milam," 3.

109. "Called Lynch-Murder," 10C; Minor, "Two Not Guilty" 5; Kempton, "2 Face Trial as 'Whistle' Kidnapers," 16; Metress, *Lynching of Emmett Till*, 102–3, 110. Chatham's son, Gerald Chatham Sr., later recalled memories of his dog, Shep, in interviews he gave over fifty years after his father told this story in court. Chatham says his father exaggerated the story, but that it was the type of anecdote, complete with embellishments, that good attorneys use in court. Shep, a large black and white woolly dog, had been hit by a car on the highway near the Chatham home. Young Gerald learned of the incident, went to the road, carried him home, and buried him. Rather than being dead for some time and decomposing, the pet had actually just died and was easily recognizable. See Gerald Chatham Sr., Oral History Interview (OH293), January 19, 2005, Charles W. Capps Jr. Archives and Museum, Delta State University, Cleveland, Miss.; Gerald Chatham Sr., author interview, February 24, 2012, Hernando, Miss.

110. Shoemaker and Featherston, "State Demands Conviction," 1; Everett, "Trial in Leflore Must Await Action," 8; "Called Lynch-Murder," 10C; Sorrels, "Two Mississippians Acquitted," 2; Metress, *Lynching of Emmett Till*, 102, 109.

111. "Called Lynch-Murder," 10C; Metress, *Lynching of Emmett Till*, 103; "Sidelights of Till Trial," 5.

112. "Called Lynch-Murder," 10C; Metress, *Lynching of Emmett Till*, 104.

113. Gunter, "Milling Throng," 4; "Called Lynch-Murder," 10C; Metress, *Lynching of Emmett Till*, 101–4.

114. Featherston and Shoemaker, "State Demands Conviction," 1, 9.

115. Everett, "Trial in Leflore," 8.

116. Everett, "Trial in Leflore," 8.

117. Everett, "Trial in Leflore," 8; Featherston and Shoemaker, "State Demands Conviction," 1; "Jury Acquits Bryant, Milam," 3; Sorrels, "Two Mississippians Acquitted," 2.

118. Featherston and Shoemaker, "State Demands Conviction," 9.

119. Featherston and Shoemaker, "State Demands Conviction," 9; Kempton, "2 Face Trial," 16; Metress, *Lynching of Emmett Till*, 110.

120. Kempton, "2 Face Trial," 16; Metress, *Lynching of Emmett Till*, 110; "Defense Lawyer Quotes Dickens in Final Plea," *Jackson State Times*, September 23, 1955, 1.

121. Featherston and Shoemaker, "State Demands Conviction," 9.

122. Kempton, "2 Face Trial," 16; Metress, *Lynching of Emmett Till*, 110; Everett, "Trial in Leflore," 8.

123. Kempton, "2 Face Trial," 16; Metress, *Lynching of Emmett Till*, 110–11. Kempton said, in reference to the above quote, that Kellum had taken it from Paul Johnson, three-time candidate for governor in Mississippi (he would finally win in 1963). Johnson himself had apparently created this quote by blending the words of William Cullen Bryant, a nineteenth-century editor of the *New York Evening Post*, and Robert Ingersoll, former Illinois politician and great defender of agnosticism.

124. Milner, "Defendants Turned Back," 1.

125. Milner, "Defendants Turned Back," 1.

126. Kempton, "2 Face Trial," 1, 16; Metress, *Lynching of Emmett Till*, 108; Wakefield, "Justice in Sumner," 285.

127. David Beito statement in Beauchamp, *Untold Story*, rough-cut version in author's possession.

128. Wakefield, "Justice in Sumner," 285; Kempton, "2 Face Trial," 16; Metress, *Lynching of Emmett Till*, 108.

129. Kempton, "2 Face Trial," 16; Metress, *Lynching of Emmett Till*, 111.

130. Milner, "Defendants Turned Back," 8; Sorrels, "Two Mississippians Acquitted," 2.

131. Kempton, "2 Face Trial," 16; Metress, *Lynching of Emmett Till*, 109; Sorrels, "Two Mississippians Acquitted," 2.

132. Trial Transcript, 351; Gunter, "Milling Throng in Courtroom," 1.

133. Clark Porteus, "Next: 2 Face Till Kidnap Charges," *Memphis Press-Scimitar*, September 24, 1955, 3; Kempton, "2 Face Trial," 16.

134. James Hicks, "Big Town," *Baltimore Afro-American*, October 8, 1955, 9.

135. Edward Murrain, "Till's Mom, Mayor Get Bomb Threats," *New York Age Defender*, October 1, 1955, 2; Gunter, "Milling Throng in Courtroom," 1.

136. Mattie Smith Colin, "Till's Mom, Diggs Both Disappointed," *Tri-State Defender* (Memphis, Tenn.), October 1, 1955, 2; Mamie Till-Mobley, author telephone interview, December 3, 1996.

137. Gunter, "Milling Throng in Courtroom," 1; Clark Porteous, "Next: Two Face Till Kidnap Charges," *Memphis Press-Scimitar*, September 24, 1955, 1, 3.

138. Gunter, "Milling Throng in Courtroom," 4; Wakefield, "Justice at Sumner," 285; Herrick, author telephone interview, January 27, 2012.

139. Kempton, "2 Face Trial," 3; Gunter, "Milling Throng in Courtroom," 1; Porteous, "Next: 2 Face Till Kidnap Charges," 3.

140. Sorrels, "Two Mississippians Acquitted," 1. The trial transcript says the deliberation took one hour and eight minutes, as does reporter Clark Porteous (Trial Transcript, 352; Porteous, "Next: 2 Face Till Kidnap Charges," 3). Bill Minor said he timed it at one hour and five minutes (Minor, "Two Not Guilty," 1; Wilson F. Minor, author interview, August 24, 2009, Jackson, Miss.). Most accounts put it at one hour and seven minutes.

141. Porteous, "Next: 2 Face Till Kidnap Charges," 3.

142. Trial Transcript, 352; Porteous, "Next: 2 Face Till Kidnap Charges," 3.

143. Porteous, "Next: 2 Face Till Kidnap Charges," 3; Sorrels, "Two Mississippians Acquitted," 1; Gunter, "Milling Throng in Courtroom," 4; James Kilgallen, "Defendants Receive Handshakes, Kisses," *Memphis Commercial Appeal*, September 24, 1955, 3.

144. Trial Transcript, 352; Sorrels, "Two Mississippians Acquitted," 1; Porteous, "Next: 2 Face Till Kidnap Charges," 3; Kilgallen, "Defendants Receive Handshakes," 3.

145. Porteous, "Next: 2 Face Till Kidnap Charges," 3; Gunter, "Milling Throng in Courtroom," 1.

146. Trial Transcript, 352–53; Gunter, "Milling Throng in Courtroom," 1; Porteous, "Next: 2 Face Kidnap Charges," 3.

147. Porteous, "Next: 2 Face Till Kidnap Charges," 3.

148. Porteous, "Next: 2 Face Till Kidnap Charges," 3; Sorrels, "Two Mississippians Acquitted," 1.

149. Kilgallen, "Defendants Receive Handshakes," 3; Milner, "Defendants Turned Back," 8; Paul Holmes, "Jury Reaches Verdict after Hour Debate," *Chicago Daily Tribune*, September 24, 1955, 2.

150. Porteous, "Next: 2 Two Face Till Kidnap Charges," 3; Sorrels, "Two Mississippians Acquitted," 2; Minor, "Two Not Guilty," 5. Hugh Stephen Whitaker, who interviewed the jurors in 1962, said one of them told him that all three ballots were unanimous for a "not guilty" verdict (Whitaker, "Case Study in Southern Justice," 154, reprint, 210). In 2005, Whitaker noted that "in retrospect, if the ballots had been unanimous, there should not have been three votes." He was later told by a son of one of the jurors "that three of the jurors voted 'guilty' on the first ballot. Two quickly changed their votes, but one held out for a while, until the others wore him down" (Hugh Stephen Whitaker, email to author, June 22, 2005). While this is certainly a possibility, it is also likely that the son simply assumed the jurors who abstained from voting on the first two ballots actually voted "guilty." Unfortunately, we will never know for sure.

151. Charles Gruenberg, "Jury Tells Why It Acquitted—'Shocking,' Says NAACP," *New York Post*, September 25, 1955, 3.

152. Gruenberg, "Jury Tells Why It Acquitted," 3.

153. Gruenberg, "Jury Tells Why It Acquitted," 3.

154. "Trial by Jury," *Time* 66, no. 14 (October 3, 1955): 19.

155. Porteous, "Next: 2 Face Till Kidnap Charges," 3; Minor, "Two Not Guilty," 1, 5.

156. Ralph Hutto, "Now Sumner Is Just Another Sleepy Delta Town," *Jackson State Times*, September 24, 1955, 1.

157. Hutto, "Now Sumner Is Just Another Sleepy Delta Town," 1; Holmes, "Jury Reaches Verdict," 2.

158. "Mamie Bradley Says She Expected Verdict," *Delta Democrat-Times* (Greenville, Miss.), September 25, 1955, 1; Porteous, "Next: 2 Face Till Kidnap Charges," 3.

159. Porteous, "Next: 2 Face Till Kidnap Charges," 3.

160. Gruenberg, "Jury Tells Why It Acquitted," 3.

161. Gruenberg, "Jury Tells Why It Acquitted," 3.

162. "Till Case Still Troubles Mississippi," *Chicago American*, September 26, 1955, 4.

163. Beito and Beito, *Black Maverick*, 129.

164. "Dr. Howard: Situation in Mississippi Extremely Serious," *Pittsburgh Courier*, October 8, 1955, 1, 4.

165. Hugh White to Armis Hawkins, September 14, 1955, James P. Coleman Papers, Accn. Z1877, box 23, fd. 3, Mississippi Department of Archives and History, Archives and Library Division, Special Collections Section, Manuscript Collection, Jackson.

166. Minor, "Two Not Guilty," 5; Bill Minor, *Eyes on Mississippi: A Fifty-Year Chronicle of Change* (Jackson, Miss.: J Prichard Morris Books, 2001), 195.

167. "Dr. Howard: Situation," 1, 4; Beito and Beito, *Black Maverick*, 129.

168. "Till Case Still Troubles Mississippi," 4.

169. R. R. Shurden to J. Edgar Hoover, September 5, 1955; Office memorandum from Mr. Parsons to Mr. Tolson, September 9, 1955; Report of the FBI laboratory to Mr. R. R. Shurden, Chief of Police, Greenwood, Mississippi, September 14, 1955, all in FBI FOIA release to Devery S. Anderson, 2006, re Emmett Till.

170. Jay Milner, "Newsmen Disagree on Protest Rallies," *Jackson Clarion-Ledger*, September 27, 1955, 1.

171. "Situation in Mississippi," 2.

172. Whitaker, "Case Study in Southern Justice," 152, reprint, 209.

173. "Situation in Mississippi," 4; "Cong. Diggs, 'Emmett Till Trial Over, but Negroes Should Never Forget Its Meaning,'" *Pittsburgh Courier*, October 8, 1955, 4.

174. Whitaker, "Case Study in Southern Justice," 147–48, reprint, 207–8.

175. Beito and Beito, *Black Maverick*, 129.

176. C. Sidney Carlton, "Defense Says Till Verdict Was Justice," *Chicago Defender*, October 1, 1955. Carlton was clearly speaking as an attorney vested in the case. He says that "the defendants were only questionably placed at Mose Wright's house," an obvious reference to Wright's testimony, which Carlton tried to rebut, but he ignores the testimonies of Sheriff George Smith and Deputy John Cothran, who both testified to receiving kidnap admissions from Milam and Bryant, and Roy Bryant himself, who admitted to the attorneys after his arrest that he was not only at the Wright home but identified himself by name. Carlton also insists that "the only expert and scientific testimony conclusively showed that the body taken from the river had been dead a minimum of eight to 10 days, while Till was missing only three days before that time." Yet under cross-examination, these witnesses admitted that an overweight body, or one that had been severely beaten, could decompose faster.

177. This insight as to ethics was given to me on July 20, 2011, in an interview with John A. Hays, a defense attorney residing in Longview, Washington.

178. Whitaker, "Case Study in Southern Justice," 147, 155, reprint, 207, 210–11.

179. Tom Brennan, "Emmett Till: More Than a Murder," *Jackson Clarion–Ledger/Jackson Daily News*, August 25, 1985, 2H.

180. Murrain, "Till's Mom, Mayor," 2.

181. Ted Poston, "Mose Wright Left Everything to Flee for Life," *New York Post*, October 3, 1955, 28; Lee Blackwell, "2 Who Fled Mississippi Tell Stories," *Chicago Defender*, October 1, 1955, 2.

182. Porteous, "Next: 2 Face Till Kidnap Charges," 3; Blackwell, "2 Who Fled Mississippi," 2.

183. Porteous, "Next: 2 Face Till Kidnap Charges," 1; Wheeler Parker Jr., Crosby Smith Jr., and Simeon Wright, author interview, February 7, 2007, Argo, Ill., comments by Wright; Paul Burton, "'Old Man Mose' Sells Out, He'll Move to New York," *Jackson Clarion-Ledger*, September 26, 1955, 1; Simeon Wright, with Herb Boyd, *Simeon's Story: An Eyewitness Account of the Kidnapping of Emmett Till* (Chicago: Lawrence Hill Books, 2010), 82; "Moses Wright Turns Down Island Job," *New York Amsterdam News*, October 8, 1955, 23.

184. Wright told this story several times, with some variations, as discussed in the next chapter. The first known account was given during a filmed interview between Wright's arrival in Chicago on Monday, September 26, and Sunday, October 2. The clip is shown in Beauchamp, *Untold Story*.

185. Burton, "Old Man Mose," 1; Poston, "Mose Wright Left Everything," 5.

Chapter 7

1. B. J. Skelton, "Visiting Newsmen Pack Typewriters, Head for Homes," *Clarksdale (Miss.) Press Register*, September 24, 1955, 1; Russell Harris, "4 Worlds of the South Highlighted by

Trial," *Detroit News*, September 24, 1955, 1; John Herbers, "Cross-Burning at Sumner Went Almost Un-Noticed Yesterday," *Delta Democrat-Times* (Greenville, Miss.), September 22, 1955, 1.

2. These descriptions of Boyack come from his son, James Edmund Boyack Jr., email to author, February 8, 2011.

3. Skelton, "Visiting Newsmen Pack," 1.

4. James E. Boyack, "Courier's James Boyack Hangs Head in Shame," *Pittsburgh Courier*, October 1, 1955, 1.

5. "New Rochelle Demos Ask Action on Mississippi," *Daily Worker* (New York), September 27, 1955, 3.

6. Virginia Gardner and Roosevelt Ward Jr., "20,000 in Harlem Flay Till Verdict," *Daily Worker* (New York), September 26, 1955, 8.

7. "3 Harlem Street Rallies Hit Terror in Mississippi," *Daily Worker* (New York), September 26, 1955, 2; "Mass Meet Crowd Bitter, Mad, Sullen," *New York Amsterdam News*, October 1, 1955, 7.

8. "Acquitted Men Stay in Jail," *Jackson State Times*, September 24, 1955, 10A; "Leflore Officials Delay Fixing Bond in Till Case," *Jackson Daily News*, September 25, 1955, 1.

9. Gardner and Ward, "20,000 in Harlem," 1; Ted Poston, "'My Son Didn't Die in Vain,' Till's Mother Tells Rally," *New York Post*, September 26, 1955, 5.

10. Poston, "My Son Didn't Die in Vain," 5.

11. Poston, "My Son Didn't Die in Vain," 5; Mattie Smith Colin, "Till's Mom, Diggs Both Disappointed," *Tri-State Defender* (Memphis, Tenn.), October 1, 1955, 1.

12. Poston, "My Son Didn't Die in Vain," 22; Gardner and Ward, "20,000 in Harlem," 1.

13. Press release by Robert L. Birchman, cochairman, Press and Publicity Committee of the NAACP, titled "NAACP to Stage Mass Protes[t] Meeting on Till Lynching." The document states that "Mrs. Mamie Bradley, mother of the Till youth will speak at the meeting" scheduled for Sunday, September 25, 1955 at 3:30 P.M. at the Metropolitan Community Church in Chicago. For Huff's account of her change of plans, see William Henry Huff to B. T. George, December 2, 1955, Papers of the NAACP: Part 18, Special Projects, 1940–1955, Series C, General Office Files, microfilm reel 15 (Bethesda, Md.: University Publications of America, 1955).

14. Carl Hirsch, "10,000 in Detroit, 10,000 in Chicago Call for U.S. Intervention in Mississippi Terror," *Daily Worker* (New York), September 27, 1955, 3 (separate articles by two different reporters share this same headline).

15. William Allan, "10,000 in Detroit, 10,000 in Chicago Call for U.S. Intervention in Mississippi Terror," *Daily Worker* (New York), September 27, 1955, 3; "Rep. Diggs Blasts Mississippi Trial," *Jackson Clarion-Ledger*, September 26, 1955, 8; "Till Trial Acquittal Protested by Rallies," *Delta Democrat-Times* (Greenville, Miss.), September 26, 1955, 1; "6000 Here Protest Mississippi Verdict," *Detroit Daily News*, September 26, 1955, 8.

16. "6000 Here Protest," 8; Arthur L. Johnson to Gloster B. Current, September 27, 1955, Papers of the NAACP: Part 18, Series C, reel 14.

17. "2500 Protest in Baltimore," *Daily Worker* (New York), September 29, 1955, 1, 3.

18. "NAACP Calls Verdict Rooted in Racist Oppression," *Daily Worker* (New York), September 26, 1955, 8.

19. "Powell Says Till Stirs All Europe," *Chicago Defender*, October 8, 1955.

20. "France Irate Over Till Case," *Jackson Clarion-Ledger*, September 26, 1955, 8; "French Hit Verdict in Till Case," *Chicago Defender*, October 1, 1955, 43.

21. "A Call for Justice," *New York Post*, September 26, 1955, 22; "Rep. Anfuso Asks Brownell Probe Sumner, Miss., Trial," *Daily Worker* (New York), September 27, 1955, 3; "Diggs Gives Far Different Appraisal of Trial at Detroit Than at Sumner," *Jackson Daily News*, September 26, 1955, 9.

22. "'Once Proud of the South' but Renounces Till Verdict," *Memphis Commercial Appeal*, September 26, 1955, 4. Hinant sent a follow-up letter to the *Commercial Appeal* two weeks later in which he apologized for destroying his Confederate flag, and also clarified his views. "I do not believe in social mixing. I do not believe in mixed marriage. I do not believe in mixed education. I do not believe in mixed neighborhoods." However, regarding the Till case, "I still do not believe it was a fair trial." After denying that he was out for publicity, was a Communist sympathizer, or was a member of the NAACP, Hinant affirmed that "I am an American and a Christian. I believe in treating others as I would like to be treated. Every man, regardless of color, has a soul. I would not want to face God on that final day and be sent to hell for mistreating a man because his color was not the same as mine" ("Hinant Explains Till Trial Views," *Memphis Commercial Appeal*, October 9, 1955, 3).

23. Grand Sheikh F. Turner El to His Excellency, the Governor of the State of Mississippi, September 28, 1955, James P. Coleman Papers, Accn. No. 21877, box 23, fd. 3, Mississippi Department of Archives and History, Archives and Library Division, Special Collections Section, Manuscript Collection, Jackson (hereafter cited as Coleman Papers).

24. Telegram of Ardie A. Halyard to Frank P. Zeidler; Frank P. Zeidler to Walter J. Kohler, September 28, 1955, both in Coleman Papers, box 23, fd. 3.

25. "A Southerner" to John Whitten, September 24, 1955, William Bradford Huie Papers, Cms 84, box 38, fd. 353a, Special Collections, Ohio State University Library, Columbus (hereafter cited as Huie Papers).

26. Mrs. Frank E. Moore to John W. Whitten, September 29, 1955, Huie Papers, box 38, fd. 353a.

27. Dana Wier to John Whitten, September 25, 1955, Huie Papers, box 38, fd. 353a.

28. A. B. Nimitz to John Whitten, September 28, 1955, Huie Papers, box 38, fd. 353a.

29. W. W. Malone to J. J. Breland, September 23, 1955, Huie Papers, box 38, fd. 353a.

30. J. J. Breland to W. W. Malone, September 26, 1955, Huie Papers, box 38, fd. 353a.

31. "Reactions Reverberate Around World on Till Trial's Outcome," *Delta Democrat-Times* (Greenville, Miss.), September 27, 1955, 1; "Thousands at Paris Till Protest Meet," *Delta Democrat-Times* (Greenville, Miss.), September 28, 1955, 1.

32. "Till Kidnap Pair May Be Out on Bond Friday," *New York Post*, September 28, 1955, 4; "Hearing Set Friday for Bryant, Milam," *Memphis Commercial Appeal*, September 28, 1955, 2.

33. Harold Foreman, "Reports Till Boy Alive in Detroit Bring 'Hoax' Comment from Mother," *Jackson Daily News*, September 29, 1955, 1.

34. Allan, "10,000 in Detroit, 10,000 in Chicago," 3; "Dixie Verdict Assailed in 24-Hr. Rally," *Detroit News*, September 30, 1955, 14.

35. "Strider Believes Till Is Still Alive," *Greenwood (Miss.) Commonwealth*, September 29, 1955, 1; "Rumors Flying That Till's Alive Somewhere in Detroit," *Jackson Clarion-Ledger*, September 30, 1955, 1.

36. "Bryant, Milam Released Under $10,000 Bond on Kidnap Charges," *Delta Democrat-Times* (Greenville, Miss.), September 30, 1955, 1.

37. "'A Cruel Hoax': Till's Mother," *Memphis Press-Scimitar*, September 29, 1955, 4; Foreman, "Reports Till Boy Alive," 1.

38. Jack Stapleton, "Query Lingers: Is Till Dead?," *Clarksdale (Miss.) Press Register*, September 30, 1955, 1.

39. "Yarn About Till Being in City Is Denied by Negro," *Delta Democrat-Times* (Greenville, Miss.), September 30, 1955, 1.

40. "2 Negro 'Whistling Killing' Witnesses Still Missing and Are Feared Slain," *New York Post*, September 29, 1955, 5; "Fate of 2 Witnesses Remains a Mystery," *Daily Worker* (New York), October 3, 1955, 2.

41. "Till Witness Under Guard," *Memphis Press-Scimitar*, September 29, 1955, 4; "Willie Reed, Till Witness, Starting Life Anew, Chicago," *Delta Democrat-Times* (Greenville, Miss.), September 29, 1955, 2.

42. Bill Spell, "Daily News Readers Offer Help to Send Willie Reed's Girl Friend to Chicago," *Jackson Daily News*, September 29, 1955, 1.

43. "Ella Mae Shuns Willie," *Jackson Daily News*, September 30, 1955, 1; Willie Reed, author interview, February 6, 2007, Chicago.

44. "Reed Boy, Bradley Woman Fled State for 'Safety' but Police Guard Homes," *Jackson Daily News*, September 30, 1955, 1.

45. Reed, author interview.

46. "Reed Boy, Bradley Woman Fled State," 1.

47. "Bryant and Milam Released on $10,000 Bonds for Appearance Before Grand Jury November 7," *Greenwood (Miss.) Commonwealth*, September 30, 1955, 1; Helen Shearon, "Bryant and Milam Freed Under Bond," *Memphis Commercial Appeal*, October 1, 1955, 1.

48. Shearon, "Bryant and Milam Freed," 1; "Till Kidnap Suspects Free on $10,000 Bond," *Jackson State Times*, September 30, 1955, 1A.

49. "Bryant and Milam Released on $10,000 Bonds," 1; William Middlebrooks, "Milam and Bryant Freed on $10,000 Bond at Hearing," *Greenwood (Miss.) Morning Star*, October 1, 1955, 1; "Till Kidnap Suspects Free on $10,000 Bond," 1A; "Bryant, Milam Released Under $10,000 Bond," 1.

50. "Milwaukee Rally Asks Intervention," *Daily Worker* (New York), September 29, 1955, 3; "U.S. Intervention in Till Case Urged in Many Cities," *Daily Worker* (New York), September 30, 1955, 3; "Powell Urges Special Session to Adopt Anti-Lynch Law," *Daily Worker* (New York), September 30, 1955, 3; "Community Leaders Protest in Buffalo," *Daily Worker* (New York), September 29, 1955, 3; "Reactions Reverberate," 1.

51. "U.S. Intervention in Till Case Urged," 1, 3.

52. Jamie L. Whitten to J. J. Breland, John Whitten, Sidney Carlton, Harvey Henderson, and J. W. Kellum, September 27, 1955, Huie Papers, box 38, fd. 353a.

53. "The Verdict at Sumner," *Jackson Daily News*, September 25, 1955, 8.

54. The Civil Rights Statute is explained in Jonathan L. Entin, "Emmett Till and Federal Enforcement of Civil Rights," paper presented on September 16, 2005, at Stillman College, Tuscaloosa, Ala., copy in author's possession.

55. The FBI probe is summarized in a memorandum from F. L. Price to Mr. [Alex] Rosen, February 29, 1956, FBI FOIA release to Devery S. Anderson, 2006, re Emmett Till (hereafter cited as FBI file on Emmett Till). Decades later, Herbert Brownell, Eisenhower's attorney general, recalled that his office entered into the matter briefly but quickly decided it had no jurisdiction. See Herbert Brownell Jr., interview, conducted by Blackside, Inc., November 15, 1985, for *Eyes on the Prize: America's Civil Rights Years (1954–1965)*, Henry Hampton Collection, Washington University, St. Louis, http://digital.wustl.edu/eyesontheprize/; Herbert Brownell and John P. Burke, *Advising Ike: The Memoirs of Attorney General Herbert Brownell* (Lawrence: University Press of Kansas, 1993), 204.

56. "Missing Till Witnesses Flight Told," *Chicago American*, October 1, 1955, 11; L. Alex Wilson, "Wilson Tells How He Found, Got Collins to Chicago," *Chicago Defender*, October 8, 1955, 1, and *Tri-State Defender* (Memphis, Tenn.), October 8, 1955, 1, reprinted in Christopher Metress, ed., *The Lynching of Emmett Till: A Documentary Narrative* (Charlottesville: University of Virginia Press, 2002), 180.

57. Wilson, "Wilson Tells How He Found," 1; Metress, *Lynching of Emmett Till*, 178–79; "Henry Loggins Looms in Case as Vital Link," *St. Louis Argus*, October 14, 1955, 1; Howard B. Woods, "Witness in Till Case Vanishes," and Steve Duncan, "Relatives of Loggins Are Worried," both *St. Louis Argus*, October 28, 1955, 1.

58. Wilson, "Wilson Tells How He Found," 1; Metress, *Lynching of Emmett Till*, 179–81.

59. Wilson, "Wilson Tells How He Found," 1; Metress, *Lynching of Emmett Till*, 181.

60. "Till's Mother Hits 'Bungling' by Prosecutor," *Chicago American*, October 4, 1955, 4. According to Bradley, "The prosecutor did not visit the places which testimony brought out at the trial were the scenes of the crime. He did not look over the truck on which my son Emmett was supposed to have been seen riding with white men, and he did not follow up many leads his office received." Bradley was not correct in most of her criticisms. As discussed in earlier chapters, state investigators *did* go to the shed in Drew where Willie Reed said he heard sounds of a beating, although they did not conduct scientific tests. Highway inspector Gwin Cole announced on the fourth day of the trial that he did find the truck, but because neither he nor the press said anything further about it, he may have discovered it was the wrong vehicle. It is also true that Chatham did not allow for the black press to check out the Charleston jail after it was rumored Collins and Loggins were incarcerated there, but this was done, he said, because prosecutors had already visited the jail and the men were not there. Robert Smith said Cole visited two jails, which clearly upset the sheriffs in charge of each of these jails. See Clark Porteous, "Officers Work All Night on Searches," *Memphis Press-Scimitar*, September 21, 1955, 7; Ralph Hutto, "NAACP Leader Says Two Witnesses Disappeared," *Jackson State Times*, September 23, 1955, 6A; L. Alex Wilson, "Reveals Two Key Witnesses Jailed," *Tri-State Defender* (Memphis, Tenn.), October 1, 1955, 2; Murray Kempton, "They Didn't Forget," *New York Post*, September 26, 1955, 22; Clark Porteous, "Mrs. Bryant on Stand," *Memphis Press-Scimitar*, September 22, 1955, 4.

61. "Till's Mother in Seclusion," *Memphis Press-Scimitar*, October 5, 1955, 7.

62. L. Alex Wilson, "Here Is What 'Too Tight' Told the Defender," *Chicago Defender*, October 8, 1955, 35; Metress, *Lynching of Emmett Till*, 182–83, 191.

63. "'Missing' Witness Denied He Saw Till Slaying," *Memphis Press-Scimitar*, October 4, 1955, 19; L. Alex Wilson, "Collins Denies Any Link to Till," *Chicago Defender*, October 8, 1955, 1, and

Tri-State Defender (Memphis, Tenn.), October 8, 1955, 1; Wilson, "Here Is What 'Too Tight' Told the Defender," 35; Metress, *Lynching of Emmett Till*, 182–94.

64. Wilson, "Here Is what 'Too Tight' Told the Defender," 35; Metress, *Lynching of Emmett Till*, 187–89.

65. Ted Poston, "'Missing' Till Witness Admits Milam Took Him Out of Town," *New York Post*, October 4, 1955, 5.

66. L. Alex Wilson, "'Too Tight' Collins Missing," *Chicago Defender*, November 12, 1955, 1, 2.

67. Wilson, "Here Is What 'Too Tight' Told the Defender," 35; Metress, *Lynching of Emmett Till*, 186, 189–90.

68. "Reporter Dares Miss. Death," *New York Age Defender*, October 8, 1955, 1, 2; Poston, "'Missing' Till Witness," 5.

69. Poston, "'Missing' Till Witness," 5.

70. Bill Spell, "A *Daily News* Newspaperman Dared to Penetrate Chicago's South Side: State Negroes Held 'Captive' in Chicago," *Jackson Daily News*, October 5, 1955, 1. In 2010, Spell said the investigation was his idea, and that his immediate supervisor, Jimmy Ward, approved it and gave him the go-ahead (Bill Spell, author telephone interview, August 20, 2010).

71. "Ignore Doctor, 2 Grill Young Reed," *Chicago Defender*, October 15, 1955, 1; Spell, author telephone interview. William Chrisler (1922–2010) later served in Korea and Vietnam, retiring as a major general in 1978 (William Julius Chrisler obituary, published by Wright and Ferguson Funeral Home, Jackson, Miss., http://obits.dignitymemorial.com).

72. Spell, "*Daily News* Newspaperman Dared," 1; Mort Edelstein, "Witnesses Called 'Prisoners,'" *Chicago American*, October 7, 1955, 1.

73. Spell, "*Daily News* Newspaperman Dared," 1.

74. Bill Spell, "Mandy Bradley Refutes NAACP Claim Her Life Was in Danger, Then," *Jackson Daily News*, October 6, 1955, 1.

75. Spell, "Mandy Bradley Refutes NAACP," 1, 7.

76. "Till Witness Threats Probed," *Chicago Defender*, October 8, 1955, 34; Spell, author telephone interview.

77. Spell, "Mandy Bradley Refutes NAACP," 7.

78. Bill Spell, "Mose Wright Couldn't Be Reached without a 'Middle Man,'" *Jackson Daily News*, October 7, 1955, 1.

79. Spell, "Mose Wright Couldn't Be Reached," 1. Spell recalled in 2010 that "word got around fast that we were there," and remembers the notes under his door as being, for the most part, from the local press (Spell, author telephone interview).

80. Spell, "Mose Wright Couldn't Be Reached," 1.

81. Spell, "Mose Wright Couldn't Be Reached," 1; Charles C. Diggs Jr., "Emmett Till Trial Over but Negros Should Never Forget Its Meaning," *Pittsburgh Courier*, October 8, 1955, 4.

82. Edelstein, "Witnesses Called 'Prisoners,'" 1; Bill Spell and W. C. Shoemaker, "Alonzo Refutes Charges Made by Congressman Diggs," *Jackson Daily News*, October 6, 1955, 1; "Witness to Get Free Glasses," *Chicago Defender*, October 8, 1955, 34.

83. Spell and Shoemaker, "Alonzo Refutes Charges," 1; James L. Hicks, open letter to US Attorney General Herbert Brownell and FBI Chief J. Edgar Hoover, in "Hicks Digs into Till Case," *Washington Afro-American*, November 19, 1955, 14, reprinted in Metress, *Lynching of Emmett Till*, 198.

84. Bill Spell, "Effort to Tell Mandy of Her Husband Fails as Phone Connection Was Cut," *Jackson Daily News*, October 8, 1955, 1.

85. "Negro 'Captive' Articles Doubted, Mandy Bradley Says Her Husband Missing," *Jackson Daily News*, October 6, 1955, 7.

86. Edleston, "Witnesses Called 'Prisoners,'" 1.

87. Edleston, "Witnesses Called 'Prisoners,'" 1, 2.

88. Edleston, "Witnesses Called 'Prisoners,'" 2.

89. To be sure, Wright's story was somewhat problematic. Shortly after the trial, he gave several speeches and interviews, and sometimes the cemetery story came up. Some details would be expected to vary in multiple accounts, but one important aspect seemed to change drastically. In at least three accounts, Wright stated or implied that he heard from a neighbor that two men went to his house, but that they did nothing more than look around outside (Mose Wright interview, archival clip shown in Keith Beauchamp, prod., *The Untold Story of Emmett Louis Till* [Till Freedom Come Productions, 2005], and Felix Wold, "Mose Tells of Sleeping in Cemetery but 'Middle Man' Attended Interview," *Jackson Daily News*, October 8, 1955, 1). In a tape-recorded account, Wright said specifically that the trespassers were spotted "flashing a light all around, but they didn't go in" (Moses Wright, "I Saw Them Take Emmett Till," *Front Page Detective*, February 1956, 28). However, on several other occasions, he said that when he came home from the cemetery in the morning, a neighbor told him the men were yelling "Preacher, Uncle Mose, come on out here." Then Wright noticed that his screen door was broken, that beds were overturned, and that his home had been "ransacked." In a telephone interview with a *New York Post* reporter published on October 3, Wright described those who vandalized his home as "three carloads of white men," similar to the version from Diggs that caught Bill Spell's eye days earlier (Ted Poston, "Mose Wright Left Everything to Flee for Life," *New York Post*, October 3, 1955, 1. See also Moses Wright, "How I Escaped from Mississippi," *Jet* 8, no. 23 [October 13, 1955]: 10).

When asked in 2007 if he recalled this incident, Wright's youngest son, Simeon, said that he remembered the version that two white men came to the house with flashlights, but that any claims saying the house had been ransacked were not true (Wheeler Parker Jr., Crosby Smith Jr., and Simeon Wright, author interview, February 7, 2007, Argo, Ill., comments by Wright). Grover Frederick, the Wrights' landlord, dismissed the account of a break-in when questioned about it also, saying that was the first he had heard about it. The day Mose Wright left the state, he visited Leflore County sheriff George Smith, telling Smith he would be back for the kidnapping trial. Smith noted that Wright did not mention the alleged incident and appeared "calm and without a worry in the world" ("Till's Uncle Says He Fled for Life after Trial," *Memphis Commercial Appeal*, October 5, 1955, 28). It remains a mystery as to what really occurred the night in question, and it is even more puzzling why Wright gave conflicting accounts of the details. Yet something happened that scared him and prompted him to leave behind his cotton and his belongings and move to Chicago weeks before he had planned. Perhaps he thought he needed to convince skeptical Mississippians that he *was* afraid for his life, and having the trespassers go into the house and vandalize it accomplished that more than if people interpreted the incident to be a harmless visit by two men who did nothing more than shine their lights and leave.

90. Edleston, "Witnesses Called 'Prisoners,'" 2.

91. "Bill Spell Answers the *American*," *Jackson Daily News*, October 7, 1955, 1; Spell, author telephone interview.

92. "Bill Spell Answers the *American*," 1.

93. "Ignore Doctor," 1.

94. Spell, author telephone interview.

95. Spell, author telephone interview.

96. The actual article is "CRC 'Festival' Opens with Theme Centered on Till," *Jackson Daily News*, October 10, 1955, 1.

97. Mamie E. Bradley to Roy Wilkins, October 10, 1955, Papers of the NAACP: Part 18, Series C, reel 15.

98. Gloster Current to Billy Jones, October 5, 1955, Papers of the NAACP: Part 18, Series C, reel 14.

99. Tarea H. Pittman to Gloster B. Current, October 14, 1955, Papers of the NAACP: Part 18, Series C, reel 14.

100. Jerry Gordon, "In Memoriam," letter to the editor, *Cleveland Call and Post*, October 15, 1955, 8C.

101. Mort Edelstein, "Till Witness Decides Not to Testify," *Chicago American*, October 10, 1955, 5; "Gov. White Tells Reed Boy's Mother Her Fears Are Based on Propaganda," *Jackson Daily News*, October 10, 1955, 1.

102. Roy Wilkins to Mamie Bradley, November 15, 1955; William Durham to Miley O. Williamson, October 8, 1955; "Agreement Between Rev. Moses Wright and the Columbus and Dayton Branches of the NAACP," signed by Barbee William Durham and Moses Wright, October 8, 1955, all in Papers of the NAACP: Part 18, Series C, reel 14.

103. Durham to Williamson, October 8, 1955.

104. For more on Roosevelt and her outspoken stance on racial issues, see Pamela Tyler, "'Blood on Your Hands': White Southerners' Criticisms of Eleanor Roosevelt during World War II," in *Before Brown: Civil Rights and White Backlash in the Modern South*, ed. Glenn Feldman (Tuscaloosa: University of Alabama Press, 2004), 96–115.

105. Eleanor Roosevelt, "I Think the Till Jury Will Have Uneasy Conscience," *Memphis Press-Scimitar*, October 11, 1955, 6, reprinted in Metress, *Lynching of Emmett Till*, 136–37. Roosevelt's "My Day" columns ran from 1936 to 1962. The entire run is available at http://www.gwu.edu/~erpapers/myday/.

106. "Roosevelt Asks Law to Prevent Till Occurrences," *Jackson Daily News*, October 12, 1955, 3; "2,000 in Frisco Hit Till Murder; Rep. Roosevelt Urges U.S. to Act," *Daily Worker* (New York), October 19, 1955, 3.

107. "Press Release, Office of Honorable Adam Clayton Powell, Jr., 11 October 1955," quoted in Metress, *Lynching of Emmett Till*, 133–36; Harry Raymond, "20,000 at Rally Cheer 'March on Washington,'" *Daily Worker* (New York), October 12, 1955, 1.

108. American Jewish Committee, memorandum, October 7, 1955, reprinted in Metress, *Lynching of Emmett Till*, 138–43. See also "Lynching Acquittal Shocks All Europe," *Daily Worker* (New York), October 11, 1955, 2, for several quotations from European papers.

109. "Minnesotan Is Using Till Case in Politics," *Jackson Daily News*, October 12, 1955, 3.

110. Ethel L. Payne, "Tom [sic] Till Died for Democracy; Son Its Victim," *New York Age Defender*, October 1, 1955, 2.

111. "Father of Young Till Died for His Country," *New York Amsterdam News*, October 1, 1955, 7.

112. Roosevelt, "I Think the Till Jury," 6.

113. "In Memoriam, Emmett Till," *Life*, October 10, 1955, 48.

114. "Mississippi Solons Bare Hanging of Till's Father," *Chicago Defender*, October 22, 1955, 1.

115. Ethel L. Payne, "Army Gave Till Facts to Eastland," *Chicago Defender*, October 22, 1955, 1; John Stennis to M. G. Vaiden, November 26, 1955, John C. Stennis Collection, Series 29, Civil Rights, box 5, fd. 24, Congressional and Political Research Center, Mitchell Memorial Library, Mississippi State University, Starkville.

116. "Till's Father Had Been Billed 'War Hero'" during Fund-Raising Drives," *Jackson Daily News*, October 15, 1955, 1.

117. "About Till's Father (an editorial)," *Jackson Daily News*, October 15, 1955, 1.

118. "Till's Father Had Been Billed 'War Hero,'" 1.

119. Lemorse Mallory and Mamie E. Till, marriage certificate, dated August 19, 1946, no. 1925866, filed August 20, 1946, Cook County Clerk's Office, Chicago; National Archives and Records Administration, *U.S. World War II Army Enlistment Records, 1938–1946* [database online], Provo, Utah, USA: Ancestry.com, Operations Inc., 2005; photocopies of documents related to Mallory's final payment and discharge were sent to author with a covering letter dated November 20, 2008, from Tina Hanson, archives technician, National Personnel Records Center.

120. Parker, Smith, and Wright, author interview, comments by Parker.

121. "GI Buddies Say Till's Dad Was 'Railroaded' in Italy," *Jet* 8, no. 26 (November 3, 1955): 4–5.

122. "Mamie Bradley's Untold Story," installment four, *Daily Defender* (Chicago), March 1, 1956, 5.

123. James G. Chesnutt to William Bradford Huie, October 18, 1945, Huie Papers, box 38, fd. 349.

124. Louis Till burial, disinterment, and reburial records, sent with a covering letter by Thomas M. Jones, Chief, Freedom of Information and Privacy Act Office, to author, March 16, 2009.

125. Ezra Pound, *Pisan Cantos*, edited and annotated with an introduction by Richard Sieburth (New York: New Directions Books, 2003), x–xii.

126. Pound, *Pisan Cantos*, lines 170–72, 269.

127. See, for example, Alice Kaplan, *The Interpreter* (New York: Free Press, 2005); J. Robert Lilly, *Taken by Force: Rape and American GIs in Europe during World War II* (New York: Palgrave MacMillan, 2007).

128. *United States v. Private Fred A. McMurray and Private Louis Till*, trial transcript; Branch Office of the Judge Advocate General with the Mediterranean Theater of Operations, U.S. Army, Board of Review, *United States v. Privates Fred A. McMurray and Louis Till (36 392 273)*, both of *177th Port Company, 379th Port Battalion, Transportation Corps*, Peninsular Base Section, Trial by G.C.M., convened at Leghorn, Italy, February 17, 1945, copies in author's possession.

129. H. S. J. Walker, M.D., to editor, *Life*, October 18, 1955, Coleman Papers, box 23, fd. 3.

130. Wade Milam to editor, *Life*, October 18, 1955, Coleman Papers, box 23, fd. 3; Wade Milam, "Writes a Letter to Life Editor," *Jackson Daily News*, October 21, 1955, 6; Houck and Grindy, *Emmett Till and the Mississippi Press*, 138. See also Ruth Feldstein, "'I Wanted the Whole World to See': Race, Gender, and Constructions of Motherhood in the Death of Emmett Till," in *Not June Cleaver: Women and Gender in Postwar America, 1945–1960*, ed. Joanne Meyerowitz (Philadelphia: Temple University Press, 1994), 275; Valerie Smith, "Emmett Till's Ring," *Women Studies Quarterly* 36, nos. 1–2 (Spring/Summer 2008): 157.

Chapter 8

1. "Till's Mother Stirs 9,500 in Washington," *Daily Worker* (New York), October 20, 1955, 3; Larry Still, "Time Out for Crying," *Washington Afro-American*, October 22, 1955, 1, 5; "Prayer Meets Planned for Six Cities," *Washington Afro-American*, October 22, 1955, 5.

2. "Uncle of Lynched Boy Tells of Death Night," *Cleveland Call and Post*, October 22, 1955, 2A; "Meetings Sponsored by NAACP Branches Featuring Speakers other than Mrs. Bradley," n.d., Papers of the NAACP: Part 18: Special Subjects, 1940–1955: Series C, General Office files, microfilm reel 14 (Bethesda, Md.: University Publications of America, 1955). Reporter James Hicks noted that "every colored woman I talked to in Mississippi was critical of Mose Wright for permitting the two white men to come into his home and take the Till boy in the first place." They praised Wright for being brave enough to come testify at the trial, but they were adamant that "he should have killed them both when they broke into his home" (James L. Hicks, "Hicks Says U.S. Ought to Act Now," *Baltimore Afro-American*, November 19, 1955, 2; see also "What the People Say: Blast Till Pacifists," letter to the editor, *Chicago Defender*, September 17, 1955, 9).

3. Ethel L. Payne, "Army Gave Till Facts to Eastland," *Chicago Defender*, October 22, 1955, 2; "Senate May Hear Till Lynch Story," *Chicago Defender*, October 29, 1955, 1, 2.

4. "Vatican Urges U.S. Catholics to Help Erase Stain of Till Murder," *Daily Worker* (New York), October 18, 1955, 3.

5. "Abe Stark Asks Anti-Lynch Law," *Daily Worker* (New York), October 19, 1955, 3.

6. "Rabb Says White House Is Concerned Over Till Case," *Chicago Defender*, October 22, 1955, 12; E. Frederic Morrow, *Black Man in the White House: A Diary of the Eisenhower Years by the Administration Officer for Special Projects, the White House, 1955–1961* (New York: Coward-McCann, 1963), 223.

7. William G. Nunn to Maxwell Rabb, October 28, 1955; Maxwell Rabb to William G. Nunn, October 31, 1955, both in Dwight D. Eisenhower Library, online documents, www.eisenhower.archives.gov/research/online_documents.html.

8. For contrasting views, see Robert Fredrick Burk, *The Eisenhower Administration and Black Civil Rights* (Knoxville: University of Tennessee Press, 1984); David A. Nichols, *A Matter of Justice: Eisenhower and the Beginning of the Civil Rights Revolution* (New York: Simon and Schuster, 2007).

9. Still, "Time Out for Crying," 5; "Prayer Meets Planned," 5.

10. Memorandum from Mr. Price to [Alex] Rosen, October 13, 1955, FBI FOIA release to Devery S. Anderson, 2006, re Emmett Till (hereafter cited as FBI file on Emmett Till).

11. Edna F. Kelly to J. Edgar Hoover, October 18, 1955; J. Edgar Hoover to Edna F. Kelly, October 24, 1955, both in FBI file on Emmett Till.

12. "Chicago Negro Group Presses FBI on Till Case," *Delta Democrat-Times* (Greenville, Miss.), October 25, 1955, 2; "Negroes Rebuffed in Asking Federal Intervention," *Greenwood (Miss.) Commonwealth*, October 25, 1955, 1.

13. Memorandum from J. Edgar Hoover to Mr. Tolson, Mr. Nichols, Mr. Boardman, Mr. [Alex] Rosen, October 24, 1955, FBI file on Emmett Till. One author has documented that during his tenure as governor, Coleman's "response to Till suggests that the struggle for racial equality also prompted a change in how Southern officials responded to racial violence. It pushed the South to centralize authority, rein in local officials, improve the administration of justice, and adopt a less violent stance towards blacks—at least publicly." See Anders Walker, "The Violent Bear It Away: Emmett Till and the Modernization of Law Enforcement in Mississippi," *San Diego Law Review* 46 (2009): 459–503.

14. Bryant store sale ad, *Greenwood (Miss.) Morning Star*, October 19, 1955, 6.

15. Joe Atkins and Tom Brennan, "Bryant Wants the Past to 'Stay Dead,'" *Jackson Clarion-Ledger/Jackson Daily News*, August 25, 1985, 1H, 3H.

16. Atkins and Brennan, "Bryant Wants the Past," 3H.

17. "Mrs. Bradley Wires Moms of 3 Slain Chicago Boys," *Chicago Defender*, October 29, 1955, 7; James A. Jack, *Three Boys Missing: The Tragedy That Exposed the Pedophilia Underworld* (Chicago: HPH Publishing, 2006), 387. For more on this case, see Gene O'Shea, *Unbridled Rage: A True Story of Organized Crime, Corruption, and Murder in Chicago* (New York: Penguin, 2005); Richard C. Lindberg and Gloria Jean Sykes, *Shattered Sense of Innocence: The 1955 Murders of Three Chicago Children* (Carbondale: Southern Illinois University Press, 2006).

18. William Henry Huff to B. T. George, December 2, 1955, Papers of the NAACP: Part 18, Series C, reel 15; Mamie Till-Mobley and Christopher Benson, *Death of Innocence: The Story of the Hate Crime That Changed America* (New York: Random House, 2003), 208. In her memoir, Till-Mobley did not recall the name of the attorney Mooty took her to see, but she wrote, "I was a little concerned when I arrived and saw a run-down building and had to climb those rickety steps." She does not mention the firing of Mooty, but describes the terms of the contract he was pressuring her to sign. She also indicates that this occurred after her November 7 dispute with the NAACP (discussed later in this chapter). In recapping Bradley's difficulties with Mooty, however, Roy Wilkins said in a letter to Bradley: "In telephone conversations with me October 20 and 21, you said you were disturbed by some development involving Mr. Mooty. . . . Later you telephoned me that you had taken care of the Mooty angle and wanted to take your father on tour as your companion" (Roy Wilkins to Mamie Bradley, November 15, 1955, Papers of the NAACP: Part 18, Series C, reel 14).

19. Roosevelt Ward, "Negro Youth Ready to Testify Again at Trial of Emmett Till's Kidnapers," *Daily Worker* (New York), October 25, 1955, 3.

20. "Report on Mamie Bradley Mass Meetings Sponsored by NAACP Branches," Papers of the NAACP: Part 18, Series C, reel 14.

21. "Miss. Killing Brings New Members, Gifts to NAACP," *Louisville Defender*, September 29, 1955, 1; "Till Protest Meetings," *Crisis*, November 1955, 547.

22. "NAACP Leader Blasts Mississippi Law Enforcement," *Clarksdale (Miss.) Press Register*, November 5, 1955, 1.

23. "Four Witnesses Called in Probe," *Chicago Defender*, November 12, 1955, 2; Gloster Current to Ruby Hurley, November 4, 1955, Papers of the NAACP: Part 18, Series C, reel 15.

24. "Marshall Says Till Case 'Horrible' Terrorist Example," *Delta Democrat-Times* (Greenville, Miss.), November 7, 1955, 1.

25. Caption accompanying photograph of Willie Reed and Mose Wright under the heading "Wait to Testify Before Grand Jury," *Greenwood (Miss.) Commonwealth*, November 7, 1955, 8; Sam Johnson, "Grand Jury Not Examined Witnesses in Till Kidnapping," *Greenwood (Miss.) Commonwealth*, November 8, 1955, 1; "Four Witnesses Called," 1–2.

26. NAACP press release, November 7, 1955, Papers of the NAACP: Part 18, Series C, reel 14.

27. Wilkins to Bradley, November 15, 1955; "Conversation with Joseph Tobias via long distance from Chicago," November 9, 1955, Papers of the NAACP: Part 18, Series C, reel 15.

28. Wilkins to Bradley, November 15, 1955; "Mrs. Bradley Says Fee NAACP Idea," *Chicago Defender*, November 19, 1955, 2.

29. Franklin H. Williams to NAACP West Coast Leadership, November 8, 1955, Papers of the NAACP: Part 18, Series C, reel 14.

30. "Four Witnesses Called," 2. Willie Reed's memory of his grand jury appearance, as evidenced in his interview in Keith Beauchamp, prod., *The Untold Story of Emmett Louis Till* (Till Freedom Come Productions, 2005), has caused some confusion. In that interview, Reed said that he and Wright went to the courthouse, but that Milam and Bryant were not there. After around twenty minutes, "we was out of there." During my interview with Reed, he said essentially the same thing, but added that because Milam and Bryant failed to appear, the trial was called off. When I pointed out that this was not a trial but only a grand jury hearing (which the defendants would not have attended), he held to his recollection that it was, indeed, a trial, and that neither he nor Wright testified because it was canceled. Press footage, as seen in *Untold Story*, shows both Wright and Reed entering the chamber for the secret grand jury hearing. This footage is not to be confused with coverage of the murder trial in Sumner, because in Greenwood, both men wore suits; in Sumner, they did not. Again, press reports at the time are clear that these two men, as well as Sheriff George Smith and Deputy John Cothran, testified before the grand jury. Reed's testimony alone lasted fifteen minutes.

31. Roy Wilkins to W. Robert Ming, November 10, 1955, Papers of the NAACP: Part 18, Series C, reel 15.

32. "Conversation with Joseph Tobias."

33. Telegram from Roy Wilkins to Lester P. Bailey, November 9, 1955, Papers of the NAACP: Part 18, Series C, reel 14.

34. "NAACP Asks Who Did It as Bryant, Milam Freed," *Jackson Daily News*, November 10, 1955, 4.

35. "Jury Refuses to Indict Emmett Till Kidnapers," *Daily Worker* (New York), November 10, 1955, 1.

36. John Herbers, "'Case Closed' as Jury Fails to Indict Pair for Till Kidnaping," *Delta Democrat-Times* (Greenville, Miss.), November 10, 1955, 1.

37. Minter Krotzer, emails to author, May 17, May 19, and June 7, 2010. Somerville died in 1976 when Krotzer was only twelve. Krotzer recalled hearing, when she was young, that her grandfather had voted for an indictment, but was not positive. During our correspondence, she confirmed through a family member that this was true.

38. Mary Lou Ray, author telephone interview, August 6, 2013. Ray is a cousin of June Broadway. Although Ray did not know Broadway personally, over the years she has known and spoken with several family members who did.

39. Herbers, "Case Closed," 1; "NAACP Asks Who Did It," 4.

40. Harry Marsh, "Sheriff Says He Got Little Cooperation," *Delta Democrat-Times* (Greenville, Miss.), November 10, 1955, 1; "Comment Continues on Till Case; Witnesses Blamed," *Delta Democrat-Times* (Greenville, Miss.), November 11, 1955, 1.

41. "Grand Jury Ignores Confession; Prefers to Query Witnesses," *Jet* 8, no. 29 (November 24, 1955): 6–7.

42. "End of Kidnaping Case Where Leflore Concerned," *Greenwood (Miss.) Commonwealth*, November 10, 1955, 1; "No Kidnap Trial for Milam, Bryant," *Chicago Defender*, November 19, 1955, 1, 2.

43. "Grand Jury Frees Accused Kidnappers," *Abilene (Tex.) Reporter*, November 10, 1955, 9; "Darkness in Mississippi," *Chicago Daily Sun-Times*, November 11, 1955, 37.

44. As quoted in Herbers, "Case Closed," 1; Jerome Bernstein, "There Is No Justice in Mississippi," *Florida Flambeau* (Tallahassee), November 15, 1955, 2; Davis W. Houck and Matthew A. Grindy, *Emmett Till and the Mississippi Press* (Jackson: University Press of Mississippi, 2008), 145.

45. Dr. T. D. Patton to John Whitten, September 28, 1955, Huie Papers, box 38, fd. 353a.

46. Russel D. Moore III to Jesse Breland, October 5, 1955, Huie Papers, box 38, fd. 353a. Moore was the father-in-law of Bobby DeLaughter, Hines County assistant district attorney who prosecuted Byron De La Beckwith in 1994 for the 1963 murder of Medgar Evers. Beckwith was found guilty in this, his third trial.

47. J. J. Breland to Russel D. Moore III, October 6, 1955, Huie Papers, box 38, fd. 353a.

48. Two writers who have examined the case note the possibility that Sheriff Smith may not have been as forthcoming in his grand jury testimony as he was in Sumner regarding the kidnap confession he received from Roy Bryant. They see his sudden belief in a conspiracy among the witnesses to free Milam and Bryant and thus embarrass Mississippi as evidence of his insincerity. "Given that grand jury statements would remain secret, we can only surmise that some things had changed since his testimony of September 22" (Houck and Grindy, *Emmett Till and the Mississippi Press*, 144).

49. Reed, author interview.

50. "Four Witnesses Called in Probe," 2.

51. "Willie Reed Gets $1,000 Elk Grant," *Chicago Defender*, November 12, 1955, 4.

52. "Huff Quits Mrs. Bradley, NAACP Cancels Tour," *Chicago Defender*, November 12, 1955, 1, 2.

53. "Says Till Funds Given to Kin," *Chicago Defender*, November 26, 1955, 36.

54. Mamie Bradley to Roy Wilkins, November 9, 1955, printed in James L. Hicks, "Why Emmett Till's Mother and NAACP Couldn't Agree," *Baltimore Afro-American*, December 31, 1955, 2.

55. Wilkins to Bradley, November 15, 1955. Mamie's later recollections over this incident are clearly incorrect. She said in 1988 that the need for more money was not only to pay her father $100 per week but also to help pay his expenses, including airfare. However, she blamed Anna Crockett for insisting on the $5,000 fee. According to Mamie, Crockett said that this figure was necessary in order to pay a salary to Crockett also and for the upkeep of Mamie's home while

she was gone. Mamie held to Crockett's 1955 story from the *Chicago Defender* that one of the NAACP leaders out west, which was certainly a reference to Franklin Williams, "was in total agreement that $5,000 was little enough to ask." She said she settled for $3,500 after talking with Wilkins but that Wilkins inexplicably "just put his foot down," ended their relationship, and accused her "of capitalizing on my son's death" (Mamie Till-Mobley and Gene Mobley, interview, in Clenora Hudson-Weems, *Emmett Till: The Sacrificial Lamb of the Civil Rights Movement*, 4th ed. [Bloomington, Ind.: AuthorHouse, 2006], 147–48).

In her 2003 memoir, Till-Mobley said that a West Coast leader, a minister (this would have been Sylvester Odum), was able to secure $3,000 and even said he would try to double that, but that Wilkins called her late that night and "bawled me out" (Till-Mobley and Benson, *Death of Innocence*, 206–7). From the many letters and telegrams between Wilkins and other NAACP leaders, Wilkins's recorded phone call with Tobias, and Wilkins's detailed letter to Mamie, it is clear that Mamie's memory is inaccurate on almost all of the details. Neither Wilkins nor Williams offered a compromise to the previously agreed upon honorarium of $1,100, and the NAACP, contrary to what Mamie thought she remembered later, had already agreed to pay her father's airfare. Mamie's air force salary was $3,900 per year. Any monies required for providing a salary for Mamie, her father, and Crockett for only a two-week period, in addition to funds covering her household bills, would hardly total $5,000, the equivalent of $40,000 today.

56. Some authors, having failed to research the entire story of the Mamie Bradley–Roy Wilkins conflict, have made erroneous conclusions about the event. See Ruth Feldstein, "'I Wanted the Whole World to See': Race, Gender, and Constructions of Motherhood in the Death of Emmett Till," in *Not June Cleaver: Women and Gender in Postwar America, 1945–1960*, ed. Joanne Meyerowitz (Philadelphia: Temple University Press, 1994), 282–87; Jacqueline Goldsby, "The High and Low Tech of It: The Meaning of Lynching and the Death of Emmett Till," *Yale Journal of Criticism* 9, no. 2 (Fall 2006): 266.

57. Evers-Williams, author telephone interview.

58. "Mother of Till Raising Money," *Memphis Press-Scimitar*, November 15, 1955, 7.

59. "Stratton Asks Federal Probe in Till Slaying," *Chicago Daily Tribune*, November 11, 1955, part 1, 2; "Brownell Rejects Request for Action in Emmett Till Case," *Clarksdale (Miss.) Press Register*, December 6, 1955, 7; Jonathan L. Entin, "Emmett Till and Federal Enforcement of Civil Rights," paper presented at Stillman College, Tuscaloosa, Ala., September 16, 2005, copy in author's possession. The only other provision that would have allowed for federal intervention was Title 18, USC, section 241, which forbade *conspiracies* to violate federal rights. In 1955, this part of the civil rights statue was not clear, and, according to Entin, "even an administration that was strongly committed to protecting African Americans might have concluded that prosecuting Emmett Till's killers would face substantial legal hurdles."

60. "Government Official Labels Till Case 'Black Mark,'" *Clarksdale (Miss.) Press Register*, November 21, 1955, 1.

61. James L. Hicks, open letter to US Attorney General Herbert Brownell and FBI Chief J. Edgar Hoover, in "Hicks Digs into Till Case," *Washington Afro-American*, November 19, 1955, 4, 14, reprinted in Christopher Metress, ed., *The Lynching of Emmett Till: A Documentary Narrative* (Charlottesville: University of Virginia Press, 2002), 194–99.

62. Office memorandum from F. L. Price to Mr. [Alex] Rosen, February 29, 1956, FBI file on Emmett Till.

63. Roy Wilkins to B. T. George, December 2, 1955, Papers of the NAACP: Part 18, Series C, reel 15.

64. L. Alex Wilson, "Gus Courts, Miss. NAACP Head Tells How He Was Shot Down," *Tri-State Defender* (Memphis, Tenn.), December 3, 1955, 1, 2; "Leader Left State after Being Shot," *Baltimore Afro-American*, November 10, 1956, 8. Courts spent twenty-one days in the hospital and then moved to Chicago, where he began working for the NAACP.

65. Milton S. Katz, "E. Frederick Morrow and Civil Rights in the Eisenhower Administration," *Phylon* 42, no. 2 (2nd Quarter 1981): 133–34.

66. Memorandum of E. Frederick Morrow to Maxell Rabb, November 29, 1955, Eisenhower Library, online documents, www.eisenhower.archives.gov/research/online_documents.html.

67. Morrow to Rabb, November 29, 1955; see also Nichols, *Matter of Justice*, 117.

68. "Dr. T. R. M. Howard to Address Ala. Omegas," *Birmingham (Ala.) World*, November 18, 1955, 1; "Famed Dr. Howard, Rights Fighter, Montgomery Speaker," *Birmingham (Ala.) World*, November 22, 1955, 1, and *Alabama Tribune* (Montgomery), November 25, 1955, 1. Two of the articles announced that the meeting would be at the Dexter Avenue Baptist Church, but a caption under Howard's photo still had it scheduled at Tillibody Auditorium.

69. Emory O. Jackson, "Howard Thinking About 'March on Washington,'" *Birmingham (Ala.) World*, December 6, 1955, 6.

70. Jackson, "Howard Thinking," 6; David T. Beito and Linda Royster Beito, *Black Maverick: T. R. M. Howard's Fight for Civil Rights and Economic Power* (Urbana: University of Illinois Press, 2009), 138.

71. Rosa Parks interview, conducted by Blackside, Inc., November 14, 1985, for *Eyes on the Prize: America's Civil Rights Years (1954–1965)*, Henry Hampton Collection, Washington University, St. Louis, http://digital.wustl.edu/eyesontheprize/.

72. Jeanne Theoharis, *The Rebellious Life of Mrs. Rosa Parks* (Boston: Beacon Press, 2013), 61–65; Rosa Parks, with Jim Haskins, *Rosa Parks: My Story* (New York: Dial Books, 1992), 113–17; Douglas Brinkley, *Rosa Parks* (New York: Penguin, 2000), 103–8; Juan Williams, *Eyes on the Prize: America's Civil Rights Years, 1954–1965* (New York: Viking Books, 1987), 66.

73. Theoharis, *Rebellious Life*, 72–115; Parks and Haskins, *Rosa Parks*, 125–60; Brinkley, *Rosa Parks*, 119–73; Williams, *Eyes on the Prize*, 60–89. For detailed studies of the boycott, see Martin Luther King Jr., *Stride toward Freedom: The Montgomery Story* (New York: Harper, 1958); Donnie Williams, with Wayne Greenhaw, *The Thunder of Angels: The Montgomery Bus Boycott and the People Who Broke the Back of Jim Crow* (Chicago: Lawrence Hill Books, 2006).

74. "Mamie Till-Mobley, Civil Rights Heroine, Eulogized in Chicago," *Jet* 103, no. 5 (January 27, 2003): 18.

75. Don Babwin, "Civil Rights Advocates Seek Historical Status for Church," *Charleston (W. Va.) Sunday Gazette-Mail*, November 20, 2005, 5A. Jackson had told this story a month earlier at Parks's funeral. In the years since, the quote, although only a secondhand statement, has been assumed to be authoritative and was placed on a marker in front of the Bryant store in Money, Mississippi, in May 2011. Mississippi state senator David Jordan recently wrote of his own encounter with Parks, which backs up the Jackson story. "I remember engaging in a conversation with Rosa Parks and hearing from her own mouth that the death of Emmett Till is what triggered her refusal to give up her bus seat to a white man. It sent a chill down my spine to be engaged in a conversation with someone so resolute, whose strong belief in a cause made

her a national heroine" (David L. Jordan, with Robert L. Jenkins, *David L. Jordan: From the Mississippi Cotton Fields to the State Senate, A Memoir* [Jackson: University Press of Mississippi, 2014], 18).

Chapter 9

1. One study of ten national publications demonstrated that they paid little attention to the case to begin with, running few stories between the murder and trial verdict. Brian Thornton examined coverage of ten magazines throughout the twelve months spanning August 28, 1955, until August 28, 1956. In general, he found coverage lacking, leading him to conclude that "despite current claims and memories that an outraged nation demanded justice for [Till] in 1955, these national magazines reveal a different reality." Thornton does not consider the role of daily or weekly newspapers that made the story international news, or the protest rallies that lasted for months after the trial. In addition, he overlooked an article in the black magazine *Ebony*, a publication that he said reported nothing on Emmett Till over the course of that year. See Clotye Murdock, "Land of the Till Murder," *Ebony*, April 1956, 91–96. Although this story was a report on the current climate and economy in the Mississippi Delta, it contained several photos with captions regarding the Till case. See Brian Thornton, "The Murder of Emmett Till: Myth, Memory, and National Magazine Response," *Journalism History* 36, no. 2 (Summer 2010): 96–104.

2. Herbert S. Parmet, *Eisenhower and the American Crusades* (New York: MacMillan, 1972), 444–45. In his State of the Union speech, delivered on January 5, 1956, President Eisenhower addressed civil rights and related issues and outlined a new civil rights bill. He said in part: "The stature of our leadership in the free world has increased through the past three years because we have made more progress than ever before in a similar period to assure our citizens equality in justice, in opportunity and in civil rights. We must expand this effort on every front. We must strive to have every person judged and measured by what he is, rather than by his color, race or religion. There will soon be recommended to the Congress a program further to advance the efforts of the Government, within the area of Federal responsibility, to accomplish these objectives." For the full speech, see "Text of President Eisenhower's Annual Message to Congress on the State of the Union," *New York Times*, January 6, 1956, 10–11; www.pbs.org.

3. Parmet, *Eisenhower and the American Crusades*, 444–45.

4. "Mississippi Again," *Baltimore Afro-American*, December 17, 1955, 1, 2; "Miss. Negro's Slayer Went to Home of Till Case Figure after Shooting," *New York Post*, December 9, 1955, 63; "Witnesses Say Slain Negro Didn't Gun-Duel White Man," *Jet* 9, no. 7 (December 22, 1955): 7.

5. "Use Milam Car in Miss. Slaying," *Chicago Defender*, December 17, 1955, 1, 2; "Mississippi Again," 1, 2; David Halberstam, "Tallahatchie County Acquits a Peckerwood," *Reporter* 14, no. 8 (April 19, 1956): 27.

6. "Miss. Negro's Slayer," 3, 63.

7. "Kimbrell Is Denied Bond in Slaying at Glendora," *Jackson Clarion-Ledger*, December 29, 1955, 1; "Judge Denies Bond for Glendora Man," *Clarksdale (Miss.) Press Register*, January 10, 1956, 1; "Miss. Negro's Slayer," 3. The accused killer's last name is spelled as both "Kimbell" and "Kimbrell" in several sources.

8. "Kimbrell Is Denied Bond," 1; "Judge Denies Bond," 1.

9. Halberstam, "Tallahatchie County Acquits," 27.

10. "Seek Atonement for Latest Mississippi Murder," *Chicago Defender*, December 24, 1955, 3; "Witnesses Say Slain Negro," 8.

11. Michael Vinson Williams, *Medgar Evers: Mississippi Martyr* (Fayetteville: University of Arkansas Press, 2011), 128.

12. "Widow Drowns as Trial of Mate's Slayer Opens," *Chicago Defender*, March 17, 1956, 1; Moses J. Newson, "Acquit Kimbell in Miss. Trial," *Daily Defender* (Chicago), March 14, 1956, 1.

13. James L. Hicks, "Why Emmett Till's Mother and NAACP Couldn't Agree," *Baltimore Afro-American*, December 31, 1955, 2; Clyde Reid, "Mamie Bradley Says NAACP Used Son," *New York Amsterdam News*, December 24, 1955, 1; Roy Wilkins to Mamie Bradley, November 15, 1955, Papers of the NAACP: Part 18: Special Projects, 1940–1955, Series C: General Office Files, microfilm reel 14 (Bethesda, Md.: University Publications of America, 1995); "Huff Quits Mrs. Bradley, NAACP Cancels Tour," *Chicago Defender*, November 12, 1955, 1, 2.

14. Hicks, "Why Emmett Till's Mother," 2; Reid, "Mamie Bradley Says NAACP Used Son," 1.

15. "Louis [*sic*] Till's Mother Sets New Jersey Tour," *Washington Afro-American*, January 3, 1956, 19.

16. "Brooklyn Audience Told How Till Died in Miss.," *Baltimore Afro-American*, January 14, 1956, 17; "Surprise Guest Stirs NAACP Annual Meeting," NAACP press release, January 5, 1956, Papers of Medgar Wiley Evers and Myrlie Beasley Evers, Mississippi Department of Archives and History, Archives and Library Division, Special Collections Section, box 2, fd. 19 (hereafter cited as Evers Papers).

17. Christopher Metress, "Truth Be Told: William Bradford Huie's Emmett Till Cycle," *Southern Quarterly* 45, no. 4 (Summer 2008): 48.

18. See, for example, *Clarksdale (Miss.) Press Register*, January 11, 1956, 6; *Chicago Daily Tribune*, January 11, 1956, 11.

19. Deirdre Coakley, "Keeper of the Flame: William Bradford Huie's Widow, Martha Hunt Huie, Works to Get His Work Back in Print," *Gadsden (Ala.) Times*, October 9, 2001, B4–B5. *The Revolt of Mamie Stover*, released by Twentieth Century Fox in 1956, starred Jane Russell in the title role. *The Execution of Private Slovik* was a 1974 made-for-TV movie featuring Martin Sheen and his young son Charlie. The others were *Wild River* (1960), *The Outsider* (1961), *The Americanization of Emily* (1964), and *Klansman* (1974).

20. David Halberstam, *The Fifties* (New York: Villard Books, 1993), 434; Bob Ward, "William Bradford Huie Paid for Their Sins," *Writer's Digest* 54, no. 9 (September 1974): 16–22.

21. William Bradford Huie, *Wolf Whistle, and Other Stories* (New York: New American Library, 1959), 16–17.

22. William Bradford Huie to Roy Wilkins, October 12, 1955, William Bradford Huie Papers, Cms 84, box 38, fd. 353a, Ohio State University Library, Columbus (hereafter cited as Huie Papers).

23. Huie to Wilkins, October 12, 1955.

24. William Bradford Huie to Basil Walters, October 18, 1955, Huie Papers, box 38, fd. 353a.

25. Huie to Wilkins, October 12, 1955.

26. William Bradford Huie to Dan Mitch, October 17, 1955, Huie Papers, box 38, fd. 353a; Huie to Walters, October 18, 1955.

27. Huie to Mitch, October 17, 1955.

28. Huie to Walters, October 18, 1955.

29. William Bradford Huie to Dan Mitch, October 21, 1955, Huie Papers, box 38, fd. 353a.

30. William Bradford Huie to Dan Mitch, October 23, 1955, Huie Papers, box 38, fd. 353a; William Bradford Huie, interview, conducted by Blackside, Inc., August 3, 1979, for *Eyes on the Prize: America's Civil Rights Years (1954–1965)*, Henry Hampton Collection, Washington University, St. Louis, http://digital.wustl.edu/eyesontheprize/.

31. Huie to Mitch, October 23, 1955.

32. Ellen Whitten, "Justice Unearthed: Revisiting the Murder of Emmett Till" (Honor's thesis, Rhodes College, 2005), 17. http://www.rhodes.edu/images/content/Academics/Ellen _Whitten.pdf.

33. As two researchers into the Till case see it, "Increasingly do we now realize that Huie had been bamboozled and *Look* hoodwinked" (Davis W. Houck and Matthew A. Grindy, *Emmett Till and the Mississippi Press* [Jackson: University Press of Mississippi, 2009], 151). Although that is one possibility, it seems to me that Huie was not deceived by Milam and Bryant, but backed off of the story for the reasons I cite above.

34. Huie to Walters, October 18, 1955.

35. William Bradford Huie to Dan Mitch, October 25, 1955, Huie Papers, box 38, fd. 353a.

36. Huie, interview, for *Eyes on the Prize*.

37. John W. Milam, signed release; Carolyn Bryant, signed release, both in Huie Papers, box 38, fd. 353b.

38. Milam, signed release; Bryant, signed release.

39. Howell Raines, *My Soul Is Rested: Movement Days in the Deep South Remembered* (New York: Putnam, 1977), 388.

40. Milam, signed release.

41. Milam, signed release; Bryant, signed release.

42. Huie, *Wolf Whistle*, 38–41.

43. John W. Whitten Jr. to William Bradford Huie, November 2, 1955, Huie Papers, box 38, fd. 353b.

44. William Bradford Huie, "The Shocking Story of an Approved Killing in Mississippi," *Look*, January 24, 1956, 46–50.

45. Roy Wilkins to Branch Officers, January 6, 1956, Evers Papers, box 2, fd. 19.

46. *Congressional Record*, January 12, 1956, Appendix, A247–49 http://www.heinonline.org; "Rep. Diggs Comments in Congress on *Look*'s Story about the Emmett Till Case," *Memphis Press-Scimitar*, January 13, 1956, 19.

47. *Congressional Record*, January 16, 1956, Appendix, A337 http://www.heinonline.org; "S-T's Reply to *Look* Read to Congressmen," *Jackson State Times*, January 17, 1956, 1A, as quoted in Metress, "Truth Be Told," 49.

48. *Congressional Record*, January 17, 1956, 697, and Appendix, A387–38 http://www.heinon line.org; "Negro's Answer to *Look* Story," *Memphis Press-Scimitar*, January 18, 1956, 8.

49. Susan M. Weill, "Mississippi's Daily Press in Three Crises," in *The Press and Race: Mississippi Journalists Confront the Movement*, ed. David R. Davies (Jackson: University Press of Mississippi, 2001), 28. In his 1954 editorial, as quoted in Weill, Lee said: "Southern Negroes may lose a lot more than they gain. Integration in the North and East is not a howling success. This movement to integrate the schools of the South is loaded with more racial dynamite than appears on the surface and the Negro will be the one who is blown away."

50. "Son No Braggart, Says Mrs. Bradley," *Chicago Defender*, January 21, 1956, 1, 2.

51. "What Milam, Bryant Say of Huie Story," *Memphis Press-Scimitar*, January 13, 1956, 19; "Milam Hires Sumner, Miss., Lawyer—Says He May Sue Look Magazine," *Memphis Press-Scimitar*, January 14, 1956, 3; "Till Exposé by Writer Shakes Dixie," *Chicago Defender*, January 21, 1956, 2.

52. Jay Milner, "Milam Says He's 'Not Sure' If He Has Grounds for Libel Suit," *Delta Democrat-Times* (Greenville, Miss.), January 15, 1956, 1.

53. W. C. Shoemaker, author telephone interview, August 20, 2010.

54. "What Huie Says," *Memphis Press-Scimitar*, January 13, 1956, 19.

55. "Ask New Till Probe," *Birmingham (Ala.) World*, January 21, 1956, 1; "Ask New Indictment in Till Kidnap Case," *Baltimore Afro-American*, January 21, 1956, 2. Four years after "Shocking Story" appeared, Huie said that Wilkins and his wife read the article and considered it to be "fair" (Huie, *Wolf Whistle*, 45).

56. "'Too Busy' to Reopen Till Kidnap Case, Judge Says," *Washington Afro-American*, January 21, 1956, 11.

57. James L. Hicks, open letter to US Attorney General Herbert Brownell and FBI Chief J. Edgar Hoover, in "Hicks Digs into Till Case," *Washington Afro-American*, November 19, 1955, 4, 14, reprinted in Christopher Metress, ed., *The Lynching of Emmett Till: A Documentary Narrative* (Charlottesville: University of Virginia Press, 2002), 194–99.

58. "Recall the Murders in Mississippi," *Baltimore Afro-American*, December 24, 1955, 6, and *Washington Afro-American*, December 17, 1955, 1, 2; "Writer Challenges Brownell to Act in Till Kidnap-Murder Case," *Baltimore Afro-American*, 2.

59. "Writer Challenges Brownell," 2.

60. "Justice Dept. Says 'No' to New Probe into Till Murder," *Delta Democrat-Times* (Greenville, Miss.), February 12, 1956, 22.

61. Huie, *Wolf Whistle*, 45; Thornton, "Murder of Emmett Till," 99.

62. "Bombshell in the Till Case," *New York Post*, January 11, 1956, 1; "New Angle to Till Case," *Greenwood (Miss.) Morning Star*, January 11, 1956, 4, both quoted in Metress, "Truth Be Told," 48–49.

63. "Till Case Film Rights Secured," *Memphis Press-Scimitar*, January 19, 1956, 29.

64. "Milam, Bryant Sign for Till Case Movie," *Baltimore Afro-American*, January 28, 1956, 1.

65. "Milam, Bryant Sign for Till Case Movie," 1.

66. Raines, *My Soul Is Rested*, 389; Sharon Monteith, "The Murder of Emmett Till in the Melodramatic Imagination: William Bradford Huie and Vin Packer in the 1990s," in *Emmett Till in Literary Memory and Imagination*, ed. Harriet Pollack and Christopher Metress (Baton Rouge: Louisiana State University Press, 2008), 36; Metress, "Truth Be Told," 60–61.

67. William Bradford Huie, "What's Happened to the Emmett Till Killers," *Look*, January 22, 1957, 63–66, 68.

68. "Say Coleman Cites NAACP, Diggs for Till Case Outcome," *Delta Democrat-Times* (Greenville, Miss.), January 12, 1956, 1, 2; "Coleman and Look at Odds on Till Case," *Memphis Press-Scimitar*, January 13, 1956, 1–2.

69. "Coleman and Look at Odds," 1–2.

70. Metress, "Truth Be Told," 50; Dave Tell, "The 'Shocking Story' of Emmett Till and the Politics of Public Confession," *Quarterly Journal of Speech* 94, no. 2 (May 2008): 158. Tell has

detailed Huie's "Shocking Story" and its evolution into a confessional piece, while pointing out that neither Huie nor Milam and Bryant intended the article to be one. In his book on public confession, Tell analyzes the story further and asks, "So how is it that despite Huie's excisions … despite the intentions of the author, the killers, and their lawyers, the 'Shocking Story' is nearly universally remembered as a confession? … The answer will come as no surprise: the 'Shocking Story' became a confession because, politically speaking, it needed to be one." See Dave Tell, *Confessional Crises and Cultural Politics in Twentieth-Century America* (University Park: Pennsylvania State University Press, 2012), 66.

71. David T. Beito and Linda Royster Beito, *Black Maverick: T. R. M. Howard's Fight for Civil Rights and Economic Power* (Urbana: University of Illinois Press, 2009), 150. I am grateful to the Beitos for making this source known and for their thoughtful analysis.

72. "Look Magazine Names Milam, Bryant in Confession Story," *Tri-State Defender* (Memphis, Tenn.), January 14, 1956, 2; Huie, "Shocking Story," 50; Beito and Beito, *Black Maverick*, 271n6.

73. Huie to Mitch, October 21, 1955.

74. "Look Magazine Names Milam, Bryant," 1, 2.

75. David A. Shostak, "Crosby Smith: Forgotten Witness to a Mississippi Nightmare," *Negro Bulletin* 38, no. 1 (December 1974–January 1975): 321.

76. "Look Magazine Names Milam, Bryant," 2.

77. "Look Magazine Names Milam, Bryant," 2; Beito and Beito, *Black Maverick*, 151–52. Reed denied this possible scenario both to the Beitos and to me. Willie Reed, author interview, February 6, 2007.

78. See Amos Dixon, "Mrs. Bryant Didn't Even Hear Emmett Till Whistle," *California Eagle*, January 26, 1956, 1–2, 4; Amos Dixon, "Milam Master-Minded Emmett Till Killing," *California Eagle*, February 2, 1956, 1–2; Amos Dixon, "Till Case: Torture and Murder," *California Eagle*, February 9, 1956, 1–2; Amos Dixon, "Till Case: Torture and Murder," *California Eagle*, February 16, 1956, 1–2; Amos Dixon, "South Wins Out in Till Lynching Trial," *California Eagle*, February 23, 1956, 2.

79. Dixon, "Mrs. Bryant Didn't Even Hear," 1.

80. Olive Arnold Adams, *Time Bomb: Mississippi Exposed and the Full Story of Emmett Till* (Mound Bayou, Miss: Regional Council of Negro Leadership, 1956), 15–21.

81. T. R. M. Howard, "Stark Terror Reigns in Mississippi Delta," *Washington Afro-American*, October 1, 1955, 19; T. R. M. Howard, "Terror Reigns in Mississippi," speech delivered October 2, 1955, Baltimore, *Washington Afro-American*, October 1, 1955, 19, and *Baltimore Afro-American*, October 8, 1955, 6, reprinted in Davis W. Houck and David E. Dixon, eds., *Rhetoric, Religion, and the Civil Rights Movement, 1954–1965* (Waco, Tex.: Baylor University Press, 2006), 125–27; "Dr. Howard: Situation in Mississippi Extremely Serious," *Pittsburgh Courier*, October 8, 1955, 4.

82. Beito and Beito, *Black Maverick*, 25–29; T. R. M. Howard, foreword, in Adams, *Time Bomb*, 6–7.

83. Chester Washington, "Howard Locates Two Men," *Pittsburgh Courier*, October 15, 1955.

84. Linda Beito, telephone interview with Henry Lee Loggins, July 21, 2001, transcript in author's possession.

85. Dixon, "Mrs. Bryant Didn't Even Hear," 2; Dixon, "Milam Master-Minded," 1–2; Adams, *Time Bomb*, 19–20.

86. Hicks, "Hicks Digs into Till Case," 4; Metress, *Lynching of Emmett Till*, 195–96.

87. Dixon, "Till Case: Torture and Murder," February 9, 1956, 2.

88. "Dr. Howard Is Selling Property," *Washington Afro-American*, December 17, 1955, 1–2; Beito and Beito, *Black Maverick*, 163.

89. Price to Rosen, February 29, 1956; Office memorandum from Mr. [F. L.] Price to Mr. [Alex] Rosen, March 1, 1956, FBI FOIA release to Devery S. Anderson, 2006, re Emmett Till (hereafter cited as FBI file on Emmett Till).

90. Office memorandum from F. L. Price to the Director [J. Edgar Hoover], February 29, 1956, FBI file on Emmett Till.

91. Louis E. Lomax, "Henry Loggins Found, but Refuses to Leave Jail Cell," *Daily Defender* (Chicago), March 12, 1955, 8; Louis E. Lomax, "Milam Jails His Handyman," *Daily Defender* (Chicago), March 20, 1956, 5. During his interview with Keith Beauchamp for the documentary *The Untold Story of Emmett Louis Till* (Till Freedom Come Productions, 2005), Loggins mentioned that Milam had accused him of stealing iron and that he had spent six months in jail. In the film, Loggins professed his innocence of the charges.

92. Lomax, "Henry Loggins Found," 8.

93. Lomax, "Milam Jails His Handyman," 5.

94. "Audience Donates to Till Witness," *Chicago Defender*, March 17, 1956, 10.

95. Martin Luther King Jr., *Stride toward Freedom: The Montgomery Story* (New York: Harper, 1959), 127.

Chapter 10

1. Mamie Till-Mobley, author telephone interview, December 3, 1996.

2. "Mrs. Bradley Bares Dawson Aid," *Daily Defender* (Chicago), October 22, 1956, 1; "Till's Mother Says Ike Ignored Pleas for Help," *Chicago Defender*, November 3, 1956, 1; Alfred Duckett, "Adlai in Tribute to Dr. Johnson," *Chicago Defender*, November 10, 1956, 10.

3. "People and Places," *Chicago Defender*, December 8, 1956, 2; Ethel L. Payne, "'Ladies' Day for Adlai Lures Smart Set from All Over to Dine, Chat," *Chicago Defender*, November 3, 1956, 15.

4. "The Till Case People One Year Later," *Ebony* 5, no. 11 (October 1956): 69; Chester Higgins, "Mrs. Bradley Becomes a Teacher," *Jet* 17, no. 18 (September 1, 1960): 13–15; Mamie Till-Mobley and Christopher Benson, *Death of Innocence: The Story of the Hate Crime That Changed America* (New York: Random House, 2003), 217–29, 251, 254.

5. Higgins, "Mrs. Bradley Becomes a Teacher," 16; Till-Mobley and Benson, *Death of Innocence*, 225, 228, 270–72; Mamie Till-Mobley, biographical summary (Emmett Till Foundation, November 1994), copy in author's possession.

6. "Look Sued for Million Libel by Till's Mother," *Chicago Daily Tribune*, January 22, 1958, 8; "Emmett Till's Mother Sues Look," *Delta Democrat-Times* (Greenville, Miss.), January 23, 1958, 14; "Emmett Till's Mom Loses Libel Suit," *Delta Democrat-Times* (Greenville, Miss.), June 23, 1959, 2; Till-Mobley and Benson, *Death of Innocence*, 215–16.

7. "Mother Says Son Libeled by Stories," *Daily Defender* (Chicago), January 22, 1958, 3; "Dismiss Appeal by Till's Mother," *Daily Defender* (Chicago), May 17, 1960, A2; "Appeal Till Case to High Court," *Daily Defender* (Chicago), October 4, 1960, 2.

8. Till-Mobley, author telephone interview; Till-Mobley and Benson, *Death of Innocence*, 232.

9. "Till's Mother Marches," caption under photo, *Jet* 39, no. 4 (October 29, 1970): 33.

10. "Emmett Till Foundation Holds Annual Banquet," *Daily Defender* (Chicago), July 25, 1966, 8; Emmett Till Foundation, Statement of Mission and Purpose, copy in author's possession.

11. Till-Mobley, author telephone interview; Till-Mobley and Benson, *Death of Innocence*, 242–43.

12. "Time Heals Few Wounds for Emmett Till's Mother," *Jet* 66, no. 5 (April 9, 1984): 55–56.

13. Till-Mobley, biographical summary.

14. Douglas Kreutz, "Hundreds Watch Unveiling of King Statue in City Park," *Rocky Mountain News* (Denver), September 6, 1976, 6; Dave Curtain, "Repaired Statue Renews Legacy of Rights Battles," *Denver Post*, May 15, 2005, A1. Ten months after the statue dedication, Ed Rose filed a $35,000 lawsuit against the Denver-backed Martin Luther King Jr. Memorial Foundation for money it still owed him. The foundation countersued Rose, saying that the statue did not resemble King, and that because of Rose's "poor workmanship" and "lackadaisical approach," the foundation lost out on a $10,000 bicentennial grant and $15,000 in other expected donations. On top of this, Philip Schiavo, president of Roman Bronze Work, the Corona, New York, foundry that cast the statue, began demanding the $13,500 he was still owed, and threatened to go to Denver City Park and "start to chop the statue down and let the police arrest me." The foundation eventually paid Rose his remaining commission. The sculpture was later replaced with a $700,000 statue of King alone, and the Rose sculpture was donated to the Martin Luther King Cultural Center in Pueblo, Colorado, in 2002. Since the move, the statue has been vandalized with racist graffiti, and in April 2005, an arm on one of the figures was nearly severed. The sculpture was repaired and rededicated in May 2005 (Curtain, "Repaired Statue Renews Legacy," A1). Rose died in 2009 at age sixty-four. See "King Statue Center of Dispute," *Greeley (Colo.) Tribune*, July 6, 1977, 1; Cinder Parmenter, "Overdue Bills Endanger Bronze of King," *Denver Post*, July 7, 1977, 17; Virginia Culver, "Statue Stirred Controversy," *Denver Post*, May 7, 2009, A-08.

15. Kreutz, "Hundreds Watch Unveiling," 6; Till-Mobley and Benson, *Death of Innocence*, 247–48.

16. Fred Grim, "Memorial to Honor Civil Rights Martyrs," *Wisconsin State Journal* (Madison), July 31, 1988, 1D; Till-Mobley and Benson, *Death of Innocence*, 257–59; Morris Dees, with Steve Fiffer, *A Lawyer's Journey: The Morris Dees Story* (Chicago: American Bar Association, 2001), 333–34; D. Michael Cheers, "Dedicate Memorial to 40 Who Died in Civil Rights Struggle," *Jet* 77, no. 7 (November 20, 1989): 4–16.

17. "Chicago's 71st Street Is Renamed for Emmett Till," *Jet* 80, no. 17 (August 12, 1991): 4–5; Till-Mobley and Benson, *Death of Innocence*, 260.

18. Till-Mobley and Benson, *Death of Innocence*, 268–70; Bill Clinton, *My Life* (New York: Alfred A. Knopf, 2004), 896–97. For more on the original Selma marches, see Juan Williams, *Eyes on the Prize: America's Civil Rights Years, 1954–1965* (New York: Viking Penguin, 1987); John Lewis, with Michael D'Orso, *Walking with the Wind: A Memoir of the Movement* (New York: Simon and Schuster, 1998); Townsend Davis, *Weary Feet, Rested Souls: A Guided History of the Civil Rights Movement* (New York: W. W. Norton, 1998); J. Mills Thornton III, *Dividing Lines: Municipal Politics and the Struggle for Civil Rights in Montgomery, Birmingham, and Selma* (Tuscaloosa: University of Alabama Press, 2002).

19. James Janega and Mathew Walberg, "Mamie Till-Mobley, 1921–2003," *Chicago Daily Tribune*, January 7, 2003, 2C; Clarence Page, "Black History Isn't Just for Blacks Anymore," *Chicago Daily Tribune*, January 15, 2003, 1.

20. "Mamie Till-Mobley, Civil Rights Heroine, Eulogized in Chicago," *Jet* 103, no. 5 (January 27, 2003): 14, 18, 52.

21. Till-Mobley, author telephone interview.

22. "Mamie Till-Mobley, Civil Rights Heroine," 52.

23. As two scholars note, "lynching images, such as those of Emmett Till, are too visually provocative, too viscerally challenging, to be contained by time or distance" (Christine Harold and Kevin Michael DeLuca, "Behold the Corpse: Violent Images and the Case of Emmett Till," *Rhetoric & Public Affairs* 8, no. 2 [Summer 2005]: 266).

24. Wheeler Parker Jr., Crosby Smith Jr., and Simeon Wright, author interview, February 7, 2007, Argo, Ill., comments by Wright.

25. Simeon Wright, with Herb Boyd, *Simeon's Story: An Eyewitness Account of the Kidnapping of Emmett Till* (Chicago: Lawrence Hill Books, 2010), 86.

26. "Till Case People," 68, 72.

27. William Parker, author telephone interview, April 30, 2014.

28. William Parker, author telephone interview; Parker, Smith, and Wright, author interview, comments by Wright; Wright and Boyd, *Simeon's Story*, 87.

29. William Parker, author telephone interview; Martha Wright Baker, author telephone interview, May 5, 2014. Baker is the daughter of Will Wright.

30. William Parker, author telephone interview.

31. Parker, Smith, and Wright, author interview, comments by Wright.

32. William Parker, author telephone interview; Wright and Boyd, *Simeon's Story*, 99; "Rites Held Saturday for Moses Wright, 85," *Chicago Defender*, August 8, 1977, 2.

33. William Parker, author telephone interview; Confidential source E to author, August 15, 2011.

34. William Parker, author telephone interview.

35. Mary Sanchez, "Murder's Horror Haunts the Living," *Kansas City Star*, April 20, 2004, B7.

36. David A. Shostak, "Crosby Smith: Forgotten Witness to a Mississippi Nightmare," *Negro Bulletin* 38, no. 1 (December 1974–January 1975): 321.

37. George Curry, "Killed for Whistling at a White Woman," *Emerge*, August 1995, 27.

38. Parker, Smith, and Wright, author interview, comments by Parker.

39. Sanchez, "Murder's Horror," B7; Wright and Boyd, *Simeon's Story*, 94; Parker, Smith, and Wright, author interview, comments by Wright.

40. Clenora Hudson-Weems, *Emmett Till: The Sacrificial Lamb of the Civil Rights Movement*, 4th ed. (Bloomington, Ind.: AuthorHouse, 2006), 134.

41. Wheeler Parker Jr., author telephone interview, October 1, 2007.

42. *Argo Temple Church of God in Christ 80-Year Celebration*, program distributed for event held October 8, 2006, 2.

43. Shostak, "Crosby Smith," 325.

44. Joe Atkins, "Slain Chicago Youth Was a 'Sacrificial Lamb,'" *Jackson Clarion–Ledger/Jackson Daily News*, August 25, 1985, 20A; Parker, Smith, and Wright, author interview, comments by Smith.

45. Parker, Smith, and Wright, author interview, comments by Parker and Wright.

46. Parker, Smith, and Wright, author interview, comments by Parker.

47. Willie Reed, author interview, February 6, 2007, Chicago.

48. Reed, author interview; Parker, Smith, and Wright, author interview, comments by Parker.

49. Reed, author interview.

50. "Till Case People," 72; Reed, author interview.

51. Reed, author interview.

52. Becky Schlikerman, "Emmett Till Witness 'Never Got Over' Case," *Chicago Sun-Times*, July 24, 2013, 13; Margalit Fox, "Willie Louis, Who Named the Killers of Emmett Till at Their Trial, Dies at 76," *New York Times*, July 24, 2013, A25; Emily Langer, "Witness Dared to Testify in Emmett Till Lynching," *Washington Post*, July 25, 2013, A6; Naomi Nix, "Willie Louis: 1937–2013," *Chicago Tribune*, July 24, 2013, 6.

53. Reed, author interview.

54. Langer, "Witness Dared to Testify," A6.

55. Reed, author interview; Add Reed death certificate, Cook County, Illinois, Death Records, state file no. 606929, filed March 27, 1977.

56. "World Eyes Mississippi Grand Jury," *Chicago Defender*, November 12, 1955, 2; Lee Blackwell, "Two Who Fled Mississippi Tell Stories," *Chicago Defender*, October 1, 1955, 1–2. The papers referred to Brooks as Mandy Bradley's granddaughter, but a confidential source told me that Brooks is indeed Bradley's daughter. Confidential source D, author telephone interview, June 6, 2014.

57. "Ticker Tape U.S.A.," *Jet* 9, no. 11 (January 19, 1956): 13; "Till Case People," 68, 72.

58. Confidential source D, author telephone interview.

59. "3 Who Refused to Testify Have Dropped Out of Sight," *Jet* 13, no. 25 (April 24, 1958): 11, 13.

60. "3 Who Refused," 12–13.

61. Marsha Gaston, author telephone interview, February 17, 2014; "3 Who Refused," 12–13.

62. Federal Bureau of Investigation, Prosecutive Report of Investigation Concerning . . . Emmett Till, Deceased, Victim, February 9, 2006, 29 (hereafter cited as Prosecutive Report; names of living people are redacted in the report); Clint Gaston and Treola Collins, marriage certificate, King County, Washington, filed August 10, 1960, no. 245340; Gaston, author telephone interview. While serving in the military, Wheeler Parker met one of Levi Collins's nieces, who told Parker that her uncle eventually "lost his mind" (Parker, Smith, and Wright, author interview, comments by Parker; Richard A. Serrano, "After 49 years, Case Reopened in Racial Slaying of Emmett Till," *Oakland [Calif.] Tribune*, May 11, 2004, 1).

63. Gaston, author telephone interview.

64. Gaston, author telephone interview.

65. David T. Beito and Linda Royster Beito, *Black Maverick: T. R. M. Howard's Fight for Civil Rights and Economic Power* (Urbana: University of Illinois Press, 2009), 151–52; Henry Lee Loggins, telephone interview with Linda Beito, July 21, 2001, transcript in author's possession; "Man's Father May Have Been Involved in Terrible History of Small Mississippi Town," *Lodi (Calif.) News-Sentinel*, August 10, 2005, 7.

66. "Man's Father," 7.

67. "Gerald Chatham Dies," *New York Times*, October 11, 1956, 39.

68. Tom Brennan, "World Watched Drama Unfold in Rural County Courtroom," *Jackson Clarion-Ledger/Jackson Daily News*, August 25, 1985, 2H; Gerald Chatham Oral History Interview (OH293), courtesy of Charles W. Capps Jr. Archives and Museum, Delta State University, Cleveland, Miss.; Gerald Chatham Sr., author interview, February 24, 2012, Hernando, Miss.

69. David Brown, "Sumner Revisited: How Several Lives Altered by Till Trial," *Delta Democrat-Times* (Greenville, Miss.), August 19, 1956, 7. The letters that Chatham received were donated to Delta State University in 2005 by his family.

70. "Prosecutor in Till Case Dies Tuesday," *Delta Democrat-Times* (Greenville, Miss.), October 10, 1956, 1; Maria Burnham, "Till Case Is Also About Attorney," *Desoto (Miss.) Appeal* (Southhaven, Miss.), May 4, 2004, DS1; "Adjourn in Honor of Gerald Chatham," *Delta Democrat-Times* (Greenville, Miss.), October 11, 1956, 3.

71. "Charleston Banker Drowns in Enid Lake," *Clarksdale (Miss.) Press Register*, September 4, 1962, 8.

72. Danny McKenzie, "Ripley Attorney Played Major Role in Till Case," *Tupelo (Miss.) Daily Journal*, September 21, 2003, 1A.

73. "Prominent Local Attorney Dies," *Southern Sentinel* (Ripley, Miss.), December 7, 1967, 1; Jak and Bruce Smith Oral History Interview (OH289), comments by Bruce Smith, courtesy of Charles W. Capps Jr. Archives and Museum. Sadly, Bruce Smith died in an auto accident on August 13, 2014.

74. "Heart Attack Is Fatal to Sumner Attorney," *Mississippi Sun* (Charleston, Miss.), June 30, 1966, 1.

75. "Jesse Breland Dies at 80," *Clarksdale (Miss.) Press Register*, March 26, 1969, 1.

76. J. W. Kellum and Amzie Moore, interview, conducted by Blackside, Inc., August 29, 1979, for *Eyes on the Prize: America's Civil Rights Years (1954–1965)*, Henry Hampton Collection, Washington University, St. Louis, http://digital.wustl.edu/eyesontheprize/, comments by Kellum.

77. Richard Rubin, "The Ghosts of Emmett Till," *New York Times*, July 31, 2005, F33.

78. Kellum and Moore, interview, for *Eyes on the Prize*.

79. "Attorney J. W. Kellum Dies," *Charleston (Miss.) Sun-Sentinel*, July 25, 1996, 1.

80. Rubin, "Ghosts of Emmett Till," F33; "Attorney J. W. Kellum Dies," 1.

81. Betty Pearson, author interview, February 6, 2006, Sumner, Miss.

82. Brennan, "World Watched Drama Unfold," 2H.

83. Paul Hendrickson, "Mississippi Haunting," *Washington Post Magazine*, February 27, 2000, 26, reprinted in *Rhetoric & Public Affairs* 8, no. 2 (Summer 2005): 185.

84. Plater Robinson, *The Murder of Emmett Till*, Soundprint, copy of audio in author's possession, http://soundprint.org/radio/display_show/ID/398/name/The+Murder+of+Emmett+Till.

85. "Retired Attorney John Whitten Dies," *Charleston (Miss.) Sun-Sentinel*, February 2003.

86. Robert H. Henderson Sr. obituary, *Charleston (Miss.) Sun-Sentinel*, October 11, 2007, 3.

87. "White Jurors Acquit Sheriff of Bludgeoning," *Morgantown (Miss.) Post*, August 8, 1958, 3.

88. "Judge Swango's Rites Held on Saturday," *Batesville (Miss.) Panolian*, December 12, 1968, 1; Chatham, author interview. For more on the sanatorium and its influence, see Ashley Baggett, "The Rise of the Surgical Age in the Treatment of Pulmonary Tuberculosis: A Case Study of the Mississippi State Sanatorium" (Master's thesis, Louisiana State University, 2003).

89. Al Kuetiner, "Till Case Rarely Discussed at Site of Famous Murder Trial," *Delta Demo-crat-Times* (Greenville, Miss.), September 4, 1957, 15.

90. "Former Sheriff Dies; Served Two Terms," *Greenwood (Miss.) Commonwealth*, October 9, 1975, 1. For an account of Cothran's term as sheriff (1960–64), see Paul Hendrickson, *Sons of Mississippi: A Story of Race and Its Legacy* (New York: Knopf, 2003), 83–113.

91. "Former Sheriff Dies," 1; "John Ed Cothran, 1914–2008; Investigated 1955 Death of Emmett Till," *Chicago Tribune*, March 21, 2008, 9; "John Ed Cothran; Investigated Till Killing," *Washington Post*, March 20, 2008, B7.

92. Hugh Stephen Whitaker, "A Case Study of Southern Justice: The Emmett Till Case" (Master's thesis, Florida State University, 1963), 164–65, reprinted as Hugh Stephen Whitaker, "A Case Study in Southern Justice: The Murder and Trial of Emmett Till," *Rhetoric & Public Affairs* 8, no. 2 (Summer 2005): 213.

93. "Ross Found Guilty, Faces Huge Fine," *Laurel (Miss.) Leader Call*, September 29, 1962, 1, 2.

94. "Lee County Runoff Vote Is Scheduled," *Delta Democrat-Times* (Greenville, Miss.), February 17, 1965, 6; "H. C. Strider Dies on Hunt," *Clarksdale (Miss.) Press Register*, December 28, 1970, 13.

95. "Mississippian Says He Paid for Votes," *New York Times*, July 6, 1968, 8; Wilson F. Minor, author interview, August 24, 2009, Jackson, Miss.

96. "Two Delta Senators Offer Negro Relocation Measure," *Hattiesburg (Miss.) American*, February 25, 1966, 1. Crook would later represent Roy Bryant in a federal criminal case. This is discussed later in this chapter.

97. "H. C. Strider Dies," 13.

98. "JBW Attends Funerals," *Delta Democrat-Times* (Greenville, Miss.), December 29, 1970, 10; Mississippi Code of 1972, as amended, http://www.lexisnexis.com/hottopics/mscode/.

99. "Witness in Till Case Vanishes," *St. Louis Argus*, October 28, 1955, 1, 10; Richard B. Henry, "Charges Milam Killed 4," *Tri-State Defender* (Memphis, Tenn.), January 21, 1956, 1, 2.

100. National Cemetery Administration. *U.S. Veterans Gravesites, ca. 1775–2006* [database online], Provo, Utah, USA: Ancestry.com Operations Inc., 2006. *California, Death Index, 1940–1997* [database on-line], Provo, Utah, USA: Ancestry.com Operations Inc, 2000; http://www.findagrave.com/cgi-bin/fg.cgi?page=gr&GRid=91930730&; www.umbcbarstow.com.

101. Brown, "Sumner Revisited," 7.

102. William Bradford Huie, "What's Happened to the Emmett Till Killers," *Look*, January 22, 1957, 65–66.

103. Huie, "What's Happened," 66; "Till Trial Defendant Refused Gun Permit in Sunflower County," *Delta Democrat-Times* (Greenville, Miss.), January 8, 1957, 1.

104. Whitaker, "Case Study in Southern Justice," 161, reprint, 212.

105. Ygondine Sturdivant, author telephone interview, August 7, 2013.

106. "Ex-Farm Manager Freed in Till Murder Now in Bread Line," *New York Post*, February 14, 1958, 20; "Till 'Suspect' on 'Breadline,'" *Pittsburgh Courier*, February 22, 1958, 30; "J. W. Milam Denies Reports He Stood in Miss. Bread Line," *Jet* 13, no. 18 (March 6, 1958): 6–7.

107. Photo and caption under the title "Honored at Reception," *Delta Democrat-Times* (Greenville, Miss.), May 6, 1962, 16; Myrtle Thompson obituary, *Delta Democrat-Times*

(Greenville, Miss.), June 23, 1963, 2; Albert Thompson obituary, *Delta Democrat-Times* (Greenville, Miss.), November 22, 1965, 2; Confidential source A, author telephone interview, April 7, 2014.

108. "City Court" section of *Delta Democrat-Times* (Greenville, Miss.), January 10, 1969, 2; May 10, 1972, 11; and August 30, 1972, 2.

109. Confidential source B, author telephone interview, June 8, 2014.

110. Joe Atkins and Tom Brennan, "Bryant Wants the Past to 'Stay Dead,'" *Jackson Clarion-Ledger/Jackson Daily News*, August 25, 1985, 3H; John William Milam obituary, *Delta Democrat-Times* (Greenville, Miss.), January 2, 1981, 2A; Confidential source A, author telephone interview.

111. J. W. Milam's obituary listed Juanita as his spouse at the time of his death. Certificate of Search sent to author from Marilyn Hansell, chancery clerk of Washington County, Mississippi, May 24, 2005, indicates that Hansell checked divorce records from 1965 to 1980 and found nothing for John W. and Juanita Milam. It was later confirmed to me that the couple remained together until J. W.'s death during my telephone interview with confidential source A.

112. Advertisement for National Beauty Salon Week, *Delta Democrat-Times* (Greenville, Miss.), February 13, 1972, 17; "Television Raffle," caption under photo, *Delta Democrat-Times* (Greenville, Miss.), February 14, 1971, 20; "Delta Diary," *Delta Democrat-Times* (Greenville, Miss.), October 2, 1973, 6; "Local Cosmetologists to Give Away Television," *Delta Democrat-Times* (Greenville, Miss.), April 13, 1975, 15; Confidential source A, author telephone interview.

113. Confidential source A, author telephone interview.

114. Confidential source A, author telephone interview.

115. Confidential source A, author telephone interview.

116. Horace William Milam obituary, *Delta Democrat-Times* (Greenville, Miss.), October 9, 2008, A6; Mary Juanita Milam obituary, *Biloxi-Gulfport (Miss.) Sun Herald*, January 14, 2014, A4; Confidential source A, author telephone interview.

117. Roy Bryant obituary, *Memphis Commercial Appeal*, September 3, 1994, A14; Roy Bryant obituary, *Bolivar Commercial* (Cleveland, Miss.), September 6, 1994, 12; Bill Minor, "Saga of Till Slaying Will Live On Despite Death of 2nd Killer," *Jackson Clarion Ledger*, September 25, 1994, C3.

118. "Ex-Farm Manager Freed in Till Murder," 20; "Bryant Sought Job as Indianola Cop; He Didn't Get It," *Delta Democrat-Times* (Greenville, Miss.), May 2, 1956, 1; Huie, "What's Happened," 65; Atkins and Brennan, "Bryant Wants the Past," 1H; *United States v. Roy Bryant Sr.*, CRG-83-55, copy of case file in author's possession.

119. "Bryant Sought Job," 1.

120. "Three Hurt in Collision Here on Sunday," *Delta Democrat-Times* (Greenville, Miss.), November 19, 1956, 1; "Till Figure Injured in Auto Crash," *Chicago Defender*, December 1, 1956, 1.

121. Comments of Carolyn Donham posted on her Facebook wall, November 19, 2010. Donham does not mention the accident but acknowledges in her comments that Frank Bryant would have turned fifty-four years old that day.

122. David Holmberg, "The Legacy of Emmett Till," *Palm Beach (Fla.) Post*, September 4, 1994, 10A; Confidential source C, author interviews, August 19 and December 3, 2014.

123. Comments of Carolyn Donham on Linda Jean Bryant Facebook wall, April 7, 2013.

124. Vinton High School, *Souvenir*, 1970, 21; Comments of Thomas Lamar Bryant posted on "Memories of Vinton [Louisiana]" Facebook wall; "About," on Carol Ann Bryant Facebook wall; Comments of Carolyn Donham posted on Linda Jean Bryant Facebook wall, June 26, 2014; www.huntingwithtom.com.

125. "Sunflower Success," *Delta Democrat-Times* (Greenville, Miss.), September 19, 1974, 31; "About," on Carol Ann Bryant Facebook wall; *Carolyn Holloway Bryant v. Roy Bryant*, Chancery Court of Sunflower County, Mississippi, complaint no. 16505, copy in author's possession provided by Plater Robinson.

126. Comments of Carolyn Donham posted on Linda Jean Bryant Facebook wall, April 7, 2013.

127. Eula Bryant obituary, *Delta Democrat-Times* (Greenville, Miss.), August 27, 1974, 2; *Carolyn Holloway Bryant v. Roy Bryant*.

128. "Sunflower Voters Have Wide Choice," *Delta Democrat-Times* (Greenville, Miss.), May 9, 1977, 12; "Sunflower Candidates Chosen," *Delta Democrat-Times* (Greenville, Miss.), May 11, 1977, 12.

129. Darren, last name withheld, telephone interview with author, February 11, 2010.

130. Roy Bryant headstone, Lerhton Cemetery, Ruleville, Mississippi, includes his and Vera Jo's marriage date; Vera Jo Bryant obituary, *Bolivar Commercial* (Cleveland, Miss.), May 3, 2012, 3.

131. *United States v. Roy Bryant Sr.*, CRG-83-55.

132. *United States v. Roy Bryant Sr.*, CRG-87-82; Holmberg, "Legacy of Emmett Till," 10A.

133. The Samuels documentary is available at www.richsamuels.com/nbcmm/till/till.html; Atkins and Brennan, "Bryant Wants the Past," 3H.

134. Atkins and Brennan, "Bryant Wants the Past," 1H–2H.

135. Clotye Murdock Larsson, "Land of the Till Murder Revisited," *Ebony* 41, no. 5 (March 1986): 57.

136. Charles Ealy, "Mother of Teen Slain in '55 Tries to Keep Case Alive," *Dallas Morning News*, December 20, 1992, 16A; Holmberg, "Legacy of Emmett Till," 10A.

137. Holmberg, "Legacy of Emmett Till," 10A; Robinson, *Murder of Emmett Till*.

138. Hendrickson, *Sons of Mississippi*, 11.

139. Holmberg, "Legacy of Emmett Till," 10A.

140. Vera Jo Bryant obituary, 3. I confirmed that she was buried in the double plot she purchased with Roy Bryant during a visit to Lehrton Cemetery in Ruleville, Mississippi, on August 17, 2014.

141. Comments of Carolyn Donham posted on her Facebook wall, November 4, 2010.

142. Confidential source C, author interview, August 19, 2014; Comments of Carolyn Donham posted on her Facebook wall, November 19, 2010.

143. Comments of Carolyn Donham posted on her Facebook wall, November 9–10, 2010; Comments of Carolyn Donham and Carol Ann Bryant posted on Thomas Lamar Bryant Facebook wall, August 12–13, 2013.

144. Griffin Chandler and Madge Carolyn Holloway Bryant, marriage certificate, November 21, 1984, state file no. 123-84-25327, Mississippi State Department of Health Vital Records; Griffin Chandler obituary, *Delta Democrat-Times* (Greenville, Miss.), May 5, 1988, 3A; Confidential source C, author interview, December 3, 2014.

145. David Alford Donham obituary, *Delta Democrat-Times* (Greenville, Miss.), April 11, 2002, A5; Confidential source C, author interviews, August 19 and December 3, 2014.

146. Comments of Carolyn Donham posted on her Facebook wall, November 11, 2010; Confidential source C, author interview, December 3, 2014.

147. Confidential source C, author interview, December 3, 2014.

148. Confidential source C, author interviews, August 19 and December 3, 2014. I first learned that Carolyn Donham and her daughter-in-law were writing a book together when Carolyn's granddaughter, Rachael Bryant, revealed that fact on the *History News Network* blog on April 13, 2008, in four separate posts: "There is a book coming out soon about the case. Look for it in about a year." "I will not comment anymore about my Grandmother. She and my mom will be releasing a book in about a year. Look out for it." "I will not comment to anything. Just look for a book to be out, written by my mom and biography of Carolyn. Be on the look out, maybe another year or so." "My mom is in the process of getting Carolyn's account published. Be on the look out. I will not comment on anything further."

Rachel Bryant began posting comments on the site two years earlier to defend her grandmother against vicious and vitriolic attacks by other commentators. See comments under David T. Beito, "60 Minutes Story on Emmett Till Targets Carolyn Bryant," *History News Network*, http://hnn.us/blog/8070. I have verified that Rachael Bryant is a granddaughter of Carolyn Donham and is the daughter of Thomas Lamar and Marsha Bryant, of Raleigh, North Carolina. In January 2011, Marsha Bryant told Davis Houck of Florida State University that nothing had been done on the book since Frank Bryant's death in April 2010 (Davis Houck, telephone conversation with author, January 25, 2011).

Chapter 11

1. John Anderson, "'Till' Reviews Social History Lesson, 30 Years Later," *Chicago Tribune*, July 11, 1985, D1; "TV Highlights: New Night Court Characters," *Chicago Tribune*, July 11, 1985, D11. Wilson, considered the best high school basketball player in the nation at the time of his death, is still being mourned and was the subject of a seventy-eight-minute documentary. See Amani Martin and Ed Schillinger, *Benji: The True Story of a Life Cut Short* (ESPN Films, 2012).

2. The documentary can currently be viewed at www.richsamuels.com/nbcmm/till/till .html.

3. Joe Atkins, "Emmett Till: More Than a Murder," *Jackson Clarion-Ledger/Jackson Daily News*, August 25, 1985, 3H; Joe Atkins and Tom Brennan, "Bryant Wants the Past to 'Stay Dead,'" *Jackson Clarion-Ledger/Jackson Daily News*, August 25, 1985, 1H.

4. See, for example, Hugh Stephen Whitaker, "A Case Study in Southern Justice: The Emmett Till Case" (Master's thesis, Florida State University, 1963), reprinted as Hugh Stephen Whitaker, "A Case Study in Southern Justice: The Murder and Trial of Emmett Till," *Rhetoric & Public Affairs* 8, no. 2 (Summer 2005); Warren Breed, "Comparative Newspaper Handling of the Emmett Till Case," *Journalism Quarterly* 35 (Summer 1958): 291–98; William M. Simpson, "Reflections on a Murder: The Emmett Till Case," in *Southern Miscellany: Essays in History in Honor of Glover Moore*, ed. Frank Allen Dennis (Jackson: University Press of Mississippi, 1981), 177–200. On the dearth of scholarship on the Till case during this period, see Clenora

Hudson, "The Unearthing of Emmett Till: A Compelling Process," *Iowa Alumni Review* 41, no. 5 (October 1988): 18–23; Clenora Hudson-Weems, "Resurrecting Emmett Till: The Catalyst of the Modern Civil Rights Movement," *Journal of Black Studies* 29, no. 2 (November 1998): 179–88.

5. Philip C. Kolin, "Forgotten Manuscripts: 'Blues for Emmett Till': The Earliest Extant Song about the Murder of Emmett Till," *African American Review* 42, nos. 3–4 (Fall–Winter 2008): 455; Philip C. Kolin, "Haunting America: Emmett Till in Music and Song," *Southern Cultures* (Fall 2009): 118–21. See also Christopher Metress, "'No Justice, No Peace': The Figure of Emmett Till in African American Literature," *MELUS* 28, no. 1 (Spring 2003): 87–103.

6. Kolin, "Haunting America," 119, 121; Frederick Bock, "A Prize Winning Poet Fails to Measure Up," *Chicago Daily Tribune*, June 5, 1960, C12; Mel Watkins, "Gwendolyn Brooks, 83, Passionate Poet, Dies," *New York Times*, December 5, 2000, C22. For a chronological sampling of many of these literary efforts, see Christopher Metress, ed., *The Lynching of Emmett Till: A Documentary Narrative* (Charlottesville: University of Virginia Press, 2002), 291–345. For a study of the Brooks pieces, see Vivian M. May, "Maids Mild and Dark Villains, Sweet Magnolias and Sleeping Blood," in *Emmett Till in Literary Memory and Imagination*, ed. Harriett Pollack and Christopher Metress (Baton Rouge: Louisiana State University Press, 2008), 98–111; Laura Dawkins, "It Could Have Been My Son: Maternal Empathy in Gwendolyn Brooks's and Audre Lorde's Till Poems," in Pollack and Metress, *Emmett Till in Literary Memory and Imagination*, 112–27.

7. For the full story of Serling's attempt to portray the Till murder on television, see Christopher Metress, "Submitted for Their Approval: Rod Serling and the Lynching of Emmett Till," *Mississippi Quarterly* 61, nos. 1–2 (Winter/Spring 2008): 143–72. After Serling's death, his wife, Carol, donated her husband's papers to Ithaca College, where Serling had taught from 1967 until 1975. Carol Serling also served on the board of the school. The original version of "Noon at Tuesday" received its first public reading at Ithaca College in March 2008. See Rebecca James, "A Tale Too Explosive for '50s TV," *Syracuse (N.Y.) Post Standard*, March 27, 2008, D1–2.

8. James Baldwin, *Blues for Mister Charlie* (New York: Dial Books, 1964), dedication page and xiv; Metress, *Lynching of Emmett Till*, 319–21; Claudia Cassidy, "Baldwin's New Play: Abuse with Tom-Toms," *Chicago Daily Tribune*, May 10, 1964, J5; Lee A. Daniels, "James Baldwin, Eloquent Writer in Behalf of Civil Rights, Is Dead," *New York Times*, December 2, 1987, A1; Howard Taubman, "Theater: Blues for Mister Charlie," *New York Times*, April 24, 1964, 24; see also Brian Norman, "James Baldwin's Unifying Polemic: Racial Segregation, Moral Integration, and the Polarizing Figure of Emmett Till," in Pollack and Metress, *Emmett Till in Literary Memory and Imagination*, 75–97.

9. See, for example, Patrick Chura, "Prolepsis and Anachronism: Emmett Till and the History of To Kill a Mockingbird," *Southern Literary Journal* 32, no. 2 (Spring 2000): 1–26. Chura notes that both the Till case and *To Kill a Mockingbird* "combine the dual icons of the 'black rapist' and concomitant fear of black male sexuality with mythologized vulnerable and sacred Southern womanhood." Also, both trials include all-male, all-white juries, made up mostly of farmers; both juries reach verdicts against the black victim/defendant despite evidence to the contrary; in each instance, a fair-minded judge presided over the proceedings and a dedicated attorney (Gerald Chatham/Atticus Finch) sought justice for the black male involved. "In both cases," continues Chura, "the black victim is a diminished physical specimen of a fully grown man. In both cases, the press or media emerge as a force for racial justice. In both cases, the

concept of child murder figures prominently in the calculus of revenge for a racial and social shame of a class of poor Southern whites."

10. Julius Thompson, "Till," in *Blues Said: Walk On* (Houston: Energy Blacksouth Press, 1977), 9–11, reprinted in Metress, *Lynching of Emmett Till*, 321–23; Audre Lorde, "Afterimages," *Cream City Review* 17, no. 2 (Fall 1981): 119–23, reprinted in Metress, *Lynching of Emmett Till*, 323–27; Dawkins, "It Could Have Been My Son," 112–27. These and dozens of other Till-inspired works published into the new millennium are referenced in "Literary Representations of the Lynching of Emmett Till," in Pollack and Metress, *Emmett Till in Literary Memory and Imagination*, 224–50.

11. Video and transcript available at *NBC Learn K–12*, http://archives.nbclearn.com; Atkins and Brennan, "Bryant Wants the Past," 1H.

12. Lee Winfrey, "'Eyes on Prize' Recommended Viewing on Civil Rights History," *Elyria (Ohio) Chronicle-Telegram*, January 21, 1987, B6; Ed Siegel, "Behind 'Eyes on the Prize' Henry Hampton Reflects on a Series 19 Years in the Making," *Boston Globe*, January 21, 1987, 6; Joseph Pryweller, "Eyes on the Prize Author Has Won Respect for His Civil Rights Work," *Newport News (Va.) Daily Press*, April 7, 1991, I1.

13. See interviews with Charles Diggs, November 6, 1986; James L. Hicks, November 2, 1985; William Bradford Huie, August 30, 1979; Rutha Mae Jackson and Willie Hill Jackson, August 29, 1979; Curtis Jones, November 12, 1985; J. W. Kellum and Amzie Moore, August 29, 1979; Rev. Fred Shuttlesworth, November 7, 1985, gathered as part of *Eyes on the Prize: America's Civil Rights Years (1954–1965)*, Blackside, Inc., Henry Hampton Collection, Washington University, St. Louis, http://digital.wustl.edu/eyesontheprize.

14. Winfrey, "'Eyes on Prize' Recommended Viewing," B6; Siegel, "Behind 'Eyes on the Prize,'" 61; Julian Bond, email to author, October 18, 2013; Pryweller, "Eyes on the Prize Author," I1. For the book, see Juan Williams, *Eyes on the Prize: America's Civil Rights Years, 1954–1965* (New York: Viking Press, 1988).

15. Pryweller, "Eyes on the Prize Author," I1; Jesse McKinley, "Henry Hampton Dies at 58; Produced 'Eyes on the Prize,'" *New York Times*, November 24, 1998, 10; "'Eyes on the Prize' Returns to PBS," *Washington Informer*, September 28, 2006, 26; "'Eyes on the Prize II' Wins Three Golden Eagle Awards," *Los Angeles Sentinel*, December 11, 1990, A8; "Landmark 'Eyes on the Prize I and II' Return to PBS," *Los Angeles Sentinel*, July 8, 1993, B3.

16. Stephen J. Whitfield, *A Death in the Delta: The Story of Emmett Till* (New York: Free Press, 1988), viii.

17. The dissertation appeared as Clenora Frances Hudson, "Emmett Till: The Impetus for the Modern Civil Rights Movement" (PhD diss., University of Iowa, 1988). For her published volume, see Clenora Hudson-Weems, *Emmett Till: The Sacrificial Lamb of the Civil Rights Movement* (Troy, Mich.: Bedford Publishers, 1994). The book is currently in a revised fourth edition, which appeared in 2006 from AuthorHouse in Bloomington, Indiana. Hudson-Weems has alienated herself from other Emmett Till scholars by proclaiming that they have largely plagiarized her work. She has self-published two volumes in which she has aggressively yet erroneously put forth this claim. See Clenora Hudson-Weems, *The Definitive Emmett Till: Passion and Battle of a Woman for Truth and Intellectual Justice* (Bloomington, Ind.: AuthorHouse, 2006); Clenora Hudson-Weems, *Plagiarism: Physical and Intellectual Lynchings: An Emmett Till Continuum* (Bloomington, Ind.: AuthorHouse, 2007).

18. See Whitfield, *Death in the Delta*, 56–57; Hudson-Weems, *Emmett Till*, 12, 26.

19. Andrea Stone and Jerry Mitchell, "Evers Case Inspires Kin of Others," *USA Today*, December 24, 1990, 3A.

20. Stone and Mitchell, "Evers Case Inspires Kin," 3A; Tony Jones, "Cochran to Reopen Infamous Till Case," *Michigan Chronicle* (Detroit), September 13, 1995, 1-A.

21. For more on the Evers case and subsequent conviction of Beckwith, see Bobby DeLaughter, *Never Too Late: A Prosecutor's Story of Justice in the Medgar Evers Case* (New York: Scribner, 2001); Myrlie Evers-Williams, with Melinda Blau, *Watch Me Fly: What I Learned on the Way to Becoming the Woman I Was Meant to Be* (Boston: Little, Brown, 1999); Willie Morris, *The Ghosts of Medgar Evers: A Tale of Race, Murder, Mississippi, and Hollywood* (New York: Random House, 1998); Maryanne Vollers, *Ghosts of Mississippi: The Murder of Medgar Evers, the Trials of Byron De La Beckwith, and the Haunting of the New South* (Boston: Little, Brown, 1995).

22. Tony Jones, "Cochran May Open Till Case," *Tri-State Defender* (Memphis, Tenn.), August 26–30, 1995, 1; "Johnnie Cochran May Reopen Emmett Till Murder Case," *San Francisco Sun-Reporter*, December 14, 1995, 3.

23. Jones, "Cochran May Open Till Case," 1.

24. "Johnnie Cochran May Reopen," 3.

25. In his autobiography, published seven years after he announced his intentions, Cochran briefly mentioned the Till case but said nothing about any plans, current or former, for reopening it. See Johnnie Cochran, with David Fisher, *A Lawyer's Life* (New York: Thomas Dunne Books, 2002), 111–12.

26. Mamie Till-Mobley, author telephone interview, December 3, 1996.

27. Keith Beauchamp, author telephone interview, November 10, 2013; Megan Scott, "Film Cracks Open '55 Racial Slaying," *Ft. Wayne (Ind.) Journal-Gazette*, February 28, 2006, 2D; Connie Bloom, "Filmmaker Delivers Message on Injustice," *McClatchy-Tribune Business News*, February 23, 2007, 1.

28. Beauchamp, author telephone interviews, November 10, 2013, and February 2, 2014; "Takes Five; Keith Beauchamp," *Milwaukee Journal Sentinel*, March 24, 2006, A2.

29. Beauchamp, author telephone interview, November 10, 2013; Felicia R. Lee, "Directors Elated by Plan to Revisit 1955 Murder," *New York Times*, May 12, 2004, B4; Mamie Till-Mobley and Christopher Benson, *Death of Innocence: The Story of the Hate Crime That Changed America* (New York: Random House, 2003), 277.

30. Dawn Turner Trice, "Renewed Focus on Till Case May Rewrite History," *Chicago Tribune*, May 12, 2004, 2C; Beauchamp, author telephone interview, November 10, 2013.

31. Beauchamp, author telephone interviews, November 10, 2013, and February 2, 2014.

32. Scott, "Film Cracks Open," 2D; Joe Neumaier, "Filmmaker's 'Untold Story' Drives Inquiry in Racial Killing," *New York Daily News*, August 16, 2005, 32; Patricia Poist, "Haunted by Ghost of Mississippi," *Lancaster (Pa.) Sunday News*, January 16, 2005, 1; Dawn Turner Trice, "Renewed Focus on Till Case May Rewrite History," *Chicago Tribune*, May 12, 2004, 2C.

33. David Holmberg, "The Legacy of Emmett Till," *Palm Beach (Fla.) Post*, September 4, 1994, 10A.

34. Beauchamp, author telephone interview, November 10, 2013.

35. Ali Rahman, "Emmett Till's Mother Speaks," *New York Amsterdam News*, November 21, 2002, 4.

36. Beauchamp, author telephone interviews, November 10, 2013, and February 2, 2014.

37. Chris Jones, "Chronicle of a Life Untold: Emmett Till's Mother Speaks," *BET Weekend*, October 1999, 4; Christopher Benson, "Troubled Waters," *Chicago*, September 1999, 26; Chris Jones, "Everyone's Child," *Chicago Tribune*, September 9, 1999, S5, 10; Richard Christiansen, "Reviving the Power of the Till Tragedy," *Chicago Tribune*, September 14, 1999, 1–2.

38. Mamie Till-Mobley and David Barr III, *The Face of Emmett Till* (Woodstock, Ill.: Dramatic Publishing, 1999), 329–31.

39. Beauchamp, author telephone interviews, November 10, 2013, and February 2, 2014; Bobby DeLaughter, email to author, June 20, 2014.

40. Kam Williams, "Discourse with the Director of Award-Winning Emmett Till Documentary," *Washington Informer*, October 13, 2005, 15.

41. William Nunnelley, "Metress Hopes Book on Emmett Till Will Clear Up Some Misconceptions," January 24, 2003, http://www.samford.edu/news/newsarticle.aspx?id=21474841550#.U-RjEPldXup.

42. See Chris Crowe, *Mississippi Trial, 1955* (New York: Phillis Fogelman Books, 2002). In January 2003, Crowe published a nonfiction title, *Getting Away with Murder: The True Story of the Emmett Till Murder* (New York: Dial Books for Young Readers, 2003). Crowe had actually stumbled across the Emmett Till case in 1998 while conducting research for his book *Presenting Mildred D. Taylor* (New York: Twayne, 1999). Taylor made a reference to the Till murder in one of her essays, which piqued Crowe's curiosity. What he learned set him on a course for a new project. Once he finished the Taylor book, he began working on a book on Emmett Till, even interviewing Mamie Till-Mobley over the telephone in the process. Jim Blasingame, "'A Crime That's So Unjust!': Chris Crowe Tells About the Death of Emmett Till," *Alan Review* 2 (Spring/Summer 2003): 22–24; Chris Crowe, author telephone interview, March 24, 2014; Crowe, *Getting Away with Murder*, 11. Two other noteworthy titles that appeared during the renewed interest in the Till case after the mid-1980s include not only fiction but poetry. See Lewis Nordan, *Wolf Whistle: A Novel* (Chapel Hill: Algonquin Books, 1993); Marilyn Nelson, *A Wreath for Emmett Till* (Boston: Houghton Mifflin, 2005).

43. Mamie Till-Mobley, author telephone interview, April 15, 2002; Till-Mobley and Benson, *Death of Innocence*, 278.

44. Rahman, "Emmett Till's Mother Speaks," 4.

45. Christopher Benson, author telephone interview, August 23, 2014.

46. "Mamie Till Mobley, Heroic Mother, Mourned," *People's World*, January 24, 2003, http://www.peoplesworld.org/mamie-till-mobley-heroic-mother-mourned; Rahman, "Emmett Till's Mother Speaks," 4. Around this time, Mississippi assistant attorney general Frank Spencer affirmed to journalists that "we welcome any evidence from any source that would let us know what happened there" (Rebecca Segall and David Holmberg, "Who Killed Emmett Till?," *Nation* 276, no. 4 [February 3, 2003]: 38).

47. Beauchamp, author telephone interview, November 10, 2013; Mike Small, author telephone interview, July 20, 2014; Mike Small, email to author, July 21, 2014.

48. Beauchamp, author telephone interview, November 10, 2013; Segall and Holmberg, "Who Killed Emmett Till?," 38.

49. Brent Staples, "The Murder of Emmett Louis Till, Revisited," *New York Times*, November 11, 2002, A16.

50. Herb Boyd, "The Lynching of Emmett Till," *New York Amsterdam News*, November 21, 2002, 4.

51. Stanley Nelson, author telephone interview, October 15, 2013; Ron Howell, "A Film with a Mission," *Newsday*, January 20, 2003, B6.

52. See Stanley Nelson, prod., *The Murder of Emmett Till* (Firelight Media, 2002); Keith Beauchamp, prod., *The Untold Story of Emmett Louis Till* (Till Freedom Come Productions, 2005).

53. Lee, "Directors Elated," B4; Keith Beauchamp, online conversation with author, June 4, 2005, transcript in author's possession; Beauchamp, author telephone interview, November 10, 2013.

54. Howell, "Film with a Mission," B6.

55. Nelson, author telephone interview; Howell, "Film with a Mission," B6.

56. Bennie M. Currie, "Films, Books Revisit Saga of Slain Teen Emmett Till," *Kansas City Call*, December 20–26, 2002, 4; Monroe Dodd, *Pursuit of Truth* (Kansas City, Mo.: Kansas City Library, 2014), 16.

57. Alvin Sykes, author telephone interview, August 17, 2013.

58. C. J. Janovy, "Justice at Last," *Pitch* (Kansas City), March 23, 2006, 16; Drew Jubera, "Civil Rights–Era Murder Cases," *Atlanta Journal-Constitution*, June 3, 2007, A1; Laura Parker, "Perseverance Pays Off for Civil Rights Activist," *USA Today*, March 19, 2007, A2; Dodd, *Pursuit of Truth*, 4–5, 7, 10.

59. Janovy, "Justice at Last," 17; Parker, "Perseverance Pays Off," A2; Alvin Sykes, author telephone interview, March 8, 2014; Dodd, *Pursuit of Truth*, 4–6.

60. Janovy, "Justice at Last," 17; Sykes, author telephone interview, August 17, 2013; Dodd, *Pursuit of Truth*, 6–8.

61. Sykes, author telephone interviews, August 17, 2013, and March 8, 2014.

62. Sykes, author telephone interviews, August 17, 2013, and March 8, 2014; Dodd, *Pursuit of Truth*, 16.

63. Sykes, author telephone interview, August 17, 2013; Dodd, *Pursuit of Truth*, 6–7. Donald Burger died in 2010 at age seventy.

64. Janovy, "Justice at Last," 13, 17; Sykes, author telephone interview, August 17, 2013; Benson, author telephone interview, August 23, 2014; Dodd, *Pursuit of Truth*, 16.

65. Sykes, author telephone interview, August 17, 2013.

66. Sykes, author telephone interviews, August 17, 2013, and June 17, 2014; Beauchamp, author telephone interview, November 10, 2013.

67. Sykes, author telephone interviews, August 17, 2013, and March 8, 2014; Segall and Holmberg, "Who Killed Emmett Till?," 38.

68. Bob Longino, "The Unfinished Story of Emmett Till," *Atlanta Journal-Constitution*, January 5, 2003, A1; Bob Longino, "Ceremony Today for Till's Mother," *Atlanta Journal-Constitution*, January 8, 2003, B1.

69. Beauchamp, author telephone interview, November 10, 2013.

70. Sykes, author telephone interview, August 17, 2013.

71. Bob Longino, "Lynching Victim Mom Dies on Eve of Atlanta Visit," *Atlanta Journal-Constitution*, January 7, 2003, A1.

72. Benson, author telephone interview, August 23, 2014.

73. Beauchamp, author telephone interview, November 10, 2013.

74. Longino, "Lynching Victim Mom Dies," A1; Beauchamp, author telephone interview, November 10, 2013.

75. Beauchamp, author telephone interview, November 10, 2013; Alvin Sykes, author telephone interview, March 8, 2014.

76. Bob Longino, "Emmett Till Documentary Previewed at King Center," *Atlanta Journal-Constitution*, January 26, 2003, C2; Bob Longino, "Telling Till's 'Untold Story,'" *Atlanta Journal-Constitution*, January 24, 2003, E5.

77. Beauchamp, author telephone interview, November 10, 2013; Longino, "Telling Till's 'Untold Story,'" E5.

78. Timothy R. Brown, "Till Film Up for Emmy Tonight," *Jackson Clarion-Ledger*, September 13, 2003, 2B; "Documentary on Till Murder Wins Emmy," *Jackson Clarion-Ledger*, September 15, 2003, 1A.

79. Beauchamp, author telephone interview, November 10, 2013.

80. Sykes, author telephone interview, March 8, 2014.

81. Alvin Sykes, email to author, May 8, 2014.

82. Alvin Sykes, email to Mehmet Yaşar İşcan, n.d., copy in author's possession.

83. Mehmet Yaşar İşcan to Alvin Sykes, April 25, 2003, copy in author's possession.

84. Sykes, email to author.

85. Beauchamp, author telephone interview, February 2, 2014; Sykes, author telephone interview, March 8, 2014; William Bradford Huie, "The Shocking Story of Approved Killing in Mississippi," *Look*, January 24, 1956, 47.

86. Sykes, author telephone interview, August 17, 2013; Janovy, "Justice at Last," 13, 15; Dodd, *Pursuit of Truth*, 17.

87. Dylan Grayson, "Sykes: It's Not too Late for Truth," *Guilfordian*, February 16, 2007, http://www.guilfordian.com/archives/2007/02/16/sykes-its-not-too-late-for-truth; Janovy, "Justice at Last," 13, 15; Sykes, author telephone interview, August 17, 2013. For the Scalia opinion and how it applied both in 1976 and 1998, go to http://www.justice.gov/sites/default/files/olc/opinions/1998/04/31/op-olc-v022-p0061.pdf.

88. Sykes, author telephone interviews, August 17, 2013, and March 8, 2014.

89. Beauchamp, author telephone interview, November 10, 2013; Jerry Walker, "Emmett Till Murder Case Presented to Delegates of the United Nations," *Kansas City Call*, June 6–12, 2003, 3.

90. Mary Sanchez, "Activist Enlists Evers Family to Solve Emmett Till Case," *Charleston (W. Va.) Sunday Gazette-Mail*, June 22, 2003, 9A; Sykes, author telephone interview, March 8, 2014.

91. Vernon Jarrett, "Emmett Till's Mom Speaks Again," *Chicago Defender*, October 15, 2003, 2; Benson, author telephone interview, August 23, 2014.

92. Beauchamp, author telephone interview, November 10, 2013.

93. Sykes, author telephone interview, August 17, 2013.

94. John Hailman, *From Midnight to Guntown: True Crime Stories from a Federal Prosecutor in Mississippi* (Jackson: University Press of Mississippi, 2013), 222–23; John Hailman, author telephone interview, June 21, 2014; John Hailman, email to author, July 2, 2014; Sykes, author telephone interviews, August 17, 2013, and June 12, 2014. Hailman incorrectly wrote that Sykes's meeting with the Civil Rights Division occurred in August 2003.

95. Hailman, *From Midnight to Guntown*, 223–24; Hailman, author telephone interview.

96. Janovy, "Justice at Last?," 15.

97. Drew Jubera, "Duty Outweighs Emotion for DA in Till Case," *Atlanta Journal-Constitution*, November 5, 2006, A1; Laura Parker, "DA Has Tough, Final Call in Till Case," *USA Today*, March 22, 2006, A3.

98. Janovy, "Justice at Last?," 15; Jim Greenlee, author telephone interview, March 11, 2014; Hailman, author telephone interview; Dodd, *Pursuit of Truth*, 17.

99. Greenlee, author telephone interviews, March 11 and July 28, 2014; Hailman, author telephone interview; Hailman, *From Midnight to Guntown*, 226.

100. Sykes, author telephone interview, June 12, 2014; Hailman, author telephone interview.

101. Hailman, *From Midnight to Guntown*, 224; Hailman, author telephone interview; Laura Parker, "Justice Pursued for Emmett Till," *USA Today*, March 11, 2004, A3.

102. Jerry Mitchell, "Filmmaker to Show Movie on Emmett Till," *Jackson Clarion-Ledger*, February 7, 2004, 1B; Bob Longino, "Group Seeks to Reopen Emmett Till Case," *Atlanta Journal-Constitution*, April 6, 2004, E2; Clarence Page, "A New Thaw Comes to a Very Old Case," *Newsday*, March 31, 2004, A42; Greenlee, author telephone interviews, March 11 and July 28, 2014.

103. Sykes, author telephone interviews, August 17, 2013, and June 12, 2014.

104. Mitchell, "Filmmaker to Show Movie," 1B; Jerry Mitchell, "Support Sought to Reopen Till Case," *Jackson Clarion-Ledger*, February 8, 2004, 5B.

105. Chinta Strausberg, "Smith's Witnesses Tell Why U.S. Should Probe Till Case," *Chicago Defender*, February 10, 2004, 3; Sykes, author telephone interview, June 12, 2014; Cate Plys, "The City Council Hears Alarms," March 18, 2004, www.chicagoreader.com/chicago/the-city-council-hears-alarms/Content?oid=914872.

106. House Congressional Resolution 360, 108th Congress, 2nd Session, February 10, 2004, https://www.congress.gov/108/bills/hconres360/BILLS-108hconres360ih.pdf.

107. George E. Curry, "Justice Department Will Investigate Emmett Till Case," *Frost* (Fort Wayne, Ind.), May 19–25, 2004, 3.

108. Beauchamp, author telephone interview, November 10, 2013. Schumer later said that he met Beauchamp through Rev. A. R. Bernard of the Christian Cultural Center in New York City. See "Senators Schumer & Talent & Representative Rangel Hold a News Conference on the Investigation into the Murder of Emmett Till," *Political Transcript Wire*, November 19, 2004, http://www.highbeam.com/doc/1P3-743021641.html.

109. For more on the Louima case, see Lynette Holloway, "Sharpton Says Brutality Issue Will Propel Him to a Victory," *New York Times*, August 31, 1997, 27; Peter Noel, "The Battle for Abner Louima," *Village Voice*, September 2, 1997, 35, 42; Fred Kaplan, "Ex-Officer Guilty of Lying in Louima Case," *Boston Globe*, July 17, 2002, A2; William H. Rashbaum, "Police Officers Later Cleared in Louima Case Seek Jobs Back," *New York Times*, December 12, 2002, B3; "Justice at Last," *New York Amsterdam News*, April 6, 2006, 1; "Two Officers in Louima Case Again Seek Re-Instatement," *New York Times*, October 7, 2006, B6; "Ex-Officer in Louima Case Is Freed from Halfway House," *New York Times*, May 5, 2007, B2; Herb Boyd, "Louima: 'God Is Good,'" *New York Amsterdam News*, August 16, 2007, 1.

110. Beauchamp, author telephone interview, November 10, 2013; Karin Lipson, "The Agents for Justice, Documentary Filmmakers Go Beyond Telling the Story of Emmett Till's Shocking

Murder by Instigating a Reopening of the 1955 Case," *Newsday*, May 23, 2004, C6; "1955 Race Killing, Film Inspires Lawmakers' Call for Probe," *Newsday*, April 14, 2004, A6.

111. Amita Neruukar, "Lawmakers Want 1955 Mississippi Murder Reopened," cnn.com/2004/ LAW/04/13/till.murder.case.

112. Longino, "Group Seeks to Reopen," E2; Frank Lombardi, "Civil Rights Slay Plea Pols Urge Reopening of 1955 Till Case," *New York Daily News*, April 7, 2004, 1.

113. Sykes, author telephone interview, June 12, 2014.

114. Curry, "Justice Department Will Investigate," 3.

115. "Justice Will Investigate Till Murder Again," CNN Live Event/Special, www.cnn.com/ TRANSCRIPTS/0405/10/se.02.html.

116. Sykes, author telephone interview, June 12, 2014.

117. Maria Newman, "U.S. to Reopen Investigation of Emmett Till's Murder in 1955," *New York Times*, May 10, 2004, http://www.nytimes.com/2004/05/10/national/10CND-TILL.html; Robert J. Garrity Jr., "Emmett Till Exhumation Is Crucial to a Just Resolution to This Case," *Tinley Park (Ill.) Daily Southtown*, May 24, 2005.

118. Herb Boyd, "Till Case Reopened," *New York Amsterdam News*, May 13, 2004, 1; Trice, "Renewed Focus on Till Case," 2C; Beauchamp, author telephone interview, November 10, 2013.

119. Keith Beauchamp, email to author, May 28, 2014.

120. Lee, "Directors Elated," B4.

121. Eric Lichtblau and Andrew Jacobs, "U.S. Reopens '55 Murder Case, Flashpoint of Civil Rights Era," *New York Times*, May 11, 2004, A19; Tara Burghart, "Family of Slain Boy Relieved at Reopening," *Cincinnati Post*, May 11, 2004, A2.

122. Lynda Edwards, "Residents of Mississippi Town Say Till Killing Not Often Discussed," *Times of Northwest Indiana* (Munster), May 17, 2004, http://www.nwitimes.com/news/local/ residents-of-mississippi-town-say-till-killing-not-often-discussed/article_1720b867-8062 -56eb-b8e2-2ae147616aba.html.

123. "Emmett Till: Blacks React to Reopening of Tragic Case," *Jet* 105, no. 22 (May 31, 2004): 6, 8.

124. Lee, "Directors Elated," B4.

125. Bob Longino, "Emmett Till Case Reopened," *Atlanta Journal-Constitution*, May 11, 2004, A1.

126. Nita Martin, "Don't Spend Money on Till Case," letter to the editor, *Jackson Clarion-Ledger*, May 25, 2004, 6A.

Chapter 12

1. Dale R. Killinger, author telephone interview, April 29, 2014; Dale R. Killinger, email to author, September 15, 2014; Robert J. Garrity Jr., author telephone interview, July 7, 2014; "27-Year Veteran to Head Mississippi FBI Offices," *Memphis Commercial Appeal*, June 30, 2004, D8; John Hailman, *From Midnight to Guntown: True Crime Stories from a Federal Prosecutor in Mississippi* (Jackson: University Press of Mississippi, 2013), 227. The Greenville and Tupelo agencies have since closed, and currently there are seven resident agencies in Mississippi. Worthington went on to head homeland security for the Mississippi Department of Public Safety.

2. Killinger, author telephone interview.

3. Dale R. Killinger remarks at panel discussion as part of Mississippi Delta Center's Landmarks in American History and Culture, http://vimeo.com/74032741; Killinger, author telephone interview.

4. Killinger, author telephone interview.

5. Steve Ritea, "Opening Old Wounds," *New Orleans Times-Picayune*, June 15, 2004, 1.

6. Killinger, author telephone interview.

7. I could not identify a man by the name of Willie Hemphill in Darling, or anywhere in Mississippi, who fit the description of the person interviewed by Ritea, an indication that Hemphill used a pseudonym during his interview. However, in an April 29, 2014, email to me, Ritea wrote that "if he was using a pseudonym, that was never disclosed to me." Hemphill's name is redacted in Killinger's report because Hemphill was still living at the time. See Federal Bureau of Investigation, Prosecutive Report of Investigation Concerning . . . Emmett Till, Deceased, Victim, February 9, 2006, 48 (hereafter cited as Prosecutive Report).

8. Ritea, "Opening Old Wounds," 1.

9. Hailman, *From Midnight to Guntown*, 227–28, 33; Hailman, author telephone interview; Garrity, author telephone interview.

10. Michael Radutzky, "The Murder of Emmett Till," *60 Minutes* (CBS, October 24, 2004).

11. Radutzky, "Murder of Emmett Till"; Clarence Page, "Full New Probe Needed in Till Murder," *Newsday*, October 26, 2004, A40.

12. Alvin Sykes, author telephone interview, June 12, 2014.

13. This criticism that the report "promised far more than it delivered" was noted by the historians David T. Beito and Linda Royster Beito, in "Why the '60 Minutes' Story on Emmett Till Was a Disappointment," *History News Network*, http://hnn.us/article/8193.

14. Keith Beauchamp, author telephone interview, August 23, 2014; David Holmberg, "Murder of Emmett Till: New Developments," *MaximsNews Network*, http://www.maximsnews.com/2005davidholmberg12may.htm.

15. Rebecca Segall and David Holmberg, "Who Killed Emmett Till?," *Nation* 276, no. 9 (February 3, 2003): 38; David Holmberg, author telephone interview, July 1, 2014.

16. Jan Hillegas, "West Point 'Desegregation' Produces Violent Reactions," *Southern Patriot* (New Orleans), February 1970; James H. Haddock to Governor John Bell Williams, February 3, 1970, both in Sovereignty Commission Online, http://mdah.state.ms.us/arrec/digital_archives/sovcom.

17. Jan Hillegas, email to author, July 7, 2014.

18. See "Miss. School Rift Brings Fire, Bombing, Shooting," *Jet* 37, no. 19 (February 12, 1970): 4; "Jet Erred in Miss. Bombing, Shooting Story," *Jet* 37, no. 25 (March 19, 1970): 4.

19. Prosecutive Report, 110–12. Because Gode Davis died in 2010, I thought Killinger might reveal to me that Davis was his source because the right to privacy does not extend to deceased individuals. However, Killinger declined to "confirm or deny who provided the FBI the information referenced" (Dale R. Killinger, email to author, July 22, 2014).

20. Prosecutive Report, 112. Betty Wilson's name was redacted from the FBI report because she was still living at the time Killinger finished it on February 9, 2006. Betty Wilson died almost a year later, on February 6, 2007.

21. Prosecutive Report, 110–13.

22. In response to the Segall and Holmberg piece cited above, Gode Davis wrote a letter to the *Nation* in which he denied naming Billy Wilson as a source and accused the authors of "a number of errors, distortions, omissions by inference and untrue statements." Davis acknowledged speaking with Holmberg twice in 2002 but said he never talked with Segall. Davis insisted that his conversations with Holmberg "were never supposed to be 'on the record.'" Davis confirmed that he had investigated the Till case for his documentary and said that "I strive to protect my sources." He maintained that he "never identified any individual when speaking to Holmberg, neither confirming nor denying his speculative assumptions. I certainly did not quote my source by name at any time." Holmberg responded to Davis in a letter published in the same issue and maintained, "At no time did I tell Gode Davis that our conversations were off the record." Holmberg showed Davis Jan Hillegas's 1970 *Southern Patriot* article that spoke of Wilson and his alleged connection to the Till case, and "Davis confirmed to me that he'd been dealing with a person by that name." See "'American Lynching' Betrayed," and "Holmberg Replies," both in *Nation* 276, no. 9 (March 10, 2003): 2, 26.

23. Killinger, author telephone interview.

24. "Senators Schumer & Talent & Representative Rangel Hold a News Conference on the Investigation into the Murder of Emmett Till," *Political Transcript Wire*, November 19, 2004, http://www.highbeam.com/doc/1p3-743021641.html; Ana Radelat, "Lawmaker Says He'll Press AG Over Till Probe," *Jackson Clarion-Ledger*, November 20, 2004, 1B, 3B.

25. C. J. Janovy, "Justice at Last?," *Pitch* (Kansas City), March 23, 2006, 15; "Senators Schumer & Talent & Representative Rangel"; 109 S. Cong. Res. 3, Introduced in the Senate, 109th Congress, January 24, 2005, www.opencongress.org/bill/sconres3-109/text; 109th H. Cong. Res. 77, Introduced in the House, February 17, 2005, http://thomas.loc.gov/cgi-bin/query/z?c109:H .CON.RES.77.IH:.

26. Dawn Turner Trice, "Rushed Action Could Jeopardize Till Case Justice," *Chicago Tribune*, December 28, 2004, 2C; Alvin Sykes, author telephone interview, August 17, 2013.

27. "Senators Schumer & Talent & Representative Rangel"; Mark Melady, "Filmmaker Says Indictments Expected; Story Told of 1955 Lynching of Black Teen," *Worcester (Mass.) Telegram & Gazette*, February 24, 1955, B1.

28. Sykes, author telephone interview, June 12, 2014; Hailman, author telephone interview.

29. Killinger, author telephone interview.

30. Page, "Full Probe Needed," A40.

31. Prosecutive Report, 97–99; Willie Reed, author interview, February 6, 2007, Chicago; Jeffrey Andrews, author telephone interview, July 13, 2014.

32. Gretchen Ruethling, "Kin Disagree on Exhumation of Emmett Till," *New York Times*, May 6, 2005, A23; Simeon Wright, with Herb Boyd, *Simeon's Story: An Eyewitness Account of the Kidnapping of Emmett Till* (Chicago: Lawrence Hill Books, 2010), 108–9; Jerry Mitchell, "Group Seeks to Exhume Till Body," *Jackson Clarion-Ledger*, October 31, 2004, 1A.

33. P. J. Huffstutter, "FBI Begins Unearthing Mystery; Officials Exhume Casket of Victim in '55 Murder," *Ft. Wayne (Ind.) Journal-Gazette*, June 2, 2005, 4A; Dawn Turner Trice, "The First and Last Chance for Emmett Till to Speak for Himself," *Chicago Tribune*, May 5, 2005, 1.

34. Roland S. Martin, "Rush Welcomes Justice Department Decision to Exhume Till," *Chicago Defender*, May 5, 2005, 2.

35. Drew Jubera, "Autopsy Sought in 50-Year-Old Crime," *Atlanta Journal-Constitution*, May 5, 2005, A1. Myisha Priest erroneously states in a scholarly article that Emmett Till's mother "objected to the exhumation," apparently not realizing that Mamie Till-Mobley had died two years earlier. The author also suggests that this was a slap in the face to Till-Mobley, who "had repeatedly confirmed [the body's] identity and did so under oath at the murder trial." "The very facts that the FBI sought in the body ... dispute and privilege knowledge in ways that preserve the utility of his body for the making of dominant power." Priest did not discuss the fact that several family members saw the importance of the exhumation and autopsy. See Myisha Priest, "'The Nightmare Is Not Cured': Emmett Till and American Healing," *American Quarterly* 62, no. 1 (March 2010): 2.

36. "Jesse Jackson Asks Mississippi, FBI to Apologize to Emmett Till Family," *New York Beacon*, May 12–18, 2005, 3; Charles Sheehan, "Till Relatives Argue Over Exhuming Body," *Chicago Tribune*, May 6, 2005, 1.

37. "Some Till Relatives Oppose Exhumation," *Chicago Tribune*, May 6, 2005, 7; Sheehan, "Till Relatives Argue," 1.

38. Dawn Turner Rice, "In Till Case, Leaders Don't Need to Weigh In," *Chicago Tribune*, May 9, 2005, 2C.

39. Garrity, author telephone interview; "Director Robert Mueller Announces Appointment of Deputy Chief Information Officer," FBI National Press Release, April 21, 2005, www.fbi.gov; "State FBI Boss Moving to Washington," *Memphis Commercial Appeal*, June 1, 2005, D8. Garrity's new job as deputy chief information officer and business process reengineering executive placed him over the FBI's technology efforts.

40. Robert J. Garrity Jr., "Exhumation of Till's Remains Is Essential," letter to the editor, *Chicago Tribune*, May 22, 2005, 10; Robert J. Garrity Jr., "Emmett Till Exhumation Is Crucial to a Just Resolution to This Case," *Tinley Park (Ill.) Daily Southtown*, May 24, 2005, A8.

41. "Professor Seeks Transcript of Till Trial," *Memphis Commercial Appeal*, February 21, 2005, B5; Davis Houck, author telephone interview, June 10, 2014. For Houck's contributions on Emmett Till, see Davis W. Houck, "Killing Emmett," *Rhetoric & Public Affairs* 8, no. 2 (Summer 2005): 225–62; Davis W. Houck and David E. Dixon, *Rhetoric, Religion, and the Civil Rights Movement, 1954–1965* (Waco, Tex.: Baylor University Press, 2006); Davis W. Houck and Matthew A. Grindy, *Emmett Till and the Mississippi Press* (Jackson: University Press of Mississippi, 2008).

42. Houck, author telephone interview; Killinger remarks at Landmarks in American History and Culture; Killinger, email to author, July 22, 2014; Lee McGarrh, email to author, June 18, 2008; Prosecutive Report, 84. McGarrh's name has been redacted from the FBI report for privacy purposes.

43. Killinger remarks at Landmarks in American History and Culture; Killinger to Anderson, July 22, 2014; Shaila Dewan and Ariel Hart, "FBI Discovers Trial Transcript in Emmett Till Case," *New York Times*, May 18, 2005, A14; McGarrh, email to author, June 18, 2008; Hailman, *From Midnight to Guntown*, 228; Hailman, author telephone interview.

44. Monica Davey and Gretchen Ruethling, "After 50 Years, Emmett Till's Body Is Exhumed," *New York Times*, June 2, 2005, A12; Wright and Boyd, *Simeon's Story*, 110; Karen E. Pride, "Federal Officials Lead Exhumation of Emmett Till," *Chicago Defender*, June 2, 2005, 3.

45. Pride, "Federal Officials Lead," 3; Anthony Rapp and Jennifer-Leigh Oprihory, "Declassified: The Real Story Behind Solving Crime," *Medill Reports*, http://newsarchive.medill.northwestern.edu/chicago/news.aspx?id=210665&print=1.

46. "Autopsy Done, Emmett Till Is Reburied," *New York Times*, June 5, 2005, 34; Natasha Korecki, "Possible Bullet Pieces Found in Till Autopsy," *Chicago Sun-Times*, June 11, 2005, 6.

47. Prosecutive Report, 99.

48. Prosecutive Report, 99, 101, 111; Killinger, author telephone interview; Hailman, author telephone interview.

49. Prosecutive Report, 106; Simeon Wright's name is redacted from the FBI report for privacy purposes. However, he explained that "they first focused on one of my sisters, but in the end the FBI selected me to be the donor. They came to my house and took blood samples, and after that, all I could do was to wait for the day of the exhumation" (Wright and Boyd, *Simeon's Story*, 109).

50. Email to Keith Beauchamp, March 11, 2003, copy in author's possession. The woman who wrote the email asked not to be identified "because it could cause me a lot of trouble."

51. Beauchamp, author telephone interview, August 23, 2014; Prosecutive Report, 97, 108; Killinger to author, September 15, 2014.

52. Prosecutive Report, 110; "Autopsy Done," 34; Korecki, "Possible Bullet Pieces Found," 6; Laura Parker, "DNA Confirms Body Is Emmett Till's," *USA Today*, August 26, 2005, A2.

53. Hailman, author telephone interview; Confidential source C, author interview, December 3, 2014.

54. Hailman, author telephone interview. Killinger was not able to discuss his interactions with Carolyn Donham with me because of confidentiality issues, which still applied in her case because she was still living. Hailman, now retired, felt free to talk.

55. Prosecutive Report, 41–42, 46–49, 95.

56. Prosecutive Report, 57–58, 95–96. Carolyn Donham's statement to Killinger is provided twice in the report. Inexplicably, Killinger redacted certain words in one of these statements but includes them in the other. What I include above is a synthesis of the two.

57. Although I did not hear this directly from Killinger, Hailman told me that Killinger "was absolutely sure that Carolyn was there," meaning she was with Roy Bryant and J. W. Milam at Mose Wright's home in the early morning hours of August 28, 1955 (Hailman, author telephone interview).

58. Prosecutive Report, 59, 80. Campbell's wife, Mary Louise, told Killinger that she did not recall Carolyn Bryant placing a call to her husband that morning (Prosecutive Report, 59). Campbell's name is redacted from the report because she was still living at the time. She died in 2009.

59. Prosecutive Report, 42; Defense notes from interview with Mrs. J. W. Milam, September 2, 1955, William Bradford Huie Papers, Cms 84, box 85, fd. 347, Ohio State University Library, Columbus (hereafter cited as Huie Papers).

60. Timothy B. Tyson, emails to author, March 31 and July 26, 2014. Tyson will discuss his interviews with Carolyn Donham in a forthcoming book on the Till case.

61. Defense notes from interview with Carolyn Bryant, September 2, 1955, Huie Papers, box 85, fd. 347.

62. Ray Brennan, "Till's Uncle Sticks to Guns, Says He'll Relate Kidnaping," *Chicago Sun-Times*, September 19, 1955, 3.

63. For a sampling of the coverage of the Edgar Ray Killen case, see James Dao, "Indictment Makes Start at Lifting 40-Year-Old Cloud Over a Mississippi County," *New York Times*, January 8, 2005, A11; Shaila Dewan, "Revisiting '64 Civil Rights Deaths, This Time in a Murder Trial,"

New York Times, June 12, 2005, 26; "Jury Selection Begins in '64 Case of Civil Rights Workers' Killings," *New York Times*, June 14, 2005, A12; Shaila Dewan and Jerry Mitchell, "A Klan Confession, but Not to 1964 Civil Rights Murders," *New York Times*, June 16, 2005, A18; Shaila Dewan, "Jury Hears Mother of Rights Worker Slain in 1964," *New York Times*, June 18, 2005, A8; Sheila Dewan, "Prosecution Completes Case in 1964 Civil Rights Killings," *New York Times*, June 19, 2005, 16; "Jury Is Split at Outset of Deliberation," *New York Times*, June 21, 2005, A12; Ariel Hart, "41 Years Later, Ex-Klansman Gets 60 Years in Civil Rights Deaths," *New York Times*, June 24, 2005, A14; Shaila Dewan, "Man Convicted in '64 Case and Out on Bail Is Rejailed," *New York Times*, September 10, 2005, A8.

64. Confidential source C, author interview, December 3, 2014.

65. This story once appeared on Barrett's Nationalist website, but that link is no longer valid. However, on October 19, 2013, I found it at https://groups.google.com/forum/#!topic/misc .legal/CdjqsQBAX6c. Jerry Mitchell, longtime reporter for the *Jackson Clarion-Ledger*, verified to me that Barrett did, in fact, consult with Frank Bryant, because Barrett discussed his conversation personally with Mitchell (Jerry Mitchell, email to author, October 19, 2013). WXVT TV, of Greenville, Mississippi, no longer has a copy of this story, unfortunately, as verified by Woodrow Wilkins, a reporter and web director at the station, in an email to the author on November 6, 2013.

66. Chris Joyner, "Black Man Suspected in Death of Mississippi White Supremacist," *USA Today*, April 23, 2010, A2; Earnest McBride, "McGee Family Decries Downplay of Racist Provocation in Barrett Murder Case," *Jackson Advocate*, August 4, 2011, 1A, 9A.

67. See Bonnie Blue, *Emmett Till's Secret Witness: FBI Confidential Source Speaks* (Park Forest, Ill.: B. L. Richey Publishing, 2013). Blue told me she recorded the conversations but would not say whether she provided Killinger with those recordings, gave him a transcript, or only gave him an oral summary of what Milam told her. Blue, who lectured on Emmett Till under the name of B. L. Richey prior to the release of her book, was once very dissatisfied with the FBI's investigation and accused Killinger of sloppiness and even dishonesty. After passage of the Emmett Till Unsolved Civil Rights Act in 2008 (discussed later), Blue wrote of her dissatisfaction with the FBI agent on a blog for the *Chicago Sun-Times*: "Now all that I wait for, is that an actual investigation to be conducted by the FBI. The 2004/2007 report was so flawed that the FBI themselves [*sic*] had to conduct their own investigation into the actions of the FBI Agent conducting the investigation." She went on to assert that the US attorney general was then looking into Killinger's alleged missteps, something Blue said she had been urging since the report came out in March 2007. "I know that it is flawed because the agent deleted important information and twisted the facts that were relayed to him by Confidential Source, 'b2,'" whom Blue claimed to be. I have found no evidence that Killinger's probe has at any time been under investigation.

In June 2014, I contacted Blue about her online criticisms of Killinger. In response to my email she wrote: "I have never posted anything of that nature. . . . As for the FBI, I am satisfied with the work that was done in this case." When I sent her the link showing her critical comments, she responded later that same day. "Wow! Very good! I had completely forgotten about that." She provided nothing to explain the discrepancy between her 2008 and 2014 assessments of Killinger's probe. For her online criticisms, see comments under http://blogs.suntimes.com/ sweet/2008/09/emmett_till_civil_rights_bill.html; author, email to Bonnie Blue, June 28, 2014;

Bonnie Blue, email to author, June 29, 2014 (first under that date); author, email to Bonnie Blue, June 29, 2014; Bonnie Blue, email to author, June 29, 2014 (second under that date).

Blue became uneasy over my continued questions about the information she provided Killinger during the investigation and promptly sent me an email threatening legal action. "Should I find that any of my information (that is not in the official FBI report) is used in any of your work concerning Emmett Till, without my permission, I will have my attorney contact you" (Bonnie Blue, email to author, July 27, 2014). I am proceeding under the assumption that Killinger accurately summarized Blue's material and will reference corresponding sections of *Secret Witness* and, where necessary, point out discrepancies between the book and the report.

68. Prosecutive Report, 90. In her novel based on her interviews with Milam, Blue writes that Milam rode out to Minter City and met up with Campbell, and the two arranged to meet later for their weekly round of drinking. Milam told Campbell to meet them at a place called Hillards. Blue, *Emmett Till's Secret Witness*, 121–22.

69. Prosecutive Report, 90. In her book, Blue says that Milam rode to Loggins's home in Milam's truck and picked up both Loggins and Collins. From there they drove to Bryant's store and picked up Roy and Carolyn. They then drove out to an old barn that had been converted into a whiskey still and met up with Hubert Clark, who had arrived at the barn just a few minutes earlier. Melvin Campbell then showed up. Milam demanded that Clark let him borrow his car because he did not want anyone noticing his new green and white pickup. J. W. Milam, Roy and Carolyn Bryant, Melvin Campbell, and Levi "Too Tight" Collins then got into Clark's car, leaving Clark and Loggins behind. The group drove to Money, and headed out to Mose Wright's house, where they kidnapped Emmett Till. Melvin Campbell and Carolyn Bryant remained in the car; when J. W. and Roy took Till outside, Carolyn identified him as the right person. Blue, *Emmett Till's Secret Witness*, 123–41, 148.

70. Prosecutive Report, 90; Blue, *Emmett Till's Secret Witness*, 148–54.

71. Prosecutive Report, 90; Blue, *Emmett Till's Secret Witness*, 155–59.

72. Prosecutive Report, 91; Blue, *Emmett Till's Secret Witness*, 160–61, 252–56, 290–94.

73. Prosecutive Report, 91; Killinger remarks at Landmarks in American History and Culture.

74. Prosecutive Report, 91–92, 98.

75. Louis E. Lomax, "Leslie Milam Quits Farm Home," *Daily Defender* (Chicago), March 5, 1956, 5.

76. "Cleveland Man Charged with Possession of Drugs," *Delta Democrat-Times* (Greenville, Miss.), February 16, 1971, 1; Leslie Milam's conviction is mentioned as one of several news items under the headline "Woman Wins Damage Suit," *Delta Democrat-Times* (Greenville, Miss.), June 11, 1971, 14. Both articles mention that Milam was free on $2,500 bail.

77. Macklyn Hubbell, author telephone interview, March 1, 2014; Prosecutive Report, 92–93; Leslie Milam obituary, *Delta Democrat-Times* (Greenville, Miss.), September 1, 1974, 3; Frances Bryant obituary, http://rayfuneralhome.net/tribute/details/443/Frances_Bryant/obituary.html.

78. Prosecutive Report, 27, 29, 31, 49, 133; Killinger, author telephone interview.

79. Prosecutive Report, 28–29; Ellen Barry, "Son Hopes Aging Father Talks About Till Murder," *Los Angeles Times*, August 14, 2005, 7A.

80. Prosecutive Report, 64–67.

81. Prosecutive Report, 112–13; Jerry Tallmer, "Documentary on the Grisly Lynching of Emmett Till," *Villager*, August 3–9, 1955, http://thevillager.com/villager_118/documentary

onthegrisly.html. For more on Peggy Morgan's life, see Carolyn Haines, *My Mother's Keeper: The Peggy Morgan Story* (Montgomery, Ala.: River City Publishing, 2003).

82. Prosecutive Report, 49–50, 114.

83. Jimmie Briggs, "Emmett Till Story at Film Forum," *New York Amsterdam News*, August 18, 2005, 20; Dwight Brown, "Film: The Untold Story of Emmett Louis Till," *New York Beacon*, August 11, 2005, 25; Beauchamp, author telephone interview, November 10, 2013. I attended the August 28, 2005, event at the Film Forum and taped the discussion featuring Simeon Wright, Roosevelt Crawford, and other guests.

84. Joyce Shelby, "More Tied to Till Death—Filmmaker," *New York Daily News*, August 30, 2005, 2.

85. Charles Sheehan, "FBI Closes Probe into Till's Death," *Chicago Tribune*, November 24, 2005, 31.

86. Killinger, author telephone interview; Dale Killinger remarks at Landmarks in American History and Culture.

87. Charles Sheehan, "Federal Report on 1955 Murder Going to D.A.," *Los Angeles Times*, November 24, 2005, A35.

88. Killinger, author telephone interview; "Mississippi Must Make Every Effort to Prosecute Till Murder," *Chicago Sun-Times*, March 20, 2006, 39; Laura Parker, "DA Has Tough, Final Call in Till Case," *USA Today*, March 22, 2006, A3; Holbrook Mohr, "No Federal Charges in Till Case, FBI Says," *Chicago Tribune*, March 17, 2006, 8.

89. "Till Report Completed," *Memphis Commercial Appeal*, November 24, 2005, B6; "Prosecutor Studying FBI's Investigative File into Till Murder," *Bay State Banner* (Boston), July 6, 2006, 2; Laura Parker, "FBI Report on Emmett Till Filed in Mississippi," *Miami Times*, March 22–28, 2006, 7A.

90. Herb Boyd, "The Untold Story of Emmett Till on Court TV," *New York Amsterdam News*, September 28, 2006, 22.

91. See http://emmyonline.com/news_28th_nominations; www.imdb.com/title/tt0475420/awards?ref_=tt_awd.

92. Drew Jubera, "Duty Outweighs Emotion for DA in Till Case," *Atlanta Journal-Constitution*, November 5, 2006, A1.

93. Jubera, "Duty Outweighs Emotion," A1.

94. Hailman, *From Midnight to Guntown*, 231.

95. These cases are summarized in Keith Beauchamp, email to author, August 23, 2014. For *Gibbs v. State*, see http://law.justia.com/cases/mississippi/supreme-court/1955/39247-0.html.

96. "Grand Jury to Look at New Till Angle," *Chicago Tribune*, February 22, 2007, 8.

97. Hailman, *From Midnight to Guntown*, 231–32; Killinger, email to author, September 15, 2014; William Browning, "Till Jury Talks: Grand Jury Says Evidence Wasn't There to Indict," *Greenwood (Miss.) Commonwealth*, September 30, 2007, 1A, 10A.

98. Browning, "Till Jury Talks," 10A.

99. Jerry Mitchell, "Grand Jury Issues No Indictment in Till Killing," *Jackson Clarion-Ledger*, February 27, 2007, 3A; Sykes, author telephone interview, June 12, 2014.

100. Sykes, author telephone interview, June 12, 2014; Allen G. Breed, "End of Till Case Draws Mixed Response," *USA Today*, March 4, 2007, http://usatoday30.usatoday.com/news/

nation/2007-03-04-till-case_N.htm.; Herb Boyd, "No Indictments in Till Case," *New York Amsterdam News*, March 8, 2007, 4.

101. Breed, "End of Till Case"; Boyd, "No Indictments," 4.

102. Hailman, *From Midnight to Guntown*, 231; Hailman, author telephone interview. In his book, Hailman said that Wright was familiar with Carolyn Bryant's voice "from weekly visits to her store." However, Hailman is mistaken in this. Wright testified at the trial that he did not trade at the Bryant store. See Trial Transcript, 12. He told defense attorneys the same thing ("Resume of Interview with Mose Wright," Huie Papers, box 85, fd. 347). The Bryants had only taken over the store within the past eighteen months.

103. Browning, "Till Jury Talks," 10A.

104. Jeff Coen, "Relatives of Emmett Till Meet with FBI," *Chicago Tribune*, March 30, 2007, 3. For the FBI documents, see http://vault.fbi.gov/Emmett%20Till%20.

Chapter 13

1. *Mississippi Code 1972*, Vol. 14, *Highways, Bridges, and Ferries* (State of Mississippi, 1972–2012), 190–91; "Renamed Roads Honor Rights Victims," *Chicago Tribune*, March 22, 2005, 12; "Emmett Till's Legacy 50 Years Later," *Jet* 108, no. 12 (September 19, 2005): 23. On this same occasion, Barbour also signed into law the renaming of a portion of Mississippi 19 as the Chaney, Goodman, and Schwerner Memorial Highway.

2. Davis W. Houck and Matthew A. Grindy, *Emmett Till and the Mississippi Press* (Jackson: University Press of Mississippi, 2008), 187n6.

3. Robert Fredrick Burk, *The Eisenhower Administration and Black Civil Rights, 1953–1961* (Knoxville: University of Tennessee Press, 1984), 205–14; David A. Nichols, *A Matter of Justice: Eisenhower and the Beginning of the Civil Rights Revolution* (New York: Simon and Schuster, 2007), 143–44. For the State of the Union speech, see "Text of President Eisenhower's Annual Message to Congress on State of the Union," *New York Times*, January 11, 1957, 10, also online at pbs.org/wgbh/americanexperience/features/primary-resources/eisenhower-state57.

4. Congressional Record—Appendix, January 10, 1957, A124, www.heinonline.org.

5. Burk, *Eisenhower Administration and Black Civil Rights*, 220–21; "Rights Hearings Will Open Today," *New York Times*, February 4, 1957, 8; "States Assured on Rights Issue," *New York Times*, February 5, 1957, 15; "Need to Protect Negro Vote Cited," *New York Times*, February 15, 1957, 15.

6. As quoted in Burk, *Eisenhower Administration and Black Civil Rights*, 225.

7. For Johnson's role in the Civil Rights Act of 1957, see Robert A. Caro, *Master of the Senate: The Years of Lyndon Johnson* (New York: Knopf, 2002), 831–1012.

8. Congressional Record—House, June 14, 1957, 9189, www.heinonline.org.

9. Congressional Record—House, June 14, 1957, 9194, www.heinonline.org; Burk, *Eisenhower Administration and Black Civil Rights*, 221; Hugh Stephen Whitaker, "A Case Study of Southern Justice: The Emmett Till Case" (Master's thesis, Florida State University, 1963), 183–85, reprinted as Hugh Stephen Whitaker, "A Case Study in Southern Justice: The Murder and Trial of Emmett Till," *Rhetoric & Public Affairs* 8, no. 2 (Summer 2005): 219–20; Stephen J. Whitfield, *A Death in the Delta: The Story of Emmett Till* (New York: Free Press, 1988), 82–83.

10. C. P. Trussell, "Civil Rights Plan Passed by House," *New York Times*, June 19, 1957, 1.

11. William S. White, "Senate, 45 to 39, Sends Rights Bill Straight to Floor," *New York Times*, June 21, 1957, 1, 16; William S. White, "Rights Struggle Opens in Senate," *New York Times*, July 9, 1957, 1, 19; William S. White, "Senate Leaning to a Compromise Over Rights Bill," *New York Times*, July 10, 1957, 1, 14; William S. White, "Senate, 51–42, Attaches Jury Trials to Rights Bill in Defeat for President," *New York Times*, August 2, 1957, 1, 8; W. H. Lawrence, "Eisenhower Irate," *New York Times*, August 3, 1957, 1; William S. White, "Senate Approves Rights Bill, 72–18, with Jury Clause," *New York Times*, August 8, 1957, 1, 12; William S. White, "Martin Rejects Civil Rights Bill Voted by Senate," *New York Times*, August 13, 1957, 1, 25; William S. White, "President Backs Jury Compromise in the Rights Bill," *New York Times*, August 22, 1957, 1, 17; William S. White, "Congress Chiefs Reach an Accord on Civil Rights," *New York Times*, August 24, 1957, 1, 34.

12. William S. White, "House Passes Rights Bill; Senators Rule Out a Delay," *New York Times*, August 28, 1957, 1, 55; "Thurmond Talks Hours on Rights," *New York Times*, August 29, 1957, 1; Jay Walz, "Carolinian Sets Talking Record," *New York Times*, August 30, 1957, 1; William S. White, "Senate Votes Rights Bill and Sends It to President," *New York Times*, August 30, 1957, 1, 20; W. H. Lawrence, "President Backs U.S. Court Order," *New York Times*, September 10, 1957, 29.

13. For a look at the final version of the Civil Rights Act of 1957, see "Text of Civil Rights Bill as Passed by Congress," *New York Times*, August 31, 1957, 6.

14. Alvin Sykes, author telephone interview, July 12, 2014; Monroe Dodd, *Pursuit of Truth* (Kansas City, Mo.: Kansas City Public Library, 2014), 17.

15. "Text of the Unsolved Civil Rights Crime Act," introduced in the US Senate on July 1, 2005, www.govtrack.us/congress/bills/109/s1369/text; H.R. 3506 (109th); "Unsolved Civil Rights Crime Act, H.R. 3506," introduced in the US House of Representatives, www.govtrack.us/congress/bills/109/hr3506/text.

16. Jubera, "Civil Rights-Era Cases," A1; Trice, "Setback on Till," 2C1; "Emmett Till Unsolved Civil Rights Crime Act," Senate, Calendar No. 211, June 22, 2007, 12; 109th Congress, 2nd Session, S.2679, in the Senate of the United States, April 27, 2006, and S.2679, Calendar No. 579, August 3, 2006; http://www.gpo.gov/fdsys/pkg/BILLS-109s2679rs/pdf/BILLS-109s2679rs.pdf.

17. Tommy Stevenson, "House Passes 'Emmett Till Bill,'" *Tuscaloosa (Ala.) News*, June 21, 2007, 1A, 2A; Dodd, *Pursuit of Truth*, 18.

18. Sykes, author telephone interview, July 12, 2014; Dodd, *Pursuit of Truth*, 18.

19. Herb Boyd, "Emmett Till Bill Stalled in Senate," *New York Amsterdam News*, July 31, 2008, 4; "Senate Kills Bill for $10B in New Spending," *USA Today*, July 26, 2008, http://usatoday30.usatoday.com/news/washington/2008-07-28-senatebill_N.htm.

20. Sykes, author telephone interview, July 12, 2014; Dodd, *Pursuit of Truth*, 18–19.

21. "Reid Statement on Passage of Emmett Till Bill," http://democrats.senate.gov/2008/09/24/reid-statement-on-passage-of-emmett-till-bill/#.VLw2AEfF-Jo; Julia Malone, "Emmett Till Act Fulfills Promise: Pledge Kept to Slain Teenager's Late Mother," *Atlanta Journal-Constitution*, October 10, 2008, A7.

22. Congressional Record—Senate, September 24, 2008, S9352, www.heinonline.org.

23. Malone, "Emmett Till Act Fulfills Promise," A7.

24. Harry N. MacLean, *The Past Is Never Dead: The Trial of James Ford Seale and Mississippi's Struggle for Redemption* (New York: Basic Civitas Books, 2009), 88; Susan Glisson, author telephone interview, July 29, 2014; Susan Glisson, email to author, July 30, 2014.

25. MacLean, *Past Is Never Dead*, 143, 146; Glisson, author telephone interview.

26. MacLean, *Past Is Never Dead*, 146; Glisson, author telephone interview; Glisson, email to author, July 30, 2014; Jerry Mitchell, "Tallahatchie County to Formally Apologize to Till's Family," *Jackson Clarion-Ledger*, October 2, 2007, 3A.

27. MacLean, *Past Is Never Dead*, 88–91, 143–46; Glisson, author telephone interview; Drew Jubera, "Decades Later, an Apology," *Atlanta Journal-Constitution*, October 2, 2007, A4.

28. Senate Bill 2689, to Judiciary, Division A, Mississippi Legislature, Regular Session 2007, http://billstatus.ls.state.ms.us/documents/2007/pdf/SB/2600-2699/SB2689IN.pdf; Mitchell, "Tallahatchie County to Formally Apologize," 3A; Glisson, author telephone interview; MacLean, *Past Is Never Dead*, 223.

29. MacLean, *Past Is Never Dead*, 223–24; Glisson, author telephone interview.

30. MacLean, *Past Is Never Dead*, 225; Glisson, author telephone interview.

31. Annette Hollowell, "Tallahatchie County Group Commemorates Emmett Till," *Wellspring*, March 2008, 2.

32. To read the resolution in full, go to etmctallahatchie.com/pages/resolution.htm.

33. Audie Cornish, "County Apologizes to Emmett Till Family," October 2, 2007, npr.org/templates/story/story.php?storyId=14904083; MacLean, *Past Is Never Dead*, 231–32.

34. Hollowell, "Tallahatchie Group Commemorates," 2–3; photo of marker taken by author on October 2, 2007, Sumner, Miss.

35. MacLean, *Past Is Never Dead*, 238.

36. The brochure may be downloaded at www.etmctallahatchie.com/documents/driving tour.pdf.

37. "Memorial to Emmett Till to Be Placed in Leflore County," *Memphis Commercial Appeal*, December 31, 2005, D1.

38. Karen E. Pride, "Commemoration of Emmett Till Lynching Anniversary Includes Renaming Expressway Bridge," *Chicago Defender*, August 29–30 2005, 3; "Chicago School Renamed in Honor of Emmett Till," *Jet* 109, no. 11 (March 20, 2006): 20, 22, 46; http://www.preservationchicago.org/success-story/11.

39. Jubera, "Decades Later," A4; MacLean, *Past Is Never Dead*, 238.

40. Yolanda Jones, "Sign Honoring Emmett Till Is Marred by Vandalism," *Memphis Commercial Appeal*, June 26, 2006, B2; "Vandals Destroy Sign Marking Emmett Till Murder Site," *USA Today*, October 27, 2007, http://usatoday30.usatoday.com/news/nation/2008-10-27 -emmett-till_N.htm.

41. These were personal observations I made during trips to the Mississippi Delta on March 15, 2013, and August 14, 2014.

42. See John Ditmer, *Local People: The Struggle for Civil Rights in Mississippi* (Urbana: University of Illinois Press, 1994); Glen Feldman, ed., *Before Brown: Civil Rights and White Backlash in the Modern South* (Tuscaloosa: University of Alabama Press, 2004).

Epilogue

1. Emmett Till Historical Museum flyer, copy sent to author by Carolyn Towns, manager of Burr Oak Cemetery.

Notes

2. Dennis Lythgoe, "The Death of Emmett Till," *Deseret News* (Salt Lake City), February 26, 1997, C1–C2.

3. Mamie Till-Mobley, letter to author and the students at Olympus Jr. High School, February 14, 2000.

4. Online at http://theburroakcemetery.com/burr-oak-history; Emmett Till Historical Museum flyer.

5. Emmett Till Historical Museum flyer.

6. Emmett Till Historical Museum flyer.

7. "Breach of Trust," *Chicago Tribune*, July 10, 2009, 7; "200–300 Bodies Disinterred in Grave-Reselling Scheme," *Seattle Times*, July 10, 2009, A2.

8. Dan Blake, "Cook County Board to Sue Cemetery Owners," *Chicago Tribune*, July 22, 2009, 8; "Here's the Cemetery Worker Who Blew the Whistle," *Arlington Heights (Ill.) Daily Herald*, July 22, 2009, 15.

9. Don Babwin, "Till Casket Found in Rusty Shed," *Charleston (W.Va.) Gazette*, July 14, 2009, B10; Lauren Fitzpatrick, "Proposed Till Museum Lost in Burr Oak Scandal," *Chicago Sun-Times*, July 11, 2011, 22.

10. Jacqueline Trescott, "National African American Museum Acquires Emmett Till's Casket," *Los Angeles Times*, August 28, 2009, A14; Wendell Hutson, "Remembering Emmett Till," *Chicago Defender*, September 2, 2009, 7.

11. Lauren Fitzpatrick, "'I Am Very Sorry': Burr Oak Manager Gets 12 Years," *Chicago Sun-Times*, July 9, 2011, 2; Lolly Bowean, "Burr Oak Director Gets 12 Years," *Chicago Tribune*, July 9, 2011, 4.

12. Dorothy Rowley, "African American Museum Groundbreaking Held on the National Mall," *Washington Informer*, February 23, 2012, 32–33; Ian Duncan, "African American History Museum Is Underway in D.C.," *Los Angeles Times*, February 23, 2012, A12.

13. Francine Knowles, "Monument Dedicated to Burr Oak Healing," *Chicago Sun-Times*, August 30, 2014, 5.

Appendix

1. William Bradford Huie, "The Shocking Story of an Approved Killing in Mississippi," *Look*, January 24, 1956, 46; "Bonnie Blue, Researcher, Author, Lecturer," http://emmetttills-secretwitness.com/index.html.

2. George Murray, "'Wolf Call' Blamed by Argo Teen," *Chicago American*, September 1, 1955, 4; William Bradford Huie, *Wolf Whistle, and Other Stories* (New York: Signet Books, 1959), 40; Devery S. Anderson, "A Wallet, a White Woman, and a Whistle: Fact and Fiction in Emmett Till's Encounter in Money, Mississippi," *Southern Quarterly: A Journal of Arts & Letters in the South* 45, no. 4 (Summer 2008): 11–12; Defense notes from interview with Carolyn Bryant, September 2, 1955, William Bradford Huie Papers, Cms 84, box 85, fd. 356, Ohio State University Library, Columbus (hereafter cited as Huie Papers).

3. "Kidnapped Boy Whistled at Woman," *Chicago Daily Tribune*, August 1955, 2; Murray, "'Wolf Call' Blamed by Argo Teen," 4; Mattie Smith Colin and Robert Elliott, "Mother Waits in Vain for Her 'Bo,'" *Chicago Defender*, September 10, 1955, 2; "Nation Horrified by Murder of Kidnapped Chicago Youth," *Jet* 8, no. 19 (September 1955): 8.

4. Huie, "Shocking Story," 46; Prosecutive Report of Investigation Concerning . . . Emmett Till, Deceased, Victim, February 9, 2009, 44 (hereafter cited as Prosecutive Report); Amos Dixon, "Mrs. Bryant Didn't Even Hear Emmett Till Whistle," *California Eagle*, January 26, 1956, 2.

5. This description of the location of the candy counter is given in defense notes of interview with Carolyn Bryant, September 2, 1955.

6. Defense notes of interview with Carolyn Bryant, September 2, 1955.

7. Prosecutive Report of Investigation Concerning . . . Emmett Till, Deceased, Appendix A—Trial Transcript, February 9, 2006, 269–75 (hereafter cited as Trial Transcript).

8. Timothy B. Tyson, emails to author, March 31 and July 26, 2014.

9. "Two Armed White Men Break into Negro Worker's Home," *Greenwood (Miss.) Morning Star*, September 1, 1955, 1; "Nation Horrified," 8; Murray, "'Wolf Call' Blamed by Argo Teen," 1; Clark Porteous, "Grand Jury to Get Case of Slain Negro Boy Monday," *Memphis Press-Scimitar*, September 1, 1955, 5.

10. Defense notes of interview with Carolyn Bryant, September 2, 1955; Huie, "Shocking Story," 47.

11. Huie, "Shocking Story," 47; Prosecutive Report, 46.

12. T. R. M. Howard, "Terror Reigns in Mississippi," speech delivered October 2, 1955, Baltimore, *Washington Afro-American*, October 1, 1955, 19, and *Baltimore Afro-American*, October 8, 1955, 6, reprinted in Davis W. Houck and David E. Dixon, eds., *Religion, Rhetoric, and the Civil Rights Movement* (Waco, Tex.: Baylor University Press, 2008), 126 (hereafter, references to this speech will cite Houck and Dixon only); Huie, "Shocking Story," 47.

13. Olive Arnold Adams, *Time Bomb: Mississippi Exposed and the Full Story of Emmett Till* (Mound Bayou, Miss.: Regional Councils of Negro Leadership, 1956), 18; Howard, "Terror Reigns," 126.

14. Dixon, "Mrs. Bryant Didn't Even Hear," 2.

15. Wheeler Parker Jr., Crosby Smith Jr., and Simeon Wright, author interview, February 7, 2007, Argo, Ill., comments by Wright; Trial Transcript, 277.

16. Prosecutive Report, 41–42.

17. David A. Shostak, "Crosby Smith: Forgotten Witness to a Mississippi Nightmare," *Negro History Bulletin* 38, no. 1 (December 1974–January 1975): 321; George F. Curry, "Killed for Whistling at a White Woman," *Emerge*, August 1995, 27; Simeon Wright, with Herb Boyd, *Simeon's Story: An Eyewitness Account of the Kidnapping of Emmett Till* (Chicago: Lawrence Hill Books, 2010), 137. Wright says nothing in his book about the accusations that Maurice told Roy Bryant about the store incident, but defends his brother against a rumor that "Maurice had told Roy Bryant how to get to our house in exchange for a fifty-cent store credit."

18. "Look Magazine Names Milam, Bryant in Confession Story," *Tri-State Defender* (Memphis, Tenn.), January 14, 1956, 1, 2.

19. Keith A. Beauchamp, "What Really Happened to Emmett Till: A Corrective to the 1956 *Look* Confession," unpublished paper, n.d., copy in author's possession.

20. Prosecutive Report, 55–56. Robert Wright's name is redacted from the report for privacy purposes, but it was confirmed to me by Simeon Wright that Robert was the one in question (Simeon Wright, author interview, October 2, 2007, Money, Miss.).

21. Wright and Boyd, *Simeon's Story*, 52, 137.

22. "Nation Horrified," 8; "Details Told of Lynching of Emmett," *Baltimore Afro-American*, September 17, 1955, 14.

23. Trial Transcript, 39; Huie, *Wolf Whistle*, 41.

24. "Resume of Interview with Mose Wright," Huie Papers, box 85, fd. 346.

25. Statements of both Ruth Crawford Jackson and Roosevelt Crawford are in Keith A. Beauchamp, prod., *The Untold Story of Emmett Louis Till* (Till Freedom Come Productions, 2005).

26. Prosecutive Report, 46.

27. Prosecutive Report, 46–47.

28. Mary Strafford, "'When I Find Time I'll Cry,' Till's Mother Tells *Afro*," *Baltimore Afro-American*, October 29, 1955, 2.

29. Steve Ritea, "Opening Old Wounds," *New Orleans Times-Picayune*, June 15, 2004, 1; Prosecutive Report, 48.

30. Michael Weissenstein, "Film Recounts Till's Untold Story; Director's First Work Helped Reopen Case," *Chicago Tribune*, August 28, 2005, 14.

31. Ruth Crawford Jackson, interview, in Beauchamp, *Untold Story*.

32. Trial Transcript, 22–23, 45–48; "Resume of Interview with Mose Wright."

33. Trial Transcript, 20, 33–38, 64–65; "Resume of Interview with Mose Wright."

34. Prosecutive Report, 90.

35. "What the Public Didn't Know About the Till Trial," *Jet* 8, no. 23 (October 13, 1955): 14.

36. Defense notes of interview with Roy Bryant, September 6, 1955, Huie Papers, box 85, fd. 346.

37. Rita Dailey, email to author, May 14, 2012. Rita Dailey wrote me after finding my website, emmetttillmurder.com. Steve Whitaker, a Charleston native who wrote his 1963 master's thesis on the Till case, vouched for Bobby Dailey's honesty (Steve Whitaker, email to author, May 14, 2012).

38. James L. Hicks, open letter to U.S. Attorney General Herbert Brownell and FBI Chief J. Edgar Hoover, in "Hicks Digs into Till Case," *Washington Afro-American*, November 19, 1955, 4, reprinted in Christopher Metress, ed., *The Lynching of Emmett Till: A Documentary Narrative* (Charlottesville: University of Virginia Press, 2002), 195–96.

39. Prosecutive Report, 58, 95–96.

40. Prosecutive Report, 58.

41. M. Susan Orr-Klopher, *The Emmett Till Book* (Parchman, Miss.: M. Susan Orr-Klopher, 2005), 7–8.

42. Prosecutive Report, 90.

43. Huie, "Shocking Story," 49–50.

44. Prosecutive Report, 92.

45. William Bradford Huie to Roy Wilkins, October 12, 1955, Huie Papers, box 38, fd. 353a.

46. Hicks, "Hicks Digs into Till Case," 4; Metress, *Lynching of Emmett Till*, 196; Prosecutive Report, 58, 90–91.

47. Adams, *Time Bomb*, 19; Amos Dixon, "Milam Master-Minded Emmett Till Killing," *California Eagle*, February 2, 1956, 2.

48. See, for example, David T. Beito and Linda Royster Beito, *Black Maverick: T. R. M. Howard's Fight for Civil Rights and Economic Power* (Urbana: University of Illinois Press, 2009), 152; Beauchamp, *Untold Story*; Willie Reed, author interview, February 6, 2007, Chicago.

49. Trial Transcript, 231.

50. T. R. M. Howard, interview, *Pittsburgh Courier*, October 8, 1955, 4; Amos Dixon, "Till Case: Torture and Murder," *California Eagle*, February 16, 1956, 2.

51. Henry Lee Loggins, telephone interview with Linda Beito, July 21, 2001, transcript in author's possession.

52. See Willie Reed interviews in Stanley Nelson, *Murder of Emmett Till* (Firelight Media, 2002), and Beauchamp, *Untold Story*.

53. Roosevelt Ward, "Negro Youth Ready to Testify Again at Trial of Emmett Till's Kidnappers," *Daily Worker* (New York), October 25, 1955, 3. See also Nelson, *Murder of Emmett Till*; Beauchamp, *Untold Story*; Michael Radutzky, "The Murder of Emmett Till," *60 Minutes* (CBS, October 24, 2004).

54. Trial Transcript, 247, 253.

55. Prosecutive Report, 112.

56. Clark Porteous, "Officers Work All Night on Searches," *Memphis Press-Scimitar*, September 21, 1955, 1, 7; Prosecutive Report, 91–92.

57. Dixon, "Emmett Till: Torture and Murder," February 16, 1956, 1.

58. Huie, "Shocking Story," 50; Prosecutive Report, 80.

59. Prosecutive Report, 91; Porteous, "Officers Work All Night," 7; Ralph Hutto, "NAACP Leader Says Two Witnesses Disappeared," *Jackson State Times*, September 23, 1955, 6A.

60. Dixon, "Torture and Murder," 2.

61. Huie, "Shocking Story," 50.

62. Prosecutive Report, 64–67.

63. Huie, "Shocking Story," 50; Prosecutive Report, 92; Porteous, "Officers Work All Night," 7; Robert Walker statement in introductory film shown at the Emmett Till Historic Intrepid Center, Glendora, Miss. Although his name is redacted from Dale Killinger's report, Walker did supply Killinger with other information, but none of his statements in the Prosecutive Report mention seeing the fan. He told Killinger that he saw the truck go in the direction of the gin (Prosecutive Report, 64–65).

64. Resume of interview with George Smith, Sheriff of Leflore County, Mississippi, Huie Papers, box 85, fd. 346; Prosecutive Report, 131.

65. Nelson, *Murder of Emmett Till*.

66. Prosecutive Report, 68, 91.

67. Dailey, emails to author, May 14, 2012, and September 7, 2013.

68. Metress, *Lynching of Emmett Till*, 159–61.

69. L. Alex Wilson, "Reveals Two Key Witnesses Jailed," *Tri-State Defender* (Memphis, Tenn.), October 1, 1955, 2.

70. Hugh Stephen Whitaker, "A Case Study in Southern Justice: The Emmett Till Case" (Master's thesis, Florida State University, 1963), 32, reprinted as Hugh Stephen Whitaker, "A Case Study in Southern Justice: The Murder and Trial of Emmett Till," *Rhetoric & Public Affairs* 8, no. 2 (Summer 2005): 208–9.

71. Henry Lee Loggins, interview, in Beauchamp, *Untold Story*.

72. Louis E. Lomax, "Henry Loggins Found, but Refuses to Leave Jail Cell," *Daily Defender* (Chicago), March 12, 1955, 8; Lomax, "Milam Jails His Handyman," *Daily Defender* (Chicago), March 20, 1956, 5.

BIBLIOGRAPHY

Books and Pamphlets

Adams, Olive Arnold. *Time Bomb: Mississippi Exposed, and the Full Story of Emmett Till*. Mound Bayou, Miss.: Regional Council of Negro Leadership, 1956.

Arnesen, Eric. *Black Protest and the Great Migration: A Brief History with Documents*. Boston: Bedford/St. Martin's, 2003.

Arnold, Helen, E. Staten, and Nick Denley, comps. *Tallahatchie County, Mississippi Marriage Records*. Carrollton, Miss.: Pioneer Publishing, 1998.

Arthur, John. *Race, Equality, and the Burdens of History*. New York: Cambridge University Press, 2007.

Baldwin, James. *Blues for Mister Charlie*. New York: Dial Books, 1964.

Beito, David T., and Linda Royster Beito. *Black Maverick: T. R. M. Howard's Fight for Civil Rights and Economic Power*. Urbana: University of Illinois Press, 2009.

Black, Timuel D., Jr. *Bridges of Memory: Chicago's First Wave of Black Migration*. Evanston, Ill.: Northwestern University Press, 2003.

Blue, Bonnie. *Emmett Till's Secret Witness: FBI Confidential Source Speaks*. Park Forest, Ill.: B. L. Richey Publishing, 2013.

Booker, Simeon. *Black Man's America*. Englewood Cliffs, N.J.: Prentice Hall, 1964.

Booker, Simeon, with Carol McCabe Booker. *Shocking the Conscience: A Reporter's Account of the Civil Rights Movement*. Jackson: University Press of Mississippi, 2013.

Brady, Tom P. *Black Monday*. Winona, Miss.: Associations of Citizens' Councils, 1955.

Brinkley, Douglas. *Rosa Parks*. New York: Viking, 2000.

Brownell, Herbert, and John P. Burke. *Advising Ike: The Memoirs of Attorney General Herbert Brownell*. Lawrence: University Press of Kansas, 1993.

Burk, Robert Fredrick. *The Eisenhower Administration and Black Civil Rights*. Knoxville: University of Tennessee Press, 1984.

Caro, Robert A. *Master of the Senate: The Years of Lyndon Johnson*. New York: Knopf, 2002.

Carter, Dan T. *Scottsboro: A Tragedy of the American South*. Rev. ed. Baton Rouge: Louisiana State University Press, 2007.

Chicago Commission on Race Relations. *The Negro in Chicago: A Study of Race Relations and a Race Riot*. Chicago: University of Chicago Press, 1922.

Clinton, Bill. *My Life*. New York: Alfred A. Knopf, 2004.

Cochran, Johnnie, with David Fisher. *A Lawyer's Life*. New York: Thomas Dunne Books, 2002.

Coffman, Edward M. *The War to End All Wars: The American Military Experience in World War I*. Lexington: University Press of Kentucky, 1988.

Crowe, Chris. *Getting Away with Murder: The True Story of the Emmett Till Case*. New York: Dial Books for Young Readers, 2003.

———. *Mississippi Trial, 1955*. New York: Phillis Fogelman Books, 2002.

———. *Presenting Mildred D. Taylor*. New York: Twayne, 1999.

Cushman, Clare, and Melvin I. Urosky, eds. *Black, White and Brown: The Landmark School Desegregation Case in Retrospect*. Washington, DC: Supreme Court Historical Society/CQ Press, 2004.

Davies, David R., ed. *The Press and Race: Mississippi Journalists Confront the Movement*. Jackson: University Press of Mississippi, 2001.

Davis, Townsend. *Weary Feet, Rested Souls: A Guided History of the Civil Rights Movement*. New York: W. W. Norton, 1998.

Dees, Morris, with Steve Fiffer. *A Lawyer's Journey: The Morris Dees Story*. Chicago: American Bar Association, 2001.

DeLaughter, Bobby. *Never Too Late: A Prosecutor's Story of Justice in the Medgar Evers Case*. New York: Scribner, 2001.

Dennis, Frank Allen, ed. *Southern Miscellany: Essays in History in Honor of Glover Moore*. Jackson: University Press of Mississippi, 1981.

Ditmer, John. *Local People: The Struggle for Civil Rights in Mississippi*. Urbana: University of Illinois Press, 1994.

Dodd, Monroe. *Pursuit of Truth*. Kansas City, Mo.: Kansas City Library, 2014.

Drake, St. Clair, and Horace R. Cayton. *Black Metropolis: A Study of Negro Life in a Northern City*. New York: Harper and Row, 1962.

Duncan, Otis Dudley, and Beverly Duncan. *The Negro Population of Chicago: A Study of Residential Succession*. Chicago: University of Chicago Press, 1957.

Evers, Myrlie, with William Peters. *For Us, the Living*. New York: Doubleday, 1967.

Evers-Williams, Myrlie, with Melinda Blau. *Watch Me Fly: What I Learned on the Way to Becoming the Woman I Was Meant to Be*. Boston: Little, Brown, 1999.

Feldman, Glen, ed. *Before Brown: Civil Rights and White Backlash in the Modern South*. Tuscaloosa: University of Alabama Press, 2004.

Forest Preserve District of Cook County (Ill.). Nature Bulletin No. 500-A, September 29, 1973.

Goodman, James. *Stories of Scottsboro*. New York: Random House, 1994.

Green, Adam. *Selling the Race: Culture, Community, and Black Chicago, 1940–1955*. Chicago: University of Chicago Press, 2007.

Grossman, James R. *Land of Hope: Chicago, Black Southerners, and the Great Migration*. Chicago: University of Chicago Press, 1989.

Hailman, John. *From Midnight to Guntown: True Crime Stories from a Federal Prosecutor in Mississippi*. Jackson: University Press of Mississippi, 2013.

Haines, Carolyn. *My Mother's Keeper: The Peggy Morgan Story*. Montgomery, Ala.: River City Publishing, 2003.

Halberstam, David. *The Fifties*. New York: Villard Books, 1993.

Hendrickson, Paul. *Sons of Mississippi: A Story of Race and Its Legacy*. New York: Alfred A. Knopf, 2003.

Henry, Lillie Neely, comp., and Jean Conger May, ed. *A History of Tallahatchie County*. Charleston, Miss.: The Mississippi Sun, 1960.

Houck, Davis W., and David E. Dixon, eds. *Rhetoric, Religion, and the Civil Rights Movement, 1954–1965*. Waco, Tex.: Baylor University Press, 2006.

Houck, Davis, and Matthew Grindy. *Emmett Till and the Mississippi Press*. Jackson: University Press of Mississippi, 2008.

Bibliography

Hudson-Weems, Clenora. *The Definitive Emmett Till: Passion and Battle of a Woman for Truth and Intellectual Justice*. Bloomington, Ind.: AuthorHouse, 2006.

———. *Emmett Till: The Sacrificial Lamb of the Civil Rights Movement*. 4th ed. Bloomington, Ind.: AuthorHouse, 2006.

———. *Plagiarism: Physical and Intellectual Lynchings: An Emmett Till Continuum*. Bloomington, Ind.: AuthorHouse, 2007.

Huie, William Bradford. *Wolf Whistle, and Other Stories*. New York: Signet Books, 1959.

Illinois Guide & Gazetteer. New York: Rand McNally, 1969.

Isserman, Maurice. *Journey to Freedom: The African-American Great Migration*. New York: Facts on File, 1997.

Jack, James A. *Three Boys Missing: The Tragedy That Exposed the Pedophilia Underworld*. Chicago: HPH Publishing, 2006.

Johnson, John H. *Succeeding against the Odds*. New York: Warner Books, 1989.

Johnston, Erle. *Mississippi's Defiant Years, 1953–1973: An Interpretive Documentary with Personal Experiences*. Forest, Miss.: Lake Harbor Publishers, 1990.

Jordan, David L., with Robert L. Jenkins. *David L. Jordan: From the Mississippi Cotton Fields to the State Senate, A Memoir*. Jackson: University Press of Mississippi, 2014.

Kaplan, Alice. *The Interpreter*. New York: Free Press, 2005.

King, Martin Luther, Jr. *Stride toward Freedom: The Montgomery Story*. New York: Harper, 1958.

Lemann, Nicholas. *The Promised Land: The Great Black Migration and How It Changed America*. New York: Alfred A. Knopf, 1991.

Lewis, John, with Michael D'Orso. *Walking with the Wind: A Memoir of the Movement*. New York: Simon and Schuster, 1998.

Lilly, J. Robert. *Taken by Force: Rape and American GIs in Europe during World War II*. New York: Palgrave MacMillan, 2007.

Lindberg, Richard C., and Gloria Jean Sykes. *Shattered Sense of Innocence: The 1955 Murders of Three Chicago Children*. Carbondale: Southern Illinois University Press, 2006.

Mace, Darryl. *In Remembrance of Emmett Till: Regional Stories and Media Responses to the Black Freedom Struggle*. Lexington: University Press of Kentucky, 2014.

MacLean, Harry N. *The Past Is Never Dead: The Trial of James Ford Seale and Mississippi's Struggle for Redemption*. New York: Basic Civitas Books, 2009.

McMillan, Stokes. *One Night of Madness*. Houston: Oak Harbor Publishing, 2009.

McMillen, Neil R. *The Citizens' Council: Organized Resistance to the Second Reconstruction, 1954–64*. Urbana: University of Illinois Press, 1971.

Mendelsohn, Jack. *The Martyrs: Sixteen Who Gave Their Lives for Racial Justice*. New York: Harper & Row, 1966.

Metress, Christopher, ed. *The Lynching of Emmett Till: A Documentary Narrative*. Charlottesville: University of Virginia Press, 2002.

Meyerowitz, Joanne, ed. *Not June Cleaver: Women and Gender in Postwar America, 1945–1960*. Philadelphia: Temple University Press, 1994.

Minor, Bill. *Eyes on Mississippi: A Fifty-Year Chronicle of Change*. Jackson, Miss.: J. Prichard Morris Books, 2001.

Mississippi Code 1972. Vol. 14, *Highways, Bridges, and Ferries*. State of Mississippi, 1972–2012.

Morris, Willie. *The Ghosts of Medgar Evers: A Tale of Race, Murder, Mississippi, and Hollywood*. New York: Random House, 1998.

Bibliography

Morrow, E. Frederic. *Black Man in the White House: A Diary of the Eisenhower Years by the Administration Officer for Special Projects, the White House, 1955–1961*. New York: Coward-McCann, 1963.

Moye, J. Todd. *Let the People Decide: Black Freedom and White Resistance Movements in Sunflower County, Mississippi, 1945–1986*. Chapel Hill: University of North Carolina Press, 2004.

Nelson, Marilyn. *A Wreath for Emmett Till*. Boston: Houghton Mifflin, 2005.

Nichols, David A. *A Matter of Justice: Eisenhower and the Beginning of the Civil Rights Revolution*. New York: Simon and Schuster, 2007.

Nordan, Lewis. *Wolf Whistle: A Novel*. Chapel Hill: Algonquin Books, 1993.

Ogletree, Charles J., Jr. *All Deliberate Speed: Reflections on the First Half-Century of Brown v. Board of Education*. New York: W. W. Norton, 2004.

Olby, Michael. *Black Press Coverage of the Emmett Till Lynching*. Koln, Germany: Lambert Academic Publishing, 2007.

Orr-Klopfer, Susan. *The Emmett Till Book*. Parchman, Miss.: M. Susan Orr-Klopher, 2005.

Orr-Klopfer, Susan, with Fred Klopfer and Barry Klopfer. *Where Rebels Roost: Mississippi Civil Rights Revisited*. 2nd ed. Parchman, Miss.: M. Susan Orr-Klopfer, 2005.

O'Shea, Gene. *Unbridled Rage: A True Story of Organized Crime, Corruption, and Murder in Chicago*. New York: Penguin, 2005.

Ottanelli, Fraser M. *The Communist Party of the United States: From the Depression to World War II*. New Brunswick, N.J.: Rutgers University Press, 1991.

Parks, Rosa, with Jim Haskins. *Rosa Parks: My Story*. New York: Dial Books, 1992.

Patterson, James T. *Brown v. Board of Education: A Civil Rights Milestone and Its Troubled Legacy*. New York: Oxford University Press, 2001.

Pollack, Harriet, and Christopher Metress, eds. *Emmett Till in Literary Memory and Imagination*. Baton Rouge: Louisiana State University Press, 2008.

Pound, Ezra. *Pisan Cantos*. Edited and annotated with an introduction by Richard Sieburth. New York: New Directions Books, 2003.

Raines, Howell. *My Soul Is Rested: Movement Days in the Deep South Remembered*. New York: Putnam, 1977.

Roberts, Gene, and Hank Klibanoff. *The Race Beat: The Press, the Civil Rights Struggle, and the Awakening of a Nation*. New York: Alfred A. Knopf, 2006.

Smith, Suzanne E. *To Serve the Living: Funeral Directors and the African American Way of Death*. Cambridge, Mass.: Belknap Press of Harvard University Press, 2010.

Stampp, Kenneth M. *The Peculiar Institution: Slavery in the Ante-Bellum South*. New York: Alfred A. Knopf, 1956.

Summit Heritage. Summit, Ill.: Summit Bicentennial Commission Heritage Committee, 1977.

Tell, Dave. *Confessional Crises and Cultural Politics in Twentieth-Century America*. University Park: Pennsylvania State University Press, 2012.

Terkel, Studs. *Race: How Blacks & Whites Think & Feel About the American Obsession*. New York: New Press, 1992.

Theoharis, Jeanne. *The Rebellious Life of Mrs. Rosa Parks*. Boston: Beacon Press, 2013.

Thompson, Julius E. *Lynchings in Mississippi: A History, 1865–1965*. Jefferson, N.C.: McFarland, 2007.

Thornton, J. Mills, III. *Dividing Lines: Municipal Politics and the Struggle for Civil Rights in Montgomery, Birmingham, and Selma*. Tuscaloosa: University of Alabama Press, 2002.

Bibliography

Till-Mobley, Mamie, and Christopher Benson. *Death of Innocence: The Story of the Hate Crime That Changed America*. New York: Random House, 2003.

Till-Mobley, Mamie, and David Barr III. *The Face of Emmett Till*. Woodstock, Ill.: Dramatic Publishing, 1999.

Tuttle, William M., Jr. *Race Riot: Chicago in the Red Summer of 1919*. New York: Atheneum, 1970.

Tyson, Timothy B. *Blood Done Sign My Name*. New York: Crown, 2004.

Vilar, Irene. *A Message from God in the Atomic Age*. New York: Pantheon Books, 1996.

Vinton High School. *Souvenir*. 1970.

Vollers, Maryanne. *Ghosts of Mississippi: The Murder of Medgar Evers, the Trials of Byron De La Beckwith, and the Haunting of the New South*. Boston: Little, Brown, 1995.

Wakefield, Dan. *Between the Lines: A Reporter's Personal Journey through Public Events*. New York: New American Library, 1966.

Warsaw, Shirley Anne, ed. *Reexamining the Eisenhower Presidency*. Westport, Conn.: Greenwood Press, 1993.

Wharton, Vernon Lane. *The Negro in Mississippi, 1865–1890*. Chapel Hill: University of North Carolina Press, 1947.

Whitfield, Stephen J. *A Death in the Delta: The Story of Emmett Till*. New York: Free Press, 1988.

Wilkerson, Isabel. *The Warmth of Other Suns: The Epic Story of America's Great Migration*. New York: Random House, 2010.

Williams, Donnie, with Wayne Greenhaw. *The Thunder of Angels: The Montgomery Bus Boycott and the People Who Broke the Back of Jim Crow*. Chicago: Lawrence Hill Books, 2006.

Williams, Juan. *Eyes on the Prize: America's Civil Rights Years, 1954–1965*. New York: Viking Books, 1987.

Williams, Michael Vinson. *Medgar Evers: Mississippi Martyr*. Fayetteville: University of Arkansas Press, 2011.

Withers, Ernest. *Complete Photo Story of Till Murder Case*. Memphis, Tenn.: Withers Photographers, 1955.

Wright, Simeon, with Herb Boyd. *Simeon's Story: An Eyewitness Account of the Kidnapping of Emmett Till*. Chicago: Lawrence Hill Books, 2010.

Journals and Magazines

"American Lynching Betrayed." *Nation* 276, no. 9 (March 10, 2003): 2, 26.

Anderson, Devery S. "A Wallet, a White Woman, and a Whistle: Fact and Fiction in Emmett Till's Encounter in Money, Mississippi." *Southern Quarterly: A Journal of Arts & Letters in the South* 45, no. 4 (Summer 2008): 10–21.

Baker, Courtney. "Emmett Till, Justice, and the Task of Reconciliation." *Journal of American Culture*, 29, no. 2 (2006): 111–24.

Benson, Christopher. "Troubled Waters." *Chicago*, September 1999, 26.

Bernstein, Daniel, and Elizabeth Loftus. "How to Tell If a Particular Memory Is True or False." *Perspectives on Psychological Science* 4, no. 4 (2009): 370–74.

Blasingame, Jim. "'A Crime That's So Unjust!': Chris Crowe Tells About the Death of Emmett Till." *Alan Review* 2 (Spring/Summer 2003): 22–24.

Booker, Simeon. "Best Civil Rights Cameraman in Business Dies." *Jet* 30, no. 2 (April 21, 1966): 28–29.

———. "A Negro Reporter at the Till Trial." *Neiman Reports*, January 1956, 13–15.

Breed, Warren. "Comparative Newspaper Handling of the Emmett Till Case." *Journalism Quarterly* 35 (Summer 1958): 291–98.

Cheers, D. Michael. "Dedicate Memorial to 40 Who Died in Civil Rights Struggle." *Jet* 77, no. 7 (November 20, 1989): 4–16.

———. "Time Heals Few Wounds for Emmett Till's Mother." *Jet* 66, no. 5 (April 9, 1984): 54–56.

"Chicago Boy, 14, Kidnaped by Miss. Whites." *Jet* 8, no. 18 (September 8, 1955): 3–4.

"Chicago School Renamed in Honor of Emmett Till." *Jet* 109, no. 11 (March 20, 2006): 20, 22, 46.

"Chicago's 71st Street Is Renamed for Emmett Till." *Jet* 80, no. 17 (August 12, 1991): 4–5.

Chura, Patrick. "Prolepsis and Anachronism: Emmett Till and the History of To Kill a Mockingbird." *Southern Literary Journal* 32, no. 2 (Spring 2000): 1–26.

Curry, George. "Killed for Whistling at a White Woman." *Emerge*, August 1995, 24–32.

Dawkins, Laura. "It Could Have Been My Son: Maternal Empathy in Gwendolyn Brooks's and Audre Lorde's Till Poems." In *Emmett Till in Literary Memory and Imagination*, ed. Harriet Pollack and Christopher Metress, 112–27. Baton Rouge: Louisiana State University Press, 2008.

"Emmett Till: Blacks React to Reopening of Tragic Case." *Jet* 105, no. 22 (May 31, 2004): 6–10, 60–62.

"Emmett Till's Legacy 50 Years Later." *Jet* 108, no. 12 (September 19, 2005): 20–25.

Fairfield, James. "Deadly Discourses: Examining the Roles of Language and Silence in the Lynching of Emmett Till and Wright's Native Son." *Arizona Quarterly: A Journal of American Literature, Culture, and Theory* 63, no. 4 (Winter 2007): 63–82.

Feldstein, Ruth. "'I Wanted the Whole World to See': Race, Gender, and Constructions of Motherhood in the Death of Emmett Till." In *Not June Cleaver: Women and Gender in Postwar America, 1945-1960*, ed. Joanne Meyerowitz, 263–303. Philadelphia: Temple University Press, 1994.

"GI Buddies Say Till's Dad Was 'Railroaded' in Italy." *Jet* 8, no. 26 (November 3, 1955): 4–5.

Goldsby, Jacqueline. "The High and Low Tech of It: The Meaning of Lynching and the Death of Emmett Till." *Yale Journal of Criticism* 9, no. 2 (Fall 1996): 245–82.

"Grand Jury Ignores Confession." *Jet* 8, no. 29 (November 24, 1955): 6–7.

Grindy, Matthew A. "Mississippi Terror, Red Pressure: The *Daily Worker*'s Coverage of the Emmett Till Murder." *Controversia: An International Journal of Debate and Democratic Renewal* 6, no. 1 (2008): 39–66.

Halberstam, David. "Tallahatchie County Acquits a Peckerwood." *Reporter* 14, no. 8 (April 19, 1956): 26–30.

Harold, Christine, and Kevin Michael DeLuca. "Behold the Corpse: Violent Images and the Case of Emmett Till." *Rhetoric & Public Affairs* 8, no. 2 (Summer 2005): 263–86.

Hendrickson, Paul. "Mississippi Haunting." *Washington Post Magazine*, February 27, 2000, 12–18, 26–27; reprinted in *Rhetoric & Public Affairs* 8, no. 2 (Summer 2005): 177–88.

Higgins, Chester. "Mrs. Bradley Becomes a Teacher." *Jet* 17, no. 18 (September 1, 1960): 15–16.

Hollowell, Annette. "Tallahatchie County Group Commemorates Emmett Till." *Wellspring*, March 2008, 2.

"Holmberg Replies." *Nation* 276, no. 9 (March 10, 2003): 26.

Houck, Davis W. "Killing Emmett." *Rhetoric & Public Affairs* 8, no. 2 (Summer 2005): 225–62.

Hudson, Clenora. "The Unearthing of Emmett Till: A Compelling Process." *Iowa Alumni Review* 41, no. 5 (October 1988): 18–23.

Hudson-Weems, Clenora. "Resurrecting Emmett Till: The Catalyst of the Modern Civil Rights Movement." *Journal of Black Studies* 29, no. 2 (November 1998): 179–88.

Huie, William Bradford. "The Shocking Story of Approved Killing in Mississippi." *Look*, January 24, 1956, 46–48, 50.

———. "What's Happened to the Emmett Till Killers." *Look*, January 22, 1957, 63–66, 68.

———. "Why the Army Hanged Emmett Till's Father!" *Confidential*, May 1956, 8–9, 50, 52.

"In Memoriam, Emmett Till." *Life*, October 10, 1955, 48.

Jackson, Donald W., and James W. Riddlesperger Jr. "The Eisenhower Administration and the 1957 Civil Rights Act." In *Reexamining the Eisenhower Presidency*, ed. Shirley Anne Warsaw, 85–101. Westport, Conn.: Greenwood Press, 1993.

Jones, Chris. "Chronicle of a Life Untold: Emmett Till's Mother Speaks." *BET Weekend*, October 1999, 4.

"J. W. Milam Denies Reports He Stood in Miss. Bread Line." *Jet* 13, no. 18 (March 6, 1958): 6–7.

Katz, Milton S. "E. Frederick Morrow and Civil Rights in the Eisenhower Administration." *Phylon* 42, no. 2 (2nd Quarter, 1981): 133–44.

Kolin, Philip C. "Forgotten Manuscripts: 'Blues for Emmett Till': The Earliest Extant Song about the Murder of Emmett Till." *African American Review* 42, nos. 3–4 (Fall–Winter 2008): 455–60.

———. "Haunting America: Emmett Till in Music and Song." *Southern Cultures* (Fall 2009): 118–21.

Larsson, Clotye Murdock. "Land of the Till Murder Revisited." *Ebony* 41, no. 5 (March 1986): 53–54, 56–58.

Loftus, Elizabeth. "Make-Believe Memories." *American Psychologist* 58, no. 11 (November 2003): 867–73.

Lorde, Audre. "Afterimages." *Cream City Review* 17, no. 2 (Fall 1981): 119–23. Reprinted in *The Lynching of Emmett Till: A Documentary Narrative*, ed. Christopher Metress, 323–27. Charlottesville: University of Virginia Press, 2002.

"Mamie Till-Mobley, Civil Rights Heroine, Eulogized in Chicago." *Jet* 103, no. 5 (January 27, 2003): 12–18, 52.

Mark, Rebecca. "Mourning Emmett: 'One Long Expansive Moment.'" *Southern Literary Journal*, 40, no. 2 (Spring 2008): 121–37.

May, Vivian M. "Maids Mild and Dark Villains, Sweet Magnolias and Sleeping Blood." In *Emmett Till in Literary Memory and Imagination*, ed. Harriet Pollack and Christopher Metress, 98–111. Baton Rouge: Louisiana State University Press, 2008.

McKibbin, Molly Littlewood. "Southern Patriarchy and the Figure of the White Woman in Gwendolyn Brooks's 'A Bronzeville Mother Loiters in Mississippi. Meanwhile, a Mississippi Mother Burns Bacon.'" *African American Review* 44, no. 4 (Winter 2011): 667–85.

Metress, Christopher. "'No Justice, No Peace': The Figure of Emmett Till in African American Literature." *MELUS* 28, no. 1 (Spring 2003): 87–103.

———. "Submitted for Their Approval: Rod Serling and the Lynching of Emmett Till." *Mississippi Quarterly* 61, nos. 1–2 (Winter/Spring 2008): 143–72.

———. "Truth Be Told: William Bradford Huie's Emmett Till Cycle." *Southern Quarterly: A Journal of Arts & Letters in the South* 45, no. 4 (Summer 2008): 48–75.

"Mississippi: Shooter's Chance." *Time* 55, no. 4 (January 23, 1950): 17.

Monteith, Sharon. "The Murder of Emmett Till in the Melodramatic Imagination: William Bradford Huie and Vin Packer in the 1990s." In *Emmett Till in Literary Memory and Imagination*, ed. Harriet Pollack and Christopher Metress, 31–52. Baton Rouge: Louisiana State University Press, 2008.

"Nation Horrified by Murder of Kidnaped Chicago Youth." *Jet* 8, no. 19 (September 15, 1955): 6–9.

Norman, Brian. "James Baldwin's Unifying Polemic: Racial Segregation, Moral Integration, and the Polarizing Figure of Emmett Till." In *Emmett Till in Literary Memory and Imagination*, ed. Harriet Pollack and Christopher Metress, 75–97. Baton Rouge: Louisiana State University Press, 2008.

Priest, Myisha. "'The Nightmare Is Not Cured': Emmett Till and American Healing." *American Quarterly* 62, no. 1 (March 2010): 1–24.

Segall, Rebecca, and David Holmberg. "Who Killed Emmett Till?" *Nation* 276, no. 4 (February 3, 2003): 37–40.

"Sex Slayer Confesses." *Jet* 8, no. 14 (August 11, 1955): 48.

Shostak, David A. "Crosby Smith: Forgotten Witness to a Mississippi Nightmare." *Negro History Bulletin* 38 (December 1974–January 1975): 320–25.

Simpson, William M. "Reflections on a Murder: The Emmett Till Case." In *Southern Miscellany: Essays in History in Honor of Glover Moore*, ed. Frank Allen Dennis, 177–200. Jackson: University Press of Mississippi, 1981.

Smith, Valerie. "Emmett Till's Ring." *Women's Studies Quarterly* 36, nos. 1–2 (Spring/Summer 2008): 151–61.

Spratt, Margaret, et al. "News, Race, and the Status Quo: The Case of Emmett Louis Till." *Howard Journal of Communications* 18, no. 2 (2007): 169–92.

"The Strange Trial of the Till Kidnapers." *Jet* 8, no. 22 (October 6, 1955): 6–11.

Tell, Dave. "The 'Shocking Story' of Emmett Till and the Politics of Public Confession." *Quarterly Journal of Speech* 94, no. 2 (May 2008): 156–78.

Thompson, Julius. "Till." In *Blues Said: Walk On*, 9–11. Houston: Energy Blacksouth Press, 1977. Reprinted in Christopher Metress, ed., *The Lynching of Emmett Till: A Documentary Narrative*, 321–23. Charlottesville: University of Virginia Press, 2002.

Thornton, Brian. "The Murder of Emmett Till: Myth, Memory, and National Magazine Response." *Journalism History* 36, no. 2 (Summer 2010): 96–104.

"3 Who Refused to Testify Have Dropped Out of Sight." *Jet* 13, no. 25 (April 24, 1958): 11, 13.

"Ticker Tape U.S.A." *Jet* 9, no. 11 (January 19, 1956): 13.

"The Till Case People One Year Later." *Ebony* 5, no. 11 (October 1956): 68–70, 72, 74.

"Till Protest Meetings." *Crisis*, November 1955, 547.

"Till's Mother Marches." *Jet* 39, no. 4 (October 29, 1970): 33.

"Till's Mother Sues Magazine." *Jet* 13, no. 4 (February 6, 1958): 17.

Tisdale, John R. "Different Assignments, Different Perspectives: How Reporters Reconstruct the Emmett Till Civil Rights Murder Trial." *Oral History Review* 29, no. 1 (Winter/Spring 2002): 39–58.

Bibliography

"Trial by Jury." *Time* 66, no. 14 (October 3, 1955): 18–19.

Tyler, Pamela. "'Blood on Your Hands': White Southerners' Criticisms of Eleanor Roosevelt during World Ward II." In *Before Brown: Civil Rights and White Backlash in the Modern South*, ed. Glen Feldman, 96–115. Tuscaloosa: University of Alabama Press, 2004.

Wagner, Terry. "America's Civil Rights Revolution: Three Documentaries About Emmett Till's Murder in Mississippi (1955)." *Historical Journal of Film, Radio and Television* 30, no. 2 (June 2010): 187–201.

Wakefield, Dan. "Justice in Sumner, Land of the Free." *Nation*, 181, no. 14 (October 1, 1955): 284–85.

Walker, Anders. "The Violent Bear It Away: Emmett Till and the Modernization of Law Enforcement in Mississippi." *San Diego Law Review* 46 (2009): 459–503.

Ward, Bob. "William Bradford Huie Paid for Their Sins." *Writer's Digest* 54, no. 9 (September 1974): 16–22.

Weill, Susan M. "Mississippi's Daily Press in Three Crises." In *The Press and Race: Mississippi Journalists Confront the Movement*, ed. David R. Davies, 17–53. Jackson: University Press of Mississippi, 2001.

"What the Public Didn't Know About the Till Trial." *Jet* 8, no. 23 (October 13, 1955): 14–15.

Whitaker, Hugh Stephen. "A Case Study in Southern Justice: The Murder and Trial of Emmett Till." *Rhetoric & Public Affairs* 8, no. 2 (Summer 2005): 189–224.

"Witnesses Say Slain Negro Didn't Gun-Duel White Man." *Jet* 9, no. 7 (December 22, 1955): 6–8.

Wood, Amy Louise, and Susan V. Donaldson. "Lynching's Legacy in American Culture." *Mississippi Quarterly* 61, nos. 1–2 (Winter/Spring 2008): 5–25.

Wright, Moses. "How I Escaped from Mississippi." *Jet* 8, no. 23 (October 13, 1955): 6–11.

———. "I Saw Them Take Emmett Till." *Front Page Detective*, February 1956, 26–29, 69.

Newspaper Articles

"Abe Stark Asks Anti-Lynch Law." *Daily Worker* (New York), October 19, 1955, 1.

"About Till's Father (an editorial)." *Jackson Daily News*, October 15, 1955, 1.

"Accused White Men Plead Innocent of Murder and Kidnap." *Greenwood (Miss.) Morning Star*, September 7, 1955, 1.

"Acquitted Men Stay in Jail." *Jackson State Times*, September 24, 1955, 1A, 10A.

Adams, Virgil. "A New Wrinkle in the Vilification of Mississippi." *Greenwood (Miss.) Morning Star*, September 27, 1955, 6.

———. "Resentment Rising against Radicals at Trial." *Greenwood (Miss.) Morning Star*, September 22, 1955, 6.

———. "State Granted Recess to Produce New Witnesses in Till Case." *Greenwood (Miss.) Morning Star*, September 21, 1955, 1.

"Adjourn in Honor of Gerald Chatham." *Delta Democrat-Times* (Greenville, Miss.), October 11, 1956, 3.

Advertisement. National Beauty Salon Week. *Delta Democrat-Times* (Greenville, Miss.), February 13, 1972, 17.

Ainsworth, A. B. "To All White Mississippians." *Greenwood (Miss.) Commonwealth*, September 8, 1955, 8.

Allan, William. "10,000 in Detroit, 10,000 in Chicago Call for U.S. Intervention in Mississippi Terror." *Daily Worker* (New York), September 27, 1955, 3.

Anderson, John. "'Till' Reviews Social History Lesson, 30 Years Later." *Chicago Tribune*, July 11, 1985, D1.

"Appeal Till Case to High Court." *Daily Defender* (Chicago), October 4, 1960, 2.

"Armed Trio Seizes Visitor in Mississippi." *Chicago Daily Tribune*, August 29, 1955, 1.

"Arrival of Victim's Mother Causes Stir." *Jackson State Times*, September 20, 1955, 1.

"Ask Ike to Act in Dixie Death of Chicago Boy." *Chicago Daily Tribune*, September 2, 1955, 2.

"Ask Mississippi Governor to Denounce Killing of Boy." *Chicago Daily Tribune*, September 1, 1955, 1.

"Ask New Indictment in Till Kidnap Case." *Baltimore Afro-American*, January 21, 1956, 2.

"Ask New Till Probe." *Birmingham (Ala.) World*, January 21, 1956.

"Asks FBI Guard Mother of Slain Boy." *New York Post*, September 13, 1955, 8.

Atkins, Joe. "Slain Chicago Youth Was a 'Sacrificial Lamb.'" *Jackson Clarion-Ledger/Jackson Daily News*, August 25, 1985, 20A.

Atkins, Joe, and Tom Brennan. "Bryant Wants the Past to 'Stay Dead.'" *Jackson Clarion-Ledger/Jackson Daily News*, August 25, 1985, 1H, 3H.

"Attala Court Judge Overrules Mistrial Motion by Defense." *Jackson Clarion-Ledger*, March 21, 1950, 1, 10.

"Attala Desperadoes Captured after Killing 3 Negro Children." *Kosciusko (Miss.) Star-Herald*, January 12, 1950, 1, 6.

"Attorney J. W. Kellum Dies." *Charleston (Miss.) Sun-Sentinel*, July 25, 1996, 1.

"Audience Donates to Till Witness." *Chicago Defender*, March 17, 1956, 10.

"Autopsy Done, Emmett Till Is Reburied." *New York Times*, June 5, 2005, 34.

Babwin, Don. "Civil Rights Advocates Seek Historical Status for Church." *Sunday Gazette-Mail* (Charleston, W.Va.), November 20, 2005, 5A.

———. "Till Casket Found in Rusty Shed." *Charleston (W.Va.) Gazette*, July 14, 2009, B10.

"Backer Says Bryant-Milam Fund Is Growing Rapidly." *Clarksdale (Miss.) Press Register*, September 13, 1955, 1.

Barrow, John. "Here's a Picture of Emmett Till Painted by Those Who Knew Him." *Chicago Defender*, September 24, 1955, 5.

Barry, Ellen. "Son Hopes Aging Father Talks About Till Murder." *Los Angeles Times*, August 14, 2005, 7A.

"Bill Spell Answers the *American*." *Jackson Daily News*, October 7, 1955, 1.

Binder, David. "Jamie Whitten, Who Served 53 Years in House, Dies at 85." *New York Times*, September 11, 1995, D13.

Blackwell, Lee. "2 Who Fled Mississippi Tell Stories." *Chicago Defender*, October 1, 1955, 1, 2.

Blake, Dan. "Cook County Board to Sue Cemetery Owners." *Chicago Tribune*, July 22, 2009, 8.

Bloom, Connie. "Filmmaker Delivers Message on Injustice." *McClatchy-Tribune Business News*, February 23, 2007, 1.

Bludeau, Glen. "10,000 View Casket of Slain Negro Boy." *Jackson State Times*, September 4, 1955, 1A, 16A.

Bock, Frederick. "A Prize Winning Poet Fails to Measure Up." *Chicago Daily Tribune*, June 5, 1960, C12.

"Body of Negro Found in River." *Jackson Clarion-Ledger*, September 1, 1955, 1, 5.

"Bombshell in the Till Case." *New York Post*, January 11, 1956, 1.

Bowean, Lolly. "Burr Oak Director Gets 12 Years." *Chicago Tribune*, July 9, 2011, 4.

Boyack, James E. "Courier's James Boyack Hangs Head in Shame." *Pittsburgh Courier*, October 1, 1955, 1, 4.

Boyd, Herb. "Emmett Till Bill Stalled in Senate." *New York Amsterdam News*, July 31, 2008, 4.

———. "Louima: 'God Is Good.'" *New York Amsterdam News*, August 16, 2007, 1.

———. "The Lynching of Emmett Till." *New York Amsterdam News*, November 21, 2002, 4.

———. "No Indictments in Till Case." *New York Amsterdam News*, March 8, 2007, 4.

———. "The Real Deal on Emmett Till." *New York Amsterdam News*, May 20, 2004, 3.

———. "Till Case Reopened." *New York Amsterdam News*, May 13, 2004, 1.

———. "The Untold Story of Emmett Till on Court TV." *New York Amsterdam News*, September 28, 2006, 22.

"Boy's Slaying Held Murder by Gov. White." *Chicago Daily Tribune*, September 2, 1955, 1, 2.

Bradley, Mamie. "I Want You to Know What They Did to My Boy." *Washington Afro-American*, November 5, 1955, 20, 21, and *Baltimore Afro-American*, November 12, 1955, 6, 7.

———. "Mamie Bradley's Untold Story." 8 parts. *Daily Defender* (Chicago), February 27, 1956–March 8, 1956.

"Breach of Trust." *Chicago Tribune*, July 10, 2009, 7.

Brennan, Ray. "Till's Uncle Sticks to Guns, Says He'll Relate Kidnapping." *Chicago Sun-Times*, September 19, 1955, 3.

———. "2 on Trial in Till Slaying." *Chicago Sun-Times*, September 18, 1955, 3.

Brennan, Tom. "World Watched Drama Unfold in Rural County Courtroom." *Jackson Clarion-Ledger/Jackson Daily News*, August 25, 1985, 2H.

Briggs, Jimmie. "Emmett Till Story at Film Forum." *New York Amsterdam News*, August 18, 2005, 20.

"Brilliant Defense Counsel Named for Three Men Accused of Massacre." *Kosciusko (Miss.) Star-Herald*, January 26, 1950, 1, 3.

"Brooklyn Audience Told How Till Died in Miss." *Baltimore Afro-American*, January 14, 1956, 17.

Brown, David. "Sumner Revisited: How Several Lives Altered by Till Trial." *Delta Democrat-Times* (Greenville, Miss.), August 19, 1956, 7.

Brown, Dwight. "Film: The Untold Story of Emmett Louis Till." *New York Beacon*, August 11, 2005, 25.

Brown, Timothy R. "Till Film up for Emmy Tonight." *Jackson Clarion-Ledger*, September 13, 2003, 2B.

"Brownell Rejects Request for Action in Emmett Till Case." *Clarksdale (Miss.) Press Register*, December 6, 1955, 7.

Browning, William. "Till Jury Talks: Grand Jury Says Evidence Wasn't There to Indict." *Greenwood (Miss.) Commonwealth*, September 30, 2007, 1A, 10A.

Bryant, Eula. Obituary. *Delta Democrat-Times* (Greenville, Miss.), August 27, 1974, 2.

"Bryant, Milam Released Under $10,000 Bond on Kidnap Charges." *Delta Democrat-Times* (Greenville, Miss.), September 30, 1955, 1.

Bryant, Roy. Obituary. *Bolivar Commercial* (Cleveland, Miss.), September 6, 1994, 12.

Bryant, Roy. Obituary. *Memphis Commercial Appeal*, September 3, 1994, A14.

Bryant, Vera Jo. Obituary. *Bolivar Commercial* (Cleveland, Miss.), May 3, 2012, 3.

"Bryant and Milam Released on $10,000 Bonds for Appearance Before Grand Jury November 7." *Greenwood (Miss.) Commonwealth*, September 30, 1955, 1.

"Bryant's Brother Claims Charges Are All 'Politics.'" *Memphis Commercial Appeal*, September 4, 1955, 19.

"Bryant Sought Job as Indianola Cop." *Delta Democrat-Times* (Greenville, Miss.), May 2, 1956, 1.

"Bryant's Store in Money Robbed Sat. Night." *Greenwood (Miss.) Morning Star*, September 20, 1955, 1.

Burghart, Tara. "Family of Slain Boy Relieved at Reopening." *Cincinnati Post*, May 11, 2004, A2.

Burnham, Maria. "Till Case Is Also About Attorney." *Desoto (Miss.) Appeal*, May 4, 2004, DS1.

Burton, Paul. "'Old Man Mose' Sells Out, He'll Move to New York." *Jackson Clarion-Ledger*, September 26, 1955, 1.

"A Call for Justice." *New York Post*, September 26, 1955, 22.

"Called Lynch-Murder, 'Morally, Legally' Wrong." *Cleveland Call and Post*, October 1, 1955, 10C.

Carlton, C. Sidney. "Defense Says Till Verdict Was Justice." *Chicago Defender*, October 1, 1955, 9.

Cassidy, Claudia. "Baldwin's New Play: Abuse with Tom-Toms." *Chicago Daily Tribune*, May 10, 1964, J5.

Chandler, Griffin. Obituary. *Delta Democrat-Times* (Greenville, Miss.), May 5, 1988, 3A.

"Charged Negro Boy Abducted." *Laurel (Miss.) Leader-Call*, August 29, 1955, 2.

"Charge Greenwood Storekeeper with Abducting Youth." *Delta Democrat-Times* (Greenville, Miss.), August 29, 1955, 2.

"Charleston Banker Drowns in Enid Lake." *Clarksdale (Miss.) Press Register*, September 4, 1962, 8.

"Charleston Sheriff Says Body in River Wasn't Young Till." *Memphis Commercial Appeal*, September 4, 1955, 1, 2.

"Chicago Negro Group Presses FBI on Till Case." *Delta Democrat-Times* (Greenville, Miss.), October 25, 1955, 2.

"Chicago Negro Youth Abducted by Three White Men at Money." *Greenwood (Miss.) Commonwealth*, August 29, 1955, 1.

Christiansen, Richard. "Reviving the Power of the Till Tragedy." *Chicago Tribune*, September 14, 1999, 1–2.

"City Court." *Delta Democrat-Times* (Greenville, Miss.), January 10, 1969, 2.

"City Court." *Delta Democrat-Times* (Greenville, Miss.), May 10, 1972, 11.

"City Court." *Delta Democrat-Times* (Greenville, Miss.), August 30, 1972, 2.

"Cleveland Man Charged with Possession of Drugs." *Delta Democrat-Times* (Greenville, Miss.), February 16, 1971, 1.

Coakley, Deirdre. "Keeper of the Flame: William Bradford Huie's Widow, Martha Hunt Huie, Works to Get His Work Back in Print." *Gadsden (Ala.) Times*, October 9, 2001, B4-B5.

Coen, Jeff. "Relatives of Emmett Till Meet with FBI." *Chicago Tribune*, March 30, 2007, 3.

"Coleman and Look at Odds on Till Case." *Memphis Press-Scimitar*, January 13, 1956, 1–2.

"Coleman Names Assistant to Aid Delta Prosecution." *Jackson Clarion-Ledger*, September 10, 1955, 1.

Colin, Mattie Smith. "Mother's Tears Greet Son Who Died a Martyr." *Chicago Defender*, September 10, 1955, 1, 2.

———. "Till's Mom, Diggs Both Disappointed." *Tri-State Defender* (Memphis, Tenn.), October 1, 1955, 1, 2.

Colin, Mattie Smith, and Robert Elliott. "Mother Waits in Vain for Her 'Bo.'" *Chicago Defender*, September 10, 1955, 1, 2.

"Collins Editor Asks U.S. Law on Dead Bodies." *Jackson Daily News*, September 8, 1955, 1.

"Comment Continues on Till Case." *Delta Democrat-Times* (Greenville, Miss.), November 11, 1955, 1.

"Community Leaders Protest in Buffalo." *Daily Worker* (New York), September 29, 1955, 3.

Cooper, James. "'Wolf Whistle' Men Are Freed." *London Express*, September 24, 1955, 1.

"Councilman Brown Urges Picketing of White House to Protest Lynching." *Daily Worker* (New York), September 9, 1955, 1.

"CRC 'Festival' Opens with Theme Centered on Till." *Jackson Daily News*, October 10, 1955, 1.

"'A Cruel Hoax': Till's Mother." *Memphis Press-Scimitar*, September 29, 1955, 4.

Culver, Virginia. "Statue Stirred Controversy." *Denver Post*, May 7, 2009, A8.

Currie, Bennie M. "Films, Books Revisit Saga of Slain Teen Emmett Till." *Kansas City Call*, December 20–26, 2002, 4.

Curry, George E. "Justice Department Will Investigate Emmett Till Case." *Frost* (Fort Wayne, Ind.), May 19–25, 2004, 3.

Curtain, Dave. "Repaired Statue Renews Legacy of Rights Battles." *Denver Post*, May 15, 2005, A1.

"Daily Worker's Reporter at Trial Is Mississippian." *Jackson Daily News*, September 20, 1955, 6.

Daniels, Lee A. "James Baldwin, Eloquent Writer in Behalf of Civil Rights, Is Dead." *New York Times*, December 2, 1987, A1.

Dao, James. "Indictment Makes Start at Lifting 40-Year-Old Cloud Over a Mississippi County." *New York Times*, January 8, 2005, A11.

Davey, Monica, and Gretchen Ruethling. "After 50 Years, Emmett Till's Body Is Exhumed." *New York Times*, June 2, 2005, A12.

"Deaf Mute Convicted of Rape-Slaying." *Spencer (Iowa) Daily Reporter*, December 13, 1955, 2.

"Defendant Carried Gun—Witness." *Chicago American*, September 22, 1955, 1, 4.

"Defendants Refuse to Pose Before TV." *Jackson State Times*, September 19, 1955, 8A.

"Defense Lawyer Quotes Dickens in Final Plea." *Jackson State Times*, September 23, 1955, 1.

"Defense Predicts State Cannot Prove Murder." *Greenwood (Miss.) Morning Star*, September 18, 1955, 1.

"Delta Diary." *Delta Democrat-Times* (Greenville, Miss.), October 2, 1973, 6.

"Delta Officers Study Abduction of Negro Youth." *McComb (Miss.) Enterprise-Journal*, August 29, 1955, 1.

"Delta Veniremen Called." *Jackson Clarion-Ledger*, September 16, 1955, 1.

"Delta White Men to Go on Trial September 19." *Jackson Daily News*, September 9, 1955, 1.

"'A Den of Snakes' Youth's Mother Calls Mississippi." *Delta Democrat-Times* (Greenville, Miss.), September 1, 1955, 2.

Desmond, James. "Old Negro Points to White Pair, Says 'That's the Men.'" *New York Daily News*, September 22, 1955, C3.

"Details Told of Lynching of Emmett." *Baltimore Afro-American*, September 17, 1955, 14.

Dewan, Shaila. "Jury Hears Mother of Rights Worker Slain in 1964." *New York Times*, June 18, 2005, A8.

———. "Man Convicted in '64 Case and Out on Bail Is Rejailed." *New York Times*, September 10, 2005, A8.

———. "Prosecution Completes Case in 1964 Civil Rights Killings." *New York Times*, June 19, 2005, 16.

———. "Revisiting '64 Civil Rights Deaths, This Time in a Murder Trial." *New York Times*, June 12, 2005, 26.

Dewan, Shaila, and Ariel Hart. "FBI Discovers Trial Transcript in Emmett Till Case." *New York Times*, May 18, 2005, A14.

Dewan, Shaila, and Jerry Mitchell. "A Klan Confession, but Not to 1964 Civil Rights Murders." *New York Times*, June 16, 2005, A18.

Diggs, Charles C., Jr. "Emmett Till Trial Over but Negros Should Never Forget Its Meaning." *Pittsburgh Courier*, October 8, 1955, 1, 4.

"Diggs Gives Far Different Appraisal of Trial at Detroit Than at Sumner." *Jackson Daily News*, September 26, 1955, 9.

"Dismiss Appeal by Till's Mother." *Daily Defender* (Chicago), May 17, 1960, A2.

"Dismiss Traffic Charge against Reporter Covering Sumner Trial." *Clarksdale (Miss.) Press Register*, September 22, 1955, 1.

"Dixie Verdict Assailed in 24-Hr. Rally." *Detroit News*, September 30, 1955, 14.

Dixon, Amos. "Milam Master-Minded Emmett Till Killing." *California Eagle* (Los Angeles), February 2, 1956, 1–2.

———. "Mrs. Bryant Didn't Even Hear Emmett Till Whistle." *California Eagle* (Los Angeles), January 26, 1956, 1, 2, 4.

———. "South Wins Out in Till Lynching Trial." *California Eagle* (Los Angeles), February 23, 1956, 2.

———. "Till Case: Torture and Murder." *California Eagle* (Los Angeles), February 9, 1956, 1–2.

———. "Till Case: Torture and Murder." *California Eagle* (Los Angeles), February 16, 1956, 1–2.

"Documentary on Till Murder Wins Emmy." *Jackson Clarion-Ledger*, September 15, 2003, 1A.

Donham, David Alford. Obituary. *Delta Democrat-Times* (Greenville, Miss.), April 11, 2002, A5.

"Dr. Howard: Situation in Mississippi Extremely Serious." *Pittsburgh Courier*, October 8, 1955, 1, 4.

"Dr. Howard Is Selling Property." *Washington Afro-American*, December 17, 1955, 1–2.

"Dr. T. R. M. Howard to Address Ala. Omegas." *Birmingham (Ala.) World*, November 18, 1955, 1.

Ducket, Alfred. "Adlai in Tribute to Dr. Johnson." *Chicago Defender*, November 10, 1956, 10.

Duncan, Ian. "African American History Museum Is Underway in D.C." *Los Angeles Times*, February 23, 2012, A12.

Duncan, Steve. "Argus Pres. On-the-Scene." *St. Louis Argus*, September 23, 1955, 13.

———. "NAACP Disavows Support of Till Fund Raising." *St. Louis Argus*, September 23, 1955, 13.

———. "Relatives of Loggins Are Worried." *St. Louis Argus*, October 28, 1955, 1, 10.

Ealy, Charles. "Mother of Teen Slain in '55 Tries to Keep Case Alive." *Dallas Morning News*, December 20, 1992, 16A.

Edelstein, Mort. "Till Witness Decides Not to Testify." *Chicago American*, October 10, 1955, 5.

———. "Witnesses Called 'Prisoners.'" *Chicago American*, October 7, 1955, 1, 2.

"8-Man Team Covers Till Case Trial." *Chicago Defender*, September 24, 1955, 5, and *Tri-State Defender* (Memphis, Tenn.), September 24, 1955, 1, 2.

"Ella Mae Shuns Willie." *Jackson Daily News*, September 30, 1955, 1.

"Emmett Till Foundation Holds Annual Banquet." *Daily Defender* (Chicago), July 25, 1966, 8.

"Emmett Till's Mom Loses Libel Suit." *Delta Democrat-Times* (Greenville, Miss.), June 23, 1959, 2.

"Emmett Till's Mother Sues *Look*." *Delta Democrat-Times* (Greenville, Miss.), January 23, 1958, 14.

"End of Kidnaping Case Where Leflore Concerned." *Greenwood (Miss.) Commonwealth*, November 10, 1955, 1.

"An Even Bigger Crime." *Scott County Times* (Forest, Miss.), September 8, 1955, 4.

"Events Night of Kidnaping Told by Slain Boy's Cousin." *Jackson Daily News*, September 1, 1955, 12.

Everett, Arthur. "Defendants Admit Kidnaping Till Boy but Deny Murder." *Jackson Clarion-Ledger*, September 22, 1955, 1, 18.

———. "Hint New Witnesses May Shed More Light on Killing." *Jackson Clarion-Ledger*, September 21, 1955, 1, 5.

———. "10 Tentative Jurors Chosen in Till Trial." *Jackson Clarion-Ledger*, September 20, 1955, 1, 12.

———. "Till Nearly Missed His Fatal Journey to Land of Cotton." *Jackson Clarion-Ledger*, September 19, 1955, 1, 12.

———. "Trial in Leflore Must Wait Action by Next Grand Jury." *Jackson Clarion-Ledger*, September 24, 1955, 1, 8.

"Ex-Farm Manager Freed in Till Murder Now in Bread Line." *New York Post*, February 14, 1958, 20.

"Ex-Officer in Louima Case Is Freed from Halfway House." *New York Times*, May 5, 2007, B2.

"'Eyes on the Prize' Returns to PBS." *Washington Informer*, September 28, 2006, 26.

"'Eyes on the Prize II' Wins Three Golden Eagle Awards." *Los Angeles Sentinel*, December 11, 1990, A8.

"Famed Dr. Howard, Rights Fighter, Montgomery Speaker." *Birmingham (Ala.) World*, November 22, 1955, 1, and *Alabama Tribune* (Montgomery), November 25, 1955, 1.

"Fate of 2 Witnesses Remains a Mystery." *Daily Worker* (New York), October 3, 1955, 2.

"Father of Young Till Died for His Country." *New York Amsterdam News*, October 1, 1955, 7.

"Faulkner Pictures Till Case as Test of Survival of White Man, America." *Jackson Daily News*, September 10, 1955, 1.

Featherston, James. "Delta Courtroom Is Packed as Murder Trial Opens." *Jackson Daily News*, September 19, 1955, 1, 14.

———. "Negro Congressman Eyes Trial—His Role Not Clear." *Jackson Daily News*, September 20, 1955, 1, 7.

———. "Slain Boy's Uncle Points Finger at Bryant, Milam but Admits Light Was Dim." *Jackson Daily News*, September 21, 1955, 1, 14.

———. "White 'Deplores' Slaying in Note to NAACP Which Is Creating National Issue." *Jackson Daily News*, September 1, 1955, 1.

Featherston, James, and W. C. Shoemaker. "State Demands Conviction." *Jackson Daily News*, September 23, 1955, 1, 9.

"1500 Hear Till's Kin Speak at Rally." *Chicago Defender*, September 24, 1955, 3.

"Find Kidnaped Chicago Boy's Body in River." *Chicago Daily Tribune*, September 1, 1955, 1, 2.

"First of Trio Goes on Trial Here for Revenge Massacre of Children." *Kosciusko (Miss.) Star-Herald*, March 16, 1950, 1, 6.

Fitzpatrick, Lauren. "'I Am Very Sorry': Burr Oak Manager Gets 12 Years." *Chicago Sun-Times*, July 9, 2011.

———. "Proposed Till Museum Lost in Burr Oak Scandal." *Chicago Sun-Times*, July 11, 2011, 22.

Foreman, Harold. "Reports Till Boy Alive in Detroit Bring 'Hoax' Comment from Mother." *Jackson Daily News*, September 29, 1955, 1.

"Former Sheriff Dies." *Greenwood (Miss.) Commonwealth*, October 9, 1975, 1.

"For Sale." *Greenwood (Miss.) Morning Star*, October 19, 1955, 6.

"Four Witnesses Called in Probe." *Chicago Defender*, November 12, 1955, 1–2.

Fox, Margalit. "Willie Louis, Who Named the Killers of Emmett Till at Their Trial, Dies at 76." *New York Times*, July 24, 2013, A25.

"France Irate Over Till Case." *Jackson Clarion-Ledger*, September 26, 1955, 8.

Franklin, William B. "Staff Photog Tells Own Story of Trip." *St. Louis Argus*, September 30, 1955, 13, 19.

"French Hit Verdict in Till Case." *Chicago Defender*, October 1, 1955, 43.

Gardner, Virginia, and Roosevelt Ward Jr. "20,000 in Harlem Flay Till Verdict." *Daily Worker* (New York), September 26, 1955, 1, 8.

Garrity, Robert J. "Emmett Till Exhumation Is Crucial to a Just Resolution to This Case." *Tinley Park (Ill.) Daily Southtown*, May 24, 2005, A8.

———. "Exhumation of Till's Remains Is Essential." *Chicago Tribune*, May 22, 2005, 10.

"Gerald Chatham Dies." *New York Times*, October 11, 1956, 39.

"Girl Honored for Saving Negro Nurse." *Clarksdale (Miss.) Press Register*, September 10, 1955, 1.

Gordon, Jerry. "In Memoriam." *Cleveland Call and Post*, October 15, 1955, 8C.

"Gov. White Orders Crackdown on Wide-Open Gambling." *Greenwood (Miss.) Morning Star*, August 25, 1955, 1.

"Gov. White Tells Reed Boy's Mother Her Fears Are Based on Propaganda." *Jackson Daily News*, October 10, 1955, 1.

"Government Official Labels Till Case 'Black Mark.'" *Clarksdale (Miss.) Press Register*, November 21. 1955, 1.

Gowran, Clay. "Urban League Asks Action in Till Case." *Chicago Daily Tribune*, September 6, 1955, 8.

"Grand Jury, District Attorney Rap 'Cover-Up' in Brookhaven Case." *Clarksdale (Miss.) Press Register*, September 21, 1955, 6.

"Grand Jury Calls Several Witnesses in Till Murder Case." *Greenwood (Miss.) Morning Star*, September 6, 1955, 1.

"Grand Jury Considers Charge in Till Case as Suspects Guarded in Greenwood Jail." *Clarksdale (Miss.) Press Register*, September 5, 1955, 1, 8.

"Grand Jury Frees Accused Kidnappers." *Abilene (Tex.) Reporter*, November 10, 1955, 9.

"Grand Jury Makes Report and Adjourns." *Sumner (Miss.) Sentinel*, September 8, 1955, 1.

"Grand Jury to Look at New Till Angle." *Chicago Tribune*, February 22, 2007, 8.

Grim, Fred. "Memorial to Honor Civil Rights Martyrs." *Wisconsin State Journal* (Madison), July 31, 1988, 1D.

Gruenberg, Charles. "Jury Tells Why It Acquitted—'Shocking,' Says NAACP." *New York Post*, September 25, 1955, 3.

Gunter, James. "Early Crowd Fills Courtroom, Unrest Mounts at Late Start." *Memphis Commercial Appeal*, September 23, 1955, 35.

———. "Jokes, Threats Are Blended at Tension-Packed Sumner." *Memphis Commercial Appeal*, September 21, 1955, 8.

———. "Judge Raps Gavel as Witness Provokes Laughter at Trial." *Memphis Commercial Appeal*, September 22, 1955, 33.

———. "Milling Throng in Courtroom Kept Eyes on Juryroom Door." *Memphis Commercial Appeal*, September 24, 1955, 1, 4.

———. "Wives Serious, Children Romp as Trial Begins." *Memphis Commercial Appeal*, September 20, 1955, 1, 11.

Hall, Rob F. "Kidnapers' Friends Fill Panel as Trial Opens in Mississippi in Child's Murder." *Daily Worker* (New York), September 20, 1955, 1, 8.

———. "Lynched Boy's Mother Sees Jurymen Picked." *Daily Worker* (New York), September 21, 1955, 1, 8.

———. "Sumner, a Good Place to Raise a Boy." *Daily Worker* (New York), September 21, 1955, 1, 8.

Harmon, George. "'Jail Raid' Has Area Tense." *Jackson State Times*, September 5, 1955, 1A, 10A.

Harris, Russell. "4 Worlds of the South Highlighted by Trial." *Detroit News*, September 24, 1955, 1, 2.

Hart, Ariel. "41 Years Later, Ex-Klansman Gets 60 Years in Civil Rights Deaths." *New York Times*, June 24, 2005, A14.

"H. C. Strider Dies on Hunt." *Clarksdale (Miss.) Press Register*, December 28, 1970, 13.

"Hearing Set Friday for Bryant, Milam." *Memphis Commercial Appeal*, September 28, 1955, 2.

Henderson, Robert H., Sr. Obituary. *Charleston (Miss.) Sun-Sentinel*, October 11, 2007, 3.

"Henry Loggins Looms in Case as Vital Link." *St. Louis Argus*, October 14, 1955, 1.

Herbers, John. "'Case Closed' as Jury Fails to Indict Pair for Till Kidnaping." *Delta Democrat-Times* (Greenville, Miss.), November 10, 1955, 1.

———. "Cross-Burning at Sumner Went Almost Un-noticed Yesterday." *Delta Democrat-Times* (Greenville, Miss.), September 22, 1955, 1.

———. "Sleepy Sumner Surprised by Way World Watching Pending Till Trial Today." *Delta Democrat-Times* (Greenville, Miss.), September 18, 1955, 1.

———. "Testimony Opens Today in Till 'Wolf-Whistle' Murder Trial." *Delta Democrat-Times* (Greenville, Miss.), September 20, 1955, 1, 2.

———. "Till Trial Bogs Down in Jury-Picking Job." *Delta Democrat-Times* (Greenville, Miss.), September 19, 1955, 1, 2.

———. "Uncle Identifies Boy's Abductors." *Jackson State Times*, September 21, 1955, 1A, 8A.

———. "Wolf Whistle Murder Case Goes to Jury in Sumner Circuit Court." *Delta Democrat-Times* (Greenville, Miss.), September 23, 1955, 1, 7.

———. "Wright Tells of Kidnaping of Till Boy." *Delta Democrat-Times* (Greenville, Miss.), September 21, 1955, 1, 2.

"Here Is What 'Too Tight' Told the *Defender*." *Chicago Defender*, October 8, 1955, 35.

"Here's Cast for Sumner, Miss. Trial." *Tri-State Defender* (Memphis, Tenn.), September 24, 1955, 1, 2.

"Here's the Cemetery Worker Who Blew the Whistle." *Arlington Heights (Ill.) Daily Herald*, July 22, 2009, 15.

Hersh, Philip. "Ligeti Has a Record Day. *Chicago Tribune*, February 16, 2013, 8.

Hicks, James L. "Big Town." *Baltimore Afro-American*, October 8, 1955, 9.

———. "Hicks Arrested in Mississippi." *Baltimore Afro-American*, October 1, 1955, 8.

———. "Hicks Says U.S. Ought to Act Now." *Baltimore Afro-American*, November 19, 1955, 1, 2.

———. "Lynch Trial Begins." *Baltimore Afro-American*, September 24, 1955, 1, 2.

———. "Reporters Segregated." *Baltimore Afro-American*, September 24, 1955, 1.

———. "Unbelievable!" *Baltimore Afro-American*, November 12, 1955, 1, 2.

———. "Why Emmett Till's Mother and NAACP Couldn't Agree." *Baltimore Afro-American*, December 31, 1955, 2.

"Hicks Digs into Till Case." *Washington Afro-American*, November 19, 1955, 4, 14.

"Hinant Explains Till Trial Views." *Memphis Commercial Appeal*, October 9, 1955, 3.

Hirsch, Carl. "10,000 in Detroit, 10,000 in Chicago Call for U.S. Intervention in Mississippi Terror." *Daily Worker* (New York), September 27, 1955, 3.

Holloway, Lynette. "Sharpton Says Brutality Issue Will Propel Him to a Victory." *New York Times*, August 31, 1997, 27.

Holmberg, David. "The Legacy of Emmett Till." *Palm Beach (Fla.) Post*, September 4, 1994, 1A, 10A, 11A.

Holmes, Paul. "Hunt Shadow Witnesses in Till Slaying." *Chicago Daily Tribune*, September 21, 1955, 3.

———. "Jurors Hear of Confession in Till Trial." *Chicago Daily Tribune*, September 22, 1955, 1, 11.

———. "Jury Reaches Verdict after Hour Debate." *Chicago Daily Tribune*, September 24, 1955, 1, 2.

———. "Uncle Tells How 3 Kidnapers Invaded Home and Seized Till." *Chicago Daily Tribune*, September 19, 1955, 2.

———. "2 Go on Trial in South for Till Murder." *Chicago Daily Tribune*, September 20, 1955, 1, 2.

———. "A Way of Life Going on Trial in Till Case." *Chicago Daily Tribune*, September 18, 1955, 1, 6.

"Honored at Reception." *Delta Democrat-Times* (Greenville, Miss.), May 6, 1962, 16.

Howard, T. R. M. "Stark Terror Reigns in Mississippi Delta." *Washington Afro-American*, October 1, 1955, 19, 21.

———. "Terror Reigns in Mississippi." *Washington Afro-American*, October 1, 1955, 19, and *Baltimore Afro-American*, October 8, 1955, 6.

Howell, Ron. "A Film with a Mission." *Newsday*, January 20, 2003, B6.

"Huff Quits Mrs. Bradley, NAACP Cancels Tour." *Chicago Defender*, November 12, 1955, 1, 2.

Huffstutter, P. J. "FBI Begins Unearthing Mystery." *Ft. Wayne (Ind.) Journal-Gazette*, June 2, 2005, 4A.

"Huff Tells Why He Didn't Attend Trial." *Chicago Defender*, September 24, 1955, 2.

Hutson, Wendell. "Remembering Emmett Till." *Chicago Defender*, September 2, 2009, 7.

Hutto, Ralph. "Defense Sees Longer Trial Than Expected." *Jackson State Times*, September 19, 1955, 1A, 8A.

———. "Dynamic Personalities Form Till Trial Cast." *Jackson State Times*, September 20, 1955, 2A.

———. "NAACP Leader Says Two Witnesses Disappeared." *Jackson State Times*, September 23, 1955, 6A.

———. "Now Sumner Is Just Another Sleepy Delta Town." *Jackson State Times*, September 24, 1955, 1.

———. "Sheriff Won't Call Guard to Preserve Order." *Jackson State Times*, September 21, 1955, 8A.

"Hypocrisy Is Attacked by Writer." *Jackson State Times*, September 10, 1955, 1, 12A.

"Ignore Doctor, 2 Grill Young Reed." *Chicago Defender*, October 15, 1955, 1, 2.

Jackson, Emory O. "Howard Thinking About 'March on Washington.'" *Birmingham (Ala.) World*, December 6, 1955, 6.

Bibliography

James, Rebecca. "A Tale Too Explosive for '50s TV." *Syracuse (N.Y.) Post Standard*, March 27, 2008, D1–2.

Janega, James, and Mathew Walberg. "Mamie Till-Mobley, 1921–2003." *Chicago Daily Tribune*, January 7, 2003, 2C.

Janovy, C. J. "Justice at Last." *Pitch* (Kansas City), March 23, 2006, 11, 13, 15, 16, 17.

Jarrett, Vernon. "Emmett Till's Mom Speaks Again." *Chicago Defender*, October 15, 2003, 2.

"JBW Attends Funerals." *Delta Democrat-Times* (Greenville, Miss.), December 29, 1970, 10.

"Jesse Breland Dies at 80." *Clarksdale (Miss.) Press Register*, March 26, 1969, 1.

"Jesse Jackson Asks Mississippi, FBI to Apologize to Emmett Till Family." *New York Beacon*, May 12–18, 2005, 3.

"John Ed Cothran." *Washington Post*, March 20, 2008, B7.

"John Ed Cothran, 1914–2008." *Chicago Tribune*, March 21, 2008, 9.

"Johnnie Cochran May Reopen Emmett Till Murder Case." *San Francisco Sun-Reporter*, December 14, 1995, 3.

Johnson, Sam. "Grand Jury Not Examined Witnesses in Till Kidnapping." *Greenwood (Miss.) Commonwealth*, November 8, 1955, 1.

———. "Jury Selection Starts Climax on Noted Case." *Jackson Daily News*, September 18, 1955, 4.

———. "State Will Not Ask Death Penalty in Trial of White Men at Sumner." *Greenwood (Miss.) Commonwealth*, September 19, 1955, 1.

Jones, Tony. "Cochran May Open Till Case." *Tri-State Defender* (Memphis, Tenn.), August 26–30, 1995, 1.

———. "Cochran to Reopen Infamous Till Case." *Michigan Chronicle* (Detroit), September 13, 1995, 1-A.

Jones, Yolanda. "Sign Honoring Emmett Till Is Marred by Vandalism." *Memphis Commercial Appeal*, June 26, 2006, B2.

Joyner, Chris. "Black Man Suspected in Death of Mississippi White Supremacist." *USA Today*, April 23, 2010, A2.

Jubera, Drew. "Autopsy Sought in 50-Year-Old Crime." *Atlanta Journal-Constitution*, May 5, 2005, A1.

———. "Civil Rights-Era Murder Cases." *Atlanta Journal-Constitution*, June 3, 2007, A1.

———. "Decades Later, an Apology." *Atlanta Journal-Constitution*, October 2, 2007, A1, A4.

———. "Duty Outweighs Emotion for DA in Till Case." *Atlanta Journal-Constitution*, November 5, 2006, A1.

"Judge Curtis Swango Draws Jury List." *Jackson Clarion-Ledger*, September 13, 1955, 1.

"Judge Denies Bond for Glendora Man." *Clarksdale (Miss.) Press Register*, January 10, 1956, 1.

"Judge in Mississippi Case Has Long Service Record." *Memphis Commercial Appeal*, September 18, 1955, 10.

"Judge Limits Sketching of Murder Trial." *Jackson State Times*, September 20, 1955, 2A.

"Judge's Skilled Handling Draws General Praise." *Jackson State Times*, September 21, 1955, 8A.

"Judge Swango's Rites Held on Saturday." *Batesville (Miss.) Panolian*, December 12, 1968, 1.

"Jury Acquits Bryant, Milam of Murder Charge as Trial Ends." *Clarksdale (Miss.) Press Register*, September 23, 1955, 1, 3.

"Jury Is Split at Outset of Deliberation." *New York Times*, June 21, 2005, A12.

"Jury Selection Begins in '64 Case of Civil Rights Workers' Killings." *New York Times*, June 14, 2005, A12.

"A Just Appraisal." *Greenwood (Miss.) Commonwealth*, September 2, 1955, 1.

"Justice at Last." *New York Amsterdam News*, April 6, 2006, 1.

"Justice Dept. Says 'No' to New Probe into Till Murder." *Delta Democrat-Times* (Greenville, Miss.), February 12, 1956, 22.

"J. W. Milam and Roy Bryant Indicted Sept. 6." *Sumner (Miss.) Sentinel*, September 8, 1955, 1.

Kaplan, Fred. "Ex-Officer Guilty of Lying in Louima Case." *Boston Globe*, July 17, 2002, A2.

Keith, Bill. "No Parole for Leon Turner, Thrice Murderer." *Jackson Clarion-Ledger*, March 23, 1950, 1, 16.

———. "Turner Guilty, Jurors Disagree on Penalty." *Jackson Clarion-Ledger*, March 22, 1950, 1, 16.

———. "Windol Whitt Gets Life Term." *Kosciusko (Miss.) Star-Herald*, March 17, 1950, 1, 16.

———. "Windol Whitt's Trial Rusumes [*sic*] Today with Surprise Testimony." *Jackson Clarion-Ledger*, March 16, 1950, 1, 7.

Kempton, Murray. "The Baby Sitter." *New York Post*, September 20, 1955, 5, 32.

———. "Heart of Darkness." *New York Post*, September 21, 1955, 3, 50.

———. "He Went All the Way." *New York Post*, September 22, 1955, 5, 36.

———. "Preacher, Preacher." *New York Post*, September 19, 1955, 3, 30.

———. "They Didn't Forget." *New York Post*, September 26, 1955, 5, 22.

———. "2 Face Trial as 'Whistle' Kidnapers—Due to Post Bond and Go Home." *New York Post*, September 25, 1955, 3, 16.

"Kidnap-Murder Case Will Be Transferred to Tallahatchie." *Greenwood (Miss.) Commonwealth*, September 1, 1955, 1.

"Kidnap Murder Stirs Delta." *Clarksdale (Miss.) Press Register*, September 2, 1955, 1, 8.

"Kidnapped Boy Whistled at Woman." *Chicago Daily Tribune* August 30, 1955, 2.

"Kidnapping Charges as Boy Seized." *Jackson State Times*, August 29, 1955, 1.

Kilgallen, James. "Defendants Receive Handshakes, Kisses." *Memphis Commercial Appeal*, September 24, 1955, 3.

———. "Expect Trial to Be Short, Tense." *Tri-State Defender* (Memphis, Tenn.), September 24, 1955, 2.

———. "Jury to Go Out as State Rests Case." *Chicago American*, September 23, 1955, 1, 4.

———. "Spectators in Dixie Court Searched for Weapons." *Chicago American*, September 19, 1955, 1.

———. "Wright Tells Story of Negro's Kidnapping." *Memphis Commercial Appeal*, September 22, 1955, 11.

"Killing of Till Listed as Lynch in Records." *Greenwood (Miss.) Morning Star*, September 7, 1955, 1.

"Kimbrell Is Denied Bond in Slaying at Glendora." *Jackson Clarion-Ledger*, December 29, 1955, 1, 10.

"King Statue Center of Dispute." *Greeley (Colo.) Tribune*, July 6, 1977, 1.

"Kin Tell How Murdered Boy Was Abducted." *Chicago Daily Tribune*, September 3, 1955, 11.

Knowles, Clayton. "Five Congressmen Shot in House by 3 Puerto Rican Nationalists." *New York Times*, March 2, 1954, 1.

Knowles, Francine. "Monument Dedicated to Burr Oak Healing." *Chicago Sun-Times*, August 30, 2014, 5.

Korecki, Natasha. "Possible Bullet Pieces Found in Till Autopsy." *Chicago Sun-Times*, June 11, 2005, 6.

Kuetiner, Al. "Till Case Rarely Discussed at Site of Famous Murder Trial." *Delta Democrat-Times* (Greenville, Miss.), September 4, 1957, 15.

Kreutz, Douglas. "Hundreds Watch Unveiling of King Statue in City Park." *Rocky Mountain News*, September 6, 1976, 6.

Langer, Emily. "Witness Dared to Testify in Emmett Till Lynching." *Washington Post*, July 25, 2013, A6.

Lawrence, W. H. "Eisenhower Irate." *New York Times*, August 3, 1957, 1.

———. "President Backs U.S. Court Order." *New York Times*, September 10, 1957, 29.

"Leader Left State after Being Shot." *Baltimore Afro-American*, November 10, 1956, 8.

Lee, Felicia R. "Directors Elated by Plan to Revisit 1955 Murder." *New York Times*, May 12, 2004, B4.

"Lee County Runoff Vote Is Scheduled." *Delta Democrat-Times* (Greenville, Miss.), February 17, 1965, 6.

"Leflore County Officers Checking Kidnap Charge." *Clarksdale (Miss.) Press Register*, August 29, 1955, 1.

"Leflore Officials Delay Fixing Bond in Till Case." *Jackson Daily News*, September 25, 1955, 1, 16.

"Leon Turner Gets Life Imprisonment without Hope of Pardon." *Kosciusko (Miss.) Star-Herald*, March 22, 1950, 1.

Lichtblau, Eric, and Andrew Jacobs. "U.S. Reopens '55 Murder Case, Flashpoint of Civil Rights Era." *New York Times*, May 11, 2004, A19.

Lipson, Karin. "The Agents for Justice, Documentary Filmmakers Go Beyond Telling the Story of Emmett Till's Shocking Murder by Instigating a Reopening of the 1955 Case." *Newsday*, May 23, 2004, C6

"Local Cosmetologists to Give Away Television." *Delta Democrat-Times* (Greenville, Miss.), April 13, 1975, 15.

Lomax, Louis E. "Henry Loggins Found, but Refuses to Leave Jail Cell." *Daily Defender* (Chicago), March 12, 1955, 8.

———. "Leslie Milam Quits Farm Home." *Daily Defender* (Chicago), March 5, 1956, 5.

———. "Milam Jails His Handyman." *Daily Defender* (Chicago), March 20, 1956, 5.

Lombardi, Frank. "Civil Rights Slay Plea Pols Urge Reopening of 1955 Till Case." *New York Daily News*, April 7, 2004, 1.

Longino, Bob. "Ceremony Today for Till's Mother." *Atlanta Journal-Constitution*, January 8, 2003, B1.

———. "Emmett Till Case Reopened." *Atlanta Journal-Constitution*, May 11, 2004, A1.

———. "Emmett Till Documentary Previewed at King Center." *Atlanta Journal-Constitution*, January 26, 2003, C2.

———. "Group Seeks to Reopen Emmett Till Case." *Atlanta Journal-Constitution*, April 6, 2004, E2.

———. "Lynching Victim Mom Dies on Eve of Atlanta Visit." *Atlanta Journal-Constitution*, January 7, 2003, A1.

———. "Telling Till's 'Untold Story.'" *Atlanta Journal-Constitution*, January 24, 2003, E5.

———. "The Unfinished Story of Emmett Till." *Atlanta Journal-Constitution*, January 5, 2003, A1.

Bibliography

"Look Magazine Names Milam, Bryant in Confession Story." *Tri-State Defender* (Memphis, Tenn.), January 14, 1956, 1, 2.

"Look Sued for Million Libel by Till's Mother." *Chicago Daily Tribune*, January 22, 1958, 8.

"Louis [*sic*] Till's Mother Sets New Jersey Tour." *Washington Afro-American*, January 3, 1956, 19.

"Lynched Boy Lived Here, Early Days on Vinewood Recalled." *Michigan Chronicle* (Detroit), September 10, 1955, 1, 6.

"Lynching Acquittal Shocks All Europe." *Daily Worker* (New York), October 11, 1955, 2.

"Lynching Post-Facto." *Delta Democrat-Times* (Greenville, Miss.), September 6, 1955, 4.

"Lynch 'Kidnap Report' False." *Washington Afro-American*, October 8, 1955, 1.

Lythgoe, Dennis. "The Death of Emmett Till." *Deseret News* (Salt Lake City), February 26, 1997, C1, C2.

Malone, Julia. "Emmett Till Act Fulfills Promise: Pledge Kept to Slain Teenager's Late Mother." *Atlanta Journal-Constitution*, October 10, 2008, A7.

"Mamie Bradley Says She Expected Verdict." *Delta Democrat-Times* (Greenville, Miss.), September 25, 1955, 1.

"Man's Father May Have Been Involved in Terrible History of Small Mississippi Town." *Lodi (Calif.) News-Sentinel*, August 10, 2005, 7.

Marsh, Harry. "Anonymous Telephone Calls Kept Sheriff Strider Awake at Night." *Delta Democrat-Times* (Greenville, Miss.), September 20, 1955, 1.

———. "Communist Writer at Trial Lauds Citizens." *Delta Democrat-Times* (Greenville, Miss.), September 23, 1955, 1.

———. "Editors Eye Clock in Awaiting Verdict." *Delta Democrat-Times* (Greenville, Miss.), September 23, 1955, 1.

———. "Hundred Newsmen Jam Scene of Till Trial." *Delta Democrat-Times* (Greenville, Miss.), September 19, 1955, 1, 2.

———. "Judge Swango Is Good Promoter for South." *Delta Democrat-Times* (Greenville, Miss.), September 21, 1955, 1, 2.

———. "Sheriff Says He Got Little Cooperation." *Delta Democrat-Times* (Greenville, Miss.), November 10, 1955, 1.

———. "Unanswered Questions Nag Newsmen at Trial." *Delta Democrat-Times* (Greenville, Miss.), September 20, 1955, 1.

Marshall, Chester, and James McBroom. "White Men Face Double Indictment for Kidnapping, Murdering Till Boy." *Jackson Daily News*, September 6, 1955, 1, 3.

"Marshall Blames Citizens Council for Till Slaying." *Jackson Daily News*, September 12, 1955, 1.

"Marshall Says Till Case 'Horrible' Terrorist Example." *Delta Democrat-Times* (Greenville, Miss.), November 7, 1955, 1.

Martin, Nita. "Don't Spend Money on Till Case." *Jackson Clarion-Ledger*, May 25, 2004, 6A.

Martin, Roland S. "Rush Welcomes Justice Department Decision to Exhume Till." *Chicago Defender*, May 5, 2005, 2.

"Mass Meet Crowd Bitter, Mad, Sullen." *New York Amsterdam News*, October 1, 1955, 7.

"Mayor Daley Protests Slaying of Chicagoan." *Chicago Sun-Times*, September 2, 1955, 3.

McBride, Earnest. "McGee Family Decries Downplay of Racist Provocation in Barrett Murder Case." *Jackson Advocate*, August 4, 2011, 1A, 9A.

McKenzie, Danny. "Ripley Attorney Played Major Role in Till Case." *Daily Journal* (Tupelo, Miss.), September 21, 2003, 1A.

Bibliography

McKinley, Jesse. "Henry Hampton Dies at 58." *New York Times*, November 24, 1998, 10.

Melady, Mark. "Filmmaker Says Indictments Expected." *Worchester (Mass.) Telegram & Gazette*, February 24, 1955, B1.

"Memorial to Emmett Till to Be Placed in Leflore County." *Memphis Commercial Appeal*, December 31, 2005, D1.

Middlebrooks, William. "Milam and Bryant Freed on $10,000 Bond at Hearing." *Greenwood (Miss.) Morning Star*, October 1, 1955, 1.

———. "Sheriff Says Body Thousands Viewed May Not Be Till's." *Delta Democrat-Times* (Greenville, Miss.), September 4, 1955, 1, 2.

"Milam, Bryant Sign for Till Case Movie." *Baltimore Afro-American*, January 28, 1956, 1.

Milam, Horace William. Obituary. *Delta Democrat-Times* (Greenville, Miss.), October 9, 2008, A6.

Milam, John William. Obituary. *Delta Democrat-Times* (Greenville, Miss.), January 2, 1981, 2A.

Milam, Leslie. Obituary. *Delta Democrat-Times* (Greenville, Miss.), September 1, 1974, 3.

Milam, Mary Juanita. Obituary. *Biloxi-Gulfport (Miss.) Sun Herald*, January 14, 2014, A4.

Milam, Wade. "Writes a Letter to Life Editor." *Jackson Daily News*, October 21, 1955, 6.

"Milam Hires Sumner, Miss., Lawyer—Says He May Sue Look Magazine." *Memphis Press-Scimitar*, January 14, 1956, 3.

"Milam Is Pictured a War Hero Who Also Snatched Negro from Drowning." *Jackson Daily News*, September 20, 1955, 6.

Milner, Jay. "Bryant Didn't Mind His Negro Non-Com during Korean War." *Jackson Clarion-Ledger*, September 20, 1955, 1, 12.

———. "Defendants Turned Back to Face Kidnap Charges by Leflore County Jury." *Jackson Clarion-Ledger*, September 25, 1955, 1, 8.

———. "Doctor's Testimony May Alter Inquiry." *Jackson Clarion-Ledger*, September 6, 1955, 1, 12.

———. "Jittery News Men at Sumner Kept in a Dither by Rumors." *Jackson Clarion-Ledger*, September 22, 1955, 2.

———. "Milam Says He's 'Not Sure' If He Has Grounds for Libel Suit." *Delta Democrat-Times* (Greenville, Miss.), January 15, 1956, 1.

———. "Negro's Funeral at Sumner Takes Spotlight from Trial." *Jackson Clarion-Ledger*, September 19, 1955, 1.

———. "Newsman Disagree on Protest Rallies." *Jackson Clarion-Ledger*, September 27, 1955, 1, 5.

———. "Sumner Folk Already Plenty Bored with All This Ruckus." *Jackson Clarion-Ledger*, September 21, 1955, 3, 5.

"Milwaukee Rally Asks Intervention." *Daily Worker* (New York), September 29, 1955, 3.

"Minnesotan Is Using Till Case in Politics." *Jackson Daily News*, October 12, 1955, 3.

Minor, Bill. "Saga of Till Slaying Will Live on Despite Death of 2nd Killer." *Jackson Clarion-Ledger*, September 25, 1994, C3.

Minor, W. F. "Two Not Guilty of Till Murder, Jury Declares." *New Orleans Times-Picayune*, September 24, 1955, 5.

"Miss. Killing Brings New Members, Gifts to NAACP." *Louisville Defender*, September 29, 1955, 1.

"Miss. Negro's Slayer Went to Home of Till Case Figure after Shooting." *New York Post*, December 9, 1955, 3, 63.

"Missing Chicago Negro Youth Found in Tallahatchie River." *Greenwood (Miss.) Commonwealth*, August 31, 1955, 1.

"Missing Till Witnesses' Flight Told." *Chicago American*, October 1, 1955, 11.

"'Missing' Witness Denied He Saw the Till Slaying." *Memphis Press-Scimitar*, October 4, 1955, 19.

"Mississippi Again." *Baltimore Afro-American*, December 17, 1955, 1, 2.

"Mississippian Says He Paid for Votes." *New York Times*, July 6, 1968, 8.

"Mississippi Must Make Every Effort to Prosecute Till Murder." *Chicago Sun-Times*, March 20, 2006, 39.

"Mississippi Sheriff Voices Doubt Body Was That of Till." *Greenwood (Miss.) Morning Star*, September 4, 1955, 1.

"Mississippi Solons Bare Hanging of Till's Father." *Chicago Defender*, October 22, 1955, 1, 2.

"Mississippi's Reaction to Boy's Death." *Memphis Press-Scimitar*, September 3, 1955, 11.

Mitchell, Jerry. "Filmmaker to Show Movie on Emmett Till." *Jackson Clarion-Ledger*, February 7, 2004, 1B.

———. "Grand Jury Issues No Indictment in Till Killing." *Jackson Clarion-Ledger*, February 27, 2007, 3A.

———. "Group Seeks to Exhume Till Body." *Jackson Clarion-Ledger*, October 31, 2004, 1A.

———. "Support Sought to Reopen Till Case." *Jackson Clarion-Ledger*, February 8, 2004, 5B.

———. "Tallahatchie County to Formally Apologize to Till's Family." *Jackson Clarion-Ledger*, October 2, 2007, 3A.

Mohr, Holbrook. "No Federal Charges in Till Case, FBI Says." *Chicago Tribune*, March 17, 2006, 8.

"'Money Jars' for Defense Delay Trial." *Jackson State Times*, September 20, 1955, 2A.

"Moses Wright Turns Down Island Job." *New York Amsterdam News*, October 8, 1955, 23.

"Mother Hysterical at Victim's Rites." *Chicago American*, September 7, 1955, 4.

"Mother of Negro Boy Advised to Stay in Chicago." *Delta Democrat-Times* (Greenville, Miss.), September 12, 1955, 1.

"Mother of Slain Chicagoan Urged to Attend Trial." *Chicago American*, September 8, 1955, 4.

"Mother of Slain Negro Is Asked to Aid in Prosecution." *Jackson Daily News*, September 8, 1955, 6.

"Mother of Till Boy Arrives in Courtroom." *Chicago American*, September 20, 1955, 4.

"Mother of Till Boy Goes to Mississippi for Trial." *Chicago American*, September 20, 1955, 4.

"Mother of Till Due Here Today on Way to Trial." *Memphis Commercial Appeal*, September 20, 1955, 15.

"Mother of Till Has a Secret." *Memphis Press-Scimitar*, September 16, 1955, 3.

"Mother of Till Raising Money." *Memphis Press-Scimitar*, November 15, 1955, 7.

"Mother of Till to Testify in Murder Trial." *Greenwood (Miss.) Morning Star*, September 13, 1955, 1.

"Mother of Till Will Attend Trial as State Witness." *Jackson Daily News*, September 13, 1955, 3.

"Mother of Till Youth Finally Agrees to Testify." *Delta Democrat-Times* (Greenville, Miss.), September 13, 1955, 1.

"Mother Says Son Libeled by Stories." *Daily Defender* (Chicago), January 22, 1958, 3.

Mother to Testify in Kidnap Trial." *Memphis Press-Scimitar*, September 13, 1955, 1.

"Mourners, Curious Mingle at Till Rites." *Clarksdale (Miss.) Press Register*, September 3, 1955, 1.

"Mrs. Bradley Bares Dawson Aid." *Daily Defender* (Chicago), October 22, 1956, 1.

"Mrs. Bradley Raps 'Expose' on Till's Father." *St. Louis Argus*, October 21, 1955, 1, 16.

"Mrs. Bradley Routs False Reports." *Washington Afro-American*, November 5, 1955, 21.

"Mrs. Bradley Says Fee NAACP Idea." *Chicago Defender*, November 19, 1955, 1, 2.

"Mrs. Bradley Wires Moms of 3 Slain Chicago Boys." *Chicago Defender*, October 29, 1955, 7.

"Muddy River Gives Up Body of Slain Negro Boy." *Memphis Commercial Appeal*, September 1, 1955, 1, 4.

"Murdered Youth's Kin Hysterical at Station." *Chicago Sun-Times*, September 2, 1955, 3.

"Murder Trial Jury Hears Wolf Whistle." *London Express*, September 23, 1955, 1.

Murrain, Edward. "Till's Mom, Mayor Get Bomb Threats." *New York Age Defender*, October 1, 1955, 1, 2.

Murray, George. "'Wolf Call' Blamed by Argo Teen." *Chicago American*, September 1, 1955, 1, 4.

"NAACP Asks Who Did It as Bryant, Milam Freed." *Jackson Daily News*, November 10, 1955, 4.

"NAACP Calls Verdict Rooted in Racist Oppression." *Daily Worker* (New York), September 26, 1955, 8.

"NAACP Leader Blasts Mississippi Law Enforcement." *Clarksdale (Miss.) Press Register*, November 5, 1955, 1.

"Need to Protect Negro Vote Cited." *New York Times*, February 15, 1957, 15.

"Negro Bishop Asks 2 Days' Mourning as Slaying Protest." *Jackson Daily News* September 2, 1955, 1.

"Negro Boy Was Killed for 'Wolf Whistle.'" *New York Post*, September 1, 1955, 5, 12.

"Negro 'Captive' Articles Doubted, Mandy Bradley." *Jackson Daily News*, October 6, 1955, 7.

"Negro Describes Boy's Abduction." *Jackson Clarion-Ledger*, September 2, 1955, 1.

"Negroes Rebuffed in Asking Federal Intervention." *Greenwood (Miss.) Commonwealth*, October 25, 1955, 1.

"Negro Leader Hails Officers for Handling of Till Slaying." *Memphis Commercial Appeal*, September 9, 1955, 1, 31.

"Negro Mass March Called Rumor." *Jackson State Times*, September 4, 1955, 1A, 16A.

"Negro's Answer to *Look* Story." *Memphis Press-Scimitar*, January 18, 1956, 8.

Neumaier, Joe. "Filmmaker's 'Untold Story' Drives Inquiry in Racial Killing." *New York Daily News*, August 16, 2005, 32.

"New Angle to Till Case." *Greenwood (Miss.) Morning Star*, January 11, 1956, 4.

"New Rochelle Demos Ask Action on Mississippi." *Daily Worker* (New York), September 27, 1955, 3.

"Newsmen and Photographers Are Frisked for Weapons." *Memphis Commercial Appeal*, September 20, 1955, 17.

Newson, Moses J. "Acquit Kimbell in Miss. Trial." *Daily Defender* (Chicago), March 14, 1956, 3.

"Newspapers Over State Blast Murder of Negro." *Jackson Daily News*, September 3, 1955, 1.

Nichols, Joseph C. "Marciano, Floored in Second Round, Stops Moore in Ninth to Keep Title." *New York Times*, September 22, 1955, 37.

"1955 Race Killing, Film Inspires Lawmakers' Call for Probe." *Newsday*, April 14, 2004, A6.

Nix, Naomi. "Willie Louis: 1937–2013." *Chicago Tribune*, July 24, 2013, 6.

"No Developments in Negro Slaying." *Greenwood (Miss.) Commonwealth*, September 2, 1955, 1.

Noel, Peter. "The Battle for Abner Louima." *Village Voice*, September 2, 1997, 42, 35.

"No Kidnap Trial for Milam, Bryant." *Chicago Defender*, November 19, 1955, 1, 2.

"'Not Bitter' Says Mother of Till." *Memphis Press-Scimitar*, September 8, 1955, 27.

"Officer Fears Actions Build up Resentment." *Jackson Clarion-Ledger*, September 4, 1955, 1.

"Officers Press Hunt in Slaying of Negro." *Memphis Commercial Appeal*, September 4, 1955, 19.

Bibliography

"'Once Proud of the South' but Renounces Till Verdict." *Memphis Commercial Appeal*, September 26, 1955, 4.

"100,000 at Last Rites on S. Side for Kidnapped Boy." *Chicago American*, September 3, 1955, 3.

Page, Clarence. "Black History Isn't Just for Blacks Anymore." *Chicago Tribune*, January 15, 2003, 1.

———. "Full New Probe Needed in Till Murder." *Newsday*, October 26, 2004, A40.

———. "A New Thaw Comes to a Very Old Case." *Newsday*, March 31, 2004, A42.

Parker, Laura. "DA Has Tough, Final Call in Till Case." *USA Today*, March 22, 2006, A3.

———. "DNA Confirms Body Is Emmett Till's." *USA Today*, August 26, 2005, A2.

———. "FBI Report on Emmett Till Filed in Mississippi." *Miami Times*, March 22–28, 2006, 7A.

———. "Justice Pursued for Emmett Till." *USA Today*, March 11, 2004, A3.

———. "Perseverance Pays Off for Civil Rights Activist." *USA Today*, March 19, 2007, A2.

Parmenter, Cinder. "Overdue Bills Endanger Bronze of King." *Denver Post*, July 7, 1977, 17.

Payne, Ethel L. "Army Gave Till Facts to Eastland." *Chicago Defender*, October 22, 1955, 1.

———. "'Ladies' Day for Adlai Lures Smart Set from All Over to Dine, Chat." *Chicago Defender*, November 3, 1956, 15.

———. "Tom [*sic*] Till Died for Democracy." *New York Age Defender*, October 1, 1955, 1, 2.

"People and Places." *Chicago Defender*, December 8, 1956, 2.

"Plan Suit If 2 Escape Death in Boy Lynching." *New York Post*, September 7, 1955, 5.

Poist, Patricia. "Haunted by Ghost of Mississippi." *Sunday News*, January 16, 2005, 1.

Popham, John. "Slain Boy's Uncle on Stand at Trial." *New York Times*, September 22, 1955, 64.

———. "Slain Boy's Uncle Ready to Testify." *New York Times*, September 19, 1955, 50.

———. "Trial Under Way in Youth's Killing." *New York Times*, September 20, 1955, 32.

Porteous, Clark. "Big Names in Nation's Press Are at Trial." *Memphis Press-Scimitar*, September 20, 1955, 1, 2.

———. "Grand Jury to Get Case of Slain Negro Boy Monday." *Memphis Press-Scimitar*, September 1, 1955, 1, 4.

———. "Instead of Lunch, Surprises." *Memphis Press-Scimitar*, September 21, 1955, 1, 2.

———. "Jury Being Chosen in Till Trial." *Memphis Press-Scimitar*, September 19, 1955, 1, 4.

———. "Kidnap Trial Delay Sure." *Memphis Press-Scimitar*, September 23, 1955, 1.

———. "Mississippi Hunt for Clews [*sic*] Goes On." *Memphis Press-Scimitar*, September 2, 1955, 5.

———. "Mrs. Bryant on Stand." *Memphis Press-Scimitar*, September 22, 1955, 1, 2, 3, 4.

———. "New Angle in Till Case Claimed." *Memphis Press-Scimitar*, September 20, 1955, 1, 4, 5.

———. "Next: 2 Face Till Kidnap Charges." *Memphis Press-Scimitar*, September 24, 1955, 1, 3.

———. "Officers Work All Night on Searches." *Memphis Press-Scimitar*, September 21, 1955, 1, 7.

———. "Proud, with Reason at Sumner." *Memphis Press-Scimitar*, September 21, 1955, 2.

———. "Till Murder Case Goes to Jury." *Memphis Press-Scimitar*, September 23, 1955, 1, 2, 8.

Poston, Ted. "'Missing' Till Witness Admits Milam Took Him Out of Town." *New York Post*, October 4, 1955, 5.

———. "Mose Wright Left Everything to Flee for Life." *New York Post*, October 3, 1955, 5.

———. "'My Son Didn't Die in Vain,' Till's Mother Tells Rally." *New York Post*, September 26, 1955, 5, 22.

"Powell Says Till Stirs All Europe." *Chicago Defender*, October 8, 1955.

"Powell Urges Special Session to Adopt Anti-Lynch Law." *Daily Worker* (New York), September 30, 1955, 3.

"Prayer Meets Planned for Six Cities." *Washington Afro-American*, October 22, 1955, 5.

"Preliminary Hearing Set Friday for Men Accused of Mass Killing." *Kosciusko (Miss.) Star-Herald*, February 2, 1950, 1.

Pride, Karen E. "Commemoration of Emmett Till Lynching Anniversary Includes Renaming Expressway Bridge." *Chicago Defender*, August 29–30 2005, 3.

———. "Federal Officials Lead Exhumation of Emmett Till." *Chicago Defender*, June 2, 2005, 3.

"Pro and Con Argued on Murder Verdict." *Lima (Ohio) News*, September 25, 1955, 3A.

"Professor Seeks Transcript of Till Trial." *Memphis Commercial Appeal*, February 21, 2005, B5.

"Prominent Local Attorney Dies." *Southern Sentinel* (Ripley, Miss.), December 7, 1967, 1.

"Prosecution Doesn't Say If Death Penalty Sought in Trial of White Men." *Jackson Daily News*, September 12, 1955, 1.

"Prosecutor in Till Case Dies Tuesday." *Delta Democrat-Times* (Greenville, Miss.), October 10, 1956, 1.

"Prosecutor Studying FBI's Investigative File into Till Murder." *Bay State Banner* (Boston), July 6, 2006, 2.

"Protest Mississippi Shame." *New York Age Defender*, September 10, 1955, 2.

Pryweller, Joseph. "Eyes on the Prize Author Has Won Respect for His Civil Rights Work." *Daily Press* (Newport News, Va.), April 7, 1991, I1.

"Rabb Says White House Is Concerned Over Till Case." *Chicago Defender*, October 22, 1955, 12.

Radelat, Ana. "Lawmaker Says He'll Press AG Over Till Probe." *Jackson Clarion-Ledger*, November 20, 2004, 1B, 3B.

Rahman, Ali. "Emmett Till's Mother Speaks." *New York Amsterdam News*, November 21, 2002, 4.

Ramstad, Evan. "Youth's Murder for Flirting Stimulated Civil Rights Drive." *Daily Journal* (Tupelo, Miss.), September 2, 1995, 1F.

"Random Thoughts by the Editor." *Yazoo City (Miss.) Herald*, September 8, 1955, 1.

Rashbaum, William H. "Police Officers Later Cleared in Louima Case Seek Jobs Back." *New York Times*, December 12, 2002, B3.

Raymond, Harry. "Cousin Tells How Negro Youth Was Kidnapped." *Daily Worker* (New York), September 2, 1955, 1, 8.

———. "20,000 at Rally Cheer 'March on Washington.'" *Daily Worker* (New York), October 12, 1955, 1.

"Reactions Reverberate Around World on Till Trial's Outcome." *Delta Democrat-Times* (Greenville, Miss.), September 27, 1955, 1.

"Recall the Murders in Mississippi." *Baltimore Afro-American*, December 24, 1955, 6, and *Washington Afro-American*, December 17, 1955, 1, 2.

"Recover Merchandise Believed Stolen from Bryant Store at Money." *Greenwood (Miss.) Morning Star*, September 22, 1955, 1.

"Reed Boy, Bradley Woman Fled State for 'Safety' but Police Guard Homes." *Jackson Daily News*, September 30, 1955, 1.

Reid, Clyde. "Mamie Bradley Says NAACP Used Son." *New York Amsterdam News*, December 24, 1955, 1.

"Renamed Roads Honor Rights Victims." *Chicago Tribune*, March 22, 2005, 12.

"Rep. Anfuso Asks Brownell Probe Sumner, Miss., Trial." *Daily Worker* (New York), September 27, 1955, 3.

"Rep. Diggs Blasts Mississippi Trial." *Jackson Clarion-Ledger*, September 26, 1955, 1.

"Rep. Diggs Comments in Congress on *Look*'s Story about the Emmett Till Case." *Memphis Press-Scimitar*, January 13, 1956, 19.

"Reporter Dares Miss. Death." *New York Age Defender*, October 8, 1955, 1, 2.

"Retired Attorney John Whitten Dies." *Charleston (Miss.) Sun-Sentinel*, February 2003, 1.

Richardson, Marty. "Clevelanders Rally Behind Mother of Lynching Victim." *Cleveland Call and Post*, September 24, 1955, 1A, 5A.

———. "Mother of Lynched Boy Here to Open 1955 NAACP Drive." *Cleveland Call and Post*, September 17, 1955, 1A, 2A.

"Rights Hearings Will Open Today." *New York Times*, February 4, 1957, 8.

"Ripley Attorney Played Major Role in Till Case." *Daily Journal* (Tupelo, Miss.), September 21, 2003, 1A, 6A.

Ritea, Steve. "Opening Old Wounds." *New Orleans Times-Picayune*, June 15, 2004, 1.

"Rites Held Saturday for Moses Wright, 85." *Chicago Defender*, August 8, 1977, 2.

Roosevelt, Eleanor. "I Think the Till Jury Will Have Uneasy Conscience." *Memphis Press-Scimitar*, October 11, 1955, 6.

"Roosevelt Asks Law to Prevent Till Occurrences." *Jackson Daily News*, October 12, 1955, 3.

"Ross Found Guilty, Faces Huge Fine." *Laurel (Miss.) Leader Call*, September 29, 1962, 1, 2.

Rowley, Dorothy. "African American Museum Groundbreaking Held on the National Mall." *Washington Informer*, February 23, 2012, 32–33.

Rubin, Richard. "The Ghosts of Emmett Till." *New York Times*, July 31, 2005, F30–F35.

Ruethling, Gretchen. "Kin Disagree on Exhumation of Emmett Till." *New York Times*, May 6, 2005, A23.

"Rumors Flying That Till's Alive Somewhere in Detroit." *Jackson Clarion-Ledger*, September 30, 1955, 1.

"Rumors Send Newsmen on 'Wild Goose' Chase." *Jackson State Times*, September 21, 1955, 8A.

Sanchez, Mary. "Activist Enlists Evers Family to Solve Emmett Till Case." *Sunday Gazette-Mail* (Charleston, W.Va.), June 22, 2003, 9A.

———. "Murder's Horror Haunts the Living." *Kansas City Star*, April 20, 2004, B7.

"Say Coleman Cites NAACP, Diggs for Till Case Outcome." *Delta Democrat-Times* (Greenville, Miss.), January 12, 1956, 1, 2.

"Says Reds Lie About Arrest in Sumner." *Jackson State Times*, October 17, 1955, 2A.

"Says Till Funds Given to Kin." *Chicago Defender*, November 26, 1955, 36.

Schlikerman, Becky. "Emmett Till Witness 'Never Got Over' Case." *Chicago Sun-Times*, July 24, 2013, 13.

Scott, Megan. "Film Cracks Open '55 Racial Slaying." *Ft. Wayne (Ind.) Journal-Gazette*, February 28, 2006, 2D.

"Seek Atonement for Latest Mississippi Murder." *Chicago Defender*, December 24, 1955, 3.

"Senate May Hear Till Lynch Story." *Chicago Defender*, October 29, 1955, 1, 2.

Serrano, Richard A. "After 49 years, Case Reopened in Racial Slaying of Emmett Till." *Oakland (Calif.) Tribune*, May 11, 2004, 1.

"70 Newsmen Cover Trial in Sumner." *Clarksdale (Miss.) Press Register*, September 20, 1955, 1.

Shearon, Helen. "Bryant and Milam Freed Under Bond." *Memphis Commercial Appeal*, October 1, 1955, 1, 14.

Sheehan, Charles. "FBI Closes Probe into Till's Death." *Chicago Tribune*, November 24, 2005, 31.

———. "Federal Report on 1955 Murder Going to D.A." *Los Angeles Times*, November 24, 2005, A35.

———. "Till Relatives Argue Over Exhuming Body." *Chicago Tribune*, May 6, 2005.

Shelby, Joyce. "More Tied to Till Death—Filmmaker." *New York Daily News*, August 30, 2005, 1, 2.

"Sheriff Believes Body Not Till's." *Jackson Clarion-Ledger*, September 4, 1955, 1, 4.

"Sheriff Won't Call Guard to Preserve Order." *Jackson State Times*, September 21, 1955, 8A.

Shoemaker, W. C. "Mrs. Bryant Won 2 Top Beauty Honors—Mother Loyally Stays at Trial." *Jackson Daily News*, September 22, 1955, 11.

———. "Reporter for Commies Relates How He Shifted to 'Left'—Says Trial 'Fair.'" *Jackson Daily News*, September 21, 1955, 14.

———. "Sumner Citizens Turn Public Relations Experts While Spotlight Beams at Them." *Jackson Daily News*, September 20, 1955, 6.

"Sidelights of Till Trial." *Tri-State Defender* (Memphis, Tenn.), October 1, 1955, 5.

Siegel, Ed. "Behind 'Eyes on the Prize' Henry Hampton Reflects on a Series 19 Years in the Making." *Boston Globe*, January 21, 1987, 6.

Singleton, Ronald. "'Dey' Done Took Him, Says Old Mose." *London Express*, September 22, 1955, 2.

"6000 Here Protest Mississippi Verdict." *Detroit News*, September 26, 1955, 8.

Skelton, B. J. "Testimony at Bryant-Milam Trial Has Left Many Questions Unanswered." *Clarksdale (Miss.) Press Register*, September 23, 1955, 7.

——— "Visiting Newsmen Pack Typewriters, Head for Homes." *Clarksdale (Miss.) Press Register*, September 24, 1955, 1.

Skelton, B. J., and Sam Johnson. "Court Completes Jury for Bryant-Milam Trial." *Clarksdale (Miss.) Press Register*, September 20, 1955, 1, 8.

———. "Prosecutor Says Case Depends on Circumstantial Evidence." *Clarksdale (Miss.) Press Register*, September 19, 1955, 1, 8.

"Slain-Boy's Body Arrives Here." *Chicago Sun-Times*, September 3, 1955, 4.

"Slain Boy's Mother Will Get Invitation to Trial of Deltans." *Jackson Clarion-Ledger*, September 8, 1955, 1.

"Slain Boy's Uncle Recalls Fatal Night." *Chicago American*, September 19, 1955, 4.

"Slain Youth's Mother to Testify at Trial." *Delta Democrat-Times* (Greenville, Miss.), September 8, 1955, 1.

"Some Till Relatives Oppose Exhumation." *Chicago Tribune*, May 6, 2005, 7.

"Son No Braggart, Says Mrs. Bradley." *Chicago Defender*, January 21, 1956, 1, 2.

Sorrels, William. "Defendants Enter Pleas of Innocence in Slaying of Youth." *Memphis Commercial Appeal*, September 7, 1955, 1, 3.

———. "Grand Jury Weighs Officers' Reports in Death of Youth." *Memphis Commercial Appeal*, September 6, 1955, 1, 8.

———. "Guards Called to Protect Men Held in Youth's Death." *Memphis Commercial Appeal*, September 5, 1955, 1, 8.

———. "New Trial Evidence Disclosed by State in a Dramatic Turn." *Memphis Commercial Appeal*, September 21, 1955, 1, 8.

———. "'Tall Man Came' with Companion, Say His Cousins." *Memphis Commercial Appeal*, September 1, 1955, 4.

———. "10 Jurymen Are Selected for Trial of 2 White Men in Slaying of Negro Youth." *Memphis Commercial Appeal* September 20, 1955, 1, 15.

———. "Two Mississippians Acquitted in Slaying of Chicago Negro." *Memphis Commercial Appeal*, September 24, 1955, 1, 2.

———. "Uncle of Slain Boy Points Out Milam, Says Body Was Till." *Memphis Commercial Appeal*, September 22, 1955, 1, 10.

"Special Prosecutor Named in Till Case." *Memphis Commercial Appeal*, September 10, 1955, 1, 2.

"Speedy Trial Planned in Kidnap-Slaying Case." *Greenwood (Miss.) Commonwealth*, September 7, 1955, 1.

Spell, Bill. "A *Daily News* Newspaperman Dared to Penetrate Chicago's South Side." *Jackson Daily News*, October 5, 1955, 1, 14.

———. "Daily News Readers Offer Help to Send Willie Reed's Girl Friend to Chicago." *Jackson Daily News*, September 29, 1955, 1.

———. "Effort to Tell Mandy of Her Husband Fails as Phone Connection Was Cut." *Jackson Daily News*, October 8, 1955, 1.

———. "Mandy Bradley Refutes NAACP Claim Her Life Was in Danger, Then." *Jackson Daily News*, October 6, 1955, 1, 7.

———. "Mose Wright Couldn't Be Reached without a 'Middle Man.'" *Jackson Daily News*, October 7, 1955, 1, 4.

Spell, Bill, and W. C. Shoemaker. "Alonzo Refutes Charges Made by Congressman Diggs." *Jackson Daily News*, October 6, 1955, 1.

Spence, John. "Till's Mother Pauses in Memphis on Way to Trial." *Memphis Press-Scimitar*, September 20, 1955, 15.

Staples, Brent. "The Murder of Emmett Louis Till, Revisited." *New York Times*, November 11, 2002, A16.

Stapleton, Jack. "Query Lingers: Is Till Dead?" *Clarksdale (Miss.) Press Register*, September 30, 1955, 1.

"State Calls Special Counsel to Assist with Prosecution." *Clarksdale (Miss.) Press Register*, September 10, 1955, 1.

"State FBI Boss Moving to Washington." *Memphis Commercial Appeal*, June 1, 2005, D8.

"States Assured on Rights Issue." *New York Times*, February 5, 1957, 15.

Stevenson, H. L. "Fisherman Finds Body of Chicago Negro Boy in Tallahatchie River." *Greenwood (Miss.) Morning Star*, September 1, 1955, 1.

Stevenson, Tommy. "House Passes 'Emmett Till Bill.'" *Tuscaloosa (Ala.) News*, June 21, 2007, 1A, 2A.

Still, Larry. "Time Out for Crying." *Washington Afro-American*, October 22, 1955, 1, 5.

Stone, Andrea, and Jerry Mitchell. "Evers Case Inspires Kin of Others." *USA Today*, December 24, 1990, 3A.

Strafford, Mary. "'When I Find Time I'll Cry,' Till's Mother Tells Afro. Baltimore Afro-American*, October 29, 1955, 1, 2.

"Strategy of Defense Attorneys Violates Every Rule in Books." *Jackson State Times*, September 19, 1955.

"Stratton Acts in Dixie Killing." *Chicago American*, September 2, 1955, 1, 2.

"Stratton Asks Federal Probe in Till Slaying." *Chicago Daily Tribune*, November 11, 1955, 2.

Strausberg, Chinta. "Smith's Witnesses Tell Why U.S. Should Probe Till Case." *Chicago Defender*, February 10, 2004, 3.

Street, William. "Emmett Till Case Suddenly Thrusts Little Sumner into Limelight." *Memphis Commercial Appeal*, September 18, 1955, 10.

"Strider Believes Till Is Still Alive." *Greenwood (Miss.) Commonwealth*, September 29, 1955, 1.

Stringfellow, Eric. "Memories Sketch Varied Portraits of Emmett Till." *Jackson Clarion-Ledger/ Jackson Daily News*, August 25, 1985, 1H.

"Sturdivants and Stepson Held for Trial." *Charleston Mississippi Sun*, August 20, 1942, 1.

"Sturdivants Now on Trial at Sumner." *Charleston Mississippi Sun*, March 11, 1943, 1.

"Sturdivant Trial Postponed Till March." *Charleston Mississippi Sun*, September 17, 1942, 5.

"Sumner Jury Acquits Sturdivants in Alexander Slaying." *Charleston Mississippi Sun*, March 19, 1943, 1.

"Sunflower Candidates Chosen." *Delta Democrat-Times* (Greenville, Miss.), May 11, 1977, 12.

"Sunflower County Sheriff Is Dead." *Greenwood (Miss.) Commonwealth*, September 19, 1955, 1.

"Sunflower Success." *Delta Democrat-Times* (Greenville, Miss.), September 19, 1974, 31.

"Sunflower Voters Have Wide Choice." *Delta Democrat-Times* (Greenville, Miss.), May 9, 1977, 12.

"Suspect Credited with Saving Lives." *Jackson State Times*, September 1, 1955, 11A.

"Takes Five; Keith Beauchamp." *Milwaukee Journal Sentinel*, March 24, 2006, A2.

Taubman, Howard. "Theater: Blues for Mister Charlie." *New York Times*, April 24, 1964, 24.

"Television Raffle." *Delta Democrat-Times* (Greenville, Miss.), February 14, 1971, 20.

"Ten Accepted on Till Jury." *Jackson State Times*, September 20, 1955, 8A.

"10,000 at Bier of Slain Boy." *Chicago American*, September 3, 1955, 1.

"Text of Civil Rights Bill as Passed by Congress." *New York Times*, August 31, 1957, 6.

"Text of President Eisenhower's Annual Message to Congress on State of the Union." *New York Times*, January 11, 1957, 10.

"3rd Lynching of Year Shocks Nation." *Baltimore Afro-American*, September 10, 1995, 1, 2.

Thompson, Albert. Obituary. *Delta Democrat-Times* (Greenville, Miss.), November 22, 1965, 2.

Thompson, Myrtle. Obituary. *Delta Democrat-Times* (Greenville, Miss.), June 23, 1963, 2.

"Thousands at Paris Till Protest Meet." *Delta Democrat-Times* (Greenville, Miss.), September 28, 1955, 1.

"Threats Are Voiced as Trial Date Nears." *Memphis Commercial Appeal*, September 11, 1955, 13.

"3 Harlem Street Rallies Hit Terror in Mississippi." *Daily Worker* (New York), September 26, 1955, 2.

"Three Hurt in Collision Here on Sunday." *Delta Democrat-Times* (Greenville, Miss.), November 19, 1956, 1.

"Thurmond Talks Hours on Rights." *New York Times*, August 29, 1957, 1.

"Till Case Film Rights Secured." *Memphis Press-Scimitar*, January 19, 1956, 29.

"Till Case Still Troubles Mississippi." *Chicago American*, September 26, 1955, 4.

"Till Exposé by Writer Shakes Dixie." *Chicago Defender*, January 21, 1956, 1, 3.

"Till Figure Injured in Auto Crash." *Chicago Defender*, December 1, 1956, 1.

"Till Kidnap Pair May Be Out on Bond Friday." *New York Post*, September 28, 1955, 4.

"Till Kidnap Suspects Free on $10,000 Bond." *Jackson State Times*, September 30, 1955, 1A.

"Till Prosecutor Will Have Help." *Memphis Press-Scimitar*, September 10, 1955, 11.

"Till Report Completed; Grand Jury May Be Next." *Memphis Commercial Appeal*, November 24, 2005, B6.

"Till's Father Had Been Billed 'War Hero' during Fund-Raising Drives." *Jackson Daily News*, October 15, 1955, 1.

"Till Slaying Trial May Be Set Thursday." *Delta Democrat-Times* (Greenville, Miss.), September 7, 1955, 1, 12.

"Till's Mother Hits 'Bungling' by Prosecutor." *Chicago American*, October 4, 1955, 4.

"Till's Mother in Seclusion." *Memphis Press-Scimitar*, October 5, 1955, 7.

"Till's Mother Is Being Urged Not to Testify." *Jackson Daily News*, September 12, 1955, 1.

"Till's Mother Says Ike Ignored Pleas for Help." *Chicago Defender*, November 3, 1956, 1.

"Till's Mother Stirs 9,500 in Washington." *Daily Worker* (New York), October 20, 1955, 3.

"Till's Mother to Testify, She Says." *Delta Democrat-Times* (Greenville, Miss.), September 16, 1955, 1.

"Till's Mother Unsure on Attending Trial." *Jackson Clarion-Ledger*, September 14, 1955, 1.

"Till's Mother 'Wary of Foes,' Keeping Her Route to Trial Secret." *Jackson Daily News*, September 16, 1955, 1.

"Till's Uncle Says He Fled for Life after Trial." *Memphis Commercial Appeal*, October 5, 1955, 28.

"Till 'Suspect' on 'Breadline.'" *Pittsburgh Courier*, February 22, 1958, 30.

"Till Trial Acquittal Protested by Rallies." *Delta Democrat-Times* (Greenville, Miss.), September 26, 1955, 1.

"Till Trial Defendant Refused Gun Permit in Sunflower County." *Delta Democrat-Times* (Greenville, Miss.), January 8, 1957, 1.

"Till Witness Threats Probed." *Chicago Defender*, October 8, 1955, 34.

"Till Witness Under Guard." *Memphis Press-Scimitar*, September 29, 1955, 4.

"Till Youth's Mom to Delay Appearing at Murder Trial." *Delta Democrat-Times* (Greenville, Miss.), September 18, 1955, 1.

"'Too Busy' to Reopen Till Kidnap Case, Judge Says." *Washington Afro-American*, January 21, 1956, 11.

Trescott, Jacqueline. "National African American Museum Acquires Emmett Till's Casket." *Los Angeles Times*, August 28, 2009, A14.

"Trial of Revenge Murderers to Be in National Spotlight." *Kosciusko (Miss.) Star-Herald*, March 9, 1950, 1.

Trice, Dawn Turner. "The First and Last Chance for Emmett Till to Speak for Himself." *Chicago Tribune*, May 5, 2005, 1.

———. "In Till Case, Leaders Don't Need to Weigh In." *Chicago Tribune*, May 9, 2005, 2C.

———. "Renewed Focus on Till Case May Rewrite History." *Chicago Tribune*, May 12, 2004, 2C.

———. "Rushed Action Could Jeopardize Till Case Justice." *Chicago Tribune*, December 28, 2004, 2C.

"Troops Posted in Delta as Mob Violence Feared in Aftermath to Slaying." *Jackson Daily News*, September 5, 1955, 1.

Trussell, C. P. "Civil Rights Plan Passed by House." *New York Times*, June 19, 1957, 1.

"Try to Determine Spot Where Negro Was Slain." *Greenwood (Miss.) Morning Star*, September 3, 1955, 1.

"Tuskegee to Probe Slayings of Three Negroes in State." *Jackson Daily News*, September 1, 1955, 12.

"TV Highlights: New Night Court Characters." *Chicago Tribune*, July 11, 1985, D11.

"27-Year Veteran to Head Mississippi FBI Offices." *Memphis Commercial Appeal*, June 30, 2004, D8.

"Two Armed White Men Break into Negro Worker's Home." *Greenwood (Miss.) Morning Star*, September 1, 1955, 1.

"Two Delta Senators Offer Negro Relocation Measure." *Hattiesburg (Miss.) American*, February 25, 1966, 1.

"200–300 Bodies Disinterred in Grave-Reselling Scheme." *Seattle Times*, July 10, 2009, A2.

"2 Negro 'Whistling Killing' Witnesses Still Missing and Are Feared Slain." *New York Post*, September 29, 1955, 5, 26.

"Two Officers in Louima Case Again Seek Re-Instatement." *New York Times*, October 7, 2006, B6.

"Two of Three Victims of Gravel Pit Accident Die of Their Injuries." *Charleston Mississippi Sun*, October 13, 1927, 1.

"2,000 in Frisco Hit Till Murder." *Daily Worker* (New York), October 19, 1955, 3.

"2500 at Rites Here for Boy, 14, Slain in South." *Chicago Daily Tribune*, September 4, 1955, 2.

"2500 Protest in Baltimore." *Daily Worker* (New York), September 29, 1955, 1, 3.

"Two White Men Charged with Kidnapping Negro." *Delta Democrat-Times* (Greenville, Miss.), August 30, 1955, 1.

"Uncle of Lynched Boy Tells of Death Night." *Cleveland Call and Post*, October 22, 1955, 2A.

"Undertaker's Story Heard." *Jackson State Times*, September 21, 1955, 1A, 12A.

"Urge Tolerance at Boy's Funeral." *Chicago Sun-Times*, September 4, 1955, 1, 3.

"U.S. Intervention in Till Case Urged in Many Cities." *Daily Worker* (New York), September 30, 1955, 1, 3.

"Use Milam Car in Miss. Slaying." *Chicago Defender*, December 17, 1955, 1, 2.

"Vatican Urges U.S. Catholics to Help Erase Stain of Till Murder." *Daily Worker* (New York), October 18, 1955, 3.

"The Verdict at Sumner." *Jackson Daily News*, September 25, 1955, 8.

"Wait to Testify Before Grand Jury." *Greenwood (Miss.) Commonwealth*, November 7, 1955, 8.

Walker, Jerry. "Emmett Till Murder Case Presented to Delegates of the United Nations." *Kansas City Call*, June 6–12, 2003, 3.

Walz, Jay. "Carolinian Sets Talking Record." *New York Times*, August 30, 1957, 1.

Ward, Roosevelt. "Negro Youth Ready to Testify Again at Trial of Emmett Till's Kidnapers." *Daily Worker* (New York), October 25, 1955, 3.

Washington, Chester. "Howard Locates Two Men." *Pittsburgh Courier*, October 15, 1955, 1, 4.

Watkins, Mel. "Gwendolyn Brooks, 83, Passionate Poet, Dies." *New York Times*, December 5, 2000, C22.

Weissenstein, Michael. "Film Recounts Till's Untold Story." *Chicago Tribune*, August 28, 2005, 14.

"'Were Never into Meanness' Says Accused Men's Mother." *Memphis Commercial Appeal*, September 2, 1955, 35.

Wesley, John Milton. "The Legacy of Emmett Till." *Washington Post National Weekly Edition*, September 4–10, 1995, 21.

"What Huie Says." *Memphis Press-Scimitar*, January 13, 1956, 19.

"What Milam, Bryant Say of Huie Story." *Memphis Press-Scimitar*, January 13, 1956, 19.

"What the People Say: Blast Till Pacifists." *Chicago Defender*, September 17, 1955, 9.

"Whistle Killing May Go to Jury Today." *New York Post*, September 23, 1955, 3, 10.

White, William S. "Congress Chiefs Reach an Accord on Civil Rights." *New York Times*, August 24, 1957, 1, 34.

———. "House Passes Rights Bill." *New York Times*, August 28, 1957, 1, 55.

———. "Martin Rejects Civil Rights Bill Voted by Senate." *New York Times*, August 13, 1957, 1, 25.

———. "President Backs Jury Compromise in the Rights Bill." *New York Times*, August 22, 1957, 1, 17.

———. "Rights Struggle Opens in Senate." *New York Times*, July 9, 1957, 1, 19.

———. "Senate, 51-42, Attaches Jury Trials to Rights Bill in Defeat for President." *New York Times*, August 2, 1957, 1, 8.

———. "Senate, 45 to 39, Sends Rights Bill Straight to Floor." *New York Times*, June 21, 1957, 1, 16.

———. "Senate Approves Rights Bill, 72-18, with Jury Clause." *New York Times*, August 8, 1957, 1, 12.

———. "Senate Leaning to a Compromise Over Rights Bill." *New York Times*, July 10, 1957, 1, 14.

———. "Senate Votes Rights Bill and Sends It to President." *New York Times*, August 30, 1957, 1, 20.

"White Calls Boy's Death 'Murder; Not Lynching.'" *Jackson Daily News* September 2, 1955, 14.

"White Jurors Acquit Sheriff of Bludgeoning." *Morgantown (Miss.) Post*, August 8, 1958, 3.

"White Man Was Hanged 65 Years Ago in Grenada for Murdering Negro." *Columbian-Progress* (Columbia, Miss.), September 29, 1955, 2.

"White Orders Full Probe of Delta's Kidnap-Murder." *Jackson Clarion-Ledger*, September 2, 1955, 1, 8.

"White Storekeeper Held in Abduction of Negro Youth." *Jackson Daily News*, August 29, 1955, 1.

"Whitt Gets 10 Years for 'Manslaughter.'" *Jackson Clarion-Ledger*, April 4, 1955, 7.

"Why Didn't They Get the Same Publicity?" *Greenwood (Miss.) Morning Star*, September 7, 1955, 4.

"Widow Drowns as Trial of Mate's Slayer Opens." *Chicago Defender*, March 17, 1956, 1.

"A Wife in Hiding Writes Back to Hubby—'Come On Up Here.'" *Tri-State Defender* (Memphis, Tenn.), September 17, 1955, 5.

Williams, Kam. "Discourse with the Director of Award-Winning Emmett Till Documentary." *Washington Informer*, October 13, 2005, 15.

"Willie Reed, Till Witness, Starting Life Anew, Chicago." *Delta Democrat-Times* (Greenville, Miss.), September 29, 1955, 2.

"Willie Reed Gets $1,000 Elk Grant." *Chicago Defender*, November 12, 1955, 4.

Wilson, L. Alex. "Collins Denies Any Link to Till." *Chicago Defender*, October 8, 1955, 1, and *Tri-State Defender* (Memphis, Tenn.), October 8, 1955, 1, 2.

———. "Gus Courts, Miss. NAACP Head Tells How He Was Shot Down." *Tri-State Defender* (Memphis, Tenn.), December 3, 1955, 1, 2.

———. "Here Is What 'Too Tight' Said." *Chicago Defender*, October 8, 1955, 1, 35.

———. "Picking of Jury Delays Opening." *Tri-State Defender* (Memphis, Tenn.), September 24, 1955, 1, 2.

Bibliography

———. "Reveals Two Key Witnesses Jailed." *Tri-State Defender* (Memphis, Tenn.), October 1, 1955, 1, 2.

———. "'Too Tight' Collins Missing." *Chicago Defender*, November 12, 1955, 1, 2.

———. "Wilson Tells How He Found, Got Collins to Chicago." *Chicago Defender*, October 8, 1955, 1, 2, and *Tri-State Defender* (Memphis, Tenn.), October 8, 1955, 1, 2.

Wilson, L. Alex, and Moses Newson. "Story of the Search for New Witnesses." *Chicago Defender*, September 24, 1955, 1, 2.

"Windol Whitt's Trial Opens Today in Attala." *Jackson Clarion-Ledger*, March 15, 1950, 1.

Winfrey, Lee. "'Eyes on Prize' Recommended Viewing on Civil Rights History." *Elyria (Ohio) Chronicle-Telegram*, January 21, 1987, B6.

"Witness to Get Free Glasses." *Chicago Defender*, October 8, 1955, 34.

Wold, Felix. "Mose Tells of Sleeping in Cemetery but 'Middle Man' Attended Interview." *Jackson Daily News*, October 8, 1955, 1.

"Wolf Whistle Kidnap Pair Indicted on Murder Count." *Memphis Press-Scimitar*, September 6, 1955, 7.

"Wolf Whistle Trial Date Set Sept. 19." *Memphis Press-Scimitar*, September 9, 1955, 34.

"Woman Wins Damage Suit." *Delta Democrat Times* (Greenville, Miss.), June 11, 1971, 14.

Woods, Howard B. "Witness in Till Case Vanishes." *St. Louis Argus*, October 28, 1955, 1, 10.

"World Eyes Mississippi Grand Jury." *Chicago Defender*, November 12, 1955, 2.

"Writer Challenges Brownell to Act in Till Kidnap-Murder Case." *Baltimore Afro-American*, January 21, 1956, 2.

"Yarn About Till Being in City Is Denied by Negro." *Delta Democrat-Times* (Greenville, Miss.), September 30, 1955, 1.

Films and Television Programs

Beauchamp, Keith A., prod. *The Untold Story of Emmett Louis Till*. Till Freedom Come Productions, 2005.

Button, Nancy, prod. *The Fifties*. Vol. 6, *The Rage Within*. History Channel, 1997.

Efros, Mel, prod. *Blood Done Sign My Name*. Paladin, 2010.

Martin, Amani, and Ed Schillinger, prods. *Benji: The True Story of a Life Cut Short*. ESPN Films, 2012.

Nelson, Stanley, prod. *The Murder of Emmett Till*. Firelight Media, 2002.

Radutzky, Michael, prod. "The Murder of Emmett Till." *60 Minutes*. CBS, October 24, 2004.

Samuels, Rich, writer. *The Murder and the Movement*. WMAQ-Channel 5, Chicago, 1985.

Vecchione, Judith, and Henry Hampton, prods. *Eyes on the Prize: America's Civil Rights Years, 1954–1964*. PBS, 1987.

Papers, Theses, Dissertations, and Other Unpublished Sources

Argo Temple Church of God in Christ 80-Year Celebration. October 8, 2006.

Baggett, Ashley. "The Rise of the Surgical Age in the Treatment of Pulmonary Tuberculosis: A Case Study of the Mississippi State Sanatorium." Master's thesis, Louisiana State University, 2003.

Bibliography

Beauchamp, Keith A. "What Really Happened to Emmett Till: A Corrective to the 1956 *Look* Confession." Privately circulated paper. Copy in author's possession.

Campbell, Yolanda Denise. "Outsiders Within: A Framing Analysis of Eight Black and White U.S. Newspapers' Coverage of the Civil Rights Movement, 1954–1964." PhD diss., University of Southern Mississippi, 2011.

Davis, Rebecca Miller. "Reporting Race and Resistance in Dixie: The White Mississippi Press and Civil Rights, 1944–1964." PhD diss., University of South Carolina, 2011.

Ealy, Charles. "The Emmett Till Case: A Comparative Analysis of Newspaper Coverage." Master's thesis, University of Texas at Dallas, 1996.

Emmett Till Foundation. Statement of Mission and Purpose, n.d.

Emmett Till Historical Museum. Flyer. Burr Oak Cemetery, 2004.

Entin, Jonathan L. "Emmett Till and the Federal Enforcement of Civil Rights." Paper presented at Stillman College, Tuscaloosa, Ala., September 16, 2005.

Flourney, Craig. "Reporting the Movement in Black and White: The Emmett Till Lynching and the Montgomery Bus Boycott." PhD diss., Louisiana State University, 2003.

Hudson, Clenora Frances. "Emmett Till: The Impetus for the Modern Civil Rights Movement." PhD diss., University of Iowa, 1988.

"Leflore County Communities and Their History." Typescript, Greenwood-Leflore, Mississippi, Library.

Mace, Darryl C. "Regional Identities and Racial Messages: The Print Media's Stories of Emmett Till." PhD diss., Temple University, 2006.

Till-Mobley, Mamie. Biographical summary. Emmett Till Foundation, November 1994.

Whitaker, Hugh Stephen. "A Case Study in Southern Justice: The Emmett Till Case." Master's thesis, Florida State University, 1963.

Whitten, Ellen. "Justice Unearthed: Revisiting the Murder of Emmett Till." Honor's thesis, Rhodes College, 2005.

Archival Collections

Chatham, Gerald. Papers. Charles W. Capps Jr. Archives and Museum, Delta State University, Cleveland, Mississippi.

Coleman, James P. Papers. Accn. no. 21877, Mississippi Department of Archives and History, Archives and Library Division, Special Collections Section, Manuscript Collection, Jackson.

Evers, Medgar Wiley, and Myrlie Beasley Evers. Papers. Accn. no. Z2231.0005, Mississippi Department of Archives and History, Archives and Library Division, Special Collections Section, Manuscript Collection, Jackson.

Hampton, Henry. Collection. Washington University, St. Louis.

Huie, William Bradford. Papers. Cms 84. Ohio State University Library, Columbus.

Papers of the NAACP, Part 18: Special Subjects, 1940–1955, Series C: General Office Files (microfilm). Bethesda, Md.: University Publications of America, 1995.

Stennis, John C. Collection. Congressional and Political Research Center, Mitchell Memorial Library, Mississippi State University, Starkville.

Bibliography

State, Federal, and Military Records

Bryant, Eula Lee Morgan v. Henry E. Bryant. Chancery Court of the Second Judicial District of Tallahatchie County, Mississippi, Case No. 2875.

Carolyn Holloway Bryant v. Roy Bryant. Chancery Court of Sunflower County, Mississippi, Complaint no. 16505.

Chandler, Griffin, and Madge Carolyn Holloway Bryant. Marriage certificate, November 21, 1984. State file no. 123-84-25327, Mississippi State Department of Health Vital Records.

Congressional Record. See online resources.

Forest Preserve District of Cook County (Ill.). Nature Bulletin No. 500-A, September 29, 1973.

Gaines, Tom. Death certificate, dated August 29, 1944, Cook County Clerk's Office, Chicago.

Gaston, Clint, and Treola Collins. Marriage certificate, King County, Washington, filed August 10, 1960, no. 245340.

Holmes County (Mississippi) Circuit Clerk. *Marriage Records, 1889–1951,* black marriages, vols. 11–12: 157. Microfilm no. 879492, Family History Library.

Mallory, Lemorse and Mamie E. Till. Marriage certificate, dated August 19, 1946, no. 1925866, filed August 20, 1946, Cook County Clerk's Office, Chicago.

Reed, Add. Death certificate. Cook County, Illinois Death Records, state file no. 606929, filed March 27, 1977.

Tallahatchie County (Mississippi) Circuit Clerk. *Marriage Records of the First District, 1856–1918,* white marriages, vol. 8, 1908–1916. Microfilm no. 894882, Family History Library.

US Federal Census. 1900, 1920, 1930. Family History Library, Salt Lake City.

US Selective Service System. *World War I Selective Service System Draft Registration Cards, 1917–1918* (Washington, DC: National Archives and Records Administration), M1509.

The United States v. Private Fred A. McMurray and Private Louis Till (36 392 273), both of 177th Port Company, 379th Port Battalion, Transportation Corps. Peninsular Base Section, Trial by G.C.M., convened at Leghorn, Italy, February 17, 1945.

United States v. Roy Bryant Sr., CRG-83-55. National Archive and Records Administration, Southeast Region, Ellenwood, Georgia.

United States v. Roy Bryant Sr., CRG-87-82. National Archive and Records Administration, Southeast Region, Ellenwood, Georgia.

Online Resources

American Experience. http://www.pbs.org/wgbh/amex/till/filmmore/ps_letters.html.

Artz, E. Interview of Moses J. Newson. "A Journalist's Perspective of the Civil Rights Movement." http://collections.digitalmaryland.org/cdm/compoundobject/collection/saac/id/20059/rec/1.

"Barrett Extends Moral-Support to Carolyn Bryant." https://groups.google.com/forum/#!topic/misc.legal/CdjqsQBAX6c.

Beito, David T. "60 Minutes Story on Emmett Till Targets Carolyn Bryant." *History News Network.* http://hnn.us/blog/8070.

Beito, David T., and Linda Royster Beito. "Why the '60 Minutes' Story on Emmett Till Was a Disappointment." *History News Network*. http://hnn.us/article/8193.

"Bonnie Blue, Researcher, Author, Lecturer." http://emmetttills-secretwitness.com/index.html.

Breed, Allen G. "End of Till Case Draws Mixed Response." *USA Today*, March 4, 2007. http://usatoday30.usatoday.com/news/nation/2007-03-04-till-case_N.htm.

Bryant, Frances. Obituary. http://rayfuneralhome.net/tribute/details/443/Frances_Bryant/obituary.html.

Bryant, Linda Jean. Facebook wall, www.facebook.com.

Bryant, Thomas Lamar. Facebook wall, www.facebook.com.

Bryant, Carol Ann. Facebook wall, www.facebook.com.

Burr Oak Cemetery. http://theburroakcemetery.com/burr-oak-history.

California, Death Index, 1940–1997 [database online]. Provo, Utah, USA: Ancestry.com Operations Inc., 2008. http://www.ancestry.com.

Chrisler, William. Obituary. *Clarion-Ledger*, Jackson, Miss. http://www.legacy.com/obituaries/clarionledger/obituary.aspx?n=william-j-crisler&pid=143583474.

Congressional Record. www.heinonline.org.

Cook County, Illinois Marriage Index, 1930–1960. Provo, Utah, USA: Ancestry.com Operations Inc. 2008. www.ancestry.com.

Cornish, Audie. "County Apologizes to Emmett Till Family." NPR, October 2, 2007. www.npr.org/templates/story/story.php?storyId=14904083.

Damms, Richard V. "World War I: Loyalty and Dissent in Mississippi during the Great War, 1917–1918." http://mshistory.k12.ms.us/articles/237/World-War-I-the-great-war-1917-1918-loyalty-and-dissent-in-mississippi.

"Director Robert Mueller Announces Appointment of Deputy Chief Information Officer." FBI National Press Release, April 21, 2005. www.fbi.gov.

Donham, Carolyn. Facebook wall, www.facebook.com.

Edwards, Lynda. "Residents of Mississippi Town Say Till Killing Not Often Discussed." *Times of Northwest Indiana* (Munster), May 17, 2004. http://www.nwitimes.com/news/local/residents-of-mississippi-town-say-till-killing-not-often-discussed/article_1720b867-8062-56eb-b8e2-2ae147616aba.html.

Eisenhower, Dwight D. Library. www.eisenhower.archives.gov/research/online_documents.html.

Eisenhower, Dwight D. State of the Union, 1956. www.pbs.org/wgbh/americanexperience/features/primary-resources/eisenhower-state56/?flavour=mobile.

Emmett Till Memorial Commission. www.etmctallahatchie.com/pages/resolution.htm.

Emmett Till Murder. http://www.emmetttillmurder.com.

"Emmett Till Unsolved Civil Rights Crime Act." Senate, Calendar No. 211, June 22, 2007. www.gpo.gov/fdsys/pkg/CRPT-110srpt88/html/CRPT-110srpt88.htm.

Federal Bureau of Investigation FOIA release to Devery S. Anderson, 2006, re Emmett Till. www.fbi.gov/foia.

Federal Bureau of Investigation, Prosecutive Report of Investigation Concerning . . . Emmett Till, Deceased, Victim, February 9, 2006. www.fbi.gov.

Federal Bureau of Investigation, Prosecutive Report of Investigation Concerning . . . Emmett Till, Deceased, Appendix A—Trial Transcript, February 9, 2006. www.fbi.gov.

Gibbs v. State. 223 Miss. 1 (1955), 77 So. 2d 705. http://law.justia.com/cases/mississippi/supreme-court/1955/39247-0.html.

Grayson, Dylan. "Sykes: It's Not Too Late for Truth." *Guilfordian*, February 16, 2007. www.guil
fordian.com/archives/2007/02/16/sykes-its-not-too-late-for-truth.

Gunsmoke. Radio information and episode list. http://comp.uark.edu/~tsnyder/gunsmoke/
gun-radio1.html

Mississippi Code of 1972. http://www.lexisnexis.com/hottopics/mscode/.

Haddock, James H. to Governor John Bell Williams, February 3, 1970. http://mdah.state.ms.us/
arrec/digital_archives/sovcom.

Hampton, Henry. Collection. Washington University. http://digital.wustl.edu/eyesontheprize.

Hillegas, Jan. "West Point 'Desegregation' Produces Violent Reactions." *Southern Patriot* (New
Orleans), February 1970. http://mdah.state.ms.us/arrec/digital_archives/sovcom.

Holmberg, David. "Murder of Emmett Till: New Developments." *MaximsNews Network*. www
.maximsnews.com/2005davidholmberg12may.htm.

House Congressional Resolution 360. 108th Congress, 2nd Session, February 10, 2004. https://
www.congress.gov/108/bills/hconres360/BILLS-108hconres360ih.pdf

Hunting with Tom. www.huntingwithtom.com.

"Mamie Till Mobley, Heroic Mother, Mourned." *People's World*, January 24, 2003. www.peoples
world.org/mamie-till-mobley-heroic-mother-mourned.

Mississippi Delta Center's Landmarks in American History and Culture. http://vimeo.com/
74032741.

National Archives and Records Administration. *U.S. World War II Army Enlistment Records,
1938–1946*. Provo, Utah, USA: Ancestry.com Operations Inc., 2005. www.ancestry.com.

National Cemetery Administration. *U.S. Veterans Gravesites, ca. 1775–2006* [database online].
Provo, Utah, USA: Ancestry.com Operations Inc., 2006. http://www.ancestry.com.

Neruukar, Amita. "Lawmakers Want 1955 Mississippi Murder Reopened." cnn.com/2004/
LAW/04/13/till.murder.case.

Nolan, Beth, "Possible Bases of Jurisdiction for the Department of Justice to Investigate Matters
Relating to the Assassination of Martin Luther King, Jr." www.justice.gov/sites/default/files/
olc/opinions/1998/04/31/op-olc-v022-p0061.pdf.

"Nominees for the 28th Annual News & Documentary Emmy Awards in 32 Categories
Announced by Natas." http://emmyonline.com/news_28th_nominations.

Nunnelley, William. "Metress Hopes Book on Emmett Till Will Clear Up Some
Misconceptions." January 24, 2003. www.samford.edu/news/newsarticle.
aspx?id=21474841550#.U-RjEPldXup.

109 S. Cong. Res. 3, Introduced in the Senate, 109th Congress, January 24, 2005. www.opencon
gress.org/bill/sconres3-109/text.

109th H. Cong. Res. 77. Introduced in the House, February 17, 2005. http://thomas.loc.gov/cgi
-bin/query/z?c109:H.CON.RES.77.IH:.

109th Congress, 2nd Session, S.2679. In the Senate of the United States, April 27, 2006, and
S.2679, Calendar No. 579. August 3, 2006. www.gpo.gov/fdsys/pkg/BILLS-109s2679rs/pdf/
BILLS-109s2679rs.pdf.

Plys, Cate. "The City Council Hears Alarms." March 18, 2004. www.chicagoreader.com/chicago/
the-city-council-hears-alarms/Content?oid=914872.

Preservation Chicago: Citizens Advocating for the Preservation of Chicago's Historic Architecture.
http://www.preservationchicago.org/success-story/11.

Bibliography

Primary Sources: Letters to Chicago. PBS., *American Experience*. http://www.pbs.org/wgbh/
amex/till/filmmore/ps_letters.html.

Rapp, Anthony, and Jennifer-Leigh Oprihory. "Declassified: The Real Story Behind Solving
Crime." *Medill Reports*. http://newsarchive.medill.northwestern.edu/chicago/news
.aspx?id=210665&print=1.

"Reid Statement on Passage of Emmett Till Bill." http://democrats.senate.gov/2008/09/24/reid
-statement-on-passage-of-emmett-till-bill/#.VLw2AEfF-Jo.

Robinson, Plater, prod. *The Murder of Emmett* Till. Soundprint. http://soundprint.org/radio/
display_show/ID/398/name/The+Murder+of+Emmett+Till.

Roosevelt, Eleanor. "My Day" column. 1936 to 1962. http://www.gwu.edu/~erpapers/myday.

Samuels, Rich, writer. *The Murder and the Movement*. www.richsamuels.com/nbcmm/till/till
.html.

Senate Bill 2689, to Judiciary, Division A, Mississippi Legislature, Regular Session 2007. http://
billstatus.ls.state.ms.us/documents/2007/pdf/SB/2600-2699/SB2689IN.pdf.

"Senate Kills Bill for $10B in New Spending." *USA Today*, July 26, 2008. http://usatoday30
.usatoday.com/news/washington/2008-07-28-senatebill_N.htm.

"Senators Schumer & Talent & Representative Rangel Hold a News Conference on the Investigation into the Murder of Emmett Till." *Political Transcript Wire*, November 19, 2004.
www.highbeam.com/doc/1P3-743021641.html.

Sovereignty Commission Online. http://mdah.state.ms.us/arrec/digital_archives/sovcom.

Spears, Patricia. "Timothy Tyson Sheds Light on His Novel." *Duke Chronicle* (Durham, N.C.),
January 26, 2014. www.dukechronicle.com/articles/2014/01/26/timothy-tyson-sheds-light
-his-novel#.VJNIrCvF-Ec.

Sweet, Lynn. "Emmett Till Civil Rights Bill Passed by Senate. Named after Chicago Youth Murdered in Mississippi in 1955." Comment section. http://blogs.suntimes.com/sweet/2008/09/
emmett_till_civil_rights_bill.html.

Talmer, Jerry. "Documentary on the Grisly Lynching of Emmett Till." *Villager*, August 3–9,
2005. http://thevillager.com/villager_118/documentaryonthegrisly.html.

Tallahatchie Civil Rights Driving Tour. www.etmctallahatchie.com/documents/drivingtour.pdf.

"Text of the Unsolved Civil Rights Crime Act." Introduced in the US Senate on July 1, 2005.
www.govtrack.us/congress/bills/109/s1369/text

Till-Mobley, Mamie. Interview, February 2001. Chicago Project. https://sites.google.com/site/
mamietillinterview/.

Union Missionary Baptist Church. http://www.umbcbarstow.com.

"Unsolved Civil Rights Crime Act, H.R. 3506." Introduced in the US House of Representatives
on July 28, 2005. www.govtrack.us/congress/bills/109/hr3506/text.

Untold Story of Emmett Louis Till, awards. IMDB. www.imdb.com/title/tt0475420/awards?ref
_=tt_awd.

US Federal Census. 1940. Leflore County, Mississippi. Beat 2, Enumeration District 42, sheet
9B. https://familysearch.org/ark:/61903/1:1:VBSH-GYR.

"Vandals Destroy Sign Marking Emmett Till Murder Site." *USA Today*, October 27, 2007. http://
usatoday30.usatoday.com/news/nation/2008-10-27-emmett-till_N.htm.

Venson, Dr. R. Q., and Ethyl H. Venson. Cotton Maker's Jubilee Collection, Memphis and
Shelby County Room, Memphis Public Library and Information Center, Memphis, Tenn.
http://memphislibrary.contentdm.oclc.org/cdm/ref/collection/p13039coll1/id/39.

Bibliography

Whitten, Ellen. "Justice Unearthed: Revisiting the Murder of Emmett Till." Honor's thesis, Rhodes College, 2005. http://www.rhodes.edu/images/content/Academics/Ellen_Whitten.pdf.

Author Interviews

Andrews, Jeffrey. July 13, 2014.

Baker, Martha Wright. May 5, 2014.

Beauchamp, Keith. June 4, 2005; November 10, 2013; February 2, August 23, 2014.

Benson, Christopher. August 23, 2014.

Bradley, Randall. February 27, 2011.

Chatham, Gerald Sr. February 24, 2012.

Confidential Source A. April 7, 2014.

Confidential Source B. June 8, 2014.

Confidential Source C. August 19, December 3, 2014.

Confidential Source D. June 6, 2014.

Colon, Doris. January 5, 2007.

Crawford, Roosevelt. August 28, 2005; October 21, 2006.

Crowe, Chris. March 24, 2014.

Darren [last name withheld]. February 11, 2010.

Evers-Williams, Myrlie. April 23, 2014.

Garrity, Robert J., Jr. July 7, 2014.

Gaston, Marsha. February 17, 2014.

Glisson, Susan. July 29, 2014.

Greenlee, Jim. March 11, July 28, 2014.

Hailman, John. June 21, 2014.

Hays, John A. July 20, 2011.

Herbers, John. December 15, 2006.

Herrick, Gene. January 27, 2012.

Holmberg, David. July 1, 2014.

Houck, Davis. January 25, 2011; June 10, 2014.

Hubbell, Macklyn. March 1, 2014.

Killinger, Dale. April 29, 2014.

Minor, Wilson F. August 24, 2009.

Nelson, Stanley. October 15, 2013.

Parker, Wheeler, Jr. February 7, October 1, 2007; July 6, 2013.

Parker, William. April 30, 2014.

Pearson, Betty. February 6, 2006.

Ray, Mary Lou. August 6, 2013.

Reed, Willie. February 6, 2007.

Shoemaker, W. C. August 21, 2009; August 20, 2010.

Small, Mike. July 20, 2014.

Smith, Crosby, Jr. February 7, 2007.

Spell, Bill. August 20, 2010.

Sturdivant, Ygondine. August 7, 2013.

Bibliography

Sykes, Alvin. August 17, 2013; March 8, June 12, 17, July 12, 2014.

Till-Mobley, Mamie. December 3, 1996; April 15, 2002.

Wakefield, Dan. November 20, 2006.

Withers, Ernest C. February 8, 2006.

Wright, Simeon. August 31, 2005; February 7, October 2, 2007; February 4, 2013.

Correspondence

Beauchamp, Keith, to author, May 28, August 23, 2014.

Blue, Bonnie, to author, June 28, June 29, July 27, 2014.

Bond, Julian, to author, October 18, 2013.

Boyack, James Edmund, Jr., to author, February 8, 2011.

Confidential Source E to author, August 15, 2011.

Confidential source to Keith Beauchamp, March 11, 2003.

Dailey, Rita, to author, May 14, 2012; September 7, 2013.

DeLaughter, Bobby, to author, June 20, 2014.

Evans, Aja, to author, April 28, 2013.

Glisson, Susan, to author, July 30, 2014.

Hailman, John R., to author, July 2, 2014.

Hansell, Marilyn, to author, May 24, 2005.

Hanson, Tina, to author, November 20, 2008.

Hillegas, Jan, to author, July 7, 2014.

İşcan, Mehmet Yaşar, to Alvin Sykes, April 25, 2003.

Jones, Thomas M., to author, March 16, 2009.

Killinger, Dale R., to author, July 22, September 15, 2014.

Krotzer, Minter, to author, May 17, May 19, June 7, 2010.

Malone-France, Katherine, to author, March 1, 2006.

McGarrh, Lee, to author, June 18, 2008.

Mitchell, Jerry, to author, October 19, 2013.

Ritea, Steve, to author, April 29, 2014.

Small, Mike, to author, July 21, 2014.

Sykes, Alvin, to author, May 8, 2014.

Sykes, Alvin, to Mehmet Yaşar İşcan, n.d.

Till-Mobley, Mamie, to author, February 14, 2000.

Tyson, Timothy B., to author, March 31, July 26, 2014.

Wakefield, Dan, to author, June 20, 2009.

Whitaker, Hugh Stephen. June 22, 2005; May 14, 2012.

Wilkins, Woodrow, to author, November 6, 2013.

Oral Histories and Interviews Conducted by Others

Chatham, Gerald Sr. Oral History Interview (OH293). Conducted by Henry Outlaw, January 19, 2005, Charles W. Capps Jr. Archives and Museum, Delta State University, Cleveland, Miss.

Bibliography

"A Journalist's Perspective of the Civil Rights Movement." E. Artz, interview of Moses J. Newson. http://collections.digitalmaryland.org/cdm/compoundobject/collection/saac/id/20059/rec/1.

Loggins, Henry Lee. Interview by Linda Royster Beito, July 21, 2001.

Newson, Moses. Interview by Marshland Boone. http://knightpoliticalreporting.syr.edu/wp-content/uploads/2012/05/Moses_Newson_oral_essay.pdf.

Smith, Jak, and Bruce Smith. Oral History Interview (OH289). Conducted by Henry Outlaw, May 7, 2005. Charles W. Capps Jr. Archives and Museum, Delta State University, Cleveland, Miss.

INDEX